Through the Global Lens

An Introduction to the Social Sciences

Third Edition

Michael J. Strada

West Liberty University

New York   San Francisco   Boston   Upper Saddle River
London   Toronto   Sydney   Tokyo   Singapore   Madrid
Mexico City   Munich   Paris   Cape Town   Hong Kong   Montreal

Library of Congress Cataloging-in-Publication Data

Strada, Michael J.
    Through the global lens : an introduction to the social sciences / Michael
J. Strada. -- 3rd ed.
        p. cm.
    Includes bibliographical references and index.
    ISBN-13: 978–0–13–603040–9 (pbk.)
    ISBN-10: 0-13-603040-8 (pbk.)
    1. Social sciences. I. Title.
    H85.S77 2008
    300--dc22
                            2008016906

Editorial Director: Leah Jewell
Editor-in-Chief: Dickson Musslewhite
Publisher: Nancy Roberts
Editorial Assistant: Nart Varoqua
Director of Marketing: Brandy Dawson
Marketing Manager: Kelly May
Marketing Assistant: Irene Fraga
Text Permission Specialist: Lisa Black
Senior Operations Supervisor: Sherry Lewis
Operations Specialist: Christina Amato
Full-Service Project Management: Jill Traut/ICC
    Macmillan Inc.

Production Liaison: Barbara Reilly
Director, Image Resource Center: Melinda Patelli
Manager, Cover Visual Research and Permissions:
    Karen Sanatar
Manager, Rights and Permissions: Zina Arabia
Manager, Visual Research: Beth Brenzel
Image Permission Coordinator: Debbie Hewitson
Image Researcher: Teri Stratford
Cover Art Director: Jayne Conte
Cover Designer: Bruce Kenselaar
Cover Illustration/Photo: Getty Images, Inc.

This book was set in 10/12 Sabon by ICC Macmillan Inc. and was printed
and bound by R.R. Donnelley & Sons. The cover was printed by Phoenix Color Corp.

Credits and acknowledgments borrowed from other sources and reproduced, with permission, in this textbook appear on
appropriate page within text (or beginning on page 446).

VangoBooks™ is an imprint of Pearson Education
Pearson® is a registered trademark of Pearson plc

Pearson Education Ltd., London
Pearson Education Singapore, Pte. Ltd
Pearson Education Canada, Inc.
Pearson Education—Japan
Pearson Education Australia PTY, Limited

Pearson Education North Asia Ltd., Hong Kong
Pearson Educación de Mexico, S.A. de C.V.
Pearson Education Malaysia, Pte. Ltd.
Pearson Education Upper Saddle River, New Jersey

10 9 8 7 6 5 4 3 2 1

ISBN 13: 978-0-13-603040-9
ISBN 10:   0-13-603040-8

To Cameron Russell Witt

BRIEF CONTENTS

CONTENTS

Unit III Subjective Influences on the Human Drama

CHAPTER 10
Sociology and Human Social Activity 245

CHAPTER 11
Comparative Cultures 282

Unit V Directing the Human Drama: Politics and Government

CHAPTER 12

Political Science: Who Gets What, When, and How   312

CHAPTER 13

The State Challenged by New Actors   339

Unit VI Producing the Human Drama: Human and Nonhuman Resources

CHAPTER 14

Macroeconomics and U.S. Economic Hegemony   366

Three related motifs highlight the content, method, and philosophy inherent in this textbook. First, regarding *content,* we will peer through the global lens in studying the human drama. In our shrinking world, what happens in Bangkok, Beirut, or Beijing resonates for North Americans more than ever; therefore, **globalization** represents motif number ONE. For most U.S. citizens, what globalization meant during the 1990s was unprecedented economic growth based largely on trade. That comfort zone buckled when globalization flashed its dark side on September 11, 2001. Paradoxically, the lone superpower appears as vulnerable as everyone else on the planet.

Second, concerning *method,* applying the knowledge and insights gleaned from each social science (anthropology, economics, geography, political science, psychology, sociology) requires genuine multi-disciplinarity. This occurs via motif number TWO, the **Stanislavsky Method.** Named for Russian director Konstantin Stanislavsky, "the method" entails dramatic training whereby actors seek to get behind the eyeballs of their characters, seeing the world as their characters would. An adaptation known as perceptual analysis is used to fathom each social science's unique vision of the human script.

Third, a particular *philosophical orientation* also permeates this text. Common-sensical thinking is good enough for some things but not the complexities of human behavior. Common sense may represent a necessary condition for sound judgment, but clearly not a sufficient condition. Therefore, social sciences come equipped with critical thinking's skepticism, refusing to accept things at face value. Critical thinking means asking questions that probe unexamined assumptions and fallacious reasoning. Common sense came apart at the seams when Copernicus refused to accept the conventional wisdom that the earth was flat.

This book works for two kinds of courses: traditional introductory social science and newer courses about globalization. Several features assist in delivering the promised goods (globalization, interdisciplinary, critical thinking). Stylistically, the prose is asked to stand up and perform accessibly without abandoning scholarship. A running glossary seamlessly blends these key conceptual building blocks into the prose. Finally, more than 70 case studies provide real-world experiences illustrating vital themes.

Supplements

WIN/MAC PH Test Manager

This computerized software allows instructors to create their own personalized exams, to edit any or all test questions, and to add new questions. Other special features of this program, which are available for Windows and Macintosh, include random generation of an item set, creation of alternate versions of the same test, scrambling question sequence, and test preview before printing.

Companion Website™

In tandem with the text, students can now take full advantage of the Internet to enrich their study of the social sciences. Features of the Website include chapter objectives, study questions, links to *The New York Times* and the USA Today Census 2000 in addition to other links on the Web that can reinforce and enhance the content of each chapter. Use of the site is free to all students and faculty. Simply visit the Website at http://www.prenhall.com/strada.

The Pearson Guide to Research Navigator™

Pearson's **Research Navigator**™ is the easiest way to start a research assignment or paper. Your students will have access to exclusive databases of credible and reliable source material, including:

- EBSCO Academic Journal and Abstract Database
- "Best of the Web" Link Library
- *Financial Times* Article Archive and Company Financials

Gain access to Research Navigator™ by using the access code found in the front of the brief guide called *The Pearson Guide to Research Navigator*™. The access code for Research Navigator™ is included with every guide and can be packaged for no extra charge with *Through the Global Lens*. Please contact your Pearson representative for more information

Acknowledgments

Thanks to incisive comments from reviewers, change permeates the third edition. This interdisciplinary text employs an adaptation of the Stanislavsky Method, which strives to get beneath the skin of a dramatic character. In the social sciences, this method uses perceptual analysis to glean each discipline's unique perspective. Therefore, the scholarly reviewers for this textbook hail from all of the social sciences.

Among anthropologists, Karen Muir (Columbus State Community College), Raymond Scupin (Lindenwood University), and Peter S. Peregrine (Lawrence University) provided keen insights. Susan Herrick (West Liberty University) represented sociology's take on human behavior adroitly. Ryan Sheppard (King's College) and William Downs (Georgia State University) clearly presented the political science vantage point. The views of psychology were left in the able hands of Judy Gentry (Columbus State Community College). Finally, geography had its angle on human behavior covered thoroughly by Brian Crawford (West Liberty University). I am beholden to each of these thoughtful colleagues. My librarian wife Linda always manages to find elusive sources, especially online. Lastly, I would like to thank the following reviewers of the second edition.

William M. Downs, *Georgia State University*
Audrey Eileen Gage, *Central Florida Community College*
James J. Sheehan, *Miami University (Ohio)*
John H. Scott, *Wheaton College*
Julie L. Smith, *University of North Carolina - Pembroke*

CHAPTER 1

Globalization

CORE OBJECTIVE

To establish that globalization profoundly affects the human condition and to assess some of its costs and benefits.

THEMATIC QUESTIONS

- What is the essence of globalization?

- How many different types of globalization exist?

- Is globalization a good thing or bad thing?

- What is meant by Global Issues (GIs)?

- How do GIs influence the future prospects for our species?

Globalization. Considerable complex meaning comes wrapped up in this single word. It enrages some people while elating others. No one, however, can completely escape globalization's reach in the contemporary era. But that does not mean that individuals and groups must remain victims of globalization, because instantaneous communication empowers people in ways that were impossible before.

Despite affecting our lives in myriad real ways, globalization sounds like an abstract concept that some students find difficult to grasp. Therefore, in addition to defining the concept, we present ten metaphors that catalyze visual imagery useful in fleshing out globalization's various meanings. We then identify five categories of globalization (economic, environmental, communications, military, and cultural).

This chapter covers several pressing Global Issues (GIs) facing humankind today. After defining the nature of GIs and identifying some of the new actors challenging states to solve them, we examine four *ecological GIs* (environment, population, food, and energy). Then, other significant GIs are divided into three *highly visible* ones (WMD, terrorism, and mobile microbes) and three *less-visible* ones (human rights, massive migration, and international drug trafficking). Each of these diverse GIs represents a credible threat to the well being of humankind. Finally, the philosophical question is posed concerning whether competition or cooperation ought to guide future efforts to manage globalization wisely.

Fleshing Out Globalization

Defining a Moving Target

We begin this look at globalization by distinguishing between three related, yet distinct, terms: **foreign, international,** and **global.** That which is foreign exists within other countries or societies, that which is international transpires between two or more countries, and that which is global differs in that it potentially involves everyone.

Foreign ■ That which occurs within countries other than one's own

International ■ Relationships between two or more countries

Global ■ Events and realities beyond the scope of countries or regions that potentially affect everyone on earth

As British international studies scholar Jan Aart Scholte points out, "Disputes and confusion about globalization often begin around the issue of definition."[1] He sees it as "the advent and spread of trans-border and trans-world social spaces."[2] One major United Nations publication refers to globalization as "shrinking time, shrinking space, and disappearing borders."[3]

Worldwatch Institute researcher Hilary French calls globalization "the stunning acceleration in the growth in trade, investment, travel, computer networking, and pollution across national boundaries."[4] Concerning world trade, she points out that it increased from $311 billion in 1950 to $5.4 trillion in 1998 and continues unabated. Similarly, foreign investment by corporations rose from $44 billion in 1970 to $644 billion in 1998. Over 2 million people now cross borders daily, whereas only 69,000 did so in 1950. Since 1995, the Internet has grown by more than 50 percent yearly. Unfortunately, however, tens of thousands of monkeys and other primates are shipped internationally for profit as another face of globalization.[5]

The Global Policy Forum notes that "Jet airplanes, cheap phone service, e-mail, computers, huge oceangoing vessels, instant capital flows, have all made the world more interdependent than ever before."[6]

American University international studies scholar James Mittelman chooses a *minimalist* approach to globalization by confining it mostly to the realm of current economics: "Globalization is a phase in the history of capital whose lineage has brought together many different societies into one system."[7] Until the disaster that descended on the United States on September 11, 2001, economic manifestations of globalization seemed most germane to Americans, but military globalization displaced all competing images of globalization for several years after that fateful date.

Thomas Friedman, foreign affairs columnist for the *New York Times*, takes a decidedly *maximalist* tack. Friedman boldly claims that globalization—"the complex, technology-driven integration of politics, financial markets, and environmentalism across national borders"—is far more than just another passing phase in a fast-paced rapidly changing world. He believes it is nothing less than a pervasive *international system* replacing the previous one that dominated world affairs for forty years: the Cold War.[8]

A Cottage Industry in Metaphor Making

Common metaphors employed to pump life into this concept include "the global village," "spaceship earth," "our shrinking world," "web of interdependence," "world without walls," "world community," "vanishing boundaries," "human family," "global commons," and "borderless athletes." Such colorful phrases enliven the panoply of statistics often relied upon to describe globalization.

The metaphor that often resonates with students is the one about borderless athletes. If you are a basketball fan, you probably know that China's Yao Ming, Canada's Steve Nash, France's Tony Parker, Germany's Dirk Nowitzky, and Nigeria's Hakeem Olajuwon rank among the top players in the NBA. U.S. college coaches now actively recruit increasing numbers of foreign players with scholarships.

The National Hockey League is filled not only with Canadian hockey players but more than one hundred Europeans, nearly half of whom hail from Russia and other parts of the former Soviet Union. The influx of talented European players brought unprecedented parity to the NHL when the league's roster expanded to thirty teams.

Even baseball, the quintessentially American sport, includes not only foreign players from Latin America but also an increasing number from Japan, Korea, and Australia. A book by John Bale and Joseph Maguire explores the economic, social, and political consequences of highly paid global athletes on the move.[9]

Master Metaphorician

No analyst of globalization matches the innovative insights found in Thomas Friedman's writings on the subject. His hit 1999 book, *The Lexus and the Olive Tree,* represented cutting-edge thinking about globalization at that point. Since then, he has kept apace of rapid developments and recently authored an even more successful update on the topic called *The Earth Is Flat,* by which Friedman essentially means "electronically connected," thus empowering new players to contribute to problem solving and to compete commercially as well. The key concept of *flatness* speaks to the leveling of the playing field whereby countless individuals now can collaborate or compete in real time globally.[10]

Friedman traces three discrete stages of globalization whose speed has increased dramatically in recent years. Stage one, which he calls globalization 1.0, occurred from Columbus' venture westward in 1492 until about 1800. Countries dominated this era, in which national muscle of varying types proved paramount. He says that 1.0 shrunk the world from a size large to a size medium. Countries broke down the walls that fostered global integration. The second stage, globalization 2.0, from 1800 until 2000, the author describes as one in which multinational corporations (MNCs) took leadership from countries, with the Dutch and British joint-stock companies the prototypical success stories. Breakthroughs in hardware typified 2.0, which shrunk the world from a size medium to a size small.

Then, around 2000, a whole new kind of globalization revolutionized everything. Dubbed 3.0, this is when the earth goes flat, enabling individuals to participate in ways that were impossible before. If horsepower drove 1.0, and hardware development drove 2.0, it is computer software driving globalization 3.0, with a shrinking effect from size small to size tiny.[11]

How did the world get this way so quickly? Friedman addresses ten "flatteners" as collectively responsible. Most essential, however, were the collapse of communism, supply-chaining (a la Wal-Mart), the dot.com bust causing overinvestment in fiber-optic telecommunications, and the outsourcing of software engineers recruited to solve a perceived Y2K problem. His epiphany concerning the flattened world occurred in Bangalore (India's Silicon Valley) while interviewing Jaithirth Rao, CEO of MphasiS, a company that pioneered a software program with a standardized format facilitating the outsourcing of tax returns.

Rao explained to Friedman that U.S. tax returns performed in India increased from 25,000 in 2003, to 100,000 in 2004, and to 400,000 in 2005. The author explains how India was well positioned to benefit not only from the dot.com boom but, ironically, more so from the dot.com bust. "The boom laid the cable that connected India to the world, and the bust made the cost of using it virtually free and also vastly increased the number of American companies wanting to use that fiber-optic cable to outsource knowledge work to India."[12]

Counterintuitive Trends: Jihad versus McWorld

Rutgers political scientist Benjamin Barber tries to place globalization (which he calls McWorld) in a wider context by examining how it collides with an opposing trend toward localization (which he calls Jihad). Although the term *Jihad* derives from Arabic and Islamic traditions, it has a variety of meanings, and Barber uses it in the sense of "dogmatic and violent particularism."[13] The quest for racial, ethnic, or religious identity at smaller and smaller levels is what drives many of the civil wars breaking out all over the globe.

The end of the Cold War loosened the American and Soviet grip over the rest of the world, allowing pent-up group identities to assert their demands for recognition as independent players. When President Woodrow Wilson championed the principle of the self-determination of nations near the beginning of the twentieth century, he surely could not have envisioned the fragmented state of the world at the end of that century. Only about 40 nation-states existed prior to the outbreak of World War I in 1914. In the post-Cold War era, the number approaches 200. Barber laments that, in its most virulent strain, Jihad is "propelled by anxiety in the face of uncertainty and relieved by self-sacrificing zealotry."[14]

Jihad's opposite, *McWorld,* results from the shrinking effect of corporations pursuing unfettered global markets for their products. The failure of global communism as an alternative to market capitalism has weakened the entire notion of governmental oversight, leaving corporations freer to seek profits than they have been in at least a century.

The fragmenting tribal loyalties of Jihad function as the diametric opposite of McWorld's homogeneity. But like many enemies, they also thrive on this relationship with their opposite. Barber says, "Jihad needs McWorld as shadows do the sun."[15] As individual citizens, this interaction leaves each of us susceptible to the influences of both forces. "Jihad pursues a bloody politics of identity, McWorld a bloodless economics of profit. Belonging by default to McWorld, everyone is a consumer; seeking a repository for identity, everyone belongs to some tribe."[16] This split is so sharp that it sometimes forces us to choose sides.

New Actors Challenging States

For three and a half centuries, states (countries) have dominated the political landscape in determining how humans go about ordering public affairs. Typically, a few states have been much more powerful in settling these questions, although American power might in the 2000s seem unprecedented in many ways. However, the late twentieth century witnessed the emergence, or reemergence, of several types of actors challenging states as competitors for winning the hearts and minds of humanity. They consist mostly of NGOs, IGOs, IFIs, and MNCs. When states fail to solve problems that concern ordinary people, competitors arise as alternatives. Globalization has empowered many individuals who were previously voiceless (especially women).

Quite possibly, the rapid growth of non-governmental organizations (NGOs) has occurred most unexpectedly among new actors (see Table 1.1). These grass-roots, often

Table 1.1

GROWTH OF INTERNATIONAL NGOs

Issue Area	1990	2000	Percentage
Culture/Recreation	2169	2733	26%
Education	1485	1839	23.8%
Research	7675	8467	10.3%
Health	1357	2036	50%
Social Services	2361	4215	78.5%
Environment	979	1170	19.5%
Economic Development	9582	9614	0.3%
Law/Policy Advocacy	2712	3864	42.5%
Religion	1407	1869	32.8%
Defense	244	234	−4.1%
Politics	1275	1240	−2.7%
Total	**31,246**	**37,281**	**19.3%**

Source: Data derived from *Yearbook of International Organizations: Guide to Civil Society Networks,* 1990 and 2000 published by Union of International Associations and republished p. 300, Table R23B in *Global Civil Society,* 2001 ed. by Helmut Anheier, Marlies Glasius, and Mary Kaldor, Centre for Civil Society and Centre for the Study of Global Governance, London School of Economics and Political Science, 2001.

spontaneous and independent bodies serve as the voices of concerned citizens, and they bring an element of the civil society to GIs and subsequent events. In addressing a 2005 forum of NGOs in Montreal, seventh U.N. Secretary General Kofi Annan characterized NGOs as "the world's new superpower." A global civil society yearbook now appears annually as a pulse on the beat of civil society.[17] Data from one of these reports, depicted in Table 1.1, shows the relative growth rate of NGOs across certain issue-areas.

Although NGOs have emerged mostly in recent decades, inter-governmental organizations (IGOs) have been around for at least 150 years. The prefix "inter" means *between,* and these institutions are called intergovernmental because they are formed by groups of governments seeking to achieve common objectives. Numbers of IGOs are measured in a few hundred, in contrast to many thousands of contemporary NGOs. The two main categories of IGOs consist of global ones (such as the U.N.) and regional ones (such as NAFTA or NATO). Similarly, their purposes consist of two key functions, namely, military/defense-related, or economic/trade-related. They vary greatly in size, membership, function, and resources.

As the largest and most influential IGO, the U.N. merits discussion in any book about globalization. It began in 1945 with 50 initial members, but today's roster has risen to 191 countries. The U.N. Charter comprises its essential blueprint, setting up its organs and procedures. The Charter charged the U.N. to maintain international peace and security, develop relations between states, solve cultural/humanitarian problems, promote human rights, and act as a forum in which key stakeholders can congregate. Six organs were established: the General Assembly, Security Council, Secretariat, International Court of Justice, and Trusteeship Council (terminated in 1994).

The world body's budget for 2000–2001 was $2,535 million, which comes mostly from the member states assessed according to their ability to pay. Equally important, states are assessed separately for the expensive peacekeeping operations attempting to separate combatants, which ran to about $2 billion during the same time period. Peace-keeping operations fall under the purview of the Security Council. What is called the U.N. family consists of several other social and humanitarian duties. The U.N. system includes an International Court of Justice, which furthers the area of international law, much of which derives from more than 500 U.N.-sponsored multilateral treaties. The U.N. was intimately involved in the process of decolonization, whereby European colonial powers granted independence to former possessions. Good statistics are crucial to good decision making, and the U.N. system is responsible for generating mounds of data to assist all players on the world stage. Secretaries General serve as chief administrator for the U.N. for one ten-year term, with African Kofi Annan as the predecessor to incumbent South Korean Ban Ki-moon, the eighth Secretaries General since 1945.[18]

As a special subcategory to IGOs, international financial institutions (IFIs) consist of relatively few huge institutions possessing massive resources and responsible for deciding how to allocate those resources. The determination of economic/financial winners and losers is much influenced by the work of IFIs. Like IGOs generally, IFIs can be divided into those that are global in scope (e.g., World Bank, International Monetary Fund, WTO) and those that are regional in scope (e.g., Inter-American Development Bank). Let's sketch briefly the profile of the IMF as our example of an IFI. "It oversees the global financial system by monitoring exchange rates and balance of payments, as well as offering technical and financial assistance when asked." All but seven U.N. members participate in the IMF system, which promotes global monetary cooperation, financial stability, international trade, high employment, poverty reduction, and sustainable development. It is one of the three main economic institutions set up at the Bretton Woods Conference in 1944. Because financial crises can erupt and spread more rapidly in the modern era, the IMF can intervene in several ways. Aid from the IMF traditionally comes with "conditionality," meaning that countries must implement IMF-approved economic reforms intended to improve their economic performance. Critics claim the IMF's "one size fits all" policies fail to recognize fundamental differences between countries.[19]

The other category of actor on the world stage, the multi-national corporations (MNCs), is not really new, yet the influence of these entities, numbering in the tens of thousands, has grown significantly as of late. Their mission bears no ambiguity: the profit motive drives everything, or the bottom line is what matters most for corporate executives. Often accused of illegal or unethical behavior by NGOs or IGOs, MNCs end up defending their behavior publicly with some regularity. Globalization magnifies the significance of decisions made in highly secretive corporate board offices. Let's sketch General Motors (GM) as an example of a powerful MNC.

GM remains the world's largest automaker after seventy-five years as such. Founded in 1908, and headquartered in Detroit, GM employed 327,000 people in 2006. It manufactures cars and trucks in thirty-three countries, and in 2005, GM sold 9.17 million vehicles under twelve brand names for a profit of $193 million. GM is majority shareholder in the GM Daewoo Auto Company of South Korea. It also has collaborative efforts with Suzuki Motors and Isuzu Motors (both of Japan). After several large oil mergers, GM fell to the fifth-largest company in America based on sales. GM is saddled with extensive "legacy" costs stemming from pension and health care obligations incurred when GM's market share was substantially higher than today. The firm's economic health has been characterized as dubious in recent years.[20]

Major Categories of Globalization

Social scientists sometimes disagree over identifying the most important forms of globalization. However, it is reasonable to suggest that the five types sketched next in Figure 1.1 represent worthy contenders: *economic* globalization, *environmental* globalization, *communications* globalization, *military* globalization, and *cultural* globalization.

Economic Globalization

Economics deals with the production, distribution, and consumption of goods and services. No other form of globalization rivals economic globalization for its ubiquity. Examine the labels on your clothing. Almost certainly, they were made in far-off places such as China, Brazil, Bangladesh, or Malaysia. If you drink coffee, it likely comes from Latin America. The number of Americans working for foreign firms doubled between 1980 and 1997 to more than five million and continues to do so.

Although you may drive a car with an American name, much of it was probably assembled outside of the United States. The Honda Accord is made in the United States, but the Dodge Stealth is not. Surprisingly, my Mazda 626 is officially classified as a U.S. domestic car, but my friend's Ford Crown Victoria (a "tuna clipper" of a vehicle), qualifies

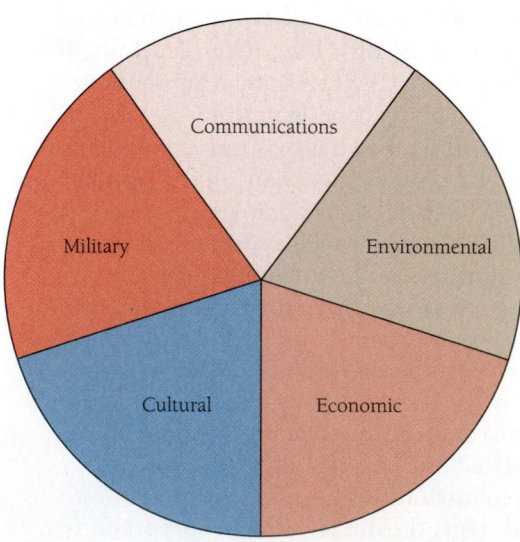

Figure 1.1
Slices of the
Globalization Pie

Case Study 1.1 Richard Leakey Lights Up the Global Economy

Exasperated over the Kenyan Wildlife Service's inability to control illegal poaching by impoverished citizens, and stung by criticism after a poacher killed an English tourist, President Daniel arap Moi turned to Richard Leakey in hopes of shaking up a corrupt and inefficient governmental wildlife department. Fully 85 percent of Kenyan elephants had already been lost to poachers and the rest were disappearing quickly.

Leakey's strategy was ambitious: he ignored the political consequences of implementing hard-nosed law enforcement, raised considerable outside money, and enlisted publicity as his ally. He succeeded in attracting $150 million to modernize the operation. He also hired and trained uncorrupted guards and employed new technologies to stay ahead of resourceful poachers. Some unfortunate poachers were killed in the process.

The impact of his next act stunned nearly everyone. Leakey gathered a pile of elephant tusks (worth millions) retrieved from poachers over the preceding year and set it ablaze while the global electronic eye chronicled every move. In this way, not only was Leakey reducing the *supply* of ivory on the world market, but he was also increasing the global *demand*. Suddenly quite unfashionable, the *price of ivory plunged* from $100 per pound to $3 per pound within days. If the story ends there, Leakey wins; case closed.

The next act in this drama on the world stage, however, features sobering reality checks for idealistic conservationists. For any reformer, succeeding where others have failed can breed a resentful backlash. In Leakey's case, high political officials were made to look bad, mid-level bureaucrats lost lucrative kickbacks, and many poachers were either dead or languishing in jail. Those who had fattened their lifestyles via the illegal ivory trade learned the meaning of downsizing the hard way.

But public fortunes can change quickly. In 1993, the Kenyan Wildlife Service was thrown into total disarray. Why? Because in very mysterious circumstances, Leakey's small plane crashed in the bush. Disgruntled poachers were suspected of sabotage, but those charges were never proven. Although he survived, Leakey lost his lower legs to amputation. He now walks using prosthetic devices from the knee down. Meanwhile, under severe attack from his political opponents, President Moi ceased backing his Director of Wildlife Services, and Richard Leakey resigned his post in 1994.

In 1999, I was preparing to host Richard Leakey when he visited our college to present a lecture. Three days before his arrival, I was surprised to learn that Leakey was asked to return to his post as Director of Kenyan Wildlife Services, and he had accepted. After I met him, such determination became more explicable because he is an intensely committed individual. After our lecture, he was flying to Washington in quest of funding from the World Bank and then on to Texas where he was to receive the Environmental Leadership Award. ■

---

as a foreign car. The American Automotive Labeling Act of 1994 defines an American car as one with 75 percent of its parts made in the United States.

Case Study 1.1 demonstrates how rapidly economic forces reverberate in the shrinking age of globalization. It involves Richard Leakey. As the son of Louis and Mary Leakey, Richard grew up in the first family of fossil hunters. Born and raised in Kenya, Richard contributed to many expeditions that piled up evidence that humans originated in Africa. But his ardent support for environmental conservation led to some extraordinary experiences in his life.

Environmental Globalization

A favorite phrase used by environmentalists is that "We all live downwind." Indeed, pollution and other consequences of industrialization respect no national boundaries, requiring us to care about what happens elsewhere on this global ecosphere. Economists typically write about record-breaking growth in global commerce during the past few decades. Yet environmental scientists counter these observations by identifying some of the costs. One is rapid deforestation, which has paralleled increased trade in the late twentieth century, as indicated in Figure 1.2.

Although studied less than deforestation, another issue gaining scholarly attention is global biodiversity, which is threatened by an increasing rate of species extinction. For example, one recent study claims that the current loss of living species represents the largest mass extinction since the dinosaurs disappeared 75 million years ago.[21]

Referred to as the sixth mass extinction, the current one differs from all others in that it results primarily from human activity. Its predecessors are called the Big Five, and

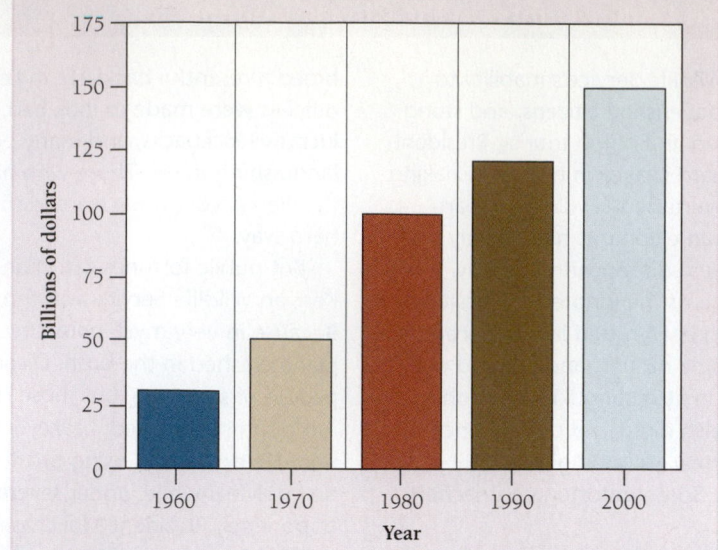

Figure 1.2
Global Trade in Forest Products, 1960–2000

Source: U.N. Food and Agricultural Administration, *FAOSTAT: Statistics Database,* http://www.apps.fao.org, October, 1999.

they certainly were big in their consequences because "during these biotic crises at least 65 percent of all species became extinct in a brief geological instant."[22] Hilary French argues that "globalization is a powerful driving force behind this biological implosion," and she bemoans the indifference of the global economy: "The new rules of the global economy pay little heed to the importance of reversing the biological impoverishment of the planet."[23]

Another example of a shrinking ecosphere is what scientists call invasive species, or "weed species" inadvertently transported into new habitats. Ships routinely suck up water for ballast in one port, and then release it in another one across the globe. Fully 40,000 tons of water per minute get dumped in U.S. ports alone. In 1988, a thumbnail-sized mollusk called the zebra mussel was taken in by a ship in the Black Sea, and then later expelled in Lake Erie, where the species had not existed previously. These few thumbnail-sized mollusks have since proliferated into billions. Scientific measurements have found as many as 60,000 zebra mussels in a square foot at the bottom of the Great Lakes. They plug up water intakes and clog canals, and it costs $30 million per year merely to monitor them. Hawaii leads all others in the United States in endangered species because of the large number of invasive species that decimate indigenous species that had developed in an isolated setting.

Globalization leads to invasive species such as zebra mussels, pests that now plug up water intakes across America's Great Lakes.

Communications Globalization

Global communications scholar Howard Frederick claims that no other species on earth is as communicative as ours, leading him to label humans as "compulsive communicators." This quality enables ideas to move about, "crashing into one another, and causing social earthquakes and revolutionary eruptions." The United States is the most communicative country, and roughly half of workers here work in information processing. Globally, information and communications are responsible for 10 percent of the total amount of goods and services produced each year.[24]

In a world of wall-to-wall communication, Frederick says that world public opinion has emerged as a meaningful force to be reckoned with by states and MNCs. This includes individual citizens. In 2006, CNN ran a special report on political dissidents in North Korea who risked their lives by criticizing the autocratic Communist regime of Kim Jong-il, even calling for his overthrow. Some of these activists became emboldened after family members died of starvation in a country where this occurred frequently. They bribed border guards to let them smuggle videos filmed in the North into China, as well as videos about the outside world into North Korea. The other vital technology aiding the dissidents includes illegal cell phones, which have expanded communications with the outside exponentially. In the nineteenth and twentieth centuries, repressive regimes held most of the resources when it came to official propaganda, as well as a monopoly of information to squelch dissidents. In this century, however, many new resources now empower individual dissidents.

In 1980, fewer than 2 million computers existed in the world, and nearly all of them were mainframes. By 1995, 150 million computers had come into use, and more than nine-tenths of them were personal computers. Not only were there many more computers around, but also companies such as Andrew Grove's Intel were churning out far more powerful ones, and at lower cost. This new computer hardware needed smart software programs to tell it what to do. Enter Bill Gates. By the mid-nineties, his prototypical software company, Microsoft, had made Gates the richest person in the world. A decade later, his philanthropic foundation led all others in assistance ($60 billion) targeted for world poverty; Gates' $30 billion was matched by an equal amount donated by Warren Buffett, who praised the work of the Gates Foundation as unique.

The Internet was developed in the late 1960s at the initiative of the U.S. Department of Defense. Its intent was to enable scientists and engineers working on military contracts to share computers, resources, and ideas via e-mail—then a new way to send messages electronically. Designed to survive a nuclear war, information was transmitted in small packages through different routes to discourage eavesdropping on these top-secret messages.

The popularity of the Internet spread slowly through the academic world, which became its main user by the mid-1980s. Two innovations then revolutionized the Internet by making it more user-friendly, thus propelling its appeal beyond the halls of academe. One was the invention by Swiss software engineer Tim Berners-Lee of the World Wide Web and hypertext to link documents with one another. The other discovery was a software program known as Mosaic (written by Illinois university undergraduate Marc Andreessen), which provided user-friendly access to the Web and the Internet. By 1994, commercial companies had surpassed universities as the leading users of the Internet.

However, while rapid communication has empowered the average person with personal computers, laptops, and cell phones, troubling trends exist in the form of merger mania among communications titans, producing what Howard Frederick calls "lords of the global village." The frenzy of media mergers includes both hardware and software, the medium and the message, respectively. Media analyst Ben Bagdikian describes the characteristics of this trend toward conglomeration; he also worries about the reduction of mass media corporations from forty-six in 1981 to twenty-three in 1991, with the number dwindling since then to six giants dominating the world's lifeblood of communication: radio and television outlets, newspapers, books, entertainment venues, and magazines.[25]

Can this trend augur well for commercial competition, which is the backbone of capitalism? What happens to the free flow of ideas when Viacom, Time Warner, Turner

Broadcasting, and Capital Cities/ABC control the bulk of the infotainment industries? What are the implications for democratic government and civil society when media moguls such as Robert Maxwell and Rupert Murdoch own not hundreds, but thousands of avenues to communicate their particular view of the world?

Examples consist of coverage of both the 1991 Persian Gulf War (Operation Desert Storm) and the 2003 Iraqi War (Operation Iraqi Freedom). The rapidly disappearing line between hard news and flashy infotainment enabled by ever-expanding technological wizardry on the battlefield and in the newsroom worries many sober observers. In both situations, viewers saw top military brass explain the game plan on the chalk board, followed by stunning visual images of sophisticated campaigns surgically executed on the ground. In 2003, the problem was exacerbated by the practice of "embedding" journalists with troops. The highly selective imagery and selective information in hindsight proved in many cases misleading. Critical thinking skills seemed absent from public discourse in those cases.

Both of these realities affect the analysis of current events commentators everywhere. Accounts of the war were well orchestrated by the U.S. government. The information monopoly forged by the U.S. military in 1991, and expanded in 2003, bears considerable risks for proscribing free expression, a core value that America espouses at home and abroad.[26] In a book and also a documentary film called *Weapons of Mass Deception,* media critic Danny Schechter dissects systematically falsehoods being carried by American mass media during the crucial prelude to the 2003 Iraqi War.

Military Globalization

Comprehending the rapid-fire changes that have globalized economics, ecology, and communications has been difficult enough. But the tragic events of September 11, 2001, underscored something that few American citizens, scholars, or policy-makers had understood: the globalization of military affairs is even more palpable than other types of globalization, especially in the form of **terrorism.**

As the sole superpower militarily, economically, and culturally, the United States probably benefits more from globalization than any other state. But this status also makes America the prime target for something that Tom Friedman warned about earlier in his 1999 book: "The greatest danger that the U.S. faces today is from Super-empowered individuals who hate Americans more than ever because of globalization, and who can do something about it on their own, more than ever, thanks to globalization."[27]

Humans are symbol-making beings for whom images resonate more than do statistics or concepts. Part of the reason that the well-orchestrated terrorist attack executed on September 11, 2001, shook the American psyche so deeply derives from the symbolic meaning associated with the respective targets. The World Trade center symbolizes America's economic power, the Pentagon symbolizes America's military power, and the intended attack on the White House symbolizes America's political power. If Hollywood resided on the East Coast rather than the West Coast, it might have been targeted as a symbol of American cultural power. Ironically, while the World Trade Center symbolized American capitalism, among its casualties were citizens from eighty other countries, underscoring globalization's pervasiveness.

Terrorism replaced Communism as an internecine threat to Western civilization. For a decade after the Cold War ended, the United States lacked a clear vision of its global mission; according to the Bush administration, that all changed on September 11, 2001.

Heading the list of global military threats is the nuclear dilemma. The creation of nuclear weapons represents a dilemma because even if we dismantle them all, we are stuck with the knowledge of how to make them. Yet, because none has been used in warfare since the United States dropped atomic weapons on Hiroshima and Nagasaki (leading to Japan's surrender ending World War II), a type of psychological firebreak—a taboo—has appeared: the more time that passes, the greater the international pressure on states to *not* use them.

The long nuclear stand-off between the United States and the Soviet Union did not represent an elegant way to deter their use, but it worked, largely because each side considered the other rational enough to avoid mutual suicide. But such confidence in the rationality of modern actors, states and nonstates alike, seems more dubious. Therefore, both the Clinton and Bush administrations placed great emphasis on efforts to prevent the proliferation of nuclear powers beyond the current number of eight states.

The contemporary agenda regarding military globalization, however, goes way beyond loose nukes. This includes other weapons of mass destruction (WMD), what some analysts call poor man's nukes, namely chemical and biological weapons. It also includes new missile technologies to deliver WMD.

Cheaper to make, easier to build and transport, and far less visible, chemical and biological weapons exacerbate the difficulties in coping with the realities of military globalization these days. Robert Joseph, Director of the Center for Counter-Proliferation Research at the National Defense University, warns that "The prospect of using chemical and biological weapons is increasing, in part because the barriers to both possession and use of these weapons have been substantially undermined in recent years."[28]

Cultural Globalization

Possibly less apparent to the casual observer is the reality of cultural globalization. Culture reflects a lifestyle, or learned way of living. In recent decades, a shared type of popular culture has seeped into even the remotest corners of the world. This newly globalized popular culture is labeled "made in the USA." From Hollywood films, to television programs, to fast foods, to MTV music, to clothing styles, to the values of consumerism, cultural globalization has a decidedly American flavor. The resources available to Warner Brothers movies, Coca-Cola products, Guess jeans, or Shakira CDs possess the economies of scale to overwhelm the markets of smaller countries.

Some critics refer to this imbalance as American **cultural imperialism.** Not surprisingly, poor Southern Hemisphere nations feel overwhelmed by the volume and slick salesmanship behind the products of American popular culture. A book called *The Ugly American* generated much attention in the 1960s as U.S. citizens traveling abroad developed a reputation for loud, arrogant, insensitive behavior. The book remains in print and continues to sell copies.[29] Some areas of Islamic culture, in particular, chafe at the decadence they perceive in the United States.

Cultural imperialism ■ An aggressive practice whereby one group attempts to impose its particular value system on other group

But even in affluent Western countries such as France, intense criticism of U.S. cultural imperialism has reached fever pitch at times. For example, the French film industry has a long, proud history of creating critically acclaimed pictures. But both the French people and their government have decried the marketing barrage pushing Hollywood's big-budget action movies that cost ten to twenty times more than French films to make.

Sociologist George Ritzer, in his provocative book, *The McDonaldization of Society,* describes the standardized and homogenized commercialization of U.S. popular culture as lowering the level of sophistication wherever its long tentacles reach.[30] The origins of this superficiality represent no mystery to journalist David Rieff. He considers America unusually "ahistorical," meaning two things: (1) the United States has relatively little historical depth when compared with older cultures; and (2) what history the United States does have is largely ignored by Americans who are more future-oriented than past-oriented. But Rieff feels that although America's "rootless character" limits its maturity in some ways, it also fits comfortably with the current global condition of change, change, change—in ways that elude more historically grounded cultures such

Mega-companies such as Nike now create more than mere products; they have become "meaning brokers" who impart social identity upon their buyers.

as Japan, China, Russia, or Brazil. The major contribution of the United States to the twentieth century, says Rieff, was the pervasiveness of a popular culture that he refers to as the "dream-scape," characterized by an "easy blending of reality and fantasy."[31]

Speaking of potent imagery, a book by Canadian journalist Naomi Klein, *No Logo*, blends seamlessly with David Rieff's writings. Klein contends that a U.S.-based explosion, in both the wealth and cultural influence of global corporations since the mid-1980s, stemmed from a little-noticed novel strategy employed by management theorists: "The belief that successful corporations must primarily produce *brands*, as opposed to products." Klein argues that a marketing renaissance resulted from adopting this mantra of "brands, not products!"

For the first time, companies saw themselves as "meaning brokers" instead of product producers. In this new branded world, labels such as Nike, Benetton, Starbucks, and Levi's were elevated to the status of lifestyle, and thus of culture. Nike so succeeded in turning Michael Jordan into a brand that his agent adopted the slogan of "superbrand" to describe his client, replacing the superstar moniker that had been commonplace before.[32]

Blessing or Curse?

Globalization produces increasingly high-stakes winners and losers, as reflected in a widening of the wealth gap, both within the United States and between the world's Northern and Southern Hemispheres. The rich are indeed getting richer, and the poor are indeed getting poorer. The relevant data suggest that these trends are consistent and compelling. Globalization is a major contributor to this phenomenon. Therefore, it comes as no surprise that some analysts love globalization while others hate it.

Globalization's Critics

Harvard political economist Dani Rodrik observes that globalization's detractors consist of a wide amalgam of "strange bedfellows" such as labor unions hoping to protect blue-collar jobs, environmentalists wanting to protect ecological integrity, pensioners desiring to protect fixed incomes, and economic nationalists looking to protect challenged domestic industries. Rodrik suggests that the cement holding such diverse interests together is opposition to unsolicited change: "backlash against having to alter traditional practices results from pressures for change that are tangible and affect all societies."[33]

Journalist Tom Friedman sees homogenization unsympathetic to local lifestyles as a better explanation for the backlash against globalization than resistance to change. "What all the backlash forces have in common is a feeling that as their countries have plugged into the globalization system, they are being forced into a Golden Straightjacket

Activist Juliette Beck engaging in the type of media-savvy behavior for which Global Exchange is famous.

that is one-size-fits-all."[34] A leader of the communitarian movement, American sociologist Amitai Etzioni, argues that an overemphasis on individualism in U.S. society contributes to a selfish obsession with accumulating wealth. Etzioni stresses the need for nurturing a countervailing sense of moral and civic virtue, values that he considers endangered by globalization's competitive agenda. He reformulates the golden rule to "respect and uphold society's moral order as you would have society respect and uphold your autonomy."[35]

A similar craving for social justice appears in the writings of Jeremy Brecher, who fuses academic analysis of globalization with grass-roots activism. He says that what has been sold under the guise of globalization is merely "globalization from *above*," as created by powerful elites. Brecher believes that the growing inequities of this type of globalization have provoked a significant resistance movement, with an alternative vision of "globalization from *below*," directed by citizen activists because "even when governments around the world are dominated by corporate interests, the world's people can act to put together their common interests."[36]

One young person who personifies Brecher's notion of globalization from below is Juliette Beck, daughter of a surgeon who went to Berkeley as a pre-med student but then changed to environmental science and graduated with honors. After working briefly in the private sector as an environmental engineer, she moved to Global Exchange, a San Francisco human rights NGO. She commented that "We feel like capitalism and buying things are just not fulfilling. Period." Beck became known to the media because of the vital role she played in organizing the 1999 Seattle protests against the World Trade Organization (WTO). She and her fellow critics argue that the international trade rules are grossly unfair and that kicking up a fuss can aid globalization's losers in changing things.[37]

The 1999 Seattle mass protests began a steady process that has persisted in the intervening years. Prague, Czech Republic, was the site of protests against the World Bank and IMF in 2000. Also in 2000, Washington, DC, witnessed protests involving about 20,000 people. Five years later, a crowd one-tenth that size resulted in 649 arrests by DC police. The four main demands involving the World Bank were to open its board meetings to the media, cancel debt of impoverished countries, end environmentally destructive projects, and cease imposing harmful economic conditions for borrowing on countries.[38] Quite violent protests against the WTO took place in Cancún, Mexico, during 2003. In 2006, similar protests targeted the WTO in Hong Kong, China, where around 10,000 gathered at the site of a WTO summit meeting.[39]

The World Development Movement released a report in 2000 suggesting that Seattle-like protests in rich countries garner media attention, but these merely represent the tip of the iceberg. "In the global south, a far deeper and wide-ranging movement has been developing for years, largely ignored by the media." Their report included at least fifty episodes of civil unrest directed at the IMF during the ten-month period following 1999's Seattle protests against the WTO. Ten people were killed and more than 300 were injured in these overlooked protests involving over a million people in thirteen poor countries such as Argentina, Ecuador, Brazil, and Zambia. The report claims to reveal the truly global scale of resistance to these powerful institutions.[40]

The International Labor Organization (ILO) created a commission in 2003 to examine fully the social dimensions of globalization. Its charge was to look at globalization from the perspective of the individual people whom it affects, shifting from the "narrow preoccupation with markets to a broader preoccupation with people." The ILO document, "A Fair Globalization: Creating Opportunities for All," runs more than 200 pages. It concluded that most of the problems stem not from globalization itself but rather from deficiencies in its governance. For example, "These rules and policies are the outcome of a system of global governance largely shaped by powerful countries and powerful players. There is a serious democratic deficit at the heart of the system." The ILO recommends socially responsible globalization based on "universal shared values, respect for human rights and individual dignity; one that is fair, inclusive, democratic with benefits for all." Nine interrelated objectives are advanced:

- Focus on people
- Effective democratic states
- Sustainable development
- Productive, equitable markets
- Fair rules
- Global solidarity
- Accountability
- Partnerships
- Effective United Nations[41]

Supporters of Globalization

Describing the "establishment" as supportive of globalization has much merit. Whenever economic globalization issues have been raised publicly in the United States, proponents have included the president, all living ex-presidents, a majority of Congress, business and corporate interests, a consensus among academic and public service economists, the military, most think tanks, and major research universities. Once largely a Republican Party platform in the United States, Democrat Bill Clinton reshaped that traditional landscape by pushing for the cause of economic globalization throughout the 1990s. Dani Rodrik notes that when business executives or government officials are asked why such changes are necessary, the same refrain is heard repeatedly: "We need to remain (or become) competitive in a global economy."[42]

One of the most enthusiastic and influential supporters has been economist Jeffrey Sachs, whose 2005 book, *An End to Poverty,* serves as the analytical framework for the conclusion to Chapter 15 here. Although the debate most often swirls around economic globalization, proponents have also praised other benefits. Globalization and falling telecommunications costs have proceeded hand-in-hand because both were built upon microchips, satellites, and the Internet. Companies may split up into components around the world, but they remain coherent cyber-businesses via teleconferencing and e-mail, thus communicating well in spite of great distances.

Tom Friedman rivals Jeffrey Sachs for his enthusiasm as to globalization's potential benefits. He points out that globalization also allows important services—such as medical, legal, entertainment, or software services—to be traded freely and efficiently in ways impossible before. Possibly the most revolutionary aspect of globalization is its *democratizing effect:* it levels many playing fields by empowering resourceful grass-roots individuals. Not only do governments and businesses benefit by "reaching farther, faster, cheaper, and deeper around the world than ever before"; many individuals likewise benefit from computers and cell phones.[43]

Other observers develop a similar theme in arguing that global communication has humanized interaction, creating a global cyber-community. The International Food Policy Research Institute contends that information/communication technologies are being harnessed in developing countries to spur efficiency and productivity. They cite the case of an Indian research center installing a computer in a village "information shop" (financed by a Canadian NGO) in the fishing village Veerampattinam, India. Before this, "locals went fishing without knowing sea conditions or the location of fish shoals. Lives were sometimes lost because of high waves and rough seas." With their new resources, "fishers now ply the seas with greater safety and efficiency." The Institute emphasizes that Veerampattinam typifies numerous examples of the Internet assisting poor people.[44]

Diverse Sets of Global Issues (GIs)

Building on the definitions of *foreign, international,* and *global* cited earlier in this chapter, note that foreign issues relate to events within other countries; international issues involve interaction between two or more countries; and global issues (GIs) potentially affect not merely countries or regions—but the world as a whole. As all of the types of globalization described previously become pervasive, the number of GIs expands accordingly because controversial issues tend to accompany public policy dilemmas. However, all GIs are not created equal.

Four of these fall under the rubric of ecological GIs: environment, population, food, and energy. Called ecological because they are interrelated aspects of humanity's relationship to the earth, these are discussed in Chapters 4 and 5. Next we examine several GIs labeled highly visible, followed by several GIs tagged as less visible. Many other GIs worthy of scholarly attention exist. Because we live in a rapidly changing world, the lineup of salient GIs is subject to change.

Ecological GIs

The concept that undergirds all of the ecological GIs is **sustainability.** The limited, or finite, nature of natural resources is a reality that humans have not easily accepted. The expansion model of progress inherent in Western civilization has traditionally promoted the unexamined assumption that "bigger is better." The contrary belief that "small is beautiful" has found itself swimming upstream throughout modern history.

Sustainability ■ Replaceability and conservation concerning the husbanding of natural resources via a lifestyle that responsibly precludes their depletion

Especially in large continental countries such as America, Russia, China, and Brazil, human stewardship over the land has proven quite wasteful. Michael H. Glantz, Director of the National Center for Atmospheric Research, warns that wanton depletion of air, land, and sea resources by ever-expanding human demands is fraught with risks and that the public must learn to see these resources as part of the "global commons," rather than the property of individual countries.[45]

This chapter identifies Websites for a variety of organizations promoting responsible ecological husbandry. For example, the Washington nonpartisan think tank called Resources for the Future (RFF) has been researching resource-depletion problems and leading public discussion for half a century. Friends of the Earth, an NGO based in Great Britain, engages in activist campaigns aimed at responsible resource use. The National Geographic Society is another NGO with sustainability on its agenda, although its role is more educational and less activist than Friends of the Earth.

The largest global body devoted to sustainability, however, is the United Nations Environmental Programme (UNEP), aimed specifically at this question. Websites for all of these organizations provide vast information promoting sustainability, as does the University of Toronto's Sustainability Archive listed among Internet resources at the end of this chapter.

ENVIRONMENT Human awareness that pollution does not respect national borders continues to increase. More and more people understand that the earth consists of one organic ecosystem. Some are sufficiently enlightened to sense that our generation has not inherited the earth from our parents, but rather, borrowed it from our children. And while sustainability is now on the lips of most key global actors, how we can best pursue such lofty goals is far from clear. Responsible spokespersons for diverse stakeholders disagree over implementing sustainable human existence on the planet.

Also quite vexing is the fact that powerful commercial forces have a vested interest in slowing the momentum of environmental protection. The authors of *Green Planet Blues* note that "American-style consumerism translates wants into needs as it spreads through sophisticated advertising and pop culture."[46] They also suggest that technology is another culprit conspiring against a green mentality superceding economic selfishness. Explosion of the world's population to more than six and one-half billion people similarly places pressure on the sufficiency of resources and the sustainability of contemporary society.

What makes environmentalism a GI is that diverse voices can be heard expressing predictably distinctive agendas, for example, the rich North versus the poor South; business groups versus citizen groups (such as the Sierra Club); car cultures (such as the U.S. and Canada) versus public transport cultures (such as Japan and Europe); scientists versus public policy makers; rural versus urban interests; proponents of renewable energy sources (such as wind and solar) versus petroleum companies; and members of the power establishment versus those wanting to upset the political applecart.

It is well known that humanity is leaving an increasingly large imprint in the ecological sand. However, no consensus exists over whether these impacts are permanent, irreversible, or excessively damaging to quality of life for future generations. Does the current rate of biodiversity loss represent a crisis for the ecosphere? Is global warming sufficient to regulate the emission of greenhouse gases? Has over-fishing by commercial fleets depleted fish stocks enough to ban fishing for certain species? Is the question of tropical rainforest destruction the responsibility of countries that possess these ecosystems, or do they represent resources of the global commons?

One fundamental question that has not been addressed sufficiently asks: exactly what is the environment *worth* to us? Because we live in a world more commercially driven than ever before, an interdisciplinary group of thirteen researchers in 1997 provided the first systematic price tag on a series of "ecological functions." Included among these services were things like flood control, pollination, genetic resources, water supply, and erosion control. The hefty annual contribution of "nature's services" was estimated at $33 trillion.[47]

POPULATION If the GIs of population and environment were any closer to each other, they would have to be Siamese twins. Their overlap is epitomized by the problem of rapid species extinction. Harvard environmental ethicist Timothy Weiskel contends that life as we know it is undergoing a massive extinction, and that unlike the previous five mass extinctions, the current one is the direct result of human activity. Technological expansion during the industrial revolution has fueled unprecedented population growth, as human civilization has devastated its environment, taking thousands of species with it. "Apparently, the right to life is defined as the right to *human* life."[48]

Since the 1960s governments, NGOs, and IGOs have funded programs aimed at slowing the rate of population growth where it is most problematic: in poor countries. Programs in places like China have succeeded while those in places such as India have failed. Paradoxically, whereas global fertility rates have dropped from 5.7 per woman in the 1960s to 2.3 per woman today, overall world population continues to grow.[49]

In fact, since 1960, world population has doubled to its current six-plus billion. The Population Council's John Bongaarts identifies three key factors for this rate of growth: (1) unmet demand for family planning in developing countries; (2) continued desire for large families by couples in developing countries; and (3) built-up population momentum: the next reproductive generation (those entering puberty or younger) is far larger than the current reproductive generation.

What governments do or fail to do matters, as the differences between Pakistan and Bangladesh attest. In 1971, both of these South Asian neighbors shown in Figure 1.3 had 66 million people, growth rates of 3 per cent annually, and were poor, rural, and Muslim

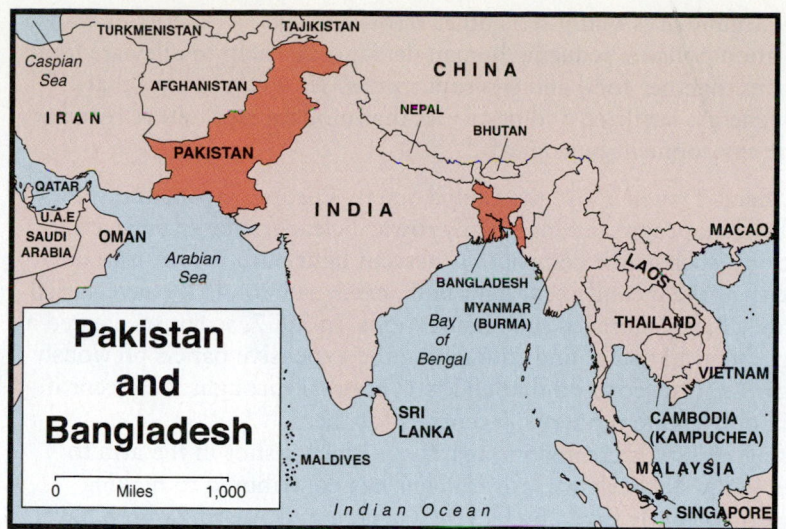

Figure 1.3

Pakistan and Bangladesh: Where did family planning fail and where it did it succeed?

Source: From Maps On File™ by Facts On File, Inc. Copyright © by Facts On File, Inc. Reprinted by permission of Facts On File, Inc.

societies. But today, Pakistan has over 20 million more citizens than its neighbor. Why? Because the Bangladesh government prioritized family planning programs while its counterpart in Pakistan did not do so.[50]

Nevertheless, scholars and policy makers differ concerning whether world population growth is out of control. Author Michael Tobias believes that decades of effort to control population have proven insufficient, yielding unprecedented environmental damage that will only increase in the future.[51] However, the Hudson Institute's Max Singer contends that as more countries achieve the benefits of modernity, the world's population will be declining in fifty years' time.[52]

FOOD Some basic facts raise concerns about food production. Worldwide grain production peaked in 1984, and the rate of increase has gradually slowed since then. Although harvests have continued to rise, they have failed to keep pace with population growth, and thus per person grain production has fallen 6 percent since 1984. By the late 1990s, it appeared that "the half century dominated by food surpluses may be coming to an end."[53] Equally troubling facts relate to the scarcity of productive new land for farming and the scarcity of water for irrigation. The vital dietary change that has occurred in the past five decades is the demand for animal protein. Livestock in the United States eat more grain each year than three-quarters of the world's people.[54]

As GIs go, few generate the consensus considering extreme hunger a scourge against humanity to be eradicated. However, a chorus of dissent arises as soon as scholars address the most basic question concerning food as a GI: what *causes* hunger?

Former World Bank Director Robert McNamara argues that overpopulation causes hunger. But the World Watch Institute's Lester Brown counters that environmental degradation erodes agricultural productivity, which results in hunger. The policies of rich northern countries cause hunger in Africa, according to John Prendergast, a researcher for a Catholic Relief organization. He attributes much hunger to the past policies of European colonialists and the continuation of unfair rules governing the international economy. Disparities in consumption patterns between the north and the south exacerbate the maldistribution of food.

Brown University's Robert Kates suggests that war is the chief cause of hunger today, and he proposes that new rules for humanitarian intervention in poor countries should be developed.[55] Activist Thomas Fenton feels that the huge corporations that dominate agribusiness these days control every facet of the production and distribution of food and that they must concern themselves with more than merely the bottom line.[56]

Almost invariably, writings about food as a GI focus on the question of increasing the *supply* to reduce food scarcity. However, economist Edward Bender notes that the other key concept of economics—*demand*—should be factored into the debate more prominently. His main argument is that just as other resources, such as energy or water, require sound conservation policies, reducing human demand can help to alleviate food shortages. Bender weaves together food and environment as GIs when he says that "intensive use of land, energy, fertilizer, and pesticides that modern agriculture requires places the health of the environment in jeopardy."[57]

ENERGY Since the first Earth Day in 1970, the United States, Europe, Japan, and some other areas of the globe have progressed marginally toward cleaner energy production and use. Novel inventions, such as the compact fluorescent light bulb, which uses only one-fourth the electricity of the incandescent light bulb, exist, but countries have varied widely as to whether they have embraced such innovations. In 2007, scientists created a new form of paint-like chemical compound eliminating the expensive panels previously needed for solar energy. Analysts contend that all kinds of breakthroughs will occur if more governments will only create economic incentives for them.

Former German Energy Minister Hermann Scheer was a visionary public official committed to a sustainable energy future wherein the public good supercedes the profits of special interest groups.

Photovoltaic roofing materials created in Japan have given a shot in the arm to solar energy use there. In the Netherlands, government has contributed to making one-third of all transport currently taken by bicycle. Canada and Australia both have sophisticated green plans identifying best practices targeted for adoption there. The former German Energy Minister, Hermann Scheer, who now heads an NGO called Eurosolar, writes in his book, *A Solar Manifesto,* that the stranglehold of corporate and governmental vested interests must be broken for the global public good. In America, however, no significant governmental incentives or rewards for sustainable energy had been established as of 2007.

As early as 1997, at least one global oil company seemed to be getting religion about some of the many renewable energy sources cited by Minister Scheer. In that year, British Petroleum (BP) invested $1 billion in wind and solar energy development and has expanded this investment substantially under the leadership of CEO John Brown.[58] In 2006, BP Solar featured a sophisticated Website providing scientific information, consultation services for prospective customers, and overall prices for solar panels and solar tiles lower than the competition.[59] Other MNCs have followed the BP lead in this regard.

No previous American administration, however, has ever been as directly tied to the oil industry as were Bush and Cheney, and after their election, they were able to forestall challenges to the fossil fuel fixation by repeating the mantra that the science was unclear about global warming.

Although some pockets of progress toward more enlightened energy policies outside of America can be identified, energy analyst Robert Fisher believes that with fossil fuels (oil, gas, coal) still dominating 90 percent of the global energy pie, humanity's lifestyle choices fail to match up with our expressed public concerns about a sustainable environment. He writes that "Changing our fuel sources requires changing our values, but it's happened before."[60] One thing that will need to change is the disparity between energy consumption in the Northern Hemisphere and energy consumption in the Southern Hemisphere. "The industrial north is glutted with energy, using seven times as much per person as the south consumes." This deprives the south of the cheap fuel it needs to lift itself from perpetual poverty.[61]

Evidence also continues to pile up regarding global warming, which a scientific consensus believes stems from increased burning of fossil fuels. Record keeping for temperatures began in 1866, but startlingly, by the late 1990s, the fourteen warmest years on record had all occurred after 1979. The footprints of global warming can also be inferred from melting icecaps in the Andes mountains, shrinking glaciers in the Alps, and reduced sea ice around Antarctica.[62] When Al Gore's documentary film about global warming, *An Inconvenient Truth,* won both an Oscar and a Nobel Peace Prize, public opinion seemed finally to be catching up with scholarly opinion about fossil fuels and global warming.

Highly Visible GIs

PROLIFERATION: WEAPONS OF MASS DESTRUCTION (WMD) PLUS MISSILES Contemporary use of the term weapons of mass destruction (WMD) speaks to concerns about the proliferation of nuclear weapons, chemical/biological weapons, and new missile technologies capable of delivering all of these. Starting in 1945, a nuclear dilemma arose concerning two intractable problems: 1) even if we were to destroy all nuclear weapons, we can never unlearn the science and technology required to build them; 2) the Cold War may be over, but the risk of nuclear attack is not. North Americans may not fear Russia lobbing intercontinental missiles at us, but loose WMD could end up in the hands of less responsible caretakers, for instance, unpredictable states such as Iran or North Korea, or terrorist groups such as Al Qaeda.

The globalized military threat concerning WMD is known as the **proliferation problem.** Eight countries currently possess nuclear weapons: the five members of the Security Council (China, France, Russia, United Kingdom, United States), as well as three open secrets (India, Israel, Pakistan). South Africa dismantled its arsenal in 1993, while both the status and intentions of Iran, and North Korea remain unclear. WMD proliferation efforts seek to halt the spread of nukes.

It is also possible for states to purchase WMD on the global black market. Former CIA director William Colby has commented that "It's a bloody miracle that one of these eggs [nukes] has not gotten loose."[63] The U.N. has gone to great lengths to prevent other states from obtaining nukes, including the 1995 extension of the Nuclear Non-Proliferation Treaty (NNPT) whereby nuclear states pledge not to give them to nonnuclear states, and nonnuclear states pledge not to build them.

A book released in 2005 by the Strategic Studies Institute emphasizes that biological weapons constitute a major security concern, spurred by diverse events. The U.S. government suggested in an official 1990 report that such programs represented a growing trend among both states and terrorist groups. In 1995, the U.N. corroborated Iraq's covert biological program; in the same year, the Japanese Aum Shinrikyo group unleashed a nerve gas attack in Tokyo's subway; shortly after 9/11, professionally prepared anthrax spores were easily distributed via the U.S. mail system; and in 2002, evidence was discovered in Afghanistan that pointed to serious efforts in this area by Al Qaeda. Between that date and 2005, $30 billion was appropriated to counter such ventures.[64]

The Center for Nonproliferation Studies maintains an impressive Website that provides extensive information regarding efforts to counter chemical/biological weapons.[65] The Federation of American Scientists contends that the "qualitative and quantitative impact" of biological agents has grown significantly in recent decades. Improved means of production create more virulent strains of organisms, and genetic modification of nonpathogenic organisms to pathogenic strains contribute to lethality. "Thus, as much as one hundred times more pathogen or toxin could be produced per cell than with naturally occurring strains."[66]

So who are some of the countries with such weapons? The Arms Control Association's "Briefing Paper on the Status of Biological Weapons Nonproliferation" identifies fifteen countries possessing or developing either biologicals or bio-defense programs. The 2006 status of seven such states is summarized in Table 1.2.

Table 1.2

GLOBAL BIOLOGICAL WEAPONS CAPABILITIES (BWC)

State	Capability
China	May have infrastructure remaining from pre-BWC program
India	Biodefense research; infrastructure for R&D pathogens
Iran	Likely has produced and weaponized limited capability
DPRK	Developed, produced, and weaponized biological agents
Pakistan	Ability to support limited weapons R&D effort
Russia	Acknowledged many illegal weaponized agents in 1992; defensive program now; unconfirmed reports of cheating
United States	1969 unilaterally gave up program; current R&D of biodefense

Source: Arms Control Association, "Briefing Paper on the Status of Biological Weapons Nonproliferation": http://www.armscontrol.org/factsheets/bwissuebrief.asp.

America monopolized atomic weapons when it leveled Hiroshima in 1945.

The Biological Weapons Convention (BWC) outlaws germ weapons and forms the basis for all nonproliferation endeavors in this area. All seven of the countries profiled in the preceding table have acceded to the BWC. Among others, Israel and Sudan have neither signed nor ratified the BWC, whereas Egypt and Syria have signed it but failed to ratify, and Taiwan has pledged to adhere to its conditions.

It took the United States four years to build the first atomic weapon during World War II, at a cost of $4 billion, for its "Manhattan Project." With a monopoly of atomic weapons at the time, America used them to end the war with Japan by dropping them on the cities of Hiroshima and Nagasaki on August 6th and 9th, 1945. But this monopoly was short-lived, as the Soviet Union exploded its first atomic bomb in 1949. Since World War II, about 30 percent of U.S. military spending has been devoted to nuclear weapons, adding up to a staggering total of more than $4 trillion.[67] Today's chief nuclear headache lies in stopping the spread of such weapons.

International efforts to dissuade other states from obtaining nuclear weapons center around the Nuclear Non-Proliferation Treaty (NNPT), which came into force in 1970 and then extended indefinitely in 1995. The NNPT prevents the nuclear "haves" from sharing their technology and raw materials with the nuclear "have-nots." The treaty also set up an Atomic Energy Agency (AEA) to conduct inspections verifying compliance by all signatories. The AEA was in and out of Iraq often in the 1990s in search of possible violations.

One potential source of loose nukes is in the former Soviet Union. Ex-CIA Director John Deutch has claimed that "Nuclear materials and technologies are more accessible now than at any other time in history—due primarily to the dissolution of the Soviet Union and that region's economic woes."[68] In hopes of preventing black market nuclear weapons escaping, the U.S. Congress allocated about $2 billion under the "Nunn-Lugar" Program to aid the former Soviet republics in dismantling and safeguarding parts of its nuclear arsenal. The measure is widely regarded among experts as successful.

Another headache for nuclear nonproliferation advocates is the "Islamic Bomb." Taken from a 1979 British documentary film of the same title, this imprecise term refers to a nuclear weapon serving the purposes of radical Islam. A few radical Muslims have suggested such a nuclear weapon would once again make Islam a force to be respected on the world stage. Consequently, one observer concludes that "Concern about the Islamic Bomb is at the heart of the intense effort to prevent the spread of nuclear weapons to Muslim countries."[69]

Growing concern over the spread of missiles to deliver WMD is traced in a 2004 Congressional Research Service report: "The primary cause for concern with missile proliferation is that missile systems can provide countries an effective vehicle for delivering nuclear, chemical, or biological weapons over long distances." They also represent status symbols for states interested in preening. The International Code of Conduct Against Ballistic Missile Proliferation operates as the chief treaty in this area. Table 1.3 identifies

Table 1.3	
MISSILES BY CATEGORIES OF RANGE	
Range	**Country**
>5,500 km	China, France, Russia, United Kingdom, United States, DPRK
3,000–5,500 km	India, Iran
1,000–3,000 km	Israel, DPRK, Saudi Arabia, China, India, Iran, Pakistan
70–1,000 km	Thirty-three countries[70]

Source: Andrew Feickert, "Missile Survey: Ballistic and Cruise Missiles of Foreign Countries," Congressional Research Service (March 2004), Order Code RL30427; received through the CRS Web.

four categories of countries by range of their missiles: ICBMs (>5,500 km); intermediate (3,000–5,500 km); medium-range (1,000–3,000 km); and short-range (70–1,000 km).

TERRORISM Adequately defining the phenomenon of **terrorism** is no simple matter. It is sometimes said that one person's terrorist is another person's freedom fighter, meaning that identifying terrorists is a very subjective process. One expert, however, specifies four elements useful in recognizing the essence of terrorism:

Terrorism ■ The indiscriminate use of violence to publicize grievances felt by powerless groups or their clandestine agents

- *Unconventional violence.* Spectacular acts designed to shock the target audience in hopes of gaining concessions.
- *Political motivation.* Ordinary criminal activity (such as the Mafia) lacks the political goals characteristic of terrorism.
- *Incidental nature of the targets.* Intended victims are only tangentially related to the aims of the terrorists and are chosen for their symbolic value.
- *Nonstate actors.* Organized terrorism tends to be the work of out-groups, or frustrated subnational entities.[71]

But a case that defied all the generalizations and conventional knowledge about terrorism is related to the 1995 attack in Oklahoma City, involving Timothy McVeigh, described in Case Study 1.2.

The U.S. State Department records reveal that during the 1980s, international terrorist events average about 500 annually, with the number peaking in 1988 at 856 incidents. Such tragedies dropped off in the 1990s with the lowest number recorded in 1998 at 273 incidents.[72] No consensus exists as to why this decrease occurred. Some observers attribute it to the end of the Cold War, which had supported clandestine activity by proxies acting on behalf of the competing superpowers. Others chalk it up to violent groups such as the IRA and the PLO rising to political respectability and renouncing the use of violence; still others think that anti-terrorist measures by target countries and by international agreements that beefed up organizations such as Interpol worked.[73]

MOBILE MICROBES AND AIDS VIRUS Many social scientists have called for expanding our notion of security beyond the Cold War fixation on national military issues. Some have written about human security, including quality of life issues such as the environment and health. Considerable new thinking has revolved about an old nemesis: mobile microbes. If WMD or environmental degradation don't wipe out our species, exposure to lethal bugs and viruses just might. Critics argue that building roads where none exist not only degrades the environment but also spreads diseases.[74]

Infectious diseases kill more people than cancer and heart disease combined; in 1993, the global loss of life amounted to 16.5 million deaths to infectious diseases.[75] At least six major bouts with lethal microbes were reported in the United States during the 1990s.[76] With the post-World War II discovery of antibiotics, it looked like bacteriological scourges such as tuberculosis, polio, diptheria, syphilis, and hepatitis had been vanquished. Not so. According to Columbia University's Dr. Harold Neu, "bacteria are cleverer than men." They have adjusted to a "world laced with antibiotics" by changes in their genetic makeup.

Case Study 1.2 Timothy McVeigh Rocks Oklahoma City

At 9:00 a.m. on Monday morning, April 19, 1995, the work week in Oklahoma City ended before it began. A massive explosion in front of the Alfred P. Murrah Building killed 168 people, physically and psychically injuring more than 500. The Alfred P. Murrah Building wasn't just *any* building, it was a federal government building. Almost overnight, the prime suspect was arrested, but unlike the 1993 World Trade Center bombing two years earlier, this was not an Islamic fundamentalist from the Middle East. Rather, he was an American Army veteran and recipient of the Bronze Star and Combat Infantry Badge for service in the Persian Gulf War. The pieces to this bizarre puzzle did not add up to a clear picture for a public looking for foreigners to blame.

Timothy McVeigh came from suburban Buffalo, New York, where he grew up in an Irish-Catholic divorced family. His teachers knew him as a computer buff and a gun aficionado. As a self-described survivalist, in his teen years, he often paraded around with bandoliers of shells, "Rambo-like." Neighbors considered him quietly introspective. After high school, he landed his first regular job as an armed guard. His favorite movie was *Red Dawn*, which he watched repeatedly.

Before long, McVeigh enlisted in the Army where he was considered an efficient and dedicated soldier. At the age of 22, he was trying out for Army Special Forces when his unit was sent in 1990 to Saudi Arabia for the Persian Gulf War. His service in the 1991 war was recognized with a Bronze Star and Combat Infantry Badge. His fellow soldiers reported that he bragged about his first kill, a rifle shot that tore off an Iraqi soldier's head at 1,000 feet. Upon returning from the war to Fort Bragg, North Carolina, he was excited about trying out for the elite Green Beret unit. However, his Saudi duty had taken its toll, and his physical conditioning was insufficient to pass the screening test.

Feeling like a failure and becoming embittered, McVeigh withdrew into himself, reading and rereading *The Turner Diaries* (1978), a novel that demonizes the U.S. government and advocates violence in pursuit of racial separation. Slowly turning to right-wing conspiracy theories, he quit the Army. When McVeigh returned home, he wrote letters to a newspaper criticizing the federal government as a threat to the Second Amendment right to bear arms. He drifted to the Midwest, where he had some Army friends.

The marker event for Timothy McVeigh's antigovernment beliefs occurred on March 19, 1993, when the FBI and ATF raided the Waco, Texas, camp of Branch Davidian religious leader David Koresh. McVeigh compared the Waco raid to China's Tiananmen Square massacre of innocents in 1989. He also said of the federal government, "when they govern by the sword, they must reckon with protest by the sword." Waco appeared to validate what had become his political Bible, William Pierce's fictional *The Turner Diaries*. And just who is this guru of right-wing extremists?[77]

Former Oregon State University physics professor William Pierce retired on 400 acres in rural West Virginia, heading an organization called the National Alliance, distributed a newsletter, wrote revolutionary fiction, and scheduled speaking engagements. Each of these activities pursued one goal: spreading his revolutionary ideas of white supremacy. His writings encourage violence against the U.S. government and against racial minorities. *The Turner Diaries* put him on the revolutionary map and made him a hero to disaffected people like Timothy McVeigh. The 1995 bombing in Oklahoma City is a carbon copy of a truck bombing of FBI headquarters on page 31 of Pierce's book. Another passage in the *Diaries* observes "There is no way we can destroy the system without many thousands of people dying."[78]

Compounding the return of these bacteriological enemies is the appearance of new viral threats such as the AIDS virus, Ebola virus, and Hanta virus. Viruses are the simplest of living organisms. In fact, they are only half-alive, but that is no reason to underestimate them.

Hollywood wasted no time in capitalizing on growing fears with a taut medical thriller, *Outbreak* (1995). Dustin Hoffman stars as a courageous American medical researcher who dives into an Ebola-infested village in Zaire to locate "ground zero," that is, to discover when and how the disease spread from primates to humans. Organisms that infect both animals and humans can't be eradicated "because the animal 'reservoir' will always persist, even if human infections are eliminated."[79]

The AIDS virus (acquired immunodeficiency syndrome) in particular has been subject to rapid mutations.[80] AIDS has another advantage as a potential threat to our species: it remains dormant, thus hiding its presence and allowing it to spread undetected. When discovered in America during the 1980s, AIDS was believed to be limited to sexual contact among homosexuals, although it was in fact already spreading through heterosexual contact in Africa and other areas. More than 40 million cases of full-blown AIDS now exist globally, mostly in poor countries where treatment regimens remain primitive.

Table 1.4

AIDS DEATHS BY COUNTRY

Rank	Country	Estimated Deaths
1	South Africa	370,000
2	India	310,000
3	Nigeria	310,000
4	Zimbabwe	170,000
5	Tanzania	160,000
6	Kenya	150,000
7	Ethiopia	120,000
8	Mozambique	110,000
9	Congo Republic	100,000
10	Zambia	89,000

Source: CIA—The World Factbook (16 May 2006):
http://www.cia.gov/cia/publications/factbook/rankorder/2157rank.html.

Although no cure exists, new antiretroviral miracle drugs have provided near-100 percent success rates for those fortunate souls receiving such treatment. Internationally based scientific research efforts are headed by the World Health Organization (WHO), the U.S. Centers for Disease Control, the U.S. National Institutes of Health (NIH), and the French Pasteur Institute.[81]

The CIA World Factbook (2006) rank orders the number of deaths attributable to AIDS by country, and Table 1.4 reveals the extent to which Sub-Saharan Africa bears a disproportionate burden in this respect, mostly due to the inability to fund the antiretroviral drug therapies available in many other places.

What accounts for the mounting world health crisis over mobile microbes? In an era of unprecedented medical advances, why should we take seriously mobile microbes as threatening to humans? The answers are not simple, but they are discernible:

- *Ecological trespassing.* As humans find new reasons to move into pristine rainforests and remote ecosystems, we encounter many of the thousands of novel microbes that are strangers to us. Some invariably prove lethal.
- *The international mixing bowl.* Modern air travel affords ample opportunities for viral hitchhikers to spread globally. This represents a palpable downside of the global commons.

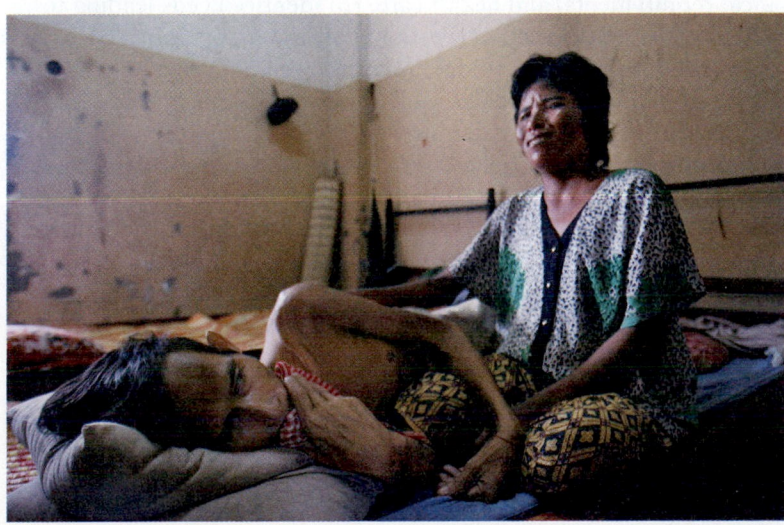

Portrait of a mother embracing her son who is afflicted with the AIDS virus.

- *Overprescription of antibiotics.* Physicians unsure of how to treat some diseases write too many prescriptions for antibiotics, even though they are useless against viruses. Not only does this practice waste money, it also weakens the patient's immune system and helps the virus to adapt (mutate) to current antivirals and vaccines.
- *Human-induced ecological disruption.* Stable ecosystems provide a set of checks and balances on the growth of microbes, but during periods of disruption, the advantage is shifted toward mobile microbes.
- *Social disruption.* Traumatic events such as civil wars uproot millions of people and place them in overcrowded situations with poor sanitation and inadequate public health services.
- *Poor countries.* The spread of infectious diseases is most acute in poor areas with bad sanitation and impure water.

Plague and pestilence are far from new problems as more humans have fallen to these forces than to warfare. Maryland political scientist Dennis Pirages notes that "History is littered with the remains of societies that have succumbed to attacks from various small organisms."[82] The agricultural revolution that occurred 10,000 years ago contributed much to human society, including the transfer of diseases from domesticated animals to humans. Public education campaigns now seek to inform citizens about the risks associated with this GI.

Less-Visible GIs

HUMAN RIGHTS Only since the end of World War II has a solid legal basis evolved to promote universal human dignity. The human rights movement begins with this proposition: simply by virtue of being human, every person is entitled to expect certain basic protections. In 1948, the United Nations General Assembly passed a comprehensive document, *The Universal Declaration of Human Rights.* Some of its principles sound similar to U.S. constitutional themes. However, in the West, we are most accustomed to thinking about human rights as freedom from specific kinds of abuses or limitations.

The U.S. Constitution's First Amendment, for instance, guarantees freedom of speech, press, religion, assembly, and petition. This way of viewing the issue revolves around *individual human rights.* However, in many other parts of the world, the issue is framed more as *collective human rights,* whereby groups of people are entitled to a certain quality of life, including a sense of human dignity.

One scholar tries to bridge both individual and collective human rights as similarly serving human *needs* that generate corresponding *rights.* He describes four such pairs of needs and rights: (1) survival needs leading to freedom from individual or collective violence; (2) well-being needs leading to the avoidance of misery, including rights to water, nutrition, biological requirements, and health care; (3) identity needs leading to the avoidance of alienation, with rights to self-expression, cultural associations, information, and a relationship to the biosphere; and (4) freedom needs leading to avoidance of repression and a right to choose in matters such as jobs, spouses, and lifestyle.[83]

Our perceptions influence how we address certain human rights questions. For example, Americans often think about human rights violations as things that happen elsewhere. Yet the human rights organization called Amnesty International considers the death penalty to constitute a violation of human rights. The United States not only has a death penalty, but the trend has been toward using it more frequently in the 38 American states where it is practiced (with Texas leading in numbers executed). No European country allows the death penalty, and global trends seem to be on their side. In 1948, only 8 countries forbade the execution of prisoners, but by 2000, that number has grown to 108 countries.[84] With whom do you agree on this issue: Amnesty International or the 38 American states employing capital punishment? The way societies think about human rights changes over time. For instance, in Western society, slavery was generally legal and considered justifiable in most countries 200 years ago. Today, it is a human rights anathema.

The United Nations measures the level of human rights and human dignity around the world with an instrument intended to get at *quality of life* issues. Called the Human Development Index (HDI), it gauges matters such as health, literacy, income, and education. Many scholars consider this indicator more meaningful than raw measures of economic output, and the HDI is referred to often in these pages.

MASSIVE MIGRATION During the Cold War era, **refugees** claiming to flee from political persecution in communist countries served as pawns in the propaganda struggle conducted by the United States and its allies. It was easy for escapees from Cuba, the Soviet Union, China, or Czechoslovakia to receive political **asylum** in the West. However, those unfortunates fleeing from noncommunist African, Asian, or Latin American countries were labeled differently as economic (not political) migrants and were often denied admission to Western countries.

> **Refugees** ■ People dislocated from their countries of origin by war, civil disturbances, and natural disasters. As they seek legal acceptance in other countries, many find tightened requirements for possible citizenship.

Sharply contrasting televised images from the Caribbean between easy admission for those displaced from Castro's Communist Cuba and a closed door for thousands of desperate Haitian "boat people" haunted presidents Ronald Reagan, George H. W. Bush, and Bill Clinton. Both Cuba and Haiti are depicted in Figure 1.4. The United States has long received more immigrants than any other country. Because U.S. immigrants include large numbers of both legal and illegal ones, exact figures remain elusive, but one million of each variety annually is often cited as an average number.

> **Asylum** ■ Different forms of this legal status exist for various circumstances, but all refer to some form of safe haven accorded persons who have fled their native country and seek sanctuary elsewhere.

Since the end of the Cold War, two developments have contributed to a growing global refugee crises: (1) the dislocation caused by many new civil wars has greatly increased the number of people fleeing from their native lands; and (2) countries to which refugees have traditionally gravitated—such as the United States, Canada, Germany, and Australia—have tightened up admission standards significantly. One of these conditions alone (increased dislocation or closing borders) would be problematic for the global refugee situation; together they equate to catastrophe.

From the mid-1970s to the mid-1990s, the number of people fleeing homelands increased tenfold. A total of 23 million left their home countries and 26 million were dislocated within their own countries. According to the main international body created to deal with these problems, the U.N. High Commission for Refugees (UNHCR), more than 80 percent of those fleeing were people of color from Africa, Asia, or the Middle East. This problem has continued to worsen since the mid-1990s.[85]

The UNHCR's budget grew from $550 million in 1990 to $2 billion by the turn of the century, employing about 6,000 staff members working in 123 countries. However, these additional resources proved incapable of handling the largest and fastest exodus in history when more than 2 million Rwandans fled the Hutu versus Tutsi ethnic violence in their country between April and August of 1994. The UNHCR's material assistance programs include emergency relief, voluntary repatriation or resettlement, social welfare services, education, and legal aid.

Figure 1.4

Geopolitics has driven U.S. refugee policy concerning Haitians and Cubans.

In addition to refugees crossing national borders, increasing numbers of people have been forced to flee local circumstances while remaining within their own country. These people on the move domestically are called displaced persons rather than refugees. Ethnic conflicts within countries have escalated in number and intensity since the Cold War ended. Some observers argue that the UNHCR was constructed for the world of 1951, not today's world, and that it is overwhelmed by contemporary migrations. One new international service supplementing the work of the UNHCR is the Worldwide Refugee Information Web, which enables the status of refugees and displaced persons in 120 countries to be traced (see the Internet list at the end of this chapter).[86]

DRUG TRAFFICKING Globalization means closer links of all kinds, including the criminal underworld. Illegal sales of armaments, spying activities, and terrorism activities have been around for some time. Only more recently has the illegal drug trade been studied seriously. International drug trafficking can be broken down into a "demand" side pulling illegal drugs into rich countries such as the United States, and a "supply" side pushing drugs out of poor countries such as Colombia, where at least one-fifth of the people rely on cocaine production to make a living. In 2006, eighty percent of the world's cocaine emanated from this South American nation. Cocaine outsells all other goods combined (including coffee) as Colombian exports. So lucrative are the payoffs on both sides of the U.S.-Colombian connection that many people are willing to run the risk of being apprehended.[87]

Unfortunately, Colombia is not only a poor country, it is also one mired in civil war. Making things worse, the leftist guerrillas who are trying to unseat the government churn out a majority of the cocaine that exits the country. Between 1995 and 2000, the United States increased tenfold its foreign aid to the Colombian government (making it the third largest recipient after Israel and Egypt). However, the American government's official estimate for cocaine in 2000 was 520 metric tons, plus 8 tons of heroin.[88]

Most of U.S. aid to Colombia is military aid, and U.S. interdiction efforts at the Mexican border have forced drug lords to vary their routine. The traffic has moved to the east, creating a Caribbean narco-economy in traditional tourist havens such as the Bahamas and Aruba, as seen in Figure 1.5. They are located neatly between Colombian supply and U.S. demand, have long and unguarded coastlines with mountain interiors, possess long-standing trade networks, and enable traffickers to get lost among hordes of *turistas*.

Estimates now suggest that one-third of drug traffic had shifted to the Caribbean route by 2001. Drug lords use high-speed "stealth boats" (made from wood and fiberglass to elude radar), new satellite-positioning systems, and sophisticated communications to make the final run to the U.S. mainland. Money laundering, repacking of the product, and protection services all bring huge profits that often dwarf the budgets of these Caribbean mini-countries.[89]

The futile American "war on drugs" is portrayed onscreen poignantly in the 2000 four-time Oscar-winning film, *Traffic* (2000), starring Michael Douglas and directed by James Cameron. Despite the creation of a cabinet-level "Drug Czar" armed with broad powers and a sizable budget, the U.S. government can't slow the steady stream of illegal drugs flooding American street life. True to real life as well as Hollywood, Douglas plays a hard-line Ohio judge who is "promoted" to serve as U.S. Drug Czar. The fact that the war on drugs is a flop comes home to roost for Douglas' character when he discovers that his honor-student, private-school daughter is hooked on cocaine.

COMPETITION OR COOPERATION? Much of human history has witnessed our reliance on *competition* and a growth model of progress to solve difficult problems. Although the competitive process does help to bring out the best in us, national competition has also led to frequent disasters. Our species has been fighting wars almost continuously,

Figure 1.5
The Caribbean interface for illegal drugs entering North America.

Source: From Maps On File™ by Facts On File, Inc. Copyright © by Facts On File, Inc. Reprinted by permission of Facts On File, Inc.

resulting in about 3.5 billion deaths (111 million in the twentieth century alone),[90] which bolsters humorist Ambrose Bierce's quip that peace is but a short period of cheating between two periods of fighting.[91]

Some idealistic observers, however, see a need for humanity to form a new *cooperative* vision that recognizes humanity as one family and everyone as a potential global citizen. This view holds that a collective future could become better than a competitive past if we become better listeners and attempt to work together when possible. Such optimists see global cooperation essential to resolving global dilemmas such as the environment, population, food, energy, WMD, human rights, terrorism, mobile microbes, massive migration, and drug trafficking.

But saying that global cooperation is a desirable goal does not make its achievement any easier. Cooperation is something our species has failed to demonstrate with consistency; thus many realists doubt that vexing GIs will be resolved by adopting a cooperative motif. Relatively few states have emphasized cooperation, ethical principles, or concern for the plight of downtrodden peoples in their foreign policies. Possibly the best such example lies just north of the U.S. border, as detailed at the end of Chapter 6.

Chapter Synopsis

The image of an interdependent world has gone from fantasy to reality in recent decades. Take a look at the clothes you wear, the car you drive, or the sports and entertainment heroes you admire, and you will discover the stuff of globalization. The communications revolution has produced e-mail, faxes, cell phones and satellite television linking all the world's continents in ways unimaginable a generation ago. Such communications treat borders as highly permeable by forging linkages based on shared values and information, not physicality. They also facilitate cooperative human endeavors differing from the competitive mind-set of the traditional state.

Five categories of globalization are examined here: economic, environmental, military, communications, and cultural globalization. In addition, a wide range of vexing Global Issues (GIs) is introduced in this chapter. They include four ecological GIs (environment, population, food, and energy), three highly visible GIs (WMD, terrorism, and mobile microbes), and three less-visible GIs (human rights, massive migration, and drug trafficking). States have had problems solving all of these GIs, leading people to look for answers from grass-roots groups such as NGOs.

Some observers view globalization as a curse, whereas others see it as a blessing. Critics consist of labor unions concerned about losing domestic jobs, environmentalists worried that other countries will not respect the earth, economic nationalists who fear that international institutions will weaken American sovereignty, and articulate proponents of social justice who contend that globalization from above should be replaced by globalization from below because the process has severely widened the gap between rich and poor.

Supporters of globalization consist of the comfortable establishment. This includes influential journalists such as Thomas Friedman, all MNCs, many politicians, most economists, and the potent military-industrial complex headed by the Pentagon. The most common theme of globalization's backers is that it is necessary to master it to remain competitive in a competitive world. Our contemporary era has witnessed the empowerment of millions of global citizens that were previously voiceless. The globalization process has also increased the importance of the diverse GIs cited earlier.

FOR DIGGING DEEPER

Arquilla, John, and David Ronfeldt. *Networks and Netwars: The Future of Terror, Crime, and Militancy*. Rand Corporation, 2001.

Bale, John, and Joseph Maguire. *The Global Sports Arena: Athletic Talent Migration in an Interdependent World*. Frank Cass, 1994.

Barber, Benjamin. *Jihad versus McWorld: How Globalism and Tribalism Are Reshaping the World*. Ballantine Books, 1996.

Broad, Robin, ed. *Global Backlash: Citizen Initiatives for a Just World Economy*. Millennium Books, 2002.

Brown, D. Clayton. *Globalization and America Since 1945*. SR Books, 2003.

Brown, Jennifer, and Peter Chalk. *The Global Threat of New and Reemerging Infectious Diseases*. Rand Corporation, 2003.

Carter, April. *Political Theory of Global Citizenship*. Routledge, 2001.

Congressional Quarterly Researcher. *Global Issues: 2005*. Congressional Quarterly, 2005.

Cornelius, Wayne A., and others, eds. *Controlling Immigration: A Global Perspective*. Stanford University Press, 2003.

Davies, John, and Edward Kaufman, eds. *Second Track/Citizen's Diplomacy*. Rowman and Littlefield, 2003.

Dunning, John H., ed. *Making Globalization Good: The Moral Challenges of Global Capitalism*. Oxford University Press, 2003.

French, Hilary. *Vanishing Borders: Protecting the Planet in the Age of Globalization*. W. W. Norton & Co., 2000.

Friedman, Thomas. *Globalization: The Lexus and the Olive Tree: Understanding Globalization*. Farrar, Strauss and Giroux, 1999.

————. *The World Is Flat: A Brief History of the Twenty-First Century*. Farrar, Strauss, and Giroux, 2006.

Gianaris, Nicholas. *Globalization: A Financial Approach*. Greenwood Publishing, 2001.

Grosse, Robert. *Drugs and Money: Laundering Latin America's Cocaine Dollars*. Greenwood Publishing, 2001.

Klein, Naomi. *No Logo: Taking Aim at the Brand-Name Bullies*. Picador Press, 2000.

Krieger, Joel. *Globalization and State Power*. Pearson Education, Inc., 2006.

Mares, David. *Drug Wars and Coffee Houses: The Political Economy of the International Drug Trade*. Congressional Quarterly Press, 2005.

Matheson, Michael. *Council Unbound: The Growth of UN Decision-Making on Conflict and Post-Conflict Issues After the Cold War*. U.S. Institute of Peace Press, 2006.

Payne, Richard, and Jamal Nassar. *Politics and Culture in the Developing World: The Impact of Globalization*. Pearson Education, Inc., 2006.

Pieterse, Jan Nederveen. *Globalization and Culture*. Rowman and Littlefield, 2003.

Rothenberg, Paula S. *Beyond Borders: Thinking Critically About Global Issues*. Worth Publishers, 2006.

Scott, Peter Dale. *Drugs, Oil, and War*. Rowman and Littlefield, 2003.

Tehranian, Majid. *Global Communication and World Politics*. Lynne Rienner, 1999.

Tetreault, Mary Ann, and Ronnie Lipschutz. *Global Politics as if People Mattered*. Rowman and Littlefield, 2005.

UNHCR. *The State of the World's Refugees 2000: Fifty Years of Humanitarian Action*. Oxford University Press, 2001.

Weimann, Gabriel. *Terror on the Internet: The New Arena, the New Challenges*. U.S. Institute of Peace Press, 2006.

Whitaker, David, ed. *Terrorism Reader*. Routledge, 2001.

INTERNET

Amnesty International (Human Rights):
http://www.amnesty.org

Care information on Global Issues:
http://www.care.org

Carnegie Endowment for International Peace:
http://www.ceip.org/

Central Intelligence Agency Factbook:
http://www.cia.gov/library/publications

Center for Immigration Studies:
http://www.cis.org

Commission on Global Governance:
http://www.cgg.ch/

Envirolink Information Resource:
http://envirolink.org

Food and Agricultural Organization (U.N.):
http://www.fao.org

Friends of the Earth:
http://www.foe.co.uk/index.html

The Hunger Project:
http://www.thp.org

Immigration and Naturalization Service (U.S.):
http://www.uscis.gov

International Institute (Canadian) for Sustainable Development:
http://www.iisd.ca

North-South Institute:
http://www.nsi-ins.c

Population and Habitat Campaign:
http://www.overpopulation.org

Rainforest Action Network:
http://www.rainforest-alliance.org

Resources for the Future:
http://www.rff.org

Statistics Canada:
http://www.statcan.ca/start.html

Sustainability Archive:
http://www.sustainabilityarchive.com

Terrorism Research Center:
http://www.terrorism.com/

United Nations Environment Program (UNEP):
http://www.unep.ch/

United Nations High Commission for Refugees (UNHCR):
http://www.unhcr.ch

United Nations Population Fund:
http://www.unfpa.org

World Health Organization:
http://www.who.ch

Worldwide Refugee Information Web:
http://www.refugees.org/world/worldmain.htm

Social Science Philosophy and Methods

CORE OBJECTIVE

To establish the historical, philosophical, and methodological foundations of the social sciences.

THEMATIC QUESTIONS

- What is the relationship between the three great bodies of knowledge?

- How did the Americanization of the social sciences affect their substance and methods?

- What characterized ancient civilizations?

- In what way did the ancient Greeks influence modern civilizations?

- How do scientific and humanistic philosophies undergird social science inquiry?

- What distinguishes the social sciences from the natural sciences and the humanities?

Social Science Roots

Three Great Bodies of Knowledge

Humanity's long struggle to understand itself and the world it inhabits has resulted in the emergence of three great bodies of knowledge: *the natural sciences, humanities,* and *social sciences*. The natural sciences consist of physics, chemistry, biology, geology, and astronomy, all of which deal with laws related to nature. These disciplines experienced tremendous advances during the European Renaissance beginning in the sixteenth century.

The humanities are made up of history, philosophy, literature, ethics, comparative religion, and criticism of the arts. Each of the humanities involves a personalized quest for insight into the human condition, particularly its aesthetic, spiritual, and emotional aspects. Their contributions to knowledge can be traced back 2,500 years to ancient Greece.

The social sciences, by contrast, have emerged as six separate disciplines (political science, economics, sociology, anthropology, psychology, and geography) much more recently. Therefore, they have freely borrowed insights, techniques, and information from their progenitors in both the natural sciences and humanities. Together the social sciences undertake the daunting task of studying the complexities of human behavior.

Modern-Day Social Sciences

One way to define the contemporary social sciences is to examine what social scientists do. This requires looking at the site of the largest concentration of social scientists, the United States, where higher education is big business. Nearly all of America's 3,000-plus colleges and universities contain departments housing social scientists who spend their time teaching, researching, writing, and consulting about myriad aspects of the human drama. In defining themselves professionally, most identify with a specific social science discipline. Typically, separate departments of political science, economics, sociology, anthropology, psychology, and geography establish lines of demarcation.

Studying people becomes very complicated. The division of mental labor allows scholars to approach human studies from a variety of perspectives. These disciplinary boundaries, however, do not prevent social scientists from pursuing topics of interest that spill over into related disciplines. Human behavior represents the crux of the social sciences. Given such a broad and elusive mandate, cross-fertilization is common among social scientists. If you ask your professors about their specialties, you are likely to uncover social psychologists, political geographers, economic psychologists, economic geographers, psycho-anthropologists, political sociologists, and anthropological geographers.

Political scientists often examine issues of power, authority, or government. As one observer put it—trying to answer the question of who gets what, when, and how? The interests of political scientists sometimes overlap with *economists* studying how people make a living. The production, distribution, and consumption of goods and services occupies the attention of economists. *Sociologists* deal with the social activity of humans, and both they and their intellectual cousins in *anthropology* share an abiding interest in the group dimension affecting our behavior. Anthropologists study humans as biocultural beings and often specialize in exploring preliterate groups. The individual's realm of inner experience (including elusive topics such as mind, motivation, and perception) intrigues today's *psychologists*. Finally, *geographers* trace the link between humans and the physical environment while concentrating on spatial analysis.

If you are tempted to take for granted this portrait of well-established, distinct, stable, and Americanized social science disciplines—don't. Its canvas has been painted mostly during the past century, which is like the blink of an eye when compared to the long haul of recorded human history during the past 10,000 years.

Recorded Human History and Ancient Civilizations

It was roughly ten millennia ago that the *agricultural revolution* dramatically transformed human existence. Its myriad effects included such milestones as populating settled communities, storing surplus crops, inventing pottery, making cloth, trading with other groups, domesticating wild animals, and record keeping. The advent of written records and accounts ended the mute days of human prehistory, ushering in the chorus of voices known as recorded history. Dogs had already been domesticated by humans prior to the agricultural revolution, and then came goats, sheep, oxen, and eventually horses.

A serendipitous set of natural and human factors combined to trigger the agricultural revolution. An explosion of new vegetation accompanied the end of the last Ice Age approximately 11,000 years ago. The most crucial genetic piece of this puzzle was the creation of a fertile wheat hybrid resulting from a cross between wild wheat and a natural goat grass. Humans first discovered how to harvest this new strain of wheat and then learned techniques for planting it themselves.

Up until this point, it is theorized that humanity's ascent consisted mainly of a biological evolution lasting millions of years. The gradual progression of this early script for humanity's performance on the world stage stood in contrast to the rapid transmutation that has dominated the last 10,000 years. The scope of humanity's relatively recent social development is best understood in the context of emerging **civilizations**.

The first civilizations following on the heels of the agricultural revolution existed in the Middle East, in what is now Iran and Iraq. Between 4000 B.C. and the time of

Civilizations ■ The agricultural revolution brought settled communities capable of reading, writing, and creating culture. Some ancient civilizations, such as Greece and Rome, contributed much to modern civilizations.

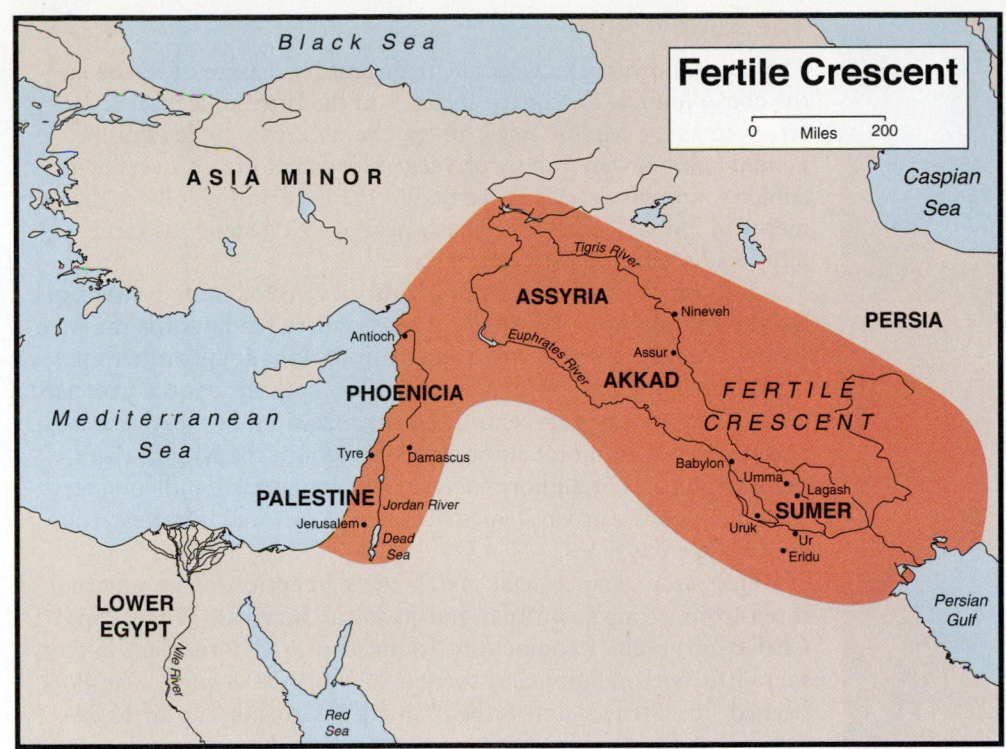

Fertile Crescent

0   Miles   200

Black Sea

ASIA MINOR

Caspian Sea

Tigris River

ASSYRIA

Nineveh

PERSIA

Antioch

Euphrates River

Assur

PHOENICIA

AKKAD

FERTILE CRESCENT

Mediterranean Sea

Tyre

Damascus

Babylon

Umma   Lagash

PALESTINE

Jordan River

SUMER

Jerusalem

Uruk   Ur

Dead Sea

Eridu

LOWER EGYPT

Nile River

Persian Gulf

Red Sea

Figure 2.1
The agricultural revolution catalyzed ancient civilizations in places like the Middle East.

Christ, major civilizations also arose in Anatolia, China, Egypt, Greece, India, and Rome. Each ancient civilization advanced human existence by organizing its residents into social classes, creating governments led by rulers considered divinely inspired, facilitating commercial trade through market forces overseen by the government, and providing for the civilization's defense. Such civilizations were to develop later in the New World (the Western Hemisphere) rather than in what is called the Old World: the Middle East, Europe, and Asia.

Humanity's creative juices had established many of the great ancient civilizations well before the birth of Christ. Some historians believe that no other advance in the human script has resulted in such a profound expansion of our species' imagination. Yet other more sanguine observers point out the dark side that accompanied this rapid social, political, and economic development. Most noticeably, a large part of the human legacy that distinguishes us from other higher order species is that recorded human history is replete with devoting time and energy to killing one other in wars.

As hunter-gatherers, humans had been relatively inefficient in this endeavor. But with the advent of complex social organization, economies producing a surplus of goods, and powerful legitimized political leaders—all the stuff of civilization—warfare expanded in scope and intensity. Some of the most brutal early wars were fought between representatives of the two contending models for human social organization at the time: the social customs of nomadic tribes versus the more orderly social existence of settlers. Despite their military successes, many nomadic invaders rode horse-back from their Central Asian homelands into Europe only to find that, after hard-won victories, their proud way of life possessed little staying power and was absorbed over time by the peoples whom they had defeated in battle. The Huns led by Attila and Genghis Khan's Mongols both experienced such ignoble fates; the settled way of life gradually took center stage in the human drama and relegated nomads to bit parts.

The age of ancient civilizations came to an end with the military defeat of the Roman Empire at the hands of Franco-Germanic tribes in the fifth century A.D. Much of the Roman way of life, however, continued to pervade the growing societies of northern Europe, which were long on power but short on culture. One of the most pervasive influences of the late Roman Empire was the Christian religion.

Christian Crusaders fought eight bloody wars with Muslims during the Middle Ages.

Feudalism ■ The economic system in Europe during the Middle Ages, relying on labor-intensive agriculture conducted by peasants tied to land owned by their feudal lords

Serfs ■ Members of the lowest feudal class who were bound to land owned by a ruling lord

Islam ■ The world's second-largest religion, with one billion believers who follow the teachings of their seventh-century prophet, Muhammad, as embodied in the holy book called the Koran

State ■ An independent political actor on the world stage characterized by territory, population, government, and recognition by its peers

Renaissance ■ From the French for rebirth, it refers to the revitalization of European intellectual life around 1500 that resulted from rekindling ancient Greek and Roman knowledge

Greek rationalism ■ Reliance on reason or critical thinking to explain the nature of life in our world, as first enunciated by Greek scholars such as Aristotle and Plato

The Middle Ages

The thousand years between the fifth-century demise of Rome and the consolidation of modern societies in the fifteenth century is referred to as the Middle Ages, an era characterized by **feudalism.** Feudal manors were run by privileged lords who ruled over their subjects, known as **serfs.** Thus tied to the land and wholly at the mercy of feudal lords, serfs lived a near-slave existence as farm laborers holding no personal rights.

Two very different levels of authority vied for more power during the Middle Ages: (1) the *local level,* where feudal lords ran their estates, loosely referred to as principalities, kingdoms, or fiefdoms; and (2) the *pan-European level* where the Catholic church exercised great power through its centralized organization, impressive wealth, and monopoly of moral authority. Throughout the Middle Ages, these rival levels of authority alternately cooperated and competed with one another as varying circumstances dictated different strategies at different times.

Few circumstances can match the perception of an external threat to a group's spiritual and physical survival. When Papal Christianity's chief competitor, **Islam,** captured Jerusalem (a city sacred to both religions), a torrent of violence ensued. The Pope begged, threatened, and bribed Christians to take up arms in defense of their faith. What resulted is called the Crusades—a recurring wave of religious military campaigns begun in 1095 and repeated eight times over the next two centuries. Carnage on an unprecedented scale left Christians and Muslims essentially where they had begun: stalemated in a bitter power struggle both temporal and spiritual.

As to the power struggle between local feudal lords and the Papacy, neither side won that long battle either. Instead, a new form of human organization gradually appeared that operated midway between the feudal lords at the local level and the Church at the all-European level, the **state.** The contemporary system of 193 competitive states began with a handful of European states in places such as Sweden, Spain, Portugal, Holland, and France. Possessing secular authority independent of the Church and able to protect their residents because of its size and resources, states ushered in the modern social organization.

Rationalism and the Renaissance

Even the briefest review of humanity's drama ought to pay homage to the pivotal role of the **Renaissance.** The Renaissance spark was lit in fourteenth-century Florence, swept across northern Italy, and then engulfed Europe by the seventeenth century. The Renaissance emphasized **Greek rationalism.** The Renaissance's classical revival of Greek rationalism expressed itself in two main areas of learning: natural science and moral philosophy.

The Greeks believed that reason could produce the "good society," which Plato (427–347 B.C.), in his manual called *Republic,* outlined for enlightened politicians. Aristotle's (384–322 B.C.) *Politics* provided a more general blueprint for an ideal, or utopian society. Critical thinking was a lynchpin of Greek rationalism, and one person who later epitomized it was Martin Luther, a free-thinking Augustinian monk. Luther ushered in the **Protestant Reformation** when he nailed his "95 Theses" to the cathedral door in Wittenberg, Germany. With unquestioned obedience to Papal authority now a relic of the Middle Ages, critical thinking settled deeply into the minds of men, and later, of women.

When Greek civilization fell in 500 B.C., most of its way of life disappeared with it. What survived to influence modernity did so ironically. What we know today of Greek philosophers such as Socrates, Plato, and Aristotle comes from unlikely middlemen: Persian (soon-to-be Muslim) conquerors of the Greeks who preserved ancient Greek knowledge for more than 1,000 years. Greek rationalism was replanted in European intellectual soil by Christian Crusaders returning from the Middle East. Slowly taking hold during the late Middle Ages, Greek rationalism failed to capture the philosophical soil of Europe's oases of learning until the Renaissance.

Intellectual History of the Social Sciences
European Enlightenment

The ideal Renaissance scholar was expected to cultivate every row of knowledge and eventually collapsed from intellectual fatigue, leading gradually to scholarly specialization during the period (1700–1800) of the **Enlightenment.** The first disciplinary earthquake severed philosophy from physics and the natural sciences; others soon followed.

Social theorizing during the Enlightenment increased in sophistication due to the powerful ideas of Enlightenment scientists such as Sir Isaac Newton. However, many social thinkers naively conceived of society as a mechanistic component of nature, bending to inexorable natural laws. Early European "system-builders" such as Auguste Comte, Herbert Spencer, and Karl Marx tried to account for all social phenomena; they represented social commentators of the broadest sort. By the eighteenth and nineteenth centuries, these theories had all firmly accepted the assumption that social progress is an historical inevitability. It is from these philosophically oriented theories of history that the modern social sciences emerged.

This optimistic notion of historical progress fits neatly with the traditional German faith in history as the grand unifying discipline of human studies. Broad-based theories of optimism dotted the German intellectual landscape right up until the outbreak of World War I in 1914. What we now conceive of as the humanities disciplines of philosophy and history were then inseparable contributors to the way Europeans thought about human affairs. When eighteenth- and nineteenth-century European scholars theorized about political matters, for example, they engaged in political philosophy.

German reformer, theologian, and originator of the Protestant Reformation, Martin Luther (1483–1546), shown in a reflective mood.

Protestant Reformation ■ The sixteenth-century rebellion against the Catholic church that unleashed the forces of individualism and rationalism in Europe

Enlightenment ■ Eighteenth-century rationalism, believing in the progressive nature of human history and leading to the diminution of religious explanations of human behavior

Political Philosophy: Hobbes, Locke, and Rousseau

Three great political thinkers stand out as pioneers. British political philosopher Thomas Hobbes (1588–1679) argued in *The Leviathan* that life in the state of nature preceding the formation of the political state (leviathan) was "solitary, poor, nasty, brutish, and short." Humans, in other words, need a government to protect them from their own worst impulses. He viewed government not as something alien imposed from above by divine authority but rather as a rational alternative that was beneficial to its citizens.

Hobbes' countryman John Locke (1632–1704) emphasized the importance of the rights of the individual citizen. Today, these are called civil liberties, as epitomized by the freedoms spelled out in the First Amendment of the U.S. Constitution: freedom of speech, press, religion, assembly, and petition. John Locke was the first to argue systematically that the rights of individuals take precedence over the rights of the government in certain circumstances and that government forfeits its right to rule if it violates the public trust. Leaders of the American revolution of 1776 took Locke's philosophical musings very seriously.

The Swiss philosopher Jean-Jacques Rousseau (1712–1778) began his political analysis with an assumption diametrically opposed to that of Thomas Hobbes: humans are essentially good at heart. Rousseau believed that the tendency of absolutist governments to abuse power must be opposed and that ultimately the power to rule needs to be traced back to the people. It did not take very long for Rousseau's ideas to be applied to real-world conditions close to home in the French revolution of 1789–1799.

Today, most social scientists think of the realms of politics and economics as related but separate. To European philosophers of the time, these endeavors seemed as complementary as symmetrical sundials. However, whereas Hobbes, Locke, and Rousseau emphasized the relationship between government and its citizens, others zeroed in on the relationship between government and the economy.

Political Economy: Adam Smith and Karl Marx

The father of classical economic theory was the Scottish philosopher Adam Smith (1723–1790). His enormously influential book, *The Wealth of Nations* (1776), argued that government should keep its hands off the economy—a *laissez-faire* approach, sharply critical of the tendency for government to use the economy as a vehicle for accumulating wealth for itself. Smith held that an "invisible hand" guided "the rules that men naturally observe in exchanging goods either for money or for one another." These self-adjusting market exchanges, according to Smith, tend to produce the greatest good for the greatest number over time *if* governments will only stay out of the way.

Not all those who theorized about free market economics, however, offered interpretations as confidently optimistic as Adam Smith's. Sitting atop the list of nay-sayers would be Karl Marx (1818–1883). When Marx looked at contemporary European economies, he saw abject poverty for the masses while the rich got much richer; he saw political systems catering exclusively to the needs of the rich elites; he saw ethical issues of social justice buried in a rush to accumulate wealth; he saw the growing inequities of market economics, leading to a violent revolution to be carried out by the many against the few. Marx was the greatest of all socialist thinkers, and his global influence proved considerable. His theories can be linked to the Russian Revolution of 1917 just as clearly as those of John Locke to the American Revolution and those of Jean-Jacques Rousseau to the French Revolution. Case Study 2.1 places Marx in the wider context of socialist thinkers.

Social Philosophy: Comte, Durkheim, and Weber

The French philosopher Auguste Comte (1798–1857) was the first to treat society as a "system" of interacting parts. He thought that politically oriented thinkers of his day failed to understand the importance of the "interconnections" between aspects of society existing apart from the political economy. Whereas political philosophers remained transfixed by the big picture of human studies, Comte preferred to examine the social system's interacting parts. In the 1830s, Comte proposed a "positive science of society," which opened the door to an increasingly independent and methodologically scientific discipline.[1]

Two later scholars, Emile Durkheim and Max Weber, agreed with Comte's plea for a separate discipline of sociology, but they epitomized the tension underlying his scientific aspirations for the discipline. Frenchman Emile Durkheim (1858–1917), a philosopher turned sociologist, objected to the historical analysis prevalent in European social thought and became one of the founders of quantitative sociology.

Durkheim's special interest lay in studying the conflicting tendencies of cohesion (unity) versus alienation (estrangement) among members of society. As the holder of the first endowed academic chair in sociology, in 1896, he soon published his landmark statistical study entitled, *Suicide: A Study in Sociology* (1897). In it, he tried to show that even highly personal and individual acts, such as the decision to commit suicide, are influenced by what he called "collective reality," or social factors.

Case Study 2.1   "Scientific Socialism"?

Writing in the middle of the 1800s, Karl Marx was critical of an earlier group of authors that he labeled "Utopian Socialists," who represented the first modern exponents of communal social thought. Marx derided their idealist hypothetical visions of egalitarian societies without identifying concrete means of getting there. Utopian Socialists have been classified as authors who published between the French Revolution (1789–1799) and the mid-1830s.

They included writers such as Robert Owen (1771–1858), a businessman who put his profits back into improving the quality of life of his textile mill employees in New Lanark, Scotland. Owen believed that humans have the freewill capacity to create any type of society that they choose, and he established a commune based on his ideas in New Harmony, Indiana. Frenchman Charles Fourier, probably the most idealistic of the early Socialists, rejected the Industrial Revolution as the dominant socioeconomic force of that era, enabling him to dream up many alternative rural scenarios for humanity.[2]

In much the same way that modern Social Scientism demeans the contributions of modern Social Humanism, Karl Marx and his followers blasted Utopian Socialists as hopelessly out of touch with reality. Marx' collaborator, fellow German Friedrich Engels, coined the moniker Scientific Socialism to describe Marxist thought. And what set apart Marxism from earlier writers was that he went beyond mere pie-in-the-sky musings to what he regarded as well-researched laws of historical development.

Marx highlighted the economic primacy inherent in historical materialism: history is driven not by abstract ideas, such as religions, but rather by concrete economic realities based on who owns the means of production during each historical stage. Marx had nothing against the visions of a perfect society conjured up by Utopian Socialists, but he believed that only through violent revolution would the capitalist stage of history give way to the socialist stage of history.

Revolution required that the proletarian masses rise up and overthrow their bourgeois oppressors. This hands-on character of Marxian thought served the needs of revolutionaries in deeply divided societies such as Vladimir Lenin's Russia, and Mao Tse-tung's China, where the first two socialist revolutions were eventually to occur. Each of these national leaders tweaked Marxist theory (better attuned to the highly developed capitalist societies such as Germany, France, or the United States) to make it fit into precapitalist societies such as Russia and China.[3]

Karl Marx was brilliantly eclectic, and he synthesized ideas from three main sources: English political economy, French socialism, and German idealist philosophy. The nineteenth-century version of capitalism brutally ignored the human rights of an oppressed working class, and Marx' well-intentioned writings aimed at improving the fate of humanity. But much like another brilliant nineteenth-century innovator in the field of psychology, Sigmund Freud, their creative prescriptions for what ailed humanity do not hold up to twenty-first-century scrutiny. Especially regarding his economic theories, Marx has proven dead wrong on most of his propositions and predictions. Countries where socialist revolutions have taken place and where leaders have implemented Marxian economic practices have faltered very, very badly. Only countries such as China, which have abandoned socialist economics, have prospered in any reasonable way. ■

Like Karl Marx before him, Max Weber (1884–1920) was a German theorist of general historical trends whose lengthy tomes often lacked clarity. Unlike the views of Marx, Weber's analysis of contemporary conditions emphasized faith in the progressive nature of the existing European sociopolitical order. Where Max Weber parted company with sociologist Durkheim, as well as with the emerging center of gravity among new sociologists, was over the growing rift between historico-philosophical methods and scientific thinking and methods. Weber remained true to the traditional German ideal of history as the vehicle for social analysis par excellence. In one book, he asks pointedly, "Can this project [science] be expected to produce useful new insights germane to concrete problems?" His answer is skeptical concerning the prospects of a scientific sociology.[4]

The Americanization of the Social Sciences

The evolution of social sciences in the United States followed a markedly different course of events than those in Europe. According to intellectual historian Dorothy Ross, the formative years for the social sciences in America were between 1870 and 1929. Unlike their European counterparts, American scholars steered the social sciences sharply away from their historico-philosophical roots and in the direction of science. The new scientific mission to discover laws of society meant ignoring subjective phenomena such as emotions, applying rigorous research methods, and remaining neutral on ethical and/or public policy questions.[5]

During the Gilded Age following the U.S. Civil War, rapidly expanding wealth, urbanization, the founding of new colleges and universities, and a growing specialization of knowledge all helped to usher in separate and viable social science disciplines in the United States. America's mostly sectarian colleges had been teaching a curriculum heavy on moral philosophy for nearly a century. But in the late 1800s it was widely believed that what America sorely lacked was a system of universities like the well-established ones found in Germany, France, Britain, or Italy.

U.S. Universities and the Paradigm of Science

Not until Baltimore's Johns Hopkins University opened its doors in 1876 could the United States boast of an American university. Even then no domestic university (or its professorate) could dream of rivaling venerable European institutions such as Cambridge, Oxford, Berlin, or the Sorbonne. But philosopher Peter T. Manicas points out that while American universities lacked tradition as a source of authority, they did not lack "science," which they came to see as their passport to respectability.[6]

The very newness of America meant freedom from tradition, and allowed American universities to reinvent themselves as paragons of progressive ideas—with science heading the agenda. Also, in sharp contrast to the muddled French Revolution, Americans viewed their own revolution as a resounding success. This perspective added to a growing suspicion among Americans that their land was an *exceptional place* able to accomplish exceptional things.

In the latter part of the nineteenth century, the action in American higher education moved swiftly and decisively away from its older undergraduate colleges to its spanking-new universities. The key feature of new private universities such as Johns Hopkins, New York University, the University of Chicago, and public land-grant universities in every state was their introduction of *graduate programs*.

The first such program in the social sciences was begun in political science at Columbia University, in 1880, by German-trained scholar John Burgess. Within a decade, Columbia's model graduate school also had departments of economics, geography, and sociology (which included anthropology at that time). A crucial innovation of U.S. graduate programs was the graduate seminar, which encouraged specialized instruction and research and was based on the laboratory model already operating in the natural sciences.

America's first university, Johns Hopkins, Americanized the social sciences with graduate programs that employed the scientific method to study human behavior.

Professionalization of the Social Sciences

American social scientists were intent on professionalizing higher education, which necessitated the creation of professional associations publishing their own specialized journals. First, the American Academy of Political and Social Science appeared in 1889, then the American Economic Association and the American Psychological Association in 1892, the American Political Science Association in 1903, the Association of American Geographers in 1904, and the American Sociological Society in 1905.

Keenly interested in separating themselves from the curriculum of moral philosophy taught in America's small colleges, the new graduate programs in U.S. universities seized upon the scientific method as their intellectual Holy Grail. "Science began to appear not only as the most authoritative modern knowledge, but as a courageous source of free inquiry, as against an authoritarian, outmoded religion."[7]

It has also been argued widely that a form of sexism contributed to American social science's fixation on scientism: at a time when almost all leading scholars were male, science seemed more acceptable to a macho-oriented, frontier-era America, than did historical or philosophical analysis. A final factor often considered to have helped to put science into the social sciences a century ago is that, as a very complex and diverse new nation, America needed a unifying symbol around which to rally, and science was it.

Before long, the top social scientists were advocating scientific approaches to the study of humans. In 1919, sociologist Luther Bernard proclaimed "We are so definitely launched upon the trend toward objectivism and definiteness of method that it is needless to argue in its defense."[8] Two years later, American Political Science Association President Charles Merriam issued a clarion call for the scientific study of politics, which he thought would enable us to exercise intelligent influence over governmental affairs. Merriam urged his colleagues to borrow the statistical techniques already in use among psychologists.

In economics, the transition to a quantitative social science was facilitated by the nature of its subject matter, and less exhortation was required. When necessary to do so, however, major economists, such as Thorstein Veblen, challenged their colleagues to become more rigorously objective. The final imprimatur sealing the success of scientism arrived in the 1920s in the form of large financial contributions for scientific research from charitable organizations with deep pockets, such as the Rockefeller and Carnegie foundations.

Philosophical Debate in the Social Sciences

It seems remarkable how little some of the underlying issues affecting the American social sciences have changed over the past century. Although much of our knowledge about human behavior has derived from the content of the humanities disciplines (especially from history and philosophy), the prevailing methodology continues to favor scientific objectivity and quantification over analytical and experiential insights. These two vastly different influences upon the American social sciences—physical sciences versus humanities—have contributed to two rival sets of philosophical lenses through which to observe human behavior. One is scientistic in outlook and called social scientism; the other is humanistic in outlook and referred to as social humanism.

Two Contending Camps

Modern social sciences owe debts to each progenitor (the natural sciences and the humanities), but only grudgingly do the proponents of either social scientism or social humanism acknowledge the existence of the other. Advocates of a more *roomy definition* of the social sciences—one involving a synthesis of scientistic and humanistic tendencies—make a logical argument.

Insights and methods from both the natural sciences and humanities are needed because the social sciences are still very young in comparison to their more experienced colleagues in the academy. They also face the daunting task of comprehending the behavior of a species as perplexing as humans. As social science philosopher Kenneth Hoover succinctly put it, "There is no particular sense in limiting the facilities of the mind in any inquiry."[9]

Social Scientism

Before a clear image of a roomy social science can be painted, however, the contrasting features of social scientism versus social humanism must be sketched in. As the prevailing approach in twentieth-century America, scientism deserves first crack at presenting its case. Scientism assumes that the differences between the natural and social sciences are merely a matter of degree, not a matter of kind. A pair of scholars provides texture to this argument: "Just as the seventeenth and eighteenth centuries saw the maturing of the physical sciences, and the nineteenth that of the biological sciences, so the twentieth century marks the coming of age of the behavioral [social] sciences."[10] Although people as subjects of study may prove more irascible than atoms, paramecia, or ozone gas, all remain ultimately amenable to the same methods of study; science is science is science.

Science gathers **facts** that help to answer the *what* type of questions. When facts are organized, they can be more abstractly analyzed to answer the complicated *why* type questions. These general explanations of specific factual realities are known as **scientific theories.**

The approach to knowledge known as *science* has been defined variously as an objective system for providing the truth, finding a pattern in a set of phenomena, insistence on systematic methodical study, a language transporting humans to new countries of the mind, and the freeing of inquiry from bias and prejudice.[11] Philosopher of science Carlo Lastrucci says that scientists make basic assumptions about their work. For example, the assumption that all objective phenomena are knowable in a world of underlying order and uniformity, and that truth must be demonstrated objectively because nothing is self-evident.[12] The rules of the scientific game are provided by a loosely structured set of procedures known as the scientific method. Most Ph.D. dissertations in the social sciences emulate these guidelines:

Facts ■ Statements whose truth or falsity can be established through empirical verification or logical analysis

Scientific theories ■ Explanatory postulates whose methodologies are grounded in science

SCIENTIFIC METHOD
- Selection of an *area to be researched* and a review of the existing literature on the subject
- Definition of the problem: forming a specific *hypothesis* (researchable question) within some explanatory theory
- Construction of the *research design:* applying a technique to measure data relevant to the study's hypothesis
- *Data collection:* observation and recording of information intended to test the hypothesis
- *Classification* and organization: after gathering data, they must be ordered properly
- *Conclusions:* evaluating the hypothesis, generalizing from the results of the study, and suggesting new research

If an objective method represents the heart of science, then its soul consists of a certain attitude—a skeptical one; science believes that things are not always what they seem to be, rendering commonsensical understanding inadequate. Common sensory perception alone may suggest to us that the earth is flat, the sun revolves around the earth, that heavy bodies always fall faster than light bodies, and that ships made of iron must head to the bottom of the sea. Yet humanity has long known all these expectations to be false. As a leading social science methodologist has argued, relying on common sense risks making inaccurate observations, overgeneralizing about the significance of our own anecdotal experiences, and making observations selectively based on the human desire to see what we either want or expect to see.[13] One historical figure who challenged common sense at his own peril was Galileo Galilei, as discussed in Case Study 2.2.

Case Study 2.2   Galileo Galilei: Scientist and/or Heretic?

In 1633, the Catholic Church condemned the Italian astronomer named Galileo Galilei (1564–1642). His crime? Galileo had relied on science to argue that the sun serves as the center of the universe. Both common sense and, not coincidentally, Church doctrine then held that the earth, not the sun, is the center of our universe.

Galileo was born in Pisa in 1564 and began his career there as a mathematics professor. He became one of the first philosophers to describe the physical world in mathematical terms and is known as the father of experimental physics. In 1609, the young scholar built a telescope and aimed it at the heavens. Seven years later, a Cardinal of the Inquisition warned the flamboyant Galileo to cease his astronomical studies. But then, in 1623, a new Pope, Urban VII, brought to his position a scientific interest rare among Pontiffs; he even admired Galileo for his keen intellect.

Eight years later, Galileo was granted permission to print his 500-page "Dialogue," which included his sacrilegious theory explaining why the earth cannot be the center of our universe. Urban VII did not read the "Dialogue," but his censors did, and they advised him to drag the brash Galileo before the Inquisition. There the scientist was forced to confess and was condemned to perpetual house arrest. His book was placed on the Church's List of Prohibited Books, where it stayed for 200 years.[14]

Since the days of early scientists such as Galileo, science has married its objective methods and a skeptical attitude to produce three scientific offspring: verifiability, systematic inquiry, and generality. *Verifiability* aims at proving the truth or falsity of statements by testing them enough times to feel confident in the results. *Systematic inquiry* consists of sorting bits of information into coherent patterns—putting the oranges with the oranges, and the bananas with the bananas. *Generality* calls for gradual movement from specific levels of explanation to broader levels. When scientific inquiry can explain things by means of laws at a general level, it then should proceed to the most challenging task of all: predicting the workings of similar phenomena in the future. ■

Research Designs

What kinds of research designs do scholars use when they study humans scientifically? The first is **survey research**. Social scientists rely on survey instruments more than any other technique to gather data about human subjects. Surveys can be mailed to subjects or derived from personal interviews. They allow researchers to tap subjective states of mind such as attitudes and beliefs in an objective fashion and to analyze the results statistically.

Survey research ■ By canvassing people via questionnaires, social scientists can generate a statistically significant sample of opinion

Voter studies by political scientists have achieved sophistication through sample surveys. Although surveys usually provide accurate readings, they are time bound because sometimes people change their minds, including for whom they intend to vote. The results of surveys also can be influenced by the way in which questions are phrased; thus researchers try to keep their personal biases from bleeding through. Second, when possible, social scientists may use **experimental design**. As the technique most directly borrowed from physical sciences such as chemistry and biology, experiments are eminently rigorous, controllable, and verifiable. Psychologists have pioneered in the use of laboratory experiments, whereas geographers and sociologists opt for loosely constructed field experiments. The popular image of the social scientist dressed in a long, white coat with clipboard in-hand and scribbling notes about human subjects fits best with experimental research design. However, critics are quick in pointing to ethical problems that can arise when experiments are conducted on unwitting human subjects, and conversely, to the possibility of self-fulfilling-prophecy, a phenomenon known as the "Hawthorne effect" when the behavior of subjects is affected by knowing they are being studied.[15]

Experimental design ■ Difficulties sometimes arise, however, in applying this theoretically attractive model to the study of humans

The third most rigorous research design involves the social scientist directly in **participant observation**. Rather than aloofly analyzing survey statistics or observing an experiment in progress, participant observation places the scholar in the midst of the action. Early anthropologists, such as Margaret Mead, who studied preliterate groups in Samoa in 1925, opened up a whole range of creative research options to fellow social scientists.

Participant observation ■ A hands-on approach pioneered by anthropological field studies of distant cultures involving a risk that the researcher may become as integrated into the culture examined as to sacrifice objectivity and analytical acuity

There simply is no equally practical way to gather information about such remote groups of people as participant observation. The fact that both similarities and dissimilarities can be found among lifestyles around the globe makes participant observation a flexible tool for comparing human societies. However, if science demands objective neutrality, participant observation suffers when the scholar becomes too personally involved with the subjects. Under such circumstances, the observer may either alter the course of events among the subjects or become biased enough to interpret the results of the investigation inaccurately.

A fourth example of social science research design is called **content analysis.** This method most often uses the written document as a source of information about the person or group responsible for a set of communications. Like the sample survey, content analysis allows for the quantification of subjective aspects of human experience such as values and beliefs, making it attractive to advocates of social scientism. In international studies, speeches made by inaccessible leaders of foreign countries represent favorite targets for content analysis.

By systematically quantifying certain characteristics of a speech, a researcher can produce insights not apparent to the casual reader. The simple act of counting (although often complexly via computer programs) can provide new insights into the state of mind of an important leader. In an era known as the age of communication, this device offers a scientific handle for us to grasp the communication process. Although very amenable to quantification, content analysis encounters problems of **validity.**

Finally, much less quantifiable and systematic is the research design known as the **case study.** The case study's utility stems largely from its concreteness. Case studies seek wider truths by dissecting what happened and why in the past and then applying relevant insights to current or future contexts. They tend to appeal to humanistic social scientists. Cases can serve a long-range purpose as building blocks for broader theories to be developed at a later date; they also represent immediate illustrations of important phenomena.

Social scientists are sometimes criticized for getting lost in abstraction, and case studies require us to ground our theoretical musings in real events. The watchword of the social scientist browsing for good case studies might be summed up by the question, "Of what is this an instance?" Professional graduate schools of business were the first to popularize the case study method of teaching. The expansion of case studies into the social sciences has been facilitated by a major funding effort from the Pew Charitable Trust, a philanthropic organization. Sometimes cases warn us to avoid glaring mistakes from the past, such as Case Study 2.3, which describes how applied social science can go very wrong.

Good Science Involving DNA

Fortunately, such abuses of science represent the exception rather than the rule, and science typically leads to more productive outcomes. One such example is the use of DNA testing for a variety of purposes. Sometimes DNA testing answers long-disputed historical questions such as the fate of the last royal family of Tsarist Russia.

For more than 300 years, the Russian monarchy had been controlled by the Romanov family, but the Russian Revolution of 1917 ended the line when Tsar Nicholas II abdicated, and the Communists soon took over. Engaged in a bitter Civil War to maintain control of Russia, the Communists held the Romanovs prisoner and vacillated about what to do with them. Then, fearing that the former Tsar might represent a threat to their shaky government, in July of 1918, the Communists executed Nicholas, his wife, son, daughters, and personal attendants.

Personal identification in those days was imprecise. Throughout Russian history, pretenders to the throne had appeared after the death of royalty. True to form, pretenders materialized for decades after 1917, but few seemed credible. One persistent rumor, however, possessed staying power: that Nicholas' youngest daughter, Anastasia, had escaped the massacre. Many women claimed to be the "real" Anastasia, but the case that fascinated journalists was that of Anna Anderson. First turning up in Berlin in 1920, she insisted that she was the youngest Romanov daughter until her 1984 death in America.

Case Study 2.3   Sloppy Science Can Hurt People

In 1965, Janet Reimer gave birth in Winnipeg, Canada, to identical twin boys, Bruce and Brian. Within a year, her sons were having trouble urinating, and her physician recommended circumcision to correct the problem. The procedure corrected Brian's problem, but not Bruce's. The surgeon botched Bruce's circumcision, destroying his penis. Into this hopeless situation stepped a Johns Hopkins University psychologist offering hope.

Dr. John Money advised Mrs. Reimer that surgery could turn her son Bruce into a girl physically, and long-term psychotherapy with parental reinforcement could turn Bruce into a girl emotionally. The path that Dr. Money advocated was radical and completely untried, yet he failed to inform them of this fact. Before Brenda turned six, Dr. Money had published scientific articles chronicling the success of what came to be known as the "twins case"—successful sexual identity change.

In 1967, Bruce Reimer had his testicles removed and a vagina surgically created. Bruce was now supposed to become *Brenda Reimer*. Regular psychotherapy would guide Brenda through these changes, and, at puberty, she would be given female hormones. The Reimers expected Brenda to grow up not only looking like a woman but feeling like one. Dr. Money gained fame, and other practitioners adopted what seemed the only hope for such children. In the interim, Dr. Money failed to learn about Brenda Reimer's actual fate.

For fourteen years, this troubled child and adolescent lived as Brenda, never accepting a feminine gender identity. In hindsight, later saying "I was never happy as Brenda. Never. I'd slit my throat before I'd go back to that." When informed of her true sex at birth, she cast off the female identity of Brenda and decided to live as a male named David. David later underwent surgeries to reconstruct his penis and for several years lived with a wife and her three children. Then, on May 4, 2004, David Reimer committed suicide in Winnipeg.

Given what science knows today, Money's prescribed treatment seems ludicrous. In the 1960s, however, his ideas were not so bizarre. Many believed that newborns represent a blank slate, onto which even gender identity could be scripted. Optimistic hopes about the power of therapy arose during this decade of optimism. Even Money's treatment for Bruce Reimer fit with the idea that nurture (experiences), not nature (heredity), shapes who we become.

Subsequent research projects, however, have established that humans are not born as sexually neutral blank slates. Structural differences between male and female brains have been discovered. But it took decades for Dr. Money's theory and therapy to be discredited. He deceived the Reimers about prior cases, failed to find out what *really* happened to Brenda, and reported prematurely on the "twins case."[16] ∎

Anastasia the escapee caught on in fictional venues such as a French play by Marcelle Maurette, then as a dramatic adaptation on the Broadway stage, later in Hollywood's *Anastasia* (starring Ingrid Bergman), and finally as an animated film in 1997. Fueling rumors was the fact that the location of the Romanov bodies was declared as unknown throughout the Communist era. But in 1989, a team of researchers claimed to have uncovered the skeletons. Traditional skeletal examination of the remains proved inconclusive, but eventually DNA testing became available.

Comparing the skeletal DNA to blood samples donated by living relatives of the Tsar's family, the mystery was solved. The bones do constitute the remains of the members of the royal family, including Anastasia. Furthermore, tests done on hair samples of Anna Anderson proved that she was *not* a blood relative of the Romanovs.[17]

This use of DNA testing, however, pales in comparison to forensic applications now routinely affecting the outcome of criminal cases. A total of twenty-eight murder and rape convictions were overturned on the basis of new DNA evidence in American courts between 1989 and 1996, and that rate has skyrocketed since then. Some Northwestern University journalism students gained the release of three men wrongfully imprisoned for a 1978 murder. Their professor, David Protess, specializes in investigating wrongful convictions.[18] So many wrongfully convicted individuals on death row in America have been released owing to DNA evidence that several states are contemplating abolishing capital punishment.

Social Humanism

The complexity of human behavior opens the door to a very different vision called *social humanism*. Social scientism and social humanism each contribute to the content and method of the modern social sciences. One pair of authors observe that "From their very inception, the social sciences have been torn between the ideals of scientific objectivity and those of humanistic reform-mindedness."[19] Social humanism emphasize humankind's aesthetic and experiential sides as providing the stuff of meaningful knowledge, and they borrow much from the humanities.

The National Endowment for the Humanities (NEH) considers the humanities to include history, philosophy, linguistics, literature, jurisprudence, comparative religion, and the criticism and theory of the arts. Social humanism offers a more personalized mirror of social reality than does social scientism. The humanities feature ideas on how to live, providing depth, texture, and meaning to routine human existence. As social beings, people face troubling moral dilemmas that creative endeavors such as literature, film, or theater can help to resolve. Life presents *Homo sapiens* with cloudy paradoxes that the humanities seek to illuminate.

Humanists believe in the value of fresh insights into the human condition as something akin to chicken soup for the spirit. They argue that the search for meaning and enjoyment serves as a palliative to over-reliance on cool, detached rationality. Humanistic appreciation of a piece of music, a painting, a film, or a ballet connects directly to human emotions. To some extent, the humanities relate to what many traditional societies considered as feminine traits, such as spirituality, emotion, and intuition.

Advocates suggest that the humanities help people to keep their values in proper perspective, a task made difficult by the materialism common in Western societies. Like the supporters of scientism, humanists see their expressions of subjective experience as means of communication among all peoples. The key difference, however, is that for the past century, scientism has held center stage in the American social sciences, with humanism relegated to a supporting role.

In Europe, no comparable triumph of scientific over humanistic social science has transpired; historical and philosophical analysis have remained paramount endeavors there. One humanities scholar decries the American divorce of history from the social sciences as responsible for a contemporary "United States of Amnesia."[20] Since star billing among the American social sciences has gone to scientism, advocates of a more humanized social science have had to serve as the critical opposition. Unlike scientism, social humanism considers the differences between natural and social sciences a serious matter of *kind,* not of degree. Much of what falls under the rubric of quantitative social science, say the humanists, is better described as **pseudo-science** practiced by those whom British philosopher of science Bertrand Russell sarcastically caricatures as "slaves of routine who would rather die than think."

Pseudo-science ■ A pejorative label describing poorly conceived, shabbily executed, or badly misinterpreted studies

Humanistic Critics of Social Scientism

It would be difficult to identify a more persistent critic of scientism than English sociologist Stan Andreski, who claims "even the old and valuable insights inherited from our illustrious ancestors are being drowned in a torrent of meaningless verbiage and useless technicalities." He considers the rush to quantification responsible for creating a methodological trap of the trivial: for human affairs to be measured, only sterile and unimportant questions get asked.[21]

The result can be an "ends–means distortion"; that which is initially valued (methodological complexity) only as a means to a greater end soon becomes valued for its own sake, with the original end (social explanation) getting lost in the shuffle. Humanists feel that such methodological exoticism springs from the mistaken belief that if certain kinds of data can be quantified and analyzed by computer, then they must be more important than mere qualitative data. To humanists, this article of scientistic faith should not be accepted without proof. British statesman Benjamin Disraeli, with tongue in cheek, once described "three kinds of lies: lies, damned lies, and statistics." The social sciences seek the nearest approximation to the truth under real-world circumstances. Sometimes that search entails quantification, but often it does not.

One of the most robust criticisms of scientism has to do with human free will. Scientific method inherently seeks to uncover regular and predictable patterns of behavior. And science seeks the discovery of underlying laws to explain such recurrent patterns. When the object of investigation is electricity, freon gas, or spiders, all seems right with this method. People, on the other hand, frequently do not follow predictable scripts. They have free will, meaning that they can change their minds, act irrationally, or behave differently than they have in the past. Rational and emotional motivations blend seamlessly together, and humans can choose to experiment with new ways of doing things, even if they seem self-defeating to an objective observer. As eighteenth-century German philosopher Immanuel Kant more colorfully put it, "Nothing straight from human timber shall ever be constructed."

The realm of human feelings is one where humanism claims special expertise. Whereas scientism appeals to the human proclivity toward order and precision, the humanities focus on our penchant for emotional and experiential meaning. Nobel Peace Prize winner and Holocaust expert Elie Wiesel has said that all of his professional activities (including thirty books, hundreds of lectures, university teaching, and the creation of international organizations) boil down to one purpose: helping people to *experience feelings* about the World War II Holocaust in which six million innocent Jews died at the hands of the Nazis.[22] Few lives stand up and perform such eloquent testimony to the humanistic spirit as does Wiesel's.

Contrasting Scientistic and Humanistic Schools

Reducing complex phenomena such as the scientistic and humanistic schools of thought to dichotomous pairs of characteristics carries a risk of oversimplification. Nevertheless, the following list, derived from the preceding discussion, may help to summarize these divergent viewpoints on the social sciences.

Social Scientism	Social Humanism
quantitative	qualitative
experimental	experiential
reality is discovered	reality is created
predictable humans	human free will
descriptive	normative
impersonal	personal
U.S.-based	European-based

Synthesis: "Roomy" Social Sciences

There is a community of scholarship between the humanities and the behavioral sciences, and the validity of one does not depend upon alienation from the other.

Leonard Broom, American philosopher

My sense of the social sciences is eclectic, one beholden to both the humanities and the natural sciences. The essence of the social sciences consists of understanding and explaining human behavior, endeavors monopolized by no single approach. Such a roomy definition of the social sciences requires peaceful coexistence between scientism and humanism, despite their differences.

Many great monuments to human ingenuity point to the fusion of scientistic and humanistic schools of thought. Consider the marriage of precision and beauty embodied in the 4,500-year-old pyramids of Egyptian civilization; or the classic Colosseum of ancient Rome, whose inspiration came partly from the mathematics of numbers considered divine and partly from emulating nature.

The great Egyptian pyramids at Giza.

Source: Alistair Duncan
© Dorling Kindersley

Architect Frank Lloyd Wright's masterpiece "Fallingwater," built during the 1930s for the Kauffman family in western Pennsylvania, is considered one of the twentieth century's works of genius. Constructed of sandstone quarried on the property, the stone functions as separate reinforced concrete trays producing three levels of rooms. The whole structure is boldly cantilevered over a stream and anchored on a natural boulder: part scientific precision, part aesthetics. The beauty of Fallingwater stems largely from the way it blends living space with natural surroundings. Only by experiencing Frank Lloyd Wright's creation can you understand the way it works both functionally and aesthetically.

It is certainly easy to split social scientism and social humanism into polar opposites: verification versus insight, objective versus subjective realities, experimental versus experiential design, and so on. Synthesizing these impulses is much harder. Yet, as the Egyptian pyramids, Roman coliseum, and Fallingwater suggest, when successfully fused, scientism and humanism can produce a dynamic synergy, tapping the best of both worlds.

Three decades ago, philosopher of science Abraham Kaplan advocated a middle position in the social science confrontation between scientists and humanists—not as a "golden mean" compromise merely to avoid strife but rather because of the intrinsic value of the synthesis.[23] A book by well-known international studies scholar Hayward Alker mines this same theme. He describes the essence of his intellectual quest as a "philosophical, methodological, and disciplinary preoccupation as a social scientist with somehow voyaging between, connecting up, or finding a bridging place between the humanities and sciences."[24]

One key policy issue looming on the horizon concerns the debate over the ethics of human cloning. Dealing with this controversy intelligently will require all of the interdisciplinary synthesis that social scientists can muster because it is such a thick tangle of unanswered questions with implications for the nature of humanity's identity as a unique species. Case Study 2.4 explores the background to the issue and presents the main arguments for and against human cloning.

Case Study 2.4   Is Cloning Humans Acceptable?

Both the science and technology of cloning animals have become nearly routine. First, scientists remove eggs from multiple donors; second, suck out the eggs' nuclei, including their DNA; third, fuse the DNA-free eggs with cells from the cloning candidate by zapping them with electricity; and fourth, allow some of the rebuilt eggs to divide and form embryos.

However, defining cloning's exact meaning in the human context is fraught with uncertainty. It is *not* organic Xeroxing or producing carbon copies of the original person. We all know about clones in the guise of identical twins, each of whom remains unique, despite many genetic similarities to its twin. Craig Venter, a pioneer in the Genome Project mapping our 30,000 humans genes, says that research thus far conducted dispels the widespread myth of genetic determinism, or the belief that heredity dwarfs human experience is shaping who we become. Venter counters that *nurture* contributes to who we become every bit as much as *nature.*

But fuzzy thinking oozes from public attitudes regarding the emotional issue of human cloning, largely because of sensational images gleaned from popular culture. Check out one of the movie versions of *Frankenstein*, based on Mary Shelley's nineteenth-century novel. Made in 1956, the first of three chilling film adaptations of *Invasion of the Body Snatchers* features furtive alien invaders inhabiting human bodies. These robotic clones lack any spark of human emotion, as one girl complains that "Uncle Ira just isn't Uncle Ira any more!" More concretely tapping historical fears is *The Boys from Brazil*, a 1978 film in which the Nazi nightmare refuses to remain buried, as neo-Nazis struggle to clone an army of little Hitlers.

That our imagery derives largely from specious origins, however, says nothing about the ethics of cloning. But it does highlight a need for *critical thinking*, or rigorous analysis, conducted with an open mind. The gravity of this subject suggests that our ethics should drive our politics, not vice versa. Often the ideological political lenses of liberalism versus conservatism are used to guide us through the turf of controversial issues that we have not yet worked our way through. However, the crutch of liberalism versus conservatism does not support us very well on this unmapped turf. Answers to vexing dilemmas may appear to be attractively simple. But thinking complexly about paradoxical questions ought to come engraved in the scholarly job description.

Although it took him 277 sheep eggs to produce one lamb, Dolly, it was Scottish scientist Ian Wilmut's 1997 successful cloning that unleashed a flood of media attention. Shortly thereafter, President Bill Clinton appointed an advisory commission, which had ninety days to study the topic. The commission recommended federal legislation to ban cloning humans. Numerous churches and politicians in America advocate banning human cloning. Countries such as Spain and France had already done so. That same year, the first major academic conference to address the subject found almost no one speaking in favor of human cloning, which also mirrored American public opinion. But in 2001, the drama continued to unfold in Rome, where researchers met to plan cloning a human. Italy currently has no ban, and if it passes one, team leader Panos Zavos hopes to perform the first clone in Israel. Zavos claims to have hundreds of infertile couples eager to clone their way into parenthood.

Common Arguments For and Against Cloning Humans

PRO:

1. *The right to personal reproductive freedom.* In America, a core value assumes that the government should be heavily limited in its ability to interfere with individual liberties, and cloning is no exception. This view is summarized by philosophy professor Gregory Pence, who writes that "The essence of democracy is that government is not a reproductive dictatorship."[25]

2. *The right to scientific inquiry.* Scientists are entitled to use scientific means in efforts to improve human existence, such as the use of cloning to treat infertility.

3. *The misguided fear factor.* Much opposition to human cloning stems from a misconception that it amounts to human Xeroxing. R. C. Lewontin notes that "Our knowledge of twins should lead us not to fear humans originated from the same gentype."[26]

4. *A higher moral standard.* The effort to reduce human suffering represents a higher ethical goal than does obedience to doctrines expressed by social or religious institutions.

5. *Futility of the Luddite option.* The knee-jerk antitechnology response typifies perennially closed Luddite minds.

CON:

1. *Honor Nature with a capital N.* Human cloning would be an abomination of Nature and the God behind it. Boston scientist George Annas avers that "Cloning would violate a barrier of natural kinds without sufficiently good reasons as moral justification."[27]

2. *Beware of the slippery slope.* Chicago philosopher, Leon Kass posits that if this practice is allowed to occur with the intention of controlling it, abuses of the original intent will inevitably develop, and unforeseen disasters will emerge.

3. *Human individuality.* Scientist James Watson sees a sacred uniqueness in what it means to be human, which cloning may threaten.

4. *Klondike capitalism.* The profit incentive will turn cloning into a commercialized human body shop encouraging many bad outcomes.[28]

5. *Embryos are humans.* Embryos (fertilized eggs) should not be used for experimental purposes because they are entitled to respect as potential humans.[29]

If you were an advisor to the president of the United States, what would you suggest should be the government's position on human cloning? Should experiments toward this end be banned? Or should they be allowed to proceed, but only with private, nonpublic funding? Or should the government support preliminary research only and then evaluate what transpires each year?

The content of the social sciences has internationalized itself significantly in recent years. The shrinking world of globalization has increased awareness of how each social science discipline is affected what happens elsewhere. Beginning with the 1979 presidential commission on international studies and foreign languages, many reports have advocated curricular internationalization, and these potent winds of change have swept across American higher education in recent decades. ■

Chapter Synopsis

The roots of the social sciences reach deeply into the soil provided by the older natural sciences and humanities. From these sources come two competing philosophical schools of thought about how to study human behavior: social scientism and social humanism. Social scientism emphasizes quantification, systematic inquiry, and a skeptical attitude concerning commonsensical beliefs. Social humanism values historico-philosophical analysis as well as insights derived from personal experience and aesthetic appreciation. Scientism has been the majority viewpoint and humanism the loyal opposition during the past hundred years in the United States. Although these two camps often ignore each other, this text seeks a roomier definition of the social sciences that recognizes their debts to both sets of intellectual progenitors.

The social sciences in Europe, however, still emphasize the tradition of historico-philosophical analysis of human affairs. It is primarily in America, where higher education is big business, that discrete professional disciplines emphasizing scientific methods have developed. Prior to the 1880s, higher education in the United States occurred in small liberal arts colleges funded and influenced by churches. As universities sprang up at the end of the nineteenth century, new graduate programs in the social sciences emulated the laboratory techniques and seminar discussions modeled by natural sciences such as chemistry and biology. Massive growth has characterized the Americanized social sciences in the past hundred years.

FOR DIGGING DEEPER

Alker, Hayward R. *Rediscoveries and Reformulations: Humanistic Methodologies for International Studies.* Cambridge University Press, 1996.

Andreski, Stanislav. *Social Science as Sorcery.* St. Martin's Press, 1973.

Babbie, Earl. *The Practice of Social Research.* Wadsworth, 1995.

———. *Observing Ourselves: Essays in Social Research.* Waveland Press, 2000.

Bannister, Robert C. *Sociology and Scientism: The American Quest for Objectivity, 1880–1940.* University of North Carolina Press, 1987.

Best, Samuel, and Brian Krueger. *Internet Data Collection.* Sage, 2004.

Calhoun, Craig, ed. *Dictionary of the Social Sciences.* Oxford University Press, 2001.

Cuba, Lee. *A Short Guide to Writing about Social Science.* Longman, 1997.

Edel, Abraham. *Relating Humanities and Social Thought.* Transaction, 1990.

Hoover, Kenneth R. *The Elements of Social Scientific Thinking.* St. Martin's Press, 1992.

Kaplan, David, ed. *The SAGE Handbook of Quantitative Methodology for the Social Sciences.* Sage, 2004.

Kirsch, George B., and others. *The West in Global Context: From 1500 to the Present.* Prentice Hall, 1997.

Kuhn, Thomas S. *The Structure of Scientific Revolutions.* University of Chicago Press, 1970.

MacKinnon, Barbara. *Human Cloning: Science, Ethics, and Public Policy.* University of Illinois Press, 2000.

Manicas, Peter T. *A History and Philosophy of the Social Sciences.* Blackwell Publishers, 1987.

Maxim, Paul S. *Quantitative Research Methods in the Social Sciences.* Oxford University Press, 1998.

Northcutt, Norvell, and Danny McCoy. *Interactive Qualitative Analysis: A Systems Method for Qualitative Research.* Sage, 2004.

Oosterhoff, Fredericka. *Ideas Have a History: Perspectives on the Western Search for Truth.* University Press of America, 2001.

Pence, Gregory. *Who's Afraid of Human Cloning?* Rowman and Littlefield, 1998.

Rosenberg, Alexander. *Philosophy of Social Science.* Westview Press, 1995.

Ross, Dorothy. *The Origins of American Social Science.* Cambridge University Press, 1991.

Silver, Lee M. *Remaking Eden: Cloning and Beyond in a Brave New World.* Hearst Books, 1997.

Van Doren, Charles. *A History of Knowledge: Past, Present, and Future.* Ballantine Books, 1992.

Yin, Robert. *Case Study Research: Design and Methods.* Sage, 2002.

INTERNET

American Scientist:
http://www.sigmaxi.org/amsci/amsci.html

Coombsweb Social Science Server:
http://coombs.anu.edu.au/

Humanities Hub:
http://www.mtute.ac.uk

Humanities on Line (H-Net):
http://h-net.msu.edu/

International Resources for the Humanities:
http://www.intute.ac.uk

Internet for Social Sciences:
http://www.unesco.org/most/brochur3.htm

NOVA Sex: Unknown:
http://www.pbs.org/wgbh/nova/transcripts/2813gender.html

Science:
http://www.science.com

Social Sciences Data on Net:
http://www.3stages.org/idata

Social Sciences Information Gateway:
http://sosig.ac.uk/

World History Links Page:
http://www.worldhistorycompass.com

CHAPTER 3

Geography and Spatial Analysis

CORE OBJECTIVE

To use geography's spatial facts, concepts, and theories in explaining the behavior of states and other actors regarding Global Issues (GIs).

THEMATIC QUESTIONS

■ How well or poorly has our species managed nature?

■ Which geographic considerations relate to the relative power of states?

■ How does geography's history illustrate both the uses and abuses of the social sciences in human affairs?

■ Which key concepts vital to addressing modern GIs were derived from the discipline of geography?

■ What does geography contribute to understanding the relationships among ecological GIs?

More than 2,000 years ago, Greek philosopher Aristotle observed that "In all things of nature, there is something of the marvelous."[1] Studying the earth as the natural home of humankind is one of geography's major tasks. However, one contemporary scholar believes that American citizens exhibit serious inadequacies when it comes to geography. According to University of Pennsylvania Professor of International Relations Walter McDougall, "Most Americans emerge from their schooling as functional illiterates in geography despite the fact that 90 percent of U.S. adults consider some geographical knowledge a prerequisite for being a well-rounded person." Professor McDougall's figures are based on a poll conducted by the National Geographic Society.[2]

Spatial ■ Having to do with a given space, and for geographers that space consists of the earth's surface

Geography is fundamentally a **spatial** discipline. Geographers rely on location, direction, and distance as the conceptual building blocks to analyze interactions that occur in or on the space of the earth.[3] Humans seem to possess a spatial concern for where something is located, how to get there, and how long it will take. Therefore, geographers see a world of *physicality* when analyzing human behavior.

The Stanislavsky method of getting behind the eyeballs of each social science means that in this chapter we must remain mindful of geography's spatial physicality. Geographers perceive human affairs differently from psychologists, anthropologists, sociologists, political scientists, and economists. Named for Russian actor and director Konstantin Stanislavsky, the "method" entails dramatic training whereby actors seek greater realism by losing themselves in a character, thus appearing as if they are part of a real world rather than a fanciful one. Stanislavsky's ideas caught on in New York beginning in the 1920s and eventually led to the famous "Actor's Studio" that produced talents such as Marlon Brando, Lee Strasberg, and Paul Newman.[4]

The spatial behavior of humans interacting with the earth, known as *ecology*, is very relevant to other social scientists. Although humanity's track record as custodian of ecological space is less than inspiring, the discipline of geography fits us with lenses calibrated to improve the record of human stewardship. Given what you learned in Chapter 2 about the fundamental differences between social scientism and social humanism, toward which of these competing philosophies do you think geography naturally gravitates, and why?

Human Mismanagement of the Earth

More than 6 billion humans exist on the face of our planet, interacting with a physical environment that affects the way we live. Although humans have been around for less than 1 percent of the Earth's history, *Homo sapiens* has managed to exert an outsized influence on the environment.[5] It is not difficult to find examples of poor human management leading to disastrous consequences for land, agriculture, and society.

Because of their isolation, islands such as Australia, Hawaii, and the Galápagos all evolved extremely different types of species, including some strange ones such as Australia's duck-billed platypus. Isolation also accounts for the absence of natural predators when humans have introduced alien species in island ecosystems. It must not have taken long for Thomas Austin, the Australian who brought jackrabbits into that country in 1859, to regret unleashing them down under because these predator-less creatures soon procreated their way to status as a pest species.

Globally, agriculture pollutes more water than any other cause, owing to fertilizers, pesticides, animal waste, and sediments. An area of 7,000 square miles known as the "dead zone" can be found in the Gulf of Mexico. Nutrients from agricultural runoff in Louisiana feed algae that bloom in summer, die and sink, and then decompose, depleting oxygen. The area is called the "dead zone" because of its disastrous effects on Gulf fishing and shrimping.[6]

In 1997, hundreds of forest fires in the Southeast Asian country of Indonesia burned more than 750,000 acres of rainforest. A haze covered an area one-third the size of the continental United States; a single day's exposure equaled smoking forty cigarettes. More than 35,000 people contracted respiratory disease from smoke during the first two weeks. What caused such a mess? One contributing factor was the existence of unusually dry conditions in the region. However, the practice of setting fires as a cheap way to clear land for subsistence farming was chiefly to blame.[7]

Also in the Pacific region in 1968, the micro-state of Nauru gained independence after decades as an Australian protectorate. For centuries, Nauru had benefited from the richest phosphate reserves on the planet. As a prime breeding ground for many bird species, massive amounts of bird guano had produced world-class phosphate deposits. After independence, Nauru's 10,000 inhabitants proceeded to over-mine these phosphates and soon had achieved the world's highest per capita income. However, it was all boom and then bust, and today its denuded landscape has been described by some as looking like a lunar landscape.[8]

Our consideration of human mismanagement concludes with a final story involving alien species related in Case Study 3.1. It involves the well-intended, yet ill-conceived, introduction during the 1940s of a toad named *Bufo marinus* into the ecological space of rural Florida.

Case Study 3.1   *Bufo Marinus*

In the 1940s, Florida had not yet become the crowded and bustling state that it is today. Farming was crucial to its economy, and sugar cane was a natural winner in Florida's warm, wet environment. But widespread use of pesticides was still in the future, and sugar cane farmers were always looking for ways to beat the beetle that was having a heyday with their crops. Desperate farmers tried some rather bizarre solutions but probably none as strange as the story of *Bufo marinus*.

The scientific (Latin-derived) name *Bufo marinus* refers to a large South American marine toad that is fond of pests such as the beetle that was infesting Florida's sugar cane fields in the 1940s. Consequently, some farmers decided to roll nature's dice, hoping for a solution to their pest problem. They brought quantities of *Bufo marinus* north to Florida and pointed them in the direction of the hated sugar cane beetles. *Bufo marinus* never did multiply sufficiently to increase the sugar cane harvest, but they certainly have become numerous enough, and nasty enough, to rank as pests themselves.

These hefty toads weigh about three pounds and measure around seven inches from stem to stern. They have been described as resembling Jabba the Hutt of *Star Wars* movie fame. *Bufo marinus* possesses large glands behind each eye that extend down its back. These glands hold a white, milky toxin that the toad can excrete when threatened. Every year, a few dogs are killed in Florida by a dose of this toxin. The curator of the Everglades National Museum, Dr. Walter Mischaka, likens the noise made by *Bufo marinus* to the sound of a distant tractor. His

description of the toad's appearance is even less flattering: "It looks like a large cow-pie."

Humans are not immune to the toxin and can become ill from exposure. Dr. Roseanne Philen, of the Centers for Disease Control in Atlanta, reports that four men in New York died in 1995 from ingesting it. They misunderstood its intended use, thinking it an oral aphrodisiac. They were supposed to rub it into the genital area, not swallow it. Its sale in the United States is now illegal. It's hoped that its users were more prudent in Mesoamerica's ancient Mayan civilization, where the toxin was taken for religious purposes as a hallucinogen.[9]

Human environmental mismanagement oozed from the introduction of a nasty toad (*Bufo marinus*) in a failed attempt by Florida farmers to get rid of a crop-devouring beetle.

Geography's Origins

Ecological courses in academia exploring the human-earth relationship are not new; they were being taught in departments of geology (earth science) in American universities more than a hundred years ago. William Morris Davis, who taught in the geology department at Harvard around 1900, is credited with starting modern geography in America. By the mid-twentieth century, geographers had begun specializing in subfields related to other social sciences, such as cultural geography, political geography, and economic geography. Geography probably represents the closest social science link to the natural sciences.

Modern geography in the United States is structured around a professional organization of 6,500 members called the Association of American Geographers (AAG). Founded in 1904, the AAG has grown to include an annual meeting, two scholarly journals and a monthly newsletter, plus nine regional and fifty-three specialization groups. By visiting the AAG Website, you can find links to the annual meeting, other conferences, Annals of the AAG, jobs and careers in geography, grants and awards, specialty groups, and information on topics such as geography and terrorism. Most interesting is an outreach service called "Ask a Geographer," which enables teachers like me and students like you to contact directly (e-mail) geographers who volunteer to provide information in their areas of expertise (such as architectural geography, cartography, climate, and environmental geography).

Although a distinct discipline of geography has occurred fairly recently, spatial analysis can be traced back to ancient Athens. The Greek scholar Eratosthenes coined the term geography, meaning "the description of the earth," as early as the third century B.C. In the second century A.D., the Roman thinker Claudius Ptolemy compiled his impressive *Geographia,* including information about sailing distances, key physical landmarks, and drawings of coastlines—all the stuff of modern geography.

Geography's interest in spatial analysis necessitates its dealing with *location, direction, and distance*—all qualities addressed by maps. The process of map making is known as cartography. A simple shorthand used by some scholars suggests that "if you can map it, it must be geography."

Mercator Projection Maps

Maps turned out to be very helpful for London officials one century ago, when they were used to track the spread of a cholera epidemic to the city's water system. Because maps aim to simulate reality, the drawing of maps may seem simple and straightforward. The process, however, is anything but simple. Part of their complexity derives from this basic fact: all maps distort reality in some way, shape, or form because they portray our round earth on flat surfaces.[10]

Consider, for example, the 400-year old Mercator projection map (see Figure 3.1), which has dominated English-language textbooks for generations. Originally intended as a navigational tool, it served that purpose admirably. However, on the Mercator map, the relative size of landmasses is all wrong: Europe and Russia appear much larger than reality, while Africa and South America seem much smaller than reality.

In recent decades, however, cartography has benefited greatly from reliance on computers. From the collection and recording of data to the creation and revision of maps, computers are intimately involved. A computer-generated set of procedures enabling assembly, storage, manipulation, analysis, and display of information, called a geographic information system (GIS), has revolutionized mapping. One very sophisticated

Ancient Greek scholar, Claudius Ptolemy, one of the pioneers who paved the way for the modern social science discipline of geography.

Source: Picture Desk, Inc./ Kobal Collection.

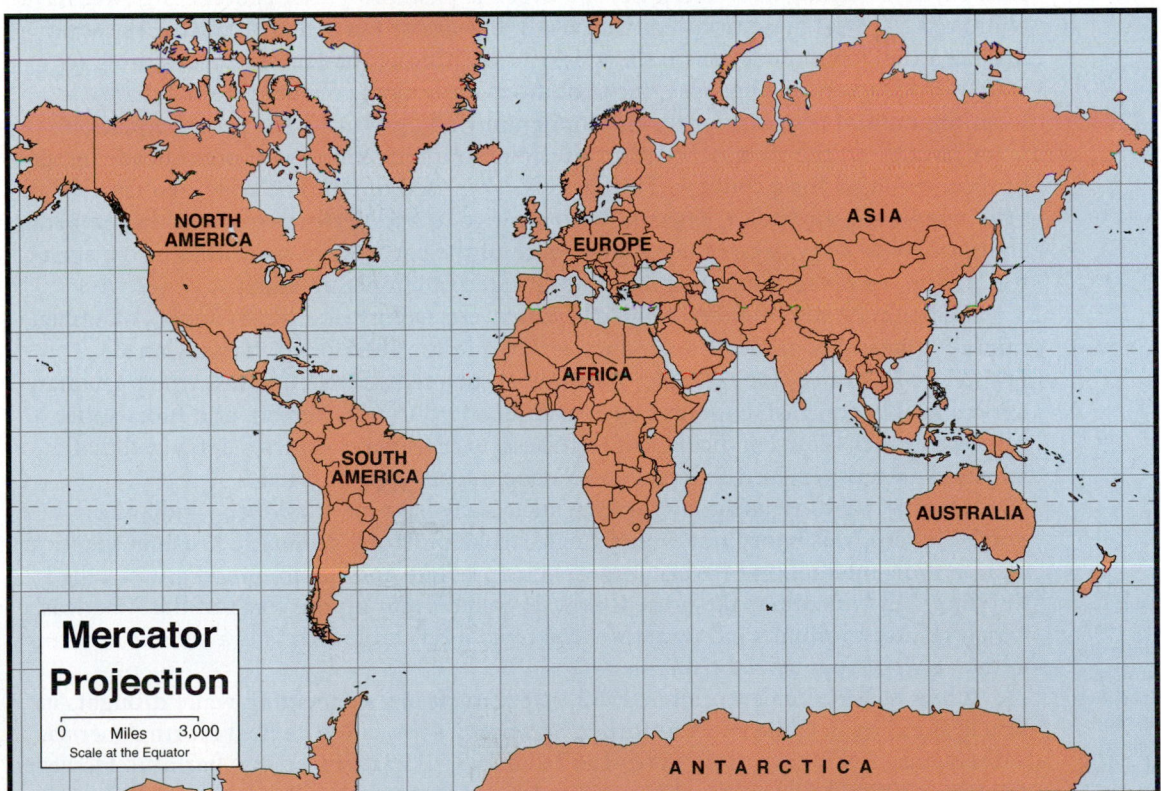

Figure 3.1

Mercator Projection map distorts reality by making Africa and South America look too small compared to the other continents.

new effort headed by Thomas Van Sant, the GeoSphere Project, resolves some of the problems inherent in mapping by linking together satellite photos, for both greater accuracy and more visually inspiring maps. The geographer's spatial perspective provides vital insights into how humanity organizes both physical and social space.[11]

Comprehending World Affairs Through Geography

Models ■ Ideational structures, similar to theories, used to explain the relationship between variables or hypotheses

Geography's contribution to our understanding of world affairs has varied according to time and circumstance. At times, social scientists have overemphasized geography's role in explaining the behavior of states in international relations. This ambitious approach led to causal **models** spouting laws of state behavior solely on the basis of geographic factors. The misuse of broad explanatory models peaked early in the twentieth century when aggressive dictators seeking to justify expansionist policies used them to offer bogus rationalizations for their imperialism.

Contemporary scholars are careful to avoid exaggerated claims about the potency of geographic explanations. If kept in proper perspective, geographic facts, concepts, and theories can help account for many aspects of human behavior at the *micro* (local), *macro* (national), and *mega* (global) levels of analysis. Geography's role in explaining behavior on the world stage can be broken down into two categories: (1) those related to a traditional emphasis on states as key actors, and (2) those germane to a new age of globalization (especially as related to ecological GIs such as environment, population, food, and energy).

Geography and State Power

Looking back over the past 4,000 years, we can map a geographic progression of power. Starting from Egypt in the Middle East, moving to Greece and Rome in Southern Europe, then settling in Western Europe over the past 500 years, centers of power have exhibited a spatial migration. For the past 350 years of Euro-centric power, the state has been the dominant actor on the world stage. Among the factors contributing to state power, a variety of geographic conditions serve as the foundation. Climate, location, natural resources, size, and topography all figure into the power equation.[12]

Climate—in the form of weather, precipitation, and wind—can provide advantages or disadvantages for a country. The earth is comprised of climatic zones: equatorial, arid, temperate, and polar. The ability to grow food and perform work in the temperate zones (forty to sixty degrees north and south of the equator) exceeds that of the equatorial, arid, or polar zones, helping states located in temperate climatic zones.[13]

Precipitation also matters. Somewhere between twenty and ninety inches of annual rainfall is generally needed for productive agriculture. The United States, Canada, France, and Ukraine, for example, all reside in such temperate climates, which facilitate agriculture. In contrast, countries such as Equador, Burundi, Yemen, and India suffer from various climatic handicaps. Nevertheless, exceptional countries defying climatic liabilities to prosper, such as Israel and Singapore, can also be cited.

Roughly 1,000 years ago, a thriving ancient civilization, the Mecho Indians of northern Peru, was wiped out with a single stroke of nature's climatic brush in the form of a periodic interaction between atmospheric pressure and ocean temperatures called **El Niño**.[14] El Niño alters the normal flow of cold current up the coast of the Americas, which reverses normal wind patterns. One of its predictable effects is a significant drop in the catch of commercial fishermen.[15]

El Niño ■ An unpredictable climatological and oceanic event occurring sporadically off the west coast of South America. It starts with a weakening of the east-west trade winds, which causes the waters of the Eastern Pacific to warm and tropical rainfall to shift from Indonesia to South America. This results in severe weather patterns in many parts of the world.

When El Niño came to call in 1982–1983, it left in its damaging wake droughts in Brazil, flooding in Chile and California, and heavy snowfall in central North America. Subsequent El Niño events in 1986–1987 and 1991–1992 proved less harmful. However, the 1997–1998 El Niño caused extremely dry conditions in the Amazon rainforest. The Brazilian city of Manaus recorded its worst smoke readings ever (and a 40 percent rise in respiratory disease) because of burning forests.[16] This particular El Niño also resulted in hundreds of deaths in California, which was inundated with quadruple the normal rainfall amounts. The term El Niño comes from the Spanish reference to the Christ child because El Niño generally arrives in Latin America during the Christmas season.[17]

The vagaries of weather were graphically portrayed in filmmaker Jan De Bont's hit adventure movie, *Twister* (1996). The film traces two young tornado-tracking scientists questing after knowledge about twisters, while experiencing frequent close calls with windblown disaster on the Oklahoma plains. In a country besieged by about 1,000 tornadoes annually, U.S. audiences proved a real pushover for *Twister's* high anxiety.

Modern humans in truth ought to feel grateful for the relatively stable and benign climate that has existed on earth during the 11,000 years since the last Ice Age. Evidence from a scientific study conducted in Greenland's ice sheet shows how relatively unusual this inter-glacial period has been. The study also shows that rapid climatic change can occur, not only over centuries, as was previously known, but over periods as brief as a decade. The evidence suggests climatic instability as the long-term norm; the stability witnessed during recent millennia is more of an exception.[18] Location can affect state power in strictly geographic terms, such as access to the sea, control of transportation routes, and availability of natural resources. Kuwait, Malta, and the United Arab Emirates, respectively, illustrate these considerations.

In an age where humanity begins to bump its head on the global ceiling by depleting nonrenewable resources, the significance of raw materials such as oil, water, soil, iron, uranium, titanium, and a clean environment becomes magnified. The earth's natural lungs, its rainforests, which are suffering from something akin to global emphysema, are now recognized as vital to our planet's survival. Saudi Arabia's oil clearly enhances its power in the world. Canada's freshwater resources make it the envy of water-poor countries such as Israel and Kazakhstan. Ukraine's dark, rich soil allows it to blossom in ways that some of its neighbors can only dream about. South Africa possesses uranium—a rare ore coveted by nuclear hopefuls such as North Korea and Iran. Yet resource-poor Japan, so often the exception, has managed to grow the world's second-largest economy without domestic energy sources or much arable land.

The sheer size of a country does not directly produce power, but it has numerous indirect influences. Size is a latent factor augmenting such things as capacity for population growth, natural resources, defensibility, and both human and ecological diversity. Russia, Canada, China, the United States, and Brazil, the world's five largest countries, seem blessed when compared to most of the world's smaller countries. Larger states also enjoy sparser population densities, as illustrated by the comparative statistics listed in Table 3.1.

Bill Paxton and Helen Hunt run from an oncoming tornado in a scene from the adventure movie, *Twister*.

Table 3.1

COMPARATIVE POPULATION DENSITIES

Country	Crude Density per Square Mile
Australia	6
Bangladesh	2,305
Canada	8
China	344
India	789
Japan	870
Nigeria	346
United States	74

Source: U.N. Food and Agriculture Organization (FAO), *Production Yearbook,* and Population Reference Bureau, *World Population Data Sheet.*

Case Study 3.2 Location, Land, and the Netherlands

States come in all shapes and sizes. The Netherlands is notable for the amount of dry land that it has created by human intervention. Fifteen million people live in the Netherlands (previously Holland) on a land area of roughly 12,500 square miles, making it continental Europe's most densely populated society (90 percent urban), depicted in Figure 3.2. Sixty percent of both its land and people lie below sea level. An ingenious and laborious system of dikes has been constructed to liberate the former sea bottom. As early as the seventeenth century, Dutch windmills were being well used to keep lowlands drained of seawater.

The Dutch war to maintain the integrity of its dikes has been a constant one, and battles have been both won and lost over the centuries. A severe storm in 1953 caused many seaward dikes to give way, drowning 1,800 unlucky victims. Property damage ran into billions of dollars. To prevent a recurrence, a massive and complex effort was undertaken to enclose the estuaries of the Rhine River at their mouths, thus reducing the amount of coastline. The Rhine now gets channeled through a series of sluices, which remove salt and polluted freshwater; the dam stays closed most of the time to hold out the seawater.

Although efforts in the Netherlands have been sophisticated and determined, the Dutch find themselves in a never-ending struggle with the natural consequences of living in an unnatural environment, namely, below sea level. Located otherwise favorably in the heart of Western Europe, next to Belgium and Germany, the Dutch have made the most of their seaward vulnerability and enjoy a world-class standard of living. Their income ranks sixteenth globally; even more impressively, the 2001 Human Development Index (HDI) rates the Netherlands eighth in the world in quality of life.[19] Since 1990, the United Nations has used the HDI to provide texture to standard economic measurements of gross output such as GNP. Do you think that humanistic social scientists would be more likely than scientistic ones to welcome the appearance of the HDI, and why?

Historically a small but great sea power, the Netherlands has been a leader among global traders for centuries; when Russia's Peter the Great traveled incognito to Europe to learn ship-building in the late 1600s, he went straight to Holland. This small country teetering on fragile stilts also became a colonial power in the eighteenth and nineteenth centuries. Although many countries have overcome geographic liabilities to prosper, the Netherlands, by creating the very soil on which to build its state, is a hard act to follow.[20]

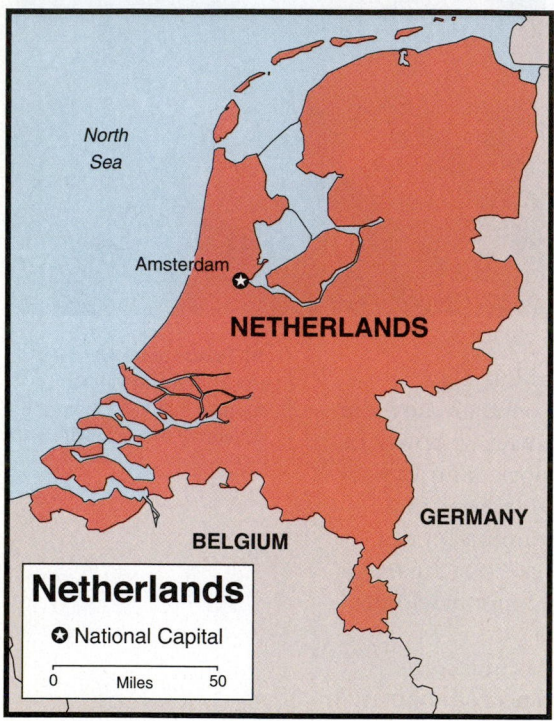

Figure 3.2

The gods of geography have smiled upon the Netherlands with the exception of the fact that it is a country located below sea level.

Decolonization ■ The process whereby colonial mother countries shed their former possessions, creating an influx of newly independent states

The proliferation of states, caused earlier by **decolonization**, but more recently by disintegration in places such as the Soviet empire, produced many countries far smaller than the Netherlands. The economic and military viability of some remain in doubt. Armenia and Kirghizia from the former Soviet Union seem small with three million residents. Yet size is a relative concept because thirty-eight micro-states have fewer than one million people.[21] Some are as small as Kiribati (76,000) and Nauru (10,000). The Maldive Islands and Andorra are nearly as tiny.

Finally, topography also affects national power. Physical features such as altitude, mountains, plains, marshes, and rivers can influence concentrations of population, agriculture, defensibility, communications, or industrial capacity—each relevant to a country's power. As a strategic factor, topography has historically made it easy for

Germans to invade Poles, Russians to invade Ukrainians, Mongols to invade Russians, Arabs to invade Persians, and Hutus to invade Tutsis. More fortunate have been the Swiss, Georgians, Chileans, and Tibetans, who have all been sheltered by impressive mountain ranges.

Geography and National Security

Location can also influence state power in strategic terms. A nation's neighbors can affect its national health or even existence. Canada and Mexico have generally benefited by bordering on a relatively peaceful United States for most of their history. Location, however, has proven less kind to Tibet (victimized by China), Poland (invaded often by Germany and Russia), or Korea (in a corridor easily accessible to China and Japan). Tiny Switzerland's location at the center of Europe surrounded by larger countries has influenced its age-old neutrality—a classic case of location shaping foreign policy.

The small city of Adrianople, located near modern Istanbul, has witnessed more great military battles (thirteen) than any other city in the world. Adrianople's unique status in military history stems directly from its precarious location where Asia and Europe meet and where the Bosporus serves as a narrow neck connecting the Atlantic Ocean and the Black Sea. In sharp contrast, the United States has traditionally felt comforted by its location. The size of the Atlantic and Pacific oceans represented physical buffer zones during those frequent occasions when war had broken out in Europe or Asia. The United States had never experienced the terror of full-scale invasion all too familiar to most other states; thus, the American mindset came to perceive wars as "away games" rather than "home games."

Actually, technological lethality had rendered Americans vulnerable to nuclear weapons delivered by intercontinental ballistic missiles from the Soviet Union ever since the 1950s. But since a U.S.-Soviet nuclear exchange *did not occur* during the forty-year Cold War, American nuclear anxiety remained dormant for decades. What, in fact, *did occur* later on September 11, 2001, seems to have expunged any sense of locational complacency in the American psyche.

Case Study 3.3   Physical Space: Russia versus America

In some respects, geography seems rather fickle because it is often kind to some states while cruel to others. Two of the largest states, Russia and the United States, make for some interesting comparisons. Another good reason to compare the geographical cards drawn by Russia and the United States is that Americans sometimes take for granted the natural bounty of their physical space.

Less modern than Western countries, Russia has been subject to the vagaries of geography. A book by historian John LeDonne makes the case that the physical environment has significantly influenced Russia's social, political, and economic development.[22] In general, the gods of geography have treated Russia about on par with America in size and natural resources but less favorably in terms of location, terrain, borders, climate, and soil quality. In no major respect does Russia enjoy a significant natural advantage over North America.

In size, the former Soviet Union took up one-sixth of the world's land mass, 8.6 million square miles, compared to 3.6 square miles for the United States. Even Russia now by itself remains the world's biggest country, spanning eleven time zones; it takes ten days to travel from St. Petersburg to Vladivostok by train. A road sign in Vladivostok identifies the motoring distance to St. Petersburg as 9,329 kilometers. The sun never sets on Russia, as indicated in Figure 3.3.

Such massiveness contributes indirectly to benefits such as diversity, natural resources, national defense, varied energy sources, ecological **carrying capacity** and potential population expansion. But its vastness becomes a liability when it comes to transporting raw materials (such as oil, coal, uranium, and bauxite) located east of the Ural Mountains in Siberia, to the people and industries west of the Urals in European Russia.

Like America, Russia's continental scope contributed to an expansionist, frontier mentality. By the middle of the seventeenth century, Russia had expanded eastward to the Pacific. Vastness also figures into what is referred to as the depth of the Russian soul: confronted with a horizon of seemingly

Carrying capacity ■ The finite amount of life that can be supported by any ecosystem

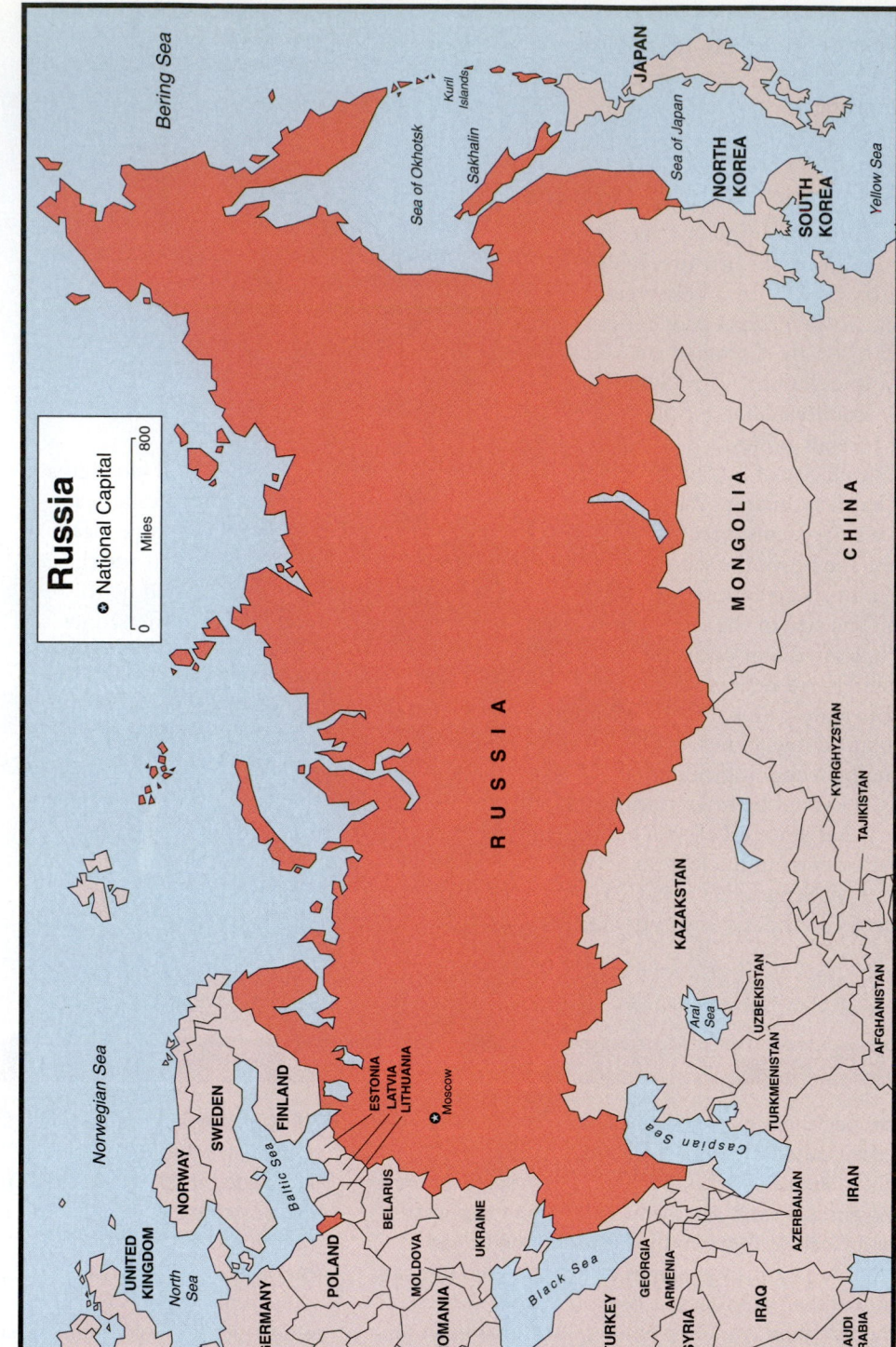

Figure 3.3
Cold climate, poor soil, and costs associated with transporting its resources from the Siberian East to the European West, in addition to bordering on thirteen potential invading countries, have historically proven problematic for Russia.

endless plains, Russians have tended to retreat within themselves. Also similar to the United States, continental vastness has encouraged wasteful practices. Ascribing infinite carrying capacity to their country, Russians and Americans have proven more wasteful than Western Europeans or Eastern Asians.

Russia has no shortage of natural resources. The twentieth century was the oil century, and Russia ranked as the top producer of crude, possessing 10 percent of world reserves. Russia also owns one-half of known iron deposits, one-fifth of hard-coal deposits, one-third of the world's water power, and one-quarter of all forests. Russia's 180,000 miles of rivers provide streams of communication as well as transportation. Lake Baikal contains 20 percent of the world's fresh water, and Lake Ladoga is the largest European lake.

Containing 20 percent of the world's fresh water, Lake Baikal symbolizes Russia's vast natural bounty that has been poorly managed by indifferent governments.

As a land of paradoxes, Russia's great resources are countered by many naturally induced problems. First is climate. Stereotypes about frigid Russian winters contain much truth because most of Russia endures extremely cold winters. One-third of the country experiences permanently frozen ground called permafrost. On occasion, the harsh Russian winter has proven beneficial, such as when it sent the invading armies of Napoleon in 1812 and Hitler in 1944 scurrying for the border.

Many of Russia's natural resources lie under the permafrost. Also frustrating is that while surrounded by 37,000 miles of coastline, most of it is ice-bound, making Russia the most landlocked nation. These realities provide insights into Tsar Peter the Great's insatiable quest for warm water ports. He carved the city of St. Petersburg out of swampland on the Baltic Sea in 1703 at great human cost.

Former KGB Colonel Mikhail Lyubimov, now a Russian novelist, wrote a doctoral dissertation on Russian national character in which he claims that climate was a major factor in forming the national psyche. Lyubimov says that "We are not systematic workers, but swing back and forth between frenzy and lethargy according to the seasons. Russians have very little sense of balance."[23]

Closely related to climate, agricultural problems have haunted Russians. Soil is poor, as 20 percent Russia is covered in marshland, and a mere 8 percent of Russian soil is suitable for cultivation. Even more troublesome is rainfall, which is inadequate and arrives at the wrong time (summer rather than spring). These conditions make for short growing seasons and low productivity.[24] Russia is a very flat country, and its only mountain ranges lie to the south, separating it from neighbors in the Caucasus (Armenia, Georgia, Azerbaijan) and Central Asia (Kazakhstan, Uzbekistan, Kirghizia, Tazikistan, Turkestan). As the only north-to-south chain, the Ural mountains separate European from Siberian Russia.

This flat Eurasian plain has produced trepidation among Russians whenever they have been weak. Attacked over the centuries by Varangians, Turks, Mongols, Poles, Swedes, Teutonic Knights, Japanese, Chinese, French, and Germans, Russians have learned to be **xenophobic.** In World War II alone, the Soviet Union lost 26 million people. U.S. history includes no remotely comparable experience, and geography helps to explain why. Russia's location is also problematic. Moscow's northern latitude equals that of Edmonton, Alberta, whereas St. Petersburg matches Anchorage, Alaska. Northern latitude contributes to many of the climatic and agricultural dilemmas cited earlier.

The loneliness of Siberia's wilderness seems palpable in this portrait of a reindeer herder in Eastern Russia.

Table 3.2

STATISTICAL COMPARISONS: RUSSIA AND AMERICA

Variable	Russia	United States
total area	17,075,200 sq km	9,629,091 sq km
bordering states	14	2
arable land	8%	19%
forest	46%	30%
irrigated land	40,000 sq km	207,000 sq km
population	146 million	278 million
pop. growth	−.38%	0.9%
age 0–14	18%	21%
age 15–64	69%	66%
age over 64	13%	13%
life expectancy	67 years	77 years
literacy	98%	97%
GDP per capita	$4,200	$36,200
pop. below poverty	40%	13%
unemployment	12%	4%

Source: CIA–The World Factbook, http://www.cia.gov/cia/publications/factbook/geos/rs.html.

Geopolitics ■ The legitimate study of how physical features affect state power became distorted from the 1880s to 1930s when pseudoscience became subverted to the political agendas of dictators looking to rationalize expansionist policies

Social Darwinism ■ Charles Darwin's theories revolutionized our understanding of biological evolution. However, when premises such as "natural selection" were carried over to analyze human affairs, they proved ripe for misuse.

Sir Halford J. Mackinder (1869–1947), whose Heartland Thesis was one of the most famous geopolitical theories during geography's infancy as a social science discipline.

Finally, the gods of location have smiled upon the United States by assigning Canada and Mexico as its neighbors. Less fortunate, Russia borders on fourteen countries, some of which bear old grievances. One of them, China, possesses nuclear weapons and claims many chunks of Russian territory. In 1969, China and the Soviet Union came to blows with hundreds of soldiers killed in battles along the Dzungarian Gates region between Soviet Kazakhstan and China's Sinkiang Province.

Historically, Russians have intimately experienced invasion, starvation, and isolation. Some of these problems are attributable to Russia's authoritarian sociopolitical system under Tsarism and Communism. However, the system has always been influenced by the harshness of existing in the geographic space known as Russia. By comparison, Americans have been guests at a cakewalk, as suggested in Table 3.2.

Critical Thinking About Grand Geopolitical Theories

Geographic considerations form a vital base for state power. Ultimately, however, people shape political events. Geography plays a supporting role in the drama taking place on the world stage. A starring role is more than it ought to aspire to currently.[25] Power is a complex, multi-faceted, and relative concept, and its presence is signaled by a country's ability to get its way in a competitive world of scarcity. Tangible attributes such as natural resources play a role but so do intangible factors such as quality of leadership, strong national will, and unifying belief systems. Critical thinking skills must pervade our assessments of geopolitical influences.

In addition to looking at how factors such as climate, natural resources, location, size, and topography affect the power status of specific states, geographers also examine mega-level questions, such as what forces shape the distribution of power in the global system? Historically, the attempt to explain world politics through geography, **geopolitics,** had its heyday during the nineteenth century's infatuation with **social Darwinism.**

American naval Admiral Alfred T. Mahan (1840–1914) looked to the seas, arguing in his twenty books that the state holding naval power would also control world power. The most-quoted geopolitician, Sir Halford J. Mackinder (1869–1947), posited that who controls the Heartland (Eastern Europe) controls the world island; who controls the world island controls the world. Neatly and concisely, his Heartland analysis provided the terra firma analogous to Mahan's oceanic vision of greatness. Mackinder's ideas attracted others, such as Yale professor Nicholas J. Spykman (1893–1943), who developed the rimland (coastlands) dictum: Who controls the Rimland rules Eurasia; who rules Eurasia controls the destinies of the world.

All of these grand geopolitical theories contained fatal flaws. First, they engaged in **reductionism** by grossly oversimplifying history. Secondly, they claimed a level of **determinism** achievable only in the natural sciences. Although probably guilty of overzealously questing for objective laws directing the human drama, the geopolitics of Mahan, Mackinder, and Spykman did little direct harm to human beings.

Not so with the German **pseudoscience** known as *Geopolitik*. This school included Frederick Ratzel (1844–1904), who viewed states as organic entities needing to expand or die. Ratzel was trained originally as a biologist, and organic metaphors flowed freely from his pen. One of this Leipzig University professor's most famous dictums held that states need food in the form of *Lebensraum* (living space).

One of Ratzel's disciples, the Germanophile Swedish professor Rudolf Kjellen (1864–1922), expressed many similar ideas in his book, *The State as a Form of Life* (1916). Whereas Ratzel argued that the state was *like* a living organism, Kjellen said that it in fact was one. After their country's defeat in World War I, Kjellen's views appealed to many Germans seeking to justify their vision of a revenge-minded German superstate rising from the ashes of degradation.

The dangers of pseudoscience masquerading as genuine science are further illustrated by Karl Haushofer (1869–1946). He believed that Germany should have won World War I, and he sought to avenge its defeat. Haushofer was a career army officer whose subsequent writings distorted the ideas of Ratzel, Mackinder, and others by bending them to the political agenda of rationalizing Germany's defeat, supporting the Nazi Party, and justifying German territorial expansion. Haushofer took a professorship at the University of Munich when the Nazis came to power in 1933, where he organized a group of disciples to propagate the so-called science of *Geopolitik*.

Disheartened by their country's malaise after World War I, many Germans latched onto Haushofer's theories. Although half-baked, his ideas about a German heartland, living space, ethnic superiority, and economic independence fed those hungering for resurgent German nationalism. Haushofer fell out of favor with German dictator Adolph Hitler near the end of World War II, and he was banished to the Dachau concentration camp, where he committed suicide. All other theories of *Geopolitik* suffer at the hands of Haushofer's misuse of scientific inquiry.

Suppose that your professor has decided to hold an in-class mock trial indicting Karl Haushofer. You have been chosen to fill the key role of prosecutor. With what sins against the brotherhood of social scientists would you charge Haushofer? In preparing your case, what line of reasoning would you expect his defense lawyer to present, and how would you counter it?

Reductionism ■ An intellectual fallacy in which the subtleties of some complex concept or theory are sacrificed to achieve a facile explanation of questionable value

Determinism ■ The belief that human behavior results directly from objective forces, not from free will. Social scientists frequently grapple with explanations that juxtapose the forces of determinism and free will.

Pseudoscience ■ A pejorative label describing poorly conceived, shabbily executed, or badly misinterpreted studies

The sad story of Nazi apologist Karl Haushofer (1869–1946) illustrates how pseudoscientific theories of national destiny were abused by some scholars to justify the aggressive ambitions of German dictator Adolf Hitler.

Jared Diamond: More Responsible Contemporary Geopolitics

Few contemporary scholars are ever accused of the abuses of geopolitics exhibited by Rudolf Kjellen or Karl Haushofer in their grandiose theories. However, any time grand claims are ascribed to one source, critical thinking social scientists ought to worry about the fallacy of single cause. An interesting example of contemporary work was the popular 1999 book by UCLA evolutionary biologist Jared Diamond, who received a Pulitzer prize for *Guns, Germs, and Steel: The Fate of Human Societies*.

One of the central questions of world history has long been, how do we account for what is called the rise of Western Civilization (starting in Europe) as the locus of power among nations during the past 500 years? Diamond takes up the challenge in the opening sentence: "This book attempts to provide a short history of everybody for the last 13,000 years. The question motivating this book is: Why did history unfold differently on different continents?"[26] Until the end of the last Ice Age, life on all continents consisted solely of hunter/gatherers; therefore, what happened between then and the year 1500, when a far different world existed?

Evolutionary biologist Diamond rejects the writings of those who argue that racial variation by continent serves to explain the West's long-term hegemony. He also criticizes journalist Thomas Sowell, who has suggested that Europe's many navigable rivers facilitated the exchange of information, which enabled European ascendancy economically and technologically over other regions.

After examining the historical development of all world regions during the past thirteen millennia, Diamond concludes that four sets of factors account for disparities in regional development:

- Continental differences in the wild plant and animal species as starting materials for domestication. He writes that "all developments of economically complex, socially stratified, politically centralized societies beyond the level of small chiefdoms were based on *food production.*"
- Varying rates of diffusion and *migration within* continents, which occurred fastest on the flat and mobile Eurasian plain but more slowly in Africa and the Americas (where significant geographic and ecological barriers existed).
- Related to diffusion of knowledge within continents was a set of variables affecting rates of *diffusion* of knowledge *between* continents. Such diffusion creates a local pool of domestication and technology. Relative isolation of the continents varies greatly. The Americas and Aboriginal Australia, for example, benefited not at all from what was transpiring on the Eurasian continent.
- Continental variation by land area or population size. Both area and population provide the *economies of scale* producing more inventors, better innovations, and more competing societies that create incentives to retain innovations (because those failing to do so become eliminated). [27]

Diamond confronts the label of "geographic determinism" slapped on his analysis by historians highly skeptical of such sweeping generalizations. He retorts confidently that "These four sets of factors constitute big environmental differences that can be quantified objectively and that are not subject to dispute." Thus, he maintains that it was *not biology, but rather geography,* that determined who domesticated plants and animals, and developed writing, government, technology, war weapons, and immunity to deadly germs (hence the book's catchy title).

Agriculture led to military prowess, which eventually produced world domination. The Eurasian landmass connects both Europe and East Asia, the two regions whose development was affected most positively by geography, according to Diamond. It was China's decision to turn inward in the 1400s that led it to lose out to Europe as competitors for world domination, and who "colonized America and Australia, took the lead in technology, became politically and economically dominant in the modern world."[28]

Diamond's work has also attracted many critics, some of whom say that he includes in his analysis only those data that support his biases, ignoring those that do not. Others charge he engages in circular reasoning that oozes with illogic and is permeated by self-fulfilling prophecies. Many suggest he describes *a useful theory but not the only useful theory.*

So what do you make of Jared Diamond's thesis regarding the trajectory of regional development in world history? Case Study 3.4 relates to some of the cruel ironies attendant to one particular world region: the Middle East.

Geography and Globalization's Web

Somewhat bruised by its maltreatment at the hands of German *Realpolitik,* contemporary geography brings new data, concepts, and theories to the modern world. Rather than focusing on state power, geographers now look more to the web of interdependence and the global issues highlighted by it.

The key insight in dealing with ecological GIs such as environment, population, food, and energy lies in their connections; they are as profoundly interrelated as strands in a spider's web. Decades ago, initial efforts to address these problems dealt with one at a time, as if they actually operated separately in the real world. Today, we better understand

Case Study 3.4   The Middle East: Nature's Cruel Ironies

The contemporary Middle East is a region with few natural treasures. Most of its soil is poor, low in both vital trace elements and organic matter. Rainfall here seldom reaches the sixteen to twenty inches required for agriculture. Direct sunlight without cloud cover and high temperatures evaporate the sparse rainfall quickly. Underground, significant mineral deposits discovered and mined during ancient times disappeared centuries ago. "Their famous shortage of water is only one among many barriers to productive farming."[29]

A bad situation continues to worsen in this region as rapidly growing human populations intensify competition between countries over water. It seems no coincidence that for all three monotheistic religions that started here, their imagery of heaven includes abundance of water and trees. For millennia, Middle East denizens adapted to desert conditions to survive, such as spelling out water rights concerning this scarce commodity from wells and springs to irrigate crops.

But twentieth century technologies produced seemingly abundant water with countless homes possessing tap water and sewerage for the first time. Irrigation made the desert bloom, and urban water use grew rapidly. For example, between 1980 and 1985, Saudi Arabia's consumption doubled. By the 1990s, several Middle Eastern countries were running out of water. "Israel, Jordan, Syria, and the Palestinian Authority face questions of water use so difficult that one of them may attempt to settle issues by force."[30] When Israel won the June 1967 War, it conquered the Golan Heights and West Bank of the Jordan River, guaranteeing its access to that body of water.

Access to safe water and sanitation constitutes one of the Millennium Development Goals set by the United Nations. People in poor countries now use about 20 liters of water daily, whereas those in rich countries use 400 to 500 liters daily. Roughly 1.2 billion people lack access to safe drinking water. Japan leads all other rich countries in water aid, giving one-third of the total aid. Five Mid-East countries have been among the top 15 recent recipients of water aid: Jordan, Egypt, Morocco, Turkey, and the Palestinian Authority.

The great exception to resource paucity in the region, however, consists of black gold: petroleum has been driving the global economy for the past century. Economic winners and losers in the region depend on who possesses oil and who does not. More than half of proven and probable oil reserves in the world are located in the sedimentary basin running from central Arabia to the mountains of Iran. Huge quantities easily extracted, piped, and shipped to refineries elsewhere occur so efficiently that pretax production costs are measured in pennies (not dollars) per gallon. For Saudi Arabia, the cost runs about $.45 for a gallon, ultimately selling for at least $4 in Europe, and about one dollar less in America. OPEC governments extract huge taxes, and MNCs (multinational corporations) take huge profits in the process.

The first wells were drilled in Europe and the United States in the nineteenth century. Gas-powered cars in the twentieth century led to voracious demand, and the search for petroleum soon turned global. Prospecting in Iraq and Iran (then Persia) began under British entrepreneur William D'Arcy, whose first commercial well was struck in 1908. His Anglo-Persian Oil Company laid a pipeline to the coast, where a refinery was established. Just before World War I, Winston Churchill convinced the British Navy to change from coal to oil, and the British government bought D'Arcy's company, which morphed into British Petroleum. In the United States, mineral rights are owned in the private sector, but in the Middle East, untilled areas belong to the government.

The "Seven Sisters" oil companies compete with host countries for lucrative payoffs. Initially, the MNCs negotiated from strength, and the rulers from weakness. Gradually, however, the balance of power shifted. Rulers proved less effective negotiating singly than collectively, and the Organization of Petroleum Exporting Countries (OPEC) arose in 1960. The intersection of supply and demand underwent a sea change in the 1970s, OPEC's golden era, which began with oil selling for about $3 per gallon, and ended at more than ten times that price.

World politics and the oil economy were now enmeshed. Major spikes again occurred during the 1990–1991 Gulf War and the 2003 Iraq War, which dragged on, exacerbating other problems, including lost refining capacity associated with the 2005 devastation of Hurricane Katrina. Oil surpassed $70 a barrel in 2006, profiting OPEC countries by more than $500 billion. Over the years, OPEC states have invested roughly $1 trillion in foreign (mostly Western) assets.[31] ■

---

ecological global issues as comprising a system: what happens to one area invariably affects the others. Geography's affinity for holistic analysis has provided conceptual tools for social scientists to comprehend the revolutionary nature of globalization.

Geography's mega-level holism also enables us to look at other long-ignored connections, such as those between culture and the environment, environment and population, population and food, and food and energy. Whereas political geography overreached in its earlier life (as geopolitics), today cultural (see Case Study 3.5), ecological, and economic geography enhance efforts to deal with the sobering complexities of all crises that are global in scope.[32]

Case Study 3.5 The Spread of English

Cultural geography looks at the link between location and human lifestyles, and the spatial distribution of languages is a topic that interests such geographers. More than 3,000 languages are in use around the world, although only about 200 are internationally significant, with 95 percent of humanity speaking fewer than 100 of these. Among the identifiable families of languages, the Indo-European is the largest group, and English is the most widely spoken Indo-European language.

The English language was brought to Britain by the Angles, Saxons, and Jutes—three Germanic tribes from whose native languages English was synthesized. When Britain was converted to Christianity in the seventh century, elements of the Greek and Latin languages drifted into the evolving English language. The French-speaking Normans conquered England in 1066, an event that resulted in a strange split: the upper classes spoke French, but the lower classes spoke English, until English became universal around 1200.[33]

From these humble origins has blossomed an extraordinary success story. If for centuries the British were proud to remind the world that the sun never set on their Empire, then the sun never set on the English language either. Seeds were sown on every continent for English to help cultivate a variety of newly emerging cultures.

Today, 350 million people speak English as their native tongue, whereas about 400 million others speak it as a second language. Perhaps more importantly, English has become the acknowledged language of international business, politics, and entertainment. English's unique international status is fortunate for North Americans, whose foreign language skills pale in comparison to people in other parts of the world.[34]

One theory explaining how the English language and English-speaking peoples managed to lead the world for the past two centuries is offered in a hefty book by American author Kevin Phillips. He contends that the two trans-Atlantic English cousins, Britain and the United States, have experienced a kind of historical synergy that has spurred both countries to greatness. Specifically, Phillips considers three brutal conflicts to have both energized and stabilized this Anglo cousin-hood: (1) the English Civil Wars of the eighteenth century, by which parliament rendered absolute monarchy illegitimate; (2) the American Revolution, establishing the two-state division that represents the genius of their cousin-ship; and (3) the American Civil War, which ended slavery and developed the principle of individual liberty. Phillips' main point is that these three revolutionary civil wars rescripted *both* societies in a productive fashion.[35] ■

Segue to Ecological Global Issues

Our mega-level comprehension of the earth as an ecosystem with regional and local subsystems stems largely from what geographers have taught us about ecological unity. Where would global consciousness be today without the array of climatic, oceanic, topographical, and planetary maps and photographs freeing us from the parochialism of our own personal and cultural experiences? Geography will help us to keep our feet planted in the physical space of planet Earth while we contemplate the rapidly changing landscape of ecological GIs discussed in Chapters 4 and 5. But in what specific stages did such a global ecological mindset develop?

Emergence of a Global Paradigm

Paradigm ■ The prevailing analytical framework used to explain some natural, social, or intellectual phenomenon. Science requires abandoning old paradigms when new data disprove previously accepted hypotheses.

Only for about sixty years have we begun thinking complexly about GIs such as environment, population, food, and energy as global rather than national or regional. Despite their newness, a genuine **paradigm** shift has washed over the intellectual turf inhabited by GIs. This new thinking has been carried ashore by the momentum of four potent conceptual waves: finiteness in the 1960s and 1970s, interdependence in the 1980s, sustainable development in the 1990s, and the Millennium Development Goals in the 2000s, as traced in Figure 3.4.

Finiteness

Biologists, ecologists, and anthropologists were among the first scholars to see beyond the national implications of environment, population, energy, and food, to the mega-level of global connections. The first wave of ideas featured the revolutionary concept

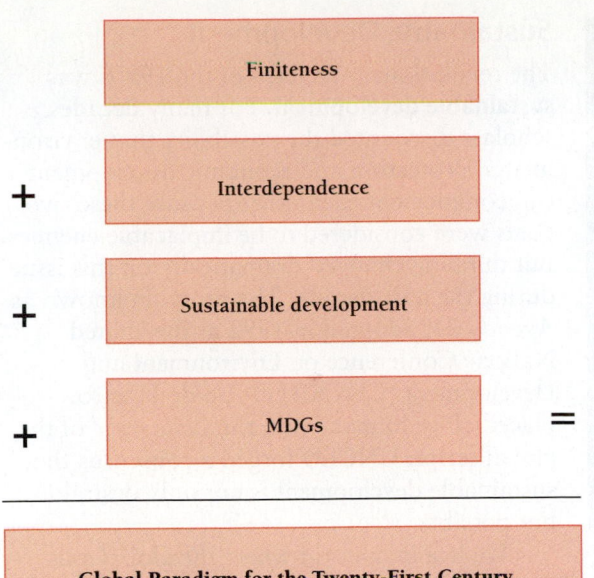

Figure 3.4
Emergence of a New Paradigm

of **finiteness.** Scientists questioned whether the earth on which we live can continue to absorb the damage that our species inflicts upon it. Are we running out of rainforests, oil, drinkable water, and arable land?

Questions about limits seemed revolutionary because they challenged one of humankind's cherished equations: *expansion equals progress.* This expansion model served us well for thousands of years. However, by relying on technological fixes to solve new problems, we bought into the dubious assumptions that bigger is always better and that resources exist for our exploitation. Problems such as hunger, global warming, dwindling petroleum reserves, and rapid population growth forced us to question the expansion model of progress and ask whether we were starting to bump our heads against the global ceiling.

In the early days of ecological awareness, research and analysis remained mostly within the confines of single disciplines. Geographers studied the environment, sociologists examined population issues, economists and political scientists looked at energy costs and policies, and food problems fell primarily to biologists. With each global issue treated as separate, defining the key problems and solutions involved little scholarly communication between different disciplines. Rather than functioning as loose membranes, disciplinary walls had hardened into formidable barriers.

Interdependence

By the 1980s, a second conceptual wave materialized: **interdependence.** An indivisible web linking us all came into sharper focus, and awareness of global interdependence developed in two categories: (1) *economic connections* through trade, international investment, and expanding corporations; and (2) profound *links between the ecological GIs of* environment, population, food, and energy—what happens to one issue affects them all.

Interdependence is an abstract concept; therefore, scholars often use metaphors to paint pictures with words intended to illustrate global indivisibility more colorfully. Some of these images included those of the global village, spaceship earth, and a shrinking world. But many national governments seemed impervious to global awareness by resisting the global insight that the fate of each individual and state is increasingly tied to the fate of all individuals and states. Thus, new actors, such as NGOs (non-government organizations), have appeared on the world stage and challenged states to a contest for the hearts and minds of humanity. It can no longer be taken for granted that the first loyalty of ecologically conscious people remains with the state to which they paid taxes.

Finiteness ■ The notion of limits, though a simple idea, has also proved a revolutionary one as applied to the carrying capacity of global ecosystems.

Interdependence ■ The multifaceted ways in which the modern world is shrinking. Economic linkages and shared fate over global issues represent two indicators of contemporary connectedness.

Delegates discussing issues at the grandest global meeting ever assembled–the 1992 Earth Summit held in Rio de Janeiro, Brazil.

Sustainable development ■
The ability to continue improving humanity's quality of life without degrading the earth's biosphere or depleting its resources

Sustainable Development

The revolutionary concept of the 1990s was **sustainable development.** For many decades, scholars discounted the possibility that environmental protection and economic development can complement each other because these two goals were considered to be implacable enemies. But thinking changed dramatically on this issue during the past decade. The program known as *Agenda 21*, adopted in 1992 at the United Nations Conference on Environment and Development (UNCED) in Rio de Janeiro, placed all of humanity on the same page of the global script; UNCED forged a consensus that sustainable development is not only desirable, but possible.

We live in a world where the global axis of conflict has shifted from East-West (U.S. versus Soviet) to North-South (rich versus poor). However, the North-South standoff entails rival visions that preen for attention just as vigorously as did those that dominated the Cold War. The rich North emphasizes environmental protection, whereas the poor South highlights its right to a higher standard of living through economic development. The northern, or more-developed countries (MDC), are more powerful, but the southern, or less-developed countries (LDC), contain two-thirds of humanity.

Under these circumstances of conflicting North-South viewpoints, do you believe that sustainable development is feasible? Or do you think the chasm separating these world-views represents an unbridgeable gap? To appreciate the extent to which sustainable development represents a dilemma, imagine what world consumption and pollution would look like if China developed economically to where its citizens consumed petroleum and emitted carbon dioxide at the rate that Americans do now.

The LDCs have a right to develop economically, but they must do so responsibly, in ways that respect the equal right of future generations to inherit a habitable earth. Sustainable development challenges human ingenuity to pursue quality of life while respecting nature's sanctity. One analogy that taps this sentiment is the idea of *living off of the interest* of an investment without disturbing the principal from which it derives. Better conservation practices, more efficient methods, and new benign technologies (such as Third World solar panels) will have to pave the way for sustainable development.

U.N. Millennium Project and MDGs

The turn of the millennium was marked by a major global town meeting, the Millennium Assembly, held in New York City. A formal statement was issued after the sessions explicating "quantified and time-bound goals to reduce extreme poverty, disease, and deprivation" by the year 2015. Eight Millennium Development Goals (MDGs) were produced:

1. Eradicate extreme hunger and poverty.
2. Achieve universal primary education.
3. Promote gender equality and empower women.
4. Reduce child mortality.
5. Improve maternal health.
6. Combat AIDS, malaria, and other diseases.
7. Ensure environmental sustainability.
8. Develop a global partnership for development.

In 2002, Secretary General Kofi Annan appointed Jeffrey Sachs (economist and Director of the Earth Institute at Columbia University) as Director of the Millennium Project, a coordinated three-year effort seeking progress toward the MDGs. The

Millennium Project observes that the world has made significant progress during the decade from 1992 to 2002. For example, average overall incomes increased by 21 percent globally, the number of people living in extreme poverty declined by 120 million people, child mortality fell from 103 to 88 deaths per 1,000 live births, life expectancy rose from 63 to 65 years of age, and 15 percent of the world's poorest people received improved sanitation services.

Small solar energy panels put to good use in rural India.

Such progress, however, has been far from uniform, and great disparities across and within countries remain to be addressed. The Millennium Project has worked with scores of countries in an advisory capacity and created user-friendly, practical "how-to formats" relevant to the wide range of stakeholders to whom the MDGs mean a great deal (states, NGOs, IGOs, IFIs, MNCs, individual citizens). At the World Summit occurring in September 2005, world leaders committed to implementing strategies to reduce global poverty by one-half within ten years (2015) and to pursue the MDGs more generally.

Each step in this evolving half-century process has broadened the scope of our vision. Each step has also illuminated the connections between phenomena previously seen as separate. Furthermore, each step has yielded a larger (yet indivisible) picture in defining human problems. Such broadened vistas facilitate interdisciplinary sharing between the various social sciences, and allow our analysis to jettison parochialism and embrace holism. A genuine ecological paradigm shift has occurred within two or three generations.

Our definition of the scope of global issues has expanded but so has the complexity of tasks requiring action. No one says that coping with agendas as ambitious as feeding the poor, fueling the global economy sustainably, managing population growth, and reversing global warming will be easy. However, at least we have all been on the same page of the script now that interdisciplinary holism has gained a solid foothold.

Chapter Synopsis

Although humans have been present for less than 1 percent of the earth's history, we have exercised an outsized influence over the natural world. Short-sighted exploitative values have shaped human management of this planet. If we continue on our current trajectory of resource depletion and pollution, a habitable planet may no longer exist. Spatial concepts and insights reside at the heart of first comprehending this extant mess and at the soul of measures intended to clean it up.

Because the possession of power affects how we exercise our free will, and states have been the key actors wielding power on the world stage, social scientists have puzzled over what makes some states more powerful than others. Toward that end, the twentieth century witnessed many mechanistic, purportedly scientific theories grounded in geography. Most were reductionist in nature; some were misused by apologists for dictators justifying the expansion of their borders. All bit off more intellectually than they could chew, giving geographic theories of national power a bad name. By falling prey to the fallacy of single cause, these ambitious accounts of national power eventually were relegated to the academic dustbin of intellectual excesses.

But as the star quality of the state has begun to wane, and as human consciousness has shifted toward solving global problems, geography's intellectual balloon once again rides high on the social science horizon. Geography contributes a rich vein of data, concepts, and theories to comprehend the linkages among ecological GIs such as population, environment, food, and energy.

FOR DIGGING DEEPER

Aguado, Edward, and James Burt. *Understanding Weather and Climate.* Prentice Hall, 2000.

Allan, John. *Student Atlas: World Geography.* McGraw-Hill Dushkin, 2007.

DeBlij, H. J., and Peter O. Muller. *Geography: Realms, Regions, and Concepts.* John Wiley and Sons, 2007.

Chaliand, Gerard, and Jean-Pierre Rageau. *Strategic Atlas: A Comparative Geopolitics of the World's Powers.* Viking Penguin, 2005.

Cutter, Susan, and William Renwick. *Exploitation, Conservation, Preservation: A Geographic Perspective on Natural Resource Use.* Wiley, 1999.

Demko, George J., and William B. Wood. *Reordering the World: Geopolitical Perspectives on the Twenty-First Century.* Westview Press, 1994.

Diamond, Jared. *Guns, Germs, and Steel: The Fate of Human Societies.* W. W. Norton, 1999.

Geography for Life: What Every American Should Know and Be Able to Do in Geography. National Geographic Society, 1994.

Getis, Arthur, Judith Getis, Victoria Getis, and Jerome Fellman. *Introduction to Geography.* McGraw-Hill, 2002.

Goudie, Andrew, and Heather Viles. *The Earth Transformed: An Introduction to the Human Impact on the Environment.* Blackwell, 1998.

Glantz, Michael. *Currents of Change: El Niño's Impact on Climate and Society.* Cambridge University Press, 1996.

LeDonne, John P. *The Russian Empire and the World, 1700–1917: The Geopolitics of Expansion.* Oxford University Press, 1997.

Livingstone, David. *The Geographical Tradition.* Blackwell, 1992.

McCrum, Robert, William Cran, and Robert MacNeil. *The Story of English.* Penguin, 2002.

Monmonier, Mark. *How to Lie with Maps.* University Chicago Press, 1996.

Phillips, Kevin. *The Cousins' Wars: Religion, Politics, and the Triumph of Anglo-America.* Penguin, 2002.

Pulsipher, Lydia M., and others. *World Regional Geography: Global Patterns, Local Lines.* W. H. Freeman, 2007.

Russell, Malcolm B. *The World Today Series: The Middle East and South Asia.* Stryker-Post, 2005.

INTERNET

American Association of Geographers:
http://www.aag.org

CIA World Factbook:
http://www.odci.gov/cia/publications/factbook

Colorado University Resources for Geographers:
http://www.Colorado.edu/geography

Earthshots: Satellite Images of Environmental Change:
http://edcwww.cr.usgs.gov/earthshots/slow/tableofcontents

EE-Link: Environmental Education:
http://eelink.net/

Geographic Names Information System:
http://www.geonames.usgs.gov

Geography Departments on the Web:
http://www.cas.sc.edu/geog/

Hunter College Map Projections:
http://www.geo.hunter.cuny.edu/

Iowa State University GPS Resources:
http://www.extension.iastate.edu/naturemapping

MapQuest:
http://www.mapquest.com

Michigan State University Geography Web Links:
http://www.geo.msu.edu/wlinks.html

National Geographic Society Maps:
http://www.nationalgeographic.com/maps/index.html

National Severe Storms Laboratory:
http://www.nssl.noaa.gov

National Spatial Data Clearinghouse:
http://www.geo-nsdi.er.usgs.gov/

Natural Resources Canada:
http://www.NRCan.gc.ca/homepage/toc_e.shtml

Peters Projection Map Site:
http://www.petersmap.com

Population Association of America:
http://www.pop.psu.edu/general/pubs/PAA_Affairs

Ryerson University Geography:
http://www.geography.ryerson.ca

GeoEye:
http://www.geoeye.com

United Nations Population Fund:
http://www.unfpa.org/

United Nations System:
http://www.unsystem.org/

University of Edinburgh Geography:
http://www.geos.ed.ac.uk

University of Texas Library, Online Map Collection:
http://www.lib.utexas.edu/maps.index.html

USGS Energy Resources Program:
http://energy.usgs.gov

CHAPTER 4

Global Ecological Problems

CORE OBJECTIVE

To show how ecological issues such as environment, population, food, and energy represent significant problems in an age of globalization.

THEMATIC QUESTIONS

- Which core elements characterize the globalist outlook?

- How does the expansion model of human progress clash with solving ecological global issues (GIs)?

- In what fundamental ways do the ecological optimists and pessimists differ?

- How is the concept of carrying capacity revolutionary when applied to the way humanity has chosen to live in societies for 10,000 years?

- Do most ecological issues have a North versus South tension lurking beneath the surface?

Environment, population, food, and energy are *ecological* issues because they relate to the physical space in which we live. What makes them global issues (GIs) as well is that they affect everyone—not just certain countries or regions. Geography's vital role in broadening the vistas of social scientists to a global paradigm was discussed in Chapter 3. Several other key concepts also covered in that context included finiteness, interdependence, sustainable development, and the Millennium Project.

Interdisciplinary Holism

Each step in this evolving process has added peripheral vision to broaden our conceptual repertoire. Each step has also illuminated the connections between phenomena previously seen as separate. Furthermore, each step has yielded a larger (yet indivisible) picture in defining human problems. Such vistas facilitate interdisciplinary sharing between social sciences and allow our analysis to jettison parochialism and embrace holism.

A genuine ecological paradigm shift has occurred within three human generations. Our definition of the scope of GIs has expanded but so has the complexity of tasks requiring action. No one claims that coping with agendas as ambitious as feeding the abjectly poor, fueling the global economy sustainably, managing population growth, or reversing global warming will be easy. However, most of the diverse set of players on the world stage (including both state and nonstate actors) now find themselves reading from the same page of the global script. The consensus forged in the 1990s at Rio de Janeiro, when sustainable development became the shared target on the horizon, was then further reinforced in the 2000s by the Millennium Development Goals (MDGs).

Optimists and Pessimists

Humanity's ecological problems are numerous and serious. Exactly how urgent, however, remains a matter of contention. Optimists such as University of Maryland Business Professor Julian Simon contend that history reflects continuous human progress in health, environmental quality, safety, welfare, and standard of living. Optimists therefore predict that ingenious technological solutions will defeat our most vexing problems. According to Simon "This is the best time on earth to have ever lived." Such optimists describe contemporary ecological "gloom and doom" as hysterical exaggeration.[1]

A more pessimistic observer is Hilary French, researcher at the environmental NGO Worldwatch Institute, who represented that organization at the 1992 Earth Summit in Rio. French warns that countries cannot continue stripping the earth's resources and polluting its environment without disastrous consequences. The pessimists believe that humanity must make drastic changes to avoid pending catastrophe.[2] The Worldwatch Institute's Director, Lester Brown, releases an annual edition, entitled *The State of the World*. Every edition warns about the shrinking window of time available to save a planet seriously at risk from multiple cases of ecological disregard.[3]

Like an eco-conscious Marco Polo, journalist Mark Hertsgaard traveled extensively around the globe looking for the environmental "dead zones" that tourists usually avoid. His book describes reed-like Dinka refugees from drought and civil war in Sudan, unbreathable air in Bangkok where a Thai love affair with cars has produced impossible traffic, and China, where newly prosperous capitalists have convinced themselves that they can get accustomed to foul air.[4]

"Tragedy of the Commons" Metaphor

Some people view ecological GIs as not only abstract but also distant from their daily lives. Scholars therefore use metaphors to bring global ecology into sharper relief. To convey the concept of finiteness (global limits), California biologist Garrett Hardin developed what he calls the "Tragedy of the Commons." In it, he asks us to imagine a medieval pasture open to herders for grazing cattle.[5] The grazing commons works well as long as the number of cattle remains within the pasture's ability to support enough grass to feed the cattle. But if no legal limits are placed on the number of cattle a herder may graze, each herder is motivated by profit to expand the herd. The individual herder thus reaps the benefits of expansion, while the ecological costs of expansion are divided among all herders.

Expansion by many herders, however, conceals an ecological trap. Tragedy looms when herders, acting in their short-term self-interest but to their ultimate detriment, overshoot the **carrying capacity** of the commons. Although there is nothing to prevent herders from limiting their cattle, thus allowing for mutual survival as well as preserving the ecosystem, the psychology of competition between humans often seems to succumb to short-term self-interest; in such cases, all herders eventually lose out. Forging an agreement to restrain herd size can work if adhered to by all, but agreements tend to break down because the system encourages taking advantage of others' self-restraint.

Geometric Progression: A Lily Pond Metaphor

Dennis Meadows' simile of a lily pond provides another conceptual hook on which to hang the idea of global limits. Concerning global population growth, the process of surpassing our planet's carrying capacity is sped up by the realities of exponential growth. Unlike the case with arithmetic progressions (e.g., 2, 4, 6, 8, 10), with geometric progressions (e.g., 2, 4, 8, 16, 32, 64, 128), subsequent doubling times become briefer in duration. The setting for Meadows' parable is a pond that we want to use for recreational purposes.

If on the first day of the month, there is one lily pad on the pond, no problem arises in the pond's use. But if the lily pads double each day, we then have two on the second day, four on the third day, eight on the fourth day, and so on. On the twenty-ninth day, half the pond is covered. At this point, there are two ways we can view the situation, each with dissimilar implications: (1) because half the pond remains empty, we seem to have nothing to worry about because plenty of space seems to exist for our use; or (2) although open pond space exists at the moment, the lilies are reproducing geometrically (not arithmetically), thus we must act immediately to prevent the pond from being covered on the next day.[6]

Deep Ecology

Deep ecology ■ The view that species have an inherent right to fight for continued existence apart from what they might do to influence the plight of humans

The way Westerners conceive of humanity's relationship with the environment has been challenged recently by another new mode of thought. Instead of considering nature an exploitable resource available to meet human needs, **deep ecology** argues that the true value of nature is intrinsic.[7] Species of flora and fauna have their own right to compete for existence, and their chances should not be precluded by human agency.

Deep ecology is closer philosophically to traditional cultures that see humans as part of the life cycle than to Western views placing humanity at the apex of creation.[8] Humanities-derived insights concerning non-Western literature's contributions to a broader perspective on humanity's interface with nature are offered in a 1,248-page source book called *Encompassing Nature*. Its editor believes that each culture's unique creation myth "is among the most revealing accounts of a culture's conception of nature and the world we live in."[9]

Inter-generational equity ■ The argument that humans have a responsibility to act as earthly stewards to bequeath a viable ecosphere to our descendants

The volatile 1960s witnessed criticism of Christianity's role in environmental degradation. The classic piece setting the parameters of the dialogue was written by a California professor of classics, Lynn White, who accused Christianity of having no green conscience. According to White, Christianity's linear sense of time (distinct beginnings and endings), its creation story (humans made in God's image), and its placing humanity above nature, all render it hostile to environmental integrity.[10]

When Christ's followers first distinguished themselves from pagans, the word "pagan" meant "country-dweller," and the pagans' otherness was bound up with being a country bumpkin. Anything connoting rural life seemed alien to the early Christians, who lived in cities of the Roman Empire, such as Antioch and Alexandria. Christianity had a decidedly urban style, and the stiffest opposition Christian proselytizers would encounter for more than a millennium was from the "tenacious nature religions of the peasantry." No other major religion matches the way Christianity bases its legitimacy on miracles that bend the laws of nature to the will of God.[11]

Nearly every responsible person involved in the *Titanic* tragedy was guilty of complacency.

As mentioned in Chapter 3, hubris about mastering nature has often landed our species in deep trouble. In Case Study 4.1, we see how humans deluded themselves in the early 1900s into believing that superior technology had rendered certain ocean vessels unsinkable.

Inter-Generational Equity

Developing alongside deep ecology has been the concept of **inter-generational equity,** asking us to look ahead to the quality of the future we

In the early 1900s, a spate of technological innovations seemed to augur human dominion over nature. U.S.-based White Star Lines, backed by financier J. P. Morgan, built the world's largest ocean vessel, the *Titanic*. Its designer, Thomas Andrews, boldly claimed that this technological marvel was unsinkable. White Star Lines built the *Titanic* and its double, the *Olympic*, to gain a competitive advantage over the Cunard Line's sleek new passenger vessels, the *Lusitania* and the *Mauritania*.

When radio reports claimed that the *Titanic* had struck an iceberg in the north Atlantic four days into its maiden voyage, White Star Lines vice president Philip Franklin's initial statement on the morning of April 15, 1912, confidently assured the world "The *Titanic* is unsinkable. Its passengers will experience nothing worse than inconvenience." But before midnight, a shaken Franklin mumbled to reporters: "I thought the *Titanic* unsinkable. I based my opinion on the best expert advice. I do not understand it."

Within hours of striking an iceberg, the supposedly invulnerable 46,000-ton *Titanic* lay broken, two miles beneath the icy Atlantic. Although 675 lucky survivors were rescued, 1,522 people died a very cold death. Many critics consider it the pinnacle of folly for nearly everyone to have believed any ship unsinkable.

Smugness contributed to a variety of inadequate safety precautions. Lifeboats existed for only one-third of those aboard. Eight telegrams warning of ice fields that tragic night were not viewed as important aboard the *Titanic*, even though other ships, such as the *Californian,* had stopped for the night while the *Titanic* steamed along at 22 knots. An unusually warm winter had loosened much ice in the north Atlantic that year. There was no public address or alarm system aboard ship, and the two lookouts on duty in the crow's nest did not have binoculars. Author Walter Lord concludes: "Complacency is written all over this story. Everyone believed that nothing bad could happen."

One manifestation of complacency consisted of the *Titanic*'s lax safety measures, which stood in sharp relief against its unprecedented shipboard luxury. This White Star Lines vessel was the world's largest passenger ship. Accordingly, it boasted the first shipboard swimming pools, Turkish baths, gymnasiums, squash courts, ballrooms, libraries, lounges with fireplaces, and world-class service—matching the world-class distortion of priorities oozing from this case study. James Cameron's blockbuster movie *Titanic* (1997) set all kinds of box office records retelling the story of disaster.

The concept of deep ecology may have come in handy, had it been rattling around in the Western mindset in 1912. Confidence in the human condition had been steadily rising since the advent of the Industrial Revolution around 1750, but this confidence showed signs of eroding. The dark cloud hovering over the *Titanic* disaster served as a harbinger of worse things to come, as the sky caved in two years later when World War I began.[12] ▪

---

will bestow on posterity. Humanity's historical ascent has generally followed an upward trajectory concerning standard of living.

Inter-generational equity argues that we owe future generations nothing less than what we inherited from our forebears. This duty of "planetary trust," says Edith Brown Weiss, requires that "each generation holds the earth as a steward in trust for its descendants, which strikes a deep chord with men and women of all cultures, religions, and nationalities."[13] The challenge laid at our feet by inter-generational equity is nothing less than taking care of today's needs without destroying the world that our grandchildren will inhabit.

Defining the Problems

Humanity has collectively left a deep footprint in the ecological sand. William Stevens revels in a little hyperbole, opining "*Homo sapiens* rivals grand forces like the movement of continents, volcanic eruptions, asteroid impacts, and ice ages as an agent of global change."[14] As was stated previously, new thinking about GIs requires us to understand them as interacting parts of a finite system. Still, to appreciate the complexity of these problems, we must examine bits and pieces of the global mosaic as discrete entities. Such atomization aids comprehension of these multidimensional problems without negating countless linkages between environment, population, food, and energy. Because each GI represents a complicated labyrinth, let's examine their factual and analytical profiles separately.

Environment
Background to the Issue

Nineteenth-century nature writers such as Henry David Thoreau and Walt Whitman planted the intellectual seeds that blossomed into what was called the "conservation" movement. The establishment of Yellowstone National Park in 1872 was a marker event, but it was the dynamic outdoorsman, President Theodore Roosevelt, who used his bully pulpit to preach the new ethic of "conservation" in the early 1900s. The first book published in the United States that captured the public's imagination was Rachel Carson's *Silent Spring* (1962). Like the canary used in coal mines to warn of pending disaster, Carson's book chronicled how pesticides such as DDT were destroying birds and other wildlife. She argued persuasively that humans are not separate from nature but part of it.

The term *environmentalist* assumed widespread use around the first Earth Day, held in 1970. Three waves of an environmental movement then appeared. The Environmental Defense Fund's (EDF) successful legal battle against DDT triggered the first wave of adversarial lawsuits against offending corporations. Describing this initial wave, one environmentalist writes "In no other social or political movement has litigation played so important a role. Not even close." A second wave soon followed, based on lobbying the government to pass far-reaching pollution control laws and regulations. Both of these strategies achieved successes, albeit rather aggressively.

Bearing emotional scars from numerous legal battles, a third wave of environmentalists began advocating in the late 1980s that negotiations might provide more constructive solutions based on compromise. Economists developed economic incentives to prod people into doing the right thing on their own. The third stage tried to dispel tensions between environmentalism and economic growth, which gets at the very soul of what sustainable development is all about.[15]

As the popular expression reminds us, "We all live downwind." Emotional attachment to the well-being of animals symbolic of environmental integrity (such as whales) runs deep. The eco-conscious film *Free Willy* (1993) extols the virtue of young people coming to the aid of a whale in distress. The credits at the end of *Free Willy* listed a phone number for information on "ways to save the whales." The weekend debut of the film produced 40,000 calls from people concerned about whales.

In many affluent countries, environmentalism has assumed the aura of a secular religion, attracting legions of followers. Green consciousness has bloomed in ways unimaginable at the first Earth Day celebration more than three decades ago. But environmental issues are often rife with paradox, and as the Worldwatch Institute's Lester Brown points out, while popular attitudes have changed, and specific improvements have occurred in many countries, the big picture continues to look grim in many ways.[16]

Perhaps the simplest way to dissect the environmental issue is to consider it as a *problem of pollution,* that is, ecological systems unable to cleanse themselves of irritants introduced by humans. Pollution threatens the viability of three interrelated physical systems: *air, land,* and *water.*

The film *Free Willy* tapped a deep reservoir of human sentiment for the plight of whales in today's world.

Air Pollution

It's hard to imagine what might rival the purity of the air we breathe as a vital issue to humans. Yet, the myriad forms of air pollution that threaten our health derive almost wholly from forces unleashed by our own species. In some places, air pollution is bad enough for locals to refer to what they breathe as "air apparent." Some forms of air pollution are not picked up by our five senses; therefore, we depend on scientists for esoteric data to verify hidden threats. If you want to know how chemical emissions in your home county compare to the rest of your state and to the United States, go to the EDF's Website (listed at the end of this chapter) for useful and accessible data. Consider these general factoids before reading about the specific problems of global warming, ozone depletion, and acid rain.

Air pollution factoids:

- Global carbon dioxide emissions have grown by 278 percent in four decades; 26 billion tons of carbon dioxide are discharged annually.
- In Mexico City, seven out of ten newborns have excessively high lead levels in their blood.
- More than 44 percent of air pollution and 85 percent of urban smog in America stems from its motor vehicles.

Not all air pollution is as readily apparent as in this smog-filled city.

Global Warming

The poor South (LDCs) criticizes the rich North (MDCs) for burning massive amounts of fossil fuels (coal, oil, gas). The Industrial Revolution that began in the eighteenth century has caused dramatic increases in the use of fossil fuels. North Americans' love affair with the private car is responsible for roughly half of its emission of **greenhouse gases.** Greenhouse gases such as carbon dioxide, methane, chlorofluorocarbons, and nitrous oxide soak up the earth's infrared radiation, trapping it close to the surface, and thus contributing to warming global temperatures.

In 2005, the National Oceanic and Atmospheric Administration reported that carbon dioxide in the atmosphere had risen to a record level of 381 parts per million. Figure 4.1's bar graph identifies the six top countries emitting carbon dioxide as of 2003, with the United States far out in front, and China, an unrivalled runner-up.

Though global warming is not normally not a very sexy issue in American politics, Al Gore never gained much traction for his obsession with it during his political candidacies. However, the 2006 release of *An Inconvenient Truth,* a documentary film about global warming that features Gore extensively, garnered not only critical acclaim but also an Oscar and a Nobel Prize. Films, whether documentary or features, can spice up an issue in ways that recitations such as those summarized in Table 4.1 simply cannot. International Energy Agency (IEA) data indicate some of the significant variation regarding carbon dioxide emissions that occur when viewed sectorally by world region. Table 4.1 uses world data as a baseline to compare emissions in Asia, Europe, Middle East, Sub-Saharan Africa, North America, and South America (as well as between MDCs and LDCs). In other words, kicking the fossil fuel habit represents a massive challenge to humanity.

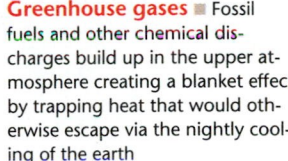

Greenhouse gases ■ Fossil fuels and other chemical discharges build up in the upper atmosphere creating a blanket effect by trapping heat that would otherwise escape via the nightly cooling of the earth

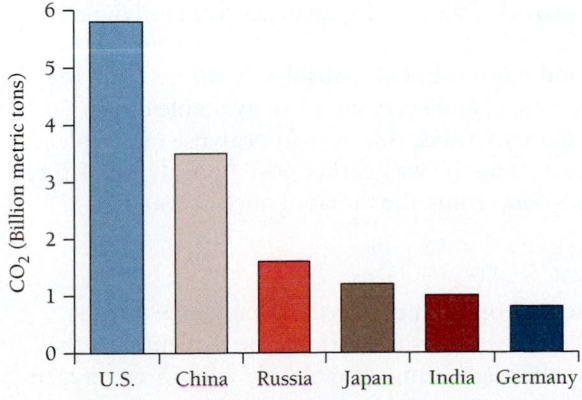

Figure 4.1

Top Country Emissions

Source: Energy Information Administration/Annual Energy Review (2004), "Carbon Dioxide Emissions": http://www.eia.doe.gov/.

Table 4.1

Carbon Dioxide Emissions by Economic Sector (2005) [million metric tons]

	CO$_2$ Total	Electric Sector	Industrial Sector	Residential Sector
World	**27,896**	**37%**	**17%**	**8%**
Africa	467	47%	17%	3%
Asia	7,402	41%	24%	7%
Europe	6,157	40%	17%	12%
Mid-Ea.	1,455	32%	21%	10%
N.A.	6,202	41%	12%	6%
S.A.	731	14%	26%	7%
MDCs	*14,719*	*41%*	*15%*	*9%*
LDCs	*8,624*	*38%*	*25%*	*7%*

Key

CO$_2$ Total: Mass of CO$_2$ released from burning fossil fuels.

Electric Sector: Percentage of CO$_2$ emissions from fuel combustion for public electricity and other public generation of power.

Industrial Sector: Percentage of CO$_2$ emissions from fuel combustion for manufacturing industries and construction.

Residential Sector: Percentage of CO$_2$ emissions from fuel combustion for households.

Source: International Energy Agency (IEA): "Carbon Dioxide Emissions by Economic Sector 2005," *EarthTrends Data Tables:* http://earthtrends.wri.org/.

Environmental authors Gareth Porter and Janet Brown claim that most experts fear that the greenhouse effect, and resultant global warming, will lead to the following:

- *Sea levels rising by five feet before the year 2050*
- *Declining nontropical forests*
- *Increasing air pollution, tropical diseases, and species extinction*
- *Shifting of arable farmland northward*[17]

Most global warming studies predicting future problems involve computer simulations of complex phenomena. However, environmental scientist Donald Wells refers to additional meteorological evidence, such as snow melting from the high Arctic earlier each year, annual thinning of Arctic icecaps, more numerous (but smaller) icebergs appearing in the North Atlantic's Labrador Current, and the U.S. experiencing a very high percentage of its hottest years on record in recent years. The severe drought of the summer of 1988 alarmed many previously unconcerned Americans about global warming.[18] Hurricane Katrina in 2005 also worried many observers. However, it is mostly small, low-lying island countries that have expressed the greatest concern about global warming because they fear it will lead to melting polar ice caps and flooding of their vulnerable coasts.

Flooding caused by global warming provided the plot for an expensive Hollywood movie, *Waterworld* (1995), directed by Kevin Costner. However, in *Waterworld*, melting polar ice caps threaten not only small island nations but also absolutely *everyone* on the planet. This climatic disaster threatens everyone, and every chunk of available dirt is fought over in Costner's disturbing film. In many ways, this post-Apocalypse movie pleads that we come to our senses about global warming the way earlier post-Apocalypse pictures tried to shock us into coming to our senses concerning the threat of nuclear war.

Ozone Depletion

Ozone layer ■ A concentration of the gas ozone in the stratosphere from about ten to thirty miles above the earth's surface

Although some minor scientific differences of opinion exist over the urgency of the fossil-fuel-induced greenhouse effect, consensus reigns concerning the depletion of the earth's protective **ozone layer**. Ironically, although ozone (a molecule with three oxygen atoms) is one of the most noxious elements contributing to urban smog, it works to our advantage in the earth's stratosphere. As chlorofluorocarbons (CFCs)—such as the freon gas found in air conditioners, refrigerators, and aerosol spray cans; Styrofoam; and some solvents—eat away at the atmosphere's protective ozone layer, humans become exposed to harmful ultraviolet (UV) radiation from the sun.

The use of CFCs is associated with the lifestyle of the MDCs. They are also *causing* lifestyle changes these days. For generations, the prescription for healthy children included lots of fresh air and sunshine. However, children are particularly susceptible to skin damage from UV radiation, and increases of skin cancer among young people are being reported around the world. Medical experts now advise parents to use protective sunscreen with a blocking factor of at least 15 to protect their children. Australia and New Zealand, where the ozone layer is being eaten away quite rapidly, have the world's highest incidence of skin cancer. Wearing hats, long-sleeved shirts, and avoiding midday sun are also recommended by dermatologists.[19] Unfortunately, the hazards of UV radiation exposure do not end with skin cancer. Exposure also weakens our immune system and is damaging to certain crops, such as beans, peas, and cotton.[20]

The most dramatic ozone depletion, however, is occurring over Antarctica, where an ozone hole the size of Europe has been measured. In the waters surrounding Antarctica, plankton organisms have declined by about 10 percent, which studies suggest results from ozone depletion. Scientists are concerned about how these losses at the bottom of the food chain will affect species residing higher on the organic food chain, initially fish, and later humans. Although the international response to ozone depletion will take time to manifest itself, the 1987 Montreal Protocol called for phasing out CFCs and creating greener technologies to replace them. The global community mobilized so quickly and successfully in responding to ozone depletion that one environmentalist concluded "The Montreal Protocol was a high point for environmental globalization."[21]

Acid Rain

To what extent **acid rain** is seen as a serious problem depends partially on where you live. Burning fossil fuels spews nitric acid and sulfuric acid into the atmosphere. This acidity is a form of air pollution that rainfall unleashes to damage forests, contaminate water resources, and kill fish living in streams and lakes. Beginning in the 1960s, taller industrial chimneys were introduced in the United States to disperse pollutants. Because of this dispersion, as well as the prevailing westerly winds, much of the pollution from industry and coal-fired electric power plants, for example, along the Ohio River, finally comes to rest in New England and Canada.

Because air pollution does not respect national boundaries, more than 10,000 acidified Canadian lakes are reportedly devoid of fish. Canadians generally become much more exercised over this issue than do U.S. residents. Acid rain is an industrial phenomenon, not a North American one, and the problem is viewed with alarm in much of northern Europe, especially in Germany, where the term *Waldsterben* (forest death) is heard increasingly. When trees die, the stability provided by their root systems dies with them, and increased soil erosion results. An estimated $23 billion in lost lumber harvest annually for Europe is widely accepted as accurate.[22]

Land Pollution

Human abuse of the land on which we live assumes many forms. One scholar refers to land as a "thin veneer of life being placed under increasing stress."[23] With a billion more mouths to feed every thirteen years, humanity needs to find ways to expand agricultural productivity. Yet nearly all such methods tend to degrade the soil. Irrigation lowers water tables, causes soil erosion, destroys wildlife habitat, salts the land, creates waterlogging, and increases the likelihood of conflict over fresh water. A fundamental problem caused by irrigation is that not all water drawn from irrigation seeps into the ground. Much of it evaporates, leaving behind salts and minerals. The greater the irrigation, the greater the salts produced, and the less effective the soil is for growing crops.[24]

The former Soviet Union was wholly oblivious to the ecological consequences of its economic development projects. To grow cotton in the dry and marginal soil of one of its former provinces, Kazakhstan, the USSR irrigated extensively. The consequences for the Aral Sea were disastrous: its level dropped 14 meters, losing 40 percent of its area and 60 percent of its volume. Mineral concentrations, such as salt, tripled, killing all marine life there. Few such stark cases of irresponsibly abusive irrigation can be cited.

When land is most seriously degraded, it becomes desert-like, and this process is called desertification. The U.N. Environmental Programme (UNEP) estimates that roughly 31,000 square miles of the earth's surface are desertified annually. This results mainly from water scarcity, deforestation, overplanting, and overgrazing. More than a hundred countries attended a U.N. Convention (global town meeting) on desertification held in Nairobi, Kenya, in 1977. You may be surprised to learn that although 1 million square kilometers of desert exists in the northeastern corner of Brazil, most North Americans associate this country primarily with rainforests. Of Brazil's five ecosystems, two are indeed rainforests, but one is a desert.

Land pollution factoids:

- Annual economic losses due to desertification are estimated at $42 billion.
- Between 1950 and 2000, the world lost one-fifth of the topsoil from its cropland.
- Land under irrigation doubled between 1900 and 1950 and has increased more than two-and-a-half-fold since then to a global level of 250 million hectares.

Deforestation

The causes of deforestation are multiple, and each exerts stress on available land resources: (1) commercial logging activity; (2) clearing of forests for human settlements; (3) slash-and-burn techniques to clear land for crop rotation; (4) large-scale, chemical-intensive agribusiness for export; and (5) overpopulation.

Deforestation factoids:[25]

- At mid-century, 12 percent of the globe was covered with tropical forest; today only 6 percent.
- Fifty million acres (78,750 sq. mi.) of forest are lost annually, and reforestation replaces only 10 percent.
- Deforestation leads to increased wood prices, loss of biodiversity, soil erosion, and global warming.

Forests are disappearing at a rate of about 6.8 million acres each year, which is the size of the state of Washington.[26] One reason this process disturbs us is that many of the trees being lost are so spectacular. The giant sequoias of northern California are the largest living things on earth, and another conifer species in that area is the oldest at 4,000-plus years. The tallest species measured is the mountain ash of Australia at 425 feet. Such old-growth forest took many hundreds of years to develop and are irreplaceable.

Brazil's Vital Rainforests

The largest-scale destruction of tropical rainforests is occurring in Brazil's massive Amazon basin, home to one-third of the globe's rainforests. However, even sadder is the decimation of Brazil's "other" rainforest, the Atlantic forest, which measured 4,500 square miles when Portuguese explorers arrived in 1500. Only 3 percent of the original Atlantic rainforest along Brazil's east coast remains today (see Figure 4.2). U.S. environmental historian Warren Dean's fascinating book on the subject chronicles a "half millennium of gluttony over a forest cursed by providing too much, too easily." Dean tells how peasants, loggers, ranchers, coffee planters, industrialists, and the Brazilian government feasted on the Atlantic forest in hopes of preventing Amazonia from suffering the same fate; because one-half of the Amazon forest still survives, there is hope for it.[27]

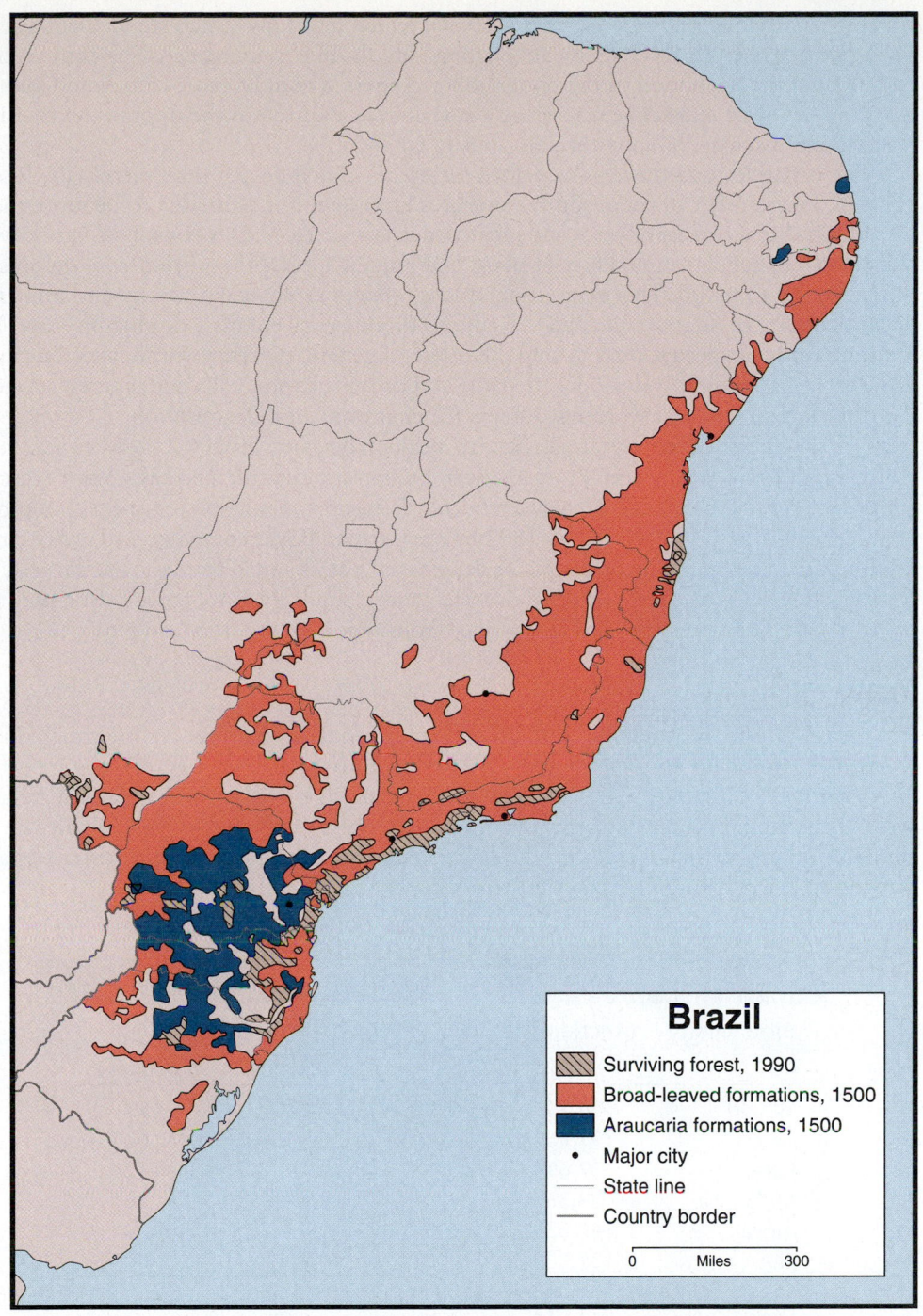

Figure 4.2
The Brazilian Atlantic
Forest over time.

Brazil's government exacerbated Amazonia's problems in 1970 when it created land incentives for farmers to colonize the basin: 100 free acres were given to anyone willing to clear the jungle to grow crops, despite the fact that such land was left nutrient-poor after the trees were gone. For a long time, it was exclusively Northern Hemisphere ecologists who complained about the global consequences of Brazil's blind eye toward slash-and-burn agriculture and its legacy of deforestation.

Then in 1988, a popular activist working in behalf of poor rubber tappers and agitating for rainforest protection, Chico Mendes, was killed to silence his voice of protest. The martyrdom of Chico Mendes helped turn the tide of public opinion in Brazil against business interests exploiting the Amazon's resources. Mendes became an international icon as both documentary and feature films told his story. Raul Julia plays the part of

Amazonian social activist Chico Mendes successfully blended the issues of worker's rights and forest conservation in gaining global recognition for his efforts.

Chico Mendes in *The Burning Season* (1994), which tells how Chico stands firm against slash-and-burn cattle ranchers by advocating Gandhi-like nonviolence. The cattle ranchers threaten the livelihood of the poor rubber tappers whom he represents, and Chico offers the idea of an extractive reserve as a sustainable solution to the impasse (extractive reserves are discussed among the solutions in Chapter 5).

The negative consequences of deforestation run much deeper than merely the loss of trees. The number of species in the world is unknown but estimated to be more than 10 million. Most consist of yet-to-be-identified insects in tropical forests. Biologist Edward Wilson calculates the annual loss of plant and animal species that result from deforestation at 4,000 to 6,000. This magnitude of loss reduces biological diversity and impedes nature's ability to adapt to change.[28] Reduced *biodiversity* entails a double hit: first, losing thousands of species; then, losing the range of genetic diversity within species. The U.S. Fish and Wildlife Website listed at the end of this chapter calls endangered species "Nature's 911," as early warning systems for environmental degradation.

The net effects of biodiversity losses are incalculable, and Table 4.2 sketches region-by-region biodiversity protection. From a strictly human standpoint, medical science's discovery of wonder drugs depends on new chemicals derived from unexplored species. Aspirin was derived from the willow tree in 1897 by the German Bayer company, and today tens of millions are taken annually by people. A drug called Taxol, taken from the Pacific yew, has performed well in treating breast and ovarian cancer. Similarly, Capoten is a drug used to control high blood pressure, and it is derived from venom of the Brazilian pit viper.

Water Pollution

American statesman Benjamin Franklin once quipped that you discover the true value of water at the moment your well runs dry. Along with oxygen, water is required by nearly all life forms. Ultimately, "The world's water system, like its air, is one great interrelated system."[29] Global demand for fresh water now doubles every twenty years while the available supply dwindles significantly in many areas of the globe. The world needs a staggering 7.1 trillion gallons a year to service expanding populations.[30]

Table 4.2

Biodiversity Protection (2005)

	Area	%	Wetlands	Biospheres
World	**806,722**	**6%**	**1,420**	**459**
Asia	191,450	8%	145	67
Europe	137,694	6%	788	172
Middle East	33,360	3%	77	26
Africa	142,025	6%	102	50
N.A.	131,738	7%	57	60
S.A.	106,018	6%	76	40
MDCs	353,555	6.3%	963	—
LDCs	454,467	5.9%	464	—

Key

Area: A protected area of land or sea dedicated to maintaining biological diversity (total in 1,000 hectares).

Percentage: Percent of total land area under protection.

Wetlands: Wetlands of international importance (based on ecology, botany, limnology, or hydrology).

Reserves: Biosphere reserves in coastal or terrestrial environments recognized under UNESCO guidelines and selected for their value to conservation.

Source: UNEP; UNESCO; World Conservation Union, "Biodiversity 2005," *EarthTrends Data Tables:* http://earthtrends.wri.org/.

Some predict that fresh water will replace oil as the liquid gold of the twenty-first century. In his book *Tapped Out,* ex-Senator Paul Simon points out that "Nations fight over oil, but valuable as it is, there are substitutes for oil. There is no substitute for water."[31] The city of Las Vegas uses 300 gallons of water per capita every day. Twenty-two countries depend on water flowing from other states, creating potential conflicts if those living upstream stem the flow to those living downstream. The regions of greatest risk include the Middle East and the south Asian triangle between India, Pakistan, and Bangladesh.[32]

Water factoids:

- Although 71 percent of the globe is water, 96.5 percent is salt water, and 2.4 percent ice or snow, leaving only 1.1 percent available to humans.
- Of the globe's fresh water, 92 percent gets used for agricultural or industrial purposes.
- More than 400,000 people worldwide live in areas on the water stress index.

Issues of both quantity and quality pervade our water-related concerns, although poor water quality (pollution) seems more immediate than quantity (volume available). Only 3 percent of the earth's water is fresh, yet that 3 percent is vital to human existence. Two-thirds of fresh water goes to agricultural irrigation, one-quarter goes to industrial use, and less than 10 percent goes to direct human consumption. Exacerbating the problem is that fresh water is very localized. For example, Lake Baikal in Russia holds 20 percent of the world's fresh water (see Figure 4.3), as do North America's five Great Lakes. Taken together, they comprise nearly half of global fresh water.

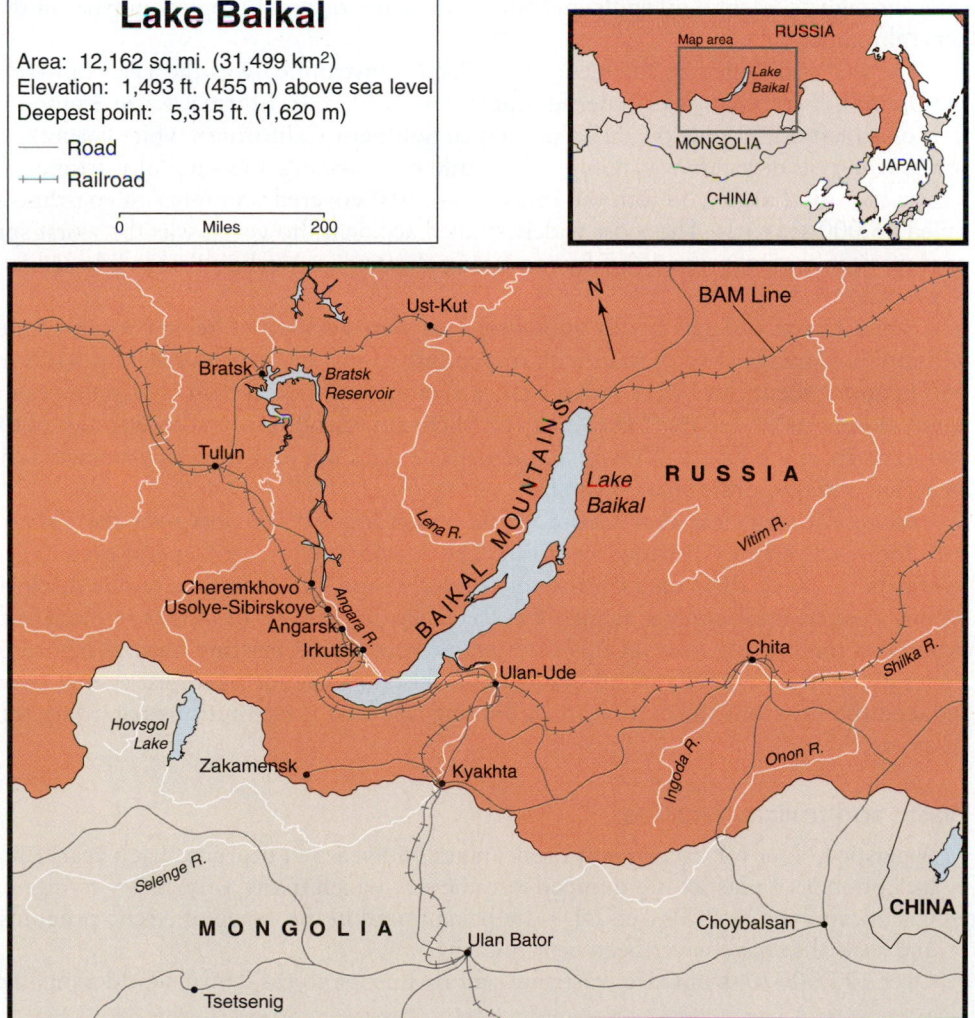

Figure 4.3

Siberia's Lake Baikal holds as much water as North America's Great Lakes combined, but has been more severely polluted.

Source: From THE WORLD BOOK ENCYCLOPEDIA. Copyright © 1997. World Book, Inc. By permission of the publisher. www.worldbookonline.com.

When such abundance is contrasted with arid African countries, the water wars on the horizon seen by some observers may be more than a mirage. In Africa's most populous state, Nigeria, only one-half of its people have access to safe drinking water, and neither Kenya nor Ethiopia fare much better. In the Middle East, Israel, Jordan, Syria, and Lebanon all draw groundwater from common underground aquifers that are being over-pumped. The Nile River runs through nine countries, whereas the Zambesi River traverses eight nations, providing flashpoints for conflicts. Egypt, for example, is completely dependent on sources of water beyond its boundaries.

How do humans pollute water supplies?

1. sediment (soil and minerals)
2. sewerage
3. infectious organisms
4. fertilizer by-products (nitrogen and phosphorus)
5. synthetic organic chemicals
6. inorganic chemicals
7. radioactivity
8. thermal (heat) pollution

About three-fourths of oceanic pollution derives from land-based sources such as industrial waste, sewerage, synthetic organic compounds, and agricultural runoff. Marine pollution is also aggravated by 3 to 4 million tons of oil discharged into the sea every year, with various aspects of marine transportation accounting for one-third of oil entering the ocean. More oil actually enters oceans through routine bilge cleaning by ships than through accidental oil spills, but spills have a major psychological impact on the general public.[33]

The first spill billed by the media as an "eco-catastrophe" was the 1969 blowout of the Union Oil Company's drilling rig near Santa Barbara, California, when 3 million gallons of oil left a 200-mile oil slick that stained Southern California's white beaches. One of the worst oil disasters was man-made—Saddam Hussein's 1991 act of wartime "eco-terrorism," discharging oil into the Persian Gulf that covered 350 miles of coastline and killed 25,000 seabirds. The most widely studied accident, however, was the worst spill on American territory, the 1989 *Exxon Valdez* disaster in Alaska's Prince Edward Sound (Case Study 4.2).

When Exxon officials finally appeared, they were accused of being concerned more with public damage control than with responding to this disaster. Eventually, $125 million in government fines were levied against Exxon, and Exxon paid civil penalties measured in billions of dollars.[34] University of Michigan scientist Garry Brewer argues that bad news from the Prince William Sound debacle does not end with environmental destruction and corporate irresponsibility.

Because it was clear that Exxon would be fending off lawsuits over the *Valdez* spill for years, secrecy became the norm. The Alaskan Attorney General even ordered scientists to "keep their data on the spill under wraps," fearing that public disclosure would weaken legal actions against Exxon. Ecologist Brewer describes free scientific inquiry as the unsung loser in this case: an unprecedented pristine natural laboratory under great stress was examined inadequately because science's greatest enemy (secrecy) reduced the flow of information, thus limiting science's contributions regarding future disasters.[35]

Waste and toxicity factoids:

- A plastic holder for beer or soft drinks takes 450 years to degrade. Each year, 100 million pounds of plastics are dumped into the sea, which many animals try to ingest.
- Chemicals such as PCBs and DDT are being found in the tissue of Arctic penguins and seals that have never been near humans.
- Over 125,000 tons of toxic waste are sent by Europe to the Third World annually.

Case Study 4.2 *Exxon Valdez*

Despite fresh memories of the 1969 Santa Barbara oil spill, reduced petroleum supplies and price increases accompanying the 1973 oil crisis fed popular fears of perpetual oil shortages. Therefore, in 1973, President Richard Nixon approved construction of an 800-mile pipeline to connect the Northern Slope of Alaska (with its 30 billion barrels of untapped oil) to the southern Alaska port at Valdez. The Alaska pipeline began carrying oil in 1977 and soon lived up to its billing as a relatively safe, efficient way to transport oil from Alaska's remote north. But after oil reaches southern Alaska at Valdez, it is shipped to its destination by commercial supertanker.

Despite calm seas and good visibility, disaster struck Prince William Sound on the night of March 24, 1989. After being at sea for only three hours, the *Exxon Valdez* struck the well-known Bligh Reef, twenty-two miles from its departure. Captain Joseph Hazelwood radioed in the leak, which eventually resulted in 20 percent of the tanker's 1.3 million barrels of oil coating the Sound and choking the life out of it. One official described it as "a fish and wildlife holocaust," in which 1.5 million birds died, including 150 bald eagles. Captain Hazelwood ended up facing criminal charges for drunkenness and negligent recklessness, with his bail set at $1 million.

The cleanup operation in Prince William Sound seemed almost as pathetic as the spill itself. Exxon did not have the

Three members of an animal recovery team dispose of the oil soaked carcasses of sea otters from the snowy ground at the edge of Prince William Sound, Alaska.

required equipment on hand to respond to the disaster. Furthermore, it took fourteen hours for Exxon's first containment team to arrive. Meanwhile, Exxon refused offers by local fishermen to assist in the cleanup; they sat by, watching in frustration as their livelihood turned belly-up in the forty-mile slick resulting from high winds and a perfunctory cleanup. ▪

North–South Environmental Debate

At the 1992 Rio Earth Summit, the primary action document produced was called *Agenda 21*, to symbolize its function as the global goal for the twenty-first century. *Agenda 21* comes down with feet planted firmly on both sides of the equator. The heart of *Agenda 21* calls for the rich countries (MDCs) to limit consumption to sustainable levels and to transfer technologies to the poor countries (LDCs), while it calls on the South to address population growth, consider market-oriented economic reforms, and increase access to natural resources for indigenous peoples in their countries. This document also recommended expenditures of $125 billion annually, with rich countries contributing 0.7 percent of their gross national product (GNP). However, fewer than ten countries have met this goal, and development aid from the MDCs has actually decreased in recent years to less than 0.3 percent of GNP.[36] In 2008, America's percentage had slipped to 0.15 percent.

Deep perceptual divisions exist between the MDCs and LDCs over ecological matters, and the plight of the rainforests is one issue that carries great symbolic meaning both north and south of the equator. Deforestation is seen by many LDCs as necessary for their economic development in much the same way as it was for the United States during the nineteenth century. Poor countries blame the rich for allowing poverty to remain the norm south of the equator, necessitating destructive practices such as deforestation. The North–South battle over rainforests entails the North contending that these resources belong to the "global commons," while the South retorts that they are resources of "sovereign discretion."

Garbage barge being loaded in New York City for transport to a destination as far away from the Big Apple as its residents can send it.

Environmental space ■ A new concept that adds a physical dimension (space) to measuring the consequences of wasting resources and creating pollution

While the MDCs fixate on conserving resources such as the rainforests, the burning environmental questions for the LDCs are urban air and water pollution, erosion and salinization of farmland, and containment of toxic chemicals.[37] From the southern perspective, wasteful northern lifestyles cause most pollution; therefore, it is the rich who should pay clean-up costs.

Poor countries have added to the dialogue the notion of **environmental space** as a criticism of wealthy "throwaway cultures" that accumulate massive amounts of waste—solid, toxic, nuclear, and industrial—and then want to ship it to the south for disposal. Less environmental space should be consumed by the North, they say, and more environmental space provided for them. Historian Paul Kennedy concurs by suggesting that the environmental issue is the first in which "what the South does can hurt the North."[38]

In 2005, a major four-year research effort involving more than 1,300 scientists worldwide was completed. The Millennium Ecosystem Assessment (MEA) gathered unprecedented data regarding the status of twenty-four ecosystems. Its chief finding is that "Unsustainable management practices have generally limited ecosystems' ability to provide goods and services for human use." Numerous examples are cited to demonstrate the human toll on ecosystems. The MEA also emphasizes how poor people are more directly dependent on ecosystem services, so that when they are degraded, the livelihoods of the poor are affected disproportionately. Disruption of coastal fisheries hurts the poor most because they are very dependent upon small-scale fisheries, and a trend toward privatization has hurt poor fishers in diverse places such as Ecuador, Thailand, Vietnam, Chile, Indonesia, the Philippines, Bangladesh, and India.[39]

America's Role

In the North–South ecological drama, the spotlight shines intently on the United States. This pivotal country epitomizes the ecological paradox: while no other country has passed as much legislation or put as many resources into environmental protection, no other country has consumed or despoiled as much. The numbers are stark: with 5 percent of world population, the United States uses one-quarter of the earth's fuel and produces one-quarter of global pollution, far outdistancing any competitor in greenhouse gas emissions.

U.S. ecosphere factoids:

- The average American uses about sixty gallons of water daily at home but only two quarts are ingested bodily.
- The average American consumes four times more steel and twenty-three times more aluminum than the average Mexican.
- One metric ton per capita of toxic waste is produced in the United States every year.

During the 1990s, the wealth gap between North and South grew considerably, yet American foreign aid diminished at about the same rate. Whereas our economy dwarfed that of Japan in the 1990s, Japan surpassed America for several years as world leader in foreign assistance. Although Al Qaeda's grievances against the West are multi-faceted, some experts refer to foreign aid as "terrorism insurance."

The American role, however, stretches beyond statistical measurement. The United States acts as symbolic leader of the world's democracies and prides itself on foreign policies blending idealism as well as *realpolitik*. America says that it tries to do the right thing ecologically. Yet, on occasion, the United States has been branded by our closest allies (the Europeans, Canadians, and Japanese) as a malingerer. In the case of the 1992 Rio Earth Summit, the United States found itself isolated when George H. W. Bush refused to sign the biodiversity agreement approved by nearly everyone else, as it did a decade later when his son, President George W. Bush, failed to honor the Kyoto Protocol on global warming.

Population

When any large population gets basic sanitation and medical services, fertility rates (births) overtake mortality rates (deaths). Put simply, more people living longer swells the size of any population. It is theorized that it required 14 million years for *Homo sapiens* to reach 1 billion in the year 1800, but only 130 years went by before humans hit the 2 billion mark in 1930. Then, 30 years passed for our population to top 3 billion in 1960; after that, only 15 years were needed to arrive at 4 billion people in 1975, and a mere 12 years later the figure of 5 billion was reached in 1987. You can refer to the World Population Clock online for the current calculation of global population.[40]

People alive today constitute a stunning one-quarter of all those humans who have ever lived because more people were added to global population in the final fifth of the twentieth century than at any other time in history.[41] Yet, some good news does exist, because the rate of annual population growth has shrunk from 2 to 1.7 percent during the past quarter century. Some analysts fear, however, that this may be a case of too little, too late. According to U.S. Census Bureau estimates, world population hit 6.5 billion earth residents on February 25, 2006, at 7:16 p.m.[42]

Because of the potency of the **momentum factor in population** growth, problems result from the time lags involved. Yale historian Paul Kennedy uses the analogy of a supertanker at sea to illustrate the momentum factor in population growth, pointing out that both a supertanker and expanding populations require a long time to slow down, and an even longer time to stop.[43] One out of three inhabitants of earth is a child, who, before long, will mature and desire to raise a family. Two well-known authors say that we will continue to see at least half a century of population growth, even after replacement-level fertility has been reached. The three main variables affecting population increases are *fertility, mortality,* and *migration*.[44]

Momentum factor in population ■ When high birth rates combine with declining death rates, large proportions of young people of childbearing age create a large population bubble that will burst forth in the future

Regional Variation

Many worldwide demographic trends are clear, but tremendous variation exists between countries and between regions. Similar to the environment, huge contrasts typify North-South population comparisons. Those inhabiting the MDCs are barely replacing themselves, whereas the **fertility rate** in many LDCs hovers around six or seven children born. In some oil-rich Arab states, governments have undertaken aggressive procreation programs, resulting in many of the world's highest fertility rates: Libya (7.6), Iraq (7.1), Jordan (7.8), Kuwait (6.9), and Oman (7.2). In Bangladesh, 768 humans cram themselves into every square kilometer, whereas population density in the United States is only 27 people in the same space.[45]

Regional variation factoids:

- The MDCs will double their population in 138 years; the LDCs in 33 years; Africa in 24 years.
- The U.N. Population Fund estimates that between now and 2025, 95 percent of world population growth will occur in the poor South.[46]
- The fertility rate for women is 2.1 in the United States, 8.5 in Rwanda, 6.4 in Saudi Arabia, 4.6 in Bolivia, and 1.3 in Italy.[47]

Table 4.3

UNPD POPULATION GROWTH

	Total Population		Fertility		% Urban	
	1975	2000	1975	2000	1975	2000
World	**4.1B**	**6.2B**	**3.9**	**2.7**	**38%**	**48%**
Africa	.33B	.68B	6.7	5.6	21%	34%
Asia	2.3B	3.5B	4.1	2.5	24%	35%
Europe	.67B	.73B	2.0	1.3	67%	75%
Middle East	.21B	.42B	5.9	3.5	43%	61%
N.A.	.24B	.32B	1.8	1.9	74%	77%
S.A.	.22B	.36B	4.3	2.4	64%	80%
MDCs	*1.1B*	*1.3B*	*2.1*	*1.6*	*69%*	*74%*
LDCs	*2.9B*	*4.9B*	*4.7*	*3.0*	*26%*	*40%*

Key

Total Population: U.N. Population Division compilation of population from all censuses and surveys.
Fertility: Average number of children per year for each woman.
% Urban: Percentage of population living in urban areas (often defined as greater than 10,000 residents).

Source: U.N. Population Division, "Demographic Indicators," *EarthTrends Data Tables:* http://earthtrends.wri.org/.

Table 4.3 illustrates more precisely the point about regional variation regarding population increases from the 1970s to 2000.

Considerable research suggests a strong correlation between the number of children borne by women and available jobs for women, education for women, and contraceptive programs.[48] One author notes that "Schooling for girls is a potent population intervention because they will also pass down what they learn to their children."[49] Poor Southern countries typically lack the resources to deliver most of these services conducive to lowering fertility rates. Therefore, other actors try to fill the gap.

Private NGOs such as the London-based International Planned Parenthood Federation (IPPF), created in 1952 and now operating in more than 150 countries, offers its own family planning services to women. The IPPF enjoys consultative status with the U.N. and participates in the global dialogue on population issues. More robust in its efforts, however, is the United Nations Population Fund (UNPF). The U.N. is a vital body in the delivery of services to people in poor countries, and the UNPF has funneled about $44 billion since it began family planning endeavors in 1969. Its annual budget is about $310 million.

Accompanying rapid increases in population has been the phenomenon of **urbanization**. There is nothing new about people living in cities. However, there are many new things about the process of urbanization. It began in earnest with the Industrial Revolution 250 years ago. Although urbanization has occurred worldwide, its rate of recent growth has been greatest in the poor South. Of the ten largest cities today, seven are found in the Southern Hemisphere, as shown in Table 4.4. In 1800, only 3 percent of human populations lived in cities, but now about one-half are urban dwellers, made up of 75 percent in the wealthy countries and 35 percent in poor states.[50]

Urbanization ■ A growing proportion of a population living in cities and those cities exerting greater influence on the societies in which they exist

Resharpening Malthusian Pencils

The U.N. Population Fund warns that "Population is intensifying hunger and poverty and straining the earth's resources."[51] The idea that population must be tied to other GIs

Table 4.4

TEN LARGEST CITIES IN THE WORLD

City	1950 Population	2000 Population
Tokyo, Japan	6.9 million	28.0 million
São Paolo, Brazil	2.0 million	22.6 million
Bombay, India	2.8 million	18.1 million
Shanghai, China	5.3 million	17.4 million
New York City, USA	12.3 million	16.6 million
Mexico City, Mexico	2.3 million	16.2 million
Beijing, China	2.8 million	14.4 million
Lagos, Nigeria	0.3 million	13.5 million
Jakarta, Indonesia	1.9 million	13.4 million
Los Angeles, USA	2.0 million	13.2 million

Source: United Nations Population Fund, 2000.

to fully comprehend its dynamics, however, is not new. Two centuries ago, British economist Thomas Malthus (1766–1834) established an innovative model portending trouble concerning the relationship between global population and global food supplies. He proposed what became known as the **Malthus theorem**, claiming that if births go unchecked, populations will outstrip their food supplies. His predictions of dire food shortages were averted by technologically based agricultural expansion. Some scholars today, called "New Malthusians," are dusting off Malthus' *Essay on the Principle of Population* (1798) and applying it to current conditions they believe warrant resurrecting Malthusian pessimism.[52]

Malthus theorem ■
Calculations made by Thomas Malthus in the eighteenth century that suggest that while the food supply increases only arithmetically, population grows geometrically

Conceptual linkages between population and other GIs are sometimes ignored in academia, where analysis is often driven by departmentalized disciplines. The most authoritative world meeting on population, however, the 1994 Cairo Conference, attempted to rectify this tendency by calling on governments "not just to make family planning services available to all but also to take measures to reduce illness and poverty, improve educational opportunity, and work toward environmentally sustainable economic development."[53]

Population Holism

The call for holistic, multifaceted approaches to the population dilemma finds a clear voice in philosopher Timothy Weiskel. In the 1950s and 1960s, simple mono-causal explanations of population growth gained currency, and a shortage of birth control techniques was branded as the culprit. They were followed in the 1970s and 1980s by the theory that poverty caused excessive population. Weiskel argues that searching for a universal "magic bullet" theory is naively unrealistic; population is a complex problem that varies from place to place according to local cultures.[54]

In traditional cultures, male social dominance often favors high fertility rates, large families, and males assuming public roles while females assume private roles. Some governments have worsened the problem through policies creating tangible incentives for large families. Why might they do so? Often they believe that large populations contribute to national power by providing large armies and labor pools that facilitate war-making. Global perspectives reveal such thinking to be short-sighted, parochial, and self-defeating. Yet, even when these governments have the right intentions, population problems can multiply. Take India's failed family planning program, for example (Case Study 4.3).

Case Study 4.3   Indian Policy and ZPG

When India's population hit 1 billion, experts predicted that it will surpass China by 2025. Fully 36 percent of Indians are in their pre-reproductive years, inflating a momentum bubble in the population pipeline. The situation can only get worse before it gets better. Ironically, India was one of the leaders among LDCs in recognizing that runaway population growth hinders economic development. India began enacting family planning policies soon after independence in 1947 that were aimed at zero population growth (ZPG).

India's first ZPG program started in 1951, but it was underfunded and limited to promotion of the rhythm method (periodic abstinence) among urban residents. It failed. When the 1961 census revealed an even higher population growth rate, it led the government to spend more money on three initiatives: (1) making intrauterine devices (IUDs) widely available; (2) expanding services to rural residents; and (3) launching a media campaign to push birth control.

Nevertheless, the 1971 census reported ever-climbing rates of growth, rendering initial visions of ZPG moot. Apparently desperate for family planning solutions, questionable new policies applied over-zealously led to grass-roots

resistance during the 1970s. A law prohibiting girls under 18 from marrying and the passage of very liberal abortion legislation produced political sparks.

However, the explosive issue that dominated family planning efforts in the 1970s was male sterilization. Public health officials were assigned quotas for vasectomies in their districts. Cash incentives were dangled before these public officials and before males agreeing to be sterilized. Some officials were accused of coercing men to go under the knife. From 1976 to 1977, vasectomies increased from 2.7 million to 8.3 million.

The 1980s ushered in a shift from male to female sterilization, which created less controversy but failed just as abjectly. Decades of policy arrows aimed at ZPG missed the target for a variety of reasons. Public policy analyst Anne Nadakavukaren believes "Over-reliance on sterilization as the chief means of limiting fertility was the main reason for the program's negative public image and failure." Nedakavukaren adds that the unavailability of condoms and birth control pills constituted major technical weaknesses, and that poor public education plagued the human resources side of Indian family planning.[55] ∎

Food

Background to the Issue

The NGO Food First calls it "a cruel paradox that 80 percent of people in the world who experience hunger make their living off the land, and 50 percent are actually independent farmers." Family farmers everywhere around the world face a dire problem because "so much food is being produced, the prices they receive are very low."[56] The process of obtaining food in the MDCs typically entails a one-hour visit to a supermarket where we gather enough to last for a week. This is possible because we have specialists who engage in intensive agriculture and produce bountiful surplus food. The commercialization of agriculture into modern **agribusiness**, which involves only 2 percent of the U.S. population, nevertheless manages to pile up major surpluses.[57]

Agribusiness ∎ Massive farming that blends economies of scale with high demand for increased agricultural products

Agribusiness allows for permanent cultivation of fields, with essential nutrients usually replaced by inorganic (chemical) fertilizers, which carry significant costs for the environment. There are certainly more benign ways of restoring fertility to the soil, but such methods do not produce the huge yields associated with agribusiness.[58] Table 4.5 relates to some of the key variables relevant to food productivity.

In the great majority of societies existing during recorded human history, food collection was not the work of specialists; rather, it fell to generalists who procured their own food through foraging activities or subsistence agriculture. Simple subsistence agriculture is what the majority of humanity still practices in the poor South. About 1 billion global citizens suffer from chronic malnutrition. Precise numbers for starvation are hard to come by because people do not officially die from starvation. Other conditions that result from weakened bodies are identified as the direct causes of death. However, it is estimated that about 15 million children die annually of causes related to hunger, translating to 41,000 every day.[59] However, a Washington-based think tank, The International Food Policy Research Institute (IFPRI), predicts about a 15 percent decline in malnourished children worldwide between 1995 and 2020. These projections are based on a 1999 computer simulation summarized in Table 4.6.[60] According to these projections, malnourishment was, and will continue to be, most severe in South Asia.

Table 4.5

COMPARATIVE FOOD AND AGRICULTURAL DATA (FAO, U.S. GOVERNMENT)

	Land	% Land	Labor	Fertilizer	Mechanization
World	**1,534,466**	**18%**	**0.87**	**90**	**18**
Africa	182,680	4%	1.02	11	1
Asia	500,878	34%	2.02	139	12
Europe	303,993	8%	0.10	73	37
Middle East	100,520	28%	0.51	67	17
N.A.	223,951	10%	0.02	99	25
S.A.	126,594	8%	0.21	79	10
MDCs	*635,324*	*11%*	*0.07*	*80*	*31*
LDCs	*904,850*	*23%*	*1.42*	*99*	*8*

Key

Land: Agricultural land, in thousand hectares, defined as total arable land and permanent cropland.

% Land: Irrigated cropland providing water to crops as a percentage of total agricultural land.

Labor: Intensity of agricultural labor input per hectare of agricultural land.

Fertilizer: Intensity of agricultural fertilizer input per hectare of agricultural land, measured as kilograms of the three nutrients: nitrogen, potash, and phosphate.

Mechanization: Intensity of agricultural mechanization, measured as number of tractors used per hectare of cropland.

Source: FAO; U.S. Agriculture Department; "Food and Agriculture," *EarthTrends Data Tables:* http://earthtrends.wri.org/.

Table 4.6

PERCENTAGE OF MALNOURISHED CHILDREN, 1995 AND 2020, BY REGION

Region	1995 Percentage	Predictions for 2020
South Asia	51%	43%
Africa	33%	29%
S.E. Asia	35%	28%
China	18%	11%
West Asia	12%	8%
Latin America	9%	4%

Source: IFPRI IMPACT simulation, July, 1999.

Because one-third of North Americans are considered obese, food insufficiency is a problem difficult for most of us to comprehend. But scholars concerned about the Malthusian relationship between population and food discussed previously can cite some ominous statistics. For example, global grain production from 1950 to 1975 exceeded population increases. But global grain production since the 1980s has grown more slowly, at an annual rate of less than 1 percent, producing a net loss of 11 percent in per capita grain supplies.[61] Furthermore, estimates suggest that the next three generations of humans will have to produce more food than all produced since the start of the Agricultural Revolution ten millennia ago.[62]

The episodic nature of our mass media also affects the food issue. During the 1990s, pictures of starving people in Somalia, Sudan, and Ethiopia pricked consciences worldwide. Media lenses almost seem magnetized to focus on short-term emergency famines to the exclusion of the deeper food problems involving the international economy,

Heart-wrenching images of starving Somali children, like this one, played a key role in mobilizing the United States and the United Nations to intervene in Somalia's bloody civil war.

Food security ■ Access of all people at all times to the food they need for an active and healthy life

environmental degradation, and civil wars. Famines used to be caused chiefly by natural disasters (droughts, floods), but most contemporary famines are attributable to human behavior.

But even media-generated food aid in response to dire disasters cannot be taken for granted in the future. The International Food Policy Research Institute warns that two factors threaten traditional food aid for emergencies. First, an increased number of *civil wars* cause great logistical complications. In Somalia's 1989 crisis when 250,000 died for lack of food, the government tried to starve the rebels into submission by cutting off shipments of food aid, while rebel factions responded by taking food from civilians to sustain themselves and to prevent it from reaching their rival factions. Second, the treaty establishing the World Trade Organization (WTO) in 1994 requires that food donor countries (such as the United States) *must slash tax and subsidy benefits* they have given to their domestic farmers to grow large surpluses; this has resulted in food aid reductions of nearly 50 percent in recent years.[63]

Just as the U.N. Population Fund leads the international community's efforts to cope with that GI, the U.N.'s Food and Agricultural Organization (FAO) spearheads a multipronged approach to problems of hunger. Founded in 1945, the FAO includes 183 countries striving to provide **food security** worldwide. This fundamental human right is expressed in international law and recognized by all states. A specific priority of the FAO is to *encourage sustainable agriculture* and rural development. The FAO Website listed at the end of this chapter provides instant access to information about the organization, statistical databases, reports on its actions, and e-mail conferencing for interested persons.[64]

Multiple Causes of Hunger

Only a small part of the hunger problem consists of what most Westerners think it is (production of sufficient food), but the problem includes quite a lot of things that are dimly understood by the public. First, *logistical problems* related to food distribution are monumental. Civil wars and natural disasters routinely prevent access to extant food supplies. Although some MDCs have standing surpluses of grain, no automatic mechanism exists for committing such supplies to the LDCs. Debt-ridden LDCs lack export-derived earnings to pay for the importation of needed food.[65]

Instead, the distribution of food depends on the vagaries of the international economy. Thus, the *inability of LDCs to pay for food imports* constitutes a second major cause of hunger. In this market-driven world, the MDCs account for the overwhelming majority of food production, distribution, and consumption. The international economy does not seem to have a special conscience when it comes to food. Global grain trade is dominated by a mere five companies, two of which (Cargill and Continental) handle one-half of the grain exported annually by the United States, which produces 25 percent of world grain exports.[66]

Third, what economists refer to as *structural trade disadvantages* contribute to inability by the LDCs to purchase food on the global market. LDCs export almost exclusively primary products extracted from the earth, such as coal, bananas, or pineapples. Conversely, the MDCs can export secondary, or manufactured products, such as automobiles, and tertiary services, such as computer software or movies. Because supply tends to be high for most primary products, the LDCs have a built-in (structural) disadvantage when competing with MDCs in the trade game. Economists refer to this unequal playing field as creating a terms-of-trade problem for the LDCs that precludes them from ever catching up.

Finally, *abuses of the land* such as over-irrigation, widespread use of pesticides, soil erosion, and slash-and-burn subsistence agriculture also contribute to global hunger. The **Green Revolution** bumped up food productivity for a few decades, particularly in Asia, but it seems to have run out of steam because no significant gains have been registered during the past ten years. In general, the high technology and intensive use of fossil fuels behind the Green Revolution produce the land abuses cited previously far more than does traditional small-scale subsistence agriculture in the LDCs.[67]

Green Revolution ■ Increased food production that occurred in East and South Asia in the 1950s and 1960s as a result of hybrid grains and advanced forms of fertilizer

Mostafa K. Tolba, former executive director of the U.N. Environment Programme, blames the Green Revolution for "making agro-ecosystems increasingly artificial, unstable, and prone to rapid degradation."[68] Current explorations of biotechnology might conceivably provide future miracles, but the use of biotechnology during the Green Revolution reduced genetic diversity among plants, leaving them more vulnerable to disease and pests. Few experts favor praying for eleventh-hour scientific discoveries to avert future hunger crises. As former U.S. Secretary of Agriculture Orville Freeman points out, it will do us no good to solve the food production problem by blithely destroying the environment, yet dealing with both issues will require a "difficult balancing act."[69]

The NGO Freedom from Hunger succinctly summarizes what it considers the chief causes of chronic hunger: (1) *Poverty* (poor lack resources to grow or buy food); (2) *Armed Conflict* (war disrupts agriculture and governments spend money on armaments); (3) *Environmental Overload* (overconsumption by MDCs and population growth in LDCs strain natural and human resources); (4) *Discrimination* (lack of access to education, credit, and employment often results from racial, ethnic, or gender discrimination); and (5) *Lack of Clout* (powerlessness renders those unable to protect their own interests, typically children, women, and the elderly).[70]

Food factoids:

- Eleven million children under the age of five die needlessly each year from hunger-related causes.
- Most child deaths result not from outright starvation but from common illnesses (diarrhea, malaria, measles, respiratory illness).
- In the LDCs, 815 million are malnourished, consuming fewer than the minimum necessary calories per day.
- Malnourishment stunts growth, slows thinking, saps energy, hinders fetal development, and leads to mental retardation.
- Pregnant women, breastfeeding mothers, and children are most at risk of malnourishment.[71]

Energy
Background to the Issue

Abundant and cheap energy in the form of oil (petroleum) helped to spur the massive economic recovery that was required in the wake of World War II's trail of devastation. In particular, the economic miracles that transformed Germany and Japan from economic basket cases into economic powerhouses could not have occurred without cheap energy fueling their recoveries. Cheap oil also got consumers worldwide accustomed to energy-intensive technologies that made life more comfortable.

At the top of this list of high-demand consumer goods sat the automobile, providing unprecedented mobility for those who could afford one. In the process, cars also triggered huge increases in the demand for oil. Economists have established a close relationship between economic growth and energy consumption.[72] Despite the central role of energy in lifting the standard of living ever since the Industrial Revolution, energy often seems like the forgotten stepchild among GIs—at least until the next *oil shock* steals our breath again. With stable oil prices and wall-to-wall economic growth in the 1990s, it seemed natural for Americans to take oil for granted, and President Bill Clinton benefited

Table 4.7

ENERGY CONSUMPTION BY SOURCE (2005) (PERCENTAGES)

	FF	Bio.	Nuclear	Hydro.	Renewables
World	**80%**	**10%**	**7%**	**2%**	**0.7%**
Africa	28%	73%	0.1%	3%	0.1%
Asia	75%	18%	4%	2%	0.5%
Europe	84%	2%	11%	2%	0.3%
Middle East	97%	2%	0.1%	0.8%	0.3%
N.A.	85%	2%	9%	2%	0.8%
S.A.	71%	15%	2%	11%	1.6%
MDCs	*84%*	*2%*	*10%*	*2%*	*0.7%*
LDCs	*74%*	*22%*	*1%*	*2%*	*0.7%*

Key

FF: Fossil fuels.

Bio.: Solid biomass, includes plant matter, wood, crop waste, animal waste, and inputs to charcoal production.

Nuclear: Nuclear fission from nuclear power plants.

Hydro.: Hydroelectric, measured as the energy content of the electricity produced in hydro power plants.

Renewables: Solar, wind, wave, biogas, liquid biomass, sewage, or crop residues.

Source: IEA; WHO; BP; "Energy 2005," *EarthTrends Data Tables:* http://earthtrends.wri.org/.

enormously. It hadn't been so easy for President Jimmy Carter in the late 1970s. Reeling from the spillover caused by sky-high oil prices, Carter declared the "moral equivalent of war" to combat the energy crisis.[73]

Table 4.7 describes the contemporary sources of global energy production, including considerable variation by region.

Oil Shocks: The Prize Oozing Through Our Fingers

Energy analyst and Pulitzer Prize-winning author Daniel Yergin argues that, "oil meant mastery during the twentieth century." The turning point, he says, occurred in 1911, when a young but already courageous First Lord of the Admiralty, Winston Churchill, overcame intense political opposition to convert Britain's war fleet from coal to oil as fuel for its ships. Vested economic interests lobbied against his plan, but he held firm. Three years later, the superior speed and power of the British fleet gave it a big edge over Germany in World War I. The stampede to petroleum had begun.[74]

Control of the "oil prize," however, has occasionally shifted hands, leaving political and economic turmoil in its wake. Several oil shocks have rocked the global economy in recent decades by reminding us that the supply and price of industrial society's black gold remain fragile. The first grew out of the 1973 Yom Kippur Arab-Israeli War. The newly united OPEC oil countries, having recently gained control of production and pricing from the big oil MNCs (such as Shell, British Petroleum, and Exxon), used oil as a diplomatic weapon. As a result, oil prices quadrupled between October 1973 and January 1974. Shortages in the United States led to rationing and long lines at gas stations, while panic gripped the national psyche.

The second oil shock occurred in 1979, in association with the Iranian Revolution. Iran, a close U.S. ally under the ruling Shah of Iran, changed political masks overnight. The Ayatollah Khomeini replaced the Shah with a fundamentalist Islamic theocracy, which branded America "the Great Satan." By the time the decade was over, world oil prices had jumped by 1,000 percent, ushering in a brief flirtation with conservation of energy and minimalist thinking in many MDCs.

The third oil shock erupted out of the Iraqi invasion of oil-rich but weak Kuwait in August of 1990. Three months before Saddam Hussein's aggressive attack on neighboring Kuwait, crude oil sold for about $15 per barrel; by September 1990, it had spiked at more than $40 per barrel. Given the importance of oil to the world economy, no wonder shock and panic ensued globally. Most intriguing is the human tendency to forget such experiences and fail to prepare for the next oil shock.[75]

A fourth oil shock took place in association with George W. Bush's prosecution of the 2003 Iraqi invasion. Oil per barrel shot up to more than $75 for the first time, and gas prices at the pump leapt by more than $1 and stayed there for more than one year.

More About King Oil

In the eighteenth century, fuelwood was the main energy source. Then coal replaced fuelwood in the nineteenth century, and by 1913, king coal accounted for 75 percent of world energy consumption. But the internal combustion engine triggered a fateful shift to oil as the energy fix of choice. In 1950, oil was only one-third of energy production, but by 1965, it had matched coal production and, by 1975, was unmatched by any other source.

Today, oil is the biggest and most pervasive business on the planet, and of the top twenty companies on the Fortune 500 list, seven are oil companies. The Middle East holds 60 percent of known reserves, with four countries (Saudi Arabia, Iraq, Iran, and Kuwait) sitting atop half of those reserves. Oil has created its own brand of hydrocarbon society, one structured around the production, distribution, and consumption of oil and its by-products. In 1991, the United States sent 500,000 of its soldiers while leading a coalition of twenty-six countries in Operation Desert Storm. This was an oil war meant to ensure the free flow of oil; it dislodged Iraq from neighboring Kuwait after Iraqi leader Saddam Hussein had seized Kuwait (and its vast reserves); the war also prevented Iraq from possible invasion of neighboring Saudi Arabia (with even larger reserves). A study by geologists Colin Campbell and Jean Laherrere estimates that the 800 billion barrels of oil already used up represents about one-half of the total supply.[76] The United States once had 262 billion barrels under its soil, but that amount has shrunk to 92 billion barrels.

Energy and LDCs

From 1980 to 1995, total energy consumed by wealthy countries increased by 20 percent. However, LDC energy consumption went up by a whopping 110 percent. The poor South now consumes about one-half of world energy, but because the LDCs seem to have a monopoly over the population explosion, analysts predict that the LDC fraction will change from one-half to two-thirds in the next generation.

Southern Hemisphere energy growth, however, is no more monolithic than is population increase in the South. The great variation that exists is illustrated by comparing West Africa's Ghana with South Asia's Pakistan. In 1992, both countries had equivalent per capita incomes, yet Pakistan consumed over 50 percent more oil than did Ghana. Pakistan's neighbor and rival, India, has tripled its oil consumption since 1970, while China's has increased twenty-fold.[77]

One hopeful sign involves *technology transfer* from North to South to reduce the technology divide existing on each side of the equator. An increasing number of "joint ventures" have created appropriate technologies helpful to poor countries. For example, the Danish and German governments have shared advanced wind turbine technology with India, allowing the latter to become a significant manufacturer of these efficient wind turbines and to emerge as the world's fifth-ranked producer of wind power.[78]

Similarly, China has benefited from a joint venture with Japan, the Netherlands, and Taiwan enabling it to become the world leader in the production of compact fluorescent light bulbs in 1997. First developed in the United States, then transferred to various southern locations, these super-efficient light bulbs are also quite environmentally benign.[79]

Barriers to Sustainable Energy

With all of the environmental problems associated with burning fossil fuels, numerous experts advocate serious development of sustainable energy. Yet calls for renewable energy sources have produced relatively little research and development (R&D) toward this end in America.

One chief reason is *political*: some of the largest corporations (automakers, oil companies, shipping companies, tire makers) have a vested interest in propping up petroleum as king of the energy hill. Their lobbying efforts work against the U.S. government's investing resources in exploring sources such as solar, wind, hydroelectric, geothermal, or hydrogen power (all known to possess considerable potential). Because we already know how to create most of these alternative sources, some of the lethargy also stems from *economics* (they have not yet proven cost-effective given subsidies provided to big oil). Actually, relatively few inherent *scientific problems,* or *technological difficulties*, attendant to well-developed scientific knowledge (such as what to do with spent nuclear fuel) can be blamed for foot dragging.

In the 1950s and 1960s, the U.S. government sold its citizens an image of atomic energy as a panacea encompassing not only national defense but commercial energy production as well. But before long, blind public trust in "our friend the atom" had vanished. The symbolic event that tarnished the benign image of atomic energy in the United States played itself out at the Three Mile Island nuclear power plant in Pennsylvania. A valve malfunction set things off at Three Mile Island on March 28, 1979, resulting in the plant's nuclear core being uncovered. Very little radioactivity escaped from the power plant, but it was enough to launch a media frenzy concerning a potential nuclear meltdown.

Coincidentally, a Hollywood movie called *The China Syndrome* (1979) premiered a few weeks prior to the events at Three Mile Island. *The China Syndrome* explored the nuclear meltdown theme and fed public awareness of the dangers associated with nuclear energy production. Jane Fonda and Michael Douglas starred as a resourceful television reporter and her cameraman uncovering unsettling details about a cover-up of nuclear malfeasance. The Three Mile Island incident and *The China Syndrome* mirrored each other, alerting people to unexamined risks. However, 7,000 miles from Pennsylvania, in a town called Chernobyl, potential risks paled in comparison to the disaster that occurred April 26, 1986. Just as quickly as the 1970s oil shocks had generated R&D money for atomic energy, the Chernobyl disaster squelched nuclear power's billing as a clean substitute for burning fossil fuels (Case Study 4.4).

What is your opinion about nuclear power as an alternative to the burning of fossil fuels? Should nuclear power carry a larger share of the energy burden in the twenty-first century? If it does, how should we dispose of radioactive spent nuclear fuel? Did Three Mile Island and Chernobyl evaporate all hopes of the atom generating widespread electricity in America? How does the nuclear option compare to solar, wind, or geothermal power as alternatives to the addition to oil.

Sustainable Futures

A 1998 U.S. national survey reported that 72 percent of Americans identify renewable and efficient energy research as energy R&D priorities for the government.[80] Two energy researchers for the Worldwatch Institute, Christopher Flavin and Seth Dunn, scoured the literature on renewable energy to produce a chapter filled with clear predictions and suggestions coalescing around kicking the fossil fuel habit. Flavin and Dunn argue that just as the Industrial Revolution created its own energy needs, so too will the current Information Revolution that was trumpeted by Thomas Friedman in Chapter 1 of *The World Is Flat.* Flavin and Dunn contend that "Our future energy economy will be highly efficient, decentralized [local], and use a range of sophisticated electronics."[81]

Various benign energy sources are already making modest contributions, including some often overlooked by observers (such as wind power, which was first used for grinding grain in Persia 1,000 years ago). Historically, technological energy innovations have

Case Study 4.4 A Glowing Achilles Heel in the Former Soviet Union

Fifty miles north of Ukraine's capital, Kiev, technicians at the Chernobyl nuclear reactor were testing how long its turbines could generate power after the steam had been shut off. Later investigations revealed six rules violations during this 1986 test. What resulted was a steam explosion that blew apart the 1,000-ton reactor as if it were made of cardboard. Thirty fires began around the power station, the worst of which was an uncontrollable blaze in the graphite core of reactor number four. Heroic firefighters became the first casualties of the disaster. Within a few days, 135,000 people were evacuated from the area around Chernobyl. Still referred to as the Dead Zone, a twenty-mile radius around the plant has become a laboratory to study the long-term ecological effects. Experts think 1,000 years will pass before people can return to live there.

A steam explosion resulted from tragic human errors at the Soviet Union's Chernobyl nuclear power plant in 1986.

The Soviet government reported only 32 immediate deaths and about 500 hospitalizations surrounding Chernobyl. But as the 1945 Hiroshima and Nagasaki experiences had earlier demonstrated, the most insidious problems derive not from the initial blast, but rather the long-term effects of radiation: genetic diseases, chromosome aberrations, and weakening of our immune system. Dangerous levels of radioactivity were reported in twenty European countries. Owing to the prevailing winds, radioactive fallout in Ukraine proved less serious than in the neighboring Soviet Republic of Belarus.

In Krypiat, a town of 45,000 people near Chernobyl, 7 cases of childhood cancer had been reported in the decade before 1986, whereas 424 occurred the decade after 1986. In 1994, Ukrainian authorities listed 8,000 deaths as attributable to radiation from Chernobyl.

The number four reactor at Chernobyl now lies under a hastily constructed cement sarcophagus. In the rest of what was the Soviet Union, 16 nuclear reactors designed identically to Chernobyl's continue churning out electricity. By 1995, more than 500 nuclear power plants operated in twenty-seven countries, including 119 in the United States. Both Belgium and the former Soviet republic of Lithuania lead the world by generating 97 percent of their electricity via nuclear energy.[82] ∎

carved out small "niches," where favorable conditions help to spur their development on a small scale. Furthermore, major changes in energy production sometimes gestate quite slowly, later exploding as big commercial successes.

The systemic shift from gas to electric lighting one century ago began very inauspiciously. Momentum for greater use of the most ubiquitous resource (solar energy) received a boost in 1997 when British Petroleum (BP) Chairman John Brown announced shortly before the Kyoto conference on global warming that his oil company now takes climate change seriously enough to invest $1 billion annually in solar energy research, which expanded further in subsequent years. Flavin and Dunn view this 1997 decision as comparable to Winston Churchill's key role in switching Britain's naval fleet from coal to oil in 1911.

One interesting technology that is aiding the solar cause is the solar voltaic cell, a semiconductor device that turns the sun's radiation directly into electric current. These cells are currently used to power pocket calculators and watches. Equally promising is the fuel cell, which uses an electrochemical process to combine hydrogen and oxygen, thus producing water and electricity. The largest current output using fuel cell is an 11-megawatt plant in Tokyo. Burning natural gas is more benign than burning oil; therefore, Flavin and Dunn see it as a likely "bridge" to widespread use of hydrogen as "a major energy carrier and storage medium" because hydrogen can be mixed with natural gas and carried in the same pipelines.[83]

Chapter Synopsis

Social scientists may overuse the phrase *paradigm shift,* but understanding the bigger picture of human connections that transcend national borders can be called little else. The key concepts of *finiteness, interdependence, sustainable development,* and *the Millennium Development Goals* liberated us from tunnel vision, helping us to face the daunting challenges posed by ecological GIs (environment, population, food, and energy).

The paradigm shift to globalization leaves humans with the inescapable conclusion that we have major ecological problems. The realization that "we all live downwind" has settled into our consciousness. Problems such as pollution, deforestation, ozone depletion, and global warming won't disappear without human activity. Compounding each issue is human population growth, whose momentum makes population look like a supertanker at sea requiring much time to halt. Current world denizens equal 25 percent of all those who have ever lived, and 100 million new people are added annually. Holistic approaches recognizing the multicausal nature of the population problem are needed.

Televised images of poor people starving to death amid civil wars often drive U.S. food policy. But the heart of the global food problem is not chiefly about producing sufficient food. Rather, it is about a complex web of political, economic, and military forces that preclude long-term food sufficiency in the LDCs. American inattention to global energy problems makes us look like amnesiacs because only when global oil shocks (1973, 1979, 1990, 2003) paralyze us with fear do we seriously engaged the issue. Even more worrisome than the dwindling oil supply are the environmental and health burdens that the oil age imposes on us. Decentralization to the local level, higher efficiency, and more sophisticated technologies for renewable energy have been recommended.

The 1992 Earth Summit in Rio de Janeiro contained something for everyone: sustainability to sate the North's desire for responsible stewardship of finite resources and development to satisfy the South's desire to grow a higher standard of living for itself. It remains to be seen whether these unlikely bedfellows can produce lifestyles amenable to the differing agendas held by the LDCs and MDCs.

FOR DIGGING DEEPER

Andrady, Anthony L. *Plastics and the Environment.* Wiley-Interscience, 2003.

Art, Henry W. *The Dictionary of Ecology and Environmental Science.* Henry Holt, 2000.

Athar, H. Syed. *The Energy Crisis in America.* Booklocker.com, Inc., 2006.

Black, Edwin. *Internal Combustion: How Corporations and Governments Addicted the World to Oil and Derailed the Alternatives.* St. Martin's Press, 2006.

Bradsher, Keith. *High and Mighty: The Dangerous Rise of the SUV.* Public Affairs, 2003.

Brennan, Scott R., and Jay Withgott. Benjamin-Cummings Publishing, 2007.

Brown, Lester R. *The State of the World 2006.* W. W. Norton, 2007.

Brune, Michael. *Coming Clean: Breaking America's Addiction to Oil and Coal.* Sierra Club/Counterpoint, 2008.

Chiras, Daniel D. *The Homeowner's Guide to Renewable Energy.* New Society Publications, 2006.

Chomat, Pierre. *Oil Addiction: The World in Peril.* Universal Publishers, 2004.

Choucri, Nazli, and others, eds. *Mapping Sustainability: Knowledge e-Networking and the Value Chain.* Springer, 2007.

Conca, Ken, and Geoffrey D. Dabelko. *Green Planet Blues: Environmental Politics from Stockholm to Kyoto.* Westview Press, 2004.

Cunningham, William P. *Understanding Our Environment: An Introduction*. William C. Brown, 2004.

Deutch, John, and others. *Energy Security and Climate Change*. Brookings Institution, 2007.

De Villiers, Marq. *Water: The Fate of Our Most Precious Resource*. Mariner, 2001.

Fenton, Thomas P., and Mary J. Heffron, eds. *Food, Hunger, Agribusiness: A Directory of Resources*. Orbis Books, 1987.

Fogel, Robert William. *The Escape from Hunger and Premature Death, 1700-2100: Europe, America, and the Third World*. Cambridge University Press, 2004.

Gardner, Gary T., and others. *Underfed and Overfed: The Global Epidemic of Malnutrition*. Worldwatch Institute, 1999.

Geist, Helmut. *The Causes and Progression of Desertification*. Ashgate Publishing, 2005.

GEO Year Book 2007: An Overview of Our Changing Environment. United Nations Publications, 2007.

Goodell, Jeff. *Big Coal: The Dirty Secret Behind America's Energy Future*. Mariner Books, 2007.

Gore, Al. *An Inconvenient Truth*. DVD. Paramount Studio, 2006.

Gorelick, Steven, and others. *Bringing the Food Economy Home: Local Alternatives to Global Agribusiness*. Zed Books, 2002.

Hardin, Garrett. *Living Within Limits: Ecology, Economics, and Population Taboos*. Oxford University Press, 1993.

Hempel, Lamont C. *Environmental Governance: The Global Challenge*. Island Press, 1996.

Hertsgaard, Mark. *Earth Odyssey*. Broadway Books, 1999.

Hesser, Leon. *The Man Who Fed the World: Nobel Peace Prize Laureate Norman Borlag and His Battle to End World Hunger*. Durban House, 2006.

Houghton, John. *Global Warming: The Complete Briefing*. Cambridge University Press, 2004.

Hughes, J. Donald, ed. *The Face of the Earth: Environment and World History*. Mitchell E. Sharpe, 1999.

Kambara, Tatsu, and Christopher Howe. *China and the Global Energy Crisis: Development and Prospects for China's Oil and Natural Gas*. Edward Elgar, 2007.

Leathers, Howard D., and Phillips Foster. *The World Food Problem: Tackling the Causes of Undernutrition in the Third World*. Lynne Reinner, 2004.

Livvi-Bacci, Massimo. *A Concise History of World Population*. Wiley-Blackwell, 2006.

Levine, Marvin J. *Pesticides: A Toxic Time Bomb in Our Midst*. Praeger Publishing, 2007.

MacFarlane, Alison M., and Rodney C. Ewing, eds. *Uncertainty Underground: Yucca Mountain and the Nation's High-Level Nuclear Waste*. MIT Press, 2006.

Malthus, Thomas R. *An Essay on the Principle of Population*. Dover Publications, 2007.

Menken, Jane, ed. *World Population and U.S. Policy*. W. W. Norton, 1986.

Menzel, Peter. *Hungry Planet: What the World Eats*. Ten Speed Press, 2007.

Miller, G. Tyler, Jr. *Living in the Environment: Principles, Connections, and Solutions*. Brooks Cole, 2004.

Moran, Matt. *Tropical Deforestation*. Rowman and Littlefield, 2006.

Morgan, Sally, and Jenny Vaughn. *Acid Rain (Earth SOS)*. Franklin Watts, Ltd., 2007.

Pahl, Greg. *The Citizen-Powered Energy Handbook: Community Solutions to a Global Crisis*. Chelsea Green Publications, 2007.

Pirages, Dennis C. *Building Sustainable Societies: A Blueprint for a Post-Industrial World*. Mitchell E. Sharp, 1996.

Porter, Gareth, and Janet Welsh Brown. *Global Environmental Politics*. Westview Press, 1996.

Raven, Peter H., and others. *Environment*. Wiley, 2008.

State of the World Population 2007: Unleashing the Potential of Urban Growth. United Nations Publications, 2007.

Swain, Brian Kenneth. *World Hunger.* iUniverse, Inc. 2007.

Redlin, Janice L. *Land Abuse and Soil Erosion.* Weigl Publishers, 2006.

Sale, Kirkpatrick. *The Green Revolution: The American Environmental Movement, 1962–1992.* Hill and Wang, 1995.

Sessions, George, ed. *Deep Ecology for the Twenty-First Century.* Random House, 1995.

Sheen, Martin. *Who Killed the Electric Car?* DVD. Sony Pictures, 2006.

Shiva, Vandana. *Water Wars: Privatization, Pollution, and Profit.* South End Press, 2002.

Swanson, Timothy. *The International Regulation of Extinction.* New York University Press, 1994.

Taylor, Milton D., and others, eds. *Pesticide Residues in Coastal Tropical Ecosystems: Distribution, Fate, and Effects.* CRC, 2002.

Tertzakin, Peter. *A Thousand Barrels a Second: The Coming Oil Break Point and the Challenges Facing an Energy Dependent World.* McGraw-Hill, 2006.

Torrance, Robert M. *Encompassing Nature: A Sourcebook, Nature and Culture from Ancient Times to the Modern World.* Counterpoint, 1998.

Vallero, Daniel. *Fundamentals of Air Pollution.* Academic Press, 2007.

Weeks, John R. *Population: An Introduction to Concepts and Issues.* Wadsworth Publishing, 2007.

Yetiv, Steve A. *Crude Awakenings: Global Oil Security and American Foreign Policy.* Cornell University Press, 2004.

Weart, Spencer R. *The Discovery of Global Warming.* Harvard University Press, 2004.

Wise, William. *Killer Smog: The World's Worst Air Pollution Disaster.* Backinprint.com, 2001.

World Population Ageing 2007. United Nations Publications, 2007.

Vandenbosch, Robert, and Suzanne E. *Nuclear Waste Stalemate: Political and Scientific Controversies.* University of Utah, 2007.

Vandermeer, John, and Yvette Perfecto. *Breakfast of Biodiversity: The Truth About Rainforest Destruction.* Food First, 1995.

Yergin, Daniel. *The Prize: The Epic Quest for Oil, Money, and Power.* Simon and Schuster, 1991.

Zedillo, Ernesto, ed. *Global Warming: Looking Beyond Kyoto.* Oxford University Press, 2007.

INTERNET

Centre for Development and Population Activities:
http://www.cedpa.org/

The Earth Times:
http://www.earthtimes.org

Energy Information Administration:
http://www.eia.doe.gov

Environmental Defense Fund (EDF):
http://www.edf.org/

EDF Chemical Scorecard:
http://www.scorecard.org

Friends of the Earth:
http://www.foe.co.uk/index.html

Global Land Information System:
http://edcwww.cr.usgs.gov

Global Warming Central:
http://www.globalwarming.net

The Hunger Project:
http://www.thp.org

Intergovernmental Panel on Climate Change:
http://www.ipcc.ch

Hybrid Fuel Cell Turbine Systems:
http://www.dodfuelcell.cecer.army.mil

International Atomic Energy Agency:
http://www.iaea.org

Migration News:
http://migration.ucdavis.edu/

The North-South Institute:
http://www.nsi-ins.ca

Office of Fossil Energy:
http://www.fe.doe.gov/

Office of Energy Efficiency and Renewable Energy:
http://www.eere.energy.gov

Planned Parenthood:
http://www.plannedparenthood.org

Population Reference Bureau:
http://www.prb.org

Resources for Energy and the Environment:
http://www.uoregonedu/energy

Resources for the Future (RFF):
http://www.rff.org

The Thirty-Hour Famine:
http://30hourfamine.org

United Nations Environment Program (UNEP):
http://www.unep.ch/

U.N. Division for Sustainable Development:
http://www.un.org/esa/sustdev/

U.N. Population Fund:
http://www.unfpa.org

U.S. Department of Energy:
http://www.doe.gov/

U.S. Fish and Wildlife Service:
http://www.fws.gov

World Conservation Monitoring Centre:
http://www.wcmc.org.uk

World Food and Agricultural Organization:
http://www.fao.org

World Population Clock:
http://www.census.gov

Zero Population Growth (ZPG):
http://www.zpg.org

Solving Ecological Problems

CORE OBJECTIVE

To identify theoretical and practical solutions to the vexing array of ecological problems.

THEMATIC QUESTIONS

- What kind of global institutions have been built in the areas of environment, population, food, and energy?

- Are there sound policy principles helpful to all actors struggling with ecological problems on the world stage?

- How do NGOs interface with civil society in solving ecological problems?

- To what extent has humanity risen to the challenge of finding creative responses to the disconcerting problems covered in Chapter 4?

- In what ways does Brazil represent a laboratory examining sustainable development's inherent tensions?

Experts concerned about environment, population, food, and energy believe that most countries have proven inept in dealing with these GIs, thus losing the confidence of many of their citizens. The traditional model of world affairs has emphasized competition as the norm and cooperation as the exception. Such narrow thinking by state leaders, however, yields piecemeal endeavors concerning ecological problems when more holistic understandings and cooperative initiatives seem more enlightened.

Solving global problems is made more urgent by the widening chasm between the rich North and poor South, a reality confirmed by an endless stream of research findings. Naiveté oozes from people who continue viewing ecological problems such as India's population explosion, or starvation in Sudan's Darfur region, or rising water levels threatening low-lying areas such as the Seychelles Islands, as someone else's problem. The revolution of rising expectations associated with communications globalization also makes the poor much better informed about their lowly status; and the wealth gap provides motivation for desperate Third Worlders to use the shrinking world's endless variety of ways to deliver terrorism. The wealth gap does not directly cause terrorist acts, but few experts dismiss its long-term significance.

The poor must obtain a better standard of living—but not at the expense of ecological integrity. Such is the dilemma confronting sustainable development. A complex mix of creative strategies must be devised. Although technology is sometimes criticized in ecological literature for contributing to environmental degradation, it also has the potential to provide part of the solution *if* used intelligently. A lot of smart people are already doing yeoman work at the grass-roots level, and if more governments provide incentives, who knows what can be accomplished? Journalist Steve Lerner offers numerous case studies of practical visionaries whom he labels *eco-pioneers,* "because they are modern pathfinders who are mapping out a sustainable future for our nation."[1] Jonathan Lash, Co-Chair of the President's Council on Sustainable Development, writes in the Foreword to Lerner's book that "*Eco-Pioneers* [the book's title] provides a new sense of hope that practical solutions to our environmental problems are already being discovered in a number of different fields."

References are often made in this textbook to the Stanislavsky Method, which requires trying to get behind the eyeballs of others to see the world as they do. When it comes to solving global ecological problems, this means appreciating the big picture provided by geography's physicality of spatial analysis, thus feeling the palpable mismanagement as humans have fouled our own nest (discussed in Chapter 4). Visionary principles of best practices must be blended with pragmatic inventions as illustrated next.

In this chapter, the ecological action agenda is divided into (1) focusing attention on serious dialogue via global town meetings and the institutions they create; (2) stipulating policy principles to guide all actors questing after ecological solutions; (3) interspersing successful case studies within the thicket of policy principles; and (4) studying Brazil in depth as a sustainable development laboratory.

Global Dialogue Institutions

The process of adapting to a changing world and adopting new attitudes and policies is an incremental one. Before consensus-based policies can be implemented, dialogue must become institutionalized. Structures are needed to give organizational life to new thinking at the mega-level. For four decades, a series of **global town meetings** have addressed vital GIs.[2] In most cases, they have grown out of special needs identified within the General Assembly of the United Nations. All global town meetings have generated heated debate, and some have produced important **treaties.**

Global town meetings ■ International conferences held under U.N. auspices to consider pressing global problems of the day, such as economic development, the environment, population, food, and energy

Treaties ■ International agreements that bind nations to responsibilities somewhat like contracts do in domestic legal practice; treaties are sometimes called conventions or pacts

United Nations Environmental Program (UNEP)

The 1972 Stockholm Conference on the Human Environment energized global activity on the environmental front when it concluded that states have the responsibility to ensure that activities occurring within their jurisdiction do not cause damage to the environment of other states. Stockholm produced what has become the leading global environmental agency, the United Nations Environmental Program (UNEP), which coordinates all U.N. matters related to the environment. The UNEP Mission Statement directs it to "play a stronger role in catalyzing effective action to protect the environment with civil society actors [NGOs] around the world," in addition to states and other actors. Some major UNEP *milestones* include the following:

- 1972: U.N. Conference recommends the creation of UNEP by the General Assembly.
- 1973: Convention on International Trade in Endangered Species is held.
- 1979: Bonn Convention on Migratory Species is held.
- 1987: Montreal Protocol on Ozone Depleting Substances treaty is created.
- 1989: Basel Convention on Movement of Hazardous Wastes takes place.
- 1992: Rio Earth Summit produces *Agenda 21,* Sustainable Development blueprint.
- 1992: Convention on Biological Diversity is held.
- 2000: Millennium Declaration and 8 MDGs are adopted.
- 2001: Stockholm Convention on Persistent Organic Pollutants occurs.
- 2002: World Summit on Sustainable Development is held.

- 2004: Bali Strategic Plan for Technology Support and Capacity Building is adopted.
- 2005: Millennium Ecosystem Assessment documents the extent of ecosystem degradation.
- 2005: World Summit documents the importance of environment to development.[3]

Earthwatch ■ A global monitoring program that compiles environmental data as an early warning signal for problems to the United Nations Environmental Program (UNEP)

UNEP also runs something akin to the function performed by canaries in nineteenth-century coalmines; **Earthwatch** reports global data tracing environmental changes. UNEP has a budget of about $50 million annually and is headquartered in Nairobi, Kenya.

UNCED: The Earth Summit

One of the greatest of all global town meetings occurred in Rio de Janeiro, Brazil, in 1992. The United Nations Conference on Environment and Development (UNCED), or the Earth Summit, brought together 178 countries and was covered by 8,000 journalists. Predictably, North–South disputes captured the headlines. The LDCs expressed their right to develop economically and sought to place the onus of responsibility for environmental decay on the rich countries producing the lion's share of global pollution. The MDCs oppose all such initiatives, killing most of them in early drafts of conference documents.

The North sought explicit restrictions on the use of forest resources, arguing that because they function as the earth's lungs, Southern Hemisphere rainforests constitute global resources subject to international regulation. The South, however, saw the issue differently, repeating its traditional claim that these forests are the independent property of each nation. Malaysia's head negotiator drew a line in the sand by asserting "Forests are clearly a sovereign resource—not like the atmosphere and oceans, which are part of a global commons."[4] The LDCs also wanted far greater financial aid for environmental cleanup, but in the end, they received only a fraction of what they requested.

Despite the North–South schism, an 800-page document dealing with 120 topics finally emerged: *Agenda 21*. A U.N. Commission on Sustainable Development was formed to implement this ambitious program. According to environmental lawyer Daniel Sitarz:

> The bold goal of *Agenda 21* is to halt and reverse the environmental damage to our planet and to promote environmentally sound and sustainable development in all countries on earth. It is a blueprint for action in all areas relating to the sustainable development of our planet into the twenty-first century.[5]

The heart of *Agenda 21* calls on MDCs to limit consumption to sustainable levels and to transfer technologies to the LDCs; conversely, it calls on the LDCs to address population growth and to institute market reforms. In 1997, the U.N. convened a special session to assess progress toward achieving the goals of *Agenda 21*. The 1997 report drew pessimistic conclusions concerning implementation of *Agenda 21* at the five-year mark. The U.N. suggested that all countries should adopt a formal National Green Plan that integrates its economic, social, and environmental objectives.[6] As of 2008, only a handful of states have done so, and the United States is not among them.

Environmental journalist Steve Lerner spent two years covering the action leading up to the Rio Earth Summit and wrote two books on the subject. Although he supports the value of the goals and principles established in Rio, when he returned home in 1992, he felt motivated to shift from the mega-level to the micro-level of environmentalism. Lerner writes "I hungered for something more grounded than international conferences—some evidence that sustainable development was indeed possible." What resulted was the important book called *Eco-Pioneers*.

The Global Environment Facility (GEF)

The most contentious aspect of solving any GI can be summed up in one word: money. Large amounts of it get distributed every year, making some states financial winners and others financial losers. In the early 1990s, a new global institution, the Global Environment Facility (GEF), was created to administer resources aimed specifically at solving ecological problems. The GEF is a by-product of the ecological spirit that led up to the Rio 1992 conference. GEF grants support projects directly related to biodiversity, global warming, international waters, land degradation, ozone depletion, and persistent organic pollutants.

Since its inception, the GEF has awarded $6.2 billion in grants for 1,300 projects conducted in more than 140 countries. Its organizational structure consists of several parts. The GEF Council represents the main governing body, consisting of thirty-two members. The GEF Assembly includes all member countries and meets once annually. The document serving as the source of authority for the GEF is called the GEF Instrument, which can be amended. The Secretariat administers all projects and reports to both the Council and the Assembly. A Scientific and Technical Advisory Panel offers its expertise, and numerous NGOs also play advisory roles.

Although technically an independent organization, the GEF is nevertheless administered by the **World Bank.** In both institutions, the World Bank and GEF, the rich MDCs exercise control through procedures called **weighted voting.** Because the MDCs put up several billion dollars annually for the GEF's budget, they desire to influence its outcomes. The LDCs, on the other hand, have argued unsuccessfully for years that the voting system should reflect the egalitarian principle of one country, one vote. They say that if equality is good enough for wealthy democratic countries as one person, one vote in their domestic elections, then it should be good enough internationally. Poor states exercise little voice in the GEF's current system of weighted voting.

Civil Society: Environmental NGOs

The list of influential environmental NGOs is long, but some of the most prominent are sketched here. We start with the oldest one, Sierra Club (1892), which was founded by legendary activist John Muir, and today remains one of the largest with 750,000 members. The phrase, "Explore, enjoy, and protect the planet" is a copyrighted trademark of the Sierra Club. Official objectives feature grass-roots activism, public education, lobbying, and litigation. Among its major cited accomplishments are establishing many national parks; enacting the U.S. Clean Water Act, Endangered Species Act, and Alaska Conservation Act (including 100 million acres of wilderness); and procuring national monument status for Utah's Grand Staircase-Escalante.

Its Website contains a primer for new volunteers called "Sierra Club 101," containing sixteen separate sections. Famous for its nature outings, Sierra offers more than 330 per year worldwide, based on its first to Yosemite National Park in 1901. Another section chronicles more than 700 titles of books and calendars since its inception, as well as a more recent television and film production company. Another section assists students participating in the Sierra Student Coalition, "the largest and most influential student environmental group in America." Also, nitty-gritty tips on distributing literature, creative protests, organizing events for children, and political activism are covered in a section.[7]

World Wildlife Fund (WWF) claims more members than Sierra, with 1.2 million in the United States and another 4 million abroad, and calls itself the largest privately financed conservation organization. WWF calls its general mission "conservation of nature," but more specifically pursues three goals: saving endangered species, protecting endangered habitats, and addressing threats such as toxic pollution, over-fishing, and global warming. Its panda bear logo is equally ubiquitous and recognized worldwide.

From its 1961 beginning, WWF has concentrated on saving endangered species, especially its "flagship species": giant pandas, tigers, whales, dolphins, rhinos, marine turtles, and great apes. WWF efforts in four central African countries have led to a 17 percent increase in the population of mountain gorillas during one decade. Claiming a reputation for acting on the basis of sound science, WWF says that by assisting these major species, a spillover effect benefits other lesser species living in the same habitats. This NGO's American headquarters reside in a wholly "green building," conserving resources while limiting waste and pollution.

World Bank ■ One of the global economic institutions set up by the Bretton Woods system in 1944 with an initial mission to finance Europe's rebuilding after World War II; today its prime function is serving as a global lending agency, especially development lending to poor countries

Weighted voting ■ In most international financial institutions (IFIs), the wealthy states tilt the decision-making process in their favor by giving themselves a greater number of votes than are given to poorer countries

Working in more than one hundred countries, WWF cites an extensive array of tangible results. Concerning wildlife, these include new fishing methods to save sea turtles; saving the tamarin; new commercial shipping lanes to assist North American right whales; innovative ways to minimize human/elephant conflict; decades of saving panda bears; reducing by-catch in shrimp trawl fisheries off Mozambique; and conserving turtles in the Guianas. Regarding wild places, WWF has contributed to saving parts of the Amazon rainforest, significant sections of the Chilean rainforest, the Yaounde Forest Summit, ending SCUBA fishing in Honduras' Cayos Cochinos, Belize's marine habitats, parks in Mozambique, and conservation in the Gulf of California. WWF's cadre of scientists has also made several landmark discoveries.[8]

Owing to its track record for boldly imaginative publicity stunts, probably the NGO with the highest profile globally is Greenpeace. To maintain this type of independence, Greenpeace does not accept donations from governments or MNCs, relying solely upon individuals and foundation grants. The NGO's name commits it to a "green and peaceful future" and represents 2.8 million supporters globally. Its very first campaign in 1971 involved a small ship venturing into Amchitka, Alaska, to protest underground nuclear testing by the United States. Other successor ships under the name *Rainbow Warrior* have engaged in similarly audacious behavior.

Greenpeace's founder, Canadian David McTaggart, parted ways with the organization in 1995, but much continuity can be chronicled during its history. Its self-described successes are many and diverse. For example, a ban on toxic waste exports to LDCs, a moratorium on commercial whaling, the U.N. fisheries management treaty, the Southern Ocean Whale sanctuary, a moratorium on mining in Antarctica, a ban on dumping radioactive and industrial wastes at sea, an end to large-scale driftnet fishing, and a ban on nuclear weapons testing.[9]

In sharp contrast to Greenpeace's in-your-face style, The Nature Conservancy works closely with varied partners, including corporations, in a "nonconfrontational, pragmatic, market-based approach to conservation challenges." In a 2006 poll, *The Chronicle of Philanthropy* rated The Nature Conservancy as the most trusted organization, similar to earlier awards such as *Forbes Magazine* rating its fundraising efficiency at 88 percent in a survey of largest American charities, and the American Institute of Philanthropy awarding it a medal of commendation.

The Nature Conservancy's e-mail newsletter, *Great Places,* helps to link together its 1 million members, 1,500 volunteers, and 3,200 employees (720 of whom are scientists). This NGO was founded in 1951, and works in all 50 states as well as 27 other countries. It has protected more than 117 million acres of land and 520 river systems around the world, and operates more than 100 marine conservation projects. In 1988, its first "debt-for-nature" swap occurred in Costa Rica's Braulio Carillo National Park with the purchase of $240,000 in Costa Rican debt. During 2002, it partnered with WWF and the U.S. AID on the Indonesia Illegal Logging Project, involving $10 million, attacking both supply-side problems in Indonesia and demand-side problems in international markets such as China and Japan.[10]

Litigation has contributed much to the environmental movement. What started out as the Sierra Club Legal Defense Fund in the 1970s, has morphed into Earthjustice, a nonprofit public law firm "dedicated to protect places, wildlife, and natural resources of this earth and to promoting a healthy environment." Earthjustice has brought precedent-setting cases covering air, forests, healthy communities, international environmental law, oceans, public lands, water, and wildlife. The organization spells out explicit criteria by which it decides what cases to pursue.[11]

Building Up to the Cairo Population Conference

The population issue emerged as part of the global agenda during the 1974 World Population Conference in Bucharest, Romania. But insistence by the LDCs on aggressive demands for a redistribution of wealth prevented any major agreements from being reached at Bucharest. Then, in 1984, another U.N. Conference on Population met in Mexico City, where North–South rancor abated considerably. General statements emanating from Mexico City emphasized the right of individual countries to deal with the population problem in ways consistent with their own social traditions.

The most influential session, however, was the 1994 Cairo International Conference on Population and Development (ICPD), attended by 11,000 registered participants, coming from more than 170 countries. The delegates' work built directly on the efforts undertaken earlier in Bucharest and Mexico City. The ICPD unanimously adopted a 113-page *Program of Action,* which pledged spending $17 billion annually on family-planning programs. The conclusion reached by many research studies that *educating poor women* leads to reduced fertility rates was prominently featured in Cairo's *Program of Action,* which called for substantial increases in funding for female education.

The *Program of Action* set out a twenty-year time frame to achieve several vital and related goals:

- *Universal Education.* Countries are to seek expansion of primary, secondary, and tertiary levels of education to females as especially critical.
- *Reduction of Infant and Child Mortality.* Countries should reduce infant and child mortality rates by fifty and seventy per live births, respectively, by 2000, and to specific other levels by 2005 and 2010.
- *Reduction of Maternal Mortality.* Countries strive to reduce mortality in 2000 to one-half the number from 1990, and half again by the year 2015.
- *Access to Reproductive and Sexual Health Services Including Family Planning.* Countries make accessible through primary health-care systems comprehensive reproductive health to all individuals of appropriate ages no later than the year 2015.[12]

The major dissenters to early drafts of the *Program of Action* struck some observers as unlikely bedfellows: Muslim fundamentalists and the Catholic Pope, both of whom criticized initial drafts relating to family planning as indirectly supporting abortion. Pope John Paul II wrote well-publicized letters to President Bill Clinton and to Pakistani physician Nafis Sadik, the Conference's Secretary General. Compromises eventually resolved most of the differences, and dissenting opinions to the final document were few.

A valuable population resource is provided by the U.N.'s Department of Economic and Social Affairs. The U.N. Population Information Network (POPIN) represents an online guide to all population material on U.N. system Websites. POPIN includes four categories of information: data, publications, organizations, and conferences. POPIN publishes annually U.N. official population estimates for all countries (1950–present) as well as future projections (present–2050). This *World Population Prospects* involves twenty-eight demographic indicators, such as birth rates, death rates, infant mortality rates, and life expectancy. Another useful annual from POPIN consists of the *U.N. Demographic Yearbooks.*[13]

As with all of the ecological GIs, good reasons exist to justify feeling worried about the state of affairs, and many facts cited in Chapter 4 suggest this applies to the population issue. However, many positive signs of progress also exist. For example, the results of a major U.N. research project released in 2004 represent a case in point. As part of the U.N.'s ongoing monitoring of contraceptive practices worldwide, this study is titled *World Contraceptive Use 2003* and covers 160 countries. Its subjects were women aged 15–49 who are married or in a consensual union because comparative data for that group is more readily available than for single women or for men.

The central conclusion is that globally "61 percent of all women of reproductive age who are married or in a consensual union are using contraception." This represents 635 million of the more than 1 billion women in this grouping. The percentage of use in MDCs is 69 percent, whereas that in LDCs is only 59 percent. Usage is lowest in Africa, where a mere 27 percent use contraception. Contraceptive usage rates are much higher in Asia and Latin America. More encouraging conclusions include the fact that 90 percent of women using contraception rely on effective modern methods generally available only at family planning clinics. Equally positive is the finding that these rates of usage "represent a substantial increase over the past decade globally." More specifically, usage has grown by at least 1 percent per year in 56 percent of all LDCs, and by at least 2 percent per year in 16 percent of LDCs. In Africa, rates increased from 17 percent in 1990 to 28 percent in 2000.[14]

Pakistani physician Nafis Sadik, Secretary General of the 1994 World Population Conference held in Cairo, Egypt.

Civil Society: Population NGOs

The number and notoriety of population NGOs pales in comparison to the environmental NGOs cited earlier. However, that does not render population NGOs insignificant. The Population Reference Bureau (PRB) "informs people around the world about population, health, and the environment, empowering them to use it to advance the well-being of current and future generations." PRB's work is funded by a combination of individuals, governments, private foundations, NGOs, and universities. It seeks partnerships with a wide range of stakeholders in the population issue and seeks to mobilize civil society.

The PRB Website includes an excellent range of resources for educators at all levels, for instance, lesson plans, resource guides, human population data, "Making Population Real" classroom exercises, teaching standards, and build-a-text. Some typical lesson plan titles organized by Martha Sharma include "Linking Population, Health, and the Environment," "The Changing Face of America," "Sports Franchises: The Demographic Dimension," "Facts in Focus—World Population Data Sheet," "Population Policy: Progress Since Cairo," "AIDS and Contemporary Population Dynamics," and "Populations in the Path of Natural Hazards."[15]

An NGO formerly known as ZPG changed its name in 2002 to Population Connection, based in Washington, DC. Despite the new name, Population Connection's mission for its 70,000 members remains untouched: "A deep and abiding concern about the critical need for population stabilization, in order to make the world better, safer, and less-crowded." A shared belief that the population issue is clearly connected to practically every other GI (such as poverty, women's rights, environment) warrants priority status for population concerns. Population Connection is well known for its useful Fact Sheets, and it conducts an extensive campus outreach program. A typical Fact Sheet released in 2001 noted that Senegal's low AIDS infection rate of 1 percent is touted by the U.N. as a huge success story. Condom promotion by the government resulted in a 1,000 percent increase in usage from 700,000 in 1988 to 8 million in 1997.[16]

Another NGO was founded in 1969 and worked with state legislatures during the 1970s to revise laws denying access to reproductive health care. Called The Population Institute, part of its mission called for reducing teen pregnancy via sex education training, creative commercials, and endorsements from celebrities. In 1978, the Institute widened its activities by adding the Population Action Council, charged with training leaders for international population programs and expanding public awareness. Shortly thereafter, it also reordered its priorities to emphasize population control efforts in LDCs, especially in the neediest regions. The Institute's commitment to "universal access to family planning information, education, and methods" puts it in close contact with many other stakeholders, and the Website provides links to many of them.[17]

Rounding out our sample of population NGOs is Population Action International (PAI), an independent policy advocacy group seeking to "strengthen political and financial support worldwide for population programs grounded in individual rights." Since 1965, PAI has pursued an integrated program of research, advocacy, and communications on behalf of population and reproductive health projects. PAI explicitly highlights the links among population, reproductive health, environment, and sustainable development.

Very active in the area of condom awareness, in a 2004 article about the devastation already wrought by AIDS, PAI cites these grim figures: 20 million dead worldwide, twice that number living with the virus, and the leading cause of death in Africa. However, API stresses that it does not have to be that way. "AIDS can be avoided, and the fact that condoms save lives is indisputable." However, public policy, attitudinal, and societal barriers work against the fully effective use of condoms. They recognize the standard ABCs of prevention: abstinence, being faithful to one's partner, and condoms for the sexually active. However, condoms represent the most efficacious underused tool currently.[18]

The FAO, Rome 1974, and the WFC

As early as 1945, the U.N. created the world's oldest food IGO—the Food and Agricultural Organization (FAO), which supplies emergency food aid and technical assistance to poor countries. FAO member states pledge to cooperate to raise the level of nutrition

and to improve the production and distribution of food where it is needed most (rural areas of LDCs, where 70 percent of the poorest and hungriest live). The FAO's four major mandates include (1) using FAO scientists to put knowledge within reach of key stakeholders; (2) sharing policy expertise with states and nonstate actors; (3) providing a neutral-forum meeting place where actors can hash out agreements on food policy; and (4) taking knowledge into the field via thousands of projects worldwide covering both emergency food aid and long-term efforts.

Based in Rome, the FAO represents 188 member countries plus the European Union, and employs more than 1,500 professional staff and 2,200 general service staff. Its 2006–2007 budget consisted of $766 million, derived from member contributions. This supported 613 field programs, 416 of which were emergency operations. *FAO milestones* include the following:

- 1945: Quebec City session opens FAO as specialized U.N. agency.
- 1960: Freedom from Hunger campaign is undertaken to generate support from food NGOs.
- 1962: FAO/WHO commission setting international food standards begins functioning.
- 1974: U.N. World Food Conference in Rome recommends mechanism for world food security.
- 1981: First World Food Day observed on October 16th.
- 1986: AGROSTAT (now FAOSTAT) is a comprehensive source of informational statistics.
- 1996: FAO hosts World Food Summit for 186 states to combat world hunger.
- 1998: FAO treaty to control trade in hazardous pesticides/chemicals is adopted.
- 2001: FAO adopts legally binding Treaty on Plant Genetic Resources.
- 2002: World Food Summit (Five Years' Assessment) attended by 179 countries.[19]

The pivotal conference regarding food was the 1974 World Food Conference in Rome, which made numerous recommendations later endorsed by the U.N. General Assembly. The most important one established a new institution, the World Food Council (WFC), created in 1975 to monitor and coordinate all aspects of the U.N. food security system. Similarly, an International Fund for Agricultural Development (IFAD) was begun in 1977 to help the rural poor in LDCs improve their food production. These recent IGOs augment the activities of the longer-standing FAO.

Civil Society: Food NGOs

Founded in 1946, Freedom from Hunger "brings innovative and sustainable self-help solutions to the fight against chronic hunger and poverty." This NGO partners with local actors providing help via international development efforts in seventeen countries. It began as Meals for Millions, and then it created Multi-Purpose Food, a high-protein powdered supplement still used in relief efforts worldwide. In 1988, however, Freedom from Hunger gained notoriety when it developed in West Africa the first integrated micro-credit/health education program, called Credit with Education, which still serves 360,000 families globally. This proven self-help program was very innovative at that time. "It combines micro-credit loans to very poor women with vital health and business education." This NGO contends that its flagship program invests in the determination of a woman to feed her children, preparing her for success via cash credit and basic education.[20]

Another food NGO with impressive credentials is called The Hunger Project, active in more than 10,000 villages in 13 LDCs, which does not provide emergency relief but rather "works in authentic partnership with the people of developing countries to address the root causes of hunger and ensure that all people have the chance to lead healthy, productive lives." The Hunger Project established a decentralized, holistic program in 1990 called Strategic Planning in Action, and like Freedom from Hunger, The Hunger Project places great emphasis on empowering poor women.

New laws enacted in Bangladesh and India guarantee one-third of local government seats for women, and this NGO has spent time and money training 35,000 grass-roots elected women in these countries. Similarly, its African Woman Food Farmer Initiative seeks to empower them economically through micro-credit, savings, and training "on behalf of the 100 million women who grow 80 percent of Africa's food." Leadership training for achieving the MDGs by 2015 constitutes another of its successes.[21]

Because only 8 percent of food-related deaths are caused by natural disasters, some NGOs leave short-term emergency relief to others. One that prioritizes emergency relief is Mercy Corps, which has provided more than $1 billion in aid to eighty-one nations since 1979. Known for its "quick-response, high impact programs," Mercy Corps was very active in the tragedy unfolding in the Darfur region of Sudan in 2006–2007 (where more than 200,000 people died). Mercy Corps founder Dan O'Neill won the 2006 Mother Theresa Award for his contributions.[22] More than 5,000 charities are rated by Charity Navigator, which "works to guide intelligent giving." Charity Navigator assigns an overall rating to each charity based on its ratings for organizational efficiency and organizational capacity. Mercy Corps received the highest (4-star) rating from Charity Navigator.[23]

In 2006, a regional food crisis in the Southern African countries of Malawi, Zambia, and Zimbabwe was going from bad to worse. Zambia declared a national state of emergency in December 2005, Malawi estimated 5 million people faced serious food shortages, and Zimbabwe estimated the number there at 4 million. Prices for staple goods had risen by as much as 700 percent. One of the leading responders to this chronic food shortage area was Africare, a food NGO. In 2006, Africare's major partner in this region was the Bill and Melinda Gates Foundation, which gave $1 million to these projects. More than half of Africans lack access to safe drinking water. Food productivity suffers greatly from water shortages, and only 4 percent of renewable water gets used (Africans lack needed wells, canals, pumps, reservoirs). For two decades, Africare has led efforts to bring water to dry places in many hundreds of African villages.[24]

A pair of more recent NGOs are Food Not Bombs and The Hunger Site. Food Not Bombs began in 1980 as an agent for nonviolent policy change in the United States. It contains hundreds of autonomous chapters that share free vegetarian food with hungry people while protesting both war and poverty, which it sees as intimately related issues.[25] The Hunger Site appeared online as a food NGO in 1999. Like Food Not Bombs, this NGO concerns itself with homelessness and food insecurity, not only abroad but also in America as well. It deals with many other issues interwoven with food insecurity.[26]

America and Energy

For a very long time, the United States enjoyed significant advantages over its competitors when it came to energy supplies. First coal in the nineteenth century, then Texas-sized oil in the twentieth century, followed by Henry Ford's mass production for the masses; the last thing America's industrial economy was worried about was energy. Europeans during the 1900s were far more concerned about petroleum, and they were the first to obsess about the Middle East.

By the 1970s, the United States had become the quintessential car culture, about the time that domestic demand outstripped domestic supply. President Jimmy Carter's woes were largely due to intractable energy crises that arose rather suddenly. During the run-up to the 2003 Iraqi War, tens of thousands of protesters gathered chanting "No Blood for Oil," meaning that neither Saddam's supposed WMDs nor democratization of the region drove U.S. Middle East policy and the pending invasion.

A 2003 labor strike in Venezuela (America's fourth largest supplier) had stopped imports from that country, and oil disruption from both Iraq and Venezuela could prove quite debilitating. By 2006, the American infatuation with SUVs and other gas-guzzlers accounted for more than half of all new car sales. And as data in Chapter 4 suggested, America continues to consume far more oil than any country on earth. During 2006–2007, we were building a log cabin and came across an article in *Popular Mechanics* that gave its annual green energy award to Southwest Windpower's innovative Skystream 3.7, a major improvement over past residential windmills at about half the price of predecessors (about $10,000). It took a while for the local zoning board to approve its first request for windpower, but eventually, they came around.

Fewer Institutions

Overall, the energy issue has historically generated little consistent attention, including less institution-building than the other ecological GIs. A rather unproductive World Energy Conference was held in 1981, but the only significant energy development was the U.S.-led construction of the International Energy Agency (IEA) in 1974. The IEA was intended to oversee sharing oil by the industrialized countries during shortages and requires member countries to stockpile oil reserves. Having grown directly out of the first oil shock of 1973, the IEA is supposedly committed to (1) foster cooperative building and sharing of oil stocks; (2) promote cost sharing for energy conservation programs; and (3) assist in developing alternative sources of energy.[27] As of 2007, it was difficult to identify any major examples of renewable energy initiatives undertaken by the IEA.

Overall, the global discourse and rate of institution-building over ecological issues has become fairly robust, especially when contrasted with the state of affairs a few decades ago. Faster-paced activity would help us to achieve enlightened stewardship over the earth, but reasons for hope do exist. Solutions to some ecological dilemmas are being crafted by a handful of governments, many creative individuals, and thousands of NGOs such as Oxfam, United Support of Artists for Africa, Live Aid, World Wildlife Fund, Greenpeace, World Conservation Union, American Forestry Association, and the Sierra Club. Some IGOs have also contributed to institution-building and dialogue, but they have often felt like Frankensteins whom their creators (states) fear will become uncontrollable.

Civil Society: Energy NGOs

Powerful people and organizations benefit so magnificently from business-as-usual in the fossil fuel energy business that cynicism dies hard. Nevertheless, some hopeful signs can be cited, for example, BP's head John Browne's noteworthy efforts on behalf of solar and other renewables mentioned in Chapter 4. Momentum stemming from the scientific community's virtual consensus that evidence establishing global warming grows stronger and stronger. The Kyoto Protocol, Case Study 5.1, and Al Gore's well-received documentary 2006 film, *An Inconvenient Truth*, provide fodder to believe that civil society exists regarding the energy issue. George W. Bush and Dick Cheney constitute the most energy-connected administration in U.S. history, yet Bush's sudden 2006 public statement that "America is addicted to oil" could conceivably represent a positive sign.

The World Resources Institute (WRI) is the source for many of the recent tables cited in this chapter and represents one major conservation-related NGO. Its *EarthTrends* publications are extremely useful. Energy Quest, an award-winning educational Website produced by the California Energy Commission, notes that "teaching an energy ethic to conserve finite resources is essential to our energy future, which is currently dependent upon fossil fuels." The Energy Quest Website includes numerous forms of resources and is especially strong on teaching aids such as lesson plans, books, videos, teacher training workshops, and higher education courses and degree programs.[28] Similarly useful are the Alliance to Save Energy and Renewable Energy Businesses in the World. Finally, the European Wind Energy Association presents much information about the underused set of technologies being pushed by European countries.[29]

The United States, responsible for one-third of global emissions, sought at Kyoto and afterwards to devise various forms of pollution trading. One called for creating a "market for emissions," enabling states to convert emissions into a budget that could be bought and sold. Another emphasized "carbon sinks," referring to this function possessed by forests, as the lungs of the earth. America wanted to trade some of its carbon excess for reforestation efforts. The Kyoto Protocol passed in 1997 but was a hollow victory, leading some to call it "Kyoto Lite."

A standoff, or agreement to disagree, had developed between Europe and the United States, which was exacerbated by the election of George W. Bush, who had ideological and political reasons to suspect it, and formally rejected Kyoto in March 2001. Bush did, however, later suggest that his administration would not interfere with countries following

Case Study 5.1 The Kyoto Protocol

The effects of global warming have become increasingly apparent. Since 1997, every year has fallen in the top ten of hottest years ever, with 2005 setting a record. The earth has warmed about 1.4 degrees F since the late nineteenth century, with an accelerated pace in the past four decades. Extreme storms such as hurricanes are more frequent, birds migrate earlier, trees bloom earlier, and increases in pests such as mosquitoes, beetles, ragweed, and poison ivy have all been traced by scientists to global warming. Polar icecaps are melting faster and permafrost disappearing more rapidly than ever before.[30]

What the international community has been doing in response to global warming can be neatly summed up by reviewing events related to the Kyoto Protocol. Only a small minority of scientists any longer dispute the connection between emission of greenhouse gases and global warming, but that small number has provided political cover. Carbon dioxide and methane gas are the chief culprits. The Tragedy of the Commons globalization metaphor introduced in Chapter 3 helps to place the significance of the battle over global warming into better perspective.

In 1988, experts were appointed to the Intergovernmental Panel of Climate Change (IPCC) in Toronto, Canada. The IPCC consisted of 2,000 climatologists from more than one hundred countries. Two years later, the IPCC issued a strong report declaring a high level of certainty that human activity is causing pollutants that will continue to worsen the greenhouse effect and resultant global warming. Two years after that, at the Rio Earth Summit, one of the major documents produced was the Framework Convention on Climate Change (FCCC). The FCCC called up states to keep emissions of global warming gases to 1990 baseline levels that had been set in that year. The signatories met again in Berlin in 1995 to specify precise targets for emissions

allowable. Then, Kyoto, Japan, was the site for the 1997 session when countries agreed to outlines of emissions (with the United States dissenting).

Four groups of states materialized at the contentious Kyoto conference:

- *The European bloc.* Led by Germany and France, Europeans called for the deepest cuts in emissions. A strong green movement had already developed in Europe that had not occurred elsewhere in the other MDCs. European per capita energy use ran about one-half that of the United States at this time.
- *Non-European MDCs.* These MDCs were unwilling to make the deep cuts in emissions desired by Europe. Critics called these the "industrial laggards," who were led by the United States and also included Japan, Canada, and Australia. The Clinton administration (prodded by Al Gore), accepted Kyoto in principle, but knew that very strong opposition in the Senate would doom any chance of gaining ratification. So the United States argued for exemptions and exceptions to finesse the issue.
- *Former members of the Soviet Union's Eastern European bloc.* These so-called countries in transition worked together at Kyoto. Their ecological profligacy during Communism was legendary, as is the daunting environmental cleanup. Post-communist countries lacked the wherewithal to add much to Kyoto's negotiations.
- *LDCs.* They argued that due to their dependence on industrialization for economic growth, it was unfair to expect them to sacrifice poverty-alleviating development at the altar of reduced carbon emissions. The MDCs had caused the problem of global warming, so they should also be expected to deal with its consequences. All LDCs taken together added little to the emissions problem. ■

Kyoto's guidelines. In December 2002, the Kyoto Protocol became international law, according to its provisions. Canada and Russia put it over the hump: when it was ratified by fifty-five states responsible for 55 percent of global emissions.[31]

Guiding Policy Principles

Merely creating dialogue within institutional forums, by itself, solves no global problems. Enlightened policies need to be pursued by all relevant actors: states, NGOs, IGOs, MNCs, and IFIs. Because countries remain the most powerful actors, their behavior is crucial, but these *sixteen principles* relate to all those operating on the world stage: deep ecology, minimalism, sustainable agriculture, creative science, grassroots initiatives, female empowerment, environmentally intelligent architecture, think globally but act locally, multilateralism, democracy and devolution, green consumerism, green justice, environmental accounting, aggressive regulation, ecological policy dialogue, and green plans.

Deep Ecology

As stated in Chapter 3, deep ecology refers to the belief that all organic creation has an inherent right to compete for existence; therefore, we should not preclude the survival chances of species wantonly for our selfish ends. Mainstream Western religions, however, have emphasized the Biblical imperative to "Be fruitful and multiply, and replenish the earth, and subdue it, and have dominion over the fish of the sea, and over the fowl of the air, and over every living thing that moveth upon the earth" (Genesis 1:28).

Consequently, religious ethicists with a green conscience, such as Jeffrey Golliher, find themselves swimming upstream. An Episcopalian priest, Rev. Golliher contends that Christians living in a time of environmental limits must say with a clear voice that "You can't love God and destroy Creation. It is a sin to destroy God's Creation." The sacred nature of Creation behooves humans to act as its stewards. He points to another passage from Genesis where Noah is instructed by God to build an ark "And of every living thing of all flesh, two of every sort shalt thou bring unto the ark, to keep them alive with thee" (Genesis 6:19–20).

Rev. Golliher is based at the Cathedral of St. John the Divine in New York City, where he preaches a green gospel about matters such as water conservation, recycling, composting, exporting hazardous waste to Africa, and self-examination through what he calls "personal environmental impact assessments." This green priest practices what he preaches, and he offers green tours of his cathedral that 500,000 tourists per year visit.

St. Francis was a rare Christian saint who cared deeply about the well-being of animals. Annually on St. Francis Day, Golliher oversees a procession of animals (elephants, camels, rats, roaches, birds, snakes, etc.) that enter his cathedral to be blessed at the altar by the bishop.[32] However, not all Christian authority figures condone expanding the umbrella of sacredness beyond humans. In a recent Earth Day sermon, the Catholic Archbishop of New York, John Cardinal O'Connor, warned that environmentalism "cannot overshadow the centrality of human beings in God's plan. The Earth exists for human persons and not vice versa."[33]

Despite opposition from powerful figures such as Archbishop O'Connor, the executive director of the National Religious Partnership for the Environment, Paul Gorman, predicts that "Church basements will increasingly look green." Gorman's group raised $4.5 million in three years to integrate scripture-based environmentalism into congregational life. One of their activities was mailing 105,000 educational packets to congregations, including every Catholic parish in the United States. In a similar vein, former Vice President Al Gore's environmental best seller stressed that "The more I search for the roots of the global environmental crisis, the more I am convinced that it is an outer manifestation of an inner spiritual crisis."[34]

Minimalism

In the 1960s, many counter-cultural values opposed the materialism of Western society, including the idea of living below your means. Some called it the Volkswagen philosophy, whereas British biologist E. E. Schumacher coined the phrase "small is beautiful" to get at the notion of doing more with less. One recent study suggests that minimalism has not dented the American youth psyche, since 93 percent of teenage girls report store-hopping as their favorite pastime.[35] Authors Vicki Robin and Joe Dominguez, however, have elevated minimalism to an art form. Robin serves as president of the New Road Map Foundation in Seattle, and she claims that spending less equals using up fewer of the earth's resources: "The single most important contribution we can make to protecting the environment is a return to frugality because money is a lien against the resources of the planet."[36] Robin grew up in an affluent Long Island family but learned about the joys of natural living while visiting a rustic cabin in Maine.

Her coauthor of the best-selling book, *Your Money or Your Life: Transforming Your Relationship with Money and Achieving Financial Independence,* Joe Dominguez, earned his frugality credentials quite differently. His parents were immigrants who settled in Harlem, and he escaped the ghetto through education. But while traveling across the country, he dropped out of college, seeking something other than a nine to five existence from life. He lived simply and saved enough money to invest wisely, retiring from full-time employment at age thirty.

Dominguez points out that two-income families now work 1,000 more hours annually than did couples twenty-five years ago. He notes that "I found I could lower my standard of living while my quality of life went up. I had more time for my friends and could do things I wanted to since I wasn't busting a gut making a living."[37] Robin and Dominguez are not the only authors promoting minimalist lifestyles. A raft of books by Juliet Schor, Amy Saltzman, Warren Johnson, Frank Levering and Wanda Urbanska, and Duane Elgin all advocate voluntary simplicity messages.[38]

Sustainable Agriculture

Modern high-tech agribusiness produces huge yields per acre. For example, agribusiness in the United States enables a mere 2 percent of its population to produce surplus food, whereas more than one-third of Russia's citizens labor unsuccessfully to feed its domestic population. But agribusiness wreaks ecological havoc: it relies chiefly on burning petroleum; it uses pesticides and chemical fertilizers, ignoring organic fertilizers; it necessitates irrigation that leads to shrinking water tables, soil erosion, and desertification; and it necessitates that food be transported an average of 1,300 miles before being consumed. Unfortunately, such methods are not sustainable over the next fifty years.[39]

Particularly when we consider the rate at which humans are propagating in the poor South, ecologically responsible methods of agriculture should be concerning our political leaders more than they are. At least in rural areas, local residents have the natural resources required to grow crops. In the burgeoning number of mega-cities containing more than 10 million people, the consequences of failing to invent sustainable agriculture will soon be serious indeed.

Two creative individuals working to make the cities of tomorrow more ecologically efficient are Paul and Julie Mankiewicz, codirectors of the Gaia Institute in New York City. Biologist Paul is developing onsite systems for composting urban food waste to use it as a nutrient base for rooftop urban agriculture. Biochemist Julie tests these compost systems and the quality of the compost produced. "By turning urban food waste into compost for agriculture, the Mankiewiczes hope to simultaneously reduce the urban waste stream and provide farmers with substitutes for chemical fertilizers."[40]

> No one questions American agribusiness' productivity, however, but its sustainability and its environmental costs produce many skeptics.

After studying current composting systems, they concluded that none was sufficiently efficient or inexpensive. They discovered that if food waste is chopped into 1-centimeter square pieces, surface area and air pockets most conducive to thriving bacteria exist. A 5-ton per day (PVC plastic) composing vessel was used to place shredded food waste and leaf mold (for bulking). Within two weeks, the compost was ready to ship off to farmers for use as fertilizer (as opposed to ending up in a landfill). Paul says that by "figuring out how to treat microbes very well, their system is more efficient than others." Their method is also cost-effective because it relies on commercial and residential basements to compost food, and small electric carts for energy-efficient transportation.

The crowning glory of the Gaia Institute's vision consists of urban rooftop agriculture (something that the city of Chicago has also embraced in a serious way). Many ecologists have ventured down this road in the past. However, each was stymied by this fact: rooftops were designed to support 30 to 40 pounds per square foot, and watered soil can weigh in at three times that amount. Mankiewicz solved this problem by inventing a super-lightweight soil (20 pounds per sq. ft.).

This soil is light enough for agriculture but heavy enough to significantly enhance a building's insulation. "Growing food in the cities not only provides a local source of nutritious sustenance, but it also reduces energy use and pollution by radically decreasing the distance over which food must be transported."[41] They estimate the cost reduction associated with their methods at 70 percent; plus, local food is much fresher. As another bonus, urban rooftop agriculture would likely create jobs for underemployed people in the inner city where they live and carve out a niche for green open space in cities.

Creative Science

Similar in many respects to the Gaia Institute's scientific mission in behalf of sustainable cities (see Figure 5.1) is the work of Canadian-born marine biologist John and his wife Nancy Jack Todd. Both of these husband-wife teams of scientists run nonprofit organizations that seek creative solutions to urban waste issues. In the case of the Todds' Center for the Restoration of Water at Ocean Arks International, located on Cape Cod, the task is building "living machines" that use plants and animals to treat municipal sewage and

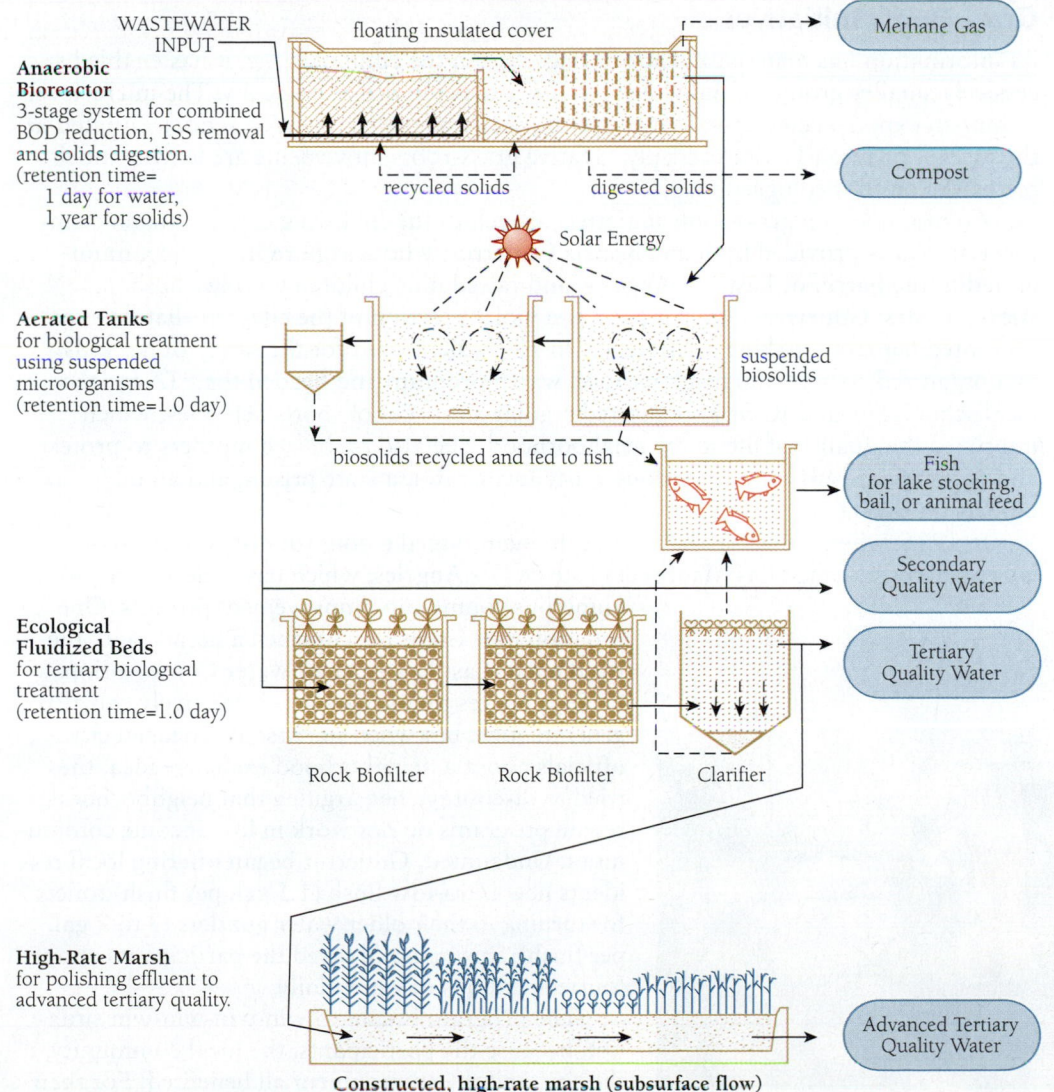

Figure 5.1

Schematic of "Living Machine"

Source: Reprinted by courtesy of John Todd from *Eco-Pioneers* by Steve Lerner.

industrial wastewater. Their elegant sewage treatment system mimics nature by "establishing a food chain in which small organisms consume the nutrients in sewage and are in turn consumed by larger, more complex organisms."[42]

Whereas standard treatment systems rely heavily on toxic chemicals to detoxify sewage, at Ocean Arks, a more organic greenhouse solution enables them to detoxify 16,000 gallons daily (about 150 households) without toxic chemicals. Inside their greenhouse, forty-eight cylindrical tanks are linked into four separate streams of twelve tanks each to move sewage from tank to tank (each with its own unique recipe of bacteria, algae, snails, plants, and fish). Toxicity is reduced with each successive tank because environments are created where increasingly complex organisms inhabit each tank.

The Todds have tested their method of creating "living machines" for years and confidently claim that greenhouse treatment of municipal sewage is superior to conventional methods for four reasons:[43] (1) greenhouse systems cost less to build; (2) theirs relies on photosynthesis and gravity rather than large mechanical devices, and therefore uses far less energy; (3) unlike standard methods, they do not use chlorine because it stresses the environment; and (4) the living machine creates only 15 percent of the amount of sludge as conventional facilities. Their living machines now operate in thirteen states and seven other countries. Among these users are very few municipalities, although some companies (such as Ben and Jerry's) have adopted it. Among their numerous honors, the Todds have received the EPA's Chico Mendes Environment Merit Award.

Grass-Roots Initiatives

As information has materialized at our fingertips in the computer age, it has enabled successively smaller groups of individuals to make a difference ecologically. The micro-level of human experience need no longer operate solely as the recipient of actions initiated at the macro- or mega-levels. Suddenly, creative grass-roots movements are leaving indelible marks on the ecological map.

An example of a grass-roots initiative, as well as the following concept (female empowerment), is provided by Juana Beatriz Gutierrez, who was born in Mexico, immigrated to the barrio of East Los Angeles, and raised nine children with her husband Ricardo. Mrs. Gutierrez lives in a poor and violent section of the city, but that has not prevented her from making a difference. In 1979, she feared for the safety of her kids and organized a successful neighborhood watch program and headed the PTA for the local school. She and Ricardo organized regular after-school sports activities, which improved the quality of life in the neighborhood. She also mobilized mothers to protest and defeat proposals for a hazardous waste incinerator, a state prison, and an oil pipeline in the barrio.

The poverty-stricken barrio of East Los Angeles provides numerous challenges for grass-roots social activists hoping to improve the quality of life for fellow residents.

In 1985, when she was in her forties, Juana founded a nonprofit organization of women activists called Las Madres del Este de Los Angeles, which has undertaken

numerous community improvement projects. One program that Gutierrez launched a decade ago, the Mothers of East Los Angeles Water Conservation Project, proves that saving water creatively can also generate jobs. But when she first approached city officials about a neighborhood exchange idea, they tried to discourage her, arguing that neighborhood rebate programs do not work in low-income communities. Undaunted, Gutierrez began offering local residents new ultra-low flush (1.5 gal. per flush) toilets for turning in their older water guzzlers (3 to 7 gal. per flush); this upgrade saved the participants about fourteen gallons of water daily.

The program became a win-win-win-win situation because the participants, the local community, the city, and the environment all benefited. For their part, the residents saved water and money. Because the city of Los Angeles is running out of water, it desperately seeks conservation measures and is appreciative enough to pay Mrs. Gutierrez's women's group $25 per toilet, which enables them to hire twenty-five full-time East Los Angles residents to work for them. In one decade, Gutierrez' brainchild has resulted in 50,000 outmoded toilets being replaced. As for Los Angeles' beleaguered environment, it not only benefits from water conservation but also from the manner in which the old toilets are recycled: they are smashed to bits with a sledge hammer, and then the crushed toilets are taken to a recycling center where they are ground up into a gravel that is used as a paving underlay by the city's street department. As single motherhood is very common in East Los Angeles, the neighbors who have assisted Mrs. Gutierrez' efforts have been mostly women, and their successes also speak to the next policy principle of female empowerment.[44]

Female Empowerment

In the poor Southern Hemisphere, which comprises two-thirds of humanity, women perform 60 percent of the work for 10 percent of the income. Consequently, female empowerment represents another key policy guideline. The inferior status to which most of the world's women are subjected is a human rights issue of gender justice in its own right, as discussed in Chapter 8. However, the unequal conditions experienced by most women globally is also a sustainable development issue because many negative social and environmental consequences result from the prevalence of gender inequality.

Attesting to this unsettling fact is a spate of recent studies finding that when female oppression is even partly lifted, good things happen, including some that foster sustainable development. For example, expanded education for Third World women slows runaway population growth because educated women have fewer children, regardless of culture or world region. Educated women are also better able to understand and practice other principles of ecological integrity. As mentioned earlier, Juana Gutierrez' story provides evidence that grass-roots initiatives by savvy and determined women with modest material resources can trigger a sense of empowerment on the part of women. But the value of education is also involved in the Gutierrez case because she and Ricardo valued formal education enough for all nine of their children to earn college degrees, some from Princeton, Berkeley, Santa Barbara, and Loyola Marymount. Education helps to empower women, whether in East Los Angeles or anywhere else.

A context about as ecologically different from East Los Angeles as you could find is Baranof Island in southeast Alaska, where we turn for another example of female empowerment in the service of ecological integrity. This is where Mary Dalton, a seventeen-year career person with the U.S. Forest Service, was assigned during the mid-1990s. Mary was described by a colleague as a "superstar" because her successful career was packed with the highest ratings by her supervisors, as well as numerous cash bonuses for jobs well done. Prior to her duty at Baranof Island, she had performed road planning, trail inspecting, and timber surveying.

At Baranof Island, she was part of a "ground reconnaissance crew" assigned to study the condition of the soil, wildlife, and habitat of a huge area (35,000 acres) following prior logging to an area proposed for new logging. The area was quite remote, and she and her colleagues traveled by helicopter and lived in a barge camp while collecting data. It took four years to complete the project, after which an Environmental Impact Statement (EIS) was filed by a base team of Forest Service colleagues who had never visited the Baranof Island site. Dalton was dismayed by much of the damage she discovered, such as "thirty-year old clear-cuts along salmon streams where literally no topsoil existed any longer."

When the base team's preliminary report was circulated in 1995, Dalton complained that they had ignored her file notes and that the report was very misleading. A year later, the final EIS appeared, but still her reports were not noted, and she began to believe that the Baranof sale must have been pushed by superiors in the Forest Service whose reasons did not include the ecological wisdom of logging this area again. Under federal ethics rules, employees are to report examples of "waste, fraud, and abuse" that they encounter on the job. Upset about her research being ignored, Dalton filed an "administrative appeal" of the Baranof sale, which federal regulations say employees may do. However, she was suspended by her supervisor for thirty days, then she was pressured to resign, and when she refused, her job was abolished, and she was reassigned to a position in Arizona at two pay grades below her rank.

Her case was taken up by the Forest Service Employees for Environmental Ethics (FSEEE), a whistle-blower defense group that accepts only one in thirty requests from Forest Service whistle-blowers. With an FSEEE lawyer at her side, the courts confirmed the legitimacy of Dalton's appeal and verified the right of agency employees to appeal questionable timber sales across the United States. Her suspension was removed from her record, and all lost pay was restored. Ecologically responsible whistle-blowers should not be punished for doing the right thing, and when an individual woman has the courage to stand up for what is right, it models female empowerment for others to emulate.[45]

Environmentally Intelligent Architecture

The inspirational work taking place at the Gaia and Ocean Arks Institutes consists largely of the *creative and intelligent design* underlying it. Sustainability resides inside our heads as much as in the physical world around us. This point also shines through the work of William McDonough, dean of the School of Architecture at the University of Virginia. As one of America's leading eco-architects, professor McDonough advocates "designing out toxins and unsustainable practices and designing in ecologically intelligent features that fit in with the cycles of nature."[46]

Architects traditionally use three design criteria: aesthetics, performance, and cost. But McDonough believes that the damage done by modern building techniques warrants two additional considerations; namely, buildings must be designed in an environmentally intelligent fashion and made of materials produced in a socially nonexploitative manner. His definition of "environmentally intelligent design" includes three key principles. First, "waste equals food" because, in nature, the waste of one species provides nutrients for others. Second, buildings need to take advantage of "current solar income" to power their heat and light. Third, building methods must respect biological and cultural diversity.

Because of these considerations, McDonough is very choosey about the building materials he will use in construction. For example, he will not merely buy paint off the shelf but often has batches mixed that contain no fungicides or biocides. Similarly, he asks brick manufacturers how they make their bricks and if they contain heavy metals or dioxins. He is even more adamant about using certified sustainably harvested lumber, and helped start a company called Forest Partnership, which promotes sustainable forestry. In a prototype "Eco-Mart" store that he built for Wal-Mart in Kansas, he invented a new type of skylight to better disperse daylight, which cut the electric bill almost in half. McDonough also used HFC-134-A rather than ozone-depleting CFCs for the cooling system, required using only recycled steel (and relying more on wood and concrete), and insisted on sustainably harvested local lumber. Wal-Mart intends to build 50 more outlets using McDonough's design features.

Professor McDonough argues that architects usually try to overwhelm nature rather than harmonize with it. He points to skyscrapers as "gas-guzzlers of the first magnitude." Manufacturing their concrete and steel takes massive energy, and reliance on glass results in excessive heating and cooling bills. Such buildings "fight the environment." A Bedouin tent, however, achieves it purposes well using minimal materials. The tent is portable, is heavy enough to

Green design pervades the "Eco-Mart" created by architect William McDonough for Wal-Mart at this Kansas site.

provide shade, light enough for breezes to penetrate, allows sunlight to penetrate, can be patched easily, and is biodegradable when no longer functional. Viewed thus, which of these building styles is primitive, and which is sophisticated?

Think Globally, Act Locally

William McDonough would applaud the efforts of Pliny Fisk III, codirector of the Center for Maximum Potential Building Systems, in Austin, Texas, who finds ways to use wastes as building products. Fisk's alternative cement, AshCrete, is made of 97 percent recycled materials and reduces carbon dioxide (a greenhouse gas) emissions, as well as reducing the waste stream of fly ash emanating from coal-fired power plants.

Fisk also personifies that ecological dictum known as think globally, act locally. He understands the nature of the global ecosphere and cares about what happens elsewhere. However, he also realizes that cutting transportation costs and using locally sustainable building materials and indigenous construction techniques represent the responsible way to build new structures. Also practicing the dictum think globally, act locally, is a group of students led by graduate student Daniel Einstein at the University of Wisconsin.

A fifth cousin of Albert Einstein, Daniel says he was motivated to counter "classes intended to expose students to information about the global environment [that] were leaving them paralyzed by the scope of the problem."[47] Einstein directs the Campus Ecology Research program, which provides students with doable local projects that yield results. He quips that professors are famous for knowing vast amounts about distant places but almost nothing about the local campus.

First, Einstein used dramatic publicity stunts to convince students to launch a recycling program for the campus newspaper (11,500 copies daily never left the newspaper racks). He also received a grant to begin a program called Solid Waste Alternatives Project (SWAP), which in its first year diverted 114,000 pounds of materials from the university waste stream.

Collected materials are entered onto a computer inventory database (including photos) from which clients can cruise the inventory to see if they want anything. To date, SWAP has moved 95 percent of materials collected. Einstein and his students have also pressured the campus procurement office to "green its purchasing procedures," and the switch to recycled plastic garbage bags alone has saved the institution $18,000 annually.

Einstein's greening efforts, however, are not only extra-curricular in nature. As the graduate assistant who heads Wisconsin's Institute for Environmental Studies (EIS) capstone certificate seminar, he oversees undergraduate academic research on the campus' environment. In all of these campus activities, he brings to life the admonition to "think globally, act locally."

Multilateralism

State leaders typically guard their autonomy, bristling at the suggestion that other entities (such as IGOs, NGOs, or MNCs) have the authority to tell them what to do. Political machismo plays especially well in individualistic polities, such as the United States. Internationally, politicians project rugged individualism through tough rhetoric and unilateral action. But going it alone runs against the grain of modern interdependence because GIs require compromise and cooperative endeavors, making multilateralism, not unilateralism, the successful motif.

In recent decades, multilateral negotiations have produced numerous influential treaties aimed at ecological integrity. Included among them is a biological security protocol, whose importance was magnified in the United States by the anthrax-tainted items that shook the Postal Service in the wake of September 11, 2001. A Law of the Sea Convention concluded decades of North versus South jockeying over the harvesting of the vast resources found in the oceans.

Achieving global consensus over the delicate balance between ecological integrity and the role of natural resources in economic development is never easy. Agreements to combat desertification, protect sea turtles in the Americas, control organic pollutants, and reduce greenhouse gas emissions to slow global warming have all emerged from painstaking multilateral negotiations.

Democracy and Devolution

Many scholars argue that democratic government acts as a check against the human and ecological abuses that have historically been associated with most authoritarian regimes. Relating to the issue of hunger, journalist Sylvia Nasar writes that "Whether or not a country starves depends more on whether it has a free press and democratic government than whether it has enough grain."[48] It has also been said often that within democratic governments (both North and South) economic development activities should devolve to local initiatives through a decentralization process. Given the poor record of countries in these economic areas, NGOs and other pressure groups have also demanded that many development activities be privatized out of the public domain in search of greater efficiency.

Green Consumerism

Another policy principle relates to the purses of private individuals and NGOs rather than the purses of governments. Positive sustainability lifestyles in the United States were discussed earlier under the rubric of voluntary simplicity, and this philosophy runs even deeper in Europe. The desire for harmonious simplicity leads citizens to engage in positive actions such as recycling, but it also contributes to more negative or aggressive ones, such as boycotting the products of polluting companies. Such assertive activities have been dubbed *green consumerism*.[49]

Public pressure for green consumerism in Germany resulted in a 1991 law that has made Germans the world's champion recyclers. This law creates market incentives for corporations to reduce the packaging around consumer products that makes up half of all residential waste in Germany. Incentives have also been given to consumers to place packages with a green dot (for ecological responsibility) in collection bins placed in each neighborhood. "In Germany, the polluter pays!" This recycling law has been so successful that France and the Netherlands have recently copied it.[50]

The red dolphin-safe labels that emerged on tuna fish cans during the 1990s in America resulted from 1980s boycotts against companies such as StarKist and Chicken of the Sea by the Sierra Club and other environmental NGOs. Assertive groups such as Greenpeace have taken even bolder actions intended to embarrass irresponsible corporations and countries alike by pulling stunts such as unfurling embarrassing banners on public buildings. Sometimes these acts of protest fit the description of "jamming," discussed in Chapter 1, whereby protesters alter the marketing slogan of a corporation with some ironic twist.

The MNC Home Depot became the target of environmentalists in 1998, when "Days of Action" were declared in seventy U.S. cities. Why did they pick out Home Depot to picket its stores? Because this mammoth building-supply chain ($25 billion annual sales) buys wood for its lumber from old-growth forests, some more than 2,000 years old. The Atlanta-based company was the target not only of picketing and a boycott, but environmental NGOs also organized "rainforest tours" where they point out to customers items such as dowels and tool handles of ramin wood from Indonesia, doors made of Amazon mahogany, and Douglas fir lumber culled from America's Northwest.

Randall Hayes, president of the Rainforest Action Network (RAN), an NGO at the forefront of hardball tactics, notes that "Home Depot is the biggest old-growth retailer in the world." The matter is urgent, says Hayes, because only 22 percent of old-growth forests remain, mostly in Brazil, Canada, and Russia. RAN has a staff of twenty-five and a budget of $2 million, is based in San Francisco, and has led tactics as diverse as running newspaper ads, teaching civil disobedience, and boycotting goods in an effort to pressure Home Depot to change its policy. Two RAN activists unfurled a banner in San Francisco saying, "Do your kids know you're buying old-growth wood?" RAN and other NGOs, such as the Washington-based American Lands Alliance, feel confident after a string of victories. Kimberley-Clark cut back its use of rainforest fiber after activists jammed their ads by depicting old-growth forests with the headline: "Oldest living things on earth or tomorrow's toilet paper?" Similarly, 3M caved in after RAN set up an 800 number for consumers to complain to the corporation over their practices.[51]

Green Justice

Another potentially contentious policy principle concerns the North–South ecological dialogue. Known as green justice, it is one that we residents of the rich MDCs tend to reject. Green justice seeks fairer allocation of responsibility for generating pollution, as well as duties (especially financial ones) for cleaning it up. The poor LDCs see a justly sustainable future depending on the rich North making three big changes: (1) reducing its occupation of environmental space; (2) taking responsibility for political and financial leadership in reversing environmental decay; and (3) giving LDCs greater representation in the institutions that distribute financial assistance for development (such as the IMF and World Bank).[52]

Green justice addresses complex problems and highly controversial solutions, and few are naive enough to expect the North fully to accept these arguments. But the MDCs have an ethical responsibility to think complexly about the implications of green justice and to discuss the topic in good faith. Just as the long-embattled factions in the Ashtabula River case, cited later in this chapter, were able to overcome suspicious hostility, so too might the LDCs and MDCs concerning green justice. Obstacles to a North–South accord on green justice are formidable, but U.S. historian Paul Kennedy believes that "The forces of change facing the world [North versus South] are so far-reaching that they call for nothing less than the reeducation of humankind."[53]

Environmental Accounting

Ecological writers have also called for innovative methods of bookkeeping to reflect the realities of long-term environmental costs associated with most economic expansion, and economists Paul Ekins, Mayer Hillman, and Robert Hutchison have answered with an impressive book about green economics.[54] Heading the list is environmental accounting, which uses resource depletion and pollution of the ecosystem in computing the bottom line of a nation's wealth. Because the modern world is largely market-driven, the more market-related principles promoting ecological awareness we can develop, the better off we will be.[55]

Economist Jonathan Rowe advocates an alternative to the standard measurement of Gross Domestic Product (total goods and services produced in a country for one year), GDP, that he calls the Index of Sustainable Progress.[56] The Human Development Index (HDI) is also superior to the sheer output measure of GDP because HDI measures general quality of life (including environment), not only output.[57] Former World Bank economist and University of Maryland professor emeritus Herman Daly, has argued most eloquently that sustainable development requires that we "conceive of the economy as *part* of the ecosystem," and thus abandon the self-defeating expansion model of progress that weds our thinking to economic growth as the ideal.[58]

If the way we price goods and services is to better reflect real environmental costs, then taxes, subsidies, and economic indicators will all have to change. For example, gasoline has always been far less expensive in the United States than in Canada, Japan, or Europe. Various governmental subsidies and tax breaks benefit corporations such as Exxon, General Motors, and Goodyear at substantial ecological cost. Foreigners blasted American policies to spend taxes building logging roads on government land, enabling trees to be sold at a loss to lumber companies engaging in clear-cutting timber. Steve Lerner notes that "The failure to shift taxes and subsidies to encourage sustainable enterprises makes the job of eco-pioneers infinitely more difficult."[59] A key recommendation made by The President's Council on Sustainable Development (PCSD) was that federal taxes and subsidies should be changed to encourage rather than discourage sustainability.[60]

Aggressive Regulation

In his analysis of American biologist Garrett Hardin's Tragedy of the Commons, political scientist Marvin Soroos examines four general strategies for avoiding a collapse of the communal pasture. In numerous similar real-world situations, Soroos believes that our policy choices boil down to (1) encouraging voluntary restraint through education and social pressure; (2) adopting regulations that limit pasture access and use, including stiff penalties for violations; (3) partitioning the pasture into fenced-in plots; or (4) abolishing private ownership in favor of communal ownership. Soroos concludes that in the hypothetical "commons," and in the real world, only the regulation of access and use, backed by penalties with teeth, stands a chance of solving ecological problems.[61]

Marvin Soroos' emphasis on aggressive regulation of access and use for our global commons (such as the oceans and the atmosphere) dovetail with biologist Donald Wells' advocacy of command-and-control ecological policies for a sustainable future. Wells' strategy entails the construction of a "large body of rules and regulations enforced through complex institutional structures." This hard-nosed approach needs to be applied inter-governmentally, that is, at all levels of government, from local to state to national to international.[62] Allowing private-sector market forces to determine social and ecological outcomes leads to human and ecological exploitation; therefore, aggressive public-sector ecological enforcement is imperative.

Ecological Policy Dialogue

We live in a world of dazzling discovery: every five years the body of scientific knowledge doubles; similarly, the wireless age creates a seemingly infinite flow of information. But problems result when a communications gap between scientific pioneers and public policy-makers occurs. Just as when Albert Einstein warned in 1949 that the creation of nuclear weapons had changed everything except the way our species thinks, today a chasm separates what scientists know about ecological problems and what policy-makers know about ecological problems.

In *The International Regulation of Extinction* (1994), Cambridge University ecologist Timothy Swanson stresses the need to build bridges between the scientific community and global policy-makers in both states and other institutions.[63] It was surely imprudent when Harry Truman assumed the U.S. presidency in 1945 not even knowing that the United States was developing an atomic bomb project, or what that term meant. Today, we likewise ought to seek to reduce ecological ignorance on the part of our contemporary policy-makers and encourage constructive dialogue between all relevant players.

Climate change expert Richard Somerville, researcher at the University of San Diego, addresses a basic dilemma concerning the science–policy linkage. Scientists are trained to be cautious about scientific results because new science often revises them. The "rigorous scrutiny of peer review" also tempers the voices of scientists. Therefore, Somerville notes that "The press conference or the congressional hearing room is not the natural habitat of active researchers." And, unfortunately, he adds, journalists hungry for sensational news gravitate toward the noisiest scientists (whom Somerville characterizes as the most self-confident but least qualified). Nevertheless, he concludes hopefully "Good science can provide the needed foundation to undergird good policy."

The representatives of countries who met at Kyoto, Japan, in 1997 were supposed to reconcile their states' interests with safeguarding global climate. The data keep changing on this issue; according to Dr. Somerville, by the time negotiators met two years later in Buenos Aires, "new science was vital to update their efforts," making good communication as essential as it is difficult to keep current.[64]

For years, the relationship between industrial polluters and environmentalists in the United States was an adversarial one that often ended up in lengthy court battles. Recently, however, cases of constructive engagement between these factions have been on the rise. One encouraging example involves the Ashtabula River in northeastern Ohio. Environmental groups had sued under the EPA's Superfund Cleanup law to force river polluters such as Alcoa Steel, Dupont Chemicals, and Exxon Oil to pay for dredging the

Ashtabula River. Decades of abusive practices had left a toxic gunk of heavy metals and carcinogenic (cancer-causing) PCB chemicals.

Recognizing that dredging the Ashtabula was not only an environmental issue but an economic one as well, John Mahan founded an NGO called the Ashtabula River Partnership. When dredged, the river would be able to accommodate more boat traffic on the channel that flows into Lake Erie, which was good for local tourism. Mahan's group succeeded in gathering together old adversaries at the negotiating table: environmental NGOs, polluting industries, EPA governmental administrators, and local city officials. None of these factions saw eye-to-eye with each other, but enough common ground was carved out to forge a cost-sharing plan to pay for dredging the polluted river. The Ashtabula River Partnership has also been using science to explore nondredging options at other local sites that aren't as bad as this one.[65]

Green Plan

The legion of eco-pioneers that inhabit Steve Lerner's book suggest that innovative Americans are at the forefront of finding practical solutions to ecological problems. However, these creative individuals from NGOs, universities, think tanks, corporations, and nonprofit organizations operate under huge handicaps. Whereas countries such as Canada, New Zealand, and the Netherlands have mapped out green plans that commit them to ecological recovery strategies based on solid financing (Netherlands spent $9.5 billion on its green plan as early as 1994), the United States has no semblance of a green plan. The Dutch green plan is backed by the public and has achieved significant results in many sectors. Environmental author Huey Johnson has studied successful green plans abroad and asserts that it is time for the United States to step up to the plate.[66] Steve Lerner concludes that the absence of an American green plan is "very curious given that U.S. diplomats are busy urging officials of developing nations to adopt sustainability to avoid the pitfalls of environmental degradation."[67]

Johnson says that states with effective green plans have "invited all stakeholders to join the process of developing, implementing, and maintaining them." They have all brought together representatives from government, industry, and environmentalist groups to debate and then implement goal-oriented activities with management-by-objective assessments. Johnson says green planning requires "comprehensiveness," involving all stakeholders. Industries are usually the most reluctant to sign on, but these countries have created incentives by streamlining the governmental regulatory systems. Although the U.S. government has gone AWOL over recommendations by the President's Council on Sustainable Development,[68] a few states have acted (e.g., Oregon, New Jersey, Connecticut, and Washington).

Debt-for-Nature Critics

University of Michigan biologists John Vandermeer and Ivette Perfecto, however, sharply criticize what they refer to in general as the Mainstream Environmental Movement, and in particular, its advocacy of debt-for-nature swaps. In their 1995 book, *Breakfast of Biodiversity: The Truth About Rainforest Destruction,* they claim that debt-for-nature swaps typify the current consensus among environmental groups, a mindset that is satisfied with "raising large sums of money to purchase and protect *islands* of rainforest with little concern for what happens *between* those islands, either to the natural world or to the social world of the people who live there."[70] Vandermeer and Perfecto argue that it is self-delusion to believe these small islands of protected land really solve anything significant. What really counts, they counter, is what happens to the land and the people *between* these protected islands.

Vandermeer and Perfecto suggest that if debt-for-nature swaps fail where they have their best chance for success, Costa Rica, what prospects can they offer in less favorable countries? The rainforests of Sarapiqui county, along Costa Rica's east coast, are especially beautiful. High temperatures and heavy rainfall in this equatorial climate create

Case Study 5.2   Win-Win Scenario? Debt-for-Nature Swaps

In Chapter 1, we talked about global trade as an example of a win-win situation or a scenario in which two or more international actors experience mutual benefit from collaboration. An ecological win-win endeavor is the creative solution falling under the rubric of *debt-for-nature swaps*. These innovations revolve around the confluence of two sets of problems found in many poor countries: first, environmental abuse, and second, a debt burden left over from heavy borrowing in the 1980s. Employing classic bargaining strategy, debt-for-nature swaps attack both of these vexing problems simultaneously.

The World Wildlife Fund's (WWF) Thomas Lovejoy devised the debt-for-nature scenario. It calls for a debtor nation to pay off part of its debt by promising to preserve a resource (such as a rainforest), which it controls and which an outside environmental group is willing to pay to protect. "In a single transaction, the debt burden of the developing nation is reduced, and global environmental protection is enhanced."[69]

Three sets of players typically negotiate debt-for-nature swaps: (1) the *debtor nation* (often represented by the national government and its central bank); (2) donor organizations, known as *debt purchasers* (usually conservation NGOs or countries with green agendas); and (3) the *creditor agency* holding the LDC's debt (such as a commercial bank). If the ensuing dialogue between these players occurs in a constructive spirit, agreements ending long-term impasses can occur. No player achieves all of its objectives, but most come to accept some compromise based on the notion that half-a-loaf is better than no loaf at all.

The flow of events often begins with a loose agreement in principle among the debtor nation, external donor, and creditor financial institution. Next, the financial transaction is carried out. This means that some part of the debt is purchased by an external donor and then traded to the debtor nation for assurances of environmental protection. Finally, the environmental agreement is implemented; this involves a long-term commitment to managing some environmental resource, usually with a local NGO serving as watchdog.

Debt-for-nature swaps have been most common in Central America (see Figure 5.2), but they have also arisen in other parts of the world. Let's examine some examples in Bolivia, Ecuador, Costa Rica, Philippines, and Madagascar.

Bolivia

In 1987, the first debt-for-nature swap occurred between Bolivia and a U.S.-based NGO called Conservation International. The Bolivian government received a reduction of its debt with a commercial bank by $650,000, which Conservation International bought for the discounted price of $100,000. Bolivia's global image was also enhanced because it served as a pioneer in this creative new endeavor.

Conservation International in turn benefited from the swap because the Bolivian government agreed to expand its Beni Biosphere Reserve (a protected zone created in 1982 and managed by its National Academy of Sciences) by 3.7 million acres. In addition, Bolivia promised to provide maximum legal protection for the Beni Biosphere Reserve and established a $250,000 endowment to fund long-term management of the protected area by both governmental and NGO overseers.

Ecuador

A few months after the Bolivian swap, a similar deal occurred in Ecuador. The World Wildlife Fund (WWF) and the Nature Conservancy, both based in the United States, purchased $10 million of Ecuadorian debt at face value, which it traded for the acquisition and management of nature preserves, management of currently protected areas, and training of environmental professionals. Implementation of the agreement was entrusted to Fundación Natura, an Ecuadorian environmental NGO.

Costa Rica

Costa Rica, one of the most environmentally astute Central American countries and the only state without a standing army, also got into the act in 1987. A consortium of international and domestic conservation groups purchased

Figure 5.2

Central American countries have been among the leading participants in debt-for-nature swaps.

$5.4 million in commercial debt from Fleet National Bank and Swiss Bank at a sharp discount. In return, the Costa Rican government established the National Resources Conservation Fund (NRCF) to finance parkland acquisition and administration, as well as training environmental professionals.

By 1996, Costa Rica was leading in the number of swaps arranged, with six transactions totaling $60 million of debt relief. Although most debt-for-nature swaps are financed by conservation NGOs, two of Costa Rica's have been funded by countries: the government of the Netherlands donated $30 million for a variety of reforestation projects, and Sweden presented a gift of $25 million to create and maintain a completely new national park.

Philippines

In 1988, the WWF bought $2 million in Philippines debt, which it traded for protection of the St. Paul Subterranean River National Park, El Nido National Marine Park, and professional training programs. The deal was overseen by a Philippine NGO called the Haribon Foundation.

Madagascar

Madagascar became the first African country to engage in a debt-for-nature swap in 1991. The WWF acquired $3 million of Madagascar's debt in exchange for commitments to long-term parkland management and hiring of park rangers. An unusual feature of this deal was the involvement of the U.S. government's Agency for International Development (AID), which also contributed $1 million to the conservation project.

Conclusion

Although the prospects for expanding debt-for-nature swaps appear promising, they do not represent the sole solution to either the LDC debt problem or the problem of environmental denigration. However, as creative responses to these global problems, they possess great symbolic value as catalysts of innovation. Past failures suggest that radically different responses to ecological dilemmas must be explored, and such win-win scenarios can help expand the envelope of human imagination. Debt-for-nature swaps also illustrate the key roles played not only by countries but also by conservation NGOs and MNCs as well. ■

---

lush tropical habitats and astonishingly varied plant and animal species. But Vandermeer and Perfecto suggest that although all may seem right with the world *within* the Sarapiqui forest, big problems loom as soon as we step *outside*.

The biggest problem, they say, is the banana because five MNCs are busily converting forest to plantation to sell this fruit abroad. Although the banana may be Costa Rica's bane, the source of exploitation in other Latin American countries may be rubber, oranges, or cattle. Vandermeer and Perfecto describe a six-stage progression that repeats itself time and again. First, MNCs identify opportunities for market expansion of an agricultural product; second, MNCs buy land and cut down everything growing on it; third, they bring in eager workers from around the country; fourth, after an initial boom period, the crop goes bust on the global market; fifth, then unemployed workers cannot find other work and seek land to grow their own subsistence crops; sixth, the only land available to them can bear fruit for a couple of years only if slash-and-burn tactics are employed in the marginally arable denuded rainforest.

In Costa Rica, Vandermeer and Perfecto believe that the government is unwittingly contributing to rainforest destruction. They do not, however, blame the debt-ridden Costa Rican government for seeking cash by exporting bananas to raise much-needed currency. They blame the few super-wealthy landowners in Costa Rica, whose possession of the land makes it impossible for the poor masses to seek food security on a small plot of their own. The authors also blame the international economic system because it forces poor countries to exploit their resources to export cash crops. Finally, they blame MNCs for luring workers to new plantations and then leaving them high-and-dry when the soil gives out or when they move their plantations.

Vandermeer and Perfecto contend that the rainforest dilemma is too complex to be solved through the approach of the Mainstream Environmental Movement. Instead, they offer a Political

The lush, raw beauty of the Sarapiqui rainforest in Costa Rica is hard to surpass.

Ecology Strategy, one that examines the role of the political economy (particularly land reform) as every bit as essential as the role of biology in finding solutions to the plight of rainforests.

What is your opinion about these conflicting visions of rainforest integrity? The Mainstream approach concentrates on protecting pristine islands of rainforests and considers the debt-for-nature swap as a viable way to do so. Conversely, Vandermeer and Perfecto's Political Ecology Strategy attacks the political and economic injustices that they see undergirding the peasant food insecurity that leads to deforestation pressures. Which vision do you find more convincing, and why?

Brazil: Pivotal Laboratory for Sustainable Development
Overview

Whereas Brazil was relegated to minor roles on the world stage during the Cold War, it finds itself under the spotlight reserved for world-class actors in the post-Cold War era. Brazil's relevance results from the new script driving the global drama, especially the widening chasm between the haves of the North and the have-nots of the South. In the space where economic and environmental issues blend together, Brazil matters. Its economic output, population, size (see Figure 5.3), and bounteous resources all rank among the world's top ten.

Brazil occupies one-half of South America, bordering on nine of the continent's eleven nations. Brazil's climate is mostly tropical or semitropical with a temperate zone

Figure 5.3
Brazil represents a giant among South American countries in many ways.

in the south. Vast forests dominate the northern region, a desert plain can be found along the northeastern coast, and mountains typify the southwest. As a frontier society that expanded aggressively across a territory seen as infinite, Brazilian culture developed a sense of profligacy, or wastefulness. In essence, believing that "bigger always means better" has caused problems for Brazil. This attitude still plagues Brazil as critics point to unsustainable practices, usually tied to massive spending on huge public projects intended to solve problems grandly.

BRAZIL'S PROFILE

Colonial ruler:	Portugal
Independence:	1822
Language:	Portuguese
Population:	183 million
Age 0–14:	29%
Area:	3,286,470 sq. mi.
Fertility rate:	2.13 children per woman
Life expectancy:	69 years
Major religion:	Catholic (80%)
GDP per capita:	$6,150
HDI ranking:	69th of 162
Inflation in 2000:	5%
Literacy:	83%
Exports:	Steel, machinery, minerals, paper products, coffee, sugar
Arable land:	5%
Forests:	58%

Source: CIA World Factbook 2004 http://www.cia.gov/cia/publications/factbook/goes/br.html.

History

Brazil was claimed by the Portuguese navigator Pedro Alvares Cabral in 1500. Colonial Brazil was ruled from the Portuguese capital of Lisbon until 1808. In that year, the Portuguese royal family fled from Napoleon's invading army and established its seat of government in Rio de Janeiro, on Brazil's Atlantic coast. Brazil became a kingdom under Dom João VI, who returned to exercise power from Lisbon in 1821. Dom João VI left his son, prince Dom Pedro, to rule as regent in Brazil. Brazil's independence was declared by the prince on September 7, 1822. He then became emperor, taking the title of Dom Pedro I. His son, Dom Pedro II, then ruled from 1831 to 1889, when a federal republic was created following a coup d'etat. Slavery had been abolished in 1888, one year before the creation of republican Brazil.[71]

From 1889 to 1930, Brazil operated as a constitutional democracy. A military coup occurred in 1930 that put Getulio Vargas in power as dictator until 1945. From 1945 until 1964, elections resulted in the presidencies of Eurico Dutra, Getulio Vargas, Juscelino Kubitschek, Janio Quadros, and João Goulart.

Economic difficulties and radical political activism in the early 1960s motivated the armed forces to once again stage a military coup in 1964. Elections failed to see the light of day until the generals relinquished power to Tancredo Neves, who was chosen by an electoral college in 1985. Brazil completed its transition to a popularly elected government in 1989 when Fernando Collor de Mello won a brief stay in the presidential palace (he was impeached for corruption in 1992). With the nation beset by economic problems such as high inflation and massive external debt, it turned to Fernando Henrique Cardoso, whose economic program, known as the *Real Plan,* pledged to reform the underlying policies causing Brazil's dysfunctional economy. Pleased with his performance, Brazilians re-elected Cardoso to another four-year term in 1998.

Brazil's great diversity is superceded by a passion for soccer in the only country to win five World Cup championships.

Society and Culture

Brazil is a heterogeneous society containing more diverse ethnic and racial groups than the United States. The four major groups are led by the descendants of Portuguese colonists who first arrived five centuries ago. Second numerically to the Portuguese are the Afro-Brazilians. The first slave ship arrived in 1538, supplying cheap labor for Brazil's profitable sugar industry. Thousands more ships followed in its wake, as 3.5 million slaves (six times the number brought to the Untied States) were imported. Brazil's abolition of slavery in 1888 created labor shortages in its coffee business, which was resolved by a massive influx of European and Asian immigrants, most notably from Japan, Germany, and Italy.

Finally, while Native peoples continue to exert a cultural influence in Brazil, their numbers have dwindled to less than 1 percent of Brazil's 175 million inhabitants. The nation's aggressive exploitation of its rainforests has historically devastated Native peoples relying on these ecosystems for their existence. Something that may prove instructive for the United States is Brazil's widespread and pacific miscegenation for the past 500 years, resulting in racial mixing among one-third of its residents.

Despite social heterogeneity, Brazil possesses a coherent national culture shared by most of its citizens. Successful racial miscegenation contributes to widespread social tolerance. Another factor binding Brazilian culture is the pervasiveness of Catholicism, to which 80 percent of the population belongs. Many nations of the world possess a passion for the game of soccer, but nowhere else as assiduously as in Brazil, partly because no other country has enjoyed comparable international soccer success. Soccer operates as more than mere entertainment in Brazil; it is a social glue binding people into a cohesive culture—a sense of Brazilian-ness.

Desenvolvimento: Bigger Is Always Better

One aspect of Brazilian culture that has often landed it in hot water is its tendency toward grandiosity, known in Portuguese as *desenvolvimento* (especially when referring to economic development ventures). Various historical experiences help to explain why the maxim that "bigger is always better" goes unchallenged in the Brazilian mind-set. The alternative viewpoint, that sometimes "small is beautiful," offers little appeal to Brazilians. Because it is inherently hostile to the values of sustainability, Brazilian *desenvolvimento* generates international criticism challenging its penchant for public mega-projects questing after quick solutions to complex problems.[72]

Many of these "pharaonic" projects have risked huge investments on dubious adventures, often resulting in massive losses. Although understandably motivated by a desire to find shortcuts to the promised land of economic development that has eluded Brazil, such big gambles have not represented sound public policy. For most of the twentieth century, Brazil's vast natural resources led observers to predict erroneously that this sleeping giant would awaken to realize its latent potential. A succession of expensive gambles based on borrowed foreign money has proven costly in more ways than one. And big-budget failures can't facilely be blamed on military regimes that dotted twentieth-century Brazilian history, because they have proven tantalizing to elected leaders as well as dictators.[73]

Kubitschek: "Fifty Years' Industrialization in Five"

The greatest proponent of *desenvolvimento,* in fact, was President Juscelino Kubitschek, elected with an industrialization mandate in 1955 of "fifty years in five." This revered leader is immortalized in a huge mausoleum in the heart of Brazil's capital city. Born of a

Czech father who died soon after his birth and a school-teacher mother, the young Kubitschek worked his way through medical school, taking internships in three European cities. After serving as governor of his native state of Minas Gerais, Kubitschek was elected to a five-year term as president of Brazil in 1955.

Shortly before assuming office, he visited the United States searching for investment money to exploit Brazil's vast natural resources. In a 1956 *Time* magazine interview, he promised that "No matter how busy I may be, any foreign investor who comes to Brazil will find my door open." Shortly thereafter, U.S. Vice President Richard Nixon visited Brazil and announced the U.S. Export-Import Bank had approved a $35 million loan to expand Brazil's steel industry. Domestic steel was sought by Kubitschek to later build his most cherished form of industrial expansion: a massive automobile industry centered around the city of São Paolo.[74]

Kubitschek's rapid industrialization also sped the process of urbanization, with concentrations of poor people living outside of Rio de Janeiro and São Paolo in giant slums known as *favelas*. Most residents of *favelas* were squatters for whom local governments could not supply basic services such as sewage collection, clean water, and electricity. Kubitschek sought to relieve some pressure from urban areas by another massive national project that drove environmentalists to despair: building paved roads into hitherto inaccessible areas of the Amazonian rainforest.

Kubitschek's largest gamble, however, was his plan to end the country's traditional concentration in the Atlantic coastal region by moving the capital city from Rio de Janeiro to a central location carved out of the high desert region. Amazingly, this ambitious project went from concept to completion during his first five-year term in office. Named Brasilia, this planned city impressed observers with in its scope and futuristic vision. Brasilia's completion bolstered Brazilian pride, but the long-term economic consequences were equally monumental and burdened Kubitschek's successors for decades.

A string of military dictators, ruling from 1964 to 1985, struggled to cope with fiscal woes unleashed by Kubitschek's spending spree. Yet this did not prevent them from succumbing to the temptation of *desenvolvimento*. In all, they initiated thirty-three mega-projects of their own. Under the catchy slogan, "Land without people for people without land," existing wilderness highways were transformed into a trans-Amazonian system, costing $1 billion. Regarding migration to the Amazon, they did Kubitschek one better by offering free one hundred-acre plots to urbanites willing to become Amazonian farmers!

The generals underwrote not only individuals, but corporations as well, in abortive Amazonian development projects such as "Grand Carajas." This huge mining project begun in 1967 in the southeastern Amazon basin was intended to produce iron ore, gold, and manganese. It is better know today for producing red ink and ecological havoc. In the same year, the military regime extended large tax incentives to lure U.S. billionaire Daniel Ludwig to purchase for $3 billion an area larger than Austria along the Jari River, a tributary of the Amazon. Ludwig hoped to harvest lumber taken from fast-growing trees imported from Asia, but this scheme also foundered when the Asian transplants died in the thin Amazonian soil.

The generals' plan to industrialize the Amazon basin required electricity, and many dams were constructed for this purpose. The Tucurui dam on the Tocantin River (the largest ever built in a tropical forest) cost $10 billion and flooded 1,000 square miles of virgin woodlands. To harvest the trees, the government subsidized the operation of a company with no experience clearing trees. The company went bankrupt and only a fraction of the wood was recovered.

Economic Fallout from *Desenvolvimento*

The negative economic consequences from myriad pharaonic projects can be easily summarized: fueling inflation, adding to the foreign debt burden, worsening socioeconomic inequality, encouraging protectionist trade policies, and discouraging foreign investment. The increased cost of goods and services in an economy (inflation) causes problems that lead most governments to undertake measures intended to keep the annual rate of inflation below 5 percent because when goods and services cost more, your money loses value. In the United States, the situation was considered very bad in the 1970s when double-digit inflation existed. In the 1980s, Brazil became one of relatively few countries in recent decades forced to deal with triple-digit inflation (over 100 percent).[75]

One of the main causes of inflation is the deficit in current accounts resulting from governments spending more money than they collect in taxes. When governments do this, they are forced to make up the shortfall in one of four ways: raising taxes, reducing spending, borrowing money, or printing significant amounts of new money. If a government lacks the political courage to either raise taxes or reduce spending, it must then borrow or print new money—either of which exacerbates inflationary pressures. Unfortunately, overspending on dubious projects by many Brazilian administrations was not followed by fiscal restraint (that is, either raising taxes or cutting spending). Instead, leaders chose the short-term response, producing deeper long-term crises. First, they borrowed foreign money once again. When borrowing failed to slow the rate of inflation, they printed new money whose worth was doomed to devaluation.[76]

When nations borrow money, they incur debt. In the 1970s, various circumstances created a global debt crisis. The key development related to the price of oil, which increased ten-fold during that decade, creating piles of "petrodollars." Oil-producing countries such as Saudi Arabia and Kuwait deposited huge amounts in Western banks; flush with petrodollars, banks aggressively sought Third World countries with development potential. Brazil sat at the top of many banks' list of borrowers to solicit. The military regime responded enthusiastically because it needed foreign money to feed the big projects described previously. Of course, few of the pharaonic projects succeeded, and Brazil exited the 1970s leading the debt parade, owing more than $120 billion. Such massive debt fed the already troublesome inflation rate eroding the nation's economy.

One of the insidious effects of inflation is that it hurts most those who can afford it least: poor people, because life's basic necessities comprise a higher percentage of their expenses. By first borrowing to fund mega-projects, then borrowing again and printing new money to service the debt, Brazilian governments condemned their impoverished citizens to even worse poverty. The rich became richer, and the poor became poorer, leading critics to call this "Hood-Robin economics": robbing from the poor and giving to the rich. By 1990, the World Bank labeled Brazil's distribution of wealth as the world's most unequal (the top 1 percent matching the poorest 50 percent).

Desenvolvimento has also fed official corruption enabling governmental officials (and their cronies) to enrich themselves at public expense. Self-serving Brazilian elites have crafted five decades of economic policies largely to benefit the powerful and the wealthy. Because many of these elites are also big-business owners in Brazil, the government has generally followed a policy of economic nationalism, which tries to protect domestic producers from foreign competition.

Economic nationalism helps domestic companies through tax breaks, taxes on imported goods (tariffs), limits on the number of imported foreign goods, assistance in researching and developing new products, and advertising campaigns telling citizens to buy domestic products. Such protectionism helps the relatively few who work for domestic manufacturers and the fewer still who own these companies. But it hurts the consumer by taking foreign producers out of the game, thus reducing competition, which is the essence of capitalism. Economists agree that economic nationalism hurt Brazil badly because it allowed Brazil's leaders to retreat into a noncompetitive protectionist shell.[77]

All of these economic difficulties (high inflation, huge foreign debt, and economic nationalism) discouraged foreign investors from risking their money in a country following unsound economic policies. Wealthy Brazilians also sought more promising venues for investment. Creditor financial organizations (the World Bank and IMF), as well as creditor states (America, Japan, and Germany), urged economic stabilization measures as a condition for further aid to Brazil. However, such external pressure required a long time to produce results in Brazil. Not until the 1994 election of Henrique Cardoso were these politically difficult, but fiscally responsible, policy choices made. Cardoso's Real

Plan sought to lower inflation, privatize many state-run companies, reduce protectionist barriers to free trade, and expand the economy modestly. The reforms introduced by Cardoso forced citizens to tighten their economic belts, but they were grounded in sound economics, and, in time, he met most of the Real Plan's objectives.

Environmental Fallout from *Desenvolvimento*

The negative economic consequences of Brazilian culture's penchant for grandiosity are matched by its outsized environmental degradation. Based on the myth of an "infinite country," Brazil's extensive natural resources have been misinterpreted as limitless. Environmental profligacy has characterized the string of developmental shortcuts financed by Brazilian leaders. Brazil's practices were sufficiently wasteful to develop an international image in the 1990s of "ecological incorrectness."[78]

Brazil's rainforests best symbolize its environmental problems. Two of Brazil's five ecosystems are forests. Fully 93 percent of its Atlantic forest had already been decimated by the 1980s. Today, 130 NGOs in Brazil deal exclusively with the Atlantic rainforest, including the largest environmental NGO, SOS Mata Atlantica, which began in 1986 and today monitors this forest by satellite. More remains of its Amazonian forest, shown in Figure 5.4, but a combination of logging, mining, cultivating, and intentional burning are reducing it; in 1998, this reduction was by an area the size of Washington state. Logging operations by wood-starved Pacific nations such as Japan, Taiwan, and South Korea were facilitated by the Brazilian government's routine approval of massive removals that environmentalists referred to as the "Asian invasion." Brazil's tropical rainforests represent one-third of those remaining on earth, leading some to describe this huge carbon sink as the "lungs of the world."[79]

The world's growing population and increased burning of fossil fuels highlight the critical role of rainforests in converting carbon dioxide into oxygen. But with the loss of rainforests also comes the loss of biodiversity. Approximately 1 million Amazonian species exist, including at least 3,000 tree species and 3,000 fish species. Because most new medical drugs used to treat diseases derive from species unknown even one generation ago, every case of species extinction equals a potential pharmacological and medical loss. Paleoanthropologist Richard Leakey says that five great mass extinctions have affected winners and losers in the game of life on earth for hundreds of millions of years. The current sixth mass extinction differs in that it is largely attributable to human action, raising the ethical question of deep ecology: do humans have the right to prevent other species from competing for survival?[80]

The majority of Brazil's mega-projects involved efforts to colonize the Amazon wilderness in the country's north via mining operations, fish farms, highway construction, electrical

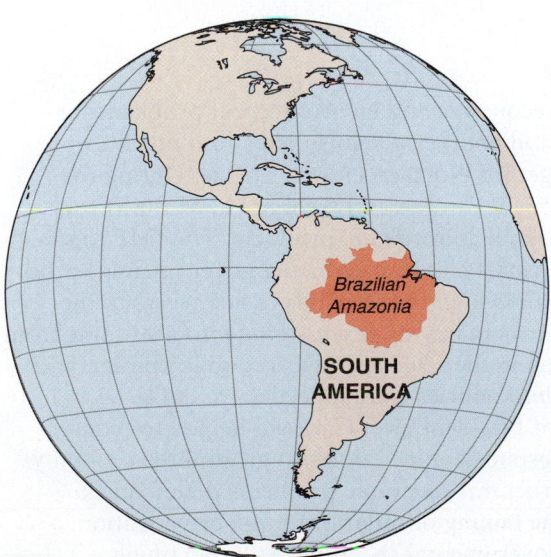

Figure 5.4
Referring to Brazilian Amazonia as the lungs of the world does not constitute hyperbole.

Source: Map, "Brazilian Amazon" p. 16 from *Vanishing Amazon* by Mirella Ricciardi. Copyright © 1991. Reprinted by permission of Mirella Ricciardi.

In 1980, the World Health Organization ranked Cubatão, Brazil, as the world's most polluted city.

projects, and timbering activities. A population explosion resulted from these endeavors. In the state of Amazonas, the headcount went from 2 million in 1960 to 20 million by 1998, which local governments were ill-prepared to cope with. Each environmentally costly migration also damages the cultural integrity of the few remaining native peoples. Although Northern Hemispheric eyes tend to focus on the rainforests, worse environmental degradation accompanied the rapid industrialization process begun in the 1960s.

No other city symbolizes urban industrial blight in Brazil as poignantly as Cubatão, which became known in the 1970s as "the valley of death." The road leading east from São Paolo crosses a beautiful mountain range on its way to the most scenic coastline in Brazil. But it runs through the denuded, brown, and barren valley of endless smokestacks—Cubatão.

In 1980, the World Health Organization described this as the most polluted spot on earth. Alarming levels of birth defects, infant mortality, and serious lung disease were chronicled. A large swamp one century ago, Cubatão was eventually drained and covered with landfill. Located strategically near both São Paolo's 10 million people and South America's largest seaport at Santos, Cubatão's geography inspired President Kubitschek to hastily install oil refineries, steel mills, fertilizer manufacturers, cement factories, and petrochemical plants. No one in 1957 worried about the inversions predictable in a tight valley like Cubatão's.[81]

Criticism of Brazilian Public Policy

Bigness and boldness have caused serious economic and environmental problems for Brazil. And in an era when the Northern and Southern Hemispheres find much to disagree about, Brazil presents a large target for Northerners to criticize. During the 1980s, free-trade American presidents (Ronald Reagan and George H. W. Bush) condemned Brazil for protectionism that closed its door to U.S. products. The IMF routinely pressured Brazil to introduce austerity measures aimed at reducing governmental spending, privatizing state-run enterprises, and allowing foreign goods easier access to the Brazilian market. Pressures to abandon the mentality of *desenvolvimento* also came from some domestic quarters. Runaway inflation in the 1980s produced public opinion backlash. Forces arrayed against *desenvolvimento* policies were indeed formidable.

The 1994 economic reform package of President-elect Cardoso helped to reduce some of the international criticism. Yet, despite genuine efforts to ground the economy in a market-oriented foundation, many structural economic problems defied quick solution. Cardoso's first term witnessed the taming of inflation, some privatization, a reduction in trade barriers, and reduced governmental spending. Still remaining, however, were large foreign debts, sizable trade deficits, stubborn pockets of governmental corruption, and the huge wealth gap. Brazilians voted in 1998 to empower Cardoso with a chance to continue his economic reforms.

Cardoso managed to reduce international criticism of Brazilian economic policy. More intractable, however, a rising crescendo of green voices condemned Brazilian environmental policy. Although Northerners consider resources such as rainforests as part of the global commons, Southerners see them as sovereign national resources. Although President Cardoso had become better at talking the environmental talk, his government was not ready to walk the environmental walk. His first administration passed considerable environmental legislation. This fact impressed many Americans, conditioned to believe from their experience that legal changes routinely produce behavioral changes. But in countries where the rule of law has emerged only recently, legislation's impact is often limited by the will, or the ability, of the governmental bureaucracy to enforce it.[82]

The Earth Summit and Sustainable Development

Given Brazil's size, vital natural resources, and economic potential, it was no coincidence that the U.N. decided to hold the historic 1992 Earth Summit in Rio. The United Nations Conference for Environment and Development (UNCED), acted like a magnet for the sharpest ecological minds on the planet. Its daunting task was to identify a blueprint balancing conflicting priorities of MDCs and LDCs. Northerners stressed environmental integrity and quality of life for current and future generations (sustainability). Conversely, Southerners saw environmentalism as secondary to the inalienable right of poor people to a higher standard of living for humanity's most disadvantaged souls (economic development).

Traditionally, these divergent goals (ecological integrity and economic growth) were seen as hopelessly inimical. It was at Rio that the concept of sustainable development achieved the status of a global vision on the horizon. The idea of environmentally benign forms of development was formalized in the document *Agenda 21,* which served to identify sustainable development as *desirable* without addressing the question of its *feasibility*.

Cardoso's Policy Dilemmas

The Cardoso administration was challenged in its second term to unleash market reforms needed for responsible economic growth without widening the wealth gap or exacerbating environmental degradation. Scholars identified a panoply of policy guidelines to aid Brazil in pursuing such difficult objectives:

- *Public Education.* Conduct a campaign to reinterpret the Brazilian cultural definition of progress in light of sustainable development.
- *Binding Social Contract.* Support sustainability as a binding new international commitment.
- *Land Reform.* The Real Plan lowered inflation and stimulated growth but did nothing about socioeconomic inequality, which requires serious land reform.
- *Free Trade.* Adhere to economically sound open trade, eschewing the politically tempting path of economic nationalism.
- *Ecological Decentralization.* Follow the advice of the World Bank by decentralizing the environmental management system.
- *Incentives for Sustainability.* Create tax breaks for initiatives such as extractive reserves, debt-for-nature swaps, trading carbon offset credits, and expanding ecotourism.
- *Aggressive Enforcement.* Pursue the application of new green laws not well enforced.
- *Curitiba, Model City.* Use the world-renowned success of Curitiba as a model of urban planning and environmental protection for other Brazilian cities to emulate.

Would new president Lula be able to maintain the momentum established by his Brazilian predecessor?

All in all, President Cardoso made considerable progress during his second term in behalf of sustainable development. Given the limitations of Brazilian cultural values, this country may never match the green plan, financial commitment, and aggressive enforcement of the Netherlands or New Zealand. Cardoso, however, moved his country forward. In 1999, he signed into force an environmental crime bill that defined pollution and deforestation as crimes punishable by stiff fines and jail sentences for the first time. Hopefully his successors will emulate the competency and decency of Cardoso's rule. Many observers have referred to Cardoso's two terms as a turning point for Brazil.

In 2002, Luiz Inácio Lula da Silva (Lula), won the presidency in a landslide election. A genuine rags-to-riches story, Lula's family or origin consisted of twenty-one siblings fathered by an illiterate farm worker. Such inspiring stories resonate politically in all areas of the world. Lula won by a huge margin of 30 million votes over his run-off election opponent. However, his left-leaning Workers' Party won only 20 percent of the seats in the Chamber of Deputies, so Lula found himself heading a four-party coalition government.

Our examination of Brazil as a vital laboratory for sustainability concludes with the very positive Case Study 5.3 about the intriguing city of Curitiba.

Case Study 5.3   Curitiba and Green Planning: Good Government in the Tropics

Located 60 miles from the Atlantic coast in a temperate southern climate, Curitiba is the capital of the state of Paraná (see Figure 5.5). Curitiba is well known for its commitment to operating as a green living space. In 1971 alone, the city planted 60,000 new trees. Anyone desiring to cut down trees requires an "in loco" site visit by a government representative and must agree to plant two new trees for every one felled. Neither wealthy nor the beneficiary of much external funding, Curitiba possesses a culture of green urban planning wholly at variance with the Brazilian knack for gigantism and spontaneity. Its recycling programs impress with both ubiquity and simplicity, which also goes for its efficient and pleasant modes of urban transport.

The genius behind Curitiba's intelligent planning regimen has been Jaime Lerner, who completed his undergraduate studies at the Sorbonne in Paris. Lerner's influential career as an architect, engineer, city planner, mayor, and state governor was profoundly affected by the earlier work of Alfred Agache and by his education in France. Lerner took Agache's inspirational ideas about planning and institutionalized them in Curitiba. One key early development was an efficient transfer system enabling residents to go anywhere in the city for a small fee, using a transport system that is privately owned but managed by the city.

In the 1960s, Lerner introduced buses that were comfortable and later added European-style accordion buses that are cheaper to run, less polluting, and reduce traffic. In the 1970s, lanes exclusively for buses improved the service. Curitiba uses a fleet of 1,550 buses along 340 routes carrying 2 million people daily (230,000 from other municipalities). For the past two decades, an alcohol fuel made from soybean (gasohol) has cut bus pollution in half. Fuel consumption in Curitiba runs 20 percent less per capita than the national average. The city's bus system consists of six types of routes:

- *Express Routes.* Red 270-passenger buses connecting transfer terminals to the city center.
- *Feeder Routes.* Orange 80-passenger buses connecting terminals to surrounding neighborhoods.
- *Inter-District Routes.* Green 110-passenger buses whose circular routes connect transfer terminals without entering the city center.
- *Direct Routes.* Silver-gray 110-passenger units linking the main districts and connecting other municipalities with Curitiba.
- *Conventional Radial Routes.* Yellow 80-passenger buses operating on the normal road network between the surrounding municipalities, the conventional terminals, and the city center.
- *City Center Circle Line.* White 30-passenger mini-buses that circle the major transport terminals and other points of interest in the traditional downtown area.

This city is as good at recycling as it is at planning. The Curitiba Green Exchange, also known as "garbage which is not garbage," was launched in 1989 and later won a U.N. award for innovative conservation. We made a field visit to a site in a poor neighborhood where twice monthly residents appear to exchange 5 kilos of recyclable garbage for 1 kilo of fruit and 1 kilo of vegetables. Currently, 25 tons per day of recyclable materials are collected by the city in seventeen specially designed bright green trucks. We made another field visit to a World Bank-funded program called "Projeto Olho d'Agua," in which school children monitor stream quality with lab kits and report back to city officials, providing useful feedback. This program also impressed us as a vehicle for ecological education for the children. Gradually, the World Bank has learned that small, micro-level projects such as this work best, whereas huge programs often go awry.[83]

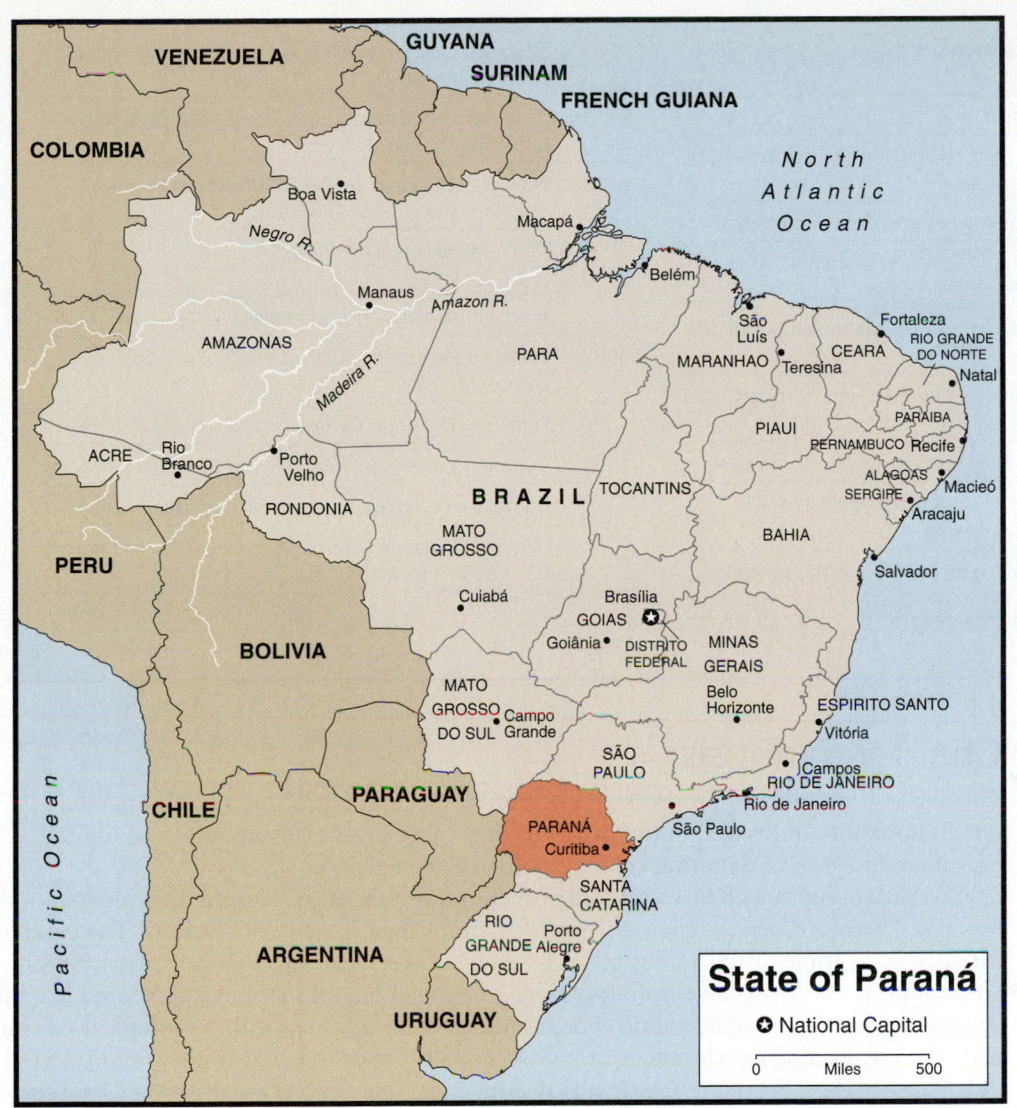

Figure 5.5

Time that I spent in the southern Brazilian city of Curitiba convinced me that its reputation for governmental best practices is well-earned.

Source: From Maps On File™ by Facts On File, Inc. Copyright © by Facts On File, Inc. Reprinted by permission of Facts On File, Inc.

Brazilian Timeline

1500 ▪ Navigator Pedro Alvares Cabral claims for Portugal what he called Terra de Vera Cruz.	**1763** ▪ Portuguese Premier Marques de Pombal expels the Jesuits from Brazil.
1501 ▪ Navigator Amerigo Vespucci returns to Portugal with a cargo of Brazilwood, used for dyeing, thus renaming Terra de Vera Cruz.	**1808** ▪ Portuguese royal family is established in Rio de Janeiro under Dom João.
	1822 ▪ Brazilian Declaration of Independence is made.
1530 ▪ Portuguese King John III begins the systematic colonization of Brazil.	**1831–89** ▪ Pedro II advances the prestige of Brazil through his statesmanship.
1532 ▪ Sugar cane is introduced at Sao Vicente.	**1850** ▪ Wave of immigrants begins to arrive as labor in coffee plantations.
1538 ▪ First slave ship arrives in Brazil.	
1693 ▪ Gold is discovered in the central Minas Gerais region.	**1853** ▪ Further importation of African slaves is outlawed.
1720 ▪ Coffee is introduced from French Guyana.	**1888** ▪ Brazil is the last country in Western Hemisphere to abolish slavery.
1729 ▪ Diamonds are found north of the gold mines in Minas Gerais.	**1889** ▪ Republic of Brazil is declared.

1898 ■ José de Moraes Barros becomes the nation's first civilian chief executive.	**1985** ■ Tancredo Neves is elected as first civilian president in twenty-one years.
1912 ■ Rubber boom goes bust.	**1987** ■ Brazil declares a moratorium on interest to preserve foreign exchange reserves.
1941 ■ After siding with the Allies in WW II, Brazil receives U.S. aid for industrial expansion.	**1988** ■ New constitution provides for direct election of president (no electoral college).
1955 ■ Juscelino Kubitschek is elected president (October).	**1988** ■ Chico Mendes is assassinated.
1956 ■ Kubitschek is inaugurated (January) and announces ambitious five-year development plan.	**1992** ■ United Nations Earth Summit held in Rio de Janeiro produces *Agenda 21* as blueprint.
1960 ■ Kubitschek makes good on his pledge to inaugurate the capital city of Brasilia.	**1992** ■ President Fernando Collor de Mello is impeached for corruption.
1964 ■ Military coup d'etat initiates two decades of military regimes (March 31).	**1994** ■ Fernando Henrique Cardoso is elected as president.
1965 ■ Law is passed that severely restricts civil liberties of citizens.	**1995** ■ Cardoso initiates his "Real Plan" of fiscal responsibility.
1970s ■ Current account deficits from mega-projects are financed by foreign borrowing.	**1998** ■ Cardoso is reelected for a second presidential term.
1982 ■ Brazil reschedules loans with creditors with new money to buy time.	**2002** ■ Luiz Inácio Lula de Silva (Lula) is elected as successor to Cardoso in a landslide victory.

Chapter Synopsis

The expansion model of progress and reliance on technological innovation may have served humanity quite well in the past, but they carry great risks in an age of limited resources and several daunting ecological GIs on the agenda.

Yet, adapting to a changing world and adopting new policies is an incremental process. Therefore, serious dialogue must be established in new institutions. The catalyst for such institutions usually consists of a "global town meeting" focusing attention on an ecological GI. Most have been sanctioned by the U.N., and all have generated heated debate. One of the most dramatic changes in recent decades regarding ecological GIs has been the astonishing development of NGOs, sometimes called civil society, and referred to by former U.N. Secretary General Kofi Annan as "the newest superpower," and they receive careful attention here.

What sound policy principles should direct the behavior of the diverse actors represented on the world stage (states, IGOs, NGOs, IFIs, and MNCs)? Sixteen such policy principles are analyzed in this chapter: deep ecology, minimalism, sustainable agriculture, creative science, grass-roots initiatives, female empowerment, environmentally intelligent architecture, think globally but act locally, multilateralism, democracy and devolution, green consumerism, green justice, environmental accounting, aggressive regulation, ecological policy dialogue, and a green plan. Examples of eco-pioneers in each policy area are also examined.

Brazil warrants attention as a laboratory for sustainable development, and is subjected to a ten-pronged examination: (1) Brazil in facts and figures; (2) its relevant historical background; (3) Brazilian society and culture; (4) *Desenvolvimento*: a Brazilian cultural value that impedes sustainable development; (5) economic and ecological consequences of *desenvolvimento*; (6) global criticism of Brazilian policy; (7) the Earth Summit and its blueprint for a sustainable future; (8) former President Cardoso's public policies; (9) Curitiba Case Study: good government in the tropics; and (10) historical timeline.

FOR DIGGING DEEPER

Ames, Barry, and Margaret Keck. "The Politics of Sustainable Development: Environmental Policy-Making in Four Brazilian States," *Journal of Inter-American Studies and World Affairs,* 1997–98, pp. 31–43.

Barnes, Pamela, and Ian Barnes. *Environmental Policy in the European Union*. Edward Elgar, 2000.

Broadhead, Lee-Ann. *International Environmental Politics: The Limits of Green Diplomacy*. Lynne Rienner, 2002.

Burns, E. Bradford. *A History of Brazil*. Columbia University Press, 1993.

Chaffee, Wilber. *Desenvolvimento: Politics and Economics in Brazil*. Lynne Rienner, 1997.

Chambers, W. Bradnee. *Interlinkages and the Effectiveness of Multilateral Environmental Agreements*. Brookings Institution, 2008.

Climate Change 2007: Impacts, Adaptation, and Vulnerability. United Nations Publications, 2007.

Daly, Herman. *Beyond Growth: The Economics of Sustainable Development*. Beacon Press, 2000.

Florini, Ann, ed. *The Third Force: The Rise of Transnational Civil Society*. Carnegie Endowment, 2000.

Gilpin, Alan. *Dictionary of Environment and Sustainable Development*. John Wiley and Sons, 1997.

Goertzel, Ted. *Fernando Enrique Cardoso: Reinventing Democracy in Brazil*. Lynne Rienner, 1999.

Goodstein, David. *Out of Gas: The End of the Age of Oil*. W. W. Norton, 2005.

Gore, Al. *Earth in the Balance: Ecology and the Human Spirit*. Plume, 1993.

Haas, Peter, ed. *Environment in the New Global Economy*. Edward Elgar, 2003.

Hinrichs, Roger A., and Merlin H. Kleinbach. *Energy: It's Use and the Environment (with InfoTrac)*. Brooks Cole, 2005.

Korppoo, Anna, and others, eds. *Russia and the Kyoto Protocol: Opportunities and Challenges*. Brookings Institution, 2005.

Layzer, Judith A. *The Environmental Case: Translating Values into Policy*. Congressional Quarterly, 2006.

Lerner, Steve. *Eco-Pioneers: Practical Visionaries Solving Today's Environmental Problems*. MIT Press, 1998.

Lipschutz, Ronnie D. *Global Environmental Politics: Power, Perspectives, and Practice*. Congressional Quarterly, 2004.

Marks, Siegfreid, ed. *Political Constraints on Brazil's Economic Development*. North-South Center Press, 1993.

Montgomery, David R. *Dirt: The Erosion of Civilization*. University California Press, 2007.

Page, Joseph. *The Brazilians*. Addison-Wesley, 1995.

Parto, Saeed, and Brent Herbert-Copley, eds. *Industrial Innovation and Environmental Regulation: Developing Workable Solutions*. Brookings Institution, 2006.

Oberthur, Sebastian, and Herman Ott. *The Kyoto Protocol: International Climate Policy for the 21st Century*. Sperlinger, 1999.

Portney, Paul, and Robert Stavins, eds. *Public Policies for Environmental Protection*. Resources for the Future, 2000.

Revkin, A. *The Burning Season: The Murder of Chico Mendes and the Fight for the Amazon Rainforest*. Houghton Mifflin Company, 1990.

Rosenbaum, Walter A. *Environmental Politics and Policy*. Congressional Quarterly, 2007.

Rothenberg, Lawrence S. *Environmental Choices: Policy Responses to Green Demands*. Congressional Quarterly, 2002.

Schneider, Ronald. *Brazil: Culture and Politics in a New Industrial Powerhouse*. Westview Press, 1996.

Stewart, Meg, and others. *Exploring Environmental Solutions with GIS with CD ROM*. McGraw-Hill Science, 2004.

Swanson, Timothy. *The International Regulation of Extinction*. New York University Press, 1994.

Tamminen, Terry. *Lives Per Gallon: The True Cost of Our Oil Addiction*. Island Press, 2006.

Vale, Brenda and Robert. *Green Architecture: Design for an Energy-Conscious Future*. Bulfinch Press, 1999.

Vandermeer, John, and Ivette Perfecto. *Breakfast of Biodiversity: The Truth About Rainforest Destruction*. Food First, 1995.

Vig, Norman J., and Regina S. Axelrod, eds. *The Global Environment: Institutions, Law, and Policy*. Congressional Quarterly, 2005.

Wells, Donald T. *Environmental Policy: A Global Perspective for the Twenty-First Century*. Prentice Hall, 2001.

Willumsen, Maria, and Eduardo Giannetti, eds. *The Brazilian Economy: Structure and Performance in Recent Decades*. North-South Center Press, 1997.

INTERNET

Africare:
http://www.africare.org/

Center of Excellence for Sustainable Development (DOE):
http://www.smartcommunities.ncat.org

Center for Renewable Energy and Sustainable Technology (CREST), "Solstice":
http://www.crest.org

CIA–The World Factbook 2000: Brazil:
https://www.cia.gov/library/publications/the-world-factbook

Earth Times Electronic Newspaper:
http://www.earthtimes.org/

Food and Agricultural Organization (FAO) of the U.N.:
http://www.fao.org/

Freedom from Hunger:
http://www.freedomfromhunger.org/

Global Land Information System:
http://www.edc.usgs.gov

Global Warming Early Warming Signs:
http://www.climatehotmap.org

Greenpeace:
http://www.greenpeace.org/

International Institute for Sustainable Development:
http://www.iisd.org/default.asp

Kyoto Treaty Text:
http://www.unfccc.int/resource/docs/convkp/kpeng.pdf

The Learning Team (DOE), "The Sun's Joules":
http://www.LearningTeam.org

National Oceanic Atmospheric Association:
http://noaa.gov/

Nature Conservancy:
http://www.nature.org/

The North-South Institute:
http://www.nsi-ins.ca

Population Action International:
http://www.populationaction.org/

Resources for Energy and the Environment:
http://www.zebu.uoregon.edu

Resources for the Future:
http://www.rff.org

Rocky Mountain Institute (100 case studies):
http://www.rmi.org

Sierra Club:
http://www.sierraclub.org/

Union of Concerned Scientists:
http://www.ucsusa.org

U.N. AIDS Campaigns:
http://www.unaids.org/

U.N. Framework Convention on Climate Change:
http://www.unfccc.int

U.N. Population Information Network (POPIN):
http://www.un.org/popin/

U.S. Environmental Protection Agency (EPA):
http://www.epa.org/

World Bank Group, "Brazil's Economy":
http://www.worldbank.org/html/extdr/offrep/lac/brazil.html

World Conservation Monitoring Center:
http://www.wcmc.org.uk

Identity Amid Human Diversity

CORE OBJECTIVE

To conceptualize the main patterns of social identity competing for the hearts and minds of humanity.

THEMATIC QUESTIONS

- Is spatial analysis sufficient to identify world regions?

- In what ways are states unique?

- Why is critical thinking vital to assessing race and ethnicity as bases for social identity?

- How likely is the development of one global community?

- Has attachment to territory figured prominently in human warfare?

- How has Canada's role on the world stage contributed to its national identity?

Consciousness

The precise interface between the human brain and mind has yet to be understood fully by researchers. Yet much has been learned in recent decades, especially using magnetic resonance imaging (MRI) and other new technologies. One of the more telling distinctions between *Homo sapiens* and other closely related species is our level of **consciousness,** contributing to both self-awareness and empathic feelings of concern for other peoples. The dual human capacities for consciousness and for empathy facilitate choosing what social groups with which to identify.

Many scholars believe that we developed consciousness to cope with the complex challenges attendant to interacting socially (both competitively and cooperatively) with our bright and adaptive fellow humans. Psychologist Nick Humphrey refers to our *empathic ability,* or predicting the behavior of others on the basis of what you would do in a similar situation, as the "Inner Eye."[1] It appears from studies, however, that while humans clearly lead the league in consciousness, we do not monopolize it. This chapter dwells on human social identity, a subject intimately linked with consciousness and empathy.

In the 1970s, psychologist Gordon Gallup created a simple means of determining whether animals possess a sense of self. Called the *mirror test,* it involves familiarizing the subject with a mirror, and then marking the animal's head with a spot. If the animal touches the spot after again looking at its reflection, it is believed to recognize the image

Consciousness ■ That dimension of intelligence involving the imagination and enabling skills such as foresight, recognition of the "self" as separate from others, and feeling empathy toward others

as its own, not merely that of some other individual. Thus far, numerous species have been given this test, but only chimpanzees and orangutans have produced positive results. Like humans, both of these species live in complex social settings involving both cooperation and competition within a group.[2] Two million years ago human ancestors experienced a single mutation that weakened jaw muscles. The downside enabled competitors to out-chew us but was countervailed by skull flexibility and subsequent brain expansion.

There is no evidence, however, that any species other than humans (not even chimpanzees or orangutans) experiences what naturalist Richard Leakey calls "the ultimate vicarious experience: fear of death. In all human societies, awareness of death has played a large part in the construction of mythology and religion. There seems, however, no comparable awareness of death among chimpanzees."[3] Evidence of human ritual burial with formalized procedures that demonstrate an awareness of death (a vital element of consciousness) can be dated back about 100,000 years.

Nature of Human Identity

The existence of consciousness provides humans with a subjective means of identifying where and with whom we fit socially. So in addition to various objective ways of classifying and categorizing human beings, we possess a sense of self and a considerable amount of free will; thus we are able to participate actively in the process of defining our social identity. In other words, we have something to say about who we are and with whom we fit. Human consciousness encourages questions such as: What am I? What are you? What are our identities? Can we hold multiple feelings of identity, and does one kind always trump other kinds? Do you think of yourself mostly as a state citizen, or by a religious identity, or by an ethic identity, and does it really matter? As practitioners of free will, humans incorporate both extremes concerning the logic and reasonableness of our beliefs: loose, common-sensical assumptions prone to fallacious reasoning, and critical thinking based on skeptical, rigorous analysis.

Studying identity is very much an interdisciplinary endeavor. Psychologists and philosophers tend to see human identity as an innate capacity that we are free as individuals to use for good or ill. Sociologists, however, contend that individual human agency concerning the formation of the self and its sense of identity results from social interactions. A century ago, sociologist Charles Horton Cooley posited that how we view ourselves does not derive from direct personal contemplation but rather from "our impressions of how others perceive us." To convey the idea that the self is a product of social interactions, Cooley coined the phrase "looking glass self."

Then, in the 1930s, sociologist George Herbert Mead paid homage to Cooley's pioneering work on the sociological sense of the self and went on to create a model of the process whereby the self emerges, which included three stages: (1) *preparatory stage:* younger children imitate the people around them (especially family); (2) *play stage:* children at age six or seven learn to take roles by mentally assuming the perspective of another person, thus enabling a response to that imagined viewpoint; and (3) *game stage:* children of eight or nine years can now respond to numerous members of the social environment, handling different tasks and relationships simultaneously.

Bases of Social Identity

Social identity facilitates the bonds of comity and cooperation that help us to feel accepted, by experiencing the we-ness of an in-group. Paradoxically, however, identity also facilitates aggression, including the dark side of civilization (warfare) when in-group identity leads to out-group hostility. Given humanity's size, complexity, and rapid expansion on the planet, it helps to mentally divide the world's 6.5 billion people into groupings of shared identity. Social scientists are accustomed to applying at least nine such conceptions of identity:

- country identity
- regional identity
- racial identity

- ethnic identity
- trade-driven super-regions
- corporate (MNC) identity
- North (MDCs) versus South (LDCs)
- mega-level cultures
- one global community

Country Identity

The world political map provides the most powerful image of how the world is divided up into 193 existing countries (states) such as Germany, Bolivia, and Vietnam (see Figure 6.1). States possess a territory and are accepted by their peers as actors on the world stage through a process of legal recognition. Humanity has ordered its public affairs through states for a very long time, and states continue to enjoy considerable loyalty from their citizens; personal loyalty and social identity are closely related phenomena.

Nations ■ A large group of people sharing feelings of common identity, usually based on historical experiences, who desire to govern themselves to some extent

Problems arise, however, when states do not mesh with **nations**. A strong feeling of identity with a nation is called *nationalism*. Problems that arise are often of two varieties: first, diversity can contribute to significant civil strife in multinational states (such as India, Somalia, and Indonesia), and, second, when nationality groups are spread around various countries, they feel frustrated by their inability to unite in one place.

In this imperfect world, far too many national identities exist for all to rule themselves. Thus, peoples such as the Kurds and the Palestinians in the Middle East, the Chechens and the Tatars in Russia, and the Tibetans in China all possess strong national loyalties and bear grievances against the states ruling over them. Since 1991, a U.N. organization called Unrepresented Nations and Peoples Organization (UNPO) has promoted the interests of minority nationalities in states where they do not rule themselves. More than 50 disgruntled nationalities seek redress of their grievances through UNPO. Their populations add up to more than 100 million, with the Kurdish people the largest (25 million) living as minorities in places such as Iraq and Turkey. Smaller ones include Australian Aborigines and Native Americans (see the UNPO Website at chapter's end).

National self-determination ■ The view that a large group of people with a common identity have the right to function independent of outside control

Because the United States' revolutionary break from Great Britain emphasized freedom and liberty (both individual and national) as its central value, Americans have always empathized with the principle of **national self-determination.** America's ideological support for national self-determination, however, comes into direct conflict with the traditional principle of sovereignty, which says that countries are free to run their internal affairs as they see fit. President Woodrow Wilson's strong advocacy of self-determination contributed to the formation of many new countries after World War I (in which the German, Austro-Hungarian, and Turkish empires were defeated). These intentions were reasonable because long-suppressed national groups were supposed to get their own states. However, some of the consequences of self-determination have proven troublesome.

The number of states increased dramatically after World War II. **Decolonization** contributed mightily to this increase. For example, when Great Britain ended its colonial administration of India in 1947, not only did the "new" sovereign state of India emerge but also civil war between Hindi and Muslim religious forces led to the separation of India from what became Pakistan, and later, Bangladesh. When founded in 1945, the U.N. had 51 members. In 2002, it accepted its 191st state (Switzerland). As of 2006, 61 colonies or dependent territories still existed around the world, held by eight countries: Australia (6), Denmark (2), Netherlands (2), France (16), New Zealand (3), Norway (3), United Kingdom (15), and United States (14).

As states proliferate, so does their diversity. The hugest countries are Russia, Canada, the United States, China, and Brazil, and the smallest are Vatican City, Monaco, Nauru, and Tuvalu. In 2006, population density was highest in Monaco, Singapore, Malta, and Maldives Islands, balancing off the sparsest ones in Western Sahara, Mongolia, Namibia, and Australia. The United States and United Kingdom possess nuclear weapons, whereas Costa Rica has no standing army whatever. Iran is a Shiite Muslim theocracy, China is officially atheistic, the United States encourages religious freedom while prohibiting any

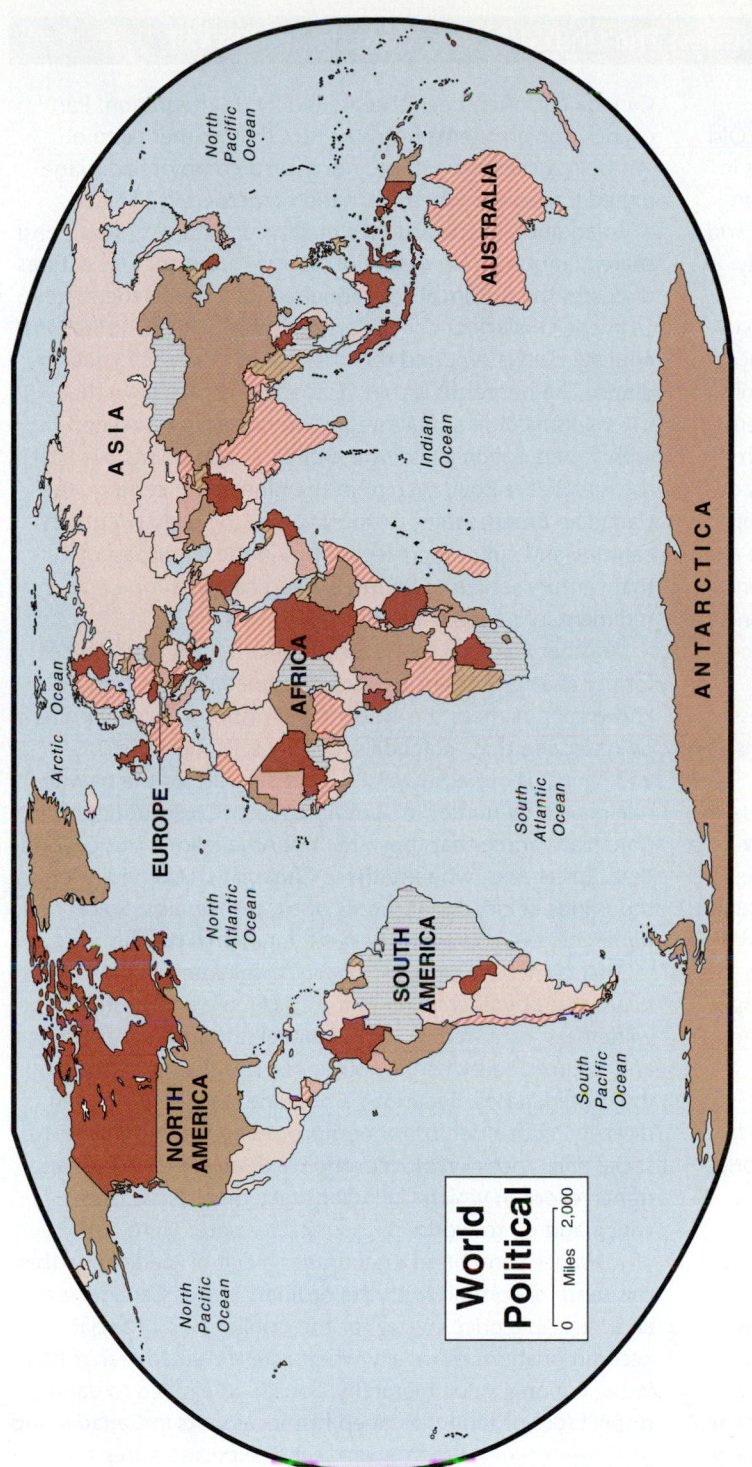

Figure 6.1
A total of 51 states
existed in 1945, but by
2007 that number had
grown to 193 states.

official state religion, and Russia gropes for a model of church-state relations appropriate to its post-communist era. Luxembourg ranked highest in per-capita income ($58,900), with the United States second ($40,100) and Norway third ($40,000). East Timor and several African countries failed to break the $600 figure.

Regional Identity

Identifying world regions requires a spatial synthesis of political, social, economic, cultural, and historical factors. No consensus exists among geographers when dividing the

Case Study 6.1   Comparative National Identities: The United States, Canada, and Brazil

The United States, Canada, and Brazil have a number of things in common. They were all New World colonies of Old World European powers, are among the largest countries in the world, possess vast stores of natural resources, used an expansionist mentality to conquer a continental frontier, and today have populations of great ethnic and racial diversity. The national identity forged by each, however, is unique.

Because the beginning of the United States occurred violently, confidently, and replete with dramatic symbols, locating the markers of American identity comes relatively easily, as compared to most other countries. Marc Pachter, external affairs officer for the Smithsonian Institution, does so with great precision and clarity. Noting that so many of Alexis de Tocqueville's observations in *Democracy in America* hold up well after 150 years, Pachter surmises the existence of an enduring "core nature" of American-ness. Americans consent to a sociopolitical compact that revolves around a passion for individual choice as the embodiment of freedom in action, including a firm belief in self-determination.

Conversely, this attachment to freedom can also necessitate a more burdensome acceptance of individual responsibility for one's personal story. According to Pachter, the American creed also involves a hunger for change because of the optimistic belief that with change comes progress. Explicit images of political freedom dot the verbal landscape with active and efficacious symbols embodied in words such as *competition, freedom, opportunity,* and *mobility.* You will observe next that whereas Canadian identity suffers from the absence of clear and direct symbols, the American identity is forced to live up to some very challenging ideals, and when it fails to do so, it finds itself vulnerable to criticism for hypocrisy. The great Achilles heel of American society is racial inequality stemming from the legacy of slavery, and Pachter predicts that it will continue to torment the national psyche for the foreseeable future.[4]

Psychologically, national identity is something Americans take for granted and Canadians obsess about. At a Canadian Studies Conference, Queens University professor C. E. S. Franks reversed a standard aphorism by quipping "Canada works well in practice, but it has a hard time in theory." While feelings of American-ness stand up and perform boldly in a whole host of ways, feelings of Canadian-ness seem reluctant to flaunt their national bona fides. American imagery employs the overtly political stars and stripes, but Canadian imagery relies on more muted symbols such as the maple leaf.

Historians suggest that Canada has never had an explicit historical mission, other than struggling for its very survival. Unlike the United States, Canadian history features no galvanizing war of independence, thus Canadians celebrate no comparably dramatic independence day. Historian Thomas Thorner uses "self-doubt" as the defining motif for the Canadian experience. His book begins by stating "Ours is a history of self-doubt. From the moment of Confederation,

Canada has often been threatened by disintegration. Part of this problem stems from the fact that neither cultural symbols, a shared heritage, nor even a common language united Canadians when the nation emerged in 1867."[5]

In addition to the absence of shared cultural symbols and shared language, University of Calgary professor David Taras discusses the historical consequences of a weak federal government, the lack of compulsory national service, no national educational system, and the absence of a core religious tradition. The net result is that "Canada does not have the mechanisms of national integration normally associated with strong nation-building." But Taras also points out that the national railroad system in the nineteenth century, the Canadian Broadcasting Corporation in the early twentieth century, and cultural protectionism in the latter part of that century served as countervailing catalysts for a rudimentary national identity.

Another voice on the subject is heard from Keith Spicer, former chair of citizens' Forum on Canada's Future and known popularly as the Spicer Commission.[6] Spicer begins by observing that "Canada's identity is its identity crisis," and "angst is our ecstasy," thus accounting for the pivotal role played by humor in venting collective insecurities. Canadians agree that they are "not Americans," but beyond that, Spicer asks, who are these Canadians? After listening to thousands of citizens at scores of town meetings, Spicer highlights five characteristics of the national psyche.

First comes the issue of *survival*, originating in the pioneer's fear of vulnerability in a cold climate and hostile wilderness, captured so well by novelist Margaret Atwood, and resurrected by contemporary fears of being crushed by the United States. Secondly, a genuine respect for human diversity, with a genius for compromising in ways that make social differences livable, contribute to an enviable human rights record in which Canadians take great pride, and which add up to world-class *social tolerance*. Third, if the cult of tolerance sometimes encourages a cult of mediocrity, then this sense of comfort with the ordinary strikes Canadians as an acceptable price to pay for the public good of social accommodation, especially when *equality* already ranks high in the national value hierarchy. Fourth, as alluded to earlier, respect for authority has deep historical roots in Canada, and unlike Americans, when given a choice between freedom and *order,* Canadians prefer the latter over the former. Finally, Spicer cites Canada's role as a beacon of peace as a source of pride. A tradition of "Pearsonian idealism," or acting as a good global citizen (the only country to serve in all thirty-four U.N. peacekeeping missions), plus its leadership in international human rights as one of the Like-Minded Nations, means "helping out abroad unites us at home."[7] The value of acting as good global citizen on the world stage in forging Canadian identity is discussed in detail at the end of this chapter.

But if American identity is confidently bold, and Canadian identity is comfortably unassuming, then Brazilian-ness is fundamentally schizoid, spontaneous, and unpredictable. And if C. E. S. Franks joked that Canada works fine in practice but has trouble in theory, quite the reverse can be said of Brazil: it often talks a good game while looking good, but somehow the results fail to match the promise. Brazilians are known for their sense of eternal optimism, yet they also are prone to great self-deprecation, typified by a common expression that theirs is a land of "unlimited impossibilities." Some observers go so far as to say Brazilians have a deep national inferiority complex. U.S. law professor and Brazilianist Joseph Page concludes that "many features of Brazilian-ness contribute significantly to the current plight of South America's ailing giant."[8]

Brazil is a nation of people who live for pleasurable experiences of the moment, rather than material possessions or planning for the future; thus it is invariably considered quite hedonistic. The most potent hedonistic symbol is Carnival week in Rio de Janeiro prior to Lent in this country of nominal Catholics. The thong bikini began in Rio, and topless beaches are common as the nation has a sensual love affair with the human body, which also shines through its entertainment industry. It is the human touch of gentleness, and the cordiality of connecting with others spontaneously, that are most prized in Brazil. Many nations are crazy about soccer, but none have enjoyed Brazil's international success or play the game with such élan. The flair oozing from Brazilian football is recognized by fans worldwide. The national fixation on grandiosity discussed in the previous chapter even appears in soccer. Maracana stadium, the world's largest, was built for the 1950 World Cup, and holds an astonishing 200,000 people.

Not to be excluded from a dissection of the national character, however, is Brazil's admirably tolerant lifestyle when it comes to race, ethnicity, and religion. In a country that is far more racially diverse than the United States, and where income distribution is more unequal than in America, considerable civil strife and violence might be predicted. However, Brazilians are famous for finding subtle ways of averting direct personal confrontations and adapting to difficult circumstances with nary a complaint. Some racism exists in all countries of diversity, but the level of overt racism in Brazil has been characterized as far below that of the United States. The Portuguese owners required their slaves to convert to Catholicism, but blacks working on sugar plantations were able to informally preserve their ancestral religious heritage and to incorporate African rituals into a superficial practice of Catholicism. ■

world, but many identify eight main regions: Europe, Eurasia, the Middle East, Asia, the Pacific Rim, Sub-Saharan Africa, Latin America, and Anglo-America.

EUROPE The 1989 collapse of communism in the eight eastern European countries rendered moot the Cold War distinction between western and eastern Europe. Europe consists of one-half billion people in thirty-eight countries, which appear increasingly similar as ex-communist countries emulate Western democratic capitalism. The more apt European dichotomy today consists of the rich Northern tier versus the poorer Southern tier (see Figure 6.2).

The world's most advanced regional cooperation is also at work in Europe. In economics, the European Union (EU) has achieved extensive cooperation among its members, thus bumping up the affluence compared to other areas of the world. The EU integrated further in January 2002 with the introduction of a single European currency, the euro, replacing all national currencies. The basic goal of the EU, crafted during the 1950s, was to prevent a reprise of the bloody wars that plagued Europe for four centuries. It was to do so by intertwining these countries in bonds of affluence, thus rendering war between them unthinkable. The EU has succeeded in creating sufficient popular loyalty for regional identity to trump national identity in this unusual region.

The 1990 reunification of a divided Germany created a country of 83 million people boasting the world's fourth-largest economy. German unification frightened some Europeans old enough to remember the devastation of WW II unleashed by Nazi dictator Adolph Hitler. But because regional integration apparently serves as an antidote to aggressive nationalism, staunch German support for EU consolidation has bolstered the optimism of other observers who believe that Europe's future will be more peaceful than its past.[9]

Europe no longer dominates other regions the way it did in previous centuries via colonialism, but Europeans continue to marshal the human resources required to succeed in global economic competition. Northern European countries make up fourteen of the top twenty in the world on the Human Development Index (HDI), measuring overall quality of life.

Figure 6.2

Europe dominated globally for much of the past 500 years, but today it leads mostly by the success of its political/economic European Union.

Wealth in this peaceful and influential part of the world runs about triple the world average, while life expectancy averages an impressive seventy-five years of age. Smaller in size than the United States, but more densely populated, three of four Europeans live in urban areas. Most European countries educate their people well, preparing them for the post-industrial age of information-intensive services. Protestantism, Catholicism, and Judaism are the region's principal religions.

America and Europe are similarly bound by countless mutually beneficial economic ties. However, the Cold War honeymoon whereby Europeans deferred to U.S. geostrategic policy is history, and on issues such as the U.S. trade embargo against Cuba, America's special relationship with Israel, genocide in Rwanda, Bush's global War on Terror, his decision to invade Iraq in 2003, and Iranian nuclear ambitions, Europeans have proven highly critical of the United States.

EURASIA (FORMER SOVIET UNION) Prior to fracturing in 1991, the Soviet Union covered one-sixth of the earth's landmass. A nuclear superpower, its population of 285 million ranked third, trailing only China and India, and it was the only country to take up an entire world region. Its fifteen Union Republics have broken apart into independent countries, with Russia as the largest and most important successor state. Russia is a Eurasian nation encompassing both European (Western) and Asian (Eastern) traits, and it has trailed eastern European states such as Poland, Hungary, and the Czech Republic in shedding its communist heritage in favor of a Western model, dangling in an uncertain limbo (see Figure 6.3).

Russia's 148 million people overshadow their Slavic brethren in neighboring Ukraine (52 million) and Belarus (12 million), although the Russian population is slowly shrinking.

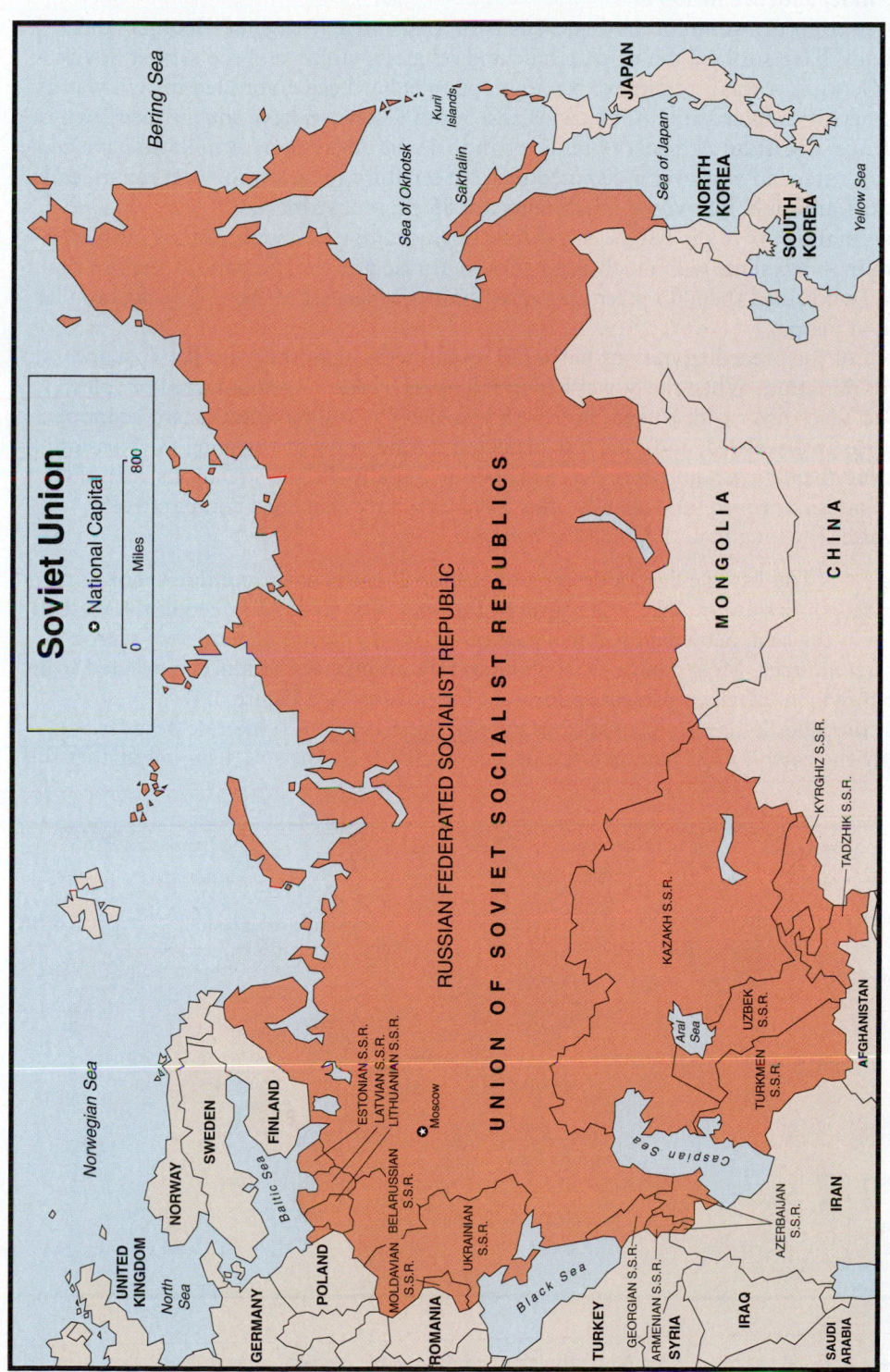

Figure 6.3

Cold War era nemesis of the United States, the former Soviet Union (FSU) now consists of 15 separate countries-in-transition.

Difficult economic circumstances have led many of its citizens to have fewer children, and because they are well educated for a country with only a middling level economy, a significant brain drain has occurred, as many of its best and brightest head for North America or Europe. The average Russian income is only about 10 percent that in the United States, and Russia's HDI (quality of life) index ranked 55th worldwide in 2001. Besides Slavs, three other main groups comprise successors to the Soviet Union. The small Baltic nations of Estonia, Latvia, and Lithuania (1.5, 2.5, and 3.5 million population, respectively) have traditional ties to Europe and were forcibly annexed by Soviet dictator Joseph Stalin in 1940. These Baltic Republics were the first Soviet Republics to achieve independence in 1991.

Three countries south of the Caucasus mountain range (Armenia, Georgia, and Azerbaijan) have suffered the worst ethnic and religious violence in the former Soviet Union. Georgia, a small country of 5 million people, has been embroiled in civil war as ethnic minorities such as the Abkhazians and South Ossetians have sought their own independence. Christian Armenia (4 million) and Islamic Azerbaijan (8 million) have conducted an extended war over a disputed piece of territory lying within Azerbaijan, called Nagorno-Karabakh, but whose inhabitants are 85 percent Armenian.

The final sector of the FSU, Central Asia, includes five Islamic countries inhabited by 50 million Muslims with much closer ties to Turkic and Asiatic nations than to the Russians who ruled them for a century and a half. The largest of these, Uzbekistan, has 24 million people.

Each of the preceding nations harbored resentments against earlier Russian and Soviet domination. When the Soviet Union fell apart, these long-subjugated peoples rushed to sever links with Russia. But these new nations still have important economic ties not easily discarded, and each has struggled to find ways of engaging the Russian bear economically without being overwhelmed politically. Russia's relations with the United States improved immediately after 1991 and have remained comparatively pacific after the long haul of Cold War tensions.

MIDDLE EAST The Middle East, a desert and semiarid region at the confluence of northern Africa, southwestern Asia, and southern Europe, runs from Morocco in the west to Pakistan in the east. Settlements in this part of the world cluster around very scarce freshwater sources. Most countries' economies rely on primary products extracted from the earth, which usually represents a formula for poverty (see Figure 6.4).

But the Middle East's oil constitutes the glaring exception to the rule because it is currently the earth's most lucrative resource extracted from the soil. King oil divides the

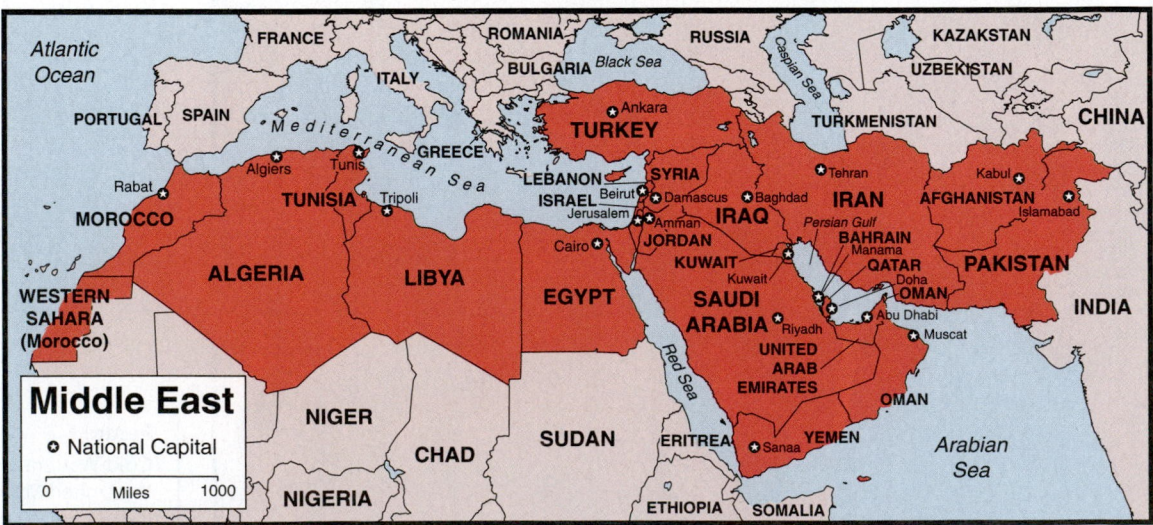

Figure 6.4

Middle Eastern identity results as much from Arab ethnicity and the Isalmic religion as from geography.

region's states into the fortunate ones that have it and the unfortunate ones that don't. Huge disparities separate rich countries such as the United Arab Emirates (GNP per capita $29,000) or Qatar (GNP per capita $26,000) from poor neighbors such as Syria (GNP per capita $1,000) or Yemen (GNP per capita $775).

The majority of the region falls below the world average on the HDI measuring quality of life, with only Bahrain and the United Arab Emirates scoring in the world's top forty-five HDI rankings. One major problem is that while democracy has flowered recently in some other regions, it has failed to firmly take root in the sands of the Middle East. In fact, Israel is the only genuine democracy in the region, a fact that frustrates many citizens desiring a voice in the affairs of their countries. Such frustration surely spawns nothing-to-lose Islamic militants.

America's motivations (either democratization or WMDs) when President George W. Bush decided to invade Iraq in 2003 were considered by much of the world as a fig leaf for other reasons (imperial or oil-related). American governments have long sought to foster democratic values and civil society in the Middle East, but they have done so via peaceful methods. The U.S.'s commitment to electoral democracy has also wavered in this region when voters have chosen fundamentalist Muslims (Iran) or radical revolutionaries bent on the destruction of Israel (Palestinians and Hamas). America is also considered throughout the region to harbor deep-seated biases toward Israel resulting in turning a blind eye toward Israeli human rights atrocities in its occupied territories.

Oil politics tend to split the region, yet the Islamic religion supersedes disparities between rich and poor countries and manages to create a sense of shared identity in the area. There are significant differences between the Sunni and Shiite sects of Islam, and even more so between moderate and fundamentalist Muslims, but as Americans became acutely aware in the wake of September 11, 2001, during crises, unity against outsiders permeates the region. That this region has frequently been dominated by powerful outsiders also feeds suspicions about foreigners' motivations.

It has been a millennium since Islam's glory days, further fueling the frustration of those desirous of an Islamic renaissance. It is no coincidence that seventeen of the nineteen Al Qaeda terrorists who attacked America were from two countries where popular frustration about governmental repression runs especially high: Saudi Arabia and Egypt. The region's minorities include religious Jews, who control the state of Israel, and ethnic Persians, who practice the Shiite version of Islam and now control the state of Iran.

Many of the borders separating Middle Eastern countries were drawn arbitrarily by European powers during their colonial control of the region, which facilitates disputes over territory. For example, when Saddam Hussein's Iraq invaded Kuwait in 1990, Saddam complained that the British colonists' borders, drawn in 1921, had cut off Iraq from the Persian Gulf, and said that he intended to rectify that colonial injustice.

Most Middle Easterners are ethnic Arabs (180 million in the region), and one reason the region is considered the world's most volatile is that it has gyrated between peace and war between Israel and its Arab neighbors. The key issue for Arabs concerns the grievances of the Palestinians, or those Arabs who in 1948 were forced into exile from what is now Israel, upon losing their war with Jews over the common turf claimed by both of these peoples. This fundamental unresolved problem of a Palestinian diaspora in the region continues to fester as the core issue spilling over to complicate all others.

ASIA Some scholars have predicted that the twenty-first century will be the Pacific century. Upbeat prognoses for Asia's health are based on an economic explosion that has been underway there, particularly in East Asia. Japan's GDP per capita ($29,000) ranks among the world's highest, and in 2001, it ranked ninth in the HDI for quality of life. A few decades ago, observers considered Japan's "economic miracle" as one unlikely to be replicated in Asia (see Figure 6.5).

But recent success in the **newly industrialized countries** (NICs), such as Taiwan, South Korea, Singapore, Malaysia, and Hong Kong, has generated considerable optimism. Following Japan's example of an export-driven, managed economy, these NICs have risen to the top one-third of nations on the HDI index and have extended life

Newly industrialized countries ■ Asian countries that have embraced the international economy by practicing export-led growth to raise the standard of living in their countries

Figure 6.5
Experts possess various good reasons for predicting that the twenty-first century will be the Asian century.

expectancies to more than seventy years. By 1996, 125 of the world's 450 billionaires came from Asia, as did 25 percent of global economic output, as compared to only 17 percent fifteen years earlier.[10]

China's growth has been equally impressive. By loosening up its rigid, communist-style planned economy, and allowing freer economic competition, it averaged 9 percent growth rates during the 1990s. Considerable urbanization has accompanied China's economic boom, which has shifted from an agricultural- to an industrial-based system. Beijing has 13 million residents, and hosting the 2008 Olympics has given the city a newer and cleaner look. The glittering new center for international commerce, Shanghai, is rapidly catching up with Beijing.

Asia stands out among former colonies for finding ways to grow its economies, producing envy in other once-colonized regions such as the Middle East, Latin America, and Africa. Asia warrants special attention for another reason: one-half of humanity resides in this region. Fully one-fifth of the world's people (1.3 billion) live in China, although India's denizens are reproducing much more rapidly, recently becoming the second billion-plus country, and expected to surpass China by 2020 in population.

Japan has only 125 million people crowded into four resource-poor islands smaller than Montana. Yet its well-educated and united society has produced the world's third-largest economy. Japan's performance in the second half of the twentieth century warrants designation as comeback actor on the world stage. The traditional religions in Japan have long been Buddhism and Shintoism. Japan's deeply ingrained work ethic, however, tempts some to jest that workaholism seems to reign there. Hinduism is the prevalent religion in culturally diverse India, whereas China remains officially atheistic under its dictatorial communist government.

Western NGOs rail about human rights abuses in China, but the U.S. government under both Clinton and Bush has allowed commerce to trump democracy and human rights in much the same way that it has overlooked egregious human rights abuses by oil giant Saudi Arabia. The price of many consumer goods—from clothing to electronics to pirated DVDs—has been kept down as China has risen to the second-largest source of U.S. (surpassing Japan and trailing only Canada). U.S. political relations with East Asia have proven relatively congenial in recent years.

PACIFIC RIM As isolated islands with small populations, economies, and militaries, the Pacific Rim often gets overlooked. This region includes Australia, New Zealand, Fiji, Micronesia, and Western Samoa (see Figure 6.6). Geography, more than culture or economics, provides the cement for this diverse Pacific Rim world region, which includes only about 35 million people.

In general, these nations tend to combine traditional, pre-industrial cultures of indigenous peoples with the ways of white European settlers. Australia dwarfs the other nations in most comparisons, with its 3 million square miles of territory, 20 million inhabitants, life expectancy of seventy-seven years, GNP per capita of $25,000, and frequent ranking

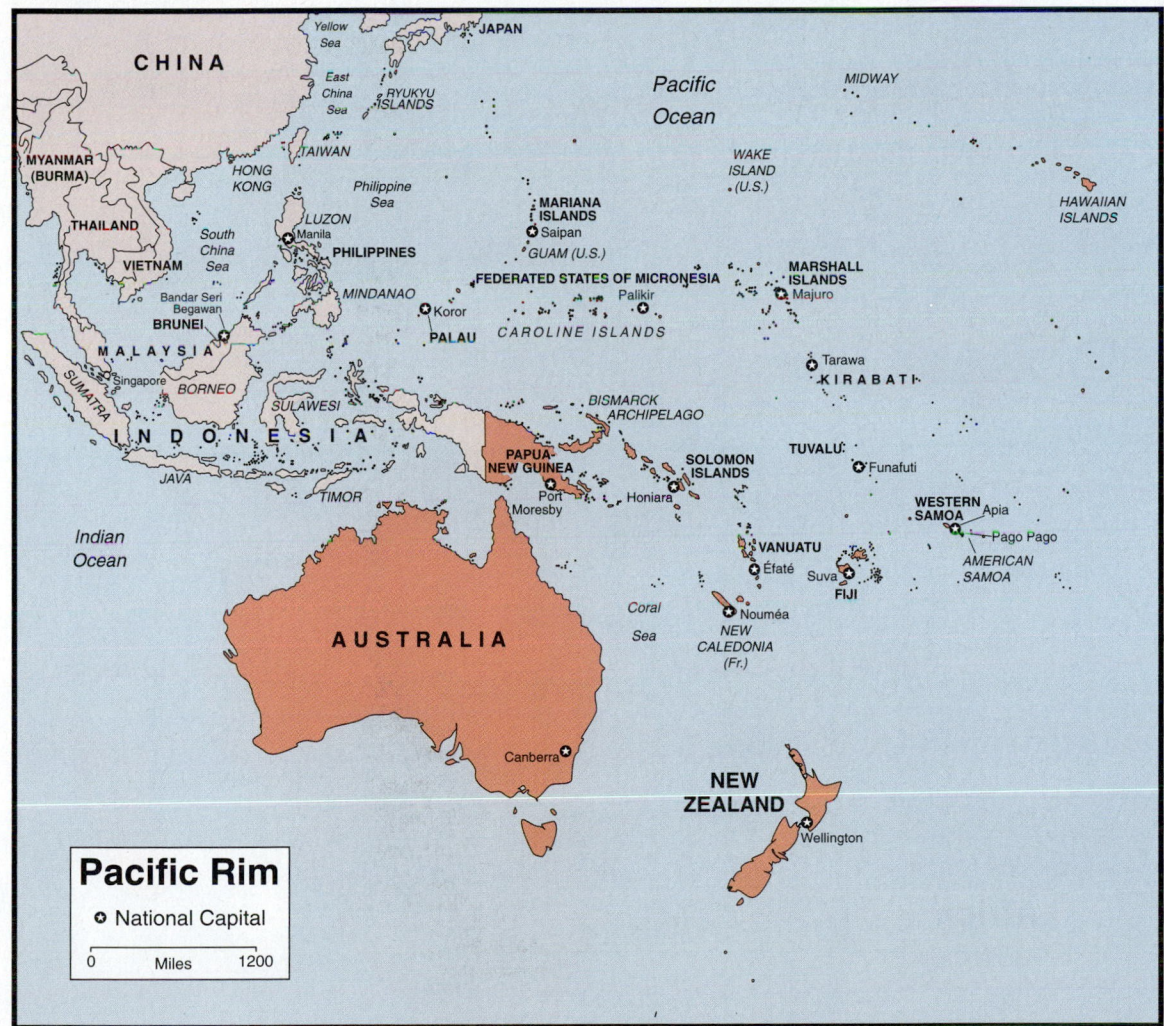

Figure 6.6
Low population, remoteness, and micro-states may contribute to the Pacific Rim being overlooked by many observers.

in the top five regarding quality of life. Nearby New Zealand shares many of Australia's quality of life benefits and also has a vibrant economy, including a vibrant wine sector.

SUB-SAHARAN AFRICA Forty-four countries comprise sub-Saharan Africa (south of the Sahara desert). All are former European colonies, and all have gained political independence since the 1960s. Most have encountered severe problems in the process of nation building, largely because the boundaries drawn by European colonial powers dating back to the Berlin conference of 1885, bear very little resemblance to traditional patterns of African tribal identity.

Many hundreds of languages are spoken. The world's very poorest people exist in countries such as Ethiopia ($125 GNP per capita), Tanzania ($120 GNP per capita), and Mozambique ($90 GNP per capita). The region's mean GNP per capita is a meager $550, which is accompanied by a brief life expectancy of fifty-two years. The twenty-five lowest-ranking countries on the 2001 HDI index were all in sub-Saharan Africa (see Figure 6.7).

Figure 6.7

No other region has been as severely decimated by the AIDS virus as sub-Saharan Africa.

The AIDS virus has devastated the African population to an extent unimaginable in other world regions. Death rates of 40 to 45 percent have been registered in some countries. The United States has marginally increased its assistance to Africa in recent years; however, the overall rate remains pitifully low. The U.N.-based Millennium Development Goals (MDGs) list number one among its eight goals for 2015 the elimination of extreme poverty now afflicting 1 billion people, mostly in Africa. Unprecedented private giving from the Bill and Melinda Gates Foundation totaling about $30 billion has been targeted largely at Africa. The continent's extensive natural wonders constitute resources with great potential for ecotourism growth.

Guarded optimism has arisen, however, in the southern cone of the continent, the Republic of South Africa. Previously condemned by the international community as a bastion of legalized racial segregation (apartheid), a very peaceful transfer of power from F. W. de Klerk's white Nationalist Party (NP) to Nelson Mandela's African National Congress (ANC) occurred in 1994, representing a very positive development.

Mandela had spent twenty-seven years as a political prisoner in Cape Town's notorious Robben Island jail. A series of "truth and reconciliation hearings" in the mid-1990s were employed to bring whites that had practiced violent oppression against blacks under the old system to account for their transgressions and, in most cases, to apologize and receive amnesty. The South African case represents a relatively rare exception in human history where a 90 percent majority of black South Africans essentially "turned the other cheek" after many decades of abuse by English and Dutch Europeans. Although that country still suffers considerable economic disparities, its political and social stories remain awe-inspiring.

LATIN AMERICA The region of Latin America (see Figure 6.8) includes Central American countries such as Guatemala, Panama, and Nicaragua, as well as South American states such as Brazil, Colombia, and Argentina. Per capita GNP and average life expectancy are very similar in both Central America and the much-larger South American continent, although South America's population doubles that of Central America.

European colonizers knowingly brought with them lethal weapons of war, as well as bringing lethal communicable diseases unwittingly (to which native peoples lacked immunity). The net result was that native peoples were more extensively wiped out by colonization in Latin America than in Africa, the Middle East, or Asia. The influence of the chief Latin American colonizers, the Spanish and the Portuguese, remains essential to understanding the common Latin American mind-set today. Overwhelmingly followers of the Roman Catholic religion, most people in the region speak the Spanish language, except in giant Brazil, which was colonized by Portugal. Although Latin Americans possess a regional identity, real differences exist nevertheless.

The region's tropical and subtropical climate contributes to an emphasis on extracting primary products from the earth, such as oil, copper, tin, and silver, in addition to growing agricultural products such as coffee, bananas, and sugar. Many observers believe the subtropical environment contributes to a slow-paced, siesta culture in which nothing work-related is so important that it cannot wait until tomorrow. For many years, undemocratic military dictatorships plagued Latin American politics. By the 1980s, however, a wave of democratization swept elected leaders into power in the region, and for the past two decades, the single glaring exception to holding democratic elections has been Fidel Castro's communist Cuba.

The United States has dominated Latin America more thoroughly, and for a longer period, than it has any other region. Well before America became a bipolar superpower in the Cold War era and then a global hegemon following the demise of the Soviet Union, geographic proximity, and the weakening grip of Spanish and Portuguese colonialists, Latin America represented a sphere of influence for the United States. The Monroe Doctrine enunciated in 1823 warned European powers to stay out of America's back yard.

An inherent tension, dilemma, or ambivalence has often confronted Latin American political leaders: whether to engage the giant to the north, seek friendly relations including

Figure 6.8

Latin American-ness derives in part from common colonial experiences with Iberian oppressors (Spain and Portugal), Catholicism, and Spanish, spoken in the great majority of countries.

foreign aid and American pressure to privatize economies and welcome international trade, or whether to play the "Yanqui Go Home" card, capitalizing on inevitable feelings of native resentment over U.S. bullydom, turn inward by engaging in self-reliance, nationalizing greater control over the ubiquitous American MNCs in the fruit, oil, or mining industries, and downplaying democratization.

NORTH AMERICA The last region, North America, consists of the United States and Canada (see Figure 6.9). However, with the 1994 initiation of the North American Free Trade Agreement (NAFTA), Mexico's classification becomes more complicated. Mexico's

Anglo-America

⊛ National Capital

| | | |
| 0 | Miles | 1,000 |

RUSSIA

Arctic Ocean

GREENLAND

CANADA

Pacific Ocean

Ottawa ⊛

UNITED STATES

Washington, D.C. ⊛

Atlantic Ocean

MEXICO

Gulf Of Mexico

Mexico City ⊛

Caribbean Sea

Figure 6.9
The United States' current economic, military, and cultural global hegemony make it seem like a region unto itself.

historical, cultural, economic, and political identity has been with Latin America. It is unclear to what extent NAFTA will bind Mexico with the United States and Canada, and whether those new links will overshadow Mexico's traditional sense of Latin identity. Mexico has undergone both economic growth and considerable democratization in recent years. Though Mexico was long a one-party system dominated by the Institutional Revolutionary Party (PRI), an upstart National Action Party (PAN) began to challenge PRI dominance in the 1980s.

This trend culminated in the 2000 election of PAN presidential candidate Vicente Fox. A former businessman and political novice, Fox promised to get rid of traditional Mexican cronyism and political corruption and run the government according to business principles such as Total Quality Management (TQM) and measurable performance factors to evaluate programmatic success or failure. He proceeded to choose a cabinet based not on personal ties but rather on merit and to create a more broadly based government of national unity. Was this the start of a new era of clean government in Mexico or just an aberration spurred by frustrated voters? The country's economy is no longer state-dominated or protectionist; in fact, it currently has a very open economy when compared to countries to its south. From 2001 to 2004, the economy under Fox grew briskly at a 7 percent pace annually, with exports keeping pace. In 2004, it ranked among the top ten leading exporter countries in the world.

Canada and the United States, already the world's largest trading partners, both enjoy moderate northern latitudes, rich arable lands, abundant natural resources, and sophisticated human resources. The U.S.'s population of 300 million towers over Canada's 30 million. Their economies rank among the world's most productive, with GNP per capita around $30,000; life expectancies average seventy-six years, and both countries routinely rank high globally in the HDI quality of life index, although the United States has never ranked first, and Canada leads all states, finishing first in HDI seven years running. The importance of Canada's role as good global citizen to its sense of national identity is analyzed in detail at the end of this chapter. Some people complain about Canada's cold winters, but with global warming, who knows how differently Canadian temperatures may appear in the year 2025?

Racial Identity

Biologists and anthropologists warn against exaggerating the significance of racial differences among *Homo sapiens* because evidence suggests that race is not a useful biological category, a view which the American Anthropological Association formalized in 1998 when it concluded that "race as a scientific fact does not exist." DNA evidence, in particular, shows that measurable human variation by race at the genetic level is very slight. Also, in the age of globalization, frequent migration has led to widespread inter-breeding between historically separate groups of people. Finally, racial classification has often contributed to discriminatory abuses against people viewed as different on the inside as well as on the outside.

Among social scientists, however, psychologists, sociologists, and political scientists are more likely to treat race as a significant factor in human affairs. Although race may not pass scientific muster as a biological fact, that does not prevent humans from believing that racial differences are more than skin deep, and that they influence human behavior accordingly. In other words, if people perceive race as more than merely superficial human variation, then those perceptions become essentially self-fulfilling; that is, by *believing* that race matters, it then *does* matter. Human definitions of social reality involve an objective dimension, but they also involve a subjective dimension.

A psychologist, then, might want to construct a laboratory research experiment to test whether subjects rate the individual attractiveness of participants in ways that reflect racially based definitions of beauty. A sociologist, on the other hand, could use a real-life research project to examine if subjects rely on racial differences to treat other subjects more, or less, favorably in their behavior toward them. Political scientists rely on extensive data banks to focus on the voting behavior of black Americans and to compare their voting patterns with those of whites and Asian-Americans, so that a great deal is now known about these comparisons.

Despite race's failure to rise to the level of a biological fact, if many humans view race as more than skin deep and therefore behave accordingly, social scientists have a legitimate interest discerning how this concept affects the human drama. And clearly one way that race matters relates to self-defined social identity. When asked the question, "With whom do you fit?" many people identify other members of a perceived racial category.

Yet race represents a problematic basis for establishing group identity credentials because absolutely no consensus whatsoever exists regarding specific categories. As few as three, and as many as twenty-nine, different races have been hypothesized by various scholars. Such designations usually rest on skin color, hair texture, facial features, and body shape. In 1758, Carolus Linnaeus, the Swedish founder of binomial nomenclature for species identification, also described four racial human categories: White (Caucasian), Red (American Indian), Yellow (Asiatic), and Black (African). How useful is Linnaeus' scheme in classifying U.S. golfer Tiger Woods, whose lineage cuts across all four of these supposed races? Furthermore, isn't it intriguing that the American news media refer to Tiger Woods as black, when that background represents a distinct minority of his heritage?

Far more troubling about seeing ourselves as members of a race, however, is that history is filled with cases of racial identity turning into the practice of racism, or discriminatory treatment of others on the basis of perceived racial identity. History's most virulent lessons warn us that racism sometimes turns into **genocide**. The 1941–1945 Nazi Holocaust slaughtering 6 million Jews represented the worst genocide on the planet, and it was not until the 1990s that the international community again held tribunals to punish genocide occurring in Rwanda and in Bosnia. Seeking to tap the mind-set of racists, Case Study 6.2 describes a clever research project undertaken by Raphael Ezekiel.

Genocide ■ The mass murder of a people on the basis of their race or other means of identity

Ethnic Identity

As Case Study 6.2 demonstrates, when it comes to human identity, employing race and **ethnicity** breeds ambiguity. Theoretically, race is supposed to relate to physical characteristics and ethnicity cultural ones, but these criteria tend to crumble when applied in real

Ethnicity ■ Human identity based on cultural heritage and common ancestry; a sense of belonging usually derives from country of origin, foods, dress, family names, language, music, or other customs

Case Study 6.2 Raphael Ezekiel: Observing Racism's Paucity of Critical Thinking

U.S. sociologist Raphael Ezekiel wanted to examine the workings of the racist mind for a sustained period of time and in close proximity. The standard social science approach for doing so is *participant observation*, where the researcher spends much time with the subjects of the study, observing them in their routine habitat. In this case, it was the leadership of the American Ku Klux Klan and neo-Nazi hate-groups that Professor Ezekiel wanted to observe. However, because Ezekiel is a Jew, he anticipated that the leaders of these groups would not cooperate with him, yet he did not want to deceive them. Therefore, he identified himself as a Jew and asked them directly if he could interview them and attend their regular meetings. To his surprise, they all consented.

The results of his research are reported in Ezekiel's book, *The Racist Mind*. He discovered that deep-seated fears about economic insecurity among unskilled whites are often exploited by hate-group leaders. Such underemployed individuals are willing to believe that a vaguely defined establishment, or system, is to blame for their poor economic prospects. This is the first core belief of hate-groups. Furthermore, as common-sensical thinkers, lacking the need for evidence demanded by critical thinkers, they readily accept the notion that the establishment is merely a set of puppets controlled from behind the scenes by an international conspiracy, usually manipulated by powerful Jews.

The essential definition of identity for hate-group members is typically race, and race is seen as an all-or-nothing category with nothing in between. People are considered members of a specific race, and their race thought of as shaping their attitudes, character, and behavior. In this simplistic world-view, you are either with us or against us, and for the neo-Nazi and Ku Klux Klan leaders whom Ezekiel studied, "us" is comprised of white Americans only.

Their leaders' minds also fixate on a second core belief: that life is war, specifically war between discrete racial groups, and this fact must be accepted realistically. Finally, any myth is plausible to these individuals (who could use a good course in critical thinking skills), and events are never what they may seem to be superficially; the schemes of the enemy are endless as they employ devious scenarios to dupe gullible whites. This is the third core belief of hate-groups.[11]

Racist leaders, of course, need common-sensical followers ready to internalize such specious ideologies. Critical thinkers represent the exception among humans, not the norm, and Ezekiel notes that "there is a ready pool of whites who will respond to the racist signal, and this population is always hungry for activity." For lives that are functioning poorly in a competitive economic environment, belonging to, and identifying with, a racist group delivers some sense of meaning. Fitting into something larger than themselves helps to rationalize away an unsatisfying personal existence in ways that conveniently place the blame on some other racial group. Racism can use various forms of social identity as a basis for hate, including ethnicity, but race generally proves easiest to employ. Scientific skepticism represents the essence of critical thinking, and it fails to register with these individuals.[12]

---

life. Both racial and ethnic ambiguities can easily be used to fuel the racist mind described by Ezekiel.

Might not Jews be better described as an ethnic group than as a race because it is mostly cultural characteristics such as religion, foods, and language (not physical traits) that bind them together? Yet they are often categorized as a separate race. Similarly, the U.S. Census Bureau uses the term "Hispanic origin" to identify people of Spanish cultural background, regardless of race. Because Hispanics are reproducing more rapidly than other ethnic groups in the United States, they are projected to become the largest ethnic or racial minority in America by the mid-twenty-first century, adding political significance to the question of how they are classified. Poverty is one of the highest barriers to quality of life, and, in America, major disparities separate whites, blacks, and Hispanics concerning poverty.

Sometimes, ethnicity can be associated with things worse than poverty. Developments in Bosnia, one of six republics that gained independence after the former Yugoslavia fractured in 1991, impressed some sobering lessons on America and its European allies. Bosnian Muslims, the largest ethnic group in Bosnia, were trapped between warring Bosnian (Eastern Orthodox) Serbs and Bosnian (Roman Catholic) Croats. In this bloody civil war, the Serbs (one-third of the population) controlled two-thirds of Bosnia's territory; the Croats (17 percent of population) held 30 percent of the land; but the Muslims (44 percent of population) possessed only 5 percent of the territory.

The Serbs engaged in widespread "ethnic cleansing," whereby they systematically deported or slaughtered Muslims as a means of negating them. Reports by neutral human rights NGOs of atrocities, including systematic rape of Muslim women, summary executions, and abusing prisoners in brutal concentration camps, revived European memories of the WW II Nazi Holocaust. Gradually, the world community became enraged and responded with economic sanctions, no-fly zones over Bosnia, and ultimate military intervention against the Serbian government and its armed forces.

For the first time in fifty years, leaders of a country (Serbia) have been arrested and indicted before an international tribunal for crimes against humanity. In 1998, the U.N. published a collection of all documents germane to the Criminal Tribunal for the Former Yugoslavia since its inception in 1993. Serbia's President, Slobodan Milosevic, was tried and convicted at The Hague (Netherlands) for war crimes against Bosnian Muslims. Possibly the most essential slogan to emerge after the 1941–1945 Nazi Holocaust was "Never Again." However, ethnic cleansing in Bosnia during the 1990s reminds us that the international community must remain ever vigilant against ethnic atrocities. Bosnia was one of two genocides to occur in the 1990s; the other was in the African country of Rwanda. Case Study 6.3 illustrates how some European colonial powers manipulated ethnicity to more effectively dominate and subjugate their colonies.

Case Study 6.3   Critical Thinking Journalism: Residue from Colonial Manipulation of Ethnic Identity

Philip Gourevitch, editor of the *Paris Review,* served as a foreign correspondent for many years, including duty in Rwanda during the 1990s. His 1998 book on the Rwandan genocide won the National Book Award for Nonfiction. Gourevitch argues that Western media too readily accept the common-sensical, unexamined assumption that contemporary conflicts in places such as Africa simply represent ancient ethnic/racial rivalries bubbling up again for the umpteenth time. His chronicling of genocide in Rwanda, however, digs deeper for more powerfully comprehensive explanations related to abuses of power for political self-interest. Common-sensical thinking just does not suffice when it comes to complex matters of human behavior, and this French journalist's stellar critical thinking skills enable us to get way beyond stereotypical thinking about ethic/racial rivalries.

The people who populate Rwanda emerged from hunter/gathers whose traditions were completely oral, not written. Therefore, accounts of Rwanda's precolonial history consist of competing mythologies, but it is the accounts of the victors that eventually subsume those of the vanquished. According to Gourevitch: "Power consists in the ability to make others inhabit your story of their reality—even when that story is written in their blood."

The uncertainty and malleability of precolonial Rwandan historical accounts enabled first German, and then Belgian, colonists to manipulate the vocabulary of national versus ethnic identity in ways congenial to the oppressors at the expense of the oppressed. The Belgian colonists in Rwanda set up a racist system strikingly similar to South Africa's notorious apartheid. In 1933, the Belgians conducted a census to create "ethnic" identity cards, categorizing all Rwandans into three categories: Hutu (85% of population), Tutsi (14% of population), or Twa (1% of population, and the few remaining indigenous pygmy peoples).

Gourevitch contends that the Belgian rulers were able to formalize and reify artificial ethnic identities (Hutu versus

Tutsi) in a country whose traditions actually consisted of long-standing nationalism and strong identity with the Rwandan state. Before colonialism, Hutus and Tutsis coexisted peacefully under a chiefdom system wherein all-powerful chiefs (considered deities) came from both Hutus and Tutsis. These subjects also spoke the same language, shared a common religion, lived in intermingled fashion, and intermarried freely. The author states "Ethnographers and historians have lately come to agree that Hutus and Tutsis cannot properly be called distinct ethnic groups."

To be sure, archetypical stereotypes existed concerning each group. Tutsis were largely herdsmen whose original possession of cattle made them wealthier than the farmers considered as Hutus. Tutsis over time came to be associated with higher political/economic status. Hutus looked squat, round-faced, dark-skinned, flat-nosed, thick-lipped, and square-jawed. The stereotypical Tutsi appeared lanky, long-faced, lighter-skinned, narrow-nosed, thin-lipped, and narrow-chinned. Like all stereotypes, such classifications broke down regarding many individuals at the margins regarding these characteristics.

Late colonialism was the heyday of "race science" in Europe. Colonial oppressors used Biblical sources or seemingly benign philosophies to mask brutalizing their colonial subjects. In Rwanda, the Belgians sent "race scientists," whose measurements of Hutu and Tutsi came to the self-fulfilling prophecy that Hutus and Tutsis were not only measurably different, but that such examination verifies the Tutsis' long-standing superiority over Hutus (which the mythology rendered supposedly traceable to a biologically based argument that the Tutsis' ancestors had emigrated southward from Ethiopia, thus possessing a more advanced bloodline of Abyssinian peoples).

This convenient fabrication enabled the Belgians to rationalize an artificial Hutu/Tutsi polarization quite at variance with the reality that Rwanda was a country possessing considerable nationalism. "Whatever Hutu and Tutsi identity may have stood for in the precolonial state no longer mattered; the Belgians had made ethnicity the defining feature of Rwandan existence." By playing upon these traditional rivalries, the Belgians were able to coopt the Tutsis into joint exploitation of the poorer and less powerful Hutus. High-sounding rhetoric was employed by the Belgians to mask their oppression, but oppression it remained.

Gourevitch dissects adroitly the relevance of this colonial backdrop to the genocide that exploded in the 1990s. So destructive was the mayhem that President Clinton traveled to Rwanda near the end of his presidency to formally apologize for not having done more to contain those events.[13] Gourevitch's careful reporting brought the same kind of critical thinking to the Rwandan genocide by cynical manipulation of ethnic identities by political elites. Gourevitch points out that even reporting by the venerable *New York Times* bit on the ancient animosities myth as a fallacy of single cause. Overt Hutu-Tutsi aggression had been the rare historical exception, not the norm. Meaningful explanations of what happened in Rwanda required more complex, nuanced critical thinking skills. And the adroit manipulation of political elites in 1994 was as important as it had been under Dutch colonialism in the 1930s.

Four films about Rwanda have appeared in recent years to provide texture and depth to the genocide story. One is a feature film by Terry George and Keir Pearson that has gotten good reviews, *Hotel Rwanda* (2004), whereas the other three are documentaries. *Shake Hands with the Devil: The Journey of Romeo Dallaire* (2004), by Canadian Peter Raymont, covers the U.N. peacekeeping force in Rwanda under the direction of this Canadian lieutenant general, in which he returns a decade later to discuss his frustrated efforts. An earlier documentary by the same filmmaker, *Rwanda: In Search of Hope* (1999), examined the plight of 500,000 children orphaned by the war. Finally, a PBS Frontline film, *Ghosts of Rwanda* (2004), contains interviews with key players such as Kofi Annan, General Romeo Dallaire, and Madeline Albright looking back at the tragic events of 1994. ◼

Trade-Driven Super Regions

There is no denying that the realm of economics has gained in relative importance globally in recent decades, nor that international trade is a big part of this process. The past three decades have seen the volume of global trade increase by 1,000 percent to more than $15 trillion per year. Today, the top four trading countries are the United States in North America, Japan and China in East Asia, and Germany in Europe. Coalescing around these four economic heavyweights are other intertwined economies (such as India) poised for more airtime in the competitive trade drama playing itself out.

In Europe, the process of regional cooperation has been underway for quite some time. Modest efforts began in 1951, with the formation of the European Coal and Steel Community (ECSC) but gathered greater momentum in 1958, when the Common Market was constructed. Step by step, by the 1990s, Europe had moved beyond this free-trade zone into genuine economic integration with the formation of the European Union (EU), including an all-European Central Bank and a single European currency called the euro. Plans were also laid for eventual political integration, leading some observers to predict that poised on the horizon was nothing less than a "United States of Europe."[14] Comparisons with the United States are apt because taken together, the EU's members at least match America in population, overall economic output, and quality of life. (EU Websites are cited at the end of the chapter.)

Public opinion surveys reveal that Europeans believe membership in the EU has improved their standard of living in ways that would not have occurred otherwise. Consequently, Europeans have augmented their national identity with a sense of European-ness.[15] If modern loyalties appear not only to follow the flag (state) but also follow the money (euro), economic integration in other regions may render regionalism increasingly relevant in defining human social identity.[16]

European integration is the prototype of an incipient triad of super-regional blocs: Japanese-led cooperative endeavors in East Asia with China challenging more each year, German-led cooperation in Europe, and U.S.-led cooperation in North America. Americans see the rival blocs as potential threats to the United States' status as the global economic hegemon. This perception contributed a sense of urgency to the Clinton Administration's mid-1990s efforts to construct a comparable trading bloc in North America (NAFTA). Until Clinton, Republicans had long owned the issue of international trade in U.S. politics, but party lines are much more difficult to discern regarding trade; in fact, momentum created by George H. W. Bush and expanded by Clinton was not picked up by George W. Bush after 2000.

Creation of the EU required four decades of incremental trust building. The United States hopes to achieve less ambitious results but more rapidly. In 1989, the United States and Canada signed a bilateral trade agreement. This arrangement was expanded in 1992, with the NAFTA agreement signed by the United States, Canada, and Mexico. All three national legislatures ratified NAFTA, and it went into effect on January 1, 1994. The NAFTA treaty totals 2,000 dense pages that stipulate schedules for reducing trade barriers gradually over a ten-year period in all but a few hundred out of more than 20,000 product categories.

Within five years, it was clear that NAFTA had succeeded in allowing a freer flow of not only goods, but also services and investments among the United States, Canada, and Mexico. Total intra-NAFTA trade for 1998 amounted to nearly $500 billion.[17] In 1994, President Bill Clinton announced that Chile would be the first country admitted into an expanded NAFTA, which might eventually encompass the entire hemisphere.

A rapidly changing world requires successful competitors to think ahead. The psychology of the trilateral economic competition (U.S. and North America, Japan and Asia, Germany and Europe), allows no one side to fall too far behind while the others embark on new paths of development. Currently, this applies to U.S. concern over exclusion from a global economy dominated by powerful regional free-trade zones. The psychological pressure to keep up with competitors in this situation resembles that which drove the spiraling arms race higher and higher during the Cold War.

Thus far, the third leg of this regional trade triangle, in Asia, has barely gotten off the ground. In 1989, the Asia-Pacific Economic Cooperation (APEC) began annual meetings aimed at growing into a regional trade organization. A total of eighteen countries participate, including Japan, China, Taiwan, and Malaysia, but according to Japanese diplomat Nobuo Matsunaga, "There are a variety of concerns, especially among the developing nations, that we proceed with caution."[18] APEC has set up a secretariat in Singapore, but symbolic of its dubious status is the fact that it has yet to tag on a word to finish off its name with a word such as Asian Pacific Economic "Organization."

Corporate Identity (MNCs)

As the new millennium dawned, a spate of corporate mergers and acquisitions left observers dizzied by merger mania. Of the one hundred largest economies on the planet, fifty-one were MNCs, and forty-nine were states. The Global Forum on Agricultural Research cited figures describing merger mania in action. Two decades prior, thousands of seed-producing companies existed, none of which controlled even 1 percent of market share. In 2000, ten companies had seized control of 30 percent of the world market. In 1980, there were sixty-five companies producing materials used in agriculture, but by 2000, ten companies remained controlling 90 percent of that market. By 2000, the number of companies alive in the world grain trade had shrunk to five, and in 2003, Cargill, Bungi, and Dreyfus had gobbled up the others so that this triptych accounts for 90 percent of world trade in corn, wheat, cocoa, coffee, and pineapples; 80 percent of trade in tea; and 70 percent in rice and bananas.

Many NGOs have been quick to point out what they consider to be a growing identity trend involving corporations (MNCs) filling some of the space left by shifting of loyalties away from states. They worry that states are becoming increasingly unwilling or unable to control powerful MNCs operating within their borders. Regulating the behavior of these profit-driven, powerful, resource-laden entities has become much more problematic than it was during the Cold War era. MNCs possess great skill at influencing popular attitudes and beliefs via public relations campaigns employing sophisticated propaganda. Does it seem plausible that MNCs might replace states as the most powerful sovereigns operating on the twenty-first century world stage?

In his book, *States Versus Markets,* economist Herman Schwartz makes two major points relative to the recent diminution of state control over MNCs. First, although those of us with relatively short historical memories dating back only to the end of WW II, may feel shocked at the recent phenomenon of markets overwhelming state policies, that actually represents going "back to the future," because it was the nature of business as usual during the global economy of the nineteenth century. In other words, the relatively high capability of states to exercise control over international commerce from 1945 to 2000 represented an aberration, not the norm. Second, identifying other economists feeling similarly, Schwartz expresses the view that not only does such MNC freedom constitute the norm, it is also preferable to scenarios in which states hamstring market forces driving corporate growth.

Tens of thousands of protestors who have demonstrated against the IMF, WTO, and World Bank in many other cities since Seattle in 1999 would disagree with Schwartz' analysis. Worried about a "race to the bottom," critics consider the outsourcing of manufacturing and service sector jobs from the MDCs to the LDCs as responsible for gross human rights abuses in Mexican, Chinese, or Indian sweatshops. Such critics have little faith in past MNC-driven globalization from above and promote solidarity aimed at globalization from below in the future.

Canadian journalist Naomi Klein's book, *No Logo,* contends that the massive wealth and cultural influence of MNCs since the mid-1980s has been based on a little-noticed corporate strategy responsible for shifting from producing products to producing *brands.* In such a brave new branded world, when people think they are buying Nike or Benetton, they do so because MNCs have become successful meaning brokers. Buyers really want the sense of identity with a brand's supposed lifestyle and status. If these purchases happen to be imitation knock-offs from China, that doesn't seem to matter much. In other words, MNCs are now selling social identity.

A documentary film by Mark Achbar and Jennifer Abbott, *The Corporation* (2004), details the rise to power of corporations and is adept at explaining the historic legal significance of defining the corporation as a "person." This legal status affords corporations the protection of the Fourteenth Amendment to the U.S. Constitution. Thus, MNCs receive the rights but not the corollary responsibilities accruing to individual persons.

North (MDCs) versus South (LDCs)

Economic concerns have received more attention in the post-Cold War era, especially the gap between the more-developed countries (MDCs) and the less-developed countries (LDCs). The MDCs, located mostly in the Northern Hemisphere, enjoy an average GDP per capita of more than $25,000 and life expectancy over seventy-five years. In sharp contrast, Southern Hemisphere LDCs have a GNP per capita of about $2,500 and average life expectancy of sixty-three years. Roughly one-fifth of humans living in the North produce about four-fifths of global wealth, whereas the poorer four-fifths of humanity produce a mere one-fifth of global income.[19]

Even worse, the gap between MDCs and LDCs continues to widen. The U.N.'s *Poverty Report 2000* concludes that "Progress toward reducing poverty has been minor, and the number of income-poor in the developing world is again on the rise after having declined slightly until 1996."[20] Another 2000 U.N. report finds that thirty-four of the forty-eight least developed countries have an "external debt burden that is unsustainable according to international criteria."[21] Debt among LDCs is a key issue because heavy foreign debt seriously inhibits the ability of those countries to develop economically. It is precisely the LDC debt issue that anti-IMF and anti-World Bank protesters highlighted when they disrupted global meetings in Seattle, Ottawa, Washington, DC, and elsewhere.

In 2001, the U.S. economy out-produced Japan's by one-third, yet Japan led the world in foreign aid. U.S. aid to the poorest forty-eight countries at the turn of the century amounted to only $3.74 per capita, with the largest U.S. recipients at that time being Israel, Egypt, and Colombia, clearly based upon geopolitical rather than economic development reasons. George W. Bush's 2003 invasion of Iraq then led to huge amounts of aid going to prop up that beleaguered state.

Poor Southern Hemisphere countries such as Somalia or Haiti or Bangladesh blame the legacy of colonial exploitation for their problems, and they have a point. Southern economies possess deep structural differences from those in the North. For example, LDCs usually rely on only a few primary products extracted from the earth for their income, whereas MDCs rely on many products, including manufactured goods and sophisticated services. Agriculture makes up 14 percent of the income of LDCs but only 2 percent of the income of MDCs. Between 1980 and 1999, the price of manufactured goods rose by 2.6 percent, whereas the price of agricultural products actually shrank by 0.2 percent.[22]

The South demands special privileges intended to make them more competitive in the global economy, akin to affirmative action programs that exist within the United States. But rich Northern countries suggest that LDCs remain poor chiefly because of their internal inefficiency and corruption, rather than their colonial legacy, and they also have a point. One such internal problem is the greater inequality of income distribution that occurs within poor countries. The World Bank measures income inequality via the Gini Index, which is expressed as a percentage in which an index of 100 implies perfect inequality, and an index of 0 implies perfect equality. The Gini index percentages for selected MDCs is consistently lower than for selected LDCs in Table 6.1. This reflects the higher income inequality that exists among poor countries.

More numerous and more agitated about the North–South gap, the LDCs bring more radical solutions to the international agenda. The MDCs, not only more wealthy but also more influential in many other ways, tread with caution in the dialogue over North–South issues. But even Northern countries realize that globalization has swept away the luxury of believing world poverty to be *their* problem.[23] Nevertheless, precious little agreement exists between rich and poor over how to deal with these disparities.

Table 6.1

GINI INDEX OF INCOME INEQUALITY FOR SELECTED MDCs AND LDCs (1.0 = PERFECT EQUALITY)

Country	Category	Gini Index
Sierra Leone	LDC	62.9%
Central African Republic	LDC	61.3%
Swaziland	LDC	60.9%
Nicaragua	LDC	60.3%
Brazil	LDC	59.1%
Honduras	LDC	59.0%
Paraguay	LDC	57.7%
Chile	LDC	57.5%
Zimbabwe	LDC	56.8%
Guinea-Bissau	LDC	56.2%
Russia	(transition)	48.7%
United States	MDC	40.8%
United Kingdom	MDC	36.1%
Australia	MDC	35.2%
Spain	MDC	32.5%
Italy	MDC	27.3%
Norway	MDC	25.8%
Japan	MDC	24.9%
Austria	MDC	23.1%

Source: World Bank, *World Development Indicators,* 2001: http://www.worldbank.org/.

Mega-Cultures

Most international conflict in centuries past was caused by territorial, political, or economic disagreements. Harvard political scientist Samuel Huntington, however, predicted in 1993 that future global conflicts will spring increasingly from differences among seven mega-cultural identities, larger than states but less than global in scope. The mega-cultures he envisions coming into conflict include Western, Confucian, Japanese, Islamic, Hindu, Slavic-Orthodox, and Latin American mega-cultures.[24]

The term Huntington used to describe the actors in such future dramas (civilizations) was possibly ill-chosen because it has multiple meanings, and many other social scientists use it differently from the way he employs it. Nevertheless, the cement holding his mega-cultures together consists of common values, beliefs, and lifestyles—the quintessential stuff of culture. Generally, religious conviction represents the highest expression of shared cultural identity that Huntington describes in each of these seven key identities.

Huntington reasons that as modern communications such as television, movies, and the Internet spread Western civilization's secular and materialistic lifestyle values worldwide, traditional mega-cultures will feel threatened and fight back, eventually resulting in a confrontation of "the West versus the rest." His bold assertion that the West would come under unprecedented frontal attack from disaffected religious traditionalists, such as conservative Muslims, was regarded as prescient by some after the September 11, 2001, assault on America, as Americans scrambled to learn more about the Islamic mega-culture.

Some other scholars, however, accepted Huntington's basic premise of likely confrontation between the West and Islam, and between the West and Confucian (Chinese) culture, but downplayed the prospects for conflict between the West and Japanese, Hindu, Slavic-Orthodox, and Latin American mega-cultures.[25] Unquestionably, Huntington's bold prognostications generated considerable scholarly discourse, and he received many critical rejoinders.

One Global Community

Some scholars see human identity as progressing from smaller to larger units: from individual to family to tribe to nation to region to planet. Ultimately, this view suggests identity will culminate in realizing that, as members of the same species, the forces that bind us supercede those that divide us. Perhaps the most popular musical expression of a global community was ex-Beatle John Lennon's song, "Imagine," in which he asks listeners to imagine a world not of countries or wars but rather of communal identity.

In a similar spirit, futurist Howard Rheingold believes that the electronic superhighway leads *not* to Samuel Huntington's nightmarish clashing mega-cultures, but rather, to a virtual community; that is, to a cooperative world of shared interests and benefits.[26] In Rheingold's idealistic vision, contemporary globalization is not the culmination of a process but merely its beginning. His Website, Electric Minds, is intended to "lead the transformation of the Web into a social Web."[27] If Rheingold is correct in predicting that the Internet will facilitate a global community, it will be laced with irony. The Internet began in the 1960s as a Pentagon-funded military communications network capable of surviving a nuclear war—an impervious decentralized fishnet. The Defense Department set up its own system in the 1980s, leaving the Internet to the universities. Harvard University Black Studies scholars Kwame Anthony Appiah and Henry Louis Gates have edited a volume that uses regional experts from all part of the globe to identify the greatest cultural achievements in each locale. Appiah and Gates contend that what is loosely referred to as "Western" culture is largely a compendium of customs absorbed from around the world during European colonial expansion, for example, the numbering system borrowed from ancient India, or the protection of Greek rationalism (that triggered the Renaissance around 1500) by Arab Muslim scholars who nurtured that intellectual flame during Europe's Dark Ages (500–1500).

Appiah and Gates point out that "Western" culture was able to usurp much from other regions because of the military and political dominance of Europe for the past 500 years. To illustrate the subtle continuation of Western influence, they cite the universality of the Christian dating system (Christ as beginning of history), despite the fact that Christians are a minority in the world.

Furthermore, they assert that a trend toward a "global culture" has been underway for the past 500 years under the guise of Western culture, leading to "the first period of a truly global human history, bringing the human species into a single political, economic, and cultural system whose details are, of course, the work of people from all around the globe." They also emphasize that if we are to celebrate the significant achievements of humanity's global culture, then we must also "more frankly acknowledge the evils that were done in the course of Europe's expansion."[28]

The spirit of global idealism has only sporadically influenced American foreign policy, but political scientist Jerel Rosati argues that the essence of U.S. President Jimmy Carter's 1970s foreign policy consisted of a "quest for global community." Although side-stepped by events and obstacles, Carter's idealistic beliefs represented an agenda to further the same spirit of global community inspiring John Lennon in the 1960s and Howard Rheingold in the 1990s.[29]

After the devastation of World War II, many thinkers advocated the creation of some kind of a world federation, or a global government, hoping to avoid a reprise of global warfare that had rocked the twentieth century. In 1947, the World Federalist Movement (WFM) was founded in Switzerland, dedicated to someday achieving the goal of world federation. Its headquarters is now in New York City, across from the U.N. complex. Its president is the British actor Peter Ustinov.

Territorial Impediments to Global Community

Optimistic one-worlders have offered some encouraging projections for the future. But good reasons can be given to question such visions of universally shared identity. One is humanity's historical penchant for *territoriality*. As individuals, we carry about "as an extension of ourselves an envelope of territory called our personal space." Although the dimensions of personal space differ from culture to culture, all humans have a sense of portable territory that we carry around with us.[30]

In the group context, humans also possess a sense of territory. Some scholars compare expressions of social space, such as street gangs using graffiti or sports teams performing better in home games than away games, as analogous to dogs urinating on trees or deer using glandular secretions to establish territorial boundaries. Scientists who study questions of territoriality borrow extensively from biology and are called *ethologists*. Modern ethologists such as English scholar Robert Ardrey emphasize the similarities between *Homo sapiens* and our primate cousins. Thus, they believe that an excellent way to learn about humans is to study closely related animals such as apes and chimpanzees. Ardrey boldly claims that "the territorial nature of humanity is genetic and ineradicable."[31]

More humanistic social scientists such as Mel Gurtov identify qualities unique to *Homo sapiens,* such as complex symbolic communication through language, artistry, spirituality, conceptualization, and consciousness, as refutations of the ethologist's assertion that humanity is but another species in the animal kingdom.[32]

Territoriality sometimes entails excessive psychological attachment to relatively worthless bits of turf. Every piece of land on the globe is

Personal space at work.

claimed by some state, regardless of its value. At times, humans have engaged in irrational and self-defeating violence to secure or maintain unimpressive territorial spoils. A study by U.S. political scientist Kal Holsti concludes that more than half of all conflicts since WW II contained a significant territorial dimension, and that since the Peace of Westphalia in 1648, "the territorial aspect of international conflict remains fairly constant."[33]

When humans engage in emotional outbursts of turfmanship, violence seems comprehensible from the ethologist's perspective as a primordial urge run amok. Take, for instance, the 1983 Falklands War between Great Britain and Argentina (two well-armed states). The Falklands Islands over which the war was fought don't amount to much militarily, economically, or geographically. But the two sides' emotional attachment to the symbolic status of the Falklands seems understandable as a brain cramp or a brief retreat from reason. More perplexing are cases of stubborn, long-term territorial fixation maintained in the face of genuinely self-defeating costs, such as Case Study 6.4's Kurile Islands saga involving Russia and Japan.

Case Study 6.4   The Kurile Islands: Still Stubborn After All These Years

When the war in the Pacific was ending in 1945, the United States asked the Soviet Union to assist in defeating Japan. Although the Soviets entered the fray only a few days prior to Japan's surrender, the Soviet Union benefited from the spoils of war, including the Kurile Islands, a small chain located only three miles from Japanese Hokkaido (see Figure 6.10). No formal treaty was ever signed between these two ex-belligerents because of Japan's unwillingness to accept losing the Kuriles.

For decades after WW II, these minor islands remained a part of the U.S.S.R. during the long East–West Cold War. Tokyo loyally supported American foreign policy at a time when the American bloc viewed the Soviets as evil incarnate. So the face-off over the Kuriles long seemed like just another example of Soviet Cold War intransigence. Then, between 1989 and 1991, communism in eastern European and the Soviet Union died, quasi-democratic systems were instituted, and Russia and the other successor states suddenly became U.S. allies and trading partners. With Cold War animosities relegated to history's dustbin, Japan hoped that its pleas for returning the Kurile Islands would finally be honored.

The relative condition of each country's economy also contributed to expectations of resolving the crisis. Russia was a post-communist basket case in the 1990s, while Japan was the second richest country on earth. Whereas Russia was resource-rich, Japan was resource-poor. Russia needed foreign assistance, and Japan was the world's number one aid donor. Such would *seem* the stuff of done deals: a win-win scenario where Japan swaps extensive development assistance to regain the Kurile spoils of WW II.

In 1990, the Japanese offered then-President Mikhail Gorbachev a $26 billion swap for the

disputed islands, as well as technical assistance to explore Russia's untapped natural resources in eastern Siberia and extensive purchases of Russian raw materials. When the Soviets balked at the deal, the patient Japanese waited two

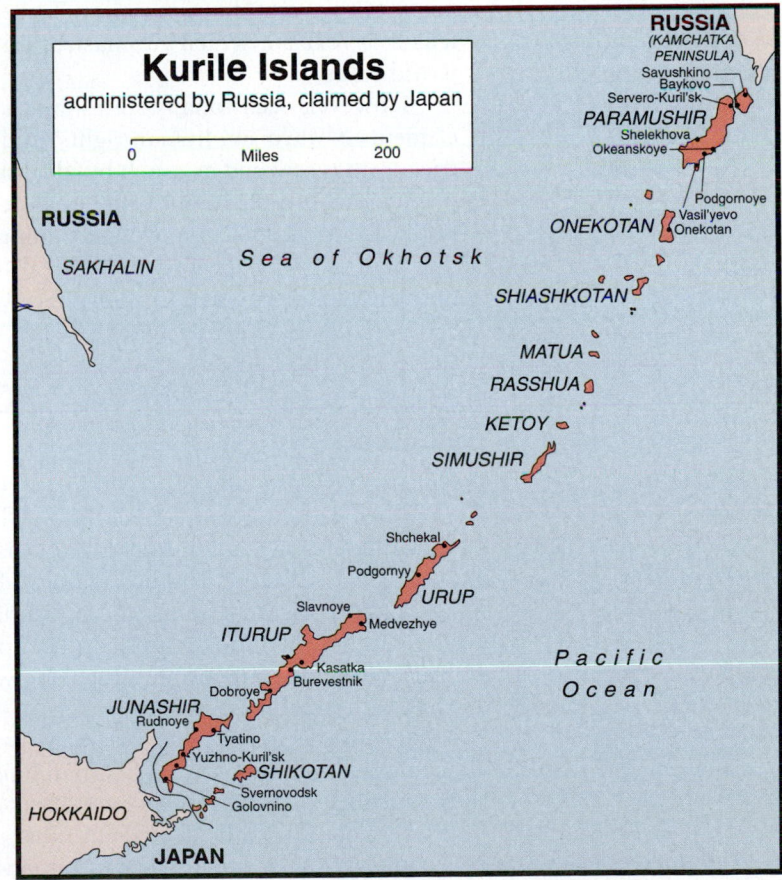

Figure 6.10
States have a long history of squabbling over the symbolic value of small pieces of turf, but it's hard to top Russia's stubbornness regarding the Kurile Islands.

more years before proposing a similar package to Gorbachev's successor, Boris Yeltsin.

However, Yeltsin had earlier pledged that Russia would never consider the transfer of "one square meter" of Russian territory; thus he too backed away from the incentives dangled before his eyes. Meanwhile, Russia's potential-laden area of eastern Siberia remained undeveloped as Moscow clung to "four rocky specks" of turf inhabited by only 50,000 people, and Japan's world-class economy looked elsewhere to invest its yen.

For more than five decades since 1945, the Kuriles saga has remained a major contentious issue for the Japanese. During the Cold War, the Russian people were subjected to communist propaganda asserting that Japan's claims to the Kuriles were specious, and that the islands had been won with Soviet blood, and thus were sacred. But since the collapse of the Soviet Union, historians and journalists have enjoyed the freedom to explore such issues more complexly, with all sides of the Kuriles debate finally being heard.

Nevertheless, even under Yeltsin's successor, Vladimir Putin, no agreement with Japan has been struck. Most outside observers believe that warmer Russo-Japanese relations would clearly serve Russia's economic and political interests because Japan is a very important player in the global economy. How do you explain the behavior of Russia in the Kuriles case, and do the views of any scholar discussed under the territoriality concept seem relevant here?[34] ■

Chapter 6 has examined various forms of human social identity as competitors for the hearts and minds of humanity in the twenty-first century. In a rapidly changing world, identities are surely in a state of flux. Despite 350 years as the dominant actor on the world stage, states can no longer assume that they will automatically warrant the default position when its comes to the loyalties of their citizens, especially when the state's track record in solving the vexing array of GIs covered in Chapter 1 appears dubious at best. It is axiomatic that states pursue a vision of their national interest when formulating foreign policy. Typically, the national interest is seen through the lenses of **realism**, which emphasizes military security while accumulating power on the world stage.

However, occasionally states take a bigger view of their national interest that entails elements of altruism, human rights, and international justice. In these rare cases, countries seem motivated as much by **idealism** as by realism. Few countries consistently demonstrate idealism, but Canada has earned a reputation for good global citizenship. In developing this theme, we will summarize the content, methods, resilience, and uniqueness of Canada's brand of idealism among states, bolstering its shaky sense of national identity discussed in Case Study 6.1.

Realism ■ A sober theory of world affairs placing a premium on competitive national interest defined as power and suspicious of cooperative endeavors among nations

Idealism ■ An optimistic approach to the world believing that human reason can find ways to avert war and promote cooperation by finding common elements uniting all peoples

Cosmopolitanism ■ An openminded and worldly set of humane values that is accepting of other lifestyles and embraces human diversity

Canadian Good Global Citizenship

Content

Greek-Cypriot scholar Costas Melakopides' book on Canadian foreign policy since WW II opens with the statement that "The idealist component of Canadian foreign policy reflects the endorsement by its makers of a set of interests conditioned by *humane values*."[35] The essence of these values Melakopides describes as the primacy of justice, satisfaction of global human needs, duties beyond Canadian borders, respect for human rights, generosity, moderation, and cooperation with other actors. The author says these principles add up to **cosmopolitanism,** which stands in sharp relief against the parochialism of most states (see Figure 6.11).

Idealism helps to temper the narrower sense of national interest that focuses more on short-term national benefits than long-term global benefits. Realists believe, pessimistically, that gains made by other countries mean equal losses for us (a win-lose situation), whereas idealists have faith that gains made by other countries will create future benefits for us as well (a win-win situation). Canada's policies on the environment, foreign aid, arms control, and human rights are widely regarded as idealist. Melakopides concludes his book suggesting that such cosmopolitanism is "the most rational and ethical policy for Canada because it strengthens its self-definition as a caring, enlightened, generous, and highly-civilized state."[36]

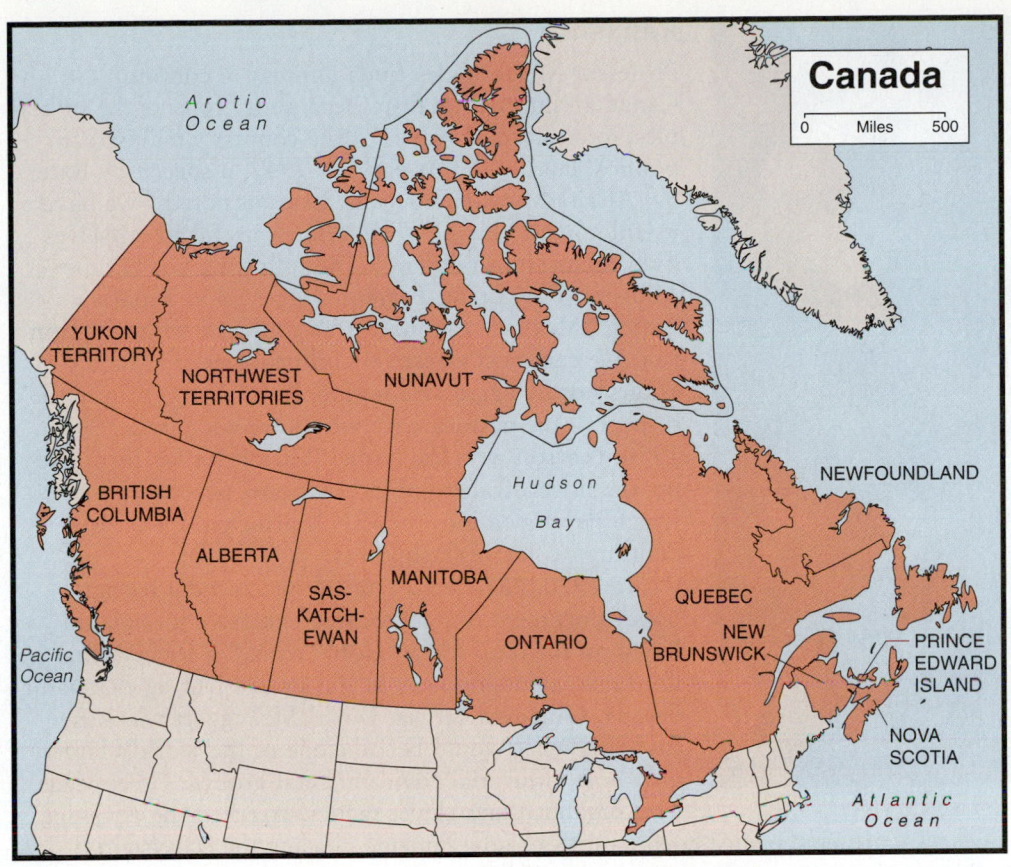

Figure 6.11
Often taken for granted by the U.S., Canada possesses a well-earned reputation among scholars and statesmen for its good global citizenship.

Methods

If humane idealism pervades the *substance* of Canadian foreign policy, then its *style* is equally well-known for its **multilateralism.** Often called multilateral diplomacy, this approach to statecraft operates collectively within international bodies and with a variety of other actors as a productive means of problem-solving. Operationally, it is the opposite of unilateral diplomacy, whereby states act alone, thus avoiding the give-and-take characteristic of multilateral diplomacy. The multilateralist approach is highly cooperative while unilateralism is typically competitive.

For six decades, multilateral diplomacy has been the style most favored by both the Canadian public and its leaders, and for a mid-level power, its influence in forums like the U.N. and the WTO has been impressive. Unlike the United States, Canada has always championed the work of the U.N. Such organizations are seen by middle powers as helpful in constraining the activities of great powers. For Canada, incentives to limit the exercise of American power are exacerbated by its proximity. The snug fit between idealism in the *content* of its foreign policy and multilateralism in the *process* of its foreign policy does not result from random chance. Rather, these two qualities complement each other as Canada projects its self-image abroad.

Early on, Canadian leaders realized that for a modest power to influence high global politics, it needed international forums to express Canadian values and to forge ties with other middle powers, often enabling it to act as "spokesman for the chorus." This philosophy has contributed to actions seeking moderation, cooperation, and mediation. Multilateralism has provided Canada with the intended diplomatic opportunities. University of Alberta political scientist Tom Keating points out that "Domestic economic interests have also been important in shaping the government's involvement in multilateral activities, since the Canadian economy is unusually dependent on international trade."[37]

Multilateralism ■ The term describing states willing to act in concert with other countries to work toward some mutually beneficial endeavor

Good global citizenship in the form of 'multilateralism' has deep roots in Canada's culture of humane values and social responsibility.

Canada's Lester Pearson won the 1956 Nobel Peace Prize for devising the clever and effective strategy of U.N. "peacekeeping" operations.

Peacekeeping ■ The process of placing U.N. troops from neutral countries in between potential combatants as a deterrent to violence

Resilience

Professor Melakopides finds impressive continuity in Canadian internationalism because it "reflects the principles, interests, and values of the country's mainstream political culture."[38] As early as 1947, a speech by External Affairs Minister Louis St. Laurent noted "We have a useful part to play in world affairs, useful to ourselves by being useful to others." The following year Prime Minister (PM) Lester Pearson suggested in a major speech "Modesty should not be confused with isolationism. We can most effectively influence international affairs not by aggressive nationalism but by earning the respect of the nations with whom we cooperate."[39] In 1956, Pearson won the Nobel Peace Prize for formulating the novel strategy of international **peacekeeping,** which developed into the U.N.'s principal means of defusing explosive flashpoints.

In 1970, PM Pierre Trudeau produced a foreign policy document that advocated extensive foreign aid based on the need for a "global ethic," a concept that he implemented assiduously in the 1970s. During that same decade, Canadian activist David McTaggart was busy founding what would become one of the world's largest and most influential environmental groups: Greenpeace. This organization's clever tactics stretched the envelope for peaceful protests against corporations or governments abusing the ecosystem.

Even in the 1980s, under conservative PM Brian Mulroney (whose election campaign favored advancing Canadian business interests), Canada was nevertheless "actively committed to human rights issues abroad." Canada exercised leadership by actively working against the legalized racial segregation (apartheid) then operating in South Africa. Canada favored strong economic sanctions against South Africa, while Great Britain did not. PM Mulroney stood up to feisty British PM Margaret Thatcher at a 1987 international meeting and asserted the morality of the Canadian position on South Africa.[40]

The 1990s witnessed probably the greatest success in Canada's history of global idealism. Its delegation was very active in setting the agenda for the 1992 Earth Summit held in Rio de Janeiro, and the director of this huge global town meeting was Canadian diplomat Maurice Strong. In 1995, the WTO was created by treaty and included nearly all countries in the world. Canada was concerned about the vulnerability of some of its trading sectors and won "a number of important victories vindicating Canadian championship of strong dispute settlement provisions."[41]

But nothing Canadian caught the world's fancy as swiftly as a policy enunciated in the mid-1990s by the Liberal Party's PM, Jean Chrétien, and his External Affairs Minister, Lloyd Axworthy. Based on the idea that the narrow Cold War view of security as merely military security must give way to what they called *human security*. The government saw human security's goal as enhancing "quality of life." According to Minister Axworthy, it includes security against economic privation, human rights guarantees, rule of law, social equity, and environmental integrity.[42] Canada has ranked number one in the world on the U.N.'s HDI seven times.

In 1995, the Government created within the Ministry of External affairs a Global Issues Bureau to coordinate Canadian policy regarding separate but related GIs. These included the environment, human rights, child protection, terrorism, drugs, health, and migration—all of which were considered by Canada as threats to human security. Sometimes average Canadian citizens assisted their government's humane agenda. In the late 1990s, thirteen-year-old Toronto schoolboy Craig Kielburger launched a fund-raising campaign to support victims of child labor practices in India. He was so successful that he ended up traveling to India to meet some of the children he had assisted. PM Chrétien was also in India at that time, and the two Canadians met in a well-publicized effort to jawbone against abusive child labor.

In 1997, Minister Axworthy led Canada's successful campaign to outlaw land mines when 122 countries signed the Anti-Personnel Mines Ban in Ottawa, Canada. Each year, 26,000 people (mostly rural farmers) are killed or maimed by land mines left over from previous wars. However, Axworthy's leadership in producing this treaty could not convince the largest makers of land mines (the United States, Russia, and China) to agree to a ban, and they did not sign it. Nevertheless, Canada immediately created a $100 million fund to support implementation of the anti-mine treaty.

Also in the late 1990s, Canada organized a dialogue group of foreign ministers to coordinate anti-drug policies, called the Hemispheric Drug Strategy. Minister Axworthy traveled to Jamaica (then a new Caribbean drug haven) to establish links between his human security policy and the illegal drug issue. Both Canadian activity and U.S. passivity were much in evidence regarding a treaty that created an International Criminal Court (ICC)—the first world court ever with power to prosecute individuals accused of war crimes and **genocide.**

Uniqueness

While American President Ronald Reagan was downplaying the significance of human rights in the 1980s, a few middle powers kept this issue on the global agenda by forming a group known as the Like-Minded Nations. Canada, Denmark, Finland, Sweden, and the Netherlands led this human rights group. To date, Canada remains the only participant in all U.N. peacekeeping endeavors. Canadian Major General Lewis McKenzie personifies his nation's commitment, as his record of serving in leadership capacities during eight different U.N. peacekeeping missions remains unrivaled.

Costas Melakopides observes that Canada's "enormous international prestige demonstrated that there was a book to be written."[43]

The United States and Canada possess the world's largest trading relationship and function as allies in most situations. However, as a more traditional practitioner of realism, the United States is sometimes discomfited by Canadian diplomacy, as evidenced in the 1997 Land-Mine Treaty mentioned previously. "Canada has used its influence, diplomatic suasion, and moral authority in multilateral forums often in opposition to American wishes."[44]

For more than forty years the United States imposed trading sanctions against Cuba and forbade its citizens from traveling there. America's Cold War strategy included leaning on its allies to isolate Cuba. Canada, however, maintained its trading relationship with Cuba, and a steady stream of Canadians have made their way to Cuba for inexpensive winter escapes during long winters.

Another Cold War example involved the Vietnam War. The Pierre Trudeau Government decided in 1966 to welcome draft resisters to Canada, and then in 1969 expanded an open door to U.S. military deserters as well. More recently, Canada's supportive leadership and America's hostility to the new International Criminal Court (ICC) under George W. Bush has garnered headlines.

The More Identities, the Merrier?

This chapter is all about human social identity in a world of flux. Many scholars believe that humans are quite capable of possessing multiple identities and that identity proliferation is occurring as a natural consequence of globalization. Some go even further to suggest that this is a very good thing and should be encouraged by states.

Two American law professors, David Martin and T. Alexander Aleinikoff, see dual citizenship as both proliferating and a good thing. They have suggested that a revolution is occurring in citizenship law and policies, spurred by increasing migration and a global economy; many states now accept and even promote dual status. Once looked down upon by states, both *host* states and *home* states now view dual citizenship much more favorably.

Countries of origin want to improve relations with their diasporas abroad, partly because these people send considerable money home to help support relatives. Many states have gotten rid of rules that strip citizenship for those naturalized in another country.

Arguing that civil societies should be in the business of not only tolerating, but even nurturing, dual citizenship, Martin and Aleinikoff believe that multiple loyalties represent the norm in the contemporary era, not an aberration, and that evidence suggests people are capable of sorting out cross currents for themselves.

The U.S. Supreme Court has gotten into the act of accepting dual status. As early as the 1960s, it maintained that Americans who take citizenship abroad cannot be stripped of U.S. citizenship. Martin and Aleinikoff sum up their opinion writing that "The growth of dual nationality presents more opportunities than dangers, freeing individuals from irreconcilable choices and fostering connections that can further travel, trade, and peaceful relations."[45]

Chapter Synopsis

The size and complexity of the human family leads social scientists to conceive of groupings based on nine shared concepts that compete for prominence: states, regions, races, ethnic groups, economic super-regions, MNCs, North/South Hemispheres, religious mega-cultures, and one global community.

First, 193 states face serious challenges in trying to meet the demands of their citizens. Second, various world regions represent an alternative source of identity, including Europe, the former Soviet Union, Middle East, Asia, Pacific Rim, Sub-Saharan Africa, Latin America, and Anglo-America. Although considered of dubious scientific validity, physical variations known as race continue to be employed as the third common form of human identity.

Fourth, cultural heritage constitutes the basis for the identity factor called ethnicity. The economic success story of the European Union in recent decades has spurred development of rival trade-driven blocs in North America and in East Asia as a fifth type of identity. Sixth, huge MNCs also vie for human identity. Seventh, a global North–South division is widening. Eighth, loosely tied mega-cultures encompassing shared values and beliefs compete. Finally, intense debate rages over whether the human species might be moving toward a genuine global community.

Optimists and pessimists among social scientists differ concerning the implications of such an emerging identity among people seeing themselves as global citizens. Humanity's historical penchant for territorial attachment raises some caveats regarding rosy one-world future scenarios. The Kurile Islands case illustrates how a state (Russia) can follow an outdated policy and be emotionally attached to a marginal piece of turf at the expense of pressing economic needs.

Most countries follow a realist foreign policy aimed at pursuing their specific national interests. A few countries, however, take a broader idealist view. Canada has developed a reputation for good global citizenship. The *content* of its foreign policy involves a commitment to humane values, and its *method* features working quietly behind the scenes multilaterally with other actors to solve global problems. *Resilience* is attested to by the consistency with which all prime ministers since WW II from various political parties have remained true to this vision. Finally, several areas unmatched by any other country speaks to this policy as *unique*.

FOR DIGGING DEEPER

Appiah, Kwame Anthony, and Henry Louis Gates, eds. *The Dictionary of Global Culture*. Alfred A. Knopf, 1997.

Bakhash, Shaul. *The Reign of the Ayatollahs: Iran and the Islamic Revolution*. Borgo Press, 1991.

Bayart, Jean-Francois. *The State in Africa: The Politics of the Belly*. Longman, 1993.

Chebel, Malek. *Symbols of Islam*. St. Martin's Press, 1997.

Chehab, Zaki. *Inside Hamas: The Untold Story of the Militant Islamic Revolution*. Nation Books, 2008.

Cleary, Thomas. *The Essential Koran: The Heart of Islam*. Harper, 1993.

Colls, Robert. *The Identity of England*. Oxford University Press, 2002.

Colovic, Ivan. *Politics of Identity in Serbia*. New York University Press, 2003.

Croucher, Sheila. *Globalization and Belonging: The Politics of Identity in a Changing World*. Millennium Books, 2003.

Davidson, Basil. *The Black Man's Burden: Africa and the Curse of the Nation-State*. Times Books, 1992.

DeBlij H. J., and Peter O. Muller. *Geography: Regions, Realms, and Concepts*. John Wiley and Sons, 2004.

Earle, Robert, and John Wirth, eds. *Identities in North America: The Search for Community*. Stanford University Press, 1995.

El-Nawawy, Mohammed, and Adel Iskander. *Al-Jazeera: The Story of the Network That Is Rattling Governments and Redefining Modern Journalism*. Basic Books, 2003.

Ezekiel, Raphael. *The Racist Mind: Portraits of American Neo-Nazis and Klansmen*. Viking, 1995.

Faist, Thomas, ed. *Dual Citizenship in Europe: From Nationhood to Societal Integration*. Perseus, 2007.

Fandy, Mamoun. *An Uncivil War of Words: Media and Politics in the Arab World*. Praeger, 2007.

Fawcett, Louise, ed. *International Relations of the Middle East*. Oxford University Press, 2005.

Felder, David. *Palestinians and Israel*. Wellington, 1996.

Glassner, Martin Ira. *Political Geography*. John Wiley and Sons, 1993.

Glenny, Misha. *The Fall of Yugoslavia: The Third Balkan War*. Viking Penguin, 1996.

Goldschmidt, Arthur, and Shibley Telhami. *The Contemporary Middle East: A Reader*. Perseus Academic, 2005.

Gurtov, Mel. *Global Politics in the Human Interest*. Lynne Rienner, 1994.

Hammond, Andrew. *What the Arabs Think of America*. Greenwood World Publishing, 2007.

Harrison, Lawrence. *The Pan-American Dream: Do Latin America's Cultural Values Discourage True Partnership with the United States and Canada?* Basic Books, 1991.

Heater, Derek. *The Idea of European Unity*. St. Martin's Press, 1992.

Hoenig, Milton, and Yonah Alexander. *The New Iranian Leadership: Ahmadinejad, Nuclear Ambition, and the Middle East*. Praeger, 2007.

Huntington, Samuel P. *Political Development and Political Decay*. Irvington Books, 1993.

Jones, Barry, ed. *The European Union and the Regions*. Oxford University Press, 1995.

Kleinschmidt, Harald. *Migration, Regional Integration and Human Security: The Formation and Maintenance of Transnational Spaces*. Oxford University Press, 2006.

Leakey, Richard, and Roger Lewin. *Origins Reconsidered: In Search of What Makes Us Human*. Anchor Books, 1992.

Lesch, David W. *The Arab-Israeli Conflict: A History*. Oxford University Press, 2007.

———. *1979: The Year That Shaped the Modern Middle East*. Westview Press, 2001.

Matthews, Mark. *Lost Years: Bush, Sharon, and Failure in the Middle East*. Nation Books, 2007.

Matthews, Richard. *Dichotomy of Power: Nation versus State in World Politics*. Lexington Books, 2002.

McCormack, Gavan. *The Emptiness of Japanese Affluence*. Sharpe, 1996.

Mitnick, Eric. *Rights, Groups, and Self-Invention: Group-Differentiated Rights in Liberal Theory*. Ashgate, 2006.

Murthy, Ranjani. *Gender, Poverty, and Human Rights in Asia*. Macmillan, 2001.

Nasiri, Omar. *Inside the Jihad: My Life with Al Qaeda*. Westview Press, 2008.

O'Connor, Brendon, ed. *Anti-Americanism: History, Causes, Themes.* Greenwood World Publishing, 2007.

Oshana, Marina. *Personal Autonomy in Society.* Ashgate, 2006.

Page, Joseph. *The Brazilians.* Addison-Wesley, 1995.

Peters, Rudolph. *Crime and Punishment in Islamic Law.* Cambridge University Press, 2005.

Primoratz, Igor, and Aleksandar Pavkovic. *Identity, Self-Determination, and Secession.* Ashgate, 2006.

Rheingold, Howard. *The Virtual Community: Homesteading on the Electronic Frontier.* Addison-Wesley, 2002.

Rosenbaum, Karen, and Toni-Michelle Travis. *The Meaning of Difference: American Constructions of Race, Sex, Gender, Social Class, and Sexual Orientation.* McGraw-Hill, 2002.

Schiller, Herbert I. *Information Inequality.* Routledge, 1996.

Sharansky, Natan. *Defending Identity: Its Indispensable Role in Protecting Democracy.* Public Affairs, 2008.

Skidmore, Thomas E., and Peter H. Smith. *Modern Latin America.* Oxford University Press, 2004.

Slider, Darrell. *The Politics of Russia's Regions.* Sharpe, 2003.

Sorenson, David S. *An Introduction to the Modern Middle East: History, Religion, Political Economy, Politics.* Westview Press, 2007.

Taras, Raymond C., and Rajit Ganguly. *Understanding Ethic Conflict: The International Dimension.* A. B. Longman, 2008.

Temple-Raston, Dina. *The Jihad Next Door: The Lackawanna Six and Rough Justice in an Age of Terror.* Public Affairs, 2007.

Triandafyllidu, Anna, and Rudy Gropas, eds. *European Immigration: A Sourcebook.* Oxford University Press, 2007.

Wresch, William. *Disconnected: Haves and Have-Nots in the Information Age.* Rutgers University Press, 1996.

Wright, Robin. *In the Name of God: The Khomeini Decade.* Simon and Schuster, 1989.

INTERNET

Africa Policy:
http://www.africapolicy.org

African Studies Institute:
http://www.sas.upenn.edu/African_Studies/AS.html

The Africa Summit:
http://www.africasummit.org

African Union:
http://www.africa-union.org/

All Africa News:
www.allafrica.com

News From Africa:
http://www.channelafrica.org/

Arab News and Information:
http://www.arab.net/

Arab-Israeli Conflict History:
http://wwwmideastweb.org

Asian Development Bank:
http://www.adb.org/

Asian News: Pacific Media Watch:
http://www.pmw.c2o.org

Asian Studies WWW Virtual Library:
http://www.ccombs.anu.edu.au/WWWVL-AsianStudies.html

Association for the Study of Ethnicity and Nationalism:
http://www.lse.ac.uk/Depts/European/Asen/

Center for European Integration:
http://www.zei.de

Electric Minds:
http://www.electricminds.org

Europe—Recent Election Results:
http://www.public.rz.uni-dusseldorf.de/~nordsiew/

European Union (EU):
http://europa.eu

Global Coalition for Africa:
http://www.gcacma.org/Privatesector.htm

International Monetary Fund (IMF):
http://www.imf.org

Internet East Asian History Sourcebook:
http://www.fordham.edu/halsall/eastasia/eastasiasbook.html

Internet Gateway to Latin America:
http://www.lanic.utexas.edu/

Japan Politics Central:
http://www.jpcentral.virginia.edu

John Fairbanks Memorial Chinese History Virtual Library:
http://www.cnd.org/fairbank/

League of Arab States:
http://www.leagueofarabstates.org/

One World Forum:
http://www.oneworld.net

Organization for Economic Cooperation and Development (OECD):
http://www.oecd.org

Organization of American States (OAS):
http://www.oas.org/

Professor Stephen Soward's Twenty-Five Lectures on Balkan History:
http://www.lib.msu.edu/sowards/balkan/

Resource Center for the Americas:
http://www.americas.org

United Nations (U.N.) Publications:
http://www.un.org/Pubs/

World Citizen Foundation:
http://www.worldcitizen.org/

World Future Society:
http://www.wfs.org/

Psychology and Human Motivation

CORE OBJECTIVE

To understand the major theories of human motivation and personality and their application to social discourse.

THEMATIC QUESTIONS

- How does psychology's mission add unique elements to the social sciences?

- From what intellectual sources does the discipline of psychology emanate?

- Which two psychological theories of motivation and personality dominated the twentieth century?

- What newer theories have challenged for preeminence?

- How have psychological theories been applied to international affairs?

- Does the passage of time facilitate assessing the War on Terror using critical thinking skills?

In 1977, Egyptian president Anwar Sadat journeyed to Israel to make a historic speech to the Knesset (parliament) in the heartland of his traditional enemy. In it, he expressed the intriguing judgment that "problems between these two nations are 70 percent psychological."[1] Three decades later, facts on the ground between Arabs and Jews have evolved significantly, yet Sadat's insight about the significance of psychology in international affairs remains valid.

Much of what happens on the world stage results from intangible, subjective forces in the human experience. Because individual human beings in group settings run the key institutions in international affairs (states, NGOs, IGOs, IFIs, and MNCs), we cannot ignore what motivates these people, including their attitudes, perceptions, beliefs, habits, brain chemistry, fears, and general mind-set. Herein lies the complex stuff that psychology unravels in explaining human behavior. Therefore, if we want to apply the Stanislavsky Method to psychology, we must become comfortable with the raw-boned emotion that often countervails rationality in the subjective experience of *Homo sapiens*.

Anwar Sadat, Egyptian president who became the first Arab leader to recognize the state of Israel.

APA Online

Psychologists outnumber their colleagues in the other social sciences, and more than 14,000 psychologists belong to the American Psychological Association (APA). The APA Website, APA Online, offers a treasure trove of information but begins with a simple definition. "Psychology is the study of the mind and behavior," an endeavor that touches on all aspects of the human experience, "from the functions of the brain to the actions of states." The Website describes a long list of fifty-five divisions of the APA. However, the only division specifically related to international content is Division 52—International Psychology—which encourages intercultural research and better understanding of the psychological problems that predominate in different world regions. Each APA division provides its own array of resources.

The lower-numbered divisions are larger and more active. For example, Division 2, Society for the Teaching of Psychology, sponsors teaching programs at conferences, disseminates pedagogical materials through a special office and its own Website, funds research about teaching psychology, gives annual teaching awards, and publishes its own quarterly journal, *Teaching of Psychology*. Links are provided for this journal, for the division's listserv, for teaching resources, for careers teaching psychology, and for its own home page.

In addition to addressing the profession of psychology, APA Online also includes direct services to readers in its Help Center. One section, "How to Find Help for Life's Problems," provides answers to a series of key questions, such as "How can you tell if it's time to ask for help?" "How does therapy work?" "What about confidentiality?" "Does my insurance cover therapy?" "How do I choose a psychologist who is right for me?"

Another section, called "Psychology in Daily Life: Get the Facts," includes timely articles by APA experts. A few months after September 11, 2001, a thoughtful piece appeared on "Coping with Terrorism." It covered who is affected directly by terrorist attacks, what those not directly affected may also experience, symptoms of stress reaction, and skills and resources for coping with such trauma. Equally relevant and useful services afforded to readers of APA Online include one called "Mind-Body Connection," which contains information about holistic health theory and methods. In 2002, this same section ran an article on the benefits of stress management for cardiac patients. A final section, "Family and Relationships," goes into universal issues concerning human relations and ways of working through their inevitable complexities.

Defining Psychology

Such disciplinary breadth led Professor Dennis Coon, author of an introductory psychology text, to observe that "psychology has become such an enormous and colorful beast that no short description can do it justice." Although unwilling to provide a pithy definition, Coon succinctly identifies psychology's goals as describing, understanding, predicting, and controlling human behavior.[2] But while succinct, Coon's goals of describing, understanding, predicting, and controlling human behavior are nevertheless gargantuan in scope.

Canadian professor Keith Stanovich's overview of the discipline, *How to Think Straight about Psychology*, provides insights into some very basic problems confronting the discipline. With so many subfields, says Stanovich, psychology cannot rely on its content alone to provide the glue to bind it together. Rather, it must also employ specific sophisticated methods of inquiry. If all college psychology departments were magically disbanded, he believes that his colleagues would easily integrate into other related departments, such as sociology, education, social work, business, or biology. This would occur because psychology overlaps with all of these other areas.

Stanovich believes that only rigorously applying the scientific method can overcome what he calls the discipline's sizable "image problem." Because the general public is exposed to "volumes of amateur psychology" by the mainstream media, he thinks that the battle against popular misconceptions requires particular vigilance: "Psychology probably more than any other science, requires *critical thinking skills* that enable students to separate the wheat from the chaff that inevitably accumulates around sciences."[3]

All social sciences are academic disciplines that conduct research to accumulate a body of knowledge for transmission. Psychology, however, is also quintessentially an **applied discipline.** Its main applied specialties include the following:

Applied discipline ■ A field of study whose theories and methods are used by society to deal directly with individual and social problems

- clinical and counseling psychology
- community psychology
- industrial/organizational psychology
- engineering psychology
- environmental psychology
- educational psychology
- consumer psychology
- legal psychology
- sports psychology[4]

Psychology's History

Like all modern social sciences, the study of human psychology can be traced to the ancient Greeks. Plato implored his students to "know thyself," acknowledging our species' impressive introspective capabilities. The Confessions of Saint Augustine (351–425 A.D.) were the first truly autobiographical writings that dwelt on analysis of the inner self as an independent consciousness of the type introduced in Chapter 6. Augustine's work served not only as a precursor to psychology but also contributed mightily to the development of the modern novel as a form of humanistic literary expression.

Much later, during the Renaissance, psychological questions of mind, motivation, character, and human consciousness became intimately bound up with the master discipline of philosophy. The first thinker to attempt systematically to divorce psychology from philosophy was the German scholar Immanuel Kant (1724–1804). By the middle of the nineteenth century, the term psychology was coming into general use, but Auguste

Comte, the Frenchman who founded sociology, argued against disciplinary status for psychology, believing that "mind, ego, and the like were but useless abstractions," meaning that they could not be readily observed and measured.[5] It was not until the start of the twentieth century that psychology emerged as a discrete discipline.

In 1875, the first psychology course was offered by the American scholar William James, who developed an approach related to the functionalist school in sociology by asking how the mind operates in ways that enable us to adapt to our environment. The first American Ph.D. in psychology was conferred three years later. However, it was at the University of Leipzig, in Germany, that Wilhelm Wundt (1832–1920) earned the status of father of psychology by establishing the first experimental laboratory in 1879. Wondering how sensations and images are formed, he developed a technique of experimental introspection, combining structured introspection with objective measurement techniques.

With the legitimacy of the discipline finally established, two main psychological theories appeared, side by side, at the turn of the century. The first wave, *psychoanalysis,* was based on observations made in the private practice of Viennese physician Sigmund Freud (1856–1939). The second wave, *behaviorism,* was first developed by John B. Watson (1878–1958), and derived much of its approach from the laboratory techniques used by biologists to study animal behavior. Contemporary U.S. neuroscientist Terrence Deacon believes that humans are above all else a symbolic species with "a compulsion to assign symbolic import to almost every aspect of the physical world."[6] If Deacon is correct, then the main symbol of psychoanalysis is Freud's couch, and its symbolic counterpart for behaviorism is the image of the black box, each of which will be explained later.

Neither psychoanalysis nor behaviorism, however, nurtured humanity with hopeful visions of our basic psychological nature, or of our ability to assuage the psychological pain of real-life patients in therapy. Therefore, in the context of the optimistic 1960s, a third wave of *humanistic* psychologies emerged as an antidote to psychoanalysis's conjectural tendencies and behaviorism's narrowly focused disregard for human free will. By the 1990s, a fourth wave, *biopsychology,* burst onto the scene and threatened to relegate all theoretical predecessors to the dustbin by its discoveries about the biochemistry of the human brain and the role of the human genome in our behavioral makeup. It is to these four amazingly different theoretical waves regarding mind, personality, and therapy that we now turn:

- psychoanalysis
- behaviorism
- humanistic psychology
- biopsychology

Psychological Theories

Psychoanalysis

Charles Darwin's nineteenth-century theories of natural selection posited the revolutionary idea that *Homo sapiens* is subject to the same developmental laws as other species. Not only were humans suddenly portrayed as less unique than generally believed, but they were also seen as legitimate objects of scientific study. One thinker greatly influenced by Darwin was the physician Sigmund Freud, who hypothesized that humans are driven by conflicting inner impulses, most of which we are unaware of. Freud was looking deeply beneath the skin in quest of the fundamental causes of behavior. Within each of us, he suggested, rages a battle involving three dynamic mental forces: id, ego, and superego.

The **id** consists of an impulsive, pleasure-seeking well of energy stemming from biological instincts. The **ego,** by contrast, is more rational. It operates according to principles of reality, not fantasy, with practical planning as part of its repertoire. The **superego** is the judge, or censor, for the plans of the ego, rendering it susceptible to feelings of

Id ■ In Freudian psychoanalysis, primal urges craving satisfaction in the human personality's struggle between competing forces

Ego ■ In Freudian psychoanalysis, the calculating part of personality that tries to mediate between the id and the superego

Superego ■ In Freudian psychoanalysis, this part of personality absorbs society's values in the form of a conscience

guilt. A constant tug-of-war takes place, with the ego in the complex position of balancing these two irreconcilable forces.

Freud believed that individuals are highly susceptible to the long-term effects of childhood trauma, and that they must develop through a series of *psychosexual stages* by age five or six to avoid unhealthy consequences in adulthood. Freud placed a great deal of emphasis on the centrality of sex in the human experience. This is partly attributable to the fact that he lived during the height of the Victorian era, which affected not only Queen Victoria's English homeland but also most of the European continent. This was a prudish period of puritanical values when polite society did not speak, hear, or see much about human sexuality, and no one studied it scientifically. Consequently, it seems that Freud may have overemphasized the impact of sexual dynamics on the human psyche.

Personality, Freud reasoned, is set in experiential concrete very early in life, when individuals fail to resolve psychosexual tensions necessary for personal development. For those carrying the ill effects of childhood trauma into adulthood, Freud created the so-called "talking cure." Clinicians try to relieve human pain, and Freud coaxed patients into lengthy dialogues to guide them ever closer to insightful recollections intended to resolve painful buried memories. To relax patients, Freud had them lie down on the couch in his office, hence the popular image of the psychoanalytic couch.[7]

Some Freudian ideas seeped quietly into American consciousness during the 1940s, 1950s, and 1960s through the writings of pediatrician Benjamin Spock. Postwar America needed a soothing voice to reassure a generation of new parents whose affluence created enough leisure time to allow them to worry about whether they were raising their kids properly. Dr. Spock preached that "what infants need most from their mothers and fathers is love. Babies are not little savages who must be broken to adult schedules as quickly as possible in matters such as potty training."[8] Spock had learned from Freud that repression during childhood could produce serious problems in adulthood. Therefore, he favored giving kids some breathing space, and strictness was not part of his repertoire. Spock underwent psychoanalysis twice in his long career, and many Freudian notions can be found in his book, *Baby and Child Care,* which has sold more than 50 million copies.

Hollywood's depiction of the vague purposes, self-absorbed characters, and elusiveness of closure associated with psychoanalysis is epitomized by the angst-riddled films of Woody Allen. Rent a video of any of Allen's movies and witness the bittersweet humor and pathos of his characters, who seem stuck on a treadmill of introspection and self-doubt. Some good examples are *Take the Money and Run* (1969), *Everything You Always Wanted to Know About Sex (but Were Afraid to Ask)* (1972), *Annie Hall* (1977), *Interiors* (1978), *Manhattan* (1979), *Stardust Memories* (1980), *Zelig* (1983), *The Purple Rose of Cairo* (1985), *Hannah and Her Sisters* (1986), and *Mighty Aphrodite* (1995).

Freud was mostly interested in the storm he observed raging within the individual psyche, not in society's collective psyche. His fullest exploration of the social implications of the battle of id versus superego found expression in his *Civilization and Its Discontents,* which analyzes the struggle between culture and the raw-boned state of nature. Typically, Freudian prognoses at both the micro and macro levels range from grim to grimmer to grimmest.

Today, Freud's theories and clinical methods are followed by less than 10 percent of psychologists in the APA. Nevertheless, Keith Stanovich laments what he calls the "Freud problem" in his profession: for most laymen, some version of Freudian theory represents the core of what they think psychology is about, despite Freud's virtual abandonment by psychologists.[9] Freud derived his theories using a loose case study method by examining the mental problems of his patients; therefore, his theories did not follow basic scientific guidelines. Somewhat like Karl Marx's analysis of social causation, Freud's analysis of psychological causation was eclectically creative for its time. For both Freud and Marx, however, what represented intriguing analysis one hundred or more years ago fails to hold up under contemporary scrutiny.

Rejected by most professional psychologists, Sigmund Freud's theories of inner turmoil continue to resonate in the popular mind-set.

Behaviorism

In 1906, Russian biologist Ivan Pavlov began publishing accounts of his experiments on animals involving conditioned response. Extrapolating some of the principles of conditioned reflex that Pavlov was applying to dogs, John B. Watson's behaviorism swept ashore as the second wave shortly after WW I. Reacting against the subjective dreamworld of Freud's psychoanalytic school, behaviorists committed themselves to operating scientifically: observability, verifiability, and quantification became their badges of objectivity.

But behaviorists believed they were armed with more than scientific methods; they believed they understood the vital role played by the social environment in influencing individual behavior. Through their strict methodology, behaviorists sought to demonstrate the potent mechanics of positive and negative conditioning, that is, of rewards and punishments. Environmental **stimuli (S)** cause behavioral **responses (R)** by the subject under examination, and the scientist's job is to record and study these observations. Behaviorists conceive of individual behavior as consisting of a black box where the vital question is not what happens inside but rather what happens on the outside. A **conditioned response** is nothing more, or less, than a learned reaction to a given stimulus. In this sense, behaviorism posits that human behavior is made up of *bundles of habits*.

Far less concerned than the Freudians about childhood trauma, behaviorists think that behavioral patterns can change because they remain subject to modification by outside influences. Unraveling personality is no inscrutable mystery to them: individual personality consists of observable behavioral habits that collectively comprise the self. Learning psychology, one of the discipline's major contemporary branches, derives from behaviorism's scientific penchant and leans toward the natural sciences in both method and content.

The most important behaviorist of the second half of the twentieth century, B. F. Skinner (1904–1990), focused more on macro-level societal issues than his more micro-oriented predecessors, and Skinner spoke of using conditioned response for social engineering purposes. By this, he meant using carefully distributed rewards and punishments to get people to do the things society wants them to do, thereby optimizing the chances for achieving the good society. First broached in fictional form via his novel *Walden Two* and then addressed more directly in *Beyond Freedom and Dignity*, Skinner attacked as anachronistic Western society's prioritization of individual rights over social rights. What is your personal assessment of Skinner's views concerning social versus individual rights?

Behaviorism satisfied a desire in the twentieth century for a psychological theory more observable and measurable than psychoanalysis. It accomplished these scientific objectives but at a significant price. Behaviorism's intellectual edifice rests on the assumption that what we know about animals is applicable to humans. Critics also contend that behaviorism treats humans like robots by ignoring the inner life of symbolic consciousness that is almost unique to our species. Behaviorism's deterministic bent also concerns philosophers of social science who focus on humanity's possession of free will, which enables us to think our way through paradoxes, rather than merely reacting to them. Some observers also consider the often-mundane questions asked by behaviorism as too sterile and mechanical to find its research agenda very inspiring.

Stimuli (S) ■ Potent events or circumstances in the environment that behaviorists see as crucial to understanding the conditioned response of subjects

Response (R) ■ Learned reactions to environmental stimuli that behaviorists believe can be measured in accordance with conditioned response

Conditioned response ■ Conduct that is motivated by a series of rewards and sanctions

Efficacy ■ The ability of human individuals or groups to exercise meaningful direction over their destinies

Behaviorist B. F. Skinner concentrated on macro-level issues relating to social engineering.

Humanistic Psychology

Neither of psychology's first two intellectual waves accorded humans much sense of **efficacy**. In the Freudian model, we find ourselves at the mercy of deep, dark forces inside us that we don't really understand. Deterministic behaviorism seems no better because it portrays our robotic behavior as resulting from external forces equally beyond our control. For anyone with a more optimistic sense of human destiny, little theoretical ammunition was provided by the discipline's first two big guns.

A key feature of America's revolutionary heyday in the 1960s was its efficacious feeling that anything is possible. At this unusual time, a third wave of **humanistic psychology** engulfed the country. Seldom in the social sciences do we find the dichotomy between social scientism and social humanism illustrated more elegantly than it is in the gap separating behaviorist and humanistic psychologies. The Association for Humanistic Psychology notes on its Website: "Its message is a response to the denigration of the human spirit that has so often been implied in the image of the person drawn by behavioral and social sciences."[10]

> **Humanistic psychology** ■ A theory of personality holding that untapped human potential includes a latent ability to adjust personality throughout our lifetime

Although numerous and diverse, all humanistic theories conceive of personality developing continuously over time. Probably the earliest to argue that "man is the origin of his actions" was the Greek philosopher Aristotle.[11] However, more than anyone else in the 1960s, psychologist Erik Erikson and his "Eight Ages of Man" convinced scholars that personality remains a work in progress until we die. Personality's ongoing nature also filtered into the popular consciousness through Daniel Levinson's *Seasons in a Man's Life* and Gail Sheehy's *Passages*.[12] According to Erikson, humans face eight common psychosocial dilemmas that we must seek to resolve for ourselves in the course of a lifetime, and how we deal with them shapes much of who we become. The long-standing Freudian principle that personality is set by age five or six was being challenged, as was his assertion that psychosexual (rather than psychosocial) dynamics shape the contours of human personality.

A belief in untapped human potential made humanistic theories both attractive and accessible during a stressful epoch when the Vietnam War and Watergate caused considerable soul-searching among Americans. For a generation that entered the 1960s believing it could change the world, the idea of individuals changing themselves was readily accepted. Fritz Perls's Gestalt therapy, Eric Berne's Transactional Analysis, Albert Ellis's Rational-Emotive therapy, Abraham Maslow's Self-Actualization therapy, and Carl Rogers's Client-Centered therapy all offered venues to cast aside self-defeating habits and embrace positive patterns of behavior.

Humanistic psychologies derive much of their inspiration from the humanities, and the influence of theater on Gestalt therapy, of philosophy on Rational-Emotive therapy, and of religious compassion on Client-Centered therapy is readily apparent. The excitement generated by humanistic psychologies during the 1960s and 1970s occurred largely because the psychoanalytic and behaviorist waves had downplayed a very meaningful part of the human experience: humanity's need for love, self-esteem, belonging, self-expression, creativity, and spirituality.[13]

Biopsychology

Most psychologists have long assumed that some combination of nurture (experience) and nature (biology) accounts for who we become, what we feel, and how we act. The contentious issue, however, concerns assessing the relative weight of each set of influences: is it 50–50, 75–25, 25–75, 90–10, or 10–90? At times, some wild gyrations have occurred regarding the conventional wisdom on this matter.

If you invert the sixties, what you discover is the nineties, a decade in psychology that truly did turn the sixties upside down. In the nurture versus nature debate, the sixties fell in love with the value of nurture, whereas scientific discoveries in the nineties revolutionized psychology with biologically based explanations for behavior and new therapies. The evidence for nature's role derives from increasingly sophisticated studies of the human mind/brain interface using MRI, exploration of DNA and mapping of the human genome, and insights about the applicability of Charles Darwin's theories of evolution not only to human bodies but also to human minds as well.

Within the framework of biopsychology, the research and writings of four major scholars will be described next. First, we'll examine the brain research of neuroscientist Vilayanur Ramachandran, which essentially treats the brain like a sophisticated computer while emphasizing the impact of its physicality on its function. Second, we will explore the antithetical views of neuroscientist Terrence Deacon, who posits that the development of language and symbolic communication among humans caused many brain traits to develop as they did. Third, the impact of the Human Genome Project's mapping of our 30,000 genes has yielded data relevant to human personality development, and the work of molecular biologist Dean Hamer will be addressed. Fourth, we will examine the work of Cornell University Professor Steven Pinker, who is probably the best-known spokesman for what has come to be known as evolutionary psychology. Pinker's fascinating book *How the Mind Works* will be summarized as a window on the relatively new subdiscipline of evolutionary psychology.

One neuroscientist, Rodolfo Llinas, explores the brain's structure, chemistry, and electrical oscillations to determine the parameters of the individual self and human consciousness itself.[14] Sharing a similar approach is San Diego State University neuroscientist Vilayanur Ramachandran, who was featured in a PBS Nova program called *Secrets of the Mind*. Ramachandran contends that his brain research reveals that biology causes many behaviors heretofore attributed to intangible rather than biological causes. For example, his research on epileptics shows that their seizures lead them to fixate on intense mystical visions that they believe represent profound supernatural truths. Ramachandran hints that such evidence may mean that religion's status as a cultural universal could ultimately be attributable to brain biochemistry.[15]

This San Diego neuroscientist thinks that human brains are hard-wired for certain types of thought, and he uses case studies taken from his work with phantom-limb patients to show how their delusional symptoms have implications for understanding humans generally. He treats patients whose parietal lobes (which control spatial understanding and visual recognition) have been damaged through injury or stroke. Four patients are especially fascinating. One man lost his arm in a motorcycle accident, yet still feels "phantom sensations" in his nonexistent limb; another young man has a head injury that causes him to believe that his parents are imposters; a third young man suffers from temporal lobe epilepsy, which produces hallucinatory seizures and profound feelings of spiritual transcendence. Finally, a female stroke victim cannot accurately sense any activity on one side of her body.[16] For researchers such as Llinas and Ramachandran, the popular expression "mind over matter" might better be reversed to "matter over mind."

Not all neuroscientists, however, agree with them. One whose research leads to markedly different conclusions about the mind–brain relationship is Boston University neuroscientist Terrence Deacon. If Linas and Ramachandran are neuroscientists who treat the brain as essentially a computer, Deacon is one who does not. His work looks like biopsychology with a resonant soul that is mostly symbolic and linguistic in nature. Deacon argues that the evolution of language did not result directly from a language organ, instinct, or simply a larger brain. Rather, "language reflected a new mode of thinking: symbolic thinking," which produced a "co-evolutionary exchange" between language and the brain that emerged over a two-million-year period.

Quite boldly, Deacon asserts that "many of the physical traits that distinguish human bodies and brains were ultimately caused by ideas shared down the generations." Symbolic thinking is regarded as an extremely potent causative agent. One reviewer of Deacon's book, *The Symbolic Species: The Co-Evolution of Language and the Brain*, observes that it aids our understanding of something quite important: "Why we are so remarkably different from other species in language learning, yet not all that different from apes in the organization and function of our primate brains."[17]

Not all biopsychological research delves into the brain. Some of it takes place at the cellular level. Cells are the fundamental working units of living systems, and the complete instructions to map their activities are contained in chemical DNA. The genome is an organism's set of DNA, and human cells all contain a complete genome.[18]

In 2001, a scientific milestone was achieved when the Human Genome Project completed mapping the 30,000 genes that comprise our genetic repertoire. One researcher at the National Institutes of Health, molecular biologist Dean Hamer, studies this research question: Does DNA influence human behavior? Hamer's ambivalent answer is that, yes, DNA does affect certain aspects of personality, but that, no, it does not act as the sole contributor to such personality traits. The issue is a complex one because although DNA is made up of only four chemicals, spelling out even a single gene can require a million combinations.[19] Hamer believes that "people are born with temperamental traits, but what they can acquire through experience is the ability to control them by exercising that intangible part of the personality called character."[20]

Hamer says he was so fascinated when he learned that Charles Darwin, 170 years ago, viewed human behavior as partially inherited, that it led Hamer to switch research fields. Among those aspects of personality being examined by Hamer are novelty-seeking, openness, anxiety, homosexuality, and nicotine addiction. His findings suggest that male homosexuality is linked to a stretch of DNA at the very tip of the X chromosome (the one inherited from mothers). Not so coincidentally, Hamer is a chain-smoking homosexual. Do you think his personal connection to these two traits either adds to or detracts from his ability to conduct scientific research in this area?

One final practitioner of biopsychology is Cornell University evolutionary psychologist Steven Pinker, who begins by noting that although science fiction brims with human-like robots, nothing approaching one has been or ever will be constructed. Pinker think this because the engineering problems required to replicate our fantastically complex feats of mental life are insurmountable. According to Pinker, "the mind is not the brain, but rather what the brain does, namely make us see, think, feel, choose, and act." To Pinker, the mind is organized into "mental organs" whose basic logic derives from our genetic program.[21]

He says that although the typical process of engineering designs a machine or an organ to do something, psychology functions as a discipline of "reverse-engineering" because it is concerned with figuring out what the prime human organ (the mind) was designed by 200,000 generations of natural selection to do. The intellectual rationale for reverse-engineering was first established by Charles Darwin, whose theories Pinker expands on here: "Our physical organs owe their complex design to the information in the human genome, and so, I believe, do our mental organs." In the case of the mind, Pinker conceives of natural selection as a "Blind Programmer" and concludes that our mental programs work as well as they do "because they were shaped by selection to allow our ancestors to master rocks, tools, plants, animals, and each other, ultimately in the service of survival and reproduction." The bottom line is that Pinker believes the mind was engineered to maximize the number of copies of its genes, and in so doing, it created a wondrously complex species.[22]

The overriding practical result of all this revolutionary research in biopsychology, however, is an entirely new generation of *prescription drugs* for psychological ailments such as **anxiety, depression,** and **obsessive-compulsive disorder.** Although psychoactive drugs have been around for decades, they have to live down a long-standing reputation for causing side effects while offering limited relief to sufferers. Symptomatic of the fast-paced Western-influenced world we live in today, that assessment seems to have changed rather quickly. New drugs raise hopes for "better living through chemistry" as they appear to work more effectively with fewer side effects than their predecessors. Today biopsychology seems to generate more sustained interest than early-childhood trauma, environmental conditioning, or self-actualization as the preferred choice for those in psychological pain, especially in an era marked by frugal managed health-care systems. However, many mental health traditionalists believe that a pill can never replace the salve of human compassion.[23]

The Cross-Cultural Perspective

For about a hundred years, the discipline of psychology has studied individual and social behavior mostly in the context of Western societies, assuming that what it discovers will apply universally. In other words, people are people everywhere. But psychologist Otto

Anxiety ■ A sense of personal dread, panic, or inordinate fear that therapists treat in a variety of ways

Depression ■ A dysfunctional condition in which someone feels inexplicably hopeless or sad for an extended period of time

Obsessive-compulsive disorder ■ The inability of an individual to break free from repetitive habits that can vary greatly by type and relative severity

Klineberg recounts an experience with colleagues from the field of cultural anthropology, which he says influenced him "like a religious conversion," and which speaks to the synergy of interdisciplinary sharing. The rhetorical question posed by Klineberg was, "How could psychologists speak of human attributes and human behavior when they knew only one kind of human being?"[24]

After surveying the cross-cultural research literature, anthropologists Carol and Melvin Ember conclude that the preliminary evidence indicates that while a few psychological universals exist, significant psychological differences between cultures are well-established. Therefore, they believe that more cross-cultural research should be pursued.[25] Donald Brown attempts to catalog research pointing to a set of psychological universals found in all cultures. Among the most interesting ones he describes are the concept of the self, inferring other people's intentions from their para-linguistics (nonverbal cues), trying to imagine the thoughts of other people, empathy with other people's feelings, and communicating by facial features emotions such as sadness, happiness, fear, and surprise. Evidence also supports the theory that human development universally proceeds according to a predictable sequence of stages featuring new mental skills in each stage.[26]

As early as Margaret Mead's Samoan field research in the 1920s, anthropologists have been indirectly challenging the assumption that human psychology is universal. Her early studies of adolescent psychology in Samoa contradicted the belief that adolescent psychology was universally a volatile one of "storm and stress" stemming from the biological effects of puberty.[27] Subsequent cross-cultural research has corroborated Mead's thesis that adolescent psychological experience is more varied than previously thought.[28] A captivating cross-cultural contrast between a society of psychologically timid people and a society of psychologically aggressive people is provided by Carol and Melvin Ember. In Malaysia live the Semai people, well known for their meekness and lack of hostility. In the words of one Semai, "We do not get angry." Their child-rearing practices involve no physical punishment and convey nonviolence through the absence of any violent behavior on the part of adults.

In bold relief to the Semai stand the Yanomamo people of Brazil's Amazon Basin. Child rearing among the Yanomamo encourages youngsters to express feelings of anger physically, including hitting another child or an adult. Parents not only tolerate such behavior but even goad children into violent outbursts. Punishment for striking others with a fist or an object is very rare. Not surprisingly, wife-beating, bloody fights, and verbal abuse are common within the Yanomamo tribe. Adversaries from outside the tribe fare even worse and fear the Yanomamo for the fierce way they fight their chronic wars.[29] Timidity versus aggressiveness represents a psychological continuum that fundamentally contrasts human behavior. If peoples like the Semai and the Yanomamo can diverge so greatly in this respect, we should exercise caution before assuming that Western psychology's theories and explanations apply to all peoples in all places at all times. Surely, these insights ought to resonate within the walls of Division 53 of the APA (International Psychology).

Psychology on the World Stage

We have characterized psychology as a diverse social science by virtue of its broad content overlapping numerous other disciplines, its large number of practitioners spanning fifty-five subfields, and its dual functions (science of behavior as well as applied therapy). But neither its diversity, size, nor status as an applied science has enabled psychological concepts and insights developed at the micro level of analysis to be routinely applied to human affairs at the macro or mega levels. One exception is the work of Canadian political psychologist Blema Steinberg. In a 1997 book, she applies principles of psychoanalytic theory to presidential decision making in the Vietnam War, and asks, "Why did Lyndon Johnson and Richard Nixon choose to escalate the conflict in Vietnam, while their predecessor, Dwight Eisenhower, desisted?" Her analysis is detailed in Case Study 7.1.

Case Study 7.1   The United States in Vietnam: To Escalate or Not to Escalate?

One of France's colonial possessions was the southeast Asian nation of Vietnam. Like most other colonial peoples, the Vietnamese conducted a campaign after WW II for their independence. Like many other colonial powers, France resisted, and a prolonged war of independence ensued. Finally, in 1954, France lost the pivotal battle of Dienbienphu and retreated in defeat. The leader of Vietnamese independence was Ho Chi Minh, whom Western countries considered a communist. At the height of the Cold War, the local issue of communist influence among Vietnamese independence fighters converted the struggle within Vietnam to the global level. As leader of the West, the United States had a decision to make in 1954: whether to fill the power vacuum left by France with a sizable American presence. President Dwight Eisenhower decided against such an escalatory move.

A civil war then developed between the North Vietnamese (supported by China and the Soviet Union) and the South Vietnamese (backed by the United States). For years, this domestic battle raged with no external powers participating directly. This typified regional struggles during the Cold War, as the major powers remained in the background, leaving military confrontation to the local forces that they backed. But by the mid-1960s, the North Vietnamese began winning the war. The United States had been supplying military hardware and advisors to South Vietnam, which nevertheless failed to keep the North from advancing.

In 1965, President Lyndon Johnson was faced with a pivotal decision: should he actively "Americanize" the war by sending large numbers of U.S. combat forces to fight? Or should he continue to allow the South Vietnamese to fight

Figure 7.1

America's blank check to go anywhere, anytime, to oppose any communist enemy was cashed in during its longest and costliest war: Vietnam (1965–1975).

their own war? Johnson chose the former path, which soon resulted in more than 500,000 combat troops in Vietnam but still no victory in sight. His policies failed so badly that in 1968, he decided not to run for a second presidential term, retiring instead to his Texas ranch. Succeeding Lyndon Johnson was President Richard Nixon, whose campaign pledged "peace with honor" in Vietnam: a gradual U.S. withdrawal without abandoning its allies.

But Vietnam proved a military and political quagmire for Nixon as well. In 1970, U.S. losses continued at an alarming pace, generating massive public protest in America's streets. Making matters worse, Nixon had not managed to coax the North Vietnamese, as promised, to the peace table for negotiations. He then decided to gamble by expanding the war in secret, bombing and invading North Vietnamese supply routes through neighboring Cambodia (see Figure 7.1).

What Blema Steinberg wanted to know was whether psychoanalytic theory helps to comprehend why Eisenhower chose not to escalate U.S. military involvement in 1954, but Johnson and Nixon chose the opposite path in 1965 and 1970. Seeking answers in the psychoanalytic garden, she needed to dig into the personalities of the three respective presidents, using as her trowel the concept of **narcissism.** Steinberg was looking especially for the impact of shameful feelings of humiliation believed common to narcissistic personalities. She argues that these cases are well suited to examining the effect of personality profiles on foreign policy decision making because no strong public opinion or advisory influences inhibited these presidents from acting pretty much as they chose.

Her sketch of narcissistic personalities draws a picture of riveting self-involvement and exaggerated concern with the achievement of success and fame to compensate for love and affection not received in childhood. Being singled out as "special" convinces such children that love depends on performance. The self-absorption of narcissists makes it difficult to see life through the eyes of others or to experience intimacy with other people. They need accomplishments for the acclaim that results from them. Not believing they are otherwise likeable, these people are subject to feelings of inferiority when they fail to live up to such unrealistic expectations.

After examining their formative years, Steinberg says that Lyndon Johnson and Richard Nixon each had mothers who conveyed to them that they were special; therefore, much was expected of them. Johnson and Nixon also both had angry and impatient fathers who were discounted by mothers who were more sophisticated. Predictably, neither man's childhood involved making many good friends. In sharp contrast, Steinberg's analysis of Dwight Eisenhower's childhood reveals a poor but loving environment that encouraged stability, with young Dwight blending in comfortably with his five brothers. He held a healthy self-concept and felt loved for who he was rather than what he might do. Professor Steinberg's comparative assessment of Nixon and

In 1954, President Dwight Eisenhower decided against expanding America's military role in the Vietnamese civil war.

Narcissism ■ An excessive fixation on oneself that psychoanalysis sees as resulting from failure in youth to develop normal feelings of self-worth

Johnson on the one hand, and Eisenhower on the other, is capsulized thus:

> Lyndon Johnson and Richard Nixon were two highly narcissistic individuals who suffered from painful feelings of shame and humiliation. It was these feelings, in the overall context of their narcissistic character structures, which played an important part in shaping their presidential decisions on Vietnam. Dwight Eisenhower, in contrast, was not a narcissistic personality. As a confident, psychologically well-adjusted individual, his political decision making in 1954 was less colored by his psychological needs and fears.[30]

Professor Steinberg's analysis is presented here as one explanation of presidential decision making concerning Vietnam, not the only one. Such matters are complex, and social scientists try to avoid what philosophers refer to as the fallacy of single cause, or treating one factor in a multicausal situation as if it were the only one. Presidents Eisenhower, Johnson, and Nixon were subject to a host of political, military, economic, and social influences on their decisions. Nonetheless, political scientist John Stoessinger's studies of U.S. foreign policy share Steinberg's view that the personality of a president is very important in shaping American policy.[31]

The other five social sciences (geography, sociology, anthropology, political science, and economics) operate mostly at the macro level (national) or the mega level (global), but psychology is more apt to study human behavior at the micro level (individual). Although social scientists examine the *behavior* of humans at all three levels, the nature of the milieu differs from the micro level to macro level to mega level. Therefore, caution should be exercised when crossing levels of analysis, especially between the micro and mega levels, although this does not mean that such jumps cannot prove fruitful. Case Study 7.2 illustrates how one social psychologist has skillfully applied psychological concepts to world affairs. ■

Case Study 7.2   From David L. Rice to Nuclear Numbing

In 1986, psychologist Sam Keen visited a Seattle prison to interview an inmate convicted of murdering an innocent family of four. What intrigued Keen was not the gruesome crime, but rather murderer David L. Rice's bizarre mind-set. According to David L. Rice's rhetoric, he did not commit murder for revenge, robbery, money, or lust for power. After extensive interviews, Keen concludes that Rice believed he was a soldier fighting against global communism, and that he killed to defeat the communist menace.

That this convicted murderer would use the global communist menace to justify murdering four peaceful family members seems absurd. They were not communists, but Rice says he was told that they were, and he seems to have simple-mindedly accepted it. However, even the most militantly anticommunist citizens do not go around killing people, and Keen emphasizes that his analysis of this case in no way justifies, minimizes, or defends such evil behavior.

David L. Rice said his anti-communist zeal led him to kill an innocent Seattle family.

Keen was struck not only by the bizarre aspects of Rice's thinking but also by how Rice's beliefs reflected general societal attitudes in the early 1980s about communism, as expressed routinely in the mass media. The Cold War still existed when Rice committed these murders, and his skewed logic interpreted this mega-level conflict as legitimizing his personal crusade against domestic communists. Both Rice and society in general viewed the world through simplistic Cold War lenses whose imagery depicted the enemy as subhuman, thus facilitating a sense of moral righteousness.

Keen suggests that in this instance, skipping across levels of analysis can provide insight into international behavior otherwise unobtainable. For example, it is dangerous for humans to numb themselves into an avoidance of reality, and he marvels at the way Rice became an unfeeling automaton. Rice's path of least resistance consisted of numbing himself by suppressing all feeling associated with his crime. Although Rice likely could never "heal" in any psychological sense without coming to grips with his feelings, numbness represented the short-term solution as his defense mechanism.

This micro-level insight is also applied to humanity's penchant for a comparable psychic numbing against feelings generated by the proliferation of WMDs. It is easier to avoid confronting the realities of the nuclear, biological, and chemical dilemmas; however, in so doing, we become less likely to grasp the true nature of their threat. We can't hope to resolve proliferation dilemmas if we fail to assess them honestly. Like David L. Rice, we numb ourselves to avoid strong feelings associated with considering the frightening WMD situation.[32] ■

Perceptual Analysis and World Affairs

Perceptual analysis ■ Studying human behavior by emphasizing the role of subjective factors such as values and beliefs that affect the way we internalize information from our environment

The study of world affairs has been enhanced in recent decades by the systematic study of **perceptual analysis**.[33] Examining the process of human perception suggests that, in addition to the objective dimension of reality we encounter, a subjective dimension also affects our behavior. The human mind does not work like an organic photocopying machine, absorbing images of everything crossing its path. Rather, the mind engages in *selective perception*. Our five senses are capable of internalizing various impressions from the present environment and storing them away, but we tend to pick and choose. While reading this sentence, you may not notice other stimuli, such as a humming air-conditioner, a fly landing on your desk, the smell of pizza down the hall, or a vibrating stereo. By perceiving one thing at a time, we exclude other things.

When we perceive more complex social phenomena, the human mind responds more complexly. For one thing, selective perception is not random but rather seeks consistency with our underlying beliefs and expectations. The ancient Greek philosopher Demosthenes provides a still-valuable insight by observing; "Nothing is easier than self-deceit. For what each man wishes, that he also believes to be true."[34] And groups of people within a society may view the world through common prisms made up of values and historical memories, all of which produce selective perception.

Certain aspects of selective perception transcend different societies, and political scientist John Rourke summarizes five universal tendencies that can affect decision-makers and citizens alike: (1) we believe that other cultures see and interpret events essentially as we do; (2) other countries are seen as inherently more hostile than ours; (3) the behavior of adversaries is thought to be more efficient and masterful than our own; (4) we assume that the sincerity of our intentions is self-evident enough to preclude being doubted by

Case Study 7.3 Perceptual Role Reversal: The Czechoslovakian and Dominican Crises

Neither the United States nor the Soviet Union had any incentive to question the validity of its Cold War mission. The enemy, by definition, was an aggressor. Perceived facts and events had to be filtered through these Cold War prisms. Given such firmly held convictions, the superpowers exhibited diametrically opposite interpretations of two serious 1960s crises.

In 1965, U.S. President Lyndon Johnson received intelligence reports that the Dominican Republic's government, headed by Juan Bosch, had fallen under the control of communists. Johnson responded by sending American marines to the tiny Caribbean nation to overthrow its leftist government and secure a regime more friendly to the United States. LBJ defended his action with an argument known as "regional sphere of influence," citing the 1823 *Monroe Doctrine* and other actions taken by U.S. presidents to protect American interests in the Western Hemisphere. He considered the Dominican invasion a regional matter, therefore not relevant to the Soviet interests.

The USSR begged to differ. Rather than viewing the Dominican crisis as local in nature, the Soviet Union interpreted it as a global matter. Taking a "universal international law" approach, the Soviets branded the invasion as a violation of the sovereign independence of the Dominican Republic. Soviet eyes perceived nothing short of naked aggression—a violation of the U.N. Charter and other international legal standards—and therefore they condemned the United States at the U.N.

Fast-forward three years to the Czechoslovakian crisis: same players, complete role reversal. With Czechoslovakia, one of the eastern European countries occupied by the Soviet Union after Germany's defeat in WW II, the Communist Party leadership of Czechoslovakia walked a tightrope. Czechoslovakian ties had historically been to the European West, not to the Soviet East. Culturally, politically, and economically, the Czechoslovakian people felt kinship with the West, and most of them hated being controlled by the Soviet Union. Czechoslovakian Party leaders dreamed of exercising some freedom from Moscow, but they knew that if they made Kremlin leaders nervous about changes to their political and economic system, they could be crushed.

Czechoslovakian leader Alexander Dubček cautiously fashioned what came to be known as the "Prague Spring": allowing limited freedom of expression and economic liberty that deviated from the Soviet authoritarian model. Dubček wanted to create "communism with a human face" rather than the rigid form pushed by the Russians. During most of 1968, euphoria swept through the capital city of Prague. Citizens enjoyed a modicum of freedom of speech, religion was practiced quietly, and farmers improved their income with profits from privately grown produce. It all seemed too good to be true—and it was. U.S. film director Philip Kaufman's tender movie *The Unbearable Lightness of Being* (1988) re-creates a poignant slice of life from 1960s Prague.

Fearing that a little freedom could spill over into other Eastern European countries and even into the Soviet Union itself, in August of 1968, Soviet leader Leonid Brezhnev sent tanks into Prague and choked Dubček's breath of fresh air, installing a regime kowtowing to the Soviet line. Espousing the new *Brezhnev Doctrine*, the Soviets warned other Eastern European communist states that no deviation from the Soviet path to communism would be tolerated. Brezhnev invoked the argument of "regional sphere of influence," calling this a local drama between socialists in which outsiders had no place. The parallels between the Monroe Doctrine and the Brezhnev Doctrine are multifaceted.

The United States perceived the invasion of Czechoslovakia quite differently. As had the Soviets in the earlier Dominican crisis, America invoked the language of "universal international law" in criticizing Brezhnev's invasion as a violation of the territorial integrity of a sovereign state.[35]

Only three years separated these two superpower crises, and so the same key decision-makers were in place for both. To objective observers, the overt behavior involved in the U.S. invasion of the Dominican Republic and the Soviet invasion of Czechoslovakia shared much in common. In each case, a superpower invaded a small country in its regional sphere of influence to further that superpower's perceived national interest. The parallels between the two situations are striking. Yet the influence of official American and Russian Cold War prisms was very potent, as each filtered reality to fit its belief system. If you were to take at face value the words spoken by U.S. and Soviet leaders, you would think that the two cases consisted of completely unrelated elements.[36] Differing perceptions over the atomic bomb leveling Hiroshima in 1945 comprise Case Study 7.4. ■

---

adversaries; and (5) two countries intensely involved with one another tend to see each other as either positive or negative mirror images of one another.[37]

The conditions for misperception are omnipresent in international affairs because the stakes are high, cultural differences between actors are often great, and accurate communication between the players is made difficult by distance, language barriers, and competing interests. The outbreak of WW I is often cited as a classic example of a war triggered by rampant misperception. If the players are global superpowers, the consequences of distorted perceptions can be especially disconcerting. Two examples from the tense Cold War days of the 1960s are discussed in Case Study 7.3. The Americans and Soviets conveniently flip-flopped their interpretations to suit their conflicting interests in the Dominican (1965) and Czechoslovakian (1968) crises.

Case Study 7.4 Textbook Spin, U.S. and Japanese Style

Events in world affairs often acquire symbolic meaning, layered onto their factual meaning, and societies struggling to deal with painful past experiences are prime candidates for distorting symbolic meaning. In such cases, we tend to find selective perception contributing to a form of cultural mythology, or shared historical blind spots. The content of public school textbooks can provide a window on the role of selective perception in coping with a society's psychic scars. Comparing American and Japanese textbooks' treatment of the August 6, 1945, dropping of the atomic bomb on the city of Hiroshima offers a peek through such a window.

This important event has been studied extensively. Although much factual information has been produced, intriguing differences of emphasis exist in textbook accounts of the Hiroshima bombing. Please read the following excerpts; then reread them, making two lists: identical elements versus different elements in the information reported. Excerpt from American textbook:

> On 6 August the first atomic bomb was dropped on Hiroshima, killing nearly eighty thousand people and reducing four square miles of the city to rubble and ashes. Still, Tokyo did not surrender, and three days later, the only other bomb that had thus far been produced was dropped on Nagasaki with similar dreadful consequences. At the same time, Soviet Russia declared war on Japan. On 14 August the Japanese at last accepted the Allies' terms of surrender, provided only that the Emperor be permitted to remain on his throne.

Excerpt from Japanese textbook

> On 6 August America dropped the world's first atomic bomb on Hiroshima. On the 8th of August the Soviet Union, breaking the Japan-Soviet Neutrality Treaty, declared war on Japan and invaded Manchuria. On the 9th, America dropped an atomic bomb on Nagasaki as well.

The atomic bombs took about 200,000 lives in Hiroshima and 100,000 in Nagasaki. Not only were there victims of the high heat and the shock wave, but also many of those exposed to radiation died within a few weeks. Moreover, for more than 20 years afterward, people continued to fall ill and die. The damage from these A-bomb after-effects shows people even today the dreadfulness of nuclear weapons. On 14 August Japan finally decided to accept the Allies' terms of surrender, and the nation was informed the next day by the Emperor's radio broadcast.[38]

Are you struck more by similarities, or differences, in these two textbook accounts? Why do you think this is so? Of what value is perceptual analysis in explaining the nature of these accounts, as well as your observations about them? Finally, how is it possible for countries such as Japan and the United States to switch so rapidly from adversaries in the 1930s, to enemies in the 1940s, then to allies after WW II?

Memorial cenotaph in Hiroshima Peace Park reminding the world about the devastation of nuclear weapons.

The Psychology of Enemy-Making

Wars have plagued human history as civilization's dark side. Because all societies express taboos against killing (often based on religious strictures), how is it that our species managed to kill more than 100 million people in the twentieth century alone?

If social taboos condemn killing, but wars require it, that presents humans with a conundrum. The psychodynamics enabling a society to create an "enemy" help explain how we have resolved this conundrum. The trip-wire that allows nations to shift (as did Japan and America) from adversaries to enemies consists of the process of **dehumanization.** Societies use dehumanization as a simple but potent tool by convincing their members that the enemy is essentially less than human: a monster, vermin, beast, madman, or demon—all of which are not only different but dangerous to us.

Dehumanization ■
Categorizing a group of people in an "out-group" as sufficiently inferior to our "in-group" as to render them sub-human

By examining diverse cultures at various times, social psychologist Sam Keen concludes that the dehumanization process is universally employed by countries preparing to fight wars. In comparing their visual imagery in posters, films, cartoons, and paintings, he marveled that it was "almost as if they all went to the same art school." Keen is not arguing for pacifism. He thinks it unlikely that states can be enemy-less and considers it equally improbable that we can eliminate this need to kill in war. However, greater awareness of the enemy-making process, Keen believes, will enable us to assess our enemies more accurately. We can then identify those who truly deserve being on our enemies list, rather than accepting all who audition for that role. States might find better ways to redress their grievances, but only if their perceptions of the motivation and behavior of other states are reasonably accurate.[39]

The Psychology/Terrorism Interface

Sam Keen's work on the psychology of enemy-making, however, was conducted in the mid-1980s, before the Cold War ended. Several more recent developments further complicate any hopes for humanity's future to prove more pacific than its violent past. Communications globalization allows obscure groups to gain worldwide notoriety for their grievances in ways impossible a generation ago. Former British Prime Minister Margaret Thatcher once urged the communications media to "starve terrorists of the oxygen of publicity!"[40] A nice sentiment, but probably futile given the growing commercialization of the news-gathering business.

Both communications globalization and military globalization serve to empower terrorists. Something else that complicates the terrorism issue is the mind-set of its perpetrators, who often consider themselves political or religious crusaders (even martyrs). Because they do not fear death, the task of stopping them is exceedingly difficult. Terrorism has long plagued many parts of the world, but not until 9/11 did Americans really understand the fear palpably.

Despite a popular assumption that terrorists are crazy people, only in rare cases have captured terrorists proven to be **clinically insane.** Walter Reich's *Origins of Terrorism* examines the motivations of terrorists and concludes that they seldom act without purposeful and consistent inner logic aimed at a sociopolitical objective. They conduct battles in a war that seeks global attention for a local cause. Because they select reprehensible means of achieving them does not mean that terrorists have no goals; but in the opinion of most of the world's people, terrorists' ends cannot justify their violent means.[41]

Soon after 9/11, President George W. Bush appointed Pennsylvania Governor Tom Ridge to head a new Office of Homeland Security, and then asked Congress for billions

Clinically insane ■ A medical diagnosis of dysfunctional mental characteristics rendering subjects not in control of their behavior

On September 11, 2001, Islamic extremists completed the destruction of the World Trade Center first attempted on February 26, 1993.

of dollars to expand the security infrastructure in the United States, as well as a host of new limitations on travel. Critics later argued that creating the Office of Homeland Security, under which the Federal Emergency Management Agency (FEMA) was subsumed, contributed significantly to the government's astonishing display of incompetence in responding to Hurricane Katrina in 2005. America represents a security nightmare because transportation routes into the United States are many and varied, lethal WMDs available to terrorists seem infinite, and the U.S. political culture (based on individual freedom) has a hard time accepting far-reaching restrictions on civil liberties.

The 9/11 attack on America has been etched into their consciousness, but the nature of the February 26, 1993, World Trade Center bombing may need retelling. It was in a plain rented yellow Ryder truck that international terrorism was delivered to America's doorstep. The truck carried 1,200 pounds of fertilizer topped with three cylinders of hydrogen gas. When detonated, it tore a five-story hole in New York City's World Trade Center (WTC), killing six, injuring more than 1,000, and filling Manhattan's financial district with scorched survivors.[42] It was a harbinger of the future, and American journalist Steven Emerson has followed the path of terrorists in the United States since the mid-1980s, and his 1998 documentary film *Jihad in America* traces a slew of clues emanating from the 1993 bombing that could have better prepared officials for 9/11.

The State as Enemy

Sometimes, however, terrorism does not involve radical Middle Eastern Muslims, and in 1995, it appeared in the American heartland at Oklahoma City, as detailed in Chapter 1's Timothy McVeigh case. During the 1990s, a growing number of disenchanted right-wing groups gained notoriety in the United States. Some operated as part of a loose Patriot movement advocating grass-roots activism against the power of the federal government. Others belonged to groups concerned about the Second Amendment's right to bear arms and are actively preparing for a confrontation with the U.S. government. Most of these disenchanted groups believe that an international conspiracy at the U.N. aims to steal America's independence.

The defining moment of their mission crystallized on September 11, 1990, when President George H. W. Bush proclaimed the Gulf War coalition as a harbinger of the "new world order" under U.N. auspices. President Bush hoped that using these words would generate public support for a war to stop Iraqi aggression against neighboring Kuwait. But the words "new world order" have been interpreted rather differently by right-wing activists fearing people of color are somehow manipulating the U.N. to control America.

Precise numbers relating to North America's right-wing extremists elude detection and vary decade-to-decade. They avoid clear organizational structures, relying mostly on "leaderless cells," thus leaving few footprints. Estimates in the 1990s suggested that about 100,000 of them were armed-to-the-teeth militia members, but as many as 12 million may see themselves as disaffected antigovernment patriots, mostly in the rural West.[43] When juxtaposed against FBI data relating to "America's bomb culture," militias seem even more ominous. Between the eighties and the nineties, a significant increase in bombings occurred: 442 in 1983, but up to 1,880 in 1993. Unfortunately, know-how is readily available today through the Internet and from mail-order publishing companies such as Paladin Press of Boulder, Colorado, whose catalog lists forty books and videos on making explosives, including *Homemade C-4: A Recipe for Survival*.[44]

How do some people become so committed to behavior so ugly? The complicated world in which we live contains many bona fide dangers. Thus, it is reasonable to fear some of those things that might threaten us individually or socially. The difficult thing to comprehend is the mental processes of those who go beyond rational fear and enter into the violent nether world of irrational **paranoia**, with its gross distortions of judgment. The paranoid personality is generally not insane but has fallen further out of touch with reality than the common forms of misperception to which all humans are susceptible.

Paranoia ■ A state of mental agitation stemming from a grossly exaggerated fear that someone very threatening intends to harm the afflicted person

Most people have felt some sense of grievance against the impersonal bureaucracies endemic to modern government. Reasonable people can recognize a kernel of truth in complaints against big government and can even empathize with brief emotional outbursts of antigovernment sentiment. Precious few, however, allow a grievance to consume their consciousness and arm themselves for a fight to the death. How do some individuals cross the line into violent paranoia?

One brick often loose in the foundation of the paranoid person relates to isolation. Alone and alienated, paranoids such as Timothy McVeigh find the acceptance they crave in radical groups. By joining a group with a siege mentality, they lose contact with outsiders who hold less pathological views. Psychiatrist Robert Jay Lifton suggests that paranoids who commit violence often consider themselves fragile and "experience feelings of falling apart."[45]

The personal identity of paranoid militia members becomes increasingly group-based. With in-group identity comes peer pressure, even peer competition, to conform to the group's stark beliefs. Repetition of its alarmist message reinforces the message's volume and intensity, and, by then, the paranoid perspective becomes routine. Yet, even after absorbing all of this hate, most militia members remain in a defensive posture, rarely switching to an offensive mode by violent attack. Sometimes those who have been kicked out of a group are pushed over the edge to commit wanton violence.[46]

This analysis does not suggest that armed insurrection is never warranted. U.S. citizens have no trouble seeing the American Revolutionary War against Great Britain as heroic resistance to oppression by freedom-seeking colonists. But separating legitimate rebellion for human rights on the one hand, from paranoid violence against legitimate governmental authority on the other hand, is not always easy. When social scientists grapple with these issues, the tools provided by psychology become just as meaningful as those offered by political science or sociology, and *critical thinking* (which derived mostly from the disciplines of psychology and philosophy) is often among those tools.

But can scientific skepticism and demands for evidence go too far, too fast? How do we balance critical thinking—a form of academic best practices praised by most professional organizations as an antidote to common sense's groupthink quality—against social expectations of loyalty to one's state? Is it proper to afford governmental officials a grace period by not asking tough or embarrassing questions when they say they're fighting an enemy? If so, what is the duration of that grace period? These difficult questions are addressed in the concluding section, "9/11, War on Terror, and David Ray Griffin's *The New Pearl Harbor*."

Griffin asks probing questions in his book about 9/11, and he claims that the Bush Administration has failed to provide credible responses to scores of unanswered questions raised about 9/11. Griffin cautions that he is not expressing final definitive conclusions about 9/11-related events, merely asking probing questions about which citizens have a right to have answers. He called for an independent inquiry based on extensive prima facie evidence that the administraton has not squared with the public about 9/11. Although prima facie evidence is not sufficient to draw final conclusions, its ubiquity in this case (similar to evidence sufficient for indictment in a criminal trial), warrants deeper and broader investigation, he contends.

After any trauma such as 9/11, diverse interpretations inevitably arise, and rigorous critical thinking is required to sort out the wheat from the chaff. Most of the alternative 9/11 interpretations I have not read; therefore, I can say nothing about their logic, academic rigor, or reliance on sound evidence. However, I have read Griffin's book completely, and hold some opinions based on close examination, but opinions nevertheless they remain. I found zero instances of hyperbole or loose rhetoric in any of its 201 pages of text, or in 717 endnotes consuming 47 pages of thorough scholarship. Too important are such issues to rely on the opinions of any authorities. Professor Emeritus at the Claremont School of Theology in California, David Ray Griffin has written about twenty books, mostly on religious and philosophical topics. More recently, however, he has spent time researching 9/11-related events, resulting in *The New Pearl Harbor: Disturbing Questions About the Bush Administration and 9/11* (Olive Branch Press, 2004).

9/11, War on Terror, and David Ray Griffin's
The New Pearl Harbor

Background

The most grievous attack ever on U.S. soil occurred on September 11, 2001. How George W. Bush decided to respond continues to ripple outward. Presidents possess vast resources to frame the public dialogue, especially during crises, when few citizens dare criticize. Bill Clinton chose to frame the matter of Osama Bin Laden and Al Qaeda as a law enforcement matter during the 1990s. President Bush, however, chose to frame it after 9/11 as part of a broader War on Terror (WOT). Griffin looks closely at the Bush Administration's official statements regarding 9/11. As of 2007, several 9/11-related questions had been considered by the mainstream media as taboo, and no mainstream media had reviewed Griffin's book.

As time passes following controversial events, assessing the validity of clashing opinions becomes less subjective and more rational. The long-term viability of civil society depends largely on an informed public acting intelligently. The Bush Administration has repeated certain claims regarding 9/11 and its responses to it. Only three issues scrutinized in Griffith's book are summarized below: (1) preparedness and military SOP; (2) Bush's behavior on 9/11, historical analogies, and preemption; (3) civil liberties and Iraq 2003/WOT.

Preparedness and Military SOP

Regarding *preparedness,* the administration claimed that: No one could have anticipated enemies flying airplanes into American skyscrapers; no credible or actionable evidence was ever presented to the administration concerning Osama Bin Laden or Al Qaeda about unusual activity in the summer of 2001; they had no foreknowledge of any pending attacks; all available evidence had been considered and it was insufficient to take extraordinary measures; the tragedy was attributable mostly to a *breakdown in communication*; rivalries between the Pentagon and intelligence agencies had contributed to the communications breakdown; more centralized bureaucratic control under one person might have proven efficacious. In other words, it was nearly impossible to have conceived of such attacks, and while problems did exist in the intelligence communities, the White House took all reasonable steps to defend America.

Griffin, however, sees the preparedness issue differently. He points to several governmental reports and academic documents in the 1990s that predicted exactly this scenario: Osama Bin Laden directing Al Qaeda-trained suicide bombers directing aerial geodes into American cultural, political, and military icons. Griffin also identifies many press articles about CIA and FBI mid-level officials submitting evidence concerning the nineteen 9/11 perpetrators that was ignored by senior officials, who rewarded their underlings' diligence by reassignment to unrelated duties or by firing. Griffin says the evidence points not to a breakdown of communications, but rather a *stand-down order* from above.

More than one hundred times annually, U.S. fighter jets scramble according to military *Standing Operating Procedure* (SOP) to intercept jets for various reasons. However, on 9/11, a unique failure to intercept flights 11, 175, and 77 allowed all three to strike their targets. Griffin claims that adherence to SOP would have allowed ample time to intercept, engage, and shoot down each plane. The world's most heavily defended building (Pentagon) was struck more than thirty minutes after the second WTC tower.

The first official account stated that no fighter jets were scrambled until after the Pentagon was hit. A second report a few days later said they had indeed scrambled planes before the Pentagon was hit, but that they arrived too late. This second White House account said planes had been scrambled to Washington from Langley AFB (130 miles away), with no reference to the closer Andrews AFB (10 miles away); and that planes had been scrambled to New York from Otis AFB (180 miles away), with no reference to the closer McGuire AFB (60 miles). Also, the scrambled planes arriving too late in New York were not redirected to the nearby capital. Despite serious SOP violations, not one instance of disciplinary action was taken after 9/11.

Bush's Behavior, Historical Analogies, and Preemption

Regarding *Bush's behavior on 9/11,* several mini-accounts have been floated and then retracted, but no full and coherent explanation exists. For example, when and how Bush learned of the attacks has varied. Griffin points out that at 8:48 a.m., two minutes after the first WTC crash, CNN was reporting the disaster. However, Bush says that he did not know for another ten minutes, despite Vice President Dick Cheney having conceded in a September 16th interview on "Meet the Press" that the Secret Service (accompanying Bush) had open lines with the Federal Aviation Administration (FAA), thus immediately recording when the first WTC tower was hit. Arriving at the Sarasota middle school just before 9:00 a.m., Bush acted unaware of the attack and claims he didn't learn of it until his arrival there, despite contrary evidence.

After being informed about the South Tower, he acted nothing like a commander-in-chief learning about a devastating terrorist attack. He reportedly told the school principal that "A commercial plane has hit the WTC and we're going to go ahead and do the reading thing, anyway" (a mere photo-op). After the second graders finished reading their story about a pet goat, Bush cracked a joke, paused to praise their skills, and advised them to remain in school and become good citizens.

When asked by a reporter if he knew about the WTC, Bush told her, "I'll talk about it later," proceeding to chat with the teacher until the press corps left. Bush's schedule had been well publicized, and Griffin asks why he and his Secret Service were not worried about an assassination attempt. Accounts from several different sources suggest that panic was oddly absent in Sarasota on 9/11. The motorcade's departure included no order for a military escort, and Air Force One took off with no jet fighter protection, even though there were two bases nearby.

Concerning *historical analogies of choice,* Bush's neo-conservative foreign policy advisors had for many years been talking about the need for a *new Pearl Harbor* to generate public support for vast expenditures (totaling over $1 trillion) for the Star Wars space-based missile system that Bush advocated. From the early 1990s, and consistently after 9/11, Bush and his advisors drew parallels between Pearl Harbor and 9/11: the United States must remain vigilant against sneak attacks of all kinds, and Al Qaeda has much in common with fascist Japan in 1941.

Griffin, however, suggests that the more apt parallel consists of the Cold War. Presidents had scared the American public excessively to maintain the military-industrial complex via record budgets during peacetime. The WOT merely substitutes for the Cold War against communism (trading one "ism" for another "ism"). The pertinent war was not WW II (the quintessentially good war), but rather the Vietnam War (the quintessentially bad war), when the United States fell prey to imperial over-stretch.

On the subject of *preemption,* Bush has contended that in a post-Cold War milieu, traditional deterrence policies no longer suffice. When varied WMDs can find their way to the "Axis of Evil Countries," or groups such as Al Qaeda, democratic leaders must act preemptively (ahead of time without overt provocation). It was clear by 2001 that the United States enjoyed global dominance unseen since the Roman Empire, so why wait for the bad guys to hurt America, asked Bush? Griffin points to protestors around the world complaining that the only rational explanation for Bush's bellicose behavior might be that he was doing it for oil or merely because he was able to.

Civil Liberties and Iraq 2003/WOT

Concerning the WOT's undeniable diminution of *civil liberties,* Bush contends that extraordinary times call for extraordinary measures. To fight the good fight against Islamic militants, his government needed to incarcerate inmates at Guantanamo Bay without recourse to Geneva Convention rights to glean information that might prevent another attack. It was also justifiable for the United States to kidnap suspects and whisk them off to opaque bases where some dubious U.S. WOT allies carried out even rougher treatment.

It was okay to eavesdrop on citizens at home without judicial warrants because they might be talking to Al Qaeda conspirators abroad. Griffin is far from alone in suggesting that America is supposed to stand for rule of law, civil society, and due process. Although many presidents have felt comfortable unilaterally expanding their power, the press, public opinion, constitutional scholars, or the Supreme Court eventually corral such hubris.

Finally, no examination of Bush's WOT is complete without noting how he has managed to fold his *2003 invasion and occupation of Iraq* into the global WOT mind-set. Saddam Hussein had nothing to do with 9/11; however, Bush's WOT justifies blurring such nuance. The fact that his rationalizations for taking Iraq all proved bogus seemed not to phase him or his advisors. Bush says that he must take on terrorists wherever they exist so that we don't have to fight them here, that we are righteous warriors against Islamic militants, and that he knows he is here for some higher purpose.

To what extent do you agree or disagree with Griffin's suggestions? Even if you disagree completely, do you consider his criticisms to represent a legitimate exercise of critical thinking skills on an inherently controversial topic? Or do you agree with those who say that books such as his constitute illegitimate inquiry tantamount to wartime disloyalty? Does the amount of time elapsing after cataclysms such as 9/11 matter when assessing the legitimacy of questions raised? Finally, do you think that psychology brings any unique insights not often applied by social scientists helpful in sorting out matters of war and peace?

Chapter Synopsis

Psychology's academic practitioners warn that critical thinking skills are required to separate the wheat from the chaff in their vast discipline. The Greek philosopher Plato struck a psychological chord in advising his students to "know thyself," but a bona fide discipline of psychology did not materialize until one century ago. By then, biologist Charles Darwin had legitimized the idea that humans obey the same developmental laws as other species, making humans fair game for scientific study. Psychological laboratory experiments borrowing heavily from natural sciences were first conducted in Leipzig, Germany, in 1879.

A Viennese physician named Sigmund Freud was much influenced by the Darwinian model of uncovering scientific laws. Freud believed that humans are driven by conflicts stemming from underlying impulses about which we are not consciously aware. Psycho-sexual childhood trauma, he argued, leads to adult dysfunctions that are hard to cure because he considered personality set in stone by age six. His psychoanalytical school used a talking cure of free association as the way to resolve painful buried memories. The subjectivity of psychoanalysis bred its chief competitor: behaviorism. Striving for a more rigorous scientific theory, behaviorists stress observation of overt human behavior, relying on positive and negative reinforcement (rewards and punishment) as the way to encourage desirable behaviors. They see human behavior as comprised of bundles of habits reinforced by the social environment.

In sharp contrast to these two theories stand two more recent challengers. The first, humanistic psychology, emerged from the idealistic 1960s in the United States. Humanistic psychology stressed free will and the lifelong evolution of personality, thus rejecting Freud's notion that the die is cast at an early age. Later, in the 1990s, rapid advances in brain research and genetics brought biopsychology to the forefront. Breakthrough chemical discoveries have resulted in many new and improved drugs to help those in psychological pain.

Psychological insights, theories, and methods also are applied to explain human behavior at the macro level. Several case studies in Chapter 7 provide fresh insights pertaining to complex questions such as nuclear numbing, selective perception, comparative textbook analysis regarding the Hiroshima bomb, and paranoia among militia members. Finally, challenges to the Bush administration's official account of 9/11-related events contained in David Ray Griffins' *New Pearl Harbor* are framed at the nexus where critical thinking skills intersect with citizenship.

FOR DIGGING DEEPER

Berkowitz, Peter, ed. *The Future of American Intelligence*. Hoover Press, 2005.

Bloom, Mia. *Dying to Kill: The Allure of Suicide Terror*. Columbia University Press, 2005.

Bouris, Erica. *Complex Political Victims*. Kumarian Press, 2007.

Brislin, Richard. *Applied Cross-Cultural Psychology*. Sage Publishing, 1990.

Buckley, Mary, ed. *The Bush Doctrine and the War on Terrorism*. Routledge, 2007.

Byman, Daniel. *Deadly Connections: States that Sponsor Terrorism*. Cambridge University, 2005.

Coates, James. *Armed and Dangerous: The Rise of the Survivalist Right*. Hill and Wang, 1996.

Coon, Dennis. *Introduction to Psychology: Exploration and Application*. West Publishing, 2004.

Deacon, Terrence. *The Symbolic Species: The Co-Evolution of Language and the Brain*. W. W. Norton, 1994.

Dutton, Donald. *The Psychology of Genocide, Massacre, and Extreme Violence: How Normal People Come to Commit War Atrocities*. Praeger, 2007.

Ember, Carol, and Melvin Ember. "Psychology and Culture," in *Cultural Anthropology*. Prentice Hall, 1996, pp. 284–304.

Forest, James J., ed. *Homeland Security: Protecting America's Targets*. Praeger, 2006.

Goodby, James E. *At the Borderline of Armageddon: How American Presidents Managed the Atomic Bomb*. Rowman and Littlefield, 2006.

Griffin, David Ray. *The New Pearl Harbor: Disturbing Questions About the Bush Administration and 9/11*. Olive Branch Press, 2004.

Hamer, Dean, and Peter Copeland. *Living with Our Genes*. Doubleday, 1998.

Hedley, R. Alan. *Running Out of Control: Dilemmas of Globalization*. Kumarian Press, 2002.

Janis, Irving L. *Groupthink*. University of Illinois Press, 1996.

Kean, Thomas H., and Lee H. Hamilton. *Without Precedent: The Inside Story of the 9/11 Commission*. Knopf, 2005.

Keen, Sam. *Faces of the Enemy: Reflections of the Hostile Imagination*. Harper and Row, 1986.

Langholtz, Harvey, ed. *The Psychology of Peacekeeping*. Greenwood Publishing, 1998.

Llinas, Rodolfo. *I of the Vortex: From Neurons to Self*. MIT Press, 2001.

Long, Austin. *On "Other War": Five Decades of RAND Counterinsurgency Research*. RAND Corporation, 2006.

Loveman, Brian, ed. *Addicted to Failure: U.S. Security Policy in Latin America and the Andean Region*. Rowman and Littlefield, 2006.

Marshall, Will, ed. *With All Our Might: A Progressive Strategy for Defeating Jihadism and Defending Liberty*. Rowman and Littlefield, 2006.

Mead, Margaret. *Coming of Age in Samoa*. Morrow, 1961.

Nasr, Vali. *The Shia Revival: How Conflicts within Islam Will Shape the Future*. Norton, 2006.

Ornstein, Robert. *The Evolution of Consciousness: Of Darwin, Freud, and Cranial Fire: The Origins of the Way We Think*. Prentice Hall, 1991.

Palmer, Monte, and Princess Palmer. *At The Heart of Terror: Islam, Jihadists, and America's War on Terrorism*. Rowman and Littlefield, 2006.

Pilon, Juliana Geran. *Why America Is Such a Hard Sell: Beyond Pride and Prejudice*. Rowman and Littlefield, 2007.

Pinker, Steven. *How the Mind Works*. W. W. Norton, 1997.

Ramachandran, Vilayanur, and Sandra Blakeslee. *Phantoms in the Brain: Probing the Mysteries of the Human Mind*. Quill/William Morrow, 1998.

Ranal, Jonathan. *Osama: The Making of a Terrorist*. Vintage, 2006.

Redlener, Irwin. *Americans at Risk: Why We Are Not Prepared for Mega-Disasters and What We Can Do*. Knopf, 2006.

Reich, Walter. *Origins of Terrorism: Psychologies, Ideologies, States of Mind*. Cambridge University Press, 1990.

Renshon, Stanley A. *Understanding the Bush Doctrine: Psychology and Strategy in an Age of Terrorism*. Routledge, 2007.

Rostker, Bernard. *I Want You! The Evolution of the All-Volunteer Force*. Rowman and Littlefield, 2006.

Schafer-Jones, Jay. *Preparing for the Worst: A Comprehensive Guide to Protecting Your Family from Terrorist Attacks, Natural Disasters, and Other Catastrophes*. Praeger, 2007.

Schultz, Richard H. *Insurgents, Terrorists, and Militias: The Warriors of Contemporary Combat*. Columbia University Press, 2006.

Segall, Marshall H., et al. *Cross-Cultural Psychology: Human Behavior in Global Perspective*. Brooks/Cole, 1979.

Singh, Robert. *Anti-Americanisms: Power, Principle, and the End of American Foreign Policy*. Routledge, 2007.

Stanovich, Keith E. *How to Think Straight about Psychology*. HarperCollins, 2006.

Steinberg, Blema S. *Shame and Humiliation: Presidential Decision Making on Vietnam*. University of Pittsburgh Press, 1996.

Taylor, Richard H., and Sandra Wright Taylor. *Homeward Bound: American Veterans Return from War*. Praeger, 2007.

Veitch, Russell, and Daniel Arkkhelin. *Environmental Psychology: An Interdisciplinary Perspective*. Prentice Hall, 1995.

Watson, Cynthia A. *Military Education: A Reference Handbook*. Praeger, 2007.

Wright, Lawrence. *The Looming Tower: Al-Qaeda and the Road to 9/11*. Knopf, 2006.

Zakaria, Fareed. *The Future of Freedom: Illiberal Democracy at Home and Abroad*. Norton, 2004.

INTERNET

American Psychological Association (APA):
http://www.apa.org/

Center for Evolutionary Psychology:
http://www.psych.ucsb.edu/research/cep/

Dehumanizing Propaganda and War:
www.classroomtools.com/faces2.htm

Encyclopedia of Psychology:
http://www.psychology.org/

From Ramachandran's Notebook:
http://www.pbs.org/wgbh/nova/mind/notebook.html

Human Genome Project Information:
http://www.ornl.gov/hgmis/

Humanistic Psychology:
http://www.ahpweb.org/aboutahp/whatis.html

Neuroscience Education:
http://faculty.washington.edu/chudler/ehceduc.html

Online Social Psychology Studies:
http://www.socialpsychology.org/expts.htm

Psychological Experiments on the Internet:
http://psych.fullerton.edu/mbirnbaum/web/IntroWeb.htm

Psychology Virtual Library:
http://www.clas.ufl.edu/users/gthursby/psi/

Remembering Nagasaki:
http://www.exploratotium.edu/nagasaki/index.html

Social Psychology Network:
http://www.socialpsychology.org/

CHAPTER 8

Global Ethics and Human Rights

CORE OBJECTIVE

To consider the relevance of ethical and humanitarian influences on human behavior.

THEMATIC QUESTIONS

- How does the domain of ethics interface with the social sciences?

- Just what does ethics mean?

- What sort of relationship exists between religion and ethical issues?

- How can the GI of human rights be seen as recent and ethics seen as ancient?

- In what ways does gender represent a controversial matter concerning human rights?

In looking at the subjective dimension of the human experience in Chapter 7, we concentrated on the discipline of psychology. In this chapter, we also include insights from philosophy, political science, and sociology because no discipline monopolizes insights pertinent to matters of right and wrong (morality). Our examination of morality's influence on human behavior on the world stage involves two categories: (1) the ancient humanities-soaked domain of ethics and (2) the contemporary evolution of a body of international law to protect a wide range of human rights.

By examining moral considerations, this chapter gives the idealist school center stage, while the realist school is relegated to the shadows. Ethics represents an area of human endeavor in which many intriguing questions arise. However, finding answers to those questions can prove very difficult. Therefore, just as we cited experts in Chapter 7 about the need for critical thinking skills in psychology, we will do so in this chapter as well.

One of the greatest twentieth-century role models for morality was the Indian social reformer M. K. Gandhi (1869–1948), called "Mahatma" (Hindi for "great soul"). His **pacifist** civil disobedience on behalf of Indian liberation from British rule influenced many idealist thinkers of the twentieth century. Among those individuals were America's Dr. Martin Luther King, Jr., and South Africa's Nelson Mandela. Gandhi's loving acceptance of Indian Muslims and Sikhs enraged Hindu fundamentalists, who assassinated him in 1948. Richard Attenborough's film *Gandhi* (1982), which won an Oscar for best picture, is one of the great film biographies, featuring British actor Ben Kingsley in the title role.

Pacifist ■ One who follows the tradition of peacefully turning the other cheek, thus refusing to meet violence with counterviolence

Economic development, as you will see in Chapters 14 and 15, contributes to higher standards of living, and in many ways, furthers overall quality of life. In other words, things such as nurturing our fragile ecosphere, promoting equal employment opportunities, protecting civil liberties such as voting, providing health care, and feeding people sufficiently all require money or other negotiable resources. Extreme poverty, which is found across great swaths of the earth, makes living a good life extremely difficult. However, in addition to standing for nonviolent civil disobedience as the path to Indian independence, Gandhi also epitomized minimalism as the path to *spiritual transcendence* of materialistic traps and temptations. He could not have lived any more simply, yet did so joyfully. The continued presence of Gandhian spiritual transcendence is something that Western observers routinely marvel at after returning from India, home of one-third of all hungry people on earth. Many say things like "These are some of the happiest people I have ever seen." India qualifies as a truly enigmatic place.

Indian holy man Mahatma Gandhi in his modest attire.

U.S. sociologist and author John Macionis writes about his 1988 research experience in the southern port city of Chennai, home to eight million residents, 500,000 of whom live in hundreds of shantytowns made out of tree branches and discarded materials. One of the most obvious realities about Madras is that you find homeless people sleeping all over the city's sidewalks. He recounts that "One immediately recoils from the smell of human sewage that hangs over the city like a malodorous cloud. Untreated sewage also renders much of its water unsafe to drink. The sights and sounds of Madras are strange and intense." There are places in India that have experienced remarkable economic booms since the early 1990s, but Madras is not among them.

Macionis also notes that U.S. students initially feel uncomfortable in Madras, probably because the poorest sections of American inner cities seem to be boiling over with frustration. But what visitors soon learn is that, philosophically, Indians in Madras interpret poverty very differently than do Westerners. The Hindu concept of dharma, or destiny, teaches Indians to accept their given fate, regardless of its travails, and to use hardship to rise above suffering. After working in India for years, Mother Teresa stated in a similar vein that "Americans have angry poverty, but the worse conditions in India result in a happy poverty." Tight families and communities also help to ease life's burdens there.[1]

More than a few scholars have drawn comparisons between Mahatma Gandhi and Jesus Christ as pacifists. Jesus Christ was the first prophet or leader in the Jewish tradition to teach "turning the other cheek to one's enemies." Considered a ground-breaker in this respect, Jesus is thought to have recognized that past revolutionaries' response to violence with violence merely served to perpetuate the spiral of violence begetting more violence. Gandhi's nonviolent civil disobedience and pacifism have also been connected with many other religious and spiritual leaders.

Ethics

Deceit and violence appear often in the script that plays itself out on the world stage, so what role can possibly exist for ethics at this level? Do global actors merely pay lip service to moral considerations, ignoring them during real-world conflicts? Do the principles and values that quietly guide the lives of most individuals disappear in the face of competition for huge stakes such as billion-dollar profits, cultural survival, and national power?

Avenues of Ethical Influence

Ethical influences on state behavior seem to manifest themselves in several ways. First, in democracies, society's moral values come through in the form of public opinion polls, to which decision-makers pay close attention. These general values help to set parameters of the acceptable in society, thus establishing general policy limitations. Just as domestic public opinion exerts influence, global public opinion represents a second ethical voice. On a day-to-day basis, leaders go to great pains to conform to international sensibilities and to convince the world that they are good global citizens. This fact is often missed because the mass media sensationalize the cases of defiance against the world community but downplay behaviors consistent with global norms.

Finally, ethics enter into the picture via the personal values of key decision-makers because they are human beings first and national leaders second. When Franklin Roosevelt decided against using gas warfare during WW II, his individual ethics played a key role, raising the question whether, if he had lived longer, he would have acted differently from Harry S. Truman in using the atomic bomb. Swedish diplomat Raoul Wallenberg was ethically motivated when he risked his life during the same war to save many thousands of European Jews scheduled for the Nazi gas chambers. Similarly, Robert F. Kennedy's account of the Cuban missile crisis, *Thirteen Days,* claims that President John F. Kennedy found morally abhorrent the military's advice to bomb Cuba as a means of getting rid of the Russian offensive missiles placed there in 1962.

In an unusual wartime situation, neither American nor world public opinion had any chance to express itself regarding the big question that faced President Harry S. Truman in 1945: how to end the Pacific war with Japan. Only the president and a small group of advisors even knew about America's possession of the new atomic bomb. A smaller circle still had any influence over what the president might choose to do with the super-weapon. Not many situations involve larger ethical implications than does Case Study 8.1 that follows. In fact, in 1999, a survey of prominent U.S. journalists and scholars concluded that Hiroshima was the top news story of the entire twentieth century.[2]

Problems in Putting Ethics into Action

Applying ethical principles to world affairs almost invariably presents serious challenges. One problem is that two or more attractive moral ideals can conflict in the real world. The very soul of the discipline of anthropology conveys the value judgment that cultural differences should be respected. However, complexities arise when the goal of allowing other cultures to do their own thing brings us face-to-face with cultures that practice activities we consider immoral, such as female genital mutilation.

Second, there is the level-of-analysis problem. Ethical philosophers have long argued that in addition to the motivation of the actor, we must take into account the relevant context when assessing the morality of decisions. The operational milieu facing common people is sufficiently different from that of the president of the United States, the head of General Motors, or the secretary general of the U.N. as to raise questions about the interchangeability of ethical principles between levels. President Truman's milieu in the Hiroshima case is something we can only imagine because we cannot re-create it.

Third, the history of the state is replete with examples of powerful countries imposing their vision of morality on simpler societies. At times, ethics have seemed nothing more than footnotes to national power considerations, seemingly validating what ethicist Joel Rosenthal calls the realist's aphorism—"that the strong do what they will, and the weak do what they must."[3] When the strong throw their weight around today, they are often accused of cultural imperialism, violating a weaker culture's right to exist on its own terms. The image of the bully is neither attractive nor amicable, and powerful Western societies such as the United States do what they can to avoid such an unflattering global image. Nevertheless, the influences that rich industrial societies exert over poor preindustrial ones remain pervasive.

Veteran American diplomat George Kennan recognizes some of the difficulties inherent in passing moral judgment on other peoples. He suggests that in world affairs we are better off leading by example, thus setting a moral tone via behavior more

Case Study 8.1   Truman's Decision to Drop the Bomb

Protagonists

- President Harry S. Truman—sworn in after the death of President Roosevelt in April 1945
- Henry L. Stimson—secretary of war and general "overseer" of the Manhattan Project
- James L. Byrnes—secretary of state
- General Leslie Groves—Army general heading the logistical side of the Manhattan Project
- Robert L. Oppenheimer—Berkeley physicist heading the scientific side of the Manhattan Project
- Otto Franck and Leo Szilard—physicists at the University of Chicago who sent a report to the president urging that the bomb not be used for military purposes against Japan
- Emperor Hirohito—Emperor of Japan with traditional status of divinity; his reign included savage aggression against Manchuria and China, alliance with the Axis, and the 1941 attack on Pearl Harbor

Prologue

The United States' entry into WW II occurred suddenly with Japan's sneak attack at Pearl Harbor on December 7, 1941, a date President Roosevelt asserted would "live in infamy." American resentment against anything Japanese ran very high, attested to by the relocation of one-quarter million Japanese-American citizens into remote and tightly controlled camps. Most lost their property as well as their freedom. This relocation was undertaken even though no Japanese-American citizen was ever convicted of espionage or sabotage during WW II. In fact, the most highly decorated unit among American forces turned out to be the "Fighting

Kiloton ■ One kiloton equals the nuclear equivalency of 1,000 tons of TNT explosive

Destroyer USS *Shaw* explodes during the Japanese invasion of Pearl Harbor, home of the American Pacific Fleet, on December 7, 1941.

442nd," made up of Japanese-Americans fighting in Europe. Interestingly, no similar denial of civil rights was even considered against German-Americans or Italian-Americans (also countries at war with America).

Victory in Europe was finally achieved in May of 1945. The war with Japan, however, dragged on, with bloody battles across the Pacific islands. Japanese atrocities against Allied forces were widely reported. The American people, ecstatic over the defeat of Hitler, wanted the "other" war to end as well. Throughout the summer of 1945, U.S. fire-bombings of Japanese cities were killing 100,000 people per day. The Japanese rulers, however, remained unwilling to accept the only terms America would offer: *total unconditional surrender*. A land invasion of Japan stayed on the back burner because military estimates had projected that U.S. casualties in such a scenario could reach 250,000 GIs.

Dramatic Plot

Into this frustrating milieu, a seeming miracle of science and technology stepped center stage. On July 16, 1945, the top-secret $4 billion Manhattan Project paid dividends as the United States successfully exploded the world's first atomic bomb in New Mexico. The huge project, headed by physicist Robert Oppenheimer on the scientific side and General Leslie Groves on the logistical side, created a super-weapon of 20 **kilotons**. With this new weapon, American leaders felt a sense of confidence about concluding the war on their terms.

A very difficult decision, however, confronted the inexperienced President Truman and his top advisors, Secretary of War Henry Stimson and Secretary of State James Byrnes—namely, how best to use this awesome weapon. Before Truman ascended to the presidency, the Manhattan Project was one of many matters that Roosevelt had kept from him.

Truman knew that his goal was to end the war as quickly as possible—on terms of unconditional surrender and with a minimum loss of American lives. The vexing question that remained, however, was how best to do this.

Seven different suggestions emanated from both the military Joint Chiefs of Staff and a special Interim Committee of advisors appointed by Truman:

1. The navy recommended a naval blockade of Japan to gradually starve the Japanese out.
2. A land invasion along the southern Kyushu region was favored by the army as the only certain guarantee of victory.
3. Continued daily fire-bombings of Japanese cities were favored by the air force as costing fewer American lives.
4. The majority of the Interim Committee advised Truman to use the A-bomb militarily by dropping it on a city with some military significance.

5. A minority on the Interim Committee preferred that the A-bomb be used in a harmless demonstration on Japanese soil—to inform the Japanese of what they were up against and why they should surrender.

6. General McCloy of the Joint Chiefs alone suggested that an explicit verbal warning about the A-bomb be given to Japan in an effort to induce surrender.

7. A final option considered was to wait the Japanese out because Allied victory was inevitable.

Each alternative possessed advantages and disadvantages. A blockade would lose few lives but would be time-consuming; loss of lives from an invasion would be great but would ensure favorable settlement terms and would be relatively fast; continued fire-bombings would cost time and great losses in Japanese civilian lives and property, but few U.S. soldiers would die; dropping the A-bomb on a city would be swift and devastating but involved ethical questions and could include unknown long-term environmental or health effects; a harmless demonstration of the A-bomb would not destroy property or lives but might fail to scare the Japanese into surrendering (and the United States had only two operational bombs); issuing a verbal warning could possibly save lives and induce surrender but might not be taken seriously by the intransigent Japanese government; waiting the Japanese out could save lives but would be politically unpopular in a country desiring the war to end quickly.

Adding to the complexity of Truman's decision was an eleventh-hour crisis of conscience for many scientists who had worked on the Manhattan Project. The program had originally been initiated at the suggestion of physicist Albert Einstein to beat Hitler to the atomic punch. Many of the scientists, so caught up in the technical challenge of creating this miracle weapon, didn't really think about the ethical dilemmas it created until faced with its possible use against Japan, which was not the original motivation for its production. For scientists such as Leo Szilard and Otto Franck, they could not accept using it against Japanese cities as ethically defensible, and they advised against this option.

President Truman decided to use the bomb militarily against a Japanese city, without warning, while continuing to demand unconditional surrender. On August 6, 1945, the first A-bomb was dropped on the city of Hiroshima, resulting in 80,000 immediate deaths and about 40,000 long-term casualties from radiation poisoning. When the Japanese still failed to accept unconditional surrender, Truman ordered a second bomb dropped on Nagasaki on August 9, 1945. Four days later, the Japanese government surrendered, ending WW II.[4]

Critical Analysis

President Truman faced a very complex decision, one that is still being debated. Given the context of the times, the central goal, and the alternatives available, which path would you have chosen? Where specifically do you agree or disagree with Truman's decision?

When Truman made his decision, the Manhattan Project was top secret, and the public was completely unaware of it, leaving no public opinion to consider. However, he would be facing an election in 1948, and how the various options would play in Peoria must have been on his mind. General Leslie Groves argued that Truman had no real choice other than military use of the A-bomb because if he had failed to use it, the mothers of all those soldiers who died invading Japan would have blamed him.

Where Truman may have been most susceptible to criticism was in clinging to total unconditional surrender from a Japanese martial culture where losing face traditionally has been looked on as worse than death. Truman also made no effort to explicitly communicate to Japan that it was up against a devastating new super-weapon, or to pursue secret feelers from the Japanese military asking for the Soviet Union to mediate an end to a war that Japan could not win. Truman adamantly stuck to unconditional surrender without diplomacy.

All such discussion is speculative. Your opinion on this question derives as much from your values as from the facts of the case. Examining our own views on Truman's decision helps in comprehending our fundamental beliefs—the ethical mind-set through which we view affairs on the world stage. For example, would you expect most realists to judge Truman's decision kindly or harshly? And would you expect most idealists to judge Truman's decision well or poorly? ■

---

than through words.[5] Or, as expressed by another scholar, as an exemplar, America should strive to represent the "shining city on the hill," which others will want to emulate.[6] In some complicated situations, however, morally exemplary behavior is as elusive as a hard rain in the desert. The Vietnam War was fraught with moral dilemmas for both American decision-makers and for individual citizens. Among those struggling with the ethics of various paths of action were America's military draftees, as detailed in Case Study 8.2.

Religion and Public Affairs

The social role of religion varies greatly around the world. The world's three largest religions differ in their involvement with public affairs. The largest religious group, 2 billion

Case Study 8.2   The Moral Dilemma of Vietnam War Draftees

America has been fortunate among democracies in enjoying a national consensus on many key foreign policy issues. American domestic politics tend toward highly charged partisanship but not typically so for world affairs. It took something as divisive as the Vietnam War to tear apart this foreign policy consensus. Divisiveness occurred partly because no public debate contributed to an explicit policy decision to "Americanize" the war in Vietnam.

Prior to his assassination, President John F. Kennedy's policy was "limited partnership," excluding American forces from combat roles in Vietnam. In his 1964 campaign, Lyndon B. Johnson portrayed Republican challenger Barry Goldwater as a warmonger capable of pushing the nuclear button on Vietnam, while he depicted himself as the peace candidate. Johnson's highest priority was his domestic *Great Society* program, which he was unwilling to sacrifice at the altar of the Vietnam War.

Some of the 100,000 demonstrators who gathered at a rally in New York City to protest against the Vietnam War.

However, the highly shaky South Vietnamese government, supported for a decade by the United States, found itself on the verge of collapse in July of 1965. Johnson's secretary of defense, Robert McNamara, returned from a tour of Vietnam concluding that the moment of decision had arrived for the United States: either abandon the South to the communists—admitting failure but cutting U.S. losses—or greatly expand its role, hoping for the best from an uncertain roll of the military dice.

During the month of July, Johnson made the critical decision. He effectively "Americanized" the war—most notably by sending more than 200,000 combat forces to replace South Vietnamese soldiers. Incredibly, these decisions were made without consultation with Congress or the public. They were, in fact, concealed and distorted. This resulted in a "credibility gap" that ultimately proved LBJ's political undoing.

Johnson also failed to finance his war honestly. Again hoping to protect his domestic Great Society, he refused to increase taxes or reduce government spending, choosing instead to print new money, resulting in rampant double-digit inflation in the 1970s.[7] The Vietnam War was not only undeclared, it soon became very unpopular. By the late 1960s, America was split—either for the war or against it—no middle ground existed. Strife-ridden college campuses imploded on themselves, going beyond debate by descending into recrimination and violence.

In this volatile political milieu, young men faced a question unusual for Americans: What to do about the military draft? U.S. ground forces in Vietnam had grown to more than 500,000, and relatively few volunteers came forward. Roughly half of college-aged males opposed the war for a combination of legal, religious, and political reasons. Five possible choices existed for those in opposition: (1) refuse induction, resulting in a likely prison sentence; (2) obtain landed immigrant status in Canada or another country welcoming American draft-dodgers; (3) if opposition was religiously based and applied to all wars, not just this one, apply for exemption as a conscientious objector; (4) swallow one's opposition to the war, accepting induction and likely Vietnam service; (5) find a way around the draft using one of the legal exemptions for things such as higher education, child dependency, sole surviving son, or alternative service in the National Guard.

Doing the right thing, or exercising what political scientist Paul Kael calls "good international citizenship," wasn't a simple matter for young men opposed to the war in the 1960s and 1970s.[8] They faced an ethical dilemma because most of them had been socialized to believe in their duty to obey the law of the land. However, because they had lost faith in a government that had deceived them on the issue of Vietnam, the legal duty argument crumbled for many young men. Yet only a few would seriously consider going to prison when they did not believe they had done anything wrong.

For the better educated, moving to Canada represented a viable—albeit disruptive—alternative. The most common means of avoidance for well-educated or well-connected young men was to obtain legal deferment status. An indisputable fact still rankles many observers: mostly poor, uneducated, minority urbanites fought the Vietnam War for the United States. The higher your socioeconomic status, the less likely you would end up being snagged by the Selective Service system. Not surprisingly, a deep sense of bitterness was shared by the families of more than 45,000 war dead and 238,000 wounded. Ethical behavior becomes hard to identify in such complicated situations, encouraging us to settle for what Kenneth Thompson calls "practical morality," or the idea that ethics can continue to function as a meaningful part of our decision making without its being the only consideration.[9] The place where people often feel safest confronting such complex questions is within the principles and rituals of their religious orientations. Not only does religion operate as a domestic agent of socialization and as a basis for just war doctrine, but it also works as part of the web of subjective forces weaving a tapestry of ethical values impinging on the behavior of actors on the world stage. ■

Christians ■ Believers in a monotheistic God whose messages were expressed in the person of Jesus Christ 2,000 years ago

Muslim ■ A monotheistic religion whose God, Allah, is believed to have expressed himself through the prophet Muhammed in 692 A.D.

Hindu ■ Native to India, a polytheistic religion emphasizing reincarnation and the need for individuals to rise spiritually above their earthly tribulations

Theocracies ■ Nonsecular governments ruled by persons believed to be wise by virtue of their holiness

Atheistic ■ Relating to the belief that no god or supernatural being exists and that monotheistic religions conjure up their own visions of a prime mover bearing the human countenance

Christians, tend to fall in the middle of the spectrum, involving religion with politics less than the world's 1 billion **Muslims** but much more than the 700 million **Hindu** adherents, whose approach to public life might be described as one of transcending politics. Historically, Roman Catholics and Muslims have confronted each other often, most notably during the eight Crusades from 1095 to 1291.

Only a few countries, such as Iran and the Taliban government in Afghanistan from 1995 to 2001, could be called modern-day **theocracies.** At the opposite extreme, we find officially **atheistic** countries treating religions with hostility. These exist today only in the four remaining communist states: China, Vietnam, North Korea, and Cuba. In places such as Spain, Russia, and the United Kingdom, an official Christian religion exists, but other religions are tolerated as well, as is the right not to practice religion at all.

The U.S. Constitution includes two notions on religion: the "establishment clause," forbidding the state from creating an official religion; and the "free exercise clause," guaranteeing the right of individuals to practice their religious beliefs. But regardless of their unique wrinkles, all societies evolved with religions operating at their foundation. Notably, almost all religions share a few basic values, such as encouraging compassion, generosity, tolerance, and honesty, as well as condemning deception, murder, torture, and selfishness. Some variation on the theme of the Golden Rule is also common among world religions.

Figure 8.1

Iran's modern-day theocracy represents an aberration in the twenty-first century.

Religion's Dual Role

As John Rourke puts it, "Religion has played a dual role in world politics." Possessing a dark side as well as a bright side, religion has at times fueled militant fanaticism, but at other times it has fostered pacifism and humanitarian understanding.[10] Since the end of the Cold War, many religions have enjoyed a renaissance, most notably in the former Soviet Union and its satellite countries in eastern Europe. In addition, world affairs scholarship has increasingly focused on the role of religious groups engaged in "peacemaking."[11] The Catholic Church played an important part in legitimizing the independent political role of the Solidarity Labor Union in Poland during the 1980s. In no other eastern European country was a religious institution so crucial to the gradual dismantling of communism as in Poland.

Scores of religiously driven grass-roots, local development initiatives in the Third World are chronicled by Mary Lean in her book *Bread, Bricks, and Belief: Communities in Charge of Their Future*. Tracing cases involving local Christian, Sikh, Hindu, Muslim, and Buddhist spiritual leaders, she draws optimistic conclusions about the impact of creative local solutions inspired by workers trusting in a higher power.[12] Accolades are justly accorded to such examples of religious inspiration contributing to grass-roots solutions to global problems. However, the darker side of religious intolerance must also be recognized.

Numerous international conflicts in recent decades have been worsened by religious tension. The Orthodox Christians of Greece and the Muslims of Turkey have conducted a long-standing battle over the disputed Mediterranean island of Cyprus, located between them. A U.N. peacekeeping force has been located there since 1964 in an effort to keep the combatants separated. India, while technically a secular state, has been experiencing a revival of Hindu fundamentalism, leading to many clashes with Pakistan, its largest Islamic neighbor. In 1993, Hindus destroyed a mosque claimed to be built on the site of an ancient Hindu temple, leading to religious rioting and conflict with Pakistan. More recently, Muslims have retaliated by setting fire to a train, which led to violent riots. Both India and Pakistan possess nuclear weapons.

A ceremony of the Russian Orthodox Church inside St. Nicholas Cathedral, St. Petersburg.

No international conflict has been fueled more by religious fervor than the face-off of the Jewish state of Israel with its Islamic-Arab neighbors. Major wars in 1948, 1956, 1967, and 1973 all involved religion in their incendiary mix. Adding to the intransigence of this religious conflict are its historical roots, traced back not centuries, but millennia, as well the intractable fact that two different peoples lay claim to the same tiny piece of sacred turf.

Almost everyone feels some sympathy for Tibet. This tiny Himalayan nation has been in and out of Chinese control over the centuries. Under their spiritual leader, the Dalai Lama, Tibet's Buddhists have often fought to establish independence from the powerful Chinese. In 1950, shortly after the communist victory in China's civil war, Tibet was reincorporated into China. In 1959, the Tibetans rose up in defiance, only to be brutally defeated by China. The Dalai Lama remains in exile today in India, while Tibetans have become a minority among the Han Chinese in their native land. When religion contributes to existing international tensions, and fighting breaks out between two countries, such situations demand attention from the international community.

Even more common in recent years has been the role of religion in igniting civil war within states. Recent examples practically jump off the page: Catholics against Protestants in Northern Ireland; Hindus versus Muslims and Sikhs in India; Sunni and Shiite Muslims in Iraq; Druse and Maronite Christians in Lebanon; Muslims and Orthodox Christians in the Chechen part of Russia; Muslims and Christians in Soviet Georgia; Buddhists

Chamulans from Mesoamerica celebrating their patron saint San Juan.

and Hindu Tamils in Sri Lanka; Christians and Muslims in Algeria; and Orthodox Christians, Catholics, and Muslims in Bosnia.

Ritual Practices

In addition to following a set of doctrinal beliefs, religious practitioners also engage in ceremonial activities. These powerful rituals are intended to bring the believer in closer contact with the sacred. When Catholics go to confession, or Muslims pray facing Mecca, or Jews perform a bar mitzvah, or Hindus bathe in the Ganges River, an internal logic renders these activities spiritually meaningful for members in ways that elude nonmembers. Sometimes spiritual rituals combine parts of seemingly disparate religions.

Among the Chamulas of Mesoamerica, it is common to borrow the worship of celestial objects from their ancient Mayan Indian ancestors and merge it with the worship of Jesus Christ, taken from the Roman Catholic Spanish conquistadors who invaded them. In the Chamula version of an afterlife, most human souls (except murderers and suicides) are transported to a pleasant underworld, an earthlike existence replete with cyclical sunlight. However, one area of human pleasure does not exist for these otherwise fortunate souls: engaging in sexual relations is believed not to be possible.[13]

Not far from where the Chamula Indians live today, the proud Aztec civilization once thrived. Like many of the most advanced ancient civilizations of both the Old and New Worlds—Mesopotamian, Greek, Viking, Celtic, Incan, and Mayan—the Aztecs engaged in a religious practice considered by contemporary Western civilization as barbarically unethical: ritual human sacrifice, as described in Case Study 8.3.

Case Study 8.3   Humans Sacrificed at the Altar of Aztec Gods

The Aztec state originated with a community of Nahuatl-speaking Amerindians in the Valley of Mexico during the early fourteenth century. Tenochtitlán developed into the grandest city in the Americas as the capital of this powerful state located in what today remains the heart of modern Mexico. The Aztec irrigation system supported organized agriculture, producing huge surpluses. The inventive Aztecs connected many of the Mexican lakes by canals, establishing regular canoe traffic that brought agricultural products such as corn, sweet potatoes, tomatoes, and tobacco to cities with skilled labor forces and well-organized economic and political institutions. An efficient bureaucracy collected taxes, delivered mail, and enforced the law. World-class science, art, architecture, and writing were also produced by this thriving empire.

But another characteristic of Aztec society was its extreme militarism. The Aztecs were intent on conquering most of their neighbors, from whom they extracted heavy taxes and tribute. As religious polytheists, the Aztecs had plenty of gods whom they believed needed appeasing, and many unfortunates defeated in war were slated for sacrifice. The protection of the gods of the sun, earth, and rivers stood at the pinnacle of Aztec beliefs and required payment in human blood. At their peak, they led possibly as many as 30,000 hapless victims per year to the sacrificial stone in Tenochtitlán.

As unnecessary as this sacrificial carnage seems to Western civilization, it made sense to the Aztecs: their gods required regular appeasement as the price for the empire's continued success. What seemed utterly without sense in Aztec logic was their own rapid butchery from 1519 to 1522 at the hands of Spain's Hernando Cortez, with his horses and thundering artillery.

An Aztec prophecy had predicted that "white gods" would appear, and at first it was believed that the arrival of the conquistadors ought to be heralded. The Aztecs were disabused of any such illusions when Cortez unleashed a holy war against religious idolatry and human sacrifice. Whereas the Spaniards found Aztec religion heretical and barbaric, many Aztecs did not find Catholic doctrine all that strange. Some of them reportedly considered the sacrifice of Jesus Christ as the path to Christian salvation quite congenial with their own notions of the relationship between salvation and human sacrifice.[14] ■

Human Rights

The GI of human rights can be viewed as a subset of the more general set of ethics in action. The core concept relevant to an understanding of human rights in international affairs is that of "inalienable rights," immediately recognizable to readers of the American Declaration of Independence. The notion of inalienable rights asserts that these rights derive from mere "human-ness"; thus, from whence they originate matters not. As members of the human species, we possess a claim on them. Inalienable rights are believed to exist prior to the existence of governments as authoritative entities. Rights based on mere human-ness, are not limited to civil rights (equity rights between societal groups, such as the right to vote) or to civil liberties (freedoms from governmental abuse such as speech, press, religion, assembly, or petition) but include both civil rights and civil liberties. Therefore, the list of human rights asserted in the modern world is a lengthy one, indeed.

In practice, however, the term human rights most often comes into play concerning the relationship between citizens and their government. We can return once again all the way back to ancient Greece for inspiration because Aristotle said that "the basis of a democratic state is liberty." Traditionally, government has held most of the power, with citizens left in a rather tenuous position. The concept of human rights provides additional ethical and legal fodder for oppressed peoples to protect themselves against the state and other potential rights violators such as MNCs.

An International Bill of Rights

The idea that every living person (human-ness) shares certain basic rights that governments cannot deny is a rather new one. Throughout most of the history of states, the key concept of **sovereignty** has meant that other governments, IGOs, and NGOs were supposed to abide by the corollary principle of **nonintervention**: Keep your nose out of the internal affairs of other states. Period.

The benchmark event that began to chip away at the old idea of nonintervention was the cataclysm known as WW II. More specifically, the Holocaust. Nazi Germany's obliteration of 6 million innocent Jews shocked the world's collective conscience into belated action. Why is the word *belated* used here? Because it is not as though the rest of the world did not know in the 1930s what Hitler meant by his "final solution" for European Jewry; nor can it be said that the world had no evidence of his death camps from 1941 to 1945. But apparently governments and church leaders found it easier to look the other way.

Between 1933 and 1945, millions of European Jews tried desperately to flee. The overwhelming majority were refused entry to other countries, and in the end, relatively few were saved. During this twelve-year period, Britain took in 70,000; Argentina opened its doors to 50,000; 27,000 entered Brazil; and Australia admitted 15,000 Jews.

The world's democracies opened their doors no wider than did hard-boiled dictatorships. The United States and Canada, whose national identities thrive on the notion of opportunity for the oppressed, mostly turned a blind eye. Canada accepted just 5,000, and the much larger United States a total of only 200,000 from 1933 to 1945—a mere fraction of those seeking a safe haven. In his book *None Is Too Many*, Canadian historian Harold Troper points out that "with no states prepared to take Jews, the Nazis could only conclude that none cared." It is myopic to blame only the Nazis for the Holocaust, suggests Troper, because "the Jews of Europe were not so much trapped in a whirlwind of systematic mass murder as they were abandoned to it."[15] The gripping story of a young girl's final days in hiding from the Nazis in

Sovereignty ■ The legal principle that asserts countries are independent actors responsible to themselves only

Nonintervention ■ A tenet of traditional international law of sovereignty saying that states should not meddle in the internal affairs of other states

Children behind a barbed wire fence at the Nazi concentration camp in Auschwitz, Poland, near the end of WW II.

an attic conveys some of the terror felt by European Jews during WW II in *The Diary of Anne Frank,* turned into a Broadway play and then into a film directed by George Stevens (1959). If you visit Amsterdam, go to the Anne Frank house (now a museum).

The old League of Nations, set up after WW I, had no legal provisions for human rights; however, the 1945 Covenant of the new United Nations would. Another important precedent was provided by the 1946 Nuremberg War Crimes Tribunal, which introduced the idea of "crimes against humanity" as a basis for trying and executing captured Nazi leaders. Equally crucial was the 1948 creation of the Universal Declaration of Human Rights as the cornerstone of specific rights accruing to all persons. The emphasis of the human rights movement was on spelling out this quite new category of rights up through the 1960s, with the adoption of what are known as the two Human Rights Covenants: (1) the International Covenant on Economic, Social, and Cultural Rights; and (2) the International Covenant on Civil and Political Rights. These two new types of human rights, when lumped with the 1948 Universal Declaration, are called the International Bill of Human Rights.

Monitoring

By the 1970s, the initial phase of spelling out specific categories of human rights gave way to efforts to check up on governments to see which were complying with human rights principles and which were not. Called *monitoring,* this activity required extensive field research. Some of it was conducted by IGOs set up for this purpose; however, the crucial role of monitoring was assumed mostly by the growing number of NGOs, such as the Ecumenical Movement for Human Rights, Human Rights Watch, or the International Commission of Jurists—all unfettered by government controls.

When the London-based NGO called Amnesty International won the Nobel Peace Prize in 1977, the status of all human rights NGOs received a major boost. Also, the 1970s witnessed several states beginning to incorporate human rights ideas into their operations. The U.S. Congress served notice in 1975 that it took human rights seriously when it formally linked U.S. foreign aid to the human rights record of recipient countries. A year later, the American public elected Jimmy Carter as the first (and only) American president for whom the moral imperatives of human rights represented a foreign policy cornerstone.

Single-Issue Human Rights Movements

In the 1980s, the human rights activities of NGOs and IGOs became increasingly well-established and dependable. In addition to these general human rights efforts, progress was made in developing institutions in five specific "single-issue" areas of concern: (1) workers' rights, (2) racial discrimination, (3) apartheid in South Africa, (4) women's rights, and (5) torture.[16] The story of nonviolent black leader Steven Biko's struggle against apartheid in South Africa is well-chronicled in another Richard Attenborough–directed film, *Cry Freedom* (1987). The young and charismatic Steven Biko (played by Denzel Washington in the film) was murdered by South African security forces, and the truth got out only because of the efforts of Biko's white friend, journalist Donald Woods, played in the movie by Kevin Kline.

Although human rights issues took a back seat in President Ronald Reagan's foreign policy, a group of smaller Western countries stepped forward during the 1980s. Known collectively as the like-minded countries, these middle-level powers integrated the values of human rights into the essence of their foreign policies. The Netherlands, Sweden, Canada, Finland, and Denmark led a half-dozen other countries that gave the highest levels of foreign aid in the world, vocally criticized human rights abuses wherever they saw them, and deviated from the U.S. tendency to see human rights issues through the ideological lenses of Cold War conflict (communism versus capitalism as a holy crusade).

Considerable progress toward the protection of human rights has been made since 1945. An International Bill of Rights now exists, and hundreds of NGOs such as Amnesty International perform the daily work needed to monitor and publicize human rights abuses. Global IGOs, such as the U.N.'s Commission on Human Rights, and regional ones, such as the European Commission of Human Rights, investigate thousands of cases of human rights abuses reported to them. Treaties have been enacted and organizations set up to protect the main single-issue areas of concern: workers' rights, racial discrimination, apartheid, women's rights, and torture. A global town meeting on the Protection of Human Rights was held in Vienna, Austria, in 1993 to mobilize world opinion in support of human rights, and two years later another on Women's Rights followed in Beijing.

Many states, NGOs, IGOs, and even some MNCs contributed to the decades-long struggle to isolate and condemn the last remaining example of legally sanctioned racism: apartheid in South Africa. It's hard to imagine the good things transpiring there in the 1990s occurring without this legacy of the gradual expansion of human rights as a legitimate global issue involving ethical and legal principles. Some observers describe the events in South Africa as miraculous, and they could not have occurred without a half-century of progress on human rights. South Africa's peaceful transition represents a model of human best practices, as described in Case Study 8.4.

Case Study 8.4   Moral Dilemma Facing Nelson Mandela's Democracy after Apartheid: Seeking Justice Responsibly

For many decades under the National Party (NP), the world's last openly racist regime, the international community considered South Africa a pariah state. The NP's apartheid policy of official racial classification, segregation, and discrimination produced widespread economic boycotts of South African goods as well as condemnation by more than one hundred U.N. resolutions. Leading the internal opposition to apartheid for the 80 percent black majority had been the African National Congress (ANC), whose inspirational head, Nelson Mandela, spent twenty-seven years as a political prisoner prior to his release in 1990.

Mandela genuinely believes in nonviolent civil disobedience, modeled by Mahatma Gandhi, who had lived in South Africa for twenty-one years. Negotiations between NP leaders and Mandela resulted in an astonishingly peaceful transition to free democratic elections in South Africa and to his winning the presidency in 1994 with 62 percent of the vote. Suddenly, the freedom fighters held power, and now they had to decide how to exercise it. Although Mandela believed in nonviolent solutions, there was no guarantee that the South African people or the newly elected parliament would follow his lead.

Apartheid had produced the same kind of brutal suppression of opponents to its policies and practices that was familiar in other authoritarian regimes, such as communist countries: torture, unwarranted arrests, indefinite detention, psychological abuse, intimidation of family members, imprisoning people for mere political opposition, physical beatings, and even murder. Except that in South Africa it was not only overt political opponents to the regime who suffered, but all of the 80 percent black, and 10 percent mixed-color minority who were required to carry internal passports, forced to live in designated crowded land areas (townships), legally classified into one of three racial groups (black, colored, white), and discriminated against with alacrity.

Myriad historical examples exist whereby oppressed peoples have gained power and used it to retaliate harshly against their former oppressors. Few examples can be cited, however, comparable to the dignified approach to thorny questions of justice taken on by the ANC post-1994. The truth had been hidden from public scrutiny by the apartheid regime, and Mandela's ANC was committed to truth telling regarding South Africa's history. Yet Mandela's years in prison had taught him the healing value of humility and compassion. Therefore, a reprise of the NP's unbridled violence was untenable. The elegant solution crafted was known as the Truth and Reconciliation Commission (TRC), and the person chosen to head the TRC was that prince of compassion, Archbishop Desmond Tutu. In effect, a trade-off was established: exchanging of truth for amnesty among former NP transgressors of human rights.[17]

Established by an act of Parliament in 1995, the TRC was to record a full picture of gross human rights abuses that had occurred between March 1, 1990, and December 5, 1992. Separate units of the commission traveled the country taking testimony from victims of atrocities; a special five-member amnesty committee took applications for amnesty, which were then heard and adjudicated by judges. Finally, a reparations committee established procedures for awarding payments to victims. The Archbishop's traveling confessionals examined 31,000 reports of abuses over three years and submitted a 1-million-word report to the government. Tutu's deputy concluded afterward "It was a ritual, deeply needed to cleanse a nation. It was a drama. The actors were in the main little people with a powerful story. But this was no brilliantly written play; it was the unvarnished truth in all its starkness."[18]

Past examples of truth commissions in places such as Chile, Argentina, and El Salvador involved secretive proceedings not open to the general public. In sharp contrast, South Africa's TRC was completely transparent. Held mostly in rural township settings where the victims lived, meeting rooms were packed with locals, and the media covered the hearings fully (including prime time Sunday night weekly summaries on national TV). And Mandela's commitment to truth telling was *not* limited to past NP abuses. After two terms in office, Mandela was replaced in 1999 by his long-time ANC colleague, Thabo Mbeki.

Shortly after his election, the TRC's final report was ready for release. However, Mbeki tried to dissuade the TRC from including information about the ANC's *own* human rights abuses while trying to overthrow apartheid, seeing it as "equating the ANC's struggle for liberation with the atrocities committed by the apartheid oppressors." But Mandela insisted, as the person who appointed the TRC, that "the TRC report should be published in full," and the moral personification of ANC nonviolent resistance got his way.[19]

The manner in which South Africa solved its moral dilemma over bringing apartheid's perpetrators of abuse to justice without rampant bloodshed, and in ways consistent with Mandela's belief in nonviolence, represents a major contribution to civilization. The human tendency to lose one's moorings by seeking revenge, retribution, and uncaring exploitation is well chronicled. By refusing to sink to the depravity of their oppressors, Mandela, the ANC, and democratic South Africa shine as a hopeful beacon for peaceful coexistence, forgiveness, and reconciliation in countless other flashpoints worldwide. ■

Human Rights Report Card

Although significant gains have been achieved in human rights, if you examine the global report card published annually by the NGO Human Rights Watch, the overall picture is grim in nearly every region of the world. For example, Human Rights Watch opened a typical report with these ominous words:

> The will to uphold human rights failed dismally in 1994. Having bound and shelved the volume of high-sounding pronouncements made the year before at the World Conference on Human Rights, the major powers led a wholesale retreat from their implementation.[20]

If specific human rights have been identified and agreed to, then what's the problem? The problem appears in a few different guises but can be traced back largely to sovereignty. At the end of the day, whether or not countries violate their citizens' rights rests in the hands of decision-makers running governments. Other countries, IGOs, and NGOs can complain and criticize, but they can't compel abusive states to clean up their acts. Political scientist and human rights expert Jack Donnelly recommends that we hold limited expectations of human rights protection, warning that "when human rights conflict with even minor security, political, economic, or ideological objectives, human rights usually lose out."[21]

Theoretical Challenges to Human Rights

In addition to the sovereign ability of country leaders to define their national interest in ways inimical to human rights, Donnelly identifies two more theoretical challenges to the interests of human rights. First is *realpolitik*, or the prevalence of the realist view of foreign policy. In seeing the essence of foreign policy as pursuing the national interest and in considering the national interest as synonymous with accumulating power, realpolitik weakens human rights by ignoring it. Human rights advocates find this attitude frustrating because it refuses to take their cause seriously.

The other challenge is that of cultural relativism, or the view that although the values of different cultures vary greatly, those values are not inherently superior or inferior to each other. Cultural relativism means that each culture should be able to operate according to its own internal logic and rules of the social game. Many of the principles of the International Bill of Rights derived from the experiences of Western democracies, where protecting individual liberties is highly valued. Problems arise when some of these principles come into conflict with the traditions of Oriental cultures where collective, societal rights are believed to take precedence over the interests of individual freedoms.

Cultural relativism views efforts to impose Western notions of individual human rights as modern cultural imperialism similar to the economic and political exploitation of the rich over the poor in past centuries.[22]

Almost no country escapes the fray concerning human rights abuses, as evidenced by the United States' frequent inclusion on Amnesty International's list of countries guilty of significant human rights abuses. In 2006, Amnesty issued a scathing report concerning the Bush Administration's four-year detention of suspected Al Qaeda sympathizers in violation of international law at Guantanamo Bay, where thousands of incarcerations had resulted in formal charges brought against fewer than ten individuals. More often than not, however, this unpleasant glare of world public disfavor is borne by Asian countries. Given its repressive communist political system, China has become accustomed to fending off charges of myriad human rights violations.

Ethnicity and Genocide

In the popular mind-set, race is often confused with ethnicity. But racial and ethnic groups do share certain things: (1) ambiguity concerning their meaning; (2) potential exacerbation of inequality via discriminatory attitudes against certain groups; and (3) their status as minority groups. Some people consider ethnicity synonymous with country of origin, but sociologists prefer to include cultural features such as dress, language, foods preferred, and historical identity, as well as national origin; "Ethnic groups share a sense of peoplehood within a larger society."[23]

It is ironic that racial identity and ethnic identity can soar as the apex of emotional pride, and then sink to the nadir of violent hatred. Who hasn't been stirred by tears streaming down the face of an Olympic athlete whose flag has just been raised? Similarly, if you visit the diverse city of Toronto, Canada, each June, you can experience the rich tapestry of racial and ethnic communities as they cling to their traditional identities. More than one hundred nationalities set up pavilions at their ethnic clubs to host thousands who attend "International Caravan Week." If only life consisted solely of such examples of ethnic comity.

Unfortunately, we all know about human history's track record for racially and ethnically motivated hatred. Yet unfathomable atrocities such as Adolf Hitler's incineration of 6 million European Jews in the 1940s, or Joseph Stalin's deliberate starvation of 7 million Ukrainian peasants in the 1930s, can be filed away as part of a remote past. More difficult to rationalize are more recent genocides such as the one that occurred in Bosnia, Yugoslavia, as described in Case Study 8.5.

Women's Rights, Sex, and Gender

Although Asia is one region of the world that has taken a verbal beating over violations of citizens' political rights, such as freedom of speech, assembly, and religion, all regions have been criticized by NGOs for the pervasive violation of women's right to equal treatment. Despite constituting a majority of the U.S. population and the world population, women experience unequal life chances and thus are considered by most sociologists as a minority group. One U.N. Human Development Report concludes that "in no society do women enjoy the same opportunities as men."[24] Why should this be the case, and from what sources does it spring? Why should it be necessary for a special treaty specifying rights of women, the 1979 Convention on the Elimination of Discrimination against Women, to exist?

One place to begin is by defining some often-misused words: **sex** and **gender**. The complex mix between nature (biology) and nurture (social experiences) in shaping human behavior makes it easy to confuse the roles of sex and gender. Sexual differences of a biological sort exist and distinguish males from females in the following ways (and others): males have greater grip strength, more body weight in muscle, larger hearts and lungs, are taller, and have heavier skeletons. Females, on the other hand, possess larger pelvic areas, more body weight in fat, and are less affected by nutritional shortages.[25]

Sex ■ The genetically determined fact of biological life that establishes a status of either male or female

Gender ■ A socially conditioned role of either masculinity or femininity tied into how we think and feel about ourselves

Case Study 8.5   Ethnic Cleansing in Bosnia

Located in the Balkan peninsula of southeastern Europe, Bosnia stands out as a pluralistic society even in this region of ethnic diversity. The mostly Muslim ethnic group known as Bosnians makes up about two-fifths of the population, whereas the mostly Eastern Orthodox ethnic Serbs comprise roughly one-third of the population, and the remaining one-third consists of mostly Roman Catholic Croatians. But these ethnic groups can be traced back for a millennium in this territory, and for most of that time, they have lived in peace. Bosnia did not erupt into a three-year (1992–1995) war producing 250,000 casualties and more than 1 million refugees by accident. Rather, this tragedy resulted from deliberate policy decisions made by dictators bent on ethnic cleansing.

One journalist who covered the Bosnian War writes that "ethnic cleansing was the goal of the War, not an unintended consequence."[26] After communist Yugoslavia's 1991 collapse, when Serbian leader Slobodan Milosevic failed to regain political control of all six former sections of Yugoslavia, he began a brutal military campaign to assure Serbian dominance via ethnic cleansing. This path resulted in concentration camps, systematic rape, massacres, torture, and mass deportations of civilians. A U.N. Special Commission found evidence suggesting that roughly 90 percent of such crimes were attributable to the Serbs, 6 percent to the Croatians, and 4 percent to the Bosnian Muslims.

Among journalists who covered the Bosnian War, consensus has emerged on a few points. They agree that the popular perception in the West of these ethnic groups as inevitably embroiled in "eternal conflict" represented a *spurious myth*. The truth, they believe, is more immediate and more sinister, and is traceable to the leaders of each ethnic group who manipulated public opinion through sensational exaggeration and emotional appeals to defend each group's culture and traditions. Most observers hold Milosevic more responsible than leaders of the Croatians and Muslims. Journalistic consensus also has coalesced around the view that Western countries and the U.N. failed to exercise legal means available to them that could have averted most of the bloodshed.[27]

When a cease-fire occurred in 1995, the United States belatedly got involved by hosting a peace conference resulting in the Dayton Accords—a major improvement over the preceding few years—but the accords were violated from time to time. Not until the North Atlantic Treaty Organization (NATO) conducted a major bombing war against Serbia in 1999 did Western nations take a firm stance against ethnic cleansing in Bosnia, a type of warfare that became the archetype for copycat dictators in other places such as Rwanda.

It took forty-five years after the 1948 Convention on Genocide for the first international criminal tribunal to be established, and among those subsequently arrested, indicted, and convicted for genocide was Slobodan Milosevic.[28] A poignant documentary film by Mandy Jacobson and Karmen Jelincic chronicles the travails of two women who, like thousands of others, were systematically raped and tortured, in *Calling the Ghosts: A Story About Rape, War, and Women* (1996). ◾

Socialization ◾ The process whereby one generation educates the next generation about how to live, think, and believe

However, when the impact of genetic, biological, sexual differences are exaggerated and spill over into the area known as gender, confusion ensues. Rather than being biologically based, gender refers to those behavioral and attitudinal characteristics that are learned through the **socialization** process. Part of what we learn from our culture has to do with gender roles that are considered typical in the mind-set of our particular culture. The concepts of masculinity and femininity socially define for us what our culture expects both attitudinally and behaviorally from each sex.

Cultural Variation in Gender Roles

Cross-cultural studies from anthropology help sort out nature (biology/sex) from nurture (socialization/gender). It is meaningful that the characteristics of sex roles vary enormously from one culture to another. Which sex is stronger, and which is weaker; which is rational, and which is intuitive; who is more aggressive, and who is more passive? As early as the 1920s, Margaret Mead's field research in New Guinea pointed to some tribes in which gender roles were dramatically different from those in the Western world.

Mead described polar opposite sex roles in the Arapesh versus the Mundugumor groups, although neither had the sharp gender separations common to Western cultures. Among the Arapesh, "both men and women behaved in ways we would consider 'feminine': cooperative, unaggressive, and responsive to the needs of others." Both Arapesh mothers and fathers engaged extensively in parenting activities. However, when Mead studied the Mundugumor, she found males and females sharing nearly the exact opposite sex roles. In this tribe of headhunters, both men and women had been socialized into roles we would typically consider as "actively masculine: ruthless, aggressive, and positively sexed." Studies by other anthropologists also emphasize how variously sex roles can be assigned in different societies.[29]

In the same part of the world where Margaret Mead conducted her field research, the French painter Paul Gauguin recorded his impressions of the Tahitian people during the 1890s. Much of the same sense of **androgyny** described by social scientist Margaret Mead was also seen through Gauguin's more artistic eyes. Of the similarities between the Tahitian sexes, Gauguin had this to say:

> Neither men nor women are sheltered from the rays of the sun nor the pebbles of the seashore. Together they engage in the same tasks with the same activity. . . . There is something virile in the women and something feminine in the men.[30]

Androgyny ■ Exhibiting characteristics considered to be both male and female

The Women's Rights Movement

A body of literature establishing the fact that women experience discrimination reaches back nearly 200 years. Louisa May Alcott's nineteenth-century novel, *Little Women*, chronicles the life of an intellectual woman forced to swim upstream against a strong male-dominated (patriarchal) current throughout her life. In 1848, the town of Seneca Falls, New York, hosted the first women's rights convention in the United States. It was organized by Lucretia Mott and Elizabeth Cady Stanton, two pioneering women whose spirit parallels that of the fictional heroine in *Little Women*. In 1995, the fifth film version retold this story of how an intellectually gifted woman was made to feel like a square peg trying to fit into a round hole.

At the turn of the twentieth century, the energies of American feminists were devoted to the cause of suffrage. Women recognized that without the right to vote, they would not be taken seriously as legitimate participants in public discourse. It was not until the cataclysmic dislocations of WW I reshuffled the deck of gender cards that the suffragist movement realized its goal: passage of the Nineteenth Amendment to the Constitution in 1920.

If WW I was the first great cataclysm of the twentieth century, WW II was the second, and even greater, one. Although women in the first great war had proven themselves by replacing men in demanding jobs on the shop floor of the civilian economy, in World War II, they went a giant step further toward equity by donning the nation's military uniforms and getting into harm's way around the periphery of the battlefield.

The 19th Amendment meant the right to vote for American women. Here Suffragettes protest in favor of its ratification at the Republican National Convention in June, 1920.

Some point to Betty Friedan's 1963 book, *The Feminine Mystique*, as the symbolic start of the women's rights movement.

With unprecedented economic growth in America after WW II, conditions were ripe for a more assertive women's rights movement to evolve. It was out of the volatile social milieu of the late 1960s and early 1970s that names and faces emerged as cultural icons of feminism. Many point to the publication of Betty Friedan's *The Feminine Mystique* (1963) as the symbolic beginning of the movement. Ms. Friedan delved into the more subtle forms of sexist attitudes preventing women from reaching their personal potential, a theme that dovetailed nicely with the early stages of the human potential movement as a component of humanistic psychology in America. Others, such as *Ms. Magazine* editor Gloria Steinem, helped to move feminism closer to the mainstream of American consciousness by demonstrating the pervasive effects of patriarchy.

In 1966, Betty Friedan helped found the National Organization for Women (NOW), a multifaceted lobbying group for women's rights. NOW has generally favored abortion rights and equitable pay for women and was instrumental in the 1970s in expanding the number of daycare centers in the United States. In the 1980s, NOW led an unsuccessful effort to pass a proposed twenty-seventh amendment—the equal rights amendment (ERA). The agenda of women's rights generated its broadest global attention during the 1995 World Conference on Women's Rights held in Beijing (the fourth such global meeting held).

As the women's movement grew larger, it became more fragmented over both philosophy and methods. But as internationalist Betty Reardon notes, all agree on the basic premise that "women throughout the world suffer sex-based discrimination."[31] Whereas many of the most creative salvos in the feminist war were fired from behind American barricades, the European countries proved somewhat more adept at institutionalizing the values of women's rights. European countries are smaller and more homogeneous than the United States, as well as more committed to equal distribution of human rights, making it easier for them to put into practice many of the egalitarian values of women's rights.

Many of the role models for feminist leaders were politically oriented intellectual activists. One of today's feminist heroes rose to prominence as a role model rather differently. Jane Goodall is a gentler, more intuitive humanist who also turned out to be very successful in firing the female imagination. Goodall left her native England for Africa in 1965, with no college education, to study animals. She worked for conservationist and archaeologist Louis Leakey in Kenya as a secretary. When Leakey suggested that she go to the Gombe Park Reserve to study chimpanzees, she jumped at the chance.

Her copious but unorthodox research methods proved that humans are much closer to chimps than scientists then believed. Within two decades she had become the world's leading authority on chimpanzees (although still with no college degree), and her books on the subject had become classics.

Sexist Ideology

One part of the discrimination problem stems from sexist ideology, or unsubstantiated beliefs that affect our thinking and behavior if left unchallenged by critical thinking. Many of these stereotypical beliefs consist of half-truths and faulty assumptions. Sexist ideologies usually stipulate rigid gender expectations that make it difficult for people holding them to accept realities such as emotionally sensitive males, homosexual football players, female athletes, or aggressive women. These sexist ideologies are not only held by individuals but can also pervade social institutions such as churches, schools, or political parties.

Sociologist Joan Ferrante cites an example in the U.S. Pentagon's military brass rejecting the results of a study they had commissioned because it concluded that "sexual orientation is unrelated to military performance." Gay men and women in the study served as well as or better than heterosexuals, but that conclusion did not fit the prevailing ideology of those who decided to bury this particular report.[32] Ideologies do not materialize from thin air. In the case of sexism, much of it can be traced back millennia to the origins of the world's great religions—all of which blithely assume males to be the leaders, prophets, and generally superior half of the species. The idea of the sexual double standard, or affording more sexual liberty to males, which appears throughout recorded human history, is illustrative.

The Gender Development Index

In 1995, the first Gender Development Index (GDI) Report was released by the U.N. Development Programme. It ranked most countries on a global scale measuring gender equity and the overall condition of women. The countries faring best in the study were the Scandinavian countries of Sweden, Finland, Norway, and Denmark. African nations mostly clustered at the bottom of the gender equity scale.

In general, it was found that during the past twenty years, women's conditions in education and health have improved considerably. Unfortunately, the same cannot be said for economic and political conditions, neither of which has advanced measurably. By region, European and North American rankings were by far the highest. Sub-Saharan Africa did worst on the GDI, with Asia, the Arab states, and Latin America appearing in that order as we move up the scale toward the developed countries.

The Gender Development Index Report concludes with a five-point plan for accelerating progress on gender equity. In essence, the strategy calls for the following:

1. Efforts to win legal equality within the next ten years, which includes (a) ratification of the women's rights monitoring organization (CEDAW) by the ninety governments that have yet to sign on, and (b) creation of an NGO—World Women's Watch—to prepare country-by-country reports.
2. Revamping economic and institutional arrangements to extend to the female workplace, especially (a) flexible work schedules, (b) tax incentives for women, and (c) changing laws on property, inheritance, and divorce.
3. A 30 percent target for female national level decision-makers, with firm timetables for achievement.
4. Government programs targeted to aid female education, reproductive health, and access to credit as three crucial areas for attention.
5. Both national and international efforts to create greater female access to economic and political opportunities.

In addition to slicing up gender equity by country, the GDI also analyzes women's rights data by region. The Arab Middle East is one region where serious discrimination against women is undeniable. The differences between the top five countries (all from North America and Europe) and the bottom five countries (all African) on the GDI are capsulized in Table 8.1, which summarizes female life expectancy and female literacy as two of the variables measured.

Women in the Middle East

The 1995 GDI reveals that on many dimensions of equity measurement, the Arab Middle East ranks low even as compared with less-developed-countries (LDCs) generally. Concerning adult female literacy, the Arab Middle East is the second-lowest region and falls a full 10 percent below all LDCs. Even worse, on the measure of female economic activity, the Arab region is by far the lowest ranked, falling well below one-half the average level for all developing countries. Likewise, for the dimension of parliamentary seats held by women, the Arab states' 4 percent is less than half the average of 10 percent for developing countries generally. One area in which the Arab states look better is in female school enrollment at all levels. Considerable progress in female education has occurred since the 1970s. Finally, on female life expectancy, these countries are average for developing countries.[33]

The NGO Human Rights Watch monitors the human rights situation in all regions of the world and publishes annual evaluations by region and by country. If anything, the

Table 8.1		
GDI TOP FIVE AND BOTTOM FIVE COUNTRIES:		
Top Five:		
Country	**Female Life Expectancy**	**Female Literacy**
Canada	82 years	99%
France	83	99
Norway	80	99
United States	80	99
Iceland	80	99
Bottom Five:		
Burundi	54 years	28%
Mali	49	23
Burkina Faso	44	10
Niger	50	7
Sierra Leone	36	19

Source: 1998 Gender-Related Development Index: http://www.undp.org/hdro/98gdi.htm.

1995 assessment of women's rights in the Arab Middle East conducted by Human Rights Watch is more negative than that of the GDI. Human Rights Watch emphasizes that in most Arab countries secular governments are being directly challenged by militant Islamic fundamentalist groups determined to assume power. With plenty of human rights abuses perpetrated by both sides, women have very often been the victims of overzealousness. The bottom line, according to the Human Rights Watch report, is that "governments in the region took few steps to end violations of women's human rights." They note that women still cannot vote or run for office in Kuwait, cannot enjoy freedom of movement in Saudi Arabia, and cannot dress as they wish in Algeria. Two women in Iran were stoned to death as the punishment for adultery.[34]

The most comprehensive report on women's rights in the Middle East comes from Amnesty International (AI), an NGO boasting a membership of over 1 million that opposes torture, incarceration of prisoners of conscience, and capital punishment. It won a Nobel Peace Prize in 1977. AI operates openly and within the laws of countries it visits, but it has nevertheless been kept out of some Arab Middle Eastern countries and harassed in others. Arab countries are particularly sensitive about the category of women's rights. The AI report finds heartening evidence of new activism on the parts of some brave women in the region. For example, the first shelter for battered women in the region was set up in the Palestinian village of Kfar; in Bahrain, Sudan, and Algeria, women have taken to the streets for peaceful demonstrations in favor of women's rights; a group of women in Tunisia signed a petition calling for respect for freedom of expression.

On balance, these favorable developments wilt in comparison with the hundreds of cases of inhumane treatment confirmed by AI. Women are caught in a relentless double bind: "In wartime, they are killed, taken hostage, raped, and driven from their homes. In peace, they are imprisoned and tortured for opposing the government, or simply for being related to political activists."[35] Often, violations of women's rights occur with the blessing of discriminatory domestic laws in Arab countries. A few factoids from the AI report convey the nature of the problem:

- In Algeria, seventeen-year-old student Katia Bengana was shot dead for not wearing the hijab (Islamic veil).
- In Bahrain, twelve were killed by security forces while demonstrating for a reopening of the National Parliament (closed since 1975).
- In Egypt, women students at the University of Cairo were held without charges for two weeks for peacefully protesting.

Chapter Synopsis

Although it can prove frustrating to pinpoint the relevance of ethics to real-world human behavior, a growing body of social science literature suggests that ethics play a meaningful role in influencing the behavior of actors on the world stage. Although history is replete with examples of both ethical and unethical uses of organized religion, ethics and religion both spill over to affect the collective mind-set in all cultures. Therefore, the ethical component of human subjective experience cannot be studied without attention to religion.

Human rights constitute a subset of the larger set of ethics in action. But the idea that every person possesses certain rights to be protected from governmental infringement has only become codified as a global principle since the Nazi Holocaust pricked the human conscience. Under traditional international law, state sovereignty made it very difficult for concerned countries or the international community to intercede in the domestic affairs of a country on behalf of aggrieved individuals. During the last sixty years, an International Bill of Rights has emerged to assert fundamental rights. Enforcing such rights is no small assignment; however, an array of new IGOs and NGOs is busy trying to do just that.

A periodic report released by a U.N. agency ranks all countries in the world according to a Gender Development Index (GDI), intended to measure the relative equality or inequality of women in the world's countries. Overall, the condition of the world's women cannot be described as good—for example, 70 percent of those living in poverty are women; two-thirds of illiterates are women; only 14 percent of managerial jobs are held by women; depression among women is twice as prevalent as among men; and one in six women gets raped in her lifetime. The GDI reveals that women in the countries of northern Europe fare best, followed by the rest of Europe and North America. Sub-Saharan Africa, South Asia, and the Arab Middle East ranked as the most discriminatory regions by gender. Some encouraging improvements in women's conditions can be cited, but the big picture reveals that many grave problems continue to be uniquely burdensome to women.

FOR DIGGING DEEPER

Ahmed, Leila. *Women and Gender in Islam*. Yale University Press, 1992.

Amnesty International. *Pakistan: Violence Against Women in the Name of Honor*. AI Press, 1999.

Amstutz, Mark. *International Ethics: Concepts, Theories, and Cases in Global Politics*. U.S. Institute of Peace, 1999.

Appleby, R. Scott. *The Ambivalence of the Sacred: Religion, Violence, and Reconciliation*. Rowman & Littlefield, 1997.

Coicaud, Jean-Marc, Michael O'Doyle, and Anne-Marie Gardner, eds. *The Globalization of Human Rights*. United Nations University Press, 2003.

Datta, Rekha, and Judith Kornberg, eds. *Women in Developing Countries: Assessing Strategies for Empowerment*. Lynne Rienner Publishers, 2001.

Donnelly, Jack. *International Human Rights*. Westview Press, 1997.

Dower, Nigel. *World Ethics: The New Agenda*. Columbia University Press, 1998.

Esposito, John L., ed. *The Oxford Encyclopedia of the Modern Islamic World*. Oxford University Press, 1995.

Freedman, Estelle B. *No Turning Back: The History of Feminism and the Future of Women*. Random House Books, 2002.

Harrod, Jeffrey, and Robert O'Brien. *Theory and Strategy of Organized Labor in the Global Political Economy*. Routledge, 2002.

Hartsock, Nancy. *The Feminist Standpoint Revisited and Other Essays*. Westview Press, 1997.

Hoffmann, Stanley. *Ethics and Politics of Humanitarian Intervention*. University of Notre Dame Press, 2001.

Hogan, Michael J. *Hiroshima in History and Memory*. Cambridge University Press, 1996.

Juviler, Peter. *Human Rights for the 21st Century*. Sharpe, 1993.

Kael, Paul, ed. *Ethics and Foreign Policy*. Paul and Company, 1995.

Kazemzadeh, Masoud. *Islamic Fundamentalism, Feminism, and Gender Inequality in Iran Under Khomeini*. University Press of America, 2002.

Kelley, Rita Mae, et al., eds. *Gender, Globalization, and Democratization*. Rowman and Littlefield, 2001.

Korey, William. *The Promises We Keep: Human Rights, the Helsinki Process, and American Foreign Policy*. St. Martin's Press, 1993.

Knudsen, Tonny Brems. *Humanitarian Intervention: Contemporary Manifestations of an Explosive Doctrine*. Routledge, 2004.

Kumar, Krishna, ed. *Women and Civil War: Impact, Organizations, and Action*. Lynne Rienner Publishers, 2001.

Lambley, Peter. *The Psychology of Apartheid*. University of Georgia Press, 1980.

Lopez, George A., and Drew Christiansen, eds. *Morals and Might: Ethics and the Use of Force in Modern International Affairs*. Westview Press, 1996.

Louie, Miriam Ching Yoon. *Sweatshop Warriors: Immigrant Women Take on the Global Factory*. South End Press, 2001.

Lukes, Steven. *Moral Conflicts and Politics*. Oxford University Press, 1991.

Mandela, Nelson. *The Struggle Is My Life*. Pathfinder Books, 1990.

Maogoto, Jackson Nyamuya. *War Crimes and Realpolitik: International Justice from World War I to the 21st Century*. Oxford University Press, 2004.

Meyer, Howard N. *The World Court in Action: Judging Among the Nations*. Rowman Littlefield, 2001.

Neier, Aryeh. *Four Decades in the Struggle for Human Rights*. Perseus Books, 2002.

Newell, Katherine et al. *Discrimination Against the Girl Child: Female Infanticide, Genital Cutting, Honor Killings*. Youth Advocacy Program International, 2000.

Nolan, Cathal J., ed. *Ethics and Statecraft: The Moral Dimension of International Affairs*. Praeger Publishers, 1995.

O'Byrne, Darren J. *Human Rights: An Introduction*. Longman Publishers, 2002.

Oppenheim, Felix. *The Place of Morality in Foreign Policy*. Lexington Books, 1991.

Parmar, Pratibha, and Alice Walker. *Warrior Marks: Female Genital Mutilation and the Sexual Blinding of Women*. Harvest Books, 1996.

Pettman, Jan Jindy. *Worlding Women: A Feminist International Politics*. Routledge, 1996.

Robertson, David. *A Dictionary of Human Rights*. Routledge/Europa Publications, 2004.

Rubenberg, Cheryl A. *Palestinian Women: Patriarchy and Resistance in the West Bank*. Lynne Rienner Publishers, 2001.

Sanday, Peggy Reeves. *Women at the Center: Life in a Modern Matriarchy*. Cornell University Press, 2004.

INTERNET

African National Congress:
http://www.anc.org.za

Carnegie Council on Ethics and International Affairs:
http://www.cceia.org/

Character Training International:
http://www.character-ethics.org/

CNN Online: Honor Killings: A Brutal Tribal Custom:
http://www2.cnn.com/WORLD/9512/honor_killings/

The Feminist:
http://www.feminist.org

Human Rights Internet:
http://www.hri.ca/welcome.cfm

Human Rights Watch/Defending Human Rights Worldwide:
http://www.hrw.org/

Human Rights Watch World Report 2002: Africa:
http://www.hrw.org/wr2k2/africa.html

Human Rights Watch World Report 2002: Women's Human Rights:
http://www.hrw.org/wr2k2/women.html

International Center for Ethics, Justice, and Public Life:
http://www.brandeis.edu/ethics/

International Court of Justice:
http://www.icj-cij.org/

International Ethics Resources:
http://www.ethics.ubc.ca/

South African Government:
http://www.gov.za

U.N. International Feminism:
http://www.unifem.undp.org

Universal Declaration of Human Rights:
http://www.un.org/Overview/rights.html

Women Watch:
http://www.womenwatch.org

Anthropology and Humans as Biocultural Beings

CORE OBJECTIVE

To explain anthropology's holistic insights regarding biological/cultural aspects of human behavior.

THEMATIC QUESTIONS

- What subfields comprise the discipline of anthropology?

- What basic laws of heredity transmit genetic traits from one generation to the next?

- How, when, where, and by whom was the scientific theory of evolution developed?

- From what hereditary tree are humans thought to have evolved?

- Is the concept of race more useful as a cultural or as a biological category?

Anthropology ■ A discipline that systematically studies human culture and the evolutionary dimensions of human biology

Societies ■ Groups of people occupying specific territories and sharing common languages; societies may, or may not, coincide with nations

Biocultural ■ The view that humans are unique in that biology and culture interact so that each influences the other in shaping human behavior

The social science discipline of **anthropology** emerged in the United States during the nineteenth century as the federal government was engaged in a colonial encounter with American Indians. The American Bureau of Ethnology's pioneering researchers in studying Native Americans were John Wesley Powell and Lewis Henry Morgan. In the early twentieth century, Franz Boas led the effort to professionalize the discipline. In Europe, anthropology developed alongside colonial encounters with non-Western peoples. Sociology and anthropology have always shared some common themes, but each came into being as a separate social science.

For the early part of the twentieth century, anthropology concerned itself with preliterate **societies**, but contemporary anthropology seeks to understand humans as **biocultural** beings, in all places and all times. Anthropology is concerned with variation in human behavior, both *across time* (e.g., human evolution; origins of domestication) and *across space* (contemporary societies all over the world). Most of this chapter explores human variation across time and thus focuses on biological anthropology (defined later). Chapter 11 deals mostly with human variation across space and thus emphasizes cultural anthropology (defined later).

As a biocultural endeavor, anthropology concerns itself with human traits that are both biological and social in origin, thus interfacing with natural sciences as well as with other social sciences. Such intellectual curiosity provides the discipline with a wide-angled

BIOLOGICAL ANTHROPOLOGY Forensic Anthropology Paleoanthropology Human Taxonomy	**ARCHAEOLOGY** Prehistoric Archaeology Historical Archaeology Underwater Archaeology
LINGUISTIC ANTHROPOLOGY Comparative Syntax Sociolinguistics Cognitive Linguistics	**CULTURAL ANTHROPOLOGY** Demographic Anthropology Economic Anthropology Religious Anthropology

Figure 9.1
Core Subfields and Some Offshoots

lens to examine the broad spectrum of human diversity. Yet students sometimes ask why study anthropology? Answers commonly provided by their professors suggest that, by examining lifestyles of different societies, students can more rigorously analyze features of their own society and develop more open-minded attitudes toward other lifestyles different from their own. Anthropologists Raymond Scupin and Christopher DeCorse argue that as the world we inhabit shrinks, the kind of global awareness engendered by their discipline becomes increasingly valuable.[1]

The Stanislavsky Method of acting suggests that by striving to get behind the eyeballs of others, we can better understand their worldview and gain a richer comprehension of our own. One group of authors unwittingly provides us with an insight enabling us to do so when they contend that all anthropological subfields attempt to employ "the anthropological perspective," which is inherently multidisciplinary, holistic, international, comparative, and imbued with critical thinking.[2] This "anthropological perspective" meshes nicely with both the "roomy" vision of the social sciences advocated in Chapter 2 and the global approach to human behavior pervading this text.

Some observers trace anthropology's lineage all the way back to the Greek philosopher Aristotle in the fourth century B.C. However, European and American scholars in the nineteenth century were the first to turn it into a systematic academic enterprise. The discipline consists of four major subfields: cultural anthropology, archaeology, linguistic anthropology, and biological anthropology. Although all anthropologists share many aspects of the "anthropological perspective," practitioners in each subfield also use distinctive concepts and methods to study human behavior. The largest anthropological organization, the American Anthropological Association (AAA), lists more than 7,000 practitioners, and its Website provides information about degree programs, fields of specialization, recent doctoral dissertations, careers, women anthropologists, professional ethics, and how to contact key individuals. Figure 9.1 categorizes the discipline's chief subfields.

Anthropological Subfields

Cultural Anthropology

Cultural anthropology examines contemporary societies as diverse as hunter-gatherers from the Amazon rainforest and homeless people in Los Angeles. Traditionally, cultural anthropologists probably logged more frequent-flyer miles than other social scientists because their work focused chiefly on non-Western societies found in the Southern Hemisphere. However, today they similarly focus on the lifestyles of groups closer to home. There are more practitioners in cultural anthropology than in any other subfield.

Cultural anthropology ■ The subfield of anthropology concerning itself primarily with contemporary societies, their belief systems, and social behavior

Professor Franz Boas of Columbia University mentored the first wave of cultural anthropologists in the 1920s; his star pupils included Margaret Mead and Ruth Benedict, harbingers of a female majority in the subfield. Such individuals employed a very distinctive form of field research known as *participant observation*. This deep-immersion strategy requires the cultural anthropologist to learn the language of a remote group and then live with the group to understand it from the inside. However, participant observation is not without its critics. For example, Mead's work in Samoa is attacked for relying heavily on interviewing subjects, rather than on objective observation.

More generally, the dilemma known as the "observer's paradox" questions the ability of researchers to remain objective while simultaneously living within a remote culture. In a multidisciplinary manner, the field researcher will record data concerning the environment, social organization, patterns of political or economic interaction, and religious beliefs. When she writes up her research findings, the report is called an **ethnography,** a document that can be used for cross-cultural studies when compared to other ethnographies.

Ethnography ■ A written anthropological description of a culture produced by a researcher conducting field research in that culture

Archaeology

Archaeology ■ The subfield of anthropology studying the lifestyles, history, and evolution of societies by examining their remaining artifacts

Artifacts ■ Physical objects created or modified by humans

The second subdiscipline, **archaeology,** specializes in the scientific recovery, analysis, and interpretation of the physical **artifacts** left by former societies. Like their cultural anthropology colleagues, archaeologists ask probing questions about culture. But rather than seeking insights from living people, they seek them from the artifacts remaining from earlier societies. In the hands of a specialist, artifacts can reveal valuable clues to human behavior in the past. Archaeologists want to know about the values, beliefs, and lifestyles of specific groups. They do not excavate field sites to collect artifacts randomly; instead, they do so systematically for a specific purpose. Researchers may want to know how people in a given society ate their meals, who exercised power there, or why a particular society disintegrated. Precise records are kept because the process of digging a site also destroys it. The film character Indiana Jones creates the popular impression that digging for artifacts is quite glamorous, yet much field research is painstakingly tedious. After artifacts are recovered, they must then be carefully categorized, interpreted, and integrated into the context of existing knowledge.

Linguistic Anthropology

Linguistic anthropology ■ The subfield of anthropology dealing with languages, their diversity and connections, as well as the interface between language and culture

Linguistic anthropology is the third subfield. It examines such diverse topics as the relationship between language and brain function, how languages change, links between specific languages and general families of languages, languages as indicators of past relationships between human populations, the symbiotic interaction between language and culture, how languages shape perceptions in certain cultures, the process of language acquisition in children, and the migration of certain societies over time. Matters as simple as vocabulary diversity can reveal the relative importance of certain concepts in different cultures. For example, in North American English, the word *snow* has few permutations, whereas among the Inuit Eskimos, the need to identify various forms of frozen precipitation results in many different terms. However, some scholars have questioned the validity of research on the Inuit. In many societies, people address others in ways tied to **social status.** The Thai language includes thirteen different forms of the pronoun *I,* and the proper form is determined by whether the person to whom one is speaking is an equal, a superior, an inferior, a male, or a female.[3]

Social status ■ A position of prestige in a given society

Biological Anthropology

Biological anthropology ■ The subfield of anthropology that explores the study of human biology within the framework of evolution and highlights the relationship between biology and culture

The fourth major subfield consists of **biological anthropology,** whose methods and content make it the subfield closest to the natural sciences. Therefore, biological anthropologists rely heavily on the scientific method: identifying a testable hypothesis, gathering and organizing empirical data, interpreting the data, and drawing conclusions from those data. Two of the most compelling issues addressed by biological anthropologists are the following:

- How do we account for the physical and genetic differences between human groups? A major conceptual tool applied in this research context is that of **variation.** By statistically analyzing measurable differences, researchers can go beyond common-sensical thinking in seeking answers to many vexing questions relating to variation. Noel Boaz and Alan Almquist note that people look different around the world "partly because they are adapted to different environmental conditions and partly because each population has a different history of migrations and infusions of peoples from elsewhere."[4] The application of variation analysis by biological anthropologists to the concept of race is examined later in this chapter.

- How did the human species originate in the animal world? The concept of biological **species** is a key building block in constructing the language of biological anthropology needed to create **taxonomy** and **phylogeny.** Taxonomy begins with species, which are designated scientifically via the system of **binomial nomenclature** based on genus and species. A genus lumps together species that are similar in adaptation; humans are classified in the genus *Homo* because we walk on two legs. Our species designation is *Homo sapiens* (human the wise). In conducting research into human origins, biological anthropologists rely greatly on **fossils,** often in the form of bones mineralized over time and resembling their original size and shape. Scientists also rely increasingly on the chemical analysis of molecules found in the body. Figure 9.2 provides a skeletal reference to where our species fits.

Yet even this description of the discipline's expansion into four major subfields does not begin to exhaust the scholarly pursuits of its modern practitioners. Some believe that applied anthropology should be recognized as a fifth major subfield. Anthropologists Carol and Melvin Ember point out that fully one-half of their colleagues hired today are in practical problem-solving areas outside of academia.[5] Case Study 9.1 illustrates Clyde Snow's fascinating work in the applied subfield known as **forensic anthropology.**

In Chapter 8, we saw how ethically compelling are the cases of verified human rights abuses perpetrated by governments around the globe. Moral indignation is a key motivator for the investigators who conduct field research for international human rights NGOs such as Amnesty International (AI), Human Rights Watch, and Physicians for Human Rights. These activists are advocates; that is, they take the side of little people suffering abuse at the hands of powerful actors (such as states). But Clyde Snow points out that the awful nature of many human rights violations denies him the luxury of advocacy because when he gets hired, he is expected to function as an expert witness objectively interpreting his findings. Human rights organizations hire lawyers as advocates

Variation ■ The range of differences in physical or genetic characteristics within or between populations of individuals

Species ■ A group of organisms similar enough to interbreed and produce fertile offspring

Taxonomy ■ The science of classification allowing a convenient means of reference and comparison involving different organisms

Phylogeny ■ Ancestor–descendant relationships usually presented chronologically, such as the lineal relationships between fossil humans and other primates

Binomial nomenclature ■ Two names whereby genus and species names are used to identify species; for example, *Homo sapiens* refers to human beings

Fossils ■ The preserved remains or traces of living creatures from past ages that are left when organisms die and are buried in soft mud or sand

Forensic anthropology ■ The anthropological subfield under biological anthropology that identifies human skeletal remains, often for legal purposes

Kingdom Animalia

Phylum Chordata

Class Mammalia

Order Primates

Infraorder Anthropoidea

Superfamily Hominoidea

Family Hominidae

Genus *Homo*

Species *Sapiens*

Figure 9.2
Taxonomy of the Human Species

Source: Noel Boaz and Alan Almquist, *Essentials of Biological Anthropology* (Prentice Hall, 1999), p. 12. Copyright © 1999. Reprinted and electronically reproduced by permission of Pearson Education, Inc., Upper Saddle River, NJ.

After receiving a master's degree in zoology, Clyde Snow intended to continue studying for a doctorate in physiology, but these plans were interrupted by military service in the 1950s. His tour in the Air Force serendipitously placed him near San Antonio, Texas. In his spare time, Snow found himself increasingly drawn to the local treasure trove of ancient artifacts in the area surrounding Lackland Air Force Base. Thus began his fascination with archaeology. He had grown up in a small Texas town where his father was a physician, and the family lived above his office, and he absorbed a very clinical view of death.

When Snow finished his military stint, he moved on to the University of Arizona, where his degree in zoology and keen interest in archaeology motivated him to complete a Ph.D. in biological anthropology. Now adept at identifying ancient bones and artifacts, Dr. Snow went to work as a forensic anthropologist for the Federal Aviation Administration (FAA), where his technical skills were tapped by identifying the victims of airplane crashes and by designing safety equipment to protect those involved in examining such accidents. A reputation for excellence in forensics resulted in numerous consultations and invitations to provide expert testimony at criminal trials.

One high-profile murder case led him to testify about evidence leading to the conviction of John Wayne Gacy, accused of killing more than thirty teenagers around the city of Chicago. Snow also participated in a reinvestigation of the assassination of President John F. Kennedy, which found no forensic evidence contradicting the Warren Commission Report's conclusion that Lee Harvey Oswald had acted alone as JFK's assassin in 1963. His most famous subject of forensic investigation consisted of the body of Nazi war criminal Josef Mengele, whom Snow identified via skeletal and dental examination, later corroborate by DNA evidence.

Soon Clyde Snow found his expertise in demand internationally, as well. From 1976 to 1983, a military dictatorship in Argentina secretly murdered thousands of citizens whom the government disliked. Known as the *saga of the desaparecidos* (the disappeared), these killings gradually received global media attention. The story made for compelling journalism. Why? Because the families of the *desaparecidos*, who slowly became emboldened to gather in the streets of Buenos Aires to demonstrate their grief, were hit with a double whammy: their loved ones were missing and probably dead, and the families could experience no psychological closure because no bodies were available to verify death. Dr. Snow conducted field research in Argentina, where he located and identified many of the bodies; Snow also testified when the nine members of the military dictatorship were eventually brought to justice in this sad affair. He believes that his work will make it more difficult for such egregious human rights atrocities to occur in the future, adding, "Bones never lie, and they never forget." ■

---

who apply Snow's expert testimony.[6] Public infatuation with scientific sleuthing has been much in evidence in recent years by the success of a spate of forensic TV programs.

Evolutionary Theory

The authors of one leading text observe that "humans are a product of the same biological forces that produced all life on earth. As such, we represent one contemporary component of a vast biological continuum at one point in time."[7] Professor Matt Cartmill adds that "evolution is the linchpin of biology; the unifying paradigm of all the life sciences."[8] Arriving at these insights, however, has come neither easily nor quickly to human comprehension.

Natural Selection

Evolution by natural selection ■ Darwin's theory that inherited variation results in differing survival rates for individuals and in their ability to contribute to offspring in succeeding generations

As soon as the topic of biological evolution is raised, many people immediately think of British biologist Charles Darwin (1809–1882) and his theory of **evolution by natural selection** (see photo drawing on the next page). However, the notion that members of a species whose traits favored success in meeting life's challenges were likely to pass along those characteristics to their progeny—"survival of the fittest"—was not new. Four centuries before Christ, the Greek philosopher Aristotle advanced the thesis that simple organisms slowly develop into more complex ones.

Closer to Darwin's day, various critical thinkers challenged the conventional wisdom about human origins. Swedish naturalist Carolus Linnaeus (1707–1778), developer of the system of binomial nomenclature, included humans within his classification of animals. Linnaeus was not trying to defy the biblical version of creation. Rather, his commitment to fixed species was based on his belief that this was how plants, animals, and humans were created by God. Another influential thinker was Georges-Louis Leclerc (1707–1788), also known by his royal title: Comte de Buffon. Leclerc served as keeper of the King's Gardens in Paris, which aided his understanding of the dynamic relationship between the environment and life forms and of its contribution to changing species.

Not coincidentally, Erasmus Darwin (1731–1802), Charles Darwin's grandfather, was a freethinking physician and an accomplished poet who expressed vague evolutionary concepts in his verse. More concrete, however, were Erasmus Darwin's personal letters, which spoke of the plausibility of human evolution specifically. Yet neither Buffon nor Erasmus Darwin organized the concept of evolution into an explanatory framework. The French scholar Jean-Baptiste Lamarck (1744–1829) tried to do so. Lamarck's theory of inheritance of acquired characteristics tried to explain why organic forms might vary because of environmental differences. But despite Lamarck's boldness, his thesis proved to be wrong.

Charles Darwin's theory of evolution by natural selection has profoundly influenced scientific inquiry for the past century and a half.

Thomas Malthus (1766–1834), an English clergyman and economist, studied issues related to the sustainability of human populations. He wrote "An Essay on the Principle of Population" (1798), which inspired both Charles Darwin and Alfred Wallace, his countrymen who later worked on the principle of natural selection. Malthus observed that in nature, living things produce more offspring than can survive to reproduce. For every 1,000 salmon that leave their birth stream for life in the oceans, only 10 complete their struggle against the current to return home to reproduce. Although thousands of tadpoles may hatch from eggs, few live to maturity. Darwin and Wallace gleaned from Malthus's work that determining which organisms survive depends on the process of selection. Thus, *variation within species* and *reproductive success* became the twin pillars of natural selection.

Unlike Alfred Wallace, Charles Darwin grew up as a privileged member of the landed gentry in nineteenth-century England. Darwin's father, like his grandfather, was a physician, and Charles developed a keen interest in both nature and science. He attended Shrewsbury boarding school, and began studying medicine in 1825 at Edinburgh University, where he absorbed the evolutionary theories already proposed by Lamarck and others. Nineteenth-century scholars were in love with the scientific revolution, and Darwin felt comfortable with it when he later matriculated at Cambridge University to further his studies, graduating in 1831 at age twenty-two. He had made friends at Cambridge with the botanist J. S. Henslow, who recommended Darwin for a scientific expedition aboard the HMS *Beagle*, which would circle the globe for five years. Although frequently seasick, Darwin collected numerous fossils and kept meticulous records of his work.

During his well-chronicled research stop in the Galápagos Islands, Darwin observed that inhabitants of the various islands differed somewhat from one another. He gathered thirteen varieties of finches in the Galápagos. Although they shared many characteristics, subtle differences in physical traits also materialized, most notably the size of their beaks. The insights that he derived from the finches proved amazingly resilient. All thirteen of them had changed, responding to varying island habitats and dietary preferences.[9] Upon returning to England, Darwin continued honing his theories but procrastinated over publishing his work, for two reasons. First, he worried that more evidence was needed to make his case, even though new evidence was difficult to come by. Second, he worried that his revolutionary ideas would dishonor him among his friends in the landed gentry of Victorian England. Most of his loved ones held biblical Christian beliefs; thus he feared that his interpretations of human origins would cause him great personal grief. In 1839, he married his cousin Emma Wedgwood, who hailed from the wealthy Wedgwood ceramics family. He started writing the first sketch of his research in 1842 but published *The Origin of Species* only in 1859, and then reluctantly. Ironically, some of the evidence that he craved was very nearby, as described in Case Study 9.2.

Case Study 9.2   Natural Selection at Work Right Under Darwin's Nose

It usually takes long years (numbered in thousands or millions) for major changes in nature to occur. Yet, during his lifetime, the most elegant example of natural selection ever documented was in full swing right in Darwin's vicinity.[10] Prior to Darwin's time, the most common variety of *peppered moth* found in northern England was colored a mottled gray. This light coloration served to camouflage the peppered moth against tree trunks covered by a light-colored lichen. At the same time, a darker, less common moth could also be found in the area. The darker, uncamouflaged moth was more visible to birds and thus was preyed upon more frequently. Consequently, the darker moths had shorter lives and produced fewer offspring than the lighter moths. But counterintuitively, by the end of the nineteenth century, the darker moths almost totally replaced the lighter variety.

How did this unexpected turn of events transpire? The explanation can be found in the rapidly changing environment that existed in nineteenth-century industrial England. Coal dust in the area around the city of Manchester was then settling heavily on trees, killing the lichen and turning the bark a darker color. As peppered moths continued to rest on trees, the lighter variety became increasingly conspicuous as the trees turned darker. Therefore, the lighter-colored moths were eaten by birds more often, thus contributing fewer genes to the next generation.

The sequel to this story brings us full circle: in the latter part of the twentieth century, tighter governmental controls on pollutants in England allowed trees to return to their earlier, and healthier, preindustrial (lichen-covered) condition. And what happened then? As would be predicted by the theory of natural selection, the lighter moths once again multiplied, replacing the darker ones. ■

The Laws of Heredity

As correct as Darwin was about the principle of natural selection, he failed to discard the common-sensical belief in the blending of parental traits: that offspring inherit traits in a form of genetic compromise. Ironically, just as Darwin could have gleaned much by knowing about the contemporaneous plight of the peppered moth discussed in Case Study 9.2, so could his scientific theories have been enriched by knowing about the discoveries of an obscure Augustinian monk living in Austria, Gregor Mendel (1822–1884). Mendel's experiments in the 1860s would eventually revolutionize biological thinking about inheritance. This Renaissance man was trained in botany, physics, and mathematics. Mendel taught at a local secondary school and carried out research independently. Most impressively, he deduced, without viewing cells through a microscope, that plants and animals possess **genes** that shape the patterns of inheritance for subsequent generations.

Genes ■ Discrete units of hereditary information determining specific physical attributes of organisms

Mendel's breeding experiments used controlled pollination to study pea plants differing from each other in some key characteristics (color, size, shape). For example, he cross-pollinated purebred plants producing only yellow peas with purebred plants yielding only green peas. Following the results through several generations, he found a distinct reproductive pattern using careful statistical analysis. Some green plants produced only yellow ones in the second generation but then reverted back to green in the third generation, and the ratio of yellow to green plants in the second generation was 3:1. After Mendel had rejected the concept of blending, he was able to discover that certain traits prevailed over others. To describe the trait that seemed to be lost but then reappeared, he used the term **recessive,** and the one that was expressed he called **dominant.** The concepts of dominance and recessiveness continue to serve as stalwart principles in modern genetics. He published his results in 1866, but they were ignored until his ideas were rediscovered in 1900 by three separate researchers.

Recessive ■ A gene that goes unexpressed when occurring in a gene pair with a dominant form

Dominant ■ The form of a gene that is expressed in a gene pair with a recessive form

Darwin's discovery that animals were variable and that much of this variability was inherited, and Mendel's unraveling of the mechanism by which variability passed from one generation to the next, still do not explain why change occurs in living organisms. To solve this piece of the evolutionary puzzle, we must turn to other concepts in molecular biology and population genetics. We now know that genes occur in a linear order and are found within units called **chromosomes,** and that humans have forty-six chromosomes arranged in matching pairs, with each offspring inheriting twenty-three chromosomes

Chromosomes ■ Structures in the nucleus of the cell that contain hereditary information

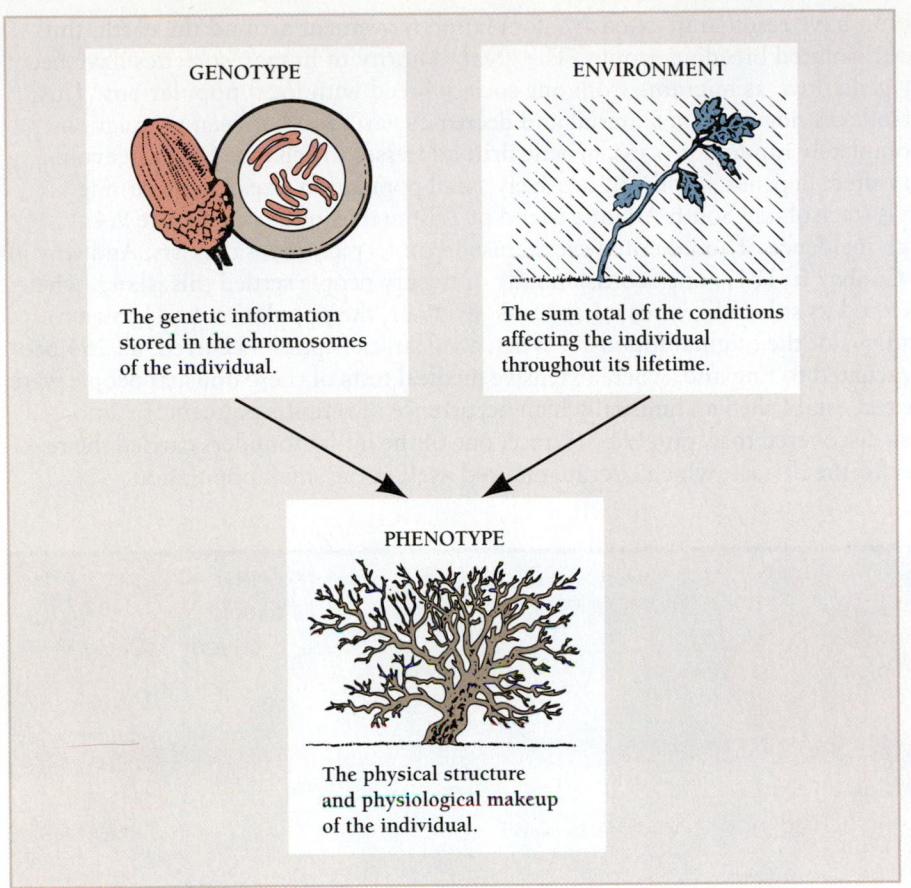

GENOTYPE

The genetic information
stored in the chromosomes
of the individual.

ENVIRONMENT

The sum total of the conditions
affecting the individual
throughout its lifetime.

PHENOTYPE

The physical structure
and physiological makeup
of the individual.

Figure 9.3

The Genotype Interacts with the
Environment to Produce the Phenotype

Source: From *The Illustrated Origin of Species*
by Charles Darwin, with an introduction by
Richard Leakey. Original publication date
1859.

from each parent, and that the nuclei of all human cells contain these chromosomes. We
also know that genes contain discrete **DNA** (**deoxyribonucleic acid**) sequences that code
for amino acids, the constituents of protein, and that DNA is the essential factor determining inherited traits. Most organisms that reproduce sexually have two genes for every
physical trait, one gene received from each parent. Biologists now distinguish between the
individual's **genotype** and its **phenotype** (see Figure 9.3).

Comprehending the theory of evolution requires that we not concentrate on individuals, but rather on the change occurring in the genetic makeup of a **population** of organisms.
Scientists studying evolution examine all of the genes, or the gene pool, of a given population. Alteration of the gene pool results from the interplay of one concept that we have discussed (natural selection) and three that we have not discussed: mutation, gene flow, and
genetic drift. One group of authors refers to these as the "four forces of evolution."[11]

Mutation, Gene Flow, and Genetic Drift

Mutation can result from environmental factors, such as radiation, or it can arise spontaneously during cell replication. By introducing variation into the gene pool, mutations
can produce either advantageous or disadvantageous new characteristics. Most mutations occur in the somatic cells of organisms, meaning they are not inheritable, and when
that individual dies, so does the mutation. But some mutations change the DNA in reproductive cells, and this type of mutation can be inherited by offspring. Although mutation alone provides variability within a population, it is unlikely by itself to unleash
evolution. However, when mutations are acted upon by natural selection, they represent
a more potent force for evolution.

Gene flow results in the introduction of new genetic material through interbreeding. Especially during the past 500 years of human history, technological advances in

**DNA (deoxyribonucleic
acid)** ■ Molecule found in the cell
containing the chemical coding
for proteins that shape traits of living organisms

Genotype ■ An individual's
actual genetic makeup

Phenotype ■ The observable
physical manifestations of genes

Population ■ Within a species,
the community of individuals in
which interbreeding occurs

Mutation ■ Alteration of genetic
material at the cellular level that
may affect both genes and chromosomes and is the source of new
variability in populations

Gene flow ■ The exchange of
genes between different populations; sometimes called migration

transportation have resulted in extensive population movement around the earth, thus leaving fewer isolated breeding groups. The great majority of human societies have been affected by gene flow, as migrants from one society breed with local populations. This process introduces new genetic material and decreases variation between populations.

As a completely random process, **genetic drift** addresses the chance factor in evolution, and its effect depends wholly on relatively small population size. An interesting illustration is the isolated South Atlantic island of Tristan da Cunha (see Figure 9.4), where a high incidence of an inherited eye disease (retinitis pigmentosa) exists. And why in Tristan da Cunha? In 1817, one Scottish family of twenty people settled this island, where they represented its sole indigenous inhabitants. By 1961, the population had grown to 294 descendants of the original founders. When a volcanic eruption occurred, all 294 people were evacuated to England, where extensive medical tests of these unusual people were taken. One test established an unusually high occurrence of retinitis pigmentosa among them. It was discovered that, purely by chance, one of the initial founders carried the recessive trait for the disease, which later manifested itself in the small population.

Genetic drift ■ Changes in gene frequency not affected by natural selection, and resulting from chance effects, and most common in small populations

Figure 9.4

The process of genetic drift is illustrated by unique events occurring on the isolated island of Tristan de Cunha.

Source: From Maps on File, by Facts on File, Inc. Copyright © by Facts on File, Inc. Reprinted by permission of Facts on File, Inc.

Biology has developed extensively since the early work of pioneers such as Charles Darwin and Gregor Mendel, and its complex understanding of these "four forces of evolution" represents great progress. However, the exact relationship between natural selection, mutation, gene flow, and genetic drift remains elusive. Another conceptual distinction capable of expanding our vision of evolution as genetic change in a population is that of **micro-evolution** versus **macro-evolution.**

Micro-Evolution Leads to Macro-Evolution

When biologists talk about changes occurring in a given population relatively quickly they use the term micro-evolution, as in the instance of the English peppered moth's alteration in color discussed in Case Study 9.2. Through micro-evolution, given populations begin differing from one another. If they vary enough, over a long enough period of time, micro-evolution may lead to macro-evolution, involving the emergence of a new species. Such macro-evolutionary change that results in a new species is called *speciation*.

And how does this process of speciation come about? Three major theories compete to explain the formation of new species. The first relates back to Darwin's intuitive assumption that the process of macro-evolution is really just micro-evolution measured over longer stretches of geological time. Darwin was influenced by geology's theories of snail-like gradual change in the physical world, and he transferred many of its assumptions to the realm of living beings. This incremental image of evolution connotes a slow and steady path to speciation. Technically known as **phyletic gradualism,** the gradualist model has been criticized for decades by scholars who believe that the fossil record contains too many large gaps—many millions of years during which archaeologists have found no fossils that identify newly emergent species. Many observers had expected that eventually, new finds would fill in the gaps, but that expectation has yet to materialize.

In an attempt to reconcile gaps in the fossil record with modern thinking about evolution, some scholars suggested that the occurrence of "sudden leaps" in evolution might account for insufficient empirical evidence supporting phyletic gradualism. Archaeologist George G. Simpson contended that large-scale mutations, or populations rapidly shifting their adaptations to the environment, could account for sudden jumps not hypothesized in the Darwinian model. This theory is called **quantum evolution.**[12] Building on these challenges to the gradualist model of evolution, Stephen Jay Gould and Niles Eldredge advanced a third theory arguing that most species experience little or no variation during their evolutionary history—a condition they referred to as stasis. On those rare occasions when adaptive change does occur, it is through short, rapid bursts, and only during the process of speciation. Gould and Eldredge coined the moniker **punctuated equilibrium** to advance their theory (see Figure 9.5).[13]

Micro-evolution ■ Small-scale evolutionary changes within a population or species over a relatively short period of time

Macro-evolution ■ Large-scale evolutionary changes over a long period of time producing changes that result in new species

Phyletic gradualism ■ The view traceable to Charles Darwin that evolution occurs piecemeal in a slow manner over long time periods

Quantum evolution ■ A theory postulating a process of stepwise evolutionary change

Punctuated equilibrium ■ A theory claiming that evolution is characterized by extended periods without change followed by bursts of quick change

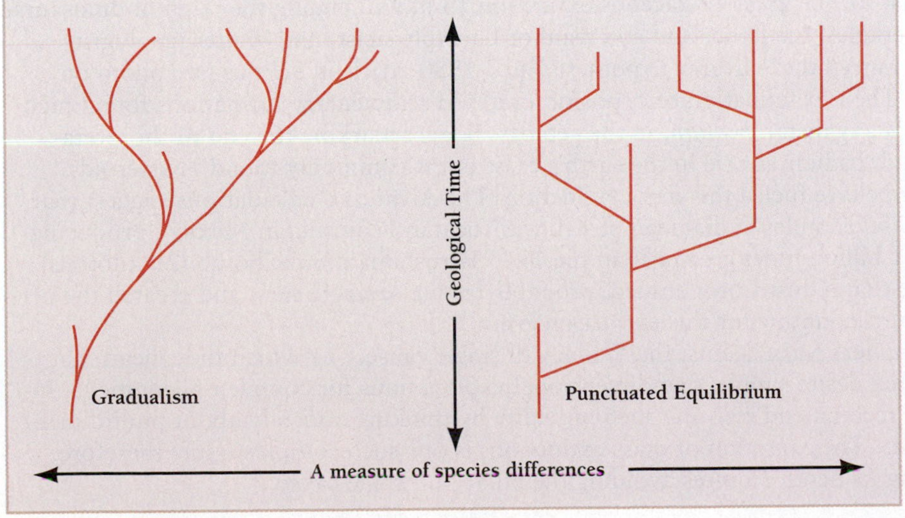

Figure 9.5

Models of Evolution: Gradualism and Punctuated Equilibrium

Source: The Record of the Past: Introduction to Physical Anthropology and Archaeology by Christopher DeCorse, Prentice Hall, 2001. Reprinted by permission of the author.

Mass Extinctions and Evolution

However, just as we seem able to wrap our minds around the various permutations of evolution, along come new findings challenging parts of it. Yet such intellectual restlessness represents the essential skepticism characteristic of scientific critical thinking. Recent evidence suggests that during certain rare events, the rules of the evolutionary game are suspended because of cataclysms known as **mass extinctions**. Five major episodes of mass extinction have occurred over the last 440 million years. Following mass extinctions, the dominant form of life on earth often changes, accompanied by a flurry of new species. The current Age of Mammals ensued after the mass extinction that took dinosaurs with it 75 million years ago (m.y.a.).

For years, biological anthropologists largely ignored the implications of mass extinctions for the process of evolution, but recently they have begun incorporating them: "Once considered a passive component in the course of evolution, mass extinction is now recognized as a major determinant of its outcome."[14] The normal rules of the game are trumped by these rare cataclysms. In other words, evolutionary winners and losers have less to do with competition, or "survival of the fittest," than with mass extinctions. As posed by David Raup, "Was it bad genes or bad luck that consigned the losers to evolutionary oblivion?"[15] The Darwinian model of survival of the fittest features both explanatory power and considerable predictability. Thus some scholars find the evidence for mass extinctions disquieting. And what causes mass extinctions that punctuate the rhythm and flow of natural selection? Probably no single explanation for mass extinctions will be discovered. One theory points to global climate change, especially global cooling, during the Ice Ages that have occurred often in our planet's history, some of which have involved glaciation. Scientist Stephen Stanley of Johns Hopkins University studies species extinction in North America and concludes that climatic cooling is the "main culprit because of the relative ease with which changes in global temperatures can occur."[16] All species are adapted to local conditions, including their usual food sources and prevailing temperatures, and if massive change occurs in either food sources or climate, mass extinction may result.

English archaeologist Paul Wignall emphasizes another plausible explanation. He believes that much evidence supports the view that all five mass extinctions have been accompanied by a significant fall in sea level—a process called *marine regression*. Polar glaciation and restructuring of the continents represent two events that can trigger marine regression. As sea level drops, continental shelves are exposed, which reduces their organic carrying capacity and puts pressure on species living in shallow waters. Because the earth comprises one interdependent ecosystem, marine regression can produce mass killings, not only along shorelines, but on land as well. If extensive oxidation of organic matter takes place, it pulls oxygen from the atmosphere, replacing it with carbon, in what Wignall calls "a story of death by suffocation for both terrestrial and marine life."[17]

The impact of giant asteroids represents another candidate for causing mass extinction, at least for the great Cretaceous extinction 75 m.y.a., ending the reign of dinosaurs. Based at Berkeley, the father-and-son team of Luis (physicist) and Walter (geologist) Alvarez advanced the "Alvarez hypothesis" in a 1980 article in *Science* (see photo on page 230). Their examination of deposition rates in sedimentary formations found high levels of a heavy metal, *iridium*, in the geological layer marking the end of the Cretaceous period. Iridium is rare in the earth's crust but is commonly found in asteroids, which they believe fueled this mass extinction. The Alvarezes' calculations suggest that an asteroid seven miles in diameter struck the Yucatán Peninsula in Mexico, producing an impact 1 billion times greater than the 1945 Hiroshima atomic bomb (20 kilotons). They argue that a dust storm ensued, probably lasting several years, and created the perpetual night accounting for this extinction event.[18]

Philosophers warn against the "fallacy of single cause," by which they mean that humans often desire simple, one-dimensional explanations for complex phenomena. Instead, they recommend resisting such unreality by thinking critically about multidimensional events. The causation of mass extinctions is one such complex issue; therefore, appreciating its depth requires avoiding the fallacy of single cause.

Mass extinctions ■ Rare biotic crises on a global scale resulting when two-thirds of extant species become extinct in a brief geological instant

Stages of Evolution

Paleoanthropologist Richard Leakey claims that all of life is something of a grand lottery, and he criticizes what he terms the "Inevitability Myth" concerning human evolution in writing that "nothing in evolution is inevitable; *Homo sapiens* was one of a range of possibilities in the evolution of the hominid group, not an inevitable product of that process."[19] Like one of those giant three-dimensional 5,000-piece puzzles, the number of pieces contributing to even a superficial appreciation of human origins can seem overwhelming. But even the most cursory reduction of prehistory may prove useful as an evolutionary timeline, which is provided by Table 9.1.

By turning the clock back about 75 million years, we can identify the appearance of mammals (Class Mammalia; see Figure 9.2) on earth. Then 20 million years later, one order of mammals, called primates, took to the trees and gradually developed into

Table 9.1

EVOLUTIONARY BENCHMARKS OF PREHISTORY[a]

Estimated Time	Life Forms or Physical Development
15 b.y.a.	Origin of the universe
4.6 b.y.a.	Origin of the earth
3.6 b.y.a.	Microscopic life on earth originates in water
1.8 b.y.a.	Oldest algae fossils
750 m.y.a.	Oldest animal fossils
450 m.y.a.	First land plants
First Mass Extinction	
438 m.y.a.	First animals (arthropods) leave sea for dry land
360 m.y.a.	Age of Reptiles begins
Second Mass Extinction	
286 m.y.a.	Mammal-like reptiles appear
Third Mass Extinction	
248 m.y.a.	First dinosaurs
Fourth Mass Extinction	
75 m.y.a.	Earliest mammals appear
Fifth Mass Extinction	
55 m.y.a.	Oldest primate (emerged from mammals) fossils
35 m.y.a.	Some tree-dwelling apes move from trees to ground
4–8 m.y.a.	Bipedalism among hominids
5 m.y.a.	First humanlike primate fossil records
2.5 m.y.a.	Stone tools appear and brain expansion originates
2 m.y.a.	Extinction of many large mammals
1.5 m.y.a.	Signs of meat eating
1.3 m.y.a.	Hominid use of fire
1 m.y.a.	*Homo erectus* leaves Africa for Eurasia
150,000 y.a.	Modern humans originate in Africa
35,000 y.a.	First art
32,000 y.a.	Neanderthals become extinct
11,000 y.a.	Last Ice Age ends
10,000 y.a.	Agricultural revolution

[a]Information derived from Christopher DeCorse, *The Record of the Past: Introduction to Physical Anthropology and Archaeology* (Prentice Hall, 2000), pp. 46–47; Edward O. Wilson, *The Diversity of Life* (Belknap Press, 1992).

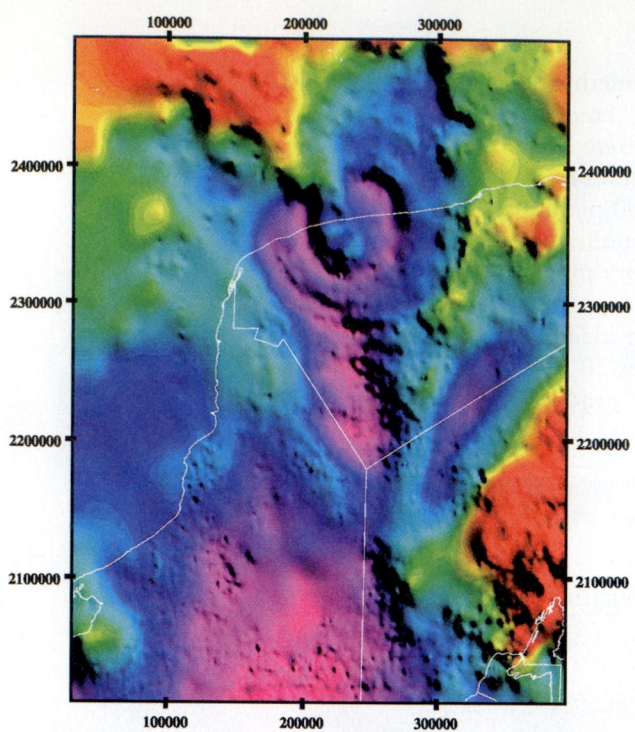

Dinosaurs were among the losers in the great Cretaceous extinction 75 m.y.a. Some scientists believe that this crater in the Yucatán peninsula was caused by a giant asteroid that also caused the Cretaceous extinction in the process.

Primates ■ The zoological order of mammals that includes monkeys, apes, and humans

Hominoids ■ Modern apes, modern humans, and their immediate ancestors

Hominids ■ Popular form of the taxonomic family *Hominidae,* including humans and ancient bipedal hominoids

warm-blooded animals. This order of mammals includes monkeys, apes, and human beings, among others. Some tree-dwelling apes eventually moved down to live on the ground about 35 m.y.a. Between 8 and 4 m.y.a., bipedalism was exhibited by some primates. The earliest humanlike creatures appeared about 5 m.y.a. This ancient prehuman line eventually divided into humans, plus at least one other species. The first stone tools and a significant brain expansion have been dated to 2.5 m.y.a., first use of fire 1.3 m.y.a., the origin of modern humans 150,000 y.a., first human art 35,000 y.a., and the agricultural revolution 10,000 y.a. Soon after the agricultural revolution, human prehistory ends as writing gradually appears.

Prequel to the Human Drama
From Early Primates to Hominoids

The first **primates** in the fossil record have been dated to 55 m.y.a. Primates emerged in tropical climates and evolved hands and feet useful for locomotion in trees. Stereoscopic vision also aided in catching prey, and an omnivorous diet characterized early primates. A key behavioral characteristic of the anthropoid primates (monkeys and apes) was living in social groups year-round, which enabled them to find solutions to reproduction, predation, and feeding problems.

Apes appear in the fossil record dating back 55 million years, representing the first humanlike hominoids, in heavily forested lowland areas. These **hominoids** were better climbers than earlier monkeys, and some scientists hypothesize that they may have used a form of knuckle-walking for locomotion. By 15 m.y.a., hominoids had migrated through much of the Old World (Europe, Africa, Asia), but by 5 m.y.a., they were mostly extinct. Four surviving groups of hominoids exist largely in African and southeast Asian rainforests: the lesser apes, gorillas, chimpanzees, and orangutans. The fossil record and molecular studies currently support the thesis that chimpanzees and modern humans took different branches of the evolutionary tree 5 to 7 m.y.a.

From Hominoids to Hominids

Hominids are those relatively large-brained members of the primate order that have adopted walking on two legs, or bipedally, as well as exhibiting larger molar teeth (relative to body size) and relatively small canine teeth, when compared with earlier hominoids. The earliest known hominid subfamily to share some significant traits with modern humans, the Australopithecines, have been traced by fossils to eastern and southern Africa between 3 and 4 m.y.a. The original Australopithicine find was made by Raymond Dart in 1925 and consisted of the skull of a juvenile hominid found in southern Africa. The specimen dates to 2.5–3 m.y.a. and has been referred to popularly as the Taung child, but in his 1925 article in *Nature,* Dart officially labeled it *Australopithecus africanus* and something of a "missing link," or an intermediary between apes and modern humans. Australopithecines seem to have been broadly adapted to savanna and woodland environments.

Dart's success in southern Africa led many fossil hunters to try their luck at other African locations. One of these was Louis Leakey, who was raised in Kenya by missionary parents and then trained as an anthropologist at Cambridge University. Alongside his archaeologist wife, Mary, and later their children, Louis Leakey began scouring geologically likely spots in northern Tanzania. At Olduvai Gorge, the Leakeys began uncovering early hominids in 1959, when Mary found a rare complete

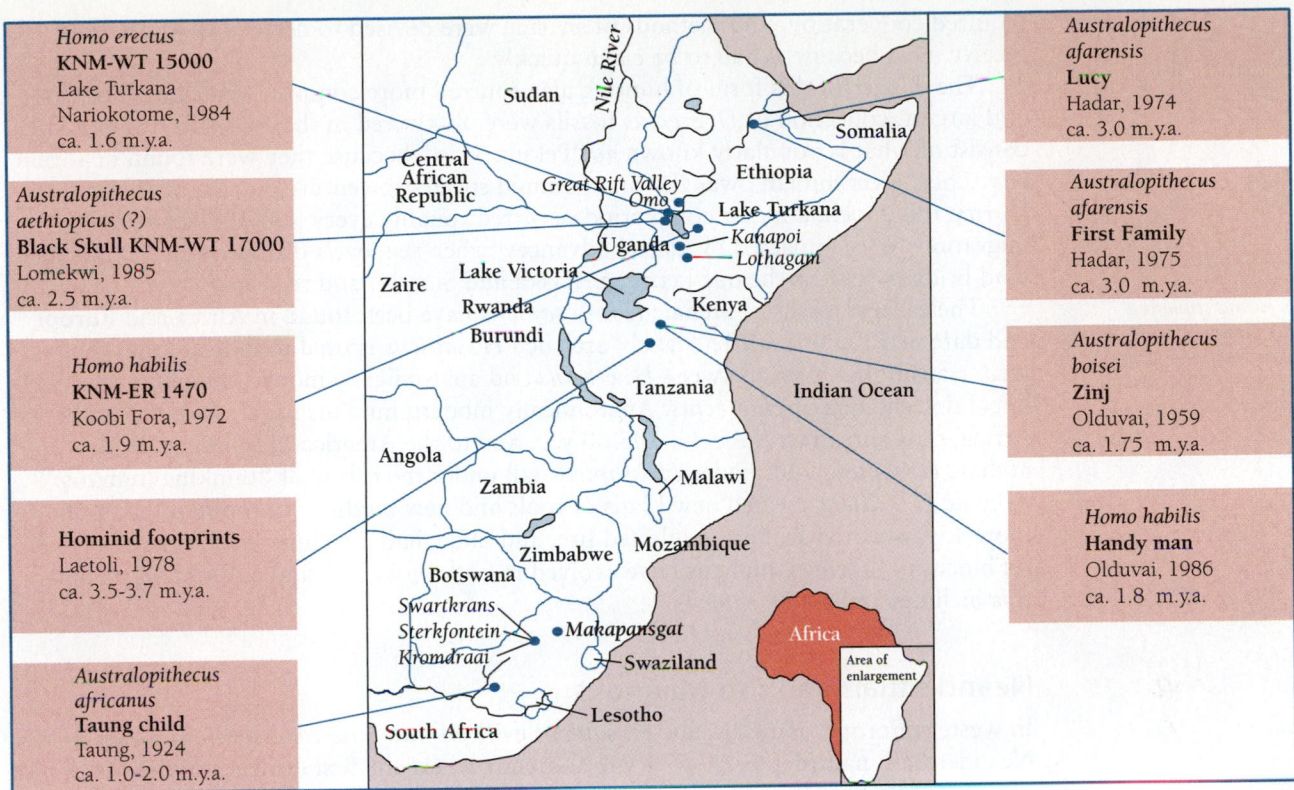

Figure 9.6
Map of African Fossil Finds

Source: From Roger Lewin, *In the Age of Mankind: A Smithsonian Book of Human Evolution* (Smithsonian Books 1988), p. 71.

Australopithecine skull. Members of the extended family continue to search to this day, finding other important bones. All Australopithecines became extinct by 1 m.y.a., and they all had much smaller brains, but larger teeth, than modern humans. What they did share with us is bipedalism.

From Hominids to the Genus *Homo*

Philosopher Jacob Bronowski pinponts a most intriguing yet elusive question in this evolutionary saga: "How did hominids come to be the kind that I honor: dexterous, observant, thoughtful, passionate, able to manipulate in the mind the symbols of language and mathematics both, the visions of art and geometry and poetry and science?"[20] Experts identify three species of the Homo family: *Homo habilis, Homo erectus,* and *Homo sapiens.* Each species is considered distinguishable from Australopithecines as stone-tool-making and culture-bearing species. **Homo habilis** is seen in the fossil record around 2.5 m.y.a. in Africa. *Homo habilis* means "handy human," a name chosen to reflect stone-tool-making capacity. The initial find of *Homo habilis* was made by the Leakeys at Olduvai Gorge in 1960, and for the first time, a new form of potassium-argon dating was employed, which placed this specimen at 1.73 m.y.a. It is not known whether *Homo habilis* ventured outside of Sub-Saharan Africa (see Figure 9.6).

The trend toward increased cranial capacity, dental reduction, and larger body size begun with *Homo habilis* remained intact in its descendants. *H. habilis* was replaced by **Homo erectus,** who moved out of Africa and into Eurasia. Fossils of *H. erectus* have been traced to 1.6 m.y.a. *H. erectus* had a larger brain, thicker cranial bones, and heavier brow ridges than *H. habilis,* and its stone tools were more sophisticated. It is believed that *H. erectus* made bifacial stone axes to hunt large animals about 500,000 y.a.—the best evidence involves tools for hunting elephants found in Spain. Hunting large animals

Homo habilis ■ The earliest recognized species of the genus Homo

Homo erectus ■ Primitive species of genus *Homo* believed to have evolved from *H. habilis* and into *H. sapiens*

required cooperation, and methods of sharing were devised to determine who would receive meat because it had to be eaten quickly.

The danger of this form of hunting also spurred more complex strategies. The first, and largest, collection of *H. erectus* fossils were discovered in the 1920s in China and consist of what is popularly known as "Peking Man" because they were found near that city. This "erect human" was the first hominid species to venture outside of Africa. During this epoch, a major cold period occurred roughly every 100,000 years, and migrations were impacted by glacial advances (when sea levels dropped, thus exposing land bridges, such as the one between Alaska and Siberia) and retreats.[21]

Archaic *Homo sapiens* ■
"Thinking humans," including all peoples on earth today as members of one interbreeding biological species

The earliest fossils of **archaic *Homo sapiens*** have been found in Africa and Europe and date to 500,000 y.a.. The label "archaic" *H. sapiens* is used to indicate that these were transitional forms between *H. erectus* and anatomically modern humans, and likely lineal descendants of *H. erectus*. Anatomically modern humans began 150,000 y.a. in Africa, then spread to Australia 50,000 y.a., and to the Americas 12,000 y.a. Both archaic *H. sapiens* and modern *H. sapiens* fall under the rubric of "thinking humans." Archaic *H. sapiens* created new kinds of tools and new methods of toolmaking, built more sophisticated shelters, exploited fire, and likely had a rudimentary form of speech. As biocultural beings, humans have evolved in both biological and cultural ways, and this includes archaic *H. sapiens*.

Neanderthals and Cro-Magnons

In western Europe, some archaic *H. sapiens* evolved into a new subspecies known as Neanderthals, named after the valley in Germany where the first evidence of their existence was discovered in 1856, three years after Darwin published *The Origin of Species*. As the first premodern humans to be found, Neanderthals immediately aroused controversy among scholars. "It took almost 100 years for scholars to accept the idea that Neanderthals were not that different from modern humans and should be classified as *Homo sapiens neanderthalensis*."[22] There is some evidence that they lived in loose settlements, sometimes near anatomically modern *H. sapiens;* they were the first to resemble modern humans closely. Disagreements abound as to whether Neanderthals should be considered a subspecies of *H. sapiens*. Something nearer to a consensus posits that they possessed shorter, more compact bodies—characteristics beneficial in the European habitat during the last Ice Age. Neanderthals were also more physically robust and made more strenuous use of their bodies. They had sloping foreheads, large brow ridges, a cranial capacity larger than that of modern humans, and larger front teeth used as tools, and they possibly were less verbally oriented than modern humans.[23]

In recent decades, scientists have provided evidence disputing the traditional view fostered in the media depicting Neanderthals as cavemen—second-rate hominids swept aside by quicker-thinking modern humans.[24] Like contemporaneous *H. sapiens,* they made tools, sought protection in caves, walked bipedally, buried their dead ceremoniously with flowers, and cared for the infirm among them. In 1997, it was discovered by German archaeologist Oscar Todkopf that Neanderthals also made musical instruments, including a six-foot-long tuba-like instrument with sixteen holes carved out of a mastodon tusk.[25] Scholars have long pondered what kinds of links may have existed between the two human cousins. DNA derived from the bones of a 30,000-year-old Neanderthal suggests that they did not interbreed with *H. sapiens* and were not our genetic ancestors, but that another subspecies (Cro-Magnons) may have been.[26] Neanderthals had migrated from Europe into the Near East and then to Asia, and existed from 130,000 y.a. to 35,000 y.a., possibly "disappearing as a result of intensive selective pressure and genetic drift."[27]

Best known of European *H. sapiens* in the Upper Paleolithic were the Cro-Magnons, who may have coexisted with Neanderthals around 60,000 to 90,000 y.a. They are named for the French village where the fragmentary remains of about six individuals were found in 1868, providing the first clear evidence of migration by modern humans into Europe. Cro-Magnons differed from Neanderthals in their higher, more bulging

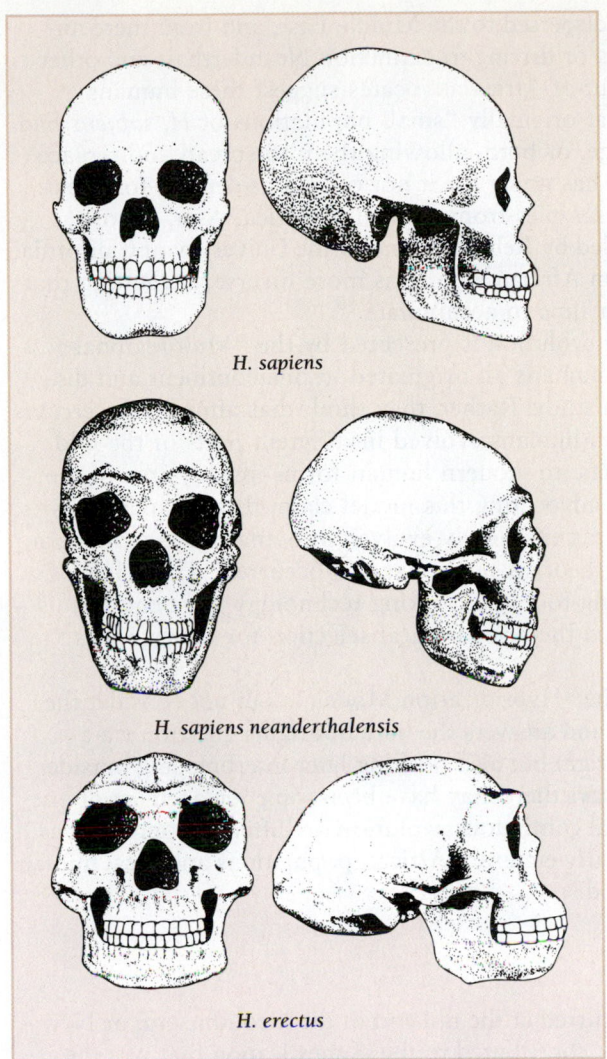

H. sapiens

H. sapiens neanderthalensis

H. erectus

Figure 9.7

Drawing: Skulls of *H. erectus, H. sapiens neanderthalensis*, Modern *H. sapiens*

Source: The Record of the Past: Introduction to Physical Anthropology and Archaeology by Christopher DeCorse, Prentice Hall, 2001. Reprinted by permission of the author.

foreheads, thinner and lighter bones, smaller faces and jaws, prominent chins, and bone ridges over the eyes.[28] Artifacts of sophisticated Cro-Magnon stone technologies—such as blades differentially made for a variety of purposes—have been found.

By 17,000 y.a., some Cro-Magnon groups began to specialize in hunting migrating reindeer herds and built highland camps overlooking migratory valleys. They made shelters for use in warm weather but then retreated to caves during cold weather. Cro-Magnons also used iron pyrite to create sparks in fire-making—an art they seem to have mastered fully. Evidence of hearths, demonstrating that they used fire for cooking as well as for heat, has been found from Belgium to Russia. They more than likely spoke languages. Possibly most impressive, however, is the wide range of artistic expression found in cave paintings located in France and Spain, and sculptures found widely, for which they used different media, such as bone, ivory, and stone. Some scholars believe that Cro-Magnon cave paintings possessed spiritual and religious significance for them (see Figure 9.7).[29]

Origins of Modern Humans

Like many other issues relating to human origins, pinpointing where anatomically modern humans came from, and when, is replete with claims and counterclaims; debate among three different models has raged for decades. The model clearly gaining the ascendancy in recent years is the "Out-of Africa Model," which posits that modern humans evolved first in Africa, then dispersed to the Middle East, and from there migrated to Europe and Asia, displacing or driving to extinction Neanderthals and other premodern humans. And how do Out-of-Africa advocates suggest these humans proved so successful? They claim that originally "small populations of *H. sapiens* had some biological or cultural advantage, or both, allowing them to spread and replace premodern *H. sapiens*." This model has going for it not only considerable fossil evidence but also DNA research using samples from women in Africa, Asia, Europe, Australia, and New Guinea. A team led by Rebecca Cann at the University of California, Berkeley, claims the DNA taken from African women is more diverse, suggesting that mutations present there had a longer time to accumulate.[30]

A quite different path to human evolution is presented by the "Multiregional Model," which rejects the idea that humans all originated in one continent and disputes the DNA findings of the Cann study. Rather, they think that after *Homo erectus* initially moved out of Africa, modern humans evolved in different parts of the Old World.[31] Thus, continuity from archaic to modern human forms in each area of the world is considered likely. Theorists advocating this model claim that Neanderthals and other archaic forms in varied locations slowly evolved into anatomically modern humans. And how do multiregional theorists posit that this occurred? They claim that "cultural improvements in cutting-tool and cooking technology were cultural improvements that could have relaxed the prior natural selection for heavy bones and musculature."[32]

An intermediate interpretation, the "Hybridization Model," does not consider the other two models mutually exclusive and answers the human origins question via a compromise—accepting an African origin but also positing later interbreeding outside of Africa. The Hybridization Model says there may have been some replacement of one population by another, plus some local continuous evolution on different continents as well as some interbreeding between early emigrant African populations and local human populations in other parts of the world.

Domestication and Settlement

Domestication ■ Adaptation or modification of plants and animals to make them more useful to humans

The conclusion of the last Ice Age occurred at the tail end of the Neolithic era, or New Stone Age, about 11,000 y.a. This fact contributed to the **domestication** that was the first solid evidence of a shift to food production in the form of agriculture. Dogs had already been domesticated by humans prior to the agricultural revolution, and then came goats, sheep, oxen, and eventually horses.

Humanity's main food crops were first domesticated in varying regions: barley, peas, and lentils in the Near East; sorghum, yams, and coffee in Africa; millet in China; rice, bananas, and sugar cane in Southeast Asia; corn, squash, and pumpkins in Mesoamerica; and lima beans, manioc, and peanuts in South America.[33] Instead of hunting migratory herds of antelope, bison, or mammoths, as their immediate predecessors had, modern humans in different regions began relying on fairly stationary sources of food—fish, wild plants, and small game. In Europe and the Middle East, an increasingly settled way of life took hold in permanent villages. In the Americas, cultivation of plants preceded settlement, but in areas such as China and the Fertile Crescent of the Middle East, settlement preceded cultivation. The agricultural revolution also enabled some communities to create surpluses, leading sometimes to the accumulation of wealth.

Anthropologists disagree as to why humans undertook domestication because significant liabilities accompanied this process along with assets such as permanent settlements and surplus wealth. Agriculture requires greater time and energy, risk-taking, and more patience than the hunter-gatherer scenario followed for most of human history.[34] In the 1930s, V. Gordon Childe proposed the first answer, known as the oasis theory. It said that major climatic changes required the creation of new subsistence strategies, as severe droughts led humans to isolated fertile oases, where they took up agriculture. This plausible-sounding thesis, however, has generated relatively little supporting field evidence (see Figure 9.8).[35]

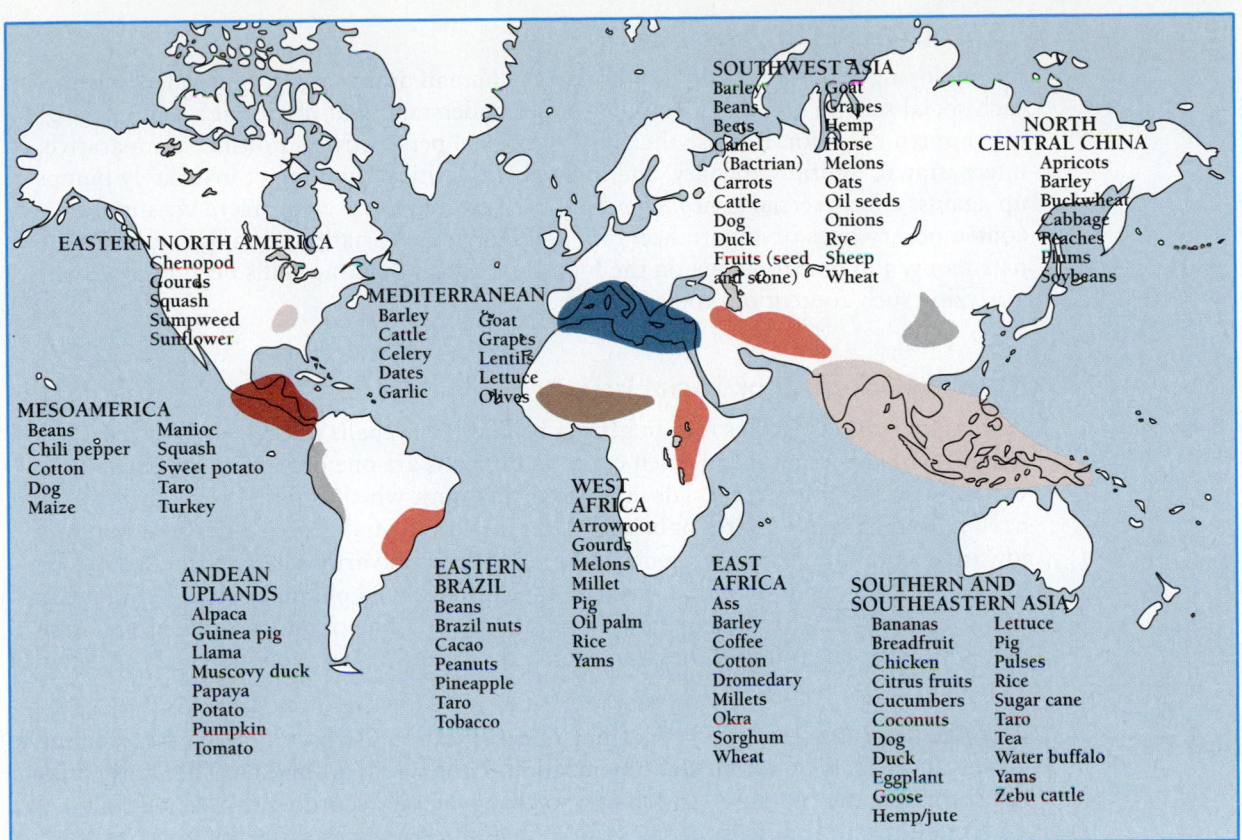

Figure 9.8
World Map showing centers of domestication

Source: Arthur Getis, et al., *Introduction to Geography*, 5th ed., Copyright © 1995, The McGraw-Hill Companies. Used by permission of The McGraw-Hill Companies.

Unlike Childe, University of Chicago archaeologist Robert Braidwood based his theory on field discoveries (in the 1950s). Braidwood thought that more than mere climate change was needed to account for why people started producing food. Called the "readiness hypothesis," it says that over an extended time, "humans became very familiar with surrounding plants and animals and eventually were prepared to domesticate them once their culture had evolved enough for them to handle such an undertaking."[36]

The work of economist Ester Boserup focuses on the interaction among three variables: population, labor, and resources. She maintains that population is the trigger factor regarding domestication, and that societies intensify cultivation activity only when increased population pressure strains available resources.[37] A number of subsequent scholars have followed in Boserup's footsteps by developing models using population analysis to explain domestication of plants and animals.

Archaeologist David Rindos attacks all of these models for their common emphasis on conscious, intentional selection. Conversely, Rindos underscores the role of subconscious human choice in the domestication process. "Unwittingly, through activities like weeding, storing, irrigating, and burning fields, humans have promoted the survival of certain types of plants."[38] Contemporary scholarship considers the domestication process more complex and multifaceted than once believed, when it was typically portrayed as a sudden "revolution" unambiguously beneficial to humans. Anthropologist Mark Cohen's research suggests that hunter-gatherers were healthier than those who developed agriculture, which limited the latter's range of vegetation and exposed them to more diseases by living in close proximity.[39]

Contemporary Issues

By employing the Stanislavsky Method to the human drama and trying to feel where each social science is coming from, we better understand that discipline's unique insights into human behavior. Because the anthropological perspective is holistic, comparative, international, multidisciplinary, and imbued with critical thinking, it invariably bumps up against controversial issues from both the past and the present. Here we survey a few contemporary ones of importance: race and individual variation, creationism, cultural patrimony, and anthropology on the Internet. Critical thinking skills become vital when analyzing such contentious topics.

Race: A Biological or Social Issue?

Race ■ A division within a species based on identifiable hereditary characteristics that is difficult to apply in the case of humans

Few issues work as well as **race** in getting behind the eyeballs of each social science's unique emphasis regarding a given concept. Humans are one of the most genetically variable species of living animals in physical anatomy, which is partly explained by our having lived in many diverse habitats. Natural selection and genetic drift go a long way toward accounting for the existence of differing traits in various geographic regions by limiting the dispersion of mutations that appear in isolated populations. Inherited variation is essential to evolution by natural selection, and some of the patterns of variation that appear are measurable ones. In general, the extent of variation increases as distance increases.[40]

PAST ARBITRARY CLASSIFICATIONS Engaging in classification has been described as a cultural universal—as part of our mental organization of the world around us. Therefore, it is not surprising that we have long sought to group people according to different races. At a common-sense level, most people believe that different races exist. But once we start categorizing real people racially, myriad problems appear. One author thinks that a proclivity toward **ethnocentrism** and the desire to delineate "in-groups from out-groups" motivates societies to invent racial categories.[41] Usually, observable traits such as skin color, nose shape, face shape, hair texture, hair color, or eye color are employed as superficial bases for separating racial groups. But such crude typologies fail to account for (1) cases at the ends of the spectrum (for example, someone whose parents come from different races); and (2) the range of variability within a given racial population. Invariably, the process ends up as an arbitrary exercise. History is filled with dubious classification schemes. The number of races varies in classifications from four to twenty-nine. Table 9.2 identifies some of the most serious efforts to categorize races.

Ethnocentrism ■ The narrow, unexamined belief that one's own culture is inherently superior to some or all other cultures

Carolus Linnaeus's 1735 taxonomy postulated four human races based on skin color: White (Europeans), Red (North American Indians), Yellow (Asiatics), and Black (Africans). Linnaeus classified each race according to perceived behavioral and intellectual attributes. Guess which race he ranked highest in intelligence? (White.) Guess which race he ranked lowest in intelligence? (Black.) In the eighteenth century, his prejudices

Table 9.2

RACIAL CLASSIFICATION SCHEMES

Proponent	Date	Number of Races	Criteria
Carolus Linnaeus	1735	4	Skin color
Johann Blumenbach	1775	5	Skin color
J. Deniker	1900	29	Hair color and texture
William Boyd	1950	6	Blood groups
Stanley Garn	1961	9	Evolutionary trends; body build; skin and facial qualities
Walter Bodmer	1976	3	Geographical groups

were shared by the majority of his fellow Europeans. Next came Johann Blumenbach, the German scholar who founded biological anthropology. He also studied variations in cranial forms among human populations, and he used these data to posit five major races: Caucasian, Mongolian, Malayan, Ethiopian, and American. However, Blumenbach did at least recognize in his writing the arbitrary nature of these categories.

In 1950, William Boyd became the first to ground racial categories in the ABO blood groups. His sixfold classification identified European, African, Asiatic, American Indian, Australoid, and Early European. It is impossible to tell from observation whether someone has A, B, or O type blood, but blood samples do reveal genetic variation, which also correlates with geographical location of populations. For instance, Native Americans exhibit a lower percentage of B types and a higher percentage of O blood types than most populations.

Unlike his predecessors, Stanley Garn did not use single, arbitrary traits, such as skin color, to develop his scheme. In 1961, he inferred how geographic isolation may have contributed to the forces of evolution. His nine geo-races consisted of populations isolated by natural barriers (oceans, mountains, deserts) because logic suggested that most individuals in these isolated populations bred within their own gene pool. His analysis led him to nine geographical races: Amerindian, Polynesian, Micronesian, Melanesian-Papuan, Australian, Asiatic, Indian, European, and African.[42]

The difficulty of identifying meaningful racial categories is illustrated by standard U.S. federal government job applications. Previously, these forms required people to identify their race, but the category of race has been supplanted by the category of ethnicity, loosely defined. Some of the choices are based on language, some on geography, some on skin color, and some on nation of origin. Applicants can pick from Hispanic; African-American; Asian-American; Native-American; White; Caucasian. Saying that all such schemes have proved inadequate masters the art of understatement.

NOT A USEFUL BIOLOGICAL CATEGORY Ember and Ember conclude that "many biological anthropologists have suggested that the term [race] should not be applied to human biological differences."[43] The American Anthropological Association (AAA) formalized this viewpoint in 1998, when it declared that race as a scientific fact does not exist. Three main reasons are responsible for scholars discounting the utility of race as a meaningful concept in describing biological variation. The first is that human history is replete with **racism.** Extraordinary misunderstanding and misuse of race by individuals and societies renders the concept fraught with potential for abuse. For example, up until 1994, the South African system of racial segregation and discrimination classified Chinese nationals as "Asian," but Japanese citizens as "White." Why? Because South Africa's government had close economic ties with Japan, but not with China. Similarly bizarre, mixed-blood South Africans were classified as "Colored," but leaders from black African countries who made an official visit were considered "White."

Second, the amount of interbreeding that has occurred in a shrinking world of travel and migration make different populations very difficult to classify racially. Third, racial categories fall apart because actual, measurable human variation at the genetic level conflicts with superficial perceptions of racial groupings. Several research studies demonstrate that, counterintuitively, the genetic diversity within the geographic population of Africans is greater than the genetic diversity between people living in England and Japan.[44] The consensus among modern anthropologists is that race should be viewed as a social category based on social perceptions, not as a biological one.

DECOUPLING RACE, LANGUAGE, AND CULTURE Great confusion has long existed among scholars and in the popular mind-set about the relationship among race, language, and culture. The preceding example concerning U.S. government job applications mixing racial, linguistic, and ethnic criteria for self-identification reinforces this fact. Although it is difficult to apply abstract concepts to real-world human beings, we cannot abandon concepts because they provide the building blocks for rigorous analysis of human complexity. The alternative is to maintain conceptual clarity about differences between the categories of race, language, and culture.

Racism ■ The unscientific policy or opinion that one perceived racial population is superior to another

Elegant theories were devised to rationalize an economically motivated system of cruel exploitation—human slavery.

They are distinct concepts that mean different things. Thus, scholars should try to "decouple" them. People with black skin may speak English and practice the Baptist religion in the United States, speak French and practice Catholicism in Algeria, and speak Swahili and practice the Islamic religion in Gabon. Confusing the variables of race, language, and culture has facilitated racism for too long and in too many places.[45] In U.S. history, dubious racial classification was used to rationalize racist public policies and discrimination by individuals. The African slave trade enriched the coffers of European slave traders and plantation owners in both North and South America. These traders and owners institutionalized the cheapest form of labor available: human slavery (see photo above). Not until the bloody Civil War of the 1860s did slavery end in the United States.

Christopher DeCorse contends that the concept of race is "too static to encompass the dynamic nature of human interaction and the consequences of varying environmental and evolutionary forces," and advises that instead of race, biological anthropologists concentrate on the adaptive aspects of human variation enabling humans to survive in extremely different places on earth.[46] What results is strong evidence that natural selection underpins much human variation. Scientists have looked at human body build and discovered that individuals living in colder climes, such as the Inuit Eskimos, have short and stocky limbs to conserve heat.

Conversely, populations existing in warmer places, such as the Masai in Tanzania, have longer limbs to dissipate heat more quickly. Although the genetic basis for skin color is complicated, some adaptive advantages are generally recognized. Darker skin conveys advantages in tropical climates by protecting from ultraviolet radiation, which causes sunburn and skin cancer. The human need for vitamin D illustrates natural selection for lighter skin in northern latitudes where fair skin possesses an adaptive advantage. Also, studies of U.S. soldiers in the Korean War showed that light-skinned soldiers were less susceptible to frostbite than dark-skinned soldiers.[47]

Although anthropologists question the validity of race as a biological reality and decry its popular confusion with language and culture, they recognize that it is still "a term with enormous social significance." Anthropologist Robert Jurmain and his colleagues trace the tendency to confuse race with cultural groups all the way back to the 1600s. When people use labels such as "the French race" or "the Japanese race," they are talking about nationality, and when they refer to "the Jewish race," they use a term with ethnic and/or religious connotations.[48] But the way we perceive reality affects our attitudes, values, and beliefs; so, if people perceive others as members of a racially defined group and react to them according to stereotypical assumptions, then those dubious perceptions have consequences. Race works particularly well in differentiating between the way anthropologists see the world and the way sociologists see the world—a distinction that will become clearer in Chapter 10.

Creationists Oppose Evolution

SCHOOLS OF THOUGHT AMONG SCIENTISTS ABOUT RELIGION The relationship between science and religion has long been a tenuous one. Representing different realms of human experience, these two explanatory systems grow out of different sets of assumptions about how to seek our best approximation of truth. One endeavor concerns itself with physical truth, whereas the other quests after spiritual truth. And when each remains within its own parameters, peaceful coexistence remains possible.

Among Western scientists, three different mind-sets about religion are discernible. An aggressively critical posture is taken by Cambridge physicist Stephen Hawking, whose quest for a "theory of everything" leads him to argue that the basic values, goals, and methods of science and religion are inherently inimical.[49] They might as well be speaking different languages because nothing but sparks will fly when they talk to, or about, one another, argues Hawking. A second view has been voiced by Harvard scientist Stephen Jay Gould. Gould says that these two discrete domains cannot be synthesized, yet neither must they come to blows because neither science nor religion represents a mortal threat to the other.[50] The late Cornell astronomer Carl Sagan has been identified as an advocate of a third (more conciliatory) opinion called transcendence—learning to rise above egocentrism to learn from the other camp's mode of thought.[51]

Sagan's transcendent approach probably has fewer adherents than either of the other two positions among scientists, but one kindred spirit is Harvard biologist Edward O. Wilson, who criticizes academics remaining prisoner to the tunnel vision fostered by never venturing outside their own academic discipline (the discipline-as-silo mentality). Wilson's own writings ambitiously aim to link all three great bodies of knowledge discussed in Chapter 2: the physical sciences, humanities, and social sciences. Wilson argues that Western science grew logically out of monotheistic religion's biblical tradition and that science and religion can complement each other elegantly.[52]

FUNDAMENTALISM AND EVOLUTION Often in the twentieth century, however, science and religion clashed over the theory of evolution. Public opinion polls in the United States continue to show that almost half of Americans do not believe in the validity of evolution. One reason sometimes given for public skepticism is that comprehending the science underlying the theory of evolution is no simple matter.

Resistance to evolution also stems from the discomfort it causes for Christians who interpret the Bible literally. For these fundamentalists, when they read in Genesis that God created the world in six days, that all species came about at once, and that all this happened 10,000 y.a.—they consider it the highest expression of truth. Called *creationists,* they reject evolution and have engaged in various political strategies aimed at preventing evolution from being taught in American schools.

In Europe, no such religious fault lines have appeared regarding evolutionary education. And while antievolutionary fundamentalists have been politically active in America, neither mainstream Catholicism, nor Protestantism, nor Judaism, nor Islam rejects the evidence for evolution. In 1996, Pope John Paul II clarified the position of the Catholic Church as accepting evolution. The pope said that such acceptance detracts nothing from Catholic belief in a human soul divinely created and not subject to the laws of evolution.[53]

TWENTIETH-CENTURY ATTACKS ON EVOLUTIONARY THEORY Between 1915 and 1922, a series of state legislatures responded to pressure from creationists by passing laws banning the teaching of evolution in public schools. Tennessee was one such state, and in 1925, biology teacher John Scopes was indicted for ignoring its antievolution law. Scopes was convicted and fined $100, and by the 1930s, textbook publishers fearing the creationists' wrath had treated evolution like the plague. Evolution education did not make a strong comeback until the late 1960s, when antievolution laws were declared, by the U.S. Supreme Court, to violate the First Amendment's protection of free speech.

In the 1980s, creationists began demanding "equal time" for what they now refer to as "creation science," claiming it deserved the same status as evolution in the science classroom. In the interests of fairness, they contend, both should be taught as alternative scientific theories. Often they argue that "evolution is just a theory," not understanding that in science the term "theory" refers to only those explanations that cannot be disproved by current evidence. Legislation was proposed in twenty-two states to give "creation science" equal status. Many biological anthropologists testified against these bills, arguing that creation science was a misnomer: religious beliefs lack the ability to be tested as hypotheses, which the scientific method demands. Only Arkansas and Louisiana passed equal time laws.[54]

In 1987, the Supreme Court agreed with these biological anthropologists, finding in *Edwards v. Aguillard* that teaching creationism was religious advocacy, not science. Having lost their battles before the Supreme Court, creationists changed tactics in the 1990s to seeking control of local school boards, sometimes via "stealth" campaigns that did not identify their agendas. In 1992, two fundamentalists were elected to the board in Vista, California, joining another creationist and giving them a majority on the five-person board. But in Vista, the plan backfired when two of the fundamentalists were recalled from office in 1993, and all five creationists running for the school board in 1994 were defeated.[55] Shortly thereafter, the ACLU successfully challenged in court equal time for creation science established by a local school board in Pennsylvania.

STRANGE BEDFELLOWS: AGENDAS OF THE FAR RIGHT AND THE FAR LEFT Most Americans know about the fundamentalist critics of evolution found on the far right of the political spectrum. However, Professor Matt Cartmill suggests that these attacks by conservative creationists have much in common with some unlikely bedfellows on the far left. In other words, evolution bashers are found on both extremes in American politics. Cartmill argues that a loose association of academic leftists, once sympathetic to Marxism, have become equally infatuated with a new ideology—"the mind-numbing jargon of postmodernism." The postmodern critique of science believes in no objective facts, only in political agendas; choosing between competing theories boils down to a political choice, and postmodernists say that science seeks to limit our free will, controlling us through biological determinism much as capitalism seeks to limit our free will, controlling us via economic determinism (Marxism).

"For postmodernists, the facts reported by science are just the surface layer that has to be scraped off to expose the underlying moral and political reality." Both the far left and far right want science to worry about each other's definition of political morality, but science worries only about truth and falsity, not what symbolic meaning people may assign to truth and falsity. Under such circumstances, it seems unlikely that the science of evolution will find itself any less beleaguered in the next century than it did in the last one.[56]

Cultural Patrimony

WHO OWNS THE PAST? FOUR STAKEHOLDERS Exactly who owns the past? This question was seldom asked by anthropologists in the past, but today it holds a firm grip on their attention. In the course of field research, many artifacts, cultural materials, and human remains are routinely collected. At least four groups of stakeholders currently assert ownership rights, or *cultural patrimony,* to such valuable objects. First, the archaeologists who research, uncover, and analyze relics from past societies claim intellectual property rights over skeletons, fossils, and cultural artifacts. Their mental and physical labor is responsible for unearthing these objects—objects that contribute to the body of scientific knowledge. Therefore, in their view the scientific imperative outweighs the claims of other interested parties. The anthropological perspective's openness concerning other cultures failed to assert itself for a long time, and only fairly recently has the discipline more sensitively heard valid counterclaims about cultural patrimony.[57]

Ethically compelling claims to ownership today come from a second group—the descendants of those whose relics were discovered archaeologically. Often these are indigenous peoples, and in North America, this means Native Americans, some of whose cultural beliefs consider collecting, studying, and displaying human and physical remains sacrilegious. In the mind-set of some Native Americans, the scientific imperative does not trump their right to safeguard their cultural integrity. However, until recent decades, their opinions were rarely considered. Often Native American spiritual beliefs are linked to the natural world, including animals, rocks, and trees. Also, they sometimes see the past and present as blending seamlessly into one another, not as separate domains.[58]

Often matters of ownership were resolved in favor of those who had greater political strength, who were sometimes owners of the land on which archaeological sites had been excavated. Prior to the twentieth century, few laws existed concerning cultural patrimony, and those that did seldom were vigorously enforced. Landowners—the third stakeholders in the ownership debate—frequently viewed artifacts as no different from any other kind of property: "If they are on my land, then of course I own them!" And property owners were often oblivious to the interests of the fourth group in this competition, namely, the general public.

When the issue of preserving important pieces of a culture's historical legacy and sacred beliefs enters the picture, the line between private and public ownership becomes nebulous. Many times, the public interest is served by transferring artifacts to public or private museums, which provide anthropological education. In a democracy, the public is represented by a government capable of defining and protecting the common good. However, powerful pressure groups in the United States often are able to lobby behind the scenes to convince legislative leaders to look the other way on matters not essential to the average citizen—a zone of apathy that cultural patrimony sometimes falls into.

NAGPRA AND ARCHAEOLOGY IN THE UNITED STATES The entire equation regarding ownership of the past changed dramatically in the United States in 1990 with the passage of the Native American Graves Protection and Repatriation Act (NAGPRA). Other relevant laws have been passed relating to Native American burials and cultural property, but none as influential as NAGPRA. It requires federal agencies to consult with the lineal descendants of Native American groups before undertaking excavations that involve Native American human remains and artifacts, whenever these sites are on federal or tribal lands.[59]

Federal agencies, including museums, are similarly required to return, or repatriate, human remains and associated artifacts at the request of Native American descendant populations. Trade in Native American human remains is now subject to criminal penalties. NAGPRA's impact has been described as profound, and nowhere is this more true than in archaeological museums, whose very function is to consider human remains and cultural artifacts as nonliving objects of study. For museum directors, returning such objects must have been about as appealing as drinking warm dishwater.

The Peabody Museum of Archaeology at Harvard University holds an estimated 10,000 human remains. Following the new NAGPRA guidelines, Peabody sent a list of its holdings to all 756 legally recognized tribal groups in the United States. If they all desire repatriation, the museum faces a daunting task. What do you think about the NAGPRA legislation? Whose rights should take precedence in cases involving conflicting claims over cultural patrimony?

CRITICAL THINKING ABOUT ANTHROPOLOGY Calls to expand efforts to teach critical thinking skills permeate academia these days. A few years ago, M. Neil Browne and Stuart M. Keeley, professors at Bowling Green State University, published a popular book called *Asking the Right Questions: A Guide to Critical Thinking,* in which Browne and Keeley systematically demonstrate how critical thinking skills can be applied to evaluating books, articles, speeches, lectures, or Internet information.

In a recent companion piece, they apply their practical guidelines specifically to assessing online anthropological resources. "Critical thinking involves rigorous evaluation of arguments, and arguments made on the Internet need especially careful evaluation."[60] This chapter on anthropology contains many conflicting anthropological interpretations, especially relating to controversial issues such as race, creationism, and cultural patrimony. All information remains contestable, but some more so than others. Browne and Keeley's principles, described next, can guide your assessment of all theories discussed in this chapter, as well as your evaluation of all Internet-derived anthropological information discussed by Browne and Keeley in their book.

They suggest that your ability to evaluate the information already at your disposal is usually more important than gathering more information because it is reliable information that you need most to understand complex anthropological issues. Avoid being a passive recipient of information overkill, and actively reflect about the reliability of particular information so that you control information, rather than vice versa. Browne and Keeley devote a chapter to each of seven critical questions, capsulized in this checklist.

CRITICAL THINKING CHECKLIST

1. What argument does the site make?
2. How dependable is the authority providing the information?
3. What ambiguity is contained in the information?
4. What values does the site reflect?
5. How good is the evidence for the information?
6. What are the rival causes behind the information?
7. What significant information is omitted?

Chapter Synopsis

This chapter focuses on anthropology's myriad contributions to understanding humans as biocultural beings in all places and all times. While it has long shared many concepts, insights, and methods with sociology, these similar disciplines nevertheless came into being via separate processes. The Stanislavsky Method requires us to get behind the eyeballs of a social science that experts have described as "inherently multi-disciplinary, holistic, international, comparative, and imbued with critical thinking." All four major sub-fields are examined here: archaeology, biological anthropology, cultural anthropology, and linguistic anthropology.

The origins, leading voices, basic principles, and detractors of the scientific theory of evolution are examined. Charles Darwin's five-year venture aboard the *H.M.S. Beagle* provided examples suggesting inherited variation resulting in differing survival rates for individuals in succeeding generations. For example, he gathered thirteen varieties of finches in the Galapagos Islands whose beaks varied according to specific island habitats and diets.

Insightful as Darwin's work proved to be, he nevertheless failed to discard the common-sensical belief that offspring inherit traits in a form of genetic compromise (referred to as blending). It remained for an obscure Augustinian monk, Gregor Mendel, to disprove blending through ingenious experiments on the size, shape, and color of peas to establish the laws of dominant and recessive traits in the 1860s. In recent decades, data concerning six mass extinctions on Earth has helped tweak the role of evolution.

Finally, anthropologists' intimate involvement regarding four contentious contemporary issues is described here. First, the extent to which race constitutes a meaningful category for scientifically studying human behavior in a rapidly shifting world. Second, creationism and efforts by fundamentalist groups in America to undermine the position of evolution by natural selection in public schools and other social institutions. Third, the issue of cultural patrimony: who owns the artifacts, cultural materials, and human remains routinely collected by archaeologists? Several stakeholders possess incompatible views on this subject. Fourth, how do critical thinking skills help us to sort through information found online regarding a seemingly inscrutable phenomenon such as female infanticide?

FOR DIGGING DEEPER

Almquist, Alan, ed. *Contemporary Readings in Physical Anthropology*. Prentice Hall, 2003.

Boaz, Noel. *Eco-Homo: How the Human Being Emerged from the Cataclysmic History of the Earth*. Basic Books, 1997.

Boaz, Noel, and Alan Almquist. *Essentials of Biological Anthropology*. Prentice Hall, 2002.

Brandon, Robert. *Adaptation and Environment*. Princeton University Press, 1990.

DeCorse, Christopher. *The Record of the Past: Introduction to Physical Anthropology and Archaeology*. Prentice Hall, 2000.

Dunbar, R. *Grooming, Gossip, and the Evolution of Language*. Harvard University Press, 1996.

Durham, William. *Coevolution: Genes, Culture, and Human Diversity*. Stanford University Press, 1991.

Ember, Carol, and Melvin Ember. *Anthropology*. Prentice Hall, 2004.

Fagan, Brian. *People of the Earth: An Introduction to World Prehistory*. HarperCollins, 1992.

Gould, Stephen Jay. *The Structure of Evolutionary Theory*. Harvard University Press, 2002.

Heider, Karl, and Carol Hermer. *Films for Anthropological Teaching*. AAA Special Publication No. 29, 1996.

Howells, W. *Getting Here: The Story of Human Evolution*. Compass Press, 1993.

Jurmain, Robert, Harry Nelson, Lynn Kilgorem, and Wenda Trevathan. *Essentials of Physical Anthropology*. Wadsworth, 2001.

Leakey, Richard, and Roger Lewin. *Origins Reconsidered: In Search of What Makes Us Human*. Anchor Books, 1992.

Mayr, Ernest. *One Long Argument: Charles Darwin and the Genesis of Modern Evolutionary Thought*. Harvard University Press, 1991.

Molnar, Stephen. *Human Variation: Races, Types, and Ethnic Groups*. Prentice Hall, 1998.

Schick, Kathy, and N. Toth. *Making Silent Stones Speak*. Simon & Schuster, 1993.

Scupin, Raymond, and Christopher DeCorse. *Anthropology: A Global Perspective*. Prentice Hall, 2004.

Shipman, Pat. *The Evolution of Racism*. Simon & Schuster, 1994.

Tattersall, Ian. *The Fossil Trail: How We Know What We Think We Know About Human Evolution*. Oxford University Press, 1995.

Trinkaus, Erik, and P. Shipman. *The Neanderthals: Of Skeletons, Scientists, and Scandals*. Vintage Books, 1992.

Watson, C. W., ed. *Being There: Fieldwork in Anthropology*. Stylus Publications, 2004.

INTERNET

American Anthropological Association:
http://www.aaanet.org

AnthroGlobe:
http://www.anthroglobe.info

Anthropological News and Events:
http://www.tamu.edu/anthropology/news.html

Anthropology Today:
http://lucy.ukc.ac.uk/rai/AnthTodayat10-12.html

Archaeology:
http://www.ipl.org

Critique of Anthropology:
http://www.sagepub.com

Cultural Anthropology Methods:
http://www.qyctc.comment.edu

Divers Uncover Cleopatra's Palace:
http://www.School.discoveryeducation.com

Evaluating Internet Resources:
http://www.library.albany.edu

Fossil Evidence for Human Evolution in China:
http://www.chineseprehistory.com

Journal of Material Culture:
http://mcu.sagepub.com

Latest Research in Anthropology:
http://www.library.ucsb.edu/subjects/anthro/anthro.html

Prominent Hominid Fossils:
http://www.talkorigins.org/faqs/homs/specimen.html

Society for Anthropology in Community Colleges:
http://webs.anokaramsey.edu/sacc

Society for Applied Anthropology:
http://www.sfaa.net

Street Gangs in Los Angeles:
http://www.csun.edu/~hcchs006/table

Woolly Mammoth Expedition:
http://news.bbc.co.uk/2/hi/science/nature/481571.stm

ANTHROPOLOGICAL DISCUSSION GROUPS

American Cultural Resource Association:
listproc@listproc.nonprofit.net

Black Anthropologists Interest Group:
listproc@mcfeelevcc.utexas.edu

Folklore:
Listserv@tamvml.tamu.edu

Human Evolutionary Research:
listserv@freya.cc.pdx.edu

Prehistoric Ceramics:
List@listservacsu.buffalo.edu

Women Anthropologists:
Majordomo@list.pitt.edu

CHAPTER 10

Sociology and Human Social Activity

CORE OBJECTIVE

To demonstrate how society and culture represent the structure and content of human social activity.

THEMATIC QUESTIONS

- What relationships exist between societies and cultures?

- How can we contrast various kinds of societies?

- Which forms of social stratification are most influential?

- What social institutions are pivotal and why?

- What do we know of cultural universals and cultural variation?

- How and why do societies and cultures change?

Sociology's membership directory is the second largest in the social sciences, with 15,000 members belonging to the American Sociological Association (ASA). The ASA Website includes a monthly employment bulletin among its resources. Roughly one in three sociology graduates find employment in business, one in three in social services, and one in five in education.[1] Sociology deals with human social activity; thus, by extending our global metaphor, sociology constitutes the players active on the world stage. Because anthropology represents humanity's biocultural background, affecting the general plot of the drama, these two disciplines routinely enrich one another.

Sociology ■ The scientific study of human social activity

Although precisely defined major subfields characterized our examination of anthropology, no such consensus exists regarding sociology's multifarious subfields. Richard Schaefer and Robert Lamb identify a stunning forty-eight different sociological subfields.[2] Little agreement exists regarding major subfields in sociology, yet consistency pervades much of its content. A perusal of several leading introductory textbooks reveals that *five substantive topics* seem to dominate thematically.

Sociology's Main Topics

First, introductory texts cover the "sociological perspective," encompassing background issues such as the discipline's vision, its intellectual origins, the three main theories that compete in sociological analysis, as well as its key research methods. Second, texts examine "organizing social life." Here they pay attention to the integrative concepts of culture, socialization, social structure, societal development, groups, and deviance. Third, conditions of human inequality take center stage in a "social stratification" unit focusing on race, ethnicity, age, gender, social mobility, global stratification, and stratification's consequences. Fourth, an examination of the "pivotal social institutions" arising to meet human needs occurs: the family, religion, education, government, and economy. Introductory texts typically conclude with a unit about "changing society," where urbanization, population, collective behavior, environment, technology, and modernization represent salient issues.

Contrasting Anthropology and Sociology

British anthropologist Brian Morris contrasts these two siblings in the social science family from a European perspective. Morris observes that *anthropology* took root in the soil of German idealism and French field studies, relies greatly on intellect, takes a holistic approach to society, prioritizes cultural content for examination, takes the human past very seriously, and is more collectivist than individualist in outlook. *Sociology,* Morris suggests, grew out of the Anglo-American tradition, relies greatly on empirical study of behavior, takes an individualistic approach to society, prioritizes social action for examination, focuses on the present, and is more individualist than collectivist in outlook.[3] Although useful, these generalizations represent oversimplifications, and several American social scientists have taken issue with his analysis.

The Sociological Perspective

The Stanislavsky Method encourages us to get behind the eyeballs of others to see the world as they see it. What has been called the sociological perspective is a good place to start. One of sociology's most inspirational visions was articulated by C. Wright Mills in 1959, when he spoke of "the sociological imagination" as revealing the relationship between social and personal patterns. Mills believed that this state of mind enables "the use of information to develop reason in order to achieve lucid summations of what is going on in the world, and what may be happening within us individually."[4]

But this kind of creative thinking does not exhaust the sociological perspective, and another vital component—"seeing the general in the particular"—was espoused by Peter Berger in 1963. Berger wanted to know how our particular, or individual, life experiences are influenced by the broader groupings to which we belong.[5] We may be unique individuals, but that does not preclude society from working on categories of people in predictable ways.

Finally, the world according to sociology also involves "seeing the strange in the familiar" by considering how society affects our behavior. Internalizing this insight may require more effort in America's individualistic culture, accustomed to believing that "human behavior is simply a matter of what we decide to do."[6] The first major empirical study to reveal how social categories impinge on a quintessentially personal decision— the decision to commit suicide—was conducted by French sociologist Emile Durkheim (1858–1917). Durkheim discovered patterns, or categories, revealing certain types of people more likely to take their own lives. Men, Protestants, wealthy individuals, and the unmarried were especially high risks for suicide. He concluded that people's "extent of social integration" was critical: those with weak social ties were more likely suicide candidates.[7]

European Origins of Sociology

Ancient thinkers such as the Chinese philosopher Confucius (551–479 B.C.), the Greek philosophers Plato (427–347 B.C.) and Aristotle (384–322 B.C.), and the Roman emperor Marcus Aurelius (121–180 A.D.) all pondered the essential qualities of ideal, or utopian, societies. But it was not until eighteenth- and nineteenth-century European analysts rigorously examined social phenomena that an independent discipline emerged. European sociology came of age trying to fathom the profound social effects of the Industrial Revolution that began in England around 1750 and then spread outward. Sociology's early shining lights were generalists employing broad historical comparisons.

The French social thinker Auguste Comte (1798–1857) first applied the rubric of "sociology" to treating society as a "system" of interacting parts. Social analysis before Comte was subsumed under either psychology or biology. Comte yearned to understand how *society really works,* not how the utopian philosophers wanted it to work. When he read earlier political philosophers, Comte concluded that they failed to appreciate the "interconnections" between aspects of society that existed apart from politics. Political philosophers had remained transfixed by the big picture of the human drama, but Comte preferred to examine smaller components of the social system.[8]

Two later scholars agreed with Comte's plea for a separate sociology, but they epitomized the tension underlying his scientific aspirations for the discipline. The French philosopher-turned-sociologist mentioned earlier, Emile Durkheim, objected to the historical analysis prevalent among European thinkers, and he became one of the founders of quantitative sociology, epitomized by his landmark statistical study of suicide.

Rejecting the empirical bent displayed by his predecessor (Comte) and his contemporary (Durkheim), the social theorist Max Weber (1884–1920) epitomized the widespread German belief that historical analysis represents the linchpin of social analysis. Weber's voluminous writings lack clarity, but they do not want for passionate faith in the progressive nature of European socio-politics. But unlike Karl Marx (1818–1883), who considered all socio-political change to derive from *economic determinism,* Weber assigned primacy to religion. His seminal work on the **Protestant ethic** proposed that the Protestant religion embraced change more readily than Catholicism, advantaging Protestants as capitalist competitors. Weber supported his thesis by comparing the relative success of capitalism in several Protestant and Catholic countries.

> **Protestant ethic** ■ An approach to life based on the belief that if one lives frugally, works hard, and invests one's money, God rewards one's efforts

Where Max Weber clearly parted company with sociologists Comte and Durkheim, and therefore with the emerging center of gravity among sociologists, was over the rift between **historicism** and **scientism.** Weber remained true to the traditional German ideal of history as the vehicle of social analysis par excellence. In one book, he pointedly asks, "Can this project [*science*] be expected to produce useful new insights germane to concrete problems?" His skeptical answer doubts the prospects for a scientific study of human behavior.[9] Had Weber lived longer, disillusionment with twentieth-century graduate education's Americanization of the social sciences—empiricism, quantification, specialization—would likely have haunted him.

> **Historicism** ■ Attachment to historico-philosophical methods, resulting in unrealistic expectations concerning the validity of conclusions reached

> **Scientism** ■ Attachment to the foundations of scientific thinking and methods, resulting in unrealistic expectations in their application to studying human behavior

Sociology's Americanization

The Americanization of the discipline produced a new breed of specialists preferring American-based social topics. The first department opened in 1893 at the University of Chicago, which eventually nurtured prominent scholars such as George Herbert Mead, John Dewey, and William F. Ogburn. However, the University of Atlanta, then a black institution, also helped to transplant the discipline to America. The founder of American sociology, Lester Ward, served as first president of the newly formed ASA in 1905. Harvard University started a department in 1930, but Chicago continued to lead the profession until the end of World War II.

Sexism permeated the early social sciences; thus few women held prominent sociological positions. The rare female with academic credentials usually came from an affluent family. They were expected to pursue the four Cs: children, church, cooking, and clothing. One American exception was Jane Addams (1860–1935), an inveterate champion of social justice. She advocated women's suffrage, aided poor immigrants, and worked for the peace movement. In 1889, she founded Hull-House, a Chicago refuge for the downtrodden that was studied by sociologists at the University of Chicago. Addams received the Nobel Peace Prize for her efforts in 1931. She epitomized the tension between social reform and sociological analysis in American sociology.

The success Addams enjoyed was matched by an equally atypical black man as a minority person bridging the academia/social activism gap. The first African-American to receive a doctorate at Harvard, W. E. B. DuBois (1868–1963) examined black–white relations while teaching at Atlanta University. His extensive writings, especially *The Souls of Black Folks* (1903), combine sociological data with eloquent insights. DuBois also helped found the National Association for the Advancement of Colored People (NAACP) and participated in sessions of the ASA, where he typically was not allowed to eat or sleep in the hotels inhabited by his white counterparts. Disillusioned with America's deep contradictions, he moved to Ghana at the age of ninety-three and died there.

In the 1940s and 1950s, the sage of American sociology was Talcott Parsons (1902–1979), whose abstract models of orderly, rather than disorderly, society influenced a generation of theoretical sociologists little concerned with social activism. However, the pendulum once again swung back toward social reform during the upheaval of the Vietnam War when the writings of C. Wright Mills (1916–1962) inspired sociologists to change society. What Mills feared most was an interlocking directorate of powerful business, political, and military leaders that he called the *power elite*. These oligarchs, charged Mills, had little use for egalitarian values and possessed the power to thwart the will of the people. Tension between academic sociology and activist sociology continues to resonate in the discipline.[10]

Sociological Methods

Because sociologists often work directly with people, ethical standards must guide their investigative projects. The medical adage "first, do no harm" also fits sociological work. At the very least, sociologists are expected to exhibit technical competence and fair-mindedness in doing research. The process of globalization in recent decades also complicates matters for researchers, demanding comprehension of the ethical norms of other cultures to avoid violating their sensibilities. The ASA's formal Code of Ethics requires that researchers do the following:

1. Maintain objectivity and integrity in research.
2. Respect the subject's right to privacy and dignity.
3. Protect subjects from personal harm.
4. Preserve confidentiality.
5. Acknowledge collaboration and assistance.
6. Disclose sources of financial support.[11]

Experiment ■ The use of control groups and experimental groups to test cause-and-effect concerning a hypothesis

Like other social scientists, sociologists sometimes test educated guesses called *hypotheses* by stipulating cause-and-effect relationships examined under controlled circumstances in **experiments**. More frequently, however, sociologists employ **survey research** methods. The investigator presents carefully worded questions to respondents in a questionnaire. Subjective variables—such as the attitudes of young women, coal miners, and elderly dentists concerning the Mbuti (pygmy) peoples of Cameroon—might be tapped in a survey targeting these populations to compare their relative degree of ethnocentrism, for example.

Survey research ■ Canvassing a large number of people via questionnaires to generate a statistically significant sample of opinion

Fieldwork called **participant observation** represents a less frequently employed research strategy pioneered by cultural anthropologists but also used by sociologists. For example, a sociologist might want to use this flexible technique to explore the lifestyle of members of a Hare Krishna commune in Kansas and compare it with one in West Virginia. Sociologists also employ **secondary analysis** by tapping existing data sources such as censuses, crime statistics, or marriage/divorce statistics. In this manner, information gets used a second time and probably in ways unforeseen by the original researcher.

Secondary analysis ■ A research technique using publicly accessible information or data

Case study ■ Grounding concepts and theories in historical situations that provide lessons generalizable to similar contexts

The **case study** is a variation of secondary analysis involving compiling information about a real historical event and then using it systematically for a heuristic purpose. Case studies facilitate learning from the past, as well as illustrating key concepts, and they do both dramatically. Sometimes abstract sociological analysis leads critics to recommend that theorists make better contact with reality, and case studies help to ground analysis in real historical events.

Research issues have changed recently because instantaneous Internet communication facilitates framing questions in comparative and cross-cultural perspective, as well as collaborating with foreign colleagues. Analytical depth is enhanced because information is available more quickly and because communications between researcher and subject need not end with a mail survey or phone interview. New methods have evolved because of online databases that now provide easy access to statistical treasure troves. In 1994, the U.S. Census Bureau opened a set of previously closed data sources. Excellent sources of information are available at the bureau's Website and at Websites for the Institute for Social Research (University of Michigan) and the National Opinion Research Center (University of Chicago)—all cited at the end of this chapter.

Organizing Social Life

Sociology is about human social activity; and analyzing such activity requires systematic comprehension of the organization of human communities. The building blocks for such analysis consist of core concepts such as culture, socialization, cultural universals and variation, social structure (and its components: status, role, group, and institution), social interaction, formal organizations, social control/deviance, and societal development.

What Is Culture?

So pervasive is **culture** in the human drama that defining it precisely is difficult. However, culture's meaning can be clarified by describing some of its central facets. First, culture is a taken-for-granted orientation to life assumed to be "normal"—thus often remaining unexamined—and forms part of our social personality. Anthropologist Ralph Linton uses a wry metaphor to suggest that we take our speech, gestures, beliefs, and customs for granted: "The last thing a fish would ever notice would be water."[12] Yet despite its invisible quality, culture's influence is indeed profound. It imparts instructions about how to act and how to see the world around us.

Several distinctions help to clarify subtler nuances regarding culture. Sociologist William F. Ogburn separates **material culture** from **nonmaterial culture**. Sociologists tend to focus more heavily on nonmaterial culture than on material culture. Because a culture aspires toward certain values and goals does not mean that it lives up to its expressed ideals; therefore, scholars differentiate between the terms **ideal culture** and **real culture** because human behavior often fails to match its vision concerning what should be done. Americans may hold high the ideal of individual freedom, but that does not prevent a majority of Americans from wishing to silence the free speech of unpopular groups such as Satanists or communists.

Another helpful distinction separates the values or behaviors of larger cultures from their **subcultures** and **countercultures**. American culture is both large and heterogeneous; therefore, it contains thousands of subcultures (such as the Amish) whose lifestyle and worldview are different yet compatible with the larger culture. A counterculture, on the other hand, conspicuously challenges core values of the dominant culture; and countercultures appeal most often to young people and to the unempowered.[13] For example, in the 1960s, disgruntled political radicals, antiwar activists, and "hippies" all rejected American consumerism, preferring alternative lifestyles aimed at self-actualization and social responsibility.[14]

Socialization

Compared with other primates, humans enter this world as very helpless beings. Other animals have built-in responses, or instincts, that satisfy survival needs such as finding food

Culture ▪ The lifestyle transmitted from one generation to the next via socialization, providing the substance to match society's institutions

Material culture ▪ The physical or technological parts of daily human living, such as foods, tools, art objects, and dwellings

Nonmaterial culture ▪ Ways humans use material objects and subjective attitudes, values, and beliefs accepted in a culture

Ideal culture ▪ The values, norms, and goals to which a society aspires but likely does not achieve

Real culture ▪ The values, norms, and goals actually practiced by a group, which often fall short of its ideal culture

Subculture ▪ A group distinguishable from the dominant culture within which it exists without directly opposing that larger culture

Counterculture ▪ A subculture with some values that stand in direct opposition to the dominant culture

or avoiding danger. It takes a long time for humans to develop into viable individuals. Fortunately, humanity's unique level of language proficiency enables **socialization** to occur, as one generation teaches a new generation what it needs to know.

Socialization requires human interaction, and it is most crucial early in the life cycle, but continues to augment learning through later stages of human development. Viewed as a micro-level process, socialization helps individuals to learn the rules of the social game. But seen as a macro-level process, it also assists the survival of societies by passing on culture. In the age-old nature (heredity) versus nurture (social experience) debate over human behavior, sociologists emphasize the centrality of socialization among the forces of nurture.

Isolated Children and Identical Twins

Sociologists know from cases involving children isolated from human contact for long periods that these unfortunate youngsters fail to develop language and other behaviors typical of humans. Isolation clearly thwarts the socialization process.[15] The painful existence of an isolated child is depicted sensitively in the feature film *Nell* (1994). Based loosely on a story about an emaciated sixteen-year-old found in Germany, *Nell* conveys the bewildered frustration of a child living in a backwoods cabin with minimal human contact. The film revolves around a small-town doctor in the American South called into the backwoods after the death of a hermit woman. Jodie Foster plays the role of Nell, who has known no one except her strange and reclusive mother. Events turn even stranger when a university researcher attempts to capture Nell for scientific study.[16]

Sociologists have also studied identical twins who share the exact genetic inheritance but are reared in separate social environments. These individuals can develop remarkably different physical skills, personal temperaments, and levels of intelligence.[17] If human behavior resulted only from nature, then neither phenomenon—undeveloped isolated children or separately reared identical twins turning out differently—would occur. When the public Human Genome Project and a private competitor finished mapping the roughly 30,000 genes that influence our biological inheritance, one of the leaders, J. Craig Venter, stated that understanding the influence of heredity will produce a richer appreciation of the sources of human behavior, but a vital lesson learned is that social experience is at least as important as heredity in accounting for what makes us human.[18] Three American professors have studied socialization cross-culturally. Through extensive filming of children in American and Chinese kindergartens, they recorded behaviors largely overlooked by the natives but meaningful in comparative perspective. For example, when American preschoolers go to the bathroom, they do so alone and at a time of their own choosing. When Chinese youngsters go to the bathroom, they do so as an orderly group at a specified time. Thousands of such vignettes add up to a picture of greater individualism in America and greater collectivism in China.[19]

Sociobiology

However, a chorus of dissent about socialization's potency can be heard from biologists who study human behavior, known as *sociobiologists*. They have been researching several types of social interaction, including aggression, dominance, altruism, courtship, and homosexuality; and they believe that our behavior mostly reflects genetically inherited traits.[20] The lead singer in the sociobiological chorus is Harvard University's Edward O. Wilson. In one of his books, *Consilience: The Unity of Knowledge,* Wilson predicts an integration of the three great bodies of knowledge (the humanities, the physical sciences, and the social sciences) based on genetic research demonstrating sociobiology's superior scope and explanatory power. Mainstream sociologists generally dispute Wilson's confident expectation that his discipline will evolve into a master science supplanting all others.

Social Structure

Sociologists believe that when you add an underlying culture to the lifelong process of socialization, what develops is **social structure**, which consists of four elements: statuses, roles, groups, and institutions. We humans spend most of our time in the company of others, and this social existence tends to be more orderly than chaotic. Social structure helps to explain this reality. Unique among introductory textbooks is one by Brian Jones, Bernard Gallagher, and Joseph McFalls, who emphasize studying social structures at the micro-level (the self), macro-level (societal-sized groups), and mega-level (globalization) of analysis. Their equal treatment of mega-level sociology sets them apart.[21]

Social structure ■ The manner in which societies become organized into predictable human relationships

Status and Social Structure

Sociologists use some common terms in special ways, **status**, for example. Colloquial usage associates a high ranking with social status, but sociologists do not necessarily equate social status with high rank. Some statuses we hold are considered ascribed statuses or those assigned arbitrarily by society at birth, such as race or ethnicity. Other statuses that we earn through our own efforts are known as achieved statuses, because of the manner in which we acquired them, such as a physician or a college baseball coach. Because all humans hold many statuses, and some of them may be considered more prestigious than others, societies resolve inconsistencies by agreeing on certain master statuses as dominating others and preempting other statuses.

Status ■ Any of the full range of socially defined positions within a group or society

Roles and Social Structure

Closely related to statuses as elements of social structure are social **roles**. Certain expectations are associated with certain roles: locksmiths ought to be able to fix locks; brain surgeons should be able to remove tumors; and New York City taxi drivers should know how to find Madison Square Garden. But the mere fact that these expectations seem reasonable does not protect those who hold them from disappointment. Roles clearly exert powerful influences on human l behavior. I have conducted many model U.N. Security Council sessions, and it amazes me how quickly and thoroughly students lose themselves in the roles of the delegates whose states they represent.

Roles ■ The action orientation of a social status: What is a person who carries out a given status expected to do?

Groups and Social Structure

The concept of the social **group** represents the third element of social structure. Societies include countless numbers of groups, and a large part of our social interaction occurs within them, partly because they convey a sense of belonging to their members. Members of a school orchestra comprise a group, as do members of a social fraternity. Scholars juxtapose the personal orientation of **primary groups**, such as family members and close friends, versus the goal orientation of **secondary groups**, such as fellow students. Table 10.1 details some of the differences.

Group ■ Any number of people who share norms, values, and expectations and interact with one another regularly

Primary groups ■ Those close associates with whom one interacts frequently and intimately

Secondary group ■ A set of people consisting of many acquaintances useful as means to an end for a brief duration

Table 10.1

CONTRASTING PRIMARY GROUPS AND SECONDARY GROUPS

Variable	Primary Group	Secondary Group
Perception of relationships	Ends in themselves	Means to an end
Breadth of relationship	Very broad; many activities	Narrow; few activities
Duration of relationships	Normally long term	Variable, but often short term
Quality of relationships	Personal orientation	Goal orientation
Examples	Families and close friends	Coworkers and fellow students

Membership groups ■ Social groups in which an individual both belongs and participates

Reference groups ■ Social groups whose perspective is adopted by individuals and subsequently guides attitudes and behaviors

Whereas this distinction is based on duration, breadth, and quality of relationships, another dichotomy drawn by sociologists is based on the nature of one's involvement in groups. Thus, "in-groups" such as basketball teams in which individuals possess a sense of group identity and actually participate as members are called **membership groups.** These are contrasted with **reference groups,** within which individuals may not participate but which they nevertheless use to assess themselves vis-à-vis other groups. For example, a music student might admire the lifestyle of professional musicians and seek to emulate them in some ways. Sociologist John Macionis contends that most types of groups foster conformist behaviors.[22]

Classifying Societies

One classification scheme is provided by sociologists Gerhard and Jean Lenski. They suggest a progression, with simpler societies gradually evolving into more complex ones. What drives this process, in the Lenskis' view? Changes in a society's "means of subsistence," or what we think of as making a living. The Lenskis describe a social evolution spanning six types of societies: *hunting and gathering, pastoral, horticultural, agricultural, industrial, and postindustrial.*[23]

Humans spent in the neighborhood of 1 million years on earth as hunters and gatherers living off the land. They hunted wild game and foraged for whatever roots, nuts, and fruits were provided by their environs. While far less than 1 percent of today's 6.5 billion global inhabitants support themselves this way, for a long time, everyone did. Nomadic bands typically not exceeding fifty members employed Stone Age tools and weapons for an important leg up against competitive species.

Then some of these bands developed a pastoral way of life built around the herding of domesticated animals such as cattle, goats, and sheep. Pastoral benefits included dairy products and meat, as well as skin and bone for making garments. Although still small by our standards, these societies proved able to support much larger groups than had the hunting and gathering life. As pastoralists accumulated surplus goods, their groups expanded into the thousands. Some remained nomadic, following migratory animals such as the northern caribou. Others in more forgiving climates settled into more restricted grazing for their domesticated animals.

At roughly the same time, horticultural societies sprang up as humans figured out how to plant and grow seeds obtained from nature. This small-scale, hands-on primitive gardening enabled humans to settle down and develop a relationship with a tract of land. The potential for expansion of the social group and for creation of surplus wealth was limited, however, because these gardeners had small digging sticks, small plots, and small harvests.

About ten millennia ago, agricultural societies honed the earlier skills of horticulture into something bigger. Animal-drawn plows expanded productivity, which wrought many changes for their inventors in agricultural societies, as described in Chapter 9. But surpluses meant wealth for only a privileged few, and unprecedented inequities sprang up in these more complicated societies. Today, most of the Southern Hemisphere consists of societies that are primarily agrarian.

But modernity becomes more recognizable in the Lenskis' next evolutionary stage: industrial society. Spreading from England during the mid-eighteenth century, the Industrial Revolution's mechanized mass production created **economies of scale** enabling entrepreneurs to become wealthy. First using wood, then coal, and later petroleum to fuel the Industrial Revolution, industrialization's influences extended beyond the economy. Urbanization, bureaucratization, impersonalization, and stratification all gathered momentum from the Industrial Revolution.

The last stop on the Lenskis' odyssey through their version of societal history is one inhabited by only a score of today's societies. Postindustrialism refers to those industrial societies that have gone beyond the manufacture of goods and leapt into high technology. They rely on computers for information, providing more services than manufactured goods. Their well-educated workers deal in service sectors such as law, trade, finance,

Economies of scale ■ The more units of a commodity one produces, the less the cost per unit, and thus the greater its profitability

tourism, health, or science. Recent trends in postindustrial societies include increased inequality, with the poor falling further behind the rich in life chances than had been the case previously.

Institutions and Social Structure

Humans clearly have fundamental needs, such as preserving order, instilling culture in the next generation, and maintaining a sense of purpose in life, which must be met by the creation of social institutions. Both the individual at the micro level and the society at the macro level have survival needs, and sociologists gain valuable insights about the structure of society by examining social institutions developed to meet these needs. The following section examines more fully the relationship between human needs and the pivotal social institutions of the family, religion, government, the economy, and education.

Pivotal Social Institutions

To live together in social settings, humans require a certain amount of predictability, which is where **social institutions** become essential. Regardless of whether people live in small-scale or large-scale societies, agricultural or industrial ones, a number of basic human needs must be met, and institutions arise to do so.

Institutions meet needs not by spurts of extraordinary effort but rather by establishing patterned, repetitive, habitual ways of getting things done: they create expectations of normality. According to sociologists Raymond Mack and Calvin Bradford, the pivotal institutions—family, religion, education, government, and the economy—are created by societies to satisfy our most essential needs. The family provides security, affection, and primary socialization; religion speaks to our spiritual longings; education formalizes whatever skills, values, and information one generation decides to teach to the next; government makes authoritative policy decisions; and the economy systematizes access to the goods and services needed to make a living. Although specific aspects of institutions vary from society to society, these cultural instruments all facilitate behaviors intended to fulfill crucial needs, as shown in Table 10.2.[24]

Social institutions ■ A patterned set of behaviors and operations constructed by societies to satisfy basic human needs

Table 10.2

HUMAN NEEDS MET BY PIVOTAL INSTITUTIONS

Pivotal Social Institution	Individual and Societal Needs Met
Family	Replenishing societal recruits; controlling sex; feeding and protecting newborn; teaching values and skills; providing security
Religion	Providing purposefulness; maintaining order via morality; assuaging fear of unknown; regularizing the sacred
Government	Setting rules that preserve order; instilling purposeful patriotism; regulating the economy; limiting societal recruits via immigration
Economy	Providing access to food, shelter, clothing; producing and distributing goods and services; providing occupational training for new recruits
Education	Teaching skills to new recruits; transmitting values, attitudes, beliefs; maintaining cultural integrity from one generation to the next

Marriage and the Family

Family ■ Two or more people considering themselves related by blood, marriage, or adoption

The bedrock social institution, and the oldest, is the ubiquitous **family.** *Homo sapiens* take so long to mature that we remain dependent on the family for many years, making the family's child-bearing and child-rearing functions the crux of the socialization process. Despite its ubiquity, the family's form and function take on endless permutations.

Variable Family Forms

Nuclear family ■ A family structure consisting exclusively of a married couple and their children, typically found in industrial societies

Extended family ■ A family structure comprised of individuals linked by blood ties (parents, children, other kin), found most frequently in preindustrial societies

Even generalizing about family membership is fraught with difficulty. The family idealized, if not actually realized, in industrial societies consists of parents and their children, or the **nuclear family.** Although North Americans, Europeans, and Japanese are accustomed to the nuclear family as an ideal type, in a majority of cultures studied by anthropologists, a larger form of family predominates. In most preindustrial societies, the **extended family** is the norm. Whereas nuclear families consist of only parent-child links, extended families involve other kin. The extended family has some built-in advantages: it allows children to forge close relationships with several people, it spreads out the difficulties of child-rearing, it provides children with more role models, and it demonstrates a lower incidence of child abuse and neglect than the nuclear family.

Industrialization Produces Changes

As societies become industrialized, people become more mobile, increasing their chances of moving away from the traditional family home—often to pursue educational or career opportunities. Social mobility helps to account for the shift from extended to nuclear families. In industrial societies, the nuclear family has also suffered from increasing divorce rates, with about one-half of all marriages terminating. Although families in preindustrial societies have often been disrupted by the death of a spouse, divorce remains the exception in those places.

Monogamy ■ The marital pattern prevalent in industrial societies that calls for union between one man and one woman at any given time

Serial monogamy ■ A form of marriage in which a person may take more than one spouse in a lifetime, but only one at a time

Polygamy ■ A form of marriage in which an individual may have several husbands or wives at the same time

Until quite recently, all industrial societies had legally required the marital pattern involving the union of one man and one woman, or **monogamy.** However, change follows marriage everywhere. Canada, the Netherlands, and several other countries, as well as some U.S. states, now accept marriage between members of the same sex. Another North American development is a significant increase the practice of **serial monogamy.** The majority of global societies allow for at least the legal possibility of **polygamy,** but economic burdens associated with this form of marriage limit its practice. Most frequently, when polygamy exists, it involves multiple females and one male, a pattern known as *polygyny.* Only rarely does polygamy entail multiple males married to one female, which is called *polyandry.* The Sinhalese of Sri Lanka, the Toda caste of India, and some Tibetan Buddhist tribes have practiced an unusual type of fraternal polyandry, in which a woman's plural husbands are all brothers.[25]

Arranged versus Choice Mating

Arranged marriage ■ The respective families play the key role in marital matchmaking

Choice mating ■ Entails discretion for prospective mates in choosing their own marital partner

Functionalism ■ All cultural characteristics found in the society serve some useful purpose, thus accounting for their existence

Because marriage usually creates a union both sexual and economic, family members have a vested interest in the outcome of mating decisions. The selection of partners occurs either through **arranged marriage** or **choice mating.** Advocates of arranged marriage believe that romantic infatuation can cause young lovers to miss the more subtle considerations making for a good long-term relationship and that family members know best. Questions of class, religion, politics, family relations, wealth, and property might not be fully appreciated by the inexperienced.

How can we account for the staying power of the family institution? The school of thought in sociology known as **functionalism** concentrates on social order and stability as motivating forces and considers society as a set of interrelated parts. Functionalism suggests that social processes enshrined as institutions are those that work well enough to satisfy human needs. Like many other animals, humans possess a sex drive. However,

Table 10.3

MARRIAGE AND FAMILY IN PREINDUSTRIAL AND INDUSTRIAL SOCIETIES

Characteristic	Preindustrial	Industrial
Family power	Patriarchal	Some patriarchal; some division of power
Family form	Extended	Nuclear
Tradition	Strong influence	Weak influence
Mate selection	Arranged	Individual choice
Descent figured	Unilateral descent	Bilateral descent
Number of spouses	Some polygamous	Monogamous
Divorce	Low rate	High rate
Where couple lives	With one set of parents	Separate from parents
View of children	Source of labor	Financial burden

humans have created restrictions concerning the expression of the sex drive. Marital relationships help to regulate human sexual behavior. Replicating itself through procreation is facilitated by the family because it restricts and limits sexual competition. Another function of the family is that it compensates for the long infant maturation process by socializing children to learn what they must know to survive in a complicated world. Finally, the family creates an environment conducive to the human need for affection.

Family Variation: Preindustrial to Industrial

Infinite global variation in the function of marriage and family is made comprehensible by the fact that certain tendencies exist in both preindustrial and industrial societies. Table 10.3 reveals that most preindustrial ones exhibit **patriarchal power,** extended, tradition-oriented families, arranged marriage, **unilateral descent,** occasional polygamy, and seldom-dissolved marriages in which newlyweds live with parents, and children are considered valuable labor resources. In sharp contrast, industrial societies feature **divided power,** nuclear, nontraditional families, individual choice, **bilateral descent,** and monogamous, frequently dissolved marriages in which newlyweds live independently, and children are seen as financially burdensome.

Even casual observers of Western industrial societies cannot help but notice the prevalence of romantic love, or sexual attraction, idealizing another person found in venues of popular culture such as movies, music, and novels. For a long time, the scholarly evidence suggested that romantic love emerged in medieval Europe and had remained primarily a Western phenomenon.[26] However, when anthropologists William Jankowiak and Edward Fischer examined data from 166 societies from all parts of the world, they found that in 88 percent of the societies, romantic love appeared prominently.[27]

Yet the specific nature of romantic love, other studies suggest, varies greatly. Whereas Americans see love as involving a passionate, mysterious element leading to marriage, South Asian Indians consider love a peaceful feeling occurring after marriage, when couples learn to share common interests and goals. In India, allowing premarital dating is believed to encourage premarital sex, and allowing marital free choice is thought to leave crucial family decisions up to emotionally immature hearts; about 95 percent of marriages there are still arranged.[28]

Marital Ceremonies

Most cultures celebrate the passage that creates a family with a ceremony mutualizing obligations. Yet for some, such as the Pukapuka of Polynesia, the ceremony typically elicits ritual insults between the yet-to-be-united families. Among the Taramiut Inuit Eskimos, however, parents arrange marriages around the time of puberty, after which

Patriarchal power ■ A system in which power is vested in men

Unilateral descent ■ A system of family lineage in which only one parent's ancestors are included

Divided power ■ A system in which power is split between men and women

Bilateral descent ■ A system of family lineage in which both parents' ancestors are included

the male moves in with his female companion; if a child is produced, they then move in with the boy's family and are considered married.[29]

Anthropologists Carol and Melvin Ember cite a nineteenth-century southern Indian caste, the Nayar, as an equally rare exception. Nayar marital unions required neither exclusive sexual activity nor binding economic responsibilities as part of their loose arrangement. Males of the Nayar caste were military specialists frequently away from home, and the Nayar bride was expected to entertain surrogate sexual partners, provided they were members of the same caste and were approved by her family.[30]

As a very heterogeneous society, India brims with interesting subcultures. In the northeastern part of the country operates one of the last remaining matrilineal cultures. In the land of 800,000 Khasi, only women inherit property, own land, run businesses, and lead clans. The Khasi way, for centuries, has required the youngest daughter to inherit the family's property and have her husband move in with her family. But the times are changing, and a group of disgruntled Khasi men have recently organized for more equal life chances. The group's leader, A. Swer, is quoted as saying, "We are sick of playing the roles of breeding bulls and baby sitters."[31] The ironic humor here stems from the fact that the situation of women in most cultures is that of baby producers and caretakers.

In Sri Lanka, not only are marriages arranged, but the key consideration for match-making is the compatibility of the candidates' horoscopes; yes, marital decisions are based on astrology. Although arranged marriages continue to thrive in India, Morocco, Sri Lanka, Saudi Arabia, and elsewhere, the more liberated lifestyles prevalent in industrial societies emphasize freedom of choice. In the United States, which prides itself on individual liberty, young people find it incongruous for society to tell them they are free to vote for whomever they want at the ballot box but that they ought to accept a family-arranged marriage.

Problems in Married Life

DIVORCE American society supports marriage, and roughly 90 percent of its citizens get married at some point. Although divorce remains much less common in preindustrial societies, its frequency in industrial societies has jumped in recent decades. The tenfold increase in divorces in the United States since World War II gives it the highest divorce rate in the world—twice as high as Canada's, four times that of Japan, and ten times Italy's.[32] But the value of critical thinking discussed in Chapter 9 is equally applicable in assessing divorce statistics in America. The popular press often reports the divorce rate as 50 percent, which is true only in that each year half as many divorces are granted as marriages performed. The more accurate statistic, however, is that the divorce rate is 2.1 percent of all married couples per year, not 50 percent per year.[33] Examined as aggregate data, not by year, about one divorce occurs for every two marriages, but only one out of four households is a single-parent one because most divorced people remarry.[34]

Why is the U.S. rate so high? Researchers identify six causes: (1) feelings of individualism are rising, and families spend less time together; (2) sexual passions fade over time, our society grounds marriage in the soil of romantic love, and most Americans believe that when romantic love subsides, it is legitimate to look elsewhere; (3) because women participate more in the labor force, they are less dependent on men and can leave unhappy marriages; (4) the majority of families now have two wage earners, which makes child-rearing more difficult and stress-producing marriages less fulfilling; (5) no stigma is attached to divorce today, removing a past deterrent; (6) technically and legally, the process of divorce is less cumbersome, and adversarial claims of infidelity are less necessary.[35]

FAMILY VIOLENCE There exists a dark side of family life. So violent is this dark side that researcher Richard Gelles describes the family as "the most violent group in society with the exception of the police and the military."[36] But Gelles cautions that family violence statistics represent educated guesses because the victims tend not to report incidents,

Table 10.4

FAMILY VIOLENCE AGAINST WOMEN GLOBALLY

Country	Study's Results
Antigua (1993)	50% of men and women report their mothers beaten
Chile (1993)	60% of women report abuse by male intimate partner
India (1990)	75% of men in lower caste admit wife-beating
Japan (1993)	59% of women report abuse by male intimate partner
Kenya (1990)	42% of women report regular physical abuse
Mexico (1992)	33% of women report abuse, and 6% report marital rape
Netherlands (1989)	21% of women report physical abuse by partner
South Korea (1988)	42% of women report regular physical abuse by partner
Tanzania (1990)	60% of women report physical abuse by partner

Source: Lori Heise, *Violence Against Women: The Hidden Health Burden* (World Bank, 1994), pp. 6–9.

possibly fearing the phenomenon of "blaming the victim" for the misdeeds of others. Extensive publicity about the 1994 murder trial of O. J. Simpson, the ex-football star accused of murdering his ex-wife, helped the efforts of some women's rights groups to convince victims not to accept such human rights abuses. The FBI estimates that each year, at least 600,000 women are domestic violence victims, while 3 million cases of child abuse are reported annually, one-third of which are substantiated.[37]

The United States is a very violent society, but domestic violence against women exists elsewhere too. In ancient Rome, men had legal authority to kill their wives not only for adultery but also for public drunkenness. The Middle Ages weren't much better because women were burned alive for nagging their husbands, masturbating, or engaging in homosexual behavior. More recently, eighteenth-century English common law stipulated that a man could beat his wife, as long as the stick used was no thicker than his thumb—thus the expression "rule of thumb."[38] Richard Schaeffer and Robert Lamb write that "drawing from studies conducted around the world, we can make the following generalizations": victims are most often female; female victims cut across all socioeconomic categories; violence in intimate relationships grows over time; psychological abuse rivals physical abuse; and alcohol worsens (but does not cause) family violence.[39] Table 10.4 capsulizes studies examining family violence against women globally.

SINGLE-PARENT FAMILIES The number of single-parent families in the United States has tripled since 1970, and two-parent families have actually decreased. One sociologist summarizes eight studies that cumulatively lead to the conclusion that "on average, children growing up in a single-parent family start out poorer, gain less schooling, and end up with lower income as adults."[40] Typically, problems center around poverty conditions, and single mothers make up the fastest-rising category among the female poor. Roughly 90 percent of single-parent families are headed by women. Although African-American women make up only 13 percent of the population, they comprise 35 percent of mother-child families.[41]

Two principal reasons appear responsible for the rapid rise in one-parent homes. First is the high divorce rate, which forces 1 million children annually from two-parent into one-parent situations. Second is the steep rise in births among unmarried women, from 20 percent to 30 percent between 1985 and 1995.[42] Societal mores matter, and in recent decades, the stigma of unwed motherhood has lost most of its sting. Again, the United States does not stand alone. Data gathered in other industrial societies in the 1990s showed that in many European societies—such as France, the United Kingdom, Denmark, and Sweden—the percentage of births to unwed mothers is higher than in the United States.[43]

Religion as a Social Institution

Basic Concepts

Supernatural ■ A force neither human nor subject to the laws of nature, usually entailing an image of a supreme spiritual being

Just as the family meets basic human needs in all societies, so does religion. If scholars consider the family the first social institution, religion is probably the second to emerge. Although religions vary tremendously, they all entail beliefs relating to some form of **supernatural** power. Most often, this involves an image of a higher spiritual entity, notions of an afterlife, ethical codes of conduct, and a sacred place where religious rituals transpire. Sociologists examine the impact of religion on both individuals and institutions. How do they account for religion's universality as a social institution?

Emile Durkheim suggested that religion performs an integrative function binding believers into a coherent social whole, thus helping meet one of the basic human needs: community. Durkheim felt that the genuine object of religious worship was actually the social unity responsible for giving people feelings of confidence.[44] Edward Tylor expressed a more direct answer in arguing that it is a basic human need for intellectual understanding that underlies human religious experience: people desire to know what life is all about.[45] An alternative interpretation by Bronislaw Malinowski emphasizes humanity's fear of death, rather than a curiosity about life, and our inability to achieve immortality in the physical realm. Because we can do nothing about our physical mortality, says Malinowski, we cope with our death anxieties by creating the therapeutic institution of religion. This viewpoint attaches great significance to religion's inclusion of a spiritual afterlife.[46]

Faith ■ Beliefs anchored in convictions rather than scientific evidence

Because religion relates to matters transcendent of everyday reality, science can neither validate nor disprove religious belief, making it a matter of **faith.** In one place, the New Testament of the Bible describes faith as "the conviction of things not seen" (Heb. 11:1), and in another it calls on Christians to "walk by faith, not by sight" (2 Cor. 5:7). After an extensive study of world religions, sociologist Emile Durkheim concluded that all religions share three key elements:

- Beliefs (faith) that certain things are sacred
- Practices (rituals) based on sacred beliefs
- A moral community (church) stemming from a group's beliefs and practices[47]

Ritual Practices

Rituals ■ Formal practices expressing and reinforcing patterns of religious belief

In addition to possessing doctrinal beliefs, practitioners also engage in ceremonial activities. These **rituals** are intended to bring the believer in closer contact with the sacred. When Catholics go to confession, or Muslims pray facing Mecca, or Jews perform a bar mitzvah, or Hindus bathe in the Ganges River, an internal logic renders these activities spiritually meaningful for members. Sometimes, spiritual rituals combine parts of seemingly disparate religions. The Chamulas of Mesoamerica commonly borrow the worship of celestial objects from their ancient Mayan Indian ancestors and merge it with the worship of Jesus Christ, taken from the Roman Catholic Spanish conquistadors. In the Chamula version of an afterlife, most human souls (except murderers and suicides) are transported to a pleasant underworld, an earthlike existence replete with cyclical sunlight. However, one area that does not exist in this afterlife is engaging in sexual relations.[48]

Religion in History

Animism ■ The belief that natural objects make up part of a spiritual world, of which the sun and moon often serve as reverential objects

Religion predates written history, and archaeologists trace religious rituals back at least 40,000 years. Early hunting and gathering societies practiced **animism,** believing in communication with ancestral spirits and worshiping natural objects. Their reverence for nature resulted in rituals worshiping the sun, moon, or mountains as spiritual forces. Many extant Native American societies hold animist views, which contribute to their respect for the natural environment. The advent of pastoral and horticultural societies witnessed the first emergence of belief in a single divine entity. The metaphor of "God as a shepherd" that continues to this day can be linked to the rise of single-God beliefs among pastoral peoples.

With the Agricultural Revolution and the emergence of ancient civilizations in places such as Egypt, Persia, Greece, and Rome, religion gained in prominence, and these societies shifted to worshiping a more abstract pantheon of gods: they practiced **polytheism**. None of the gods inhabiting the heavens of polytheistic religion was seen as superior, but nearly every civilization had its own gods. Some of these gods, such as Vishnu the creator god in Hinduism, are impersonal. But, in some cases, polytheistic gods began taking on an anthropomorphic (human) countenance. This anthropomorphic tendency was later to dominate the development of the three **monotheistic** religions of modernity: Judaism, Christianity, and Islam.

The Scientific Revolution ushered in the scientific age of critical thinking, eroding religion's monopoly in answering the big questions. However, science deals only with how our world operates, not why it works the way it does, or what design might underlie our presence here.

Polytheism ▪ The recognition of numerous gods without considering any of them as supremely ordained

Monotheistic ▪ Believing in one supreme being, as in Christianity, Judaism, and Islam

Functionalism versus Conflict Theory

Two theories mentioned earlier, functionalism and conflict theory, vie for air time on almost all sociological issues. Regarding religion, Durkheim's analysis fits snugly within the functionalist view because he explained religion's ubiquity according to its contribution to social survival in these ways: (1) social cohesion, (2) social control, (3) sense of purpose. By sharing ethical beliefs and engaging in ritual behaviors, members of a religion strengthen society. Functionalists such as Durkheim concentrate on the positive side of religion as a creator of community. But another set of theorists describes a negative, dysfunctional side of religion.

Conflict theorists believe that exploitation by the strong over the weak typifies human behavior, including religious behavior. The existence of a social hierarchy lubricates the social control exercised by the power elite, and religion legitimizes the status quo by diverting people's eyes from immediate injustices to the long-term goal of reaching heaven through humble obedience. Conflict theorists observe that nearly all the world's religions are patriarchal, thereby aiding and abetting social inequality for more than one-half of humanity. If Durkheim is an oft-quoted functionalist voice, Karl Marx (1818–1883) holds a similar distinction among conflict theorists.

Greatly influenced by the Darwinian revolution in biological science, Marx believed he was discovering equally definitive laws of society. An avowed atheist, Marx described religion as the "opium of the masses" because it intoxicates the downtrodden with fanciful visions of a sweet hereafter. Instead, the masses should recognize economic determinism: all aspects of the social "superstructure" (religion, philosophy, politics, art) are shaped by the prevailing "economic substructure," enabling the rich to exploit the poor.[49]

Some other conflict theorists focus on war as one of two major religious dysfunctions. Roughly a thousand wars were fought between the years 1000 and 2000 A.D., and religion factored into many of them. Europe's Christian monarchs supported eight invasions against Islam during the Crusades from the eleventh to the fourteenth centuries. Today, Jews and Muslims oppose each other in the Middle East while Catholics and Protestants do likewise in Northern Ireland.

A second major religious dysfunction cited by conflict theorists is its use in justifying the persecution of heretics and nonbelievers. Starting in the thirteenth century and continuing into the nineteenth, a series of special commissions established by the Roman Catholic Church—the Inquisition—made a habit of torturing women into confessing witchcraft, after which they were burned at the stake. Protestants have also engaged in religious persecution over alleged witchcraft, as in the 1692 case in Salem, Massachusetts, when drowning was the method of choice for purifying alleged witches. The last recorded case of execution for witchcraft occurred in Scotland in 1722.[50]

Table 10.5

COMPARISON OF CHURCH, SECT, AND CULT BY FOUR ORGANIZATIONAL VARIABLES

	Church	Sect	Cult
Integration into mainstream	high	moderate	low
Bureaucratic complexity	high	moderate	low
Personalization of experience	high	moderate	low
Proselytizing new members	high	moderate	low

Religious Organization

Sociologists have discovered that religious groups exhibit a broad range of social organizations. Western societies, in particular, contain striking religious diversity. Each group's beliefs, rituals, and membership composition help to shape structures that meet its needs. Max Weber suggested that, over time, the structure of a religious group can influence the nature of the interaction between its members, as well as its relationship to society in general.[51]

In industrial societies, religion has become increasingly formalized, and impressive edifices are constructed as places of worship. Sociologists identify three major categories of religious organization—church, sect, and cult—with each demonstrating different degrees of integration, bureaucracy, personalization, and conversion activity. Table 10.5 capsulizes these analytical distinctions.

Church ■ A formal religious organization that is well-integrated into the mainstream of society

CHURCHES Ernst Troeltsch says that well-established **churches,** such as the Catholic Church, can span many centuries.[52] Such well-structured churches develop their own bureaucracies composed of trained pastors, priests, and other officials who establish policies and rules of behavior. Churches may be ecclesias, which are formally allied with the state, such as Spain's Catholic Church, Sweden's Lutheran Church, Saudi Arabia's Islam, and Thailand's Buddhism. Or churches may be denominations, which are not allied with the state and generally recognize religious pluralism, as in Canada or the United States.

Sect ■ An informal religious group not closely integrated into the mainstream of society

SECTS Breakaway groups from established churches sometimes develop into **sects,** which differ in that informal religious practice lies at their core, with ecstatic experiences actively sought. Supernatural feelings are seen as manifestations of faith that purify practitioners. Sects also lack tight integration with the broader society, which they reject. Lay members often assume leadership roles, as personal charisma or emotional fervor compensate for lack of training. Furthermore, sects have no formalized rules of behavior and no hierarchy of officials. Their very informality requires sects to devote much effort to converting new members. Because of these factors, Max Weber argued that sects typically last for one generation only. However, on rare occasions, sects become large and structured enough to become churches; one example is the Society of Friends (Quakers), which broke away from the Church of England.

An unusually stable, long-term sect, the Amish communities in places like rural Pennsylvania have isolated themselves from their neighbors. They reject modern conveniences such as electricity, automobiles, television, radio, and newspapers. The German Bible that their ancestors brought from the old country is the sole book found in most Amish homes. They remain aloof from a country that many people worldwide find quite alluring because they consider the Amish religion the one and only true religion.[53]

Cult ■ A religious movement that is extremely unorthodox vis-à-vis the mainstream society

CULTS Whereas sects frequently emerge from rebellions against established churches, **cults** generally seek to found novel religious groups without links to existing churches. Cults coalesce around a charismatic leader claiming divine inspiration and pointing

Case Study 10.1 Heaven's Gate: A Cyber Cult?

In an exclusive San Diego suburb, police were called to a sprawling, immaculate home on March 26, 1997. When they entered Rancho Santa Fe, officials discovered thirty-nine dead bodies—twenty-one women and eighteen men, whose ages ranged from twenty-six to seventy-two. All were identically dressed in black unisex shirts; had purple, diamond-shaped shrouds over their faces; wore new Nike running shoes; and were clutching bags of clothing, several five-dollar bills, some quarters, and a valid passport. Some of the men had been castrated, but the police found no signs of struggle.

What conceivable logic could unravel the bizarre facts of this case? Marshall Herff Applewhite, seventy-two, founded a religious cult in the early 1970s called Heaven's Gate, in the Southwest—a region thick with reported UFO sightings. At times, as many as 1,000 members participated in the secluded life of Heaven's Gate.

Applewhite, also known as "Do," preached that he was a Christlike extraterrestrial who had taken human form. Since 1975, he had been predicting that a spaceship would arrive to take believers to a more evolved level of existence. Like all cults, Heaven's Gate needed to recruit mew members, and it was the first to use cyberspace extensively for recruitment. In 1997, its Website announced that the approach of the Hale-Bopp comet was the "marker event" they had been awaiting to signal the arrival of a spacecraft from the "level above to take us home to their world." This revelation enabled him to convince thirty-eight adults to commit suicide with him at Rancho Santa Fe in 1997.

Duke University researcher Wendy Gale Robinson says that Applewhite was influenced by science fiction literature and millennial prophecies more than by biblical sources. She criticizes the media for exaggerating the extent to which the cult was integrated into the Internet culture. True, they did use their Website to recruit members, and they possessed a modicum of computer skills enabling a few members to open a Web consulting business, but she believes Heaven's Gate is better described as a "UFO cult rather than a Web cult."

Robinson blasts the media for jumping to conclusions with scant evidence that "Heaven's Gate was part of the online community and therefore representative of cyberculture," and says that "the press acted irresponsibly by hastily pointing the finger at the Net, although many factors influenced the decision of Applewhite and his followers to end their lives." She also accuses the media of lying in wait for an Internet-related bad-news story to sensationalize cyber perils, fantasizing these cult members as "celebrated Webmasters."[54] ■

---

toward salvation. One sociologist believes that those most susceptible to cult messages are people who are desperately questing after personal meaning in their lives and thus are primed for life-changing experiences.[55] Cult members often adopt lifestyle changes such as eating exotic foods and living communally in remote areas while rejecting the dominant culture.[56] Late-sixties and early-seventies rebelliousness in Western societies created a heyday for cults. Occasionally, cults result from the movement of religious ideals to new territory, such as the changes that were grafted onto the Asian worship of Krishna (a meditative religion practiced by retired affluent men) when it spread to the United States (practiced by rebellious youth wearing saffron-colored robes and handing out literature in airports).[57]

Because cults swim furthest from the mainstream, their distinctive behaviors often become sensationalized by the news media. Coverage of Heaven's Gate is a case in point, as described in Case Study 10.1.

The Great World Religions

Counted globally, the number of religious churches, sects, and cults runs well into the thousands. U.N. figures indicate that about 80 percent of the world's people profess religious belief, two-thirds of whom report they are active in their faith. In the United States, 95 percent describe themselves as believers, with about two-thirds belonging to a religious group.[58] America is atypical in the composition of its Christian community, which has a majority of Protestants, whereas globally Catholics outnumber Protestants substantially. Because size matters when it comes to the relative influence enjoyed by world religions, Table 10.6 identifies the world's religions by size.

Table 10.6

PERCENTAGE OF BELIEVERS IN MAJOR WORLD RELIGIONS

World Religion	Percentage of World Population
Roman Catholics	18.7%
Muslims	18.3
Nonreligious	16.3
Hindus	13.5
All other Christians	8.0
Protestants	6.9
Buddhists	6.0
Other religionists	4.7
Atheists	4.2
Chinese folk religionists	2.6
Sikhs	0.4
Jews	0.2
Confucians	0.1
Shintoists	0.1
Total	**100%**

Source: Adapted from David B. Barrett, "Worldwide Adherents of All Religions by Seven Continental Areas," *Encyclopaedia Britannica Book of the Year*, 1995, p. 275.

HINDUISM Another way to categorize major world religions is by age, and Hinduism is probably the oldest, originating in the Indus Valley of India about 4,500 years ago. Whereas some other world religions have expanded globally, Hinduism has not done so, and most of its practitioners live in India and Pakistan.[59] So seamlessly do Hinduism and Indian society blend together that it is hard to tell where one ends and the other begins. This is surely the case with the caste system of rigid classes, with its four hierarchical castes based on heredity, making it nearly impossible for Hindus to move from one caste to another.

Hinduism is also distinctive in that its precepts cannot be traced to the teachings of a single individual or even reduced to a single book of sacred knowledge. Not surprisingly, then, great variation exists between different interpretations of holy texts such as the Vedas, Upanishads, and Sutras. But a few generalizations can be made.

All life is considered sacred because all life contains a spiritual soul, including the ubiquitous sacred cows one sees dotting the Indian landscape. Endemic to most Hindu worship is the concept of *dharma,* which specifies broad ethical duties and obligations. Another fundamental concept, *karma,* says that human actions have spiritual consequences, and people accumulate both good and bad *karma. Karma* also entails belief in the spiritual progress experienced by individual souls, and such progress is considered vital because Hindus also believe in reincarnation—new birth springing from death—and the nature of each new reincarnation depends on the morality of behavior, good *karma* and bad, from previous lives.[60]

The ultimate goal is *moksha,* or a paradise of the soul representing a reward for good earthly deeds. Hindus believe in at least three main gods: Brahma (the Creator); Vishnu (the Sustainer); and Siva (the Destroyer). Hindus typically inherit the religion of their families and practice private rituals—such as cleaning their bodies after contact with nonbelievers or lower-caste members—but other rituals are highly public, as with the *Kumbh Mela,* in which Hindus travel to the Ganges River every twelve years to bathe in its sacred waters.[61]

BUDDHISM Buddhism developed in India about two millennia after Hinduism, or 2,500 years ago. Found chiefly in diverse parts of Asia, Buddhism has roughly 350 million adherents today. In many ways, Buddhism grew out of Hinduism; thus the two religions share several values. However, Buddhism clearly stands apart by originating in the experiences of one man: Siddhartha Gautama, who was born in 563 B.C. to a high-caste Indian family. At the age of twenty-nine, he committed himself to a spiritual life of self-denial, spending much time in solitary, trancelike meditation.

As he began traveling widely, Gautama preached the virtue of seeking attainment of *bodhi,* or a transcendent state of enlightenment. Meditative insights about the essence of life resulted in Gautama becoming a Buddha (enlightened one), as he attracted many followers who helped spread his *dharma,* or set of spiritual doctrines. In essence, Buddha preached rationality, moderation, compassion, and gentleness.

By the third century B.C., India's ruler accepted the Buddhist religion, declared India a Buddhist state, or ecclesia, and dispatched missionaries around Asia to spread Buddhist teachings. Buddhism believes in reincarnation, except that with the achievement of full enlightenment, the cycle of birth and rebirth ends, thus liberating the enlightened Buddhists from physical suffering. This key difference from Hinduism appealed to believers desiring a vision of an end to suffering. However, it conceives of no god interfering by keeping track of the righteousness of people's lives.[62]

Buddha's travels were difficult. They also exposed him to India's abject poverty, resulting in the tenet that existence consists mostly of suffering. His personal suffering en route to enlightenment led him to consider material wealth as the prime obstacle to spiritual growth. Therefore, Buddhists are exhorted to rise above earthly problems through personal transcendence. Buddhism espouses right thinking and worldly rejection as supportive of mystical illumination, or nirvana. Buddha was quite explicit in identifying eight specific stages required to reach the state of nirvana.

JUDAISM Traced to its animist roots worshiping animal spirits (about 4000 B.C.) in ancient Mesopotamia, Judaism stretches back further than Buddhism. However, when Jacob, grandson of Abraham, led his Hebrew tribe into Egypt, animism began to fade. In Egypt, the Jews suffered centuries of servitude under Egyptian kings. Then, in the thirteenth century B.C., Moses (the adopted son of an Egyptian princess) led the Jews on a mass exodus.

Afterwards, to honor the single omnipotent God who had answered their prayers for freedom, the Jewish nation embraced monotheism. Moses is therefore considered the founder of religious Judaism and thus began the first of the three major monotheistic religions in the world. Following the exodus from Egypt, biblical tradition states that when Moses climbed Mount Sinai, God appeared and made a formal covenant with the Jewish nation: for recognizing Yahweh, the God of Israel, as supreme ruler, Yahweh acknowledged the status of Jews as a "chosen people." Yahweh also transmitted the Ten Commandments to Moses on two stone tablets.

For thousands of years, Judaism has maintained a solid core of beliefs and rituals and has exerted much influence over the other two monotheistic religions that grew out of the same spiritual soil, namely Christianity and Islam. And if it can be said that Buddhism is a world-denying faith, then it must be said that Judaism represents a world-affirming religion as its creed emphasizes that good deeds must be performed to benefit one's fellow human beings on this planet because it does not entail a vision of eternal peace in a nirvana or heaven.[63]

Today, a majority of the world's 18 million Jews are found in North America, Europe, and the Middle East. Historically discriminated against, and killed in pogroms—organized massacres conducted with the blessing of eastern European governments—Jews know too well the sting of anti-Semitism. However, no injustice rises to the level of Adolf Hitler's World War II Holocaust, incinerating 6 million innocent Jews in Nazism's sick spasm of Aryan superiority. Largely an urban, well-educated, affluent people with strong group identity, Jews exert a cultural influence that belies their small numbers—only two-tenths of 1 percent of the global population. Three main groups exist today: Orthodox Jews—who follow traditional beliefs and rituals such as eating kosher foods only, dressing modestly, and separating the sexes at synagogue services; Reform Jews—who began in the nineteenth century to ease rules on diet, dress, and sexual segregation; and

Conservative Jews—who stake out a practical compromise position between the more extreme views of their Orthodox and Reform brethren.[64]

CHRISTIANITY Christianity follows Judaism in our discussion because it originally grew out of Judaism, as a cult. The majority of the Christian Bible, known as the Old Testament, comes straight out of Judaic sacred tradition. In what is now part of Israel, in the year 1 A.D., Judaism was a long-established religion based on traditional family ties, whereas the message of Jesus Christ must have sounded like a revolutionary cult. Charismatic leaders of cults preach their vision of salvation, and for Jesus of Nazareth, eternal salvation depended on righteousness that could only come by believing in Jesus as the Son of God and savior of man. Judaism contained no doctrine of an eternal afterlife—but for Christianity, Jesus Christ came to make a way for believers to access the eternal afterlife.

Traditional Judaism was not the only part of the establishment that was threatened by Christianity. For centuries, the last great ancient civilization, the Roman Empire, had been founded on polytheistic recognition of various supernatural entities. Typical of revolutionary cults, Jesus and his followers were persecuted by the Romans. Nevertheless, Christianity slowly spread around the Mediterranean rim, and in the fourth century A.D., the Roman emperor Constantine converted Christianity from cult to church by making it the official state religion. For the next millennium, the Roman Catholic Church dominated the political and religious scene in Europe.[65]

But in the fifteenth century, charismatic and revolutionary religious thinkers in northern Europe, such as Martin Luther and John Calvin, sought to dismantle the bureaucratized and rigid Catholic Church. Thus began the Protestant Reformation that continues to splinter Christianity today. However, Christianity has not only fragmented, it has also grown tremendously to the point where it now outnumbers any other great world religion, with about 1.6 billion adherents. Most of them reside in the Americas and Europe.[66]

Neither Jesus nor any of his disciples recorded his teachings during Jesus' lifetime. All four Gospels of the New Testament and the letters, or epistles, of the disciples are believed to have been written between fifty and one hundred years after Jesus' death. They describe crucial stories such as the Last Supper between Jesus and his twelve disciples; his crucifixion the next day, atoning for humanity's sins; and Jesus' resurrection from the dead and ascension into heaven, three days later. Like most world religions, Christianity finds many ways to implore followers to accept the golden rule: "Do unto others as you would have them do unto you."

Also like many religions, Christianity reflects the patriarchal attitudes of the societies that influenced it. Although it is true that Christians revere Jesus' mother, Mary, the New Testament conveys in many places what is said most succinctly in I Corinthians 11:7–9: "A man . . . is the image and glory of God; but woman is the glory of man. For man was not made from woman, but woman from man." But in the modern era, probably no world religion has been accused of sexism as often as the one that forms the third chapter of monotheism's story, Islam.

ISLAM Just as Christianity's roots grew out of Jewish soil, so did Islam spring from both of its monotheistic progenitors. Just as Judaism began with divine revelation to Moses, so did Islam start with divine revelation from the Islamic God (Allah) to its prophet, Muhammad, considered the final prophet. Unlike Christianity, however, which projected an afterlife based on righteousness that comes from believing in Jesus Christ as Savior, Islam envisioned eternal bliss as the reward for accepting Allah's will. Islam means "submission." Born around 570 A.D. in the Arab city of Mecca, now in Saudi Arabia, Muhammad said that Islam's holy book, the Koran, was recited to him by Allah during twenty-two years. Thus, Muslims believe the Koran is infallible and should be followed as God's inspiration. Rather unlike the other monotheistic religions, Islam can be boiled down to a few tenets—its so-called Five Pillars:

1. *Faith.* Allah is the one true God, and Muhammad is His messenger.
2. *Prayer.* Five times daily, face Mecca, kneeling in prayer.

3. *Almsgiving.* Charity to the poor is Allah's will.
4. *Fasting.* During the holy month of Ramadan, fast until dark.
5. *Pilgrimage.* Once in a lifetime, journey to Mecca, if possible.

Islam's believers, or Muslims, belong to one of three sects: an orthodox branch (Sunni) comprising about 85 percent of Muslims worldwide; a sectarian 10 percent faction (Shiite) who accept the descendants of Muhammad's cousin, Ali, as the rightful successor; and a spiritually intriguing, but tiny, mystical branch (Sufi) that engages in trance-inducing dance. The world's second-largest religion, with one billion devotees, Islam bears a proselytizing mission, and conflicts have occurred both between its sects and with other religions, principally Christianity. Shiite Iran and Sunni Iraq fought a nonsectarian bloody war from 1980 to 1988, ending in a standstill. Islam requires defense of the faith via holy wars (jihad), and its spread was, like Christianity, sometimes achieved by the sword, but sometimes not.

Islam's clear and simple doctrine also helps to spread its message, especially to the marginally literate. Two prominent scholars also evoke images of its commercial success in making converts, claiming that "Islam was the religion of the marketplace, the bazaar, the caravan."[67] Modernity has probably brought fewer changes to Islam than to its monotheistic counterparts. One constant is its fusion of religion and politics, put adroitly by medieval Muslim philosopher Ali-Ghazali: "Religion and temporal power are twins." Not surprisingly, this concept confuses many Christians, who were socialized under a quite different dictum, "Render unto Caesar the things that are Caesar's, and unto God the things that are God's." Such Islamic thinking helps to account for the consistent failure to democratize Islamic states. After its 1979 revolution, Iran was ruled by religious leaders as a medieval-style theocracy. Most Muslims live in the Middle East, India, Pakistan, Kazakhstan, and Indonesia (the largest Muslim country). Growing adoption of Islam by African-Americans has brought its numbers in the United States to about 4 million.[68]

Winds of Religious Change

Like all social institutions, religious experiences change. Five manifestations of contemporary religion are discussed here: secularization, civil religion, inclusion and women's roles, fundamentalism and the electronic church, and invisible religion.

With an overall decline in the authority of religion, **secularization** has occurred in many pluralistic societies where evidence of declining church attendance exists. Religious institutions seem less able to justify certain beliefs and practices as traditional religion's sphere of influence shrinks.[69] The critical thinking that accompanied the scientific revolution set the stage for secularization. But this process does not preclude a human need for a rich spiritual life; it only means that in pluralistic societies more people seem to be seeking such sustenance in new ways. Harvard theologian Harvey Cox observes that "the world looks less and less to religious rules and rituals for its morality or its meaning."[70] However, three sociologists temper religious pessimism by vigorously suggesting that "secularization is not a progressive elimination of religion; rather it is an uneven process of change, in which some aspects of religion may ebb while others flourish."[71]

One change to American society that countervails secularization is what sociologist Robert Bellah calls **civil religion.** Because the United States has never wanted a national church, it serves as a model of the separation of church and state, and sacredness is attached to symbols of national pride, superseding America's religious diversity.[72] Sociologist Will Herberg notes that patriotic Fourth of July celebrations share much in common emotionally and psychologically with many religious services,[73] and three textbook authors conclude that "empirical studies have demonstrated widespread acceptance of these [civil religion] beliefs among the American people."[74]

The United States was also the hub of rebelliousness against the establishment during the late sixties and early seventies. Various minorities sought to be heard, and the largest of these was women. Churches were among the first bastions of patriarchy challenged by assertive feminists not content with the traditionally passive role played by

Secularization ■ Decreasing general authority of religion often found in technological societies

Civil religion ■ Values, beliefs, and practices providing sacred meaning to a nation and its citizens

women in the pews. If priests, ministers, and rabbis provided the conduit to divinity, then the exclusion of women was an injustice intolerable to activists. The Catholic Church has proven the least responsive major religion in the West, with the pope stonewalling pleas for females in the priesthood and church hierarchy. Results in Judaism have been more mixed, with Reform Jews accepting rabbinical females, Orthodox Jews failing to bend at all on the issue, and Conservative Jews ambivalent. Only among Protestant churches have women witnessed significant liberalization, with women gaining access to ordination among Presbyterians, Anglicans, Methodists, and others.

In the United States, liberalization has produced its own backlash—namely, the revival of old-time religion or fundamentalism. It is something akin to a "back to basics" movement. One researcher cites four qualities of U.S. fundamentalists. First, they adhere to a literal interpretation of the Bible. When Genesis says that God made the world in seven days—end of story. Second, fundamentalists have no use for religious tolerance because they consider their biblical text to emanate straight from God. Third, they engage in an experiential, sectlike "personal relationship with Jesus." Fourth, fundamentalists exhibit another sectlike quality: hostility toward modernization and secularization as twin evils.[75]

In the 1980s, fundamentalists became much more directly involved in politics, raising large sums of money for favorite candidates such as Ronald Reagan for president. The 1980s also witnessed the emergence of the "electronic church," a form of religious activity linking mass television and radio audiences into something new. Critics claimed it was pitched to the intellectual level of a soap opera, but the electronic church delivered both converts and contributors. The electronic church sputtered after television evangelist Jim Bakker was caught paying blackmail to a woman he had a sexual liaison with and was imprisoned in 1989 for defrauding his contributors.[76]

Education as a Pivotal Social Institution

Education ■ The pivotal social institution enabling society to impart to its members the knowledge, skills, and values needed to function

Schooling ■ Formal educational instruction provided to students by trained professionals

Credentialing ■ A sorting process used to recruit personnel by diplomas or degrees, thus identifying potential employees

In preindustrial societies, **education** often occurs informally in places such as the family setting. But as societal complexity increases, so does formal education. Industrial societies formalize education through **schooling,** which carries considerable consequences affecting the individual's life chances. Because such societies operate somewhat anonymously, they use what one sociologist calls **credentialing.**[77] Industrial societies generally enjoy two major contributors to successful educational systems: cultural values conducive to schooling, and an economy large enough to afford substantial human and nonhuman resources for education.

Functions of Education

Functionalists analyze society's macro level and believe that when its parts work properly, they produce balance and stability. Functionalism sees education as meeting a panoply of vital social needs. First, as hinted earlier, many aspects of the *socialization* process handled by the family in preindustrial societies are performed by educational specialists in industrial societies. Second, most industrial societies have diverse populations, and schooling helps create shared cultural values that enhance *social integration*.

Third, schooling creates culture, and *cultural innovation* occurs as a by-product of the critical thinking and scientific research undertaken by institutions of higher education. Fourth, meritocracy is augmented by formal education's gatekeeping function of *social placement,* whereby successful students are rewarded for their ability and initiative. Fifth, society's increasing number of single parents are helped by schooling's *child care* role; it keeps kids occupied while parents earn a living. And finally, education forges both professional and *personal networks,* including the recruitment of a potential spouse.[78]

Conflict Theory and Education

Conflict theorists analyze social inequality and power relations perpetuating the status quo. They view formal education as serving the interests of dominant classes in five ways. The first of these is *social control*. Schooling began to burgeon in industrial countries in the late nineteenth century, just when the owners of the means of production needed a reliable and docile labor force to fuel capitalist enterprises, which public schooling provided.[79] The second is discrimination by IQ, or the use of *tests bolstering social inequality*. Intelligence tests were devised to identify innate ability, not social background, but conflict theorists argue that such biased tests favor the socially dominant class, as privilege gets disguised as merit.[80]

The third way education serves the interests of the dominant class is *social inequality through tracking*. In most formal schooling, students are assigned at an early stage to differing types of programs, which undermines meritocracy and leaves late-blooming students out of higher education. Dual school systems (vocational versus academic) are thus formed.[81] The fourth way is *unequal educational resources* for students from poorer school districts, which becomes increasingly vital in a wired age of high technology where a digital divide exists. The fifth way is through *the hidden curriculum*. Overt school curricula represent only part of the story because covert ones shadow overt curricula. Esoteric communication understood by members of the same social class, but eluding outsiders, facilitates the hidden curriculum.

Comparative Education

The point was made earlier that a society's educational system reflects its culture and its economy. In this section, we demonstrate the point with some examples. Pakistan illustrates the dilemmas facing poor preindustrial societies lacking egalitarian values; Japan represents rich Northern Hemisphere societies with strong social responsibility; Case Study 10.2 on Russia speaks for ex-communist countries now in transition and struggling to match the educational successes of societies such as Japan; and finally, the United States demonstrates that even the world's largest economy, based on a strong tradition of the Protestant work ethic, cannot resolve all problems and controversies surrounding education.

PAKISTANI EDUCATION Roughly two-thirds of humanity lives in poor, agricultural societies such as Pakistan. In such places, much of education consists of informal skills passed along during the course of daily living by family members or others in the local community. Schooling remains the privilege of a wealthy few. Pakistani citizens earn wages averaging less than 5 percent of those earned by Americans, and parents often depend on the wages of their children, some of whom labor for more than fifty hours per week. Such circumstances make a mockery of efforts to school the children of the poor. Barely half of Pakistanis are literate.[82]

For those fortunate enough to attend school, a residue of the British colonial presence remains in Pakistani schools: strict dress codes, corporal punishment, tracking at an early age into sciences (top students) or arts (mediocre students) programs, plus an emphasis on instilling discipline early. It is believed by school officials that this rigid regimen—one that American students would think of as boot camp—produces a work ethic transferable to work settings or to higher education.

But while the British colonial legacy matters in present-day Pakistani education, it pales in comparison with the influence of another factor: the Islamic religion. Above all, Pakistan's undemocratic, patriarchal, and hierarchical society is traceable to the prescriptive nature of its religion, which spills over into all areas of life. The Koran prescribes ethical behavior in a detailed manner not present in the Christian Bible. Elders are to be respected, and females must know their secondary place in society, including the classroom. A day at school begins with students actively participating in an assembly featuring both religious and patriotic singing. This is a highly dictatorial system uninterested in the problems or disadvantages that some students may bring to school. Conform or suffer the consequences of nonconformity—and this is for the affluent few attending formal schooling.

JAPANESE EDUCATION As in contemporary Pakistan, schooling was reserved for the privileged few in Japan, until industrialization brought mandatory education along with it in 1872. Today, the Japanese educational system is highly regarded by comparative education scholars. Japan's culture balances adroitly the old and the new. Primary school education focuses on traditional Japanese values, such as group identity, respect for elders, social guilt for individualism, and strong family loyalty.[83]

Secondary schools emphasize an achievement ethic, and earnest competition becomes the norm at this level; this includes rigorous courses, long school days, hours of homework nightly, and extensive tutoring for the crucial week of pre-collegiate sorting known as "examination hell." Students are expected by society to act like adults regarding schoolwork, and as the pressure mounts, so do teen suicides in Japan. It is not hyperbole to say that these final exams determine the futures of Japanese students because only a small minority of them will be accepted by the relatively few Japanese universities. Compared with U.S. students, Japanese secondary students do particularly well in standardized math and science exams.[84]

With a population less than half that of the United States, Japan's economy produces two-thirds the wealth, and this affluence contributes to an educational system that meets its objectives efficiently. But in addition to national wealth, certain Japanese cultural values must also be examined when accounting for Japan's educational success. Its culture expects unselfishness, respect for authority figures, family loyalty, fitting in with the group, earnest effort, and humility from its citizens. These values contribute to a high level of maturity on the part of secondary school students in Japan.[85]

RUSSIAN EDUCATION

Case Study 10.2   A Decade of Educational Reform: Idealism Yields to Realism

The dual factors cited previously as lubricants for educational systems running on all cylinders (work-oriented cultural values and economic productivity) drive education in the right direction in industrial powerhouses such as Japan but leak profusely in preindustrial societies such as Pakistan. Among societies that lie between the Japanese and Pakistani extremes are more than twenty societies that twist in a novel kind of limbo. Some observers call them "countries in transition." The 1991 disintegration of the Soviet Union, as well as of its eight eastern European allies, left Russia as the most influential successor state to Soviet-style communism.

After seventy-four stifling years of Communist Party rule, most Russian citizens hungered for freedom, which they hoped would improve the quality of their lives. In the late 1980s, Soviet leader Mikhail Gorbachev uncorked freedoms unknown under twentieth-century communism and unprecedented during a millennium of Russian culture. Realizing that the Soviet Union was falling further behind the West, Gorbachev tried to energize stodgy Soviet political and economic institutions through waves of reform. His gravest concern rested with the economy, but all sectors of society needed "democratization, diversification, and humanization," although most were easier to energize than the fossilized socialist economy.

Indiana University historian Ben Eklof argues that the daunting task of converting Soviet citizens from passive cogs in the machine to critically thinking global citizens fell to the educational system; the schools became change agents for societal modernization. This pedagogical mission represented a heavy burden indeed. A Soviet system long infamous for lying to its citizens about their own history now

found Gorbachev imploring educators "to tell the truth [about Russian history] because it will free us all."[86]

The legacy of Soviet education, however, had not been devoid of achievement. Eklof points out that the communists had extended free schooling throughout society, equalized access to higher education for women, and improved math and science instruction sufficiently to produce world-class achievements in space and military technologies. But cumbersome inefficiencies held back Soviet education just as the West began soaring into the lofty information age. Both outdated content and top-down rote learning methods permeated the system. Students were discouraged from thinking creatively or critically and were rewarded for old-fashioned memorization. Gorbachev listened to educational reformers represented by more than 500 "informal groups" that had formed by 1989. The journal *Teacher's Gazette* sponsored "Eureka societies" with reform agendas, and in 1988, an official-but-independent organization, VNIK-shkola, had assumed leadership of educational reform.

In 1988, the State Committee on Education called for drastic systemic change. Then in 1990, a professor of educational history who had led VNIK-shkola toward decentralization and democratization, Edward Dneprov, became Russia's minister of education. The educational rebels had taken over officialdom. In 1991, the president of a newly independent Russia, Boris Yeltsin, issued Decree Number One, which declared education a "top priority" of his government, and a new Law on Education was enacted in 1992. These were days of heady idealism concerning education's change-agentry role, with new levels of sophistication the expected result.[87]

Boris Yeltsin ruled Russia during the 1990s. He had entered the first of his two terms in office favoring economic reform intended to convert Russia into a quasi-capitalist system by following the advice of Western advisors. But who could have anticipated how badly these policies would fare? Russians experienced an economic collapse more severe than the one Americans faced during the Great Depression of the 1930s—a time when U.S. capitalism was shaken to its very foundation. Life expectancy for Russian males had been sixty-five years in 1985, but it dropped to fifty-seven years by 2000. The Russian economy shrank by roughly one-third as compared with the Soviet economy of the 1980s, and as this pie downsized, so too did the budgetary percentage allocated for education (from 6 percent under communism to 3 percent under Yeltsin).[88]

In 1996 and 1997, economists reported better numbers for the economy, and some optimistically predicted that the darkest hours had passed. Wealth was being generated by the Russian economy—but it was going to very few ultra-rich "oligarchs," who invested most of it abroad. Meanwhile, the majority of Russians slid further into a free-market black hole. Then, in 1998, even the oligarchs were burned by the financial conflagration that had ignited first in Asia and then spread to Russia. Relying on what one historian called a "pyramid scheme where only ever-new international loans [from the International Monetary Fund] kept the economic machinery going," Yeltsin had been able to avoid politically unpopular austerity measures—that is, until the crash of August 1998.[89]

Although Yeltsin had entered office audaciously, he left in failure, with public approval ratings around 2 percent. Personal illness, rampant corruption, a weak grasp of economic principles, a revolving-door Yeltsin-appointed cabinet, failure to collect taxes aggressively (especially from the oligarchs), and a zigzagging policy similar to what he had once excoriated Gorbachev for—all these doomed Yeltsin's reform agenda.

Economic failure has prevented the idealism of Mikhail Gorbachev, and of educational reformers such as Edward Dneprov, from materializing. Education will surely not serve as the change agent for a rapidly modernizing society. Neither the economic infrastructure nor cultural attitudes (a work ethic, adherence to society's rules, adaptability to new ideas, widespread civic participation) seem sufficient to catapult Russian society in the direction of the Japanese model. Such realism has replaced 1980s idealism. Nevertheless, Professor Eklof concludes that Russian educators are coping with this crisis by doing what they have done many times before: persevering by joining together to perform their duties under trying circumstances. Creative, inquiry-based teaching approaches have been established and meaningful content improvements introduced by a core of dedicated teachers often working two or three jobs to survive. Eklof suggests that "their self-sacrifice and commitment to children have been truly heroic," and that "they tend to see themselves as culture-bearers entrusted with the sacred tasks of nurturance and upbringing, as well as instruction."[90] ■

AMERICAN EDUCATION'S PROMISES Whereas Russia currently spends only 3 percent of its relatively small economic pie on education, and Japan spends roughly 12 percent of the world's second-largest economy on education, the United States spends 14 percent of the number one economy. Any comparative analysis of education must factor in these influences on the allocation of human and nonhuman resources for educational purposes in these societies. The impact of tangible economic realities, such as the U.S. GDP, are surely easier to grasp than intangible cultural values, but both realms contribute to understanding American education.

Heading the list of relevant American values is the belief that education serves as the basis for effective democracy. As early as 1776, the American political creed stated in the Declaration of Independence that all men are created equal—a revolutionary visionary principle. Thomas Jefferson argued that this new kind of society would become democratic only if schooling taught citizens to "read and understand what is going on in the world."[91] The fact that universal political participation has never been realized does not detract from its appealing imagery—an imagery at variance with humanity's inegalitarian track record.

Closely related to democracy is the value of equal opportunity for all in the American civic creed. This value may also remain unrealized, but that does not prevent public opinion polls reporting that a majority of citizens believe that all should enjoy a chance to receive an education commensurate with their ability.[92] Americans think primarily in terms of individuals rather than groups, love competition, and revere winners. Therefore, they want to believe that their society operates as a meritocracy in which talent and perseverance produce results. The idea that winning results merely from privileged status seems repugnantly Old World to the American creed.

Since the work of American educational philosopher John Dewey (1859–1952), practical learning has set the United States apart from the European intellectual traditions from which it emerged. Dewey's pragmatic faith in teaching relevant skills rather than a core of classic great books, or a body of humanities content, fit nicely with the American penchant for producing results. American cultural icons have always been silently rugged individuals—action heroes more than smooth talkers. The greatest expansion in U.S. education during the twentieth century was in higher education, as the number of institutions grew to more than 3,200 and the percentage of college graduates exceeded that of all other countries at 25 percent.[93] A related manifestation of American pragmatism has been the growth of community college education. Evolving from the concept of the junior college preparing students for entry into four-year institutions, the mission of today's community colleges is driven largely by the technological and vocational needs of local communities.

AMERICAN EDUCATION'S PROBLEMS Most disconcerting about the American system from a comparative perspective is the poorer performance of U.S. students when compared with those in other industrialized societies, especially in math and science. Many employers corroborate these concerns by reporting that high school graduates lack basic skills in reading, writing, and computation. In one study, U.S. eighth graders scored twenty-eighth in math and seventeenth in science, and the researchers concluded that school curricula are too easy and teacher expectations of student performance too low.[94] Scores on the Scholastic Aptitude Test (SAT) dropped slowly from the 1960s to the 1990s. Grade inflation and the practice of social promotion of students lacking basic skills have also been criticized.

Also intractable is the problem of unequal financial resources stemming from reliance on local property taxes to fund public education. Good schools cost money, and those local school districts willing and able to pay higher property taxes are likely to send their children to better schools than residents of poorer districts. At a time when the gap between rich and poor in America is widening, such disparities fly in the face of egalitarian values espoused by Americans. So wide is the performance gap between rich and poor school districts that many state supreme courts have declared unequal funding formulas to be in violation of state constitutional mandates. Courts have ordered state legislatures to find remedies for this injustice through legislation, but in most cases, legislatures have vacillated about this quagmire of redistributing resources.

Traditionally, education has fallen within the purview of states and localities, with the federal government in the background. But public concerns about poor performance and unequal resources have activated both the executive and legislative branches, epitomized by George W. Bush's *No Child Left Behind* program enacted in his first term.

The Economy as a Social Institution

We examine the economy in detail in Chapters 14 and 15, but here we focus on its function as a social institution enabling people to satisfy their wants in a world of scarcity. The economy represents a blueprint for the production, distribution, and consumption of goods and services. Each society must decide how it plans to meet its people's routine economic wants—a process requiring regularized patterns of social arrangements. In essence, what people expect from the economy is the removal of obstacles to perceived human happiness.

As humans moved from one stage of preindustrial society to the next (hunting and gathering to pastoral to horticultural to agricultural), increasing levels of material surplus were created that led to increasing trade with other societies. These changes fostered social inequality. Then machines run by fossil fuels ushered in the industrial age, which expanded surpluses of manufactured goods and caused even greater inequality. The Industrial Revolution's surpluses also shifted attention from the production of goods to their consumption. More recently, postindustrialism has ushered in an information age of high technology in which services supplant manufactured goods as producers of surplus and inequality. If General Motors and Exxon were corporate symbols of industrialism, then Microsoft and Google are symbols of postindustrialism.

Competing Global Economic Systems

During the twentieth century, two rival economic *isms* competed for the hearts and minds of humanity: **capitalism** and **socialism.** Capitalism begins with the principle of *private ownership,* meaning that individuals posses the land, machines, and factories, and make decisions about what goods and services get produced. The dynamic interactions of capitalism occur through the process of *market competition,* whereby goods and services are exchanged between willing buyers and sellers. The incentive driving capitalism's market process derives from selling goods and services for more than they cost to create, known as the *profit motive.* Capitalists share an ideological view that striving for profit is good for society because it provides people with what they desire. A key criticism of capitalism is that it causes social inequality.

In sharp contrast, socialism starts with the principle of *public ownership,* meaning that the government possesses the land, machines, and factories, and makes decisions about what goods and services are produced. Socialism's dynamic interaction occurs through the process of *central planning,* whereby government officials decide what goods and services get produced and distributed, and at what price. The incentive driving socialism's central planning is *rational distribution of goods and services,* designed to avoid the unpredictability of free markets. This is supposed to provide the greatest good for the greatest number of people, not the few, in society. Socialists share an ideology suggesting that striving for profits is bad for society because it leads to greed and exploitation. A common criticism made against socialism is that it fails to honor the rights of the individual.

Capitalism ■ An economic system favoring free-market forces, competition, and private ownership of the means of production

Socialism ■ An economic system based on government ownership of the means of production and a planned economy

Evolution of Capitalism and Socialism

In the twenty-first century, two main conclusions seem evident regarding these rival economic systems for producing, distributing, and consuming goods and services. First, capitalism surely has the upper hand and has even been declared the outright winner by some observers. With the disintegration of the Soviet Union and its eight eastern European satellite states, only four communist states claim to possess socialist economies (China, Vietnam, North Korea, and Cuba), two of which show signs of abandoning socialism.

Second, sociologists have suggested that "as nations industrialize, they grow alike."[95] The former Soviet Union and Eastern Europe offer the obvious example of states engaged in a difficult transition to something new. Other sociologists go further, arguing that something deeper than the collapse of the Soviet empire is at work. *Convergence theory* says that, in addition to socialist economies adopting capitalist practices, capitalist economies have similarly borrowed socialist principles such as welfare benefits, subsidized housing, social security, unemployment insurance, and a minimum wage—all of which exist in the United States. According to some, a hybrid, or mixed economy, may be the look of the future.[96]

Economic Globalization

Globalization creates constant change, and economic ones are among the most profound. The micro-level (individual and small-scale) economy and the macro-level (national) economy still matter greatly, but the action recently has shifted toward the mega-level (global) economy. Partly responsible are new technologies that speed information, goods, services, and capital across national boundaries. In pursuing the profit motive, corporations become multinational corporations (MNCs) shifting investments and production from one corner of the world to another at will.

A tension exists between the pull of micro-level and macro-level loyalties on the one hand, and the pull of mega-level commercialization on the other hand.[97] The perceived defeat of socialism as an alternative to capitalism has led one sociologist to conclude that "today we see an almost frantic embrace of capitalism by the world's nations."[98] The role of the United States as global hegemon only adds to the appeal of commercialization among the poor people making up two-thirds of world population.

Government as a Pivotal Social Institution

So intertwined are the economy and government as social institutions that one major textbook blends them together under the rubric of "political economy."[99] These pivotal institutions can be viewed from many different angles, but it is the sociological perspective that asks how social institutions meet basic human needs. As humans moved from nomadic to settled societies, they created authoritative structures for making key decisions. "From ancient times to the present, people have had to make important decisions about how to spend their time and resources."[100]

Legitimate and Illegitimate Power

Government ■ An institution set up by societies to order their public affairs

Max Weber wrote that the **government** holds a monopoly of legitimate force, and he differentiated between employing legitimate power, which he called *authority,* and employing illegitimate power, which he labeled *coercion.*[101] Elsewhere, Weber elaborated on this theme by answering the question: "Why do people accept power as legitimate?" First, the commonest historical basis for authority, especially among preliterate groups, was what he called *traditional authority,* or custom. The second, *rational-legal authority,* is based on written rules rather than custom, and written rules are supposed to be reasonable (rational) and part of law (legal). Third, he discusses *charismatic authority,* or someone perceived by people as gifted by nature with extraordinary leadership qualities. Such leaders can, of course, run the ethical gamut from Mahatma Gandhi at one extreme to Adolf Hitler at the other.[102]

Politics ■ Competition between different actors using power and influence to achieve their respective goals

The contentious process called **politics** enables individuals and groups in society with conflicting opinions about desirable policies to resolve their differences peacefully. One scholar refers to this process as the "authoritative allocation of values."[103] And as seventeenth-century English philosopher Thomas Hobbes pointed out, the alternative to compromise and accommodation is a state of chaos—"a war of every man against every other man."[104]

Functions of Government

Avoiding Hobbes's nightmarish state of nature by promoting *domestic order* is the most basic governmental function. Government establishes, enforces, and adjudicates the rules of the social game. If it fails to keep domestic order, then this failure threatens to sabotage government's other functions. Almost as basic as domestic order is government's external security function. The safety of every society must be guarded against potential enemies, and the state system has sought for more than three centuries to inspire popular confidence using a military shell protecting society. Increasingly vital in industrial and postindustrial societies has been the function of intervening to *regulate the economy.*

As legal efforts to protect human rights have grown since World War II, governments guilty of abuses against their citizens have been subjected to thorough and efficient criticism by NGOs, IGOs, and other governments possessing information once unimaginable. Thus, *protecting individual freedoms* as the essence of civil society is another function of modern government. Closely related is government's function of inspiring confidence in society's ability to *deliver justice*—that is, fairness in meting out awards and punishments according to the rule of law. Finally, government must insure an orderly *transfer of authority* from one group of leaders to the next.

Types of Government

Four major governmental variants have existed historically: monarchies, dictatorships, oligarchies, and democracies. Initially, societies were small, functioning like extended families. In a *monarchy,* an extended royal family held a monopoly on political power, with a king or queen (monarch) at the pinnacle. The monarch's authority was then passed on to the children of the royal family.

In a *dictatorship,* an individual seizes the reigns of power, often violently, and then dictates his will over the society. As in a monarchy, neither the populace nor political parties representing them have anything to say about the policies adopted by a dictatorship. This top-down and authoritarian rule by one individual usually serves to prove the point made long ago by British political observer Lord Acton, who suggested that "power corrupts, and absolute power corrupts absolutely." A close cousin of dictatorship is another form of authoritative and arbitrary exercise of power, called an *oligarchy.* Here the ruling motif consists not of an individual, but of a small group, or clique, of elites. The typical scenario finds oligarchy resulting from a violent military coup. The world region where this type of government was most common in the past was Latin America, where nominal presidents may be appointed by the oligarchy, but often military leaders control power.

Human existence in the preceding types of governments could be brutish and short-lived. But the idea that in some way, shape, or form power ought to reside with the people took a long time to develop. The best example of evolutionary popular rule, or *democracy,* is Great Britain, where the voice of the people has grown in volume for nearly a millennium. But even Great Britain routinely squelched democratic expression in its colonies, and, in America, this led to the violence of the American Revolution two centuries ago. With victory won, American colonists had enough of monarchical rule and set out to establish a bold democratic experiment. Ancient Greek city-states such as Athens had practiced popular representation but on a far smaller scale. Democracy carries expectations for responsible citizenship, namely, that members of society are more than mere residents—they are citizens with rights (such as freedom of religion) and responsibilities (such as understanding public issues).

U.S. Politics: Pluralism or Power Elite?

The latter part of the twentieth century witnessed an expansion of democracies around the world. The demise of the Soviet Union deflated not only communism's socialist economics but its oligarchical politics as well. Western-style democratic capitalism has been the beneficiary, as various countries in all world regions have emulated that model. The United States has increasingly found itself in the spotlight, but what do the sociological perspective's main theories have to say about the reality of American democracy?

Functionalists see government as the natural response to humanity's need for a system to order its public affairs. The problem is that if not limited, government can also turn into a social mugger. This requires a *delicate balance:* fearing both the chaos accompanying no government and the unchecked reign of dictatorships, society seeks a middle ground with limited government—and the United States is one of the beacons on the hill when it comes to limited government, according to functionalists. They consider *pluralism,* or a diffusion of power between many competing interest groups, as the essence of American constitutional democracy. Americans' penchant for joining groups that battle it out for political influence gives the people a voice in the system. Functionalists also point to the constitutional division of power between three competing branches creating checks and balances, preventing any one branch from dominating the other two. Functionalists share confidence in the U.S. system as responsive to the people.[105]

Conflict theorists, however, are much less sanguine about the health of American democracy. They view the representatives of interest groups scurrying around Washington trying to influence government officials as mere window-dressing. The real action, they suggest, occurs more subtly in private. Building on the work of C. Wright Mills, conflict theorists argue that a *power elite* composed of leaders of the largest MNCs, top military generals, and select elite politicians actually wield power behind the scenes. It is they who make really crucial decisions, such as whether or not to go to war.

But this political domination is not a grand conspiracy among the power elite meeting secretly behind closed doors. Rather, it springs naturally from the privileged backgrounds that lead to common life experiences, such as education at the elite universities, membership in exclusive clubs, and a vested interest in protecting the status quo that has made them very wealthy. Because they all share the same broad values and goals, it should come as no surprise when they also agree on specific political and economic issues of the day. These elites maintain an interlocking directorate covering all powerful sectors of society—corporate, military, and political. Conflict theory, then, harbors far greater suspicions concerning the value of American democracy.[106]

Social Inequality

Whether sociologists are studying micro-level, macro-level, or mega-level human relations, they discover *social inequality* as a universal phenomenon affecting the life chances of all peoples. Here social stratification is first defined and its relationship to social mobility explored. Second, various dimensions of inequality—race, ethnicity, and gender—are analyzed. Third, global inequality, as manifested in stratification and poverty, is explored. And fourth, stratification and poverty in the United States are examined.

Social Stratification

Social stratification ■ Any system characterized by the grouping of people into unequal layers based on some having more power, money, schooling, and health than others

What has been called the sociological perspective owes much to insights from **social stratification,** which asks how groups are arranged hierarchically and how this reality influences relative life chances. In Chapter 3, the 1912 *Titanic* tragedy illustrated the human folly of considering any ship "unsinkable," leading to inadequate safety precautions. Sociologist John Macionis uses the *Titanic*'s story to illustrate social stratification. The life chances of *Titanic*'s passengers were shaped by stratification because more than 60 percent of first-class ticket holders (housed on upper decks with accessible lifeboats) survived, whereas only 36 percent of second-class passengers lived to tell about it, and a paltry 24 percent of those in third class escaped.[107]

The Harvard sociobiologist mentioned in Chapter 9, Edward O. Wilson, provides vivid imagery taken from his study of ant colony behavior. Classified technically as "social insects," Wilson writes of ants that "groups of workers specialize as castes for particular tasks, and their activities are subordinated to the needs of the whole colony." The tasks performed by individual castes are called their *roles,* and colony members communicate in visual, tactile, and chemical ways that form a social unit, according to Wilson.[108] With both ants and humans, then, it appears that relative position in the social hierarchy greatly influences the individual's experience.

Race and Inequality

As societies evolve, they develop unique senses of identity, including the ambiguous notion of race. "Throughout time, race has been defined along *biological, legal,* and *social* lines—each of which has its own set of limitations." *Biologically,* race refers to a breeding population with a common genetic heritage. *Legally,* racial distinctions have historically been used to officially discriminate against certain people. South Africa was the last country with a pervasive legal system of racial discrimination. This leads a group of authors to conclude that "clearly biology and the law have failed to provide a satisfactory definition of race. This is because race is merely a *social concept,* not a biological or legal one. Race is simply what people say it is."[109]

In Chapter 9, we wore anthropological lenses that focused on race as a hereditary division so difficult to apply that the AAA declared that "race as a scientific fact does not exist." Anthropologists Carol and Melvin Ember were quoted as saying: "Many biological anthropologists have suggested that the term race should not be applied to human biological differences." Anthropologists also argue that greater conceptual clarity should be sought by scholars in differentiating among the variables of race, language, and culture.

Many sociologists, however, assume that things in society are not what they seem to be common sensically and that hidden meaning influences human behavior profoundly. Similarly, sociological lenses see human behavior as quite prone to irrationality. Sociologists seem intrigued by the potent relationship between two semi-hidden realities: (1) the subjective whims of human perceivers continue to arbitrarily assign groups of people to racial categories; and (2) while spurious racial categories may seldom result in *de jure* (overt legal) discrimination today, nevertheless, racial classification still contributes to cause *de facto* (covert) discrimination resulting in subtler inequities.

Gender and Inequality

If asked the question, "Does something innate lead men to pursue wealth and women to pursue beauty disproportionately?" most sociobiologists, interested in the role of heredity, would likely answer this question affirmatively. However, most sociologists, favoring the role of culture, would likely answer this question negatively. The former scientists care more about sex than about gender roles, whereas the latter scientists emphasize **gender roles** more than sex.

Like race and ethnicity, gender influences social inequality. Although progress toward equal life chances for women has been made in some areas, much evidence points to the persistence of **gender stratification** both in the United States and globally. Just under half of the U.S. paid labor force is female, compared with one-third in other post-industrialized countries and less than one-fourth in Southern Hemisphere countries (where women work very hard but are seldom paid for their efforts).[111]

Gender inequality is also reflected in what is called women's "second shift," or the unpaid housework that still remains mostly their province throughout the world. Despite moving rapidly into the labor force, women have experienced only a slight decline in the demands of housework. Because discrimination is illegal in many places, it often occurs subtly. For instance, in the corporate phenomenon known as the *glass ceiling*, women seldom rise above middle management because although the formal policies forbid discrimination on paper, the corporate male culture creates practical obstacles for ambitious women.[112]

Gender stratification in the workplace tells only part of the tale. Women lag far behind men when it comes to amount and quality of schooling, portrayal in the mass media, and holding political office, but many more of them live in poverty and are victims of violent crimes. However, some sociologists contend that technological innovations have always reduced gender stratification and that the emerging cyber-society may prove beneficial for women. Whereas women were disadvantaged in the industrial age of making *things*, cyber-society prioritizes the manipulation of *ideas*, where women compete on equal footing. Cyber-work lends itself to working at home, which helps women raising children who are unable to travel to an office. Cyber-work also encourages flexible scheduling and results-oriented assessment rather than clock punching. Finally, electronic communications such as e-mail obscure gender, which was not possible in face-to-face work settings.[113]

Global Stratification and Poverty

Economic development is not the only factor contributing to inequality globally, but it does influence relative standard of living. And although social inequality certainly

Gender roles ■ Socially conditioned roles of masculinity or femininity that are tied to how we think and feel about ourselves

Gender stratification ■ The unequal distribution of power, money, schooling, and health by sex

exists within domestic societies, its disparities show up even more strongly when comparing different societies. For example, Americans who qualify as living below the official U.S. poverty line live far better than the majority of people in the world. Therefore, sociologists distinguish between *relative poverty,* meaning lacking resources taken for granted by others in rich countries, and *absolute poverty,* denoting a life-threatening lack of resources in poor countries. In classifying countries economically, sociologists have argued aggressively for a more value-neutral terminology than the distinction among First World, Second World, and Third World countries prevalent during the Cold War. Today, more scholars refer to upper-, middle- and lower-income countries.

The group of about forty upper-income countries are mostly in North America, Europe, and East Asia. Their GDP per capita averages more than $25,000. When quality of life is measured by the United Nations using the Human Development Index (HDI), Canada has been ranked number one in the world for seven consecutive years. Countries such as Australia, France, Japan, Italy, and Canada rank high economically because they have roughly two centuries of industrial development under their belts. Because of industrialization, about 75 percent of residents in these mostly Northern Hemisphere states live in urban areas.

The category of *middle-income countries* consists of approximately ninety states averaging about $7,500 GDP per capita, where limited industrialization has occurred, and half the population still lives in rural areas as agricultural workers. In rural areas, decent medical care, schooling, and housing are rather scarce. Brazil and Russia typify the center of middle-income countries, and most of the successors to the Soviet Union and its satellite states can be found here. At the upper end of this group are countries such as South Korea and Greece, whereas the lower end is represented by Ecuador and Albania.

Agrarian economics with minimal industrialization characterize the low-income countries, such as India and Bangladesh in South Asia, and Ethiopia and Congo in Africa. Only those with GDP per capita of less than $2,500 fall in this group of sixty societies. Urban residents make up only 25 percent of the citizens in these poorest states because agriculture still dominates these traditional societies. Peasants make up fully one-half of the world's population, and most of them live in low-income countries.

Table 10.7 identifies factors other than strictly economic ones that feed social inequality.

Table 10.7

NON-INCOME CONTRIBUTORS TO GLOBAL POVERTY

Contributor	Nature of Contribution
Technology	Human labor devoted to agriculture inhibits development of human skill levels.
Population growth	The poorest countries have the highest birth rates, which inhibits economic growth.
Cultural patterns	By clinging to tradition and resisting innovation, people's attitudes in poor countries inhibit economic growth.
Social stratification	Poor agrarian societies distribute wealth less equally than industrial ones.
Gender inequality	Women lacking life chances have many children, exacerbating the vicious cycle of poverty.
Neocolonialism	Exploitation of the poor by the rich continues informally after the formal end of colonialism.

Stratification and Poverty in America

As mentioned previously, it is the concept of relative poverty rather than absolute poverty that fits American society. The nature of U.S. social stratification is measured chiefly in terms of wealth, power, and prestige.

WEALTH   *Wealth* refers both to *property* (land, machinery, stocks, businesses) and *income* (money received as wages, interest, rents, or business proceeds). Most wealth in the United States consists of real estate, stocks, and business assets and adds up to an impressive total of more than $25 trillion.[114] This amazing wealth, however, does not trickle down very far in America, as 68 percent of it is owned by only 10 percent of America's families, and the super-rich, or the top 1 percent, are worth more than the less wealthy 90 percent of Americans.[115]

The distribution of income is similarly lopsided, with the top 20 percent receiving almost half of the nation's income, while the bottom 20 percent takes home a paltry 4 percent of income. Possibly even more disconcerting is that the gap between the rich and the poor has continued to increase since the end of World War II.[116] Heads of U.S. corporations have the highest median pay: over $6 million annually, which is 200 times higher than that of the average U.S. worker.[117]

POWER   As C. Wright Mills argued as early as the 1950s, wealth and another stratification variable—power—go hand in hand in the United States. *Power* entails the ability to achieve goals in the face of considerable opposition. One sociologist following in the footsteps of C. Wright Mills, G. William Domhoff, contends that no significant decisions in U.S. politics get made without the approval of corporate, military, and governmental elites.[118]

PRESTIGE   The third intertwined stratification variable is *prestige,* meaning social respect. Prestige may be rather abstract but that does not detract from its importance to people. When most European countries were monarchies, only the emperor and his family members were allowed to wear the color purple, and, in France, only the nobility could wear lace. When China battled to have Beijing named to host the 2008 Olympic Games, its motivations seem to have been driven by a desire for respect as much as for economic growth. Much prestige in America comes from attending an elite college. Some people associate clothes bearing "designer" labels with prestige and gladly pay inflated prices for them. Studies measuring the prestige of different occupations in sixty countries show that the high-prestige jobs share four qualities: high pay, high education, abstract thought, and personal autonomy. Therefore, the professions and white-collar jobs rank high.

Occupational Prestige Globally

One sociologist concludes that "prestige rankings are very consistent across countries and over time."[119] Using measurement scales where 0 means least prestigious and 100 means most prestigious, many continuities have been identified. In some areas, U.S. prestige rankings and those of other countries are perfectly identical. For example, the rankings for astronaut (80), college professor (78), and garbage collector (13) are the same for the United States and for the average of all other countries. In a few other areas, however, significant disparities can be seen; the average in other countries for accountant (55) is lower than in the United States (65), as is the case for undertaker internationally (34) versus in the United States (51), and for welfare recipient internationally (16) and in the United State (25).[120] What conclusions can you draw from this information?

U.S. Social Classes

Examining each rung of the American social class ladder provides greater specificity in understanding the trend in which the rich have been getting richer and the poor getting poorer. Typically, six classes are described in modern America, from top to bottom, as

Table 10.8

RUNGS ON THE AMERICAN SOCIAL CLASS LADDER

Class Name	Percent of Population	Education	Occupation	Income
Capitalist	1%	exclusive university	investors	$600,000+
Upper-middle	14	postgraduate	professionals	$110,000+
Lower-middle	30	some college	craftspeople, foreman	$ 45,000
Working class	30	high school	clerical, factory	$ 35,000
Working poor	22	some high school	laborers, low-paid sales	$ 20,000
Underclass	3	grade school	welfare or part-time	$ 10,000

shown in Table 10.8: the capitalist class, upper-middle class, lower-middle class, working class, working poor, and underclass.[121]

The capitalist class's super-rich can be "old money" such as the Rockefellers, or "new money" such as Bill Gates. To most citizens, such distinctions may seem meaningless, but the longer a family's money has been around, the greater its prestige. Time also helps to erase memories of the unsavory way in which many families first made their money. For example, the Kennedy fortune came first from bootlegging, whereas the Bush family's banking interests included laundering money for Adolf Hitler's Nazis. Today such old money often facilitates public service (holding political office) or philanthropic causes.

The class whose fate is most shaped by education is the upper-middle class, whose members own their own business or profession, or manage corporations owned by the capitalist class. Well-educated professionals from the upper-middle class give the orders that are followed by the lower-middle class. The fuzziest demarcation is that between lower-middle class and the unskilled working class, but usually the former hold jobs that are moderately better paying and more prestigious. The working poor have to worry much more about the chances of being laid off during an economic downturn.

Functional illiteracy is rampant among the working poor, who hold unskilled and often seasonal jobs such as migrant worker, day laborer, or house cleaner. About 7 million working poor hold full-time jobs but depend on programs such as food stamps to make ends meet. Prospects for any social mobility are nonexistent among most of the underclass, a segment of U.S. society that has grown in recent decades. Only menial work with menial pay is available to them, and while in the past nearly all of them received welfare benefits, cutbacks and time limits on welfare imposed in the 1990s have trimmed the number of recipients. Some refer to the homeless of the underclass as the "fallout of industrialization."[122]

Once a university sociologist, then a U.S. senator, Daniel Patrick Moynihan long campaigned against what he called the nation's shame: children living in poverty, who have suffered from what he called "a general breakdown in the U.S. family," especially the tendency toward births outside marriage. One out of six white children, as well as two out of five Latino and African-American children, are now poor. The consequences of child poverty are far-reaching and include going hungry, dying in infancy, delayed development, health problems, dropping out of school, and higher risk of criminal activity. Moynihan worked for legislation intended to fund child nutrition and health care as steps in the right direction.[123]

Chapter Synopsis

In this chapter, we look at how society and culture represent the structure and content of human social activity. The section on the "sociological perspective" includes the discipline's vision of its mission (for example, "seeing the general in the particular"), its intellectual origins in Europe and America, the tenets of two of its prime theories (functionalism and conflict theory), and its chief research methods (experiment, survey research, participant observation, case study, and secondary analysis).

Under "organizing social life," the crucial concept of culture is dissected. Distinctions are made between material and nonmaterial culture, ideal and real culture, in addition to subculture and counterculture. The contributions of norms, mores, folkways, and values to culture are specified, and the complex relationship between culture and society is discussed. Vital to the perpetuation of a culture within a society is the process of socialization, or the social experience whereby individuals learn the attitudes and behaviors necessary to function in a given culture. Socialization produces social structure that expresses itself in the form of statuses, roles, groups, and institutions.

Social structure results in "pivotal institutions" meeting basic human needs. The pivotal institutions feature the bedrock institution of the family, which meets our considerable child-bearing and child-rearing needs. Religion is a second pivotal institution, and it provides an image of a supreme spiritual being, ideas about an afterlife, ethical codes of conduct, and a sacred place for rituals. The third pivotal institution is education. In preindustrial societies, education often occurs informally, but industrial societies rely on formal schooling that greatly affects an individual's life chances. The fourth pivotal institution studied is the economy, which enables people to satisfy their wants in a world of scarcity, as societies institute the production, distribution, and consumption of goods and services. The final pivotal institution is government. As humans moved from nomadic to settled milieus, we set up authoritative structures to make decisions on behalf of society. This is the stuff of government, including the competitive political process that affects society's winners and losers.

Social inequality at the micro- macro- and mega levels comprises the last part of Chapter 10. "Social stratification" is defined as well as its relationship to social mobility. Then important dimensions of inequality—race, ethnicity, and gender—are analyzed. Stratification's consequences at the global level are also detailed. Finally, the nature of stratification and poverty in America is placed under the comparative microscope.

FOR DIGGING DEEPER

Bannister, Robert. *Sociology and Scientism: The American Quest for Objectivity, 1880–1940.* University of North Carolina Press, 1987.

Barker, Eileen. *The Making of a Moonie: Brainwashing or Choice?* Basil Blackwell, 1984.

Berger, Peter. *Invitation to Sociology.* Anchor Books, 1963.

Browne, M. Neil, and Stuart Keeley. *Sociology on the Internet: Evaluating Online Resources.* Prentice Hall, 2001.

Bulliet, Richard W. *The Case for Islamo-Christian Civilization.* Columbia University, 2006.

Crone, Patricia. *God's Rule—Government and Islam: Six Centuries of Medieval Islamic Political Thought.* Columbia University, 2005.

Dneprov, Edward, and Ben Eklof. *Democracy in the Russian School.* Westview Press, 1993.

Domhoff, G. William. *Who Rules America? Power and Politics in the Year 2000.* Mayfield Publishing, 1998.

Donohue, John J., and John L. Esposito. *Islam in Transition: Muslim Perspectives.* Oxford University, 2006.

Ferrante, Joan. *Sociology: A Global Perspective.* Wadsworth, 2002.

Gelles, R. J., and C. Pedrick-Cornell. *Intimate Violence in Families.* Sage Publications, 1990.

Haines, Annette. "Targeting Sociology on the Internet Using Gateway Directories," *Teaching Sociology*, vol. 27, no. 3 (July 1999), pp. 31–37.

Heise, Lori. *Violence Against Women: The Hidden Health Burden.* World Bank, 1994.

Henslin, James. *Essentials of Sociology: A Down to Earth Approach.* Allyn and Bacon, 2000.

Hirschkind, Charles. *The Ethical Soundscape: Cassette Sermons and Islamic Counterpublics*. Columbia University, 2006.

Jones, Brian, Bernard Gallagher, and Joseph A. McFalls. *Sociology: Micro, Macro, and Mega Structures*. Harcourt Brace, 2003.

Kelso, William. *Poverty and the Underclass: Changing Perceptions of the Poor in America*. New York University Press, 1995.

Kling, Rob, "The Culture of Cyberspace: The Internet for Sociologists," *Contemporary Sociology*, vol. 26, no. 4 (July 1997), pp. 434–44.

Kurland, Daniel. *The Internet Guide for Sociology*. Wadsworth, 1997.

Lenski, Gerhard, and Jean Lenski. *Human Sociology: An Introduction to Macrosociology*. McGraw-Hill, 1987.

Macionis, John. *Society: The Basics*. Prentice Hall, 2004.

Marty, Martin. *The Christian World: A Global History*. Random House, 2005.

McAuliffe, Jane Dammen, ed. *The Cambridge Companion to the Qur'an*. Cambridge University, 2005.

Mills, C. Wright. *The Sociological Imagination*. Oxford University Press, 1959.

Mount, Ferdinand. *The Subversive Family: An Alternative History of Love and Marriage*. Free Press, 1992.

Murdock, George Peter. *Social Structure*. Macmillan, 1949.

O'Dea, Thomas, and J. O. Ariad. *The Sociology of Religion*. Prentice Hall, 1983.

Palmer, Monte, and Princess Palmer. *Islamic Extremism: Causes, Diversity, and Challenges*. Rowman and Littlefield, 2007.

Schaefer, Richard, and Robert Lamb. *Sociology*. McGraw-Hill, Inc., 1998.

Vaughn, Angela, and Joan Ferrante. *Sociology: Travel on the Internet*. Prentice Hall, 1999.

Weber, Max. *The Sociology of Religion*. Beacon Press, 1922.

Wickham, Carrie Rosefsky. *Mobililizing Islam: Religion, Activism, and Political Change in Egypt*. Columbia University, 2002.

Wilson, Edward O. *On Human Nature*. Bantam Books, 1979.

INTERNET

American Sociological Association:
http://www.asanet.org

ASA Human Subjects Guidelines:
http://www.theasa.org/ethics/guidelines.htm

Cyberspace Religions:
http://www.kenrickparish.com/gresham/contents.htm

Dead Sociologists' Society:
http://media.pfeiffer.edu/lridener/DSS/DEADSOC.HTML

Institute for Social Research:
http://www.isr.umich.edu/

International Child Labor Program:
http://www.dol.gov/ILAB/progrmas/iclp/

MNCs and Global Inequality:
http://www.stwr.net/content/view/1164/

My Family Tree:
http://www.usgenweb.org

National Opinion Research Center:
http://www.norc.uchicago.edu/

Online Norms: "Netiquette":
http://www.yahoo.com/society_and_culture

Sexual Assault Information Page:
http://www.4woman.gov/FAQ/sexualassault.html

Social Statistics Briefing Room:
http://www.whitehouse.gov/fsbr/ssbr.html

Sociological Research:
http://www.socresonline.org.uk/

Sociological Tour Through Cyberspace:
http://www.trinity.edu/~mkearl/index.html

Sociology Dictionary:
http://www.webref.org/links/sociology.htm

Sociosite: Journals:
http://www.sociosite.net

The Socioweb:
http://www.socioweb.com/~markbl/socioweb/

U.S. Census Bureau:
http://www.census.gov/

Webring: Sociology:
http://a.webring.com/hub?ring=sociology

World Hunger:
http://www.bread.org/learn/hunger-basics/hunger-facts-

CHAPTER 11

Comparative Cultures

CORE OBJECTIVE

To establish the vital importance of culture to the social sciences by comparing selected micro-, macro-, and mega-level cultures.

THEMATIC QUESTIONS

- Why identify levels of analysis in studying cultures?

- What are some key elements of American macro-level culture?

- How does collectivism characterize Japanese and Chinese macro-level cultures?

- In what ways can Russian and Brazilian macro-level cultures be described as mixed in character?

- Of what utility is comparing the Baka and Arara micro-cultures?

- How does the Islamic tradition of *Ummah* represent a form of mega-culture?

The comparative method of analysis fosters critical thinking skills by expanding our definitions of normality. The more real-life case studies that we understand, the more perspective we possess in considering the relative worth of competing social phenomena; and, in Chapter 11, the comparative motif is applied to one of the most potent concepts in the social sciences: culture. The essence of culture has to do with transmitting a lifestyle from one generation to the next generation through a process of socialization.

One issue that arises in studying cultures is the "level of analysis question" because the concept of culture manifests itself at all three levels discussed in this book: micro, macro, and mega levels. For well over three centuries, states (countries) have represented the dominant players on the world stage. Therefore, it's tempting to focus on some of the fascinating macro-level societies, which in this chapter includes Japan, China, Russia, and Brazil. But hundreds of micro-cultures, such as the Arara tribe in Brazil, also have something to teach us. Likewise, at the mega level, Islamic culture is expanding globally and increasing its influence. The distinction made in Chapter 10 between "ideal" culture and "real" culture comes in handy here.

The range of cultural diversity seems nearly infinite, but the U.N. estimates the number of distinct cultures at 10,000 and warns that many are being marginalized or eliminated in the rush toward modernization, as "many countries try to artificially fuse different ethnic groups into one cohesive nation by submerging cultural differences."[1] If we think of cultures as possessing personalities, then awareness of cultural traits can aid us in comparing them. By comparing cultural patterns, we reduce some of the confusion created by their multiplicity. Cultural comparisons also help us to apply critical thinking skills by analyzing the unexamined assumptions inherent in our own cultural lenses. Philosophers have long argued that knowledge of the self occurs partly through knowledge of others—which is one reason the comparative method is employed often in these pages.[2]

Elements of Culture

Robust forces enmesh members of a culture to the point where they consider their ways of handling life's tasks as normality itself. First comes language, the soul of each culture's unique shared symbolism. Australians, South Asians, and North Americans may all speak the English language, but they do so in ways that create pockets of esoteric communication misunderstood by outsiders. Language conveys the priorities of a culture, and vital phenomena are accompanied by a multitude of words capable of great subtlety. In the United States, the quintessential automotive culture, the meaning of the word "convertible" is crystal clear to its residents but may mystify an English speaker from India. Language also allows shared human experience to build cumulatively over time.

Forms of symbolic communication other than language represent another element of culture, from popular film images, to traffic signs, to the lyrics of popular music. All humans are symbol-making creatures, but symbols may communicate different meanings to different people depending on their cultural background. Some symbols, such as national flags or photos of martyred heroes, may evoke strong emotional responses. Common hand gestures often convey unintended symbolic meanings cross-culturally. For example, to North Americans, the hand gesture "thumbs up," in which you point your thumb upward, conveys positive meaning akin to "all right," "I agree with you," or "way to go." However, to Australians, the identical hand gesture means "up yours!"

Third, we can learn something important about a culture by studying its norms. Cultural **norms** separate proper behavior from improper behavior, and they promote predictability when encountering other people. Norms that society considers moral imperatives—**mores**—are so serious that violation may be punishable by law. An example of mores in U.S. society would be any form of physical, mental, or sexual abuse of a child.

> **Norms** ■ Codes of social behavior that influence us in both formal and informal contexts

> **Mores** ■ Strictly enforced norms thought essential to protecting society's core values

Much less imperative are norms governing everyday behavior whose violation does not invoke punishment but may upset others around you, such as walking up a down escalator or wearing sexually provocative clothing to a formal church service. These lesser transgressions are called **folkways**. Most people obey them most of the time, despite their not being backed by the threat of punishment. No folkway in China proscribes people from asking others how much money they earn. In U.S. culture, to the contrary, a widely shared folkway considers it gauche to inquire about salary, making people less likely to do so than in China.

> **Folkways** ■ Norms that are not strictly enforced by society

Whereas norms operate with specificity and immediacy, another subjective element of culture, **values**, function more generally. These abstract standards contribute to the formation of beliefs. Some cultural values that are often attributed to ideal American culture include faith in hard work yielding success; considering all people as deserving equal opportunity in society; and assuming that everyone has a right to act freely, so long as it does not infringe on the equivalent rights of others.

> **Values** ■ Culturally defined general standards of beauty, goodness, and desirability that undergird social living

These are broad, abstract American values, but they nevertheless resonate to inspire many U.S. citizens. All individuals develop personal ambitions; but the sociological perspective says that such ambitions are filtered through general cultural values. Many U.S. citizens assume that little difference exists between their values and the values of Canadians. However, researchers, including sociologist Seymour Martin Lipset, have found the values of Canadians exhibiting less concern about personal freedom and more about orderly society, less prudishness and more tolerance concerning human sexuality, as well as less parochialism and more globalism characterizing their worldview than their neighbors to the south.[3]

Culture and Society

Sociology and anthropology both examine society's social structure and culture's social content. Although closely intertwined, society and culture do not mean the same thing. The dichotomous pairs listed next are intended to show how society and culture are both similar and dissimilar. Keep in mind, however, that concepts relating to human behavior cannot be defined with the precision of material objects such as automotive mufflers, carburetors, or windshields.

Society	Culture
structure	content
organization	lifestyle
objective	subjective
social building blocks	social codes
people on a territory	people with an identity
social interaction	social thought

Because we normally observe societies and cultures operating in tandem, it's easy to overlook the subtle nuances separating them. There exists an inner logic possessed by the people who, over time, construct a society and its culture. If you visit Mexico, you are likely to notice many things that seem different from the United States. The Spanish-style architecture, spicy foods, siestas taken by some people after lunch, people gesturing with hands and standing close enough to touch while conversing, friends embracing in public, and brightly colored visual art in public display—all convey a palpable Mexican-ness. Where this palpable Mexican-ness comes from leads to a discussion of the socialization process.

Macro-Level Cultural Diversity

Macro-level cultures intrigue the human imagination. Germany, for example, tends toward an active lifestyle, whereas some countries' cultures, such as Sri Lanka, feel comfortable with greater passivity. Some Western cultures focus on the present, whereas many Oriental cultures have more of a sense of their historical past. Cultures based on the Judeo-Christian religious heritage consider humans to stand above nature, whereas most indigenous peoples, such as Native Americans, see humanity as part of a cyclical natural order. Islamic-world societies involve religion directly in public life, whereas most Western countries lean toward secularism.

The culture of the United States is imbued with an optimistic sense of efficacy, whereas Italians are somewhat more pessimistic in outlook. Heterogeneous cultures such as India vary much more than homogeneous ones such as Korea. Some, such as Australia, are quite egalitarian, whereas England remains more stratified. Some can stay fairly static, such as Tibet, but others, such as Malaysia, are quite dynamic. The Persians of Iran constitute an ancient culture, whereas Canada's macro-level culture is relatively young. Such generalizations simplify complex realities, enabling us to conceptualize global phenomena in ways that facilitate communication.

SEXUAL VARIATION Norms about human sexuality vary greatly by culture. Sociologists William Kephart and William Zellner have developed a continuum for comparing degrees of sexual permissiveness versus restrictiveness in various societies (see Figure 11.1). They cite an American religious subculture, the Shakers, as probably the most anti-sex

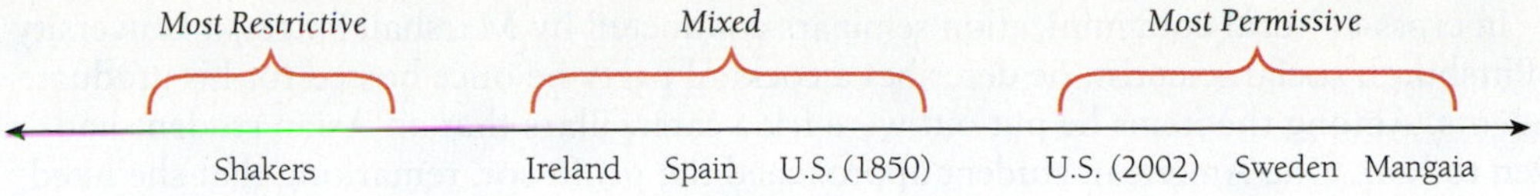

Most Restrictive   *Mixed*   *Most Permissive*

Shakers   Ireland   Spain   U.S. (1850)   U.S. (2002)   Sweden   Mangaia

Figure 11.1
Sexual Attitudes Among Cultures

group on record.[4] Like the Cathars who lived in medieval Europe, Shakers believe that sex is the root of all evil. Having children produces additional holy spirits trapped in human flesh and subject to the temptations of sexuality. Therefore, sex and all other forms of contact between men and women are forbidden. Only the recruitment of new converts prevents small celibate groups like the Shakers from disappearing completely.[5]

At the other end of Kephart and Zellner's continuum, we find the highly pro-sex group known as the Mangaia. Sex is the pivotal life experience for the Mangaians, whose average rate of sexual intercourse is three times nightly, every night of the week, on their Polynesian island. Public nudity is common and most forms of sexuality are encouraged in this extremely permissive society. Premarital intercourse occurs spontaneously and is also abetted by a practice called "night crawling" in which adolescent males visit various huts and have sex with adolescent girls without parental interference.[6]

And where does the United States fall on Kephart and Zellner's continuum? They categorize America in 1850 right about in the center of this permissive/restrictive range but say that the contemporary United States falls in a moderately permissive (but not highly permissive) range and surely is not among the most pro-sex, even though evidence of sexuality in American popular culture is omnipresent. Most affluent societies fall fairly near the United States, although some such as Spain and Ireland are more restrictive and others such as Sweden and the Netherlands are more permissive.[7]

FIRE-WALKING Sometimes cultural differences may even challenge our definition of reality. Once, during a group trip to Taiwan, some students returned from a field trip with film footage they had taken of Buddhist fire-walkers. About fifteen Buddhists had worked themselves into a meditative state by chanting and dancing, and then repeatedly walked across a large pit of burning coals at least ten feet square. None was harmed in any way. A physician from our group was present and examined the white-hot bed of coals as closely as possible but reported that they felt too hot for him to get near. The students were excited about this experience, yet confused because it represented an intellectual dilemma.

Individual personality traits may complement cultural differences in explaining how people react to such unusual experiences. Would a German person, for example, likely bring different cultural baggage to this issue than a Tibetan? One possible response is to regard fire-walking as trickery, akin to a magical act. Those comfortable with social scientism might consider it impossible and, therefore, outside the bounds of serious consideration. Skepticism is a core attitude of science, and anyone with a scientific bent would likely cast a dubious eye in the direction of fire-walking.

Those who lean toward social humanism might be willing to consider fire-walking as an exhibition of mind over matter: untapped human potential producing phenomena beyond most people's comprehension. Social humanists might point to other examples of feats considered impossible by scientific reckoning. Neither of these perspectives is demonstrably false. How do you account for this fire-walking episode? Does the type of explanation most plausible to you say anything about your general outlook on life?

CULTURE SHOCK Sometimes the practices of other cultures are so different that exposure to them produces **culture shock.** Some Westerners traveling to China find it offensive to discover dogs—which are regularly eaten there—hanging outside butcher shops. I have known students from conservative Islamic countries who have expressed shock at sexually provocative dress and public kissing in the United States.

Culture shock ■ Personal disorientation experienced by many people who travel to a foreign culture for the first time

In cross-cultural communication seminars conducted by Marshall Singer, a University of Pittsburgh social scientist, he describes a cocktail party he once hosted for his graduate students. Among the items he put out were fried caterpillars that an Asian student had given to him. One American student approached the professor, remarking that she liked the shrimp on the table in the corner.

Professor Singer then informed the student that, in fact, she had eaten an Oriental delicacy: fried caterpillars. The student immediately turned away and vomited on the living room carpet. Had the fried caterpillars made her sick? Not really; her culture-laden perceptions produced that result. Psychologist Steven Pinker notes that in Africa, Asia, and Australia, insects are seen by many as both a delicacy and a source of protein. Pinker writes that, actually, "Insects, worms, toads, maggots, caterpillars, and grubs are highly nutritious and have been eaten by the majority of peoples throughout human history."[8]

A helpless sense of culture shock permeates the Hollywood film *Not Without My Daughter* (1991), based on a book recounting the story of an American woman named Betty (played by Sally Fields).[9] Betty's husband, Moody, is an Iranian-born physician; the movie begins with them living happily in America with their four-year-old daughter, Mahtob. When they visit Iran, Moody secretly decides that the family will remain there. To Betty's horror, she finds that women have no rights in this conservative Islamic culture. Moody changes greatly while in Iran, including beating her, to which no one objects. Kidnapped in body and spirit, Betty begins a desperate effort to save her daughter by fleeing from Iran's dark side.

CULTURAL UNIVERSALS Differences between cultures seem to jump out at us, while subtly shared cultural traits may go unnoticed, leading to an exaggeration of differences and underestimation of similarities. Below the surface, there are numerous ways in which different cultures resemble one another, and such shared traits are called *cultural universals*. They exist because humans have common basic needs, and cultures represent strategies developed to meet those needs.

After examining hundreds of cultures, anthropologist George Murdock compiled a list of a few dozen cultural universals, including cooking, dancing, folklore, gestures, music, funerals, and sexual restrictions. Each society finds its own ways of adapting to human needs, so the exact manifestations of cooking, gestures, or music may diverge appreciably. For example, the functionalist perspective holds that while funerals seek to convey respect for the deceased, they also serve a key social function by reaffirming group unity during a time of separation and loss.[10]

A practice such as dancing may differ greatly among teenagers in the United States, Tanzania, and Japan. Cultures also evolve over time, largely through the processes of **innovation** and **diffusion,** so that a comparison of dancing among American teenagers today with their predecessors in the 1950s and their predecessors in the 1930s may reveal equally sharp differences.[11]

Innovation ■ The introduction of new ideas or objects into a culture

Diffusion ■ The process whereby an aspect of culture—such as an idea, technology, or custom—spreads from one society to another

Micro-, Macro-, and Mega-Level Cultures

Like a rubber band, the concept of culture seems elastic by first contracting to the level of micro-cultures, then expanding to the level of macro-cultures, and finally stretching even further to the level of mega-cultures. Cultural elasticity oozes from this chapter. We begin by examining two macro-level Oriental cultures—Japan and China—with collectivist values quite different from North America's more individualistic values.

Second, we will look at two macro-level cultures—Russia and Brazil—that fall in between Western individualism and Eastern collectivism. Third, the mega level of analysis is applied to Islamic culture. And fourth, two micro-level cultures—the Arara people of the Amazon rainforest and the Baka people of the African Ituri River forest—are described. Figure 11.2 lists the cultures examined in this chapter. In all of these comparisons, the United States serves as a rather different baseline.

Later in the chapter, an explanatory model seeks to ferret out the cultural essences of each culture.

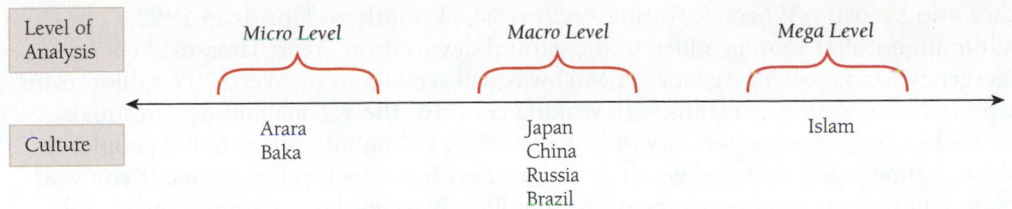

Level of Analysis		*Micro Level*	*Macro Level*	*Mega Level*	
Culture		Arara Baka	Japan China Russia Brazil	Islam	

Figure 11.2

Comparing Cultures: Micro, Macro, and Mega Levels

Comparative Baseline: America

Few macro-level cultures set themselves up with as many idealistic values as the United States. Consequently, any gap between promise and performance (between ideal and real culture) provides a convenient target for critics. It has been said that American-ness entails thinking that anything worth doing must be worth overdoing. So ambitious is the American dream that some elements of its self-identity may appear incompatible with one another. But the sheer heterogeneity of U.S. culture, replete with diverse subcultures, provides considerable wiggle room.

A book by Robert Bellah and others argues that individualism is the quintessential American value, bar none.[12] John Hewith, by contrast, suggests that the "core objects" in American culture consist of freedom, responsibility, independence, choice, security, limits, authority, happiness, duty, and the future.[13] Cultural values can change, and pollster Daniel Yankelovich concludes from survey data that the vaunted American work ethic—long emulated globally—has eroded in recent decades; now challenging hard work as a civic religion, Yankelovich says, is a stronger desire for self-fulfillment and creative expression.[14]

The United States is a nation of immigrants, and the prospect of upward social mobility has always attracted those in quest of the land of opportunity. The egalitarian belief that everyone has a chance to improve is quintessential Americana. And surely faith in American exceptionality and competitiveness contribute to a preoccupation with "being number one," something not discernible in most cultures. All of these lofty visions are fueled by a resilient feeling of efficacy, or "American can-doism."

Research by sociologist Michael Josephson, however, suggests that American competitiveness and individualism seem to be promoting selfishness and cheating as the way to get ahead in society. His findings are based on a one-hundred-question survey completed by about 7,000 college and high school students. Josephson says he has "mapped a hole in the moral ozone layer of American youth" that reveals a troubling decline in honesty, trustworthiness, and responsibility.[15]

Bikes parked casually at a train station in suburban Tokyo.

Asian Collectivist Cultures

Japanese Culture

Japan holds a paradoxical position in being both crucial to the United States yet fundamentally different from it in lifestyle. In the 1990s, it was the United States' second-leading trade partner after Canada, but a decade later, it had fallen behind China. The Japanese and American economies, however, remain interwoven in many ways. Because their cultures are so different, misperception and resentment often lurk beneath the surface of economic issues. Robert Christopher's book *The Japanese Mind* explores the many ironies pervading this relationship between what he calls the "oddest couple."[16]

PEACE AND SECURITY When Hurricane Andrew struck southern Florida in 1992, multimillion-dollar looting added to the natural devastation. Years later, the Federal Emergency Management Agency (FEMA) was still seeking to recover $209 million from suspected false insurance claims.[17] In striking contrast, the 7.2-magnitude earthquake that rocked the Japanese port city of Kobe in 1995, killing more than 6,000 people, resulted in almost no looting of goods and almost no fraud by local residents. If you visit Japan, you will surely notice some of the 3 million bicycles daily left unlocked at rail stations in this nation of commuters. They almost never get stolen. Would you advise a Japanese exchange student at your institution to do the same thing here?

Tokyo has the lowest rates of murder, rape, and theft of any major city in the world—despite Japan's having far fewer police officers per capita than the United States. What explains Japan's enviable safety numbers? Although Japan has fewer police, the citizens trust the police implicitly and cooperate with them. Police kiosks in urban neighborhoods (the Koban system) serve as effective information brokers. Gun control also matters. Only hunting rifles, which are strictly regulated, may be kept at home, and the bane of American cities—the handgun—is nonexistent. Japan is also socially cohesive because of its relatively equal distribution of wealth, its low unemployment, and its harmonious cultural values. In this society, socially deviant behavior brings strong community disapproval.[18]

WA: JAPANESE HARMONY Japan is a homogeneous society and is more closed to outsiders than the United States, which is a highly heterogeneous and open society. One reason is that the Japanese value *wa,* or maintaining harmony, in social relations. *Wa* manifests itself in gentle, conciliatory, moderate, and orderly behavior by the Japanese people.[19] If you saw a fellow American student wearing a surgical face mask in public, you would probably assume it was to protect the wearer from the germs of others. However, the visitor to Japan will notice many commuters with the sniffles riding crowded trains wearing masks to protect other people from catching the wearer's cold. Valuing *wa* also helps to account for the fact that so few disputes in Japan end up in court for resolution. America has fifteen times the number of lawyers per capita that does Japan.

The potency of group responsibility in Japan is supported by *wa.* Whether at the level of the family, the corporation, or the nation, Japanese willingness to sacrifice personal interests to those of the group confounds Americans, noted for profound individualism. Attendance at a Japanese baseball game is a marvelous way for Americans to appreciate the impact of cultural differences, such as *wa,* on a game that is technically the same but under the surface operates quite differently.

In his book *You Gotta Have Wa* (1989), Robert Whiting discusses the existence of tie games in Japan and quotes the president of the Pacific League: "Ties are suited to the Japanese character. That way nobody loses."[20] I found cheering by the crowd at a Japanese ball game more akin to the kind that occurs at a high school football game in the United States, using organized cheers complete with cheerleaders armed with megaphones and a band backing them up. The emphasis is on inspiring team effort and cohesion, not on individual heroics.

By contrast, North American baseball crowds cheer more as individuals than as a group, and their cheers are aimed to exhort individual star players to live up to their exalted billing (and salaries). North Americans also resort to jeers when cheers fail, by booing or verbally skewering their fallen heroes. Such emotionally negative behavior in public would seem crude to the Japanese. The documentary film *Baseball in Japan* (1994) is the next best thing to seeing a game in Tokyo or Kobe.[21]

STRONG WORK ETHIC Like many other East Asian cultures, the Japanese are proud of their work ethic and self-discipline, which some observers consider as essential to Japanese culture as *wa.*[22] In Whiting's analysis of baseball, he suggests that while Americans "play" baseball, the Japanese "work" baseball like an assembly-line job. The vaunted Japanese work ethic paid tangible dividends in national pride in 2006 when Ichiro Suzuki led his compatriots to victory in the first ever World Baseball Classic. However, grim evidence of overachievement at work is the sensitive issue of *karoshi,* or death from overwork, now a diagnosable cause of death in Japan. Estimates of *karoshi* cases run into the thousands annually. In one case, a corporate manager who died had worked one hundred hours of overtime per month for the preceding year.[23]

One reason that Japanese males are able to take on the role of "corporate warriors," working long hours followed by more hours of dining and drinking with coworkers, is that wives agree to run the household and stay at home raising the kids.[24] Raising families gives wives some free time, the scarcest of commodities in this driven society. The world of work is also unkind to Japanese women, who earn only one-half of men's wages, and less than 10 percent of managers are female (one of the world's lowest ratios).[25]

Japan has an extremely low violent crime rate. One innovation aiding communication between citizens and police is the Koban system of neighborhood kiosks like this one.

Often arranged, Japanese marriages are viewed more pragmatically than the U.S. version of romantic love in marriage. One study finds that many couples spend less than 30 minutes per week talking to each other, and it concludes that this cool indifference toward each other is what most Japanese spouses want.[26]

SOCIAL GUILT IN A SHAME CULTURE Exactly how and why the *karoshi* phenomenon exists in Japan is a complex question with no facile answers. However, one element may consist of the concept of a "shame culture" first introduced to Western anthropology in Ruth Benedict's classic, *The Sword and the Chrysanthemum* (1946). Benedict was criticized severely for suggesting that a shame culture leads Japanese people to do their duty not so much because it is the right thing to do but mainly because they dread dishonor. Fearing the loss of face, she found, Japanese are motivated to comply with the social norms of a group-oriented and status-conscious society.[27]

ODDEST COUPLE: UNITED STATES AND JAPAN As the oddest couple, according to Robert Christopher's description, Japan and the United States exhibit differing styles in their business relations. The Japanese penchant for patiently planning for the long term is well chronicled, as is the American fixation on immediacy. U.S. business culture obsesses over the bottom line for the current quarter, and hence planning for twenty years simply does not compute. When negotiating, Americans consider a formal agreement final, with implementation resulting naturally. Their Japanese counterparts see a negotiation as part of an ongoing process in which implementation requires future negotiation.[28]

Whereas Japan's higher education system suffers from an inability to accommodate all those wanting to attend college in the modern democratic era, as pointed out in Chapter 10, its public education system exhibits some impressive qualities. Parents, students, and teachers work hard to meet the expectations of a culture that considers success in school and success in life as nearly coterminous.[29] Fitting in is imperative, as symbolized by the school uniforms worn by all students. Student discipline, study habits, and time spent both in school and doing homework rank very high. But as with workplace *karoshi*, negative consequences accompany the overachievement expected in Japanese schools. The need to succeed places pressure on youngsters wanting desperately not to disappoint their families. The comprehensive tests taken after high school are dreaded as "examination hell" by students competing for very few university slots.[30]

HUMAN RESOURCES? YES; NATURAL RESOURCES? NO Smaller than the state of Montana, Japan's four islands equal 4 percent of U.S. territory, yet support a population more than one-third of the American population, with 130 million Japanese citizens. Nearly half are packed into the cities of Tokyo, Osaka, and Nagoya in a country with a high population density of 860 per square mile. An amazing 99.4 percent are ethnic Japanese, with Chinese and Koreans making up most of the remainder. Japan's fast-aging society and mere trickle of immigrants allowed into the country portend significant future problems.

Over half of Japan's land is mountainous, of which only 11 percent is arable, requiring it to import nearly half of its food. Farming efficiency is stretched by terracing steep slopes, by mechanization among the 8 percent of its people who farm, by heavy irrigation, by development of hybrid rices, and by multiple cropping. Its vibrant fishing industry provides protein by taking one-seventh of the world's total catch. To top it off, Japan has few natural resources, no oil fields, and very little coal.

Yet Japan has created the world's second-largest economy, and in 2000, its GNP per capita of $25,000 and its rank in the top five countries on the Human Development Index (HDI) were impressive.[31] Japanese people weigh less on average than in any industrialized country, and average life expectancy of eighty-one years (eighty-four for women, seventy-eight for men) leads the world. Few cultures have managed to blend the modern and the traditional as well as Japan.

This economic miracle has inspired other East Asian countries. Part of Japan's secret lies in its efficient use of human resources to compensate for physical weaknesses. Author Michio Morishima attributes economic success mostly to cultural values. A well-educated, hardworking, loyal, and unselfish workforce surely contributes, as do its close management–worker relations, managed economic policies, and U.S. assistance since 1945 (Japan's average defense expenditure: a minuscule 1 percent of GNP).[32]

Chinese Culture

Just as individual people differ in personality, leading them to perceive reality somewhat differently, cultures possess personalities that serve as giant lenses through which they see the world. From the U.S. perspective, Japan and China, as Asian cultures, seem quite similar. However, viewed from the inside of Japanese or Chinese cultural prisms, they exhibit quite different style and substance (see Figure 11.3).[33] What do North Americans tend to notice when considering Japan and China? Old cultures with strong group identities, homogeneous peoples, and certain common values; we might take note of their formal and conservative rituals, such as bowing to show deference or discomfort at being touched by strangers, respect for the elderly, and an aversion to losing face (honor). And, oh yes, both eat with chopsticks. American cultural lenses magnify all these genuine similarities.

Contrarily, Chinese and Japanese cultural lenses highlight equally real but quite different qualities of their cultures. For example, compare the situation in Japan to these Chinese realities: China's rural populace, its authoritarian communist government,

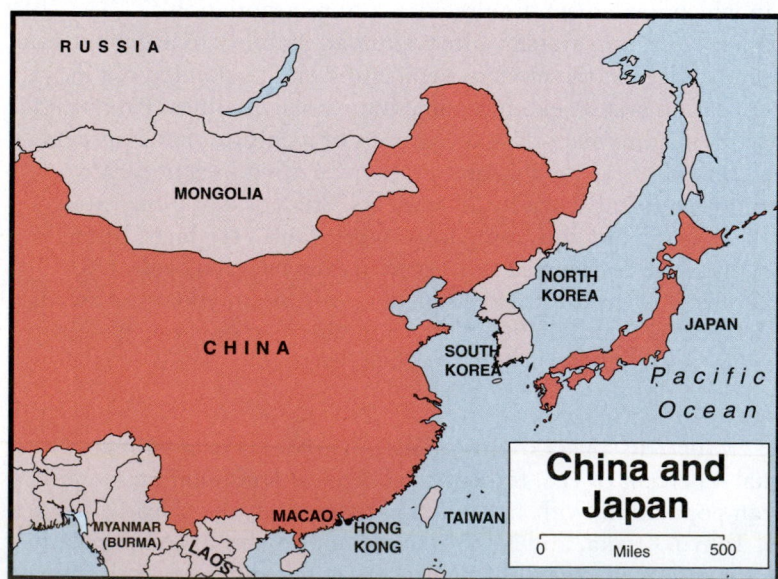

Figure 11.3

Through American lenses, Chinese and Japanese cultures appear as similarly collectivist macro-level cultures.

Source: From Maps on File, by Facts on File, Inc. Copyright © by Facts on File, Inc. Reprinted by permission of Facts on File, Inc.

preindustrial economy, official atheism, Confucian conservatism, moral Puritanism, rudimentary education system, and attempts by the government to weaken family loyalties. On such issues, no divining rod is required to locate significant differences. The question about a glass being half full or half empty is instructive here. An interesting argument can be made that Chinese and Japanese cultures are very similar; yet an equally impressive argument can be made that Chinese and Japanese cultures are very different.

CONFUCIAN VALUES As one of the world's oldest continuous cultures, China (Chinese People's Republic, or CPR) has long been influenced by a traditional philosophy valuing social stability and order, **Confucianism,** which dominated Chinese life for over twenty centuries. One of Confucius's most famous observations was that "The cautious seldom err." Confucius (551–479 B.C.) wrote during China's classical Zhou dynasty and urged the emperor, who was more than autocratic—he was considered divine—to encourage education by using meritocracy based on national examinations to select his governing ministers. Confucius stressed the role of the family and respect for both parents and the elderly as the crux of Chinese values.

Whereas in the United States, the term "old person" is considered derogatory, in China "old person" is a sign of respect comparable to our calling a judge "your honor."[34] Elderly persons are considered fonts of wisdom, given honored seating in public gatherings, expected to begin eating first at Chinese dinner tables, and continue being venerated after death through ancestor worship. Sociologist Gary Huang surveyed the scholarly literature to see whether these traditions consisted mostly of real culture or ideal culture. He concluded that respect for the elderly remains an important cultural norm in China and thus qualifies as real culture.[35]

But another sociologist emphasizes cultural change discernible in the academic literature. "As China industrializes, the bonds between generations are weakening," and caring for an aging population is becoming more difficult in this country without a social security system.[36] Some Chinese Communist Party (CCP) officials have introduced policies intended to pressure young Chinese people to meet their obligations to their aging relatives. In one province, a young couple cannot get a marriage license until they sign a contract promising to support their parents after age sixty.[37]

COMMUNIST ERA I: MAO ZEDONG For many centuries, Confucianism served China well, and Chinese culture led the world in many of the arts and sciences. However, civil unrest, military defeats, and foreign occupation characterized what the Chinese referred to as the Century of Humiliation (1842–1949). Not until after World War II did China throw off foreign dominance and regain national sovereignty. The CCP, led by Mao Zedong, won a civil war (1945–1949) against domestic rivals and then set up a strict dictatorship similar to that of the Soviet Union at that time. Mao ruled with an iron fist until his 1976 death.

The totality of Mao's power over Chinese life fit the tradition of Chinese emperors who ruled by divine right—except that in Mao's case, his source of infallibility was the secular religion of Marxism. Communism is one of the few secular ideologies that have at times equaled world religions in ideological fervor. And nowhere did communist ideology work overtime the way it did under Mao's CPR. Communism derived from the writings of German philosopher Karl Marx and was grounded in the industrialism experienced in nineteenth-century Europe. Socioeconomic conditions in China were vastly different, but Mao was determined to bend Marxism to match the peasant contours of rural China.

For three decades, the "Great Helmsman" held the power to put forward any policies he desired, but converting policy to reality proved elusive. Mao tried to replace millennia of Confucian influence with communist ideology. He grossly underestimated the staying power of conservative Confucian principles, which contributed heavily to the failure of his socioeconomic programs. Yet failed programs did not diminish his arbitrary and capricious exercise of power.

Mao hated Western influences and sought to turn the CPR inward, hoping to propel the country into the industrial era. A veritable "bamboo curtain" separated the Chinese

Confucianism ■ A conservative perspective emphasizing strong family ties and respect for the elderly, and urging individuals to rise above difficult social conditions

For more than two millennia, the philosophy of Confucius has taught Chinese people to value social order and to respect authority figures.

people from the outside world as Mao touted "self-reliance" as China's salvation. Mao disliked the West's technological complexity, but what especially riled him was its undisciplined decadence. Ideological purity was to sanctify the people's sacrifices in building a communist paradise, and this purity was personified by Mao's Little Red Book, a compendium of his most cherished sayings. Anyone daring to question Mao's orthodoxy was immediately branded a "revisionist." Religious analogies flow easily concerning Mao's CPR, and comparing his "infallible" book to the Koran among Muslim fundamentalists, or to the Bible among Christian fundamentalists, is not an imaginative stretch. Not only was Mao's thought considered unquestionably true, it was also to be memorized and publicly recited.

ANTI-WESTERN HYSTERIA: PROLETARIAN CULTURAL REVOLUTION The cacophony of devoted voices praising the "Great Helmsman" reached a crescendo from 1966 to the early 1970s, during the heyday of the Great Proletarian Cultural Revolution. In this period, the definition of acceptable social behavior shrank to a point where only overt devotion to Mao passed political muster. At the vanguard of the Cultural Revolution were the strident paramilitary Red Guards, millions of zealous youth ready to humiliate anyone not loyal enough to their leader. During the Cultural Revolution, "any person who held a position of authority, showed the slightest leaning toward foreign ways, or had academic interests was subject to interrogation, arrest, and punishment." Most typically abused were scientists, teachers, athletes, performers, artists, writers, private business owners, and people who had relatives living outside China.[38]

Reliable figures on the human costs of the Cultural Revolution remain elusive, but some observers estimate that 10 million people may have perished.[39] Undoubtedly, the toll was enormous, as individuals and families suffered under abject conditions. Those sent into rural exile were far more numerous. Social institutions, such as hospitals and schools, were closed arbitrarily. Economic productivity plummeted for China's lost generation. The hangover from this ideological binge lasted beyond Mao's death, leaving headaches for the leaders who later attempted to catch up with the rest of the world.[40]

COMMUNISM II: DENG XIAOPING By 1978, Mao's successor, Deng Xiaoping, had embarked on a dramatic new course. Having experienced Mao's prisons, Deng cut back the scale of political repression in China. But the crux of his policies featured economic change, which required opening up to the world once again. Saddled with a sluggish centrally planned economy, Deng borrowed market-oriented principles from the capitalist West that Mao despised. Both in agriculture and industry, the changes produced a quadrupling of economic output by the end of the century, when China took over as the world's second-largest economy. In the post-Mao era, China's annual economic growth rate led the world, averaging 8 percent.[41]

From the mid- to late 1980s, it also appeared that Deng's economic liberalization might be matched by loosening of political restrictions. As Soviet-style communist countries were opening up, many observers predicted that those reforms would spill over to China. The argument was that China could not open up economically without also doing so politically. Reports suggested that the CCP leadership was deeply divided over how to respond to the Student Democracy Movement that had arisen in the mid-1980s.

TIANANMEN SQUARE, JUNE 1989 The year 1989 was a watershed year. Repressive European communism died symbolically with the fall of the Berlin Wall on November 11. But five months earlier, repressive Chinese communism was reborn in its own riveting symbolic event on June 4, known simply as Tiananmen Square. On that day, the hard-liners won the policy battle in the CCP and unleashed troops on thousands of students peacefully demonstrating for democratic expression in a new China. Many thousands were killed, injured, or imprisoned. The CCP had served notice

Members of China's Red Guard, wearing armbands and carrying books containing the sayings of Mao Zedong, parade through the streets of Beijing during the Cultural Revolution. The portraits they carry also pay homage to Chairman Mao.

that dictatorial business-as-usual still reigned in China, a fact that continued to resonate after the death of Deng in 1997.

A more recent example of oppression appears even more baffling to many Westerners. In July of 1999, China made illegal the spiritual movement known as Falun Gong, which merges traditional Chinese exercises with elements of Buddhism and Taoism. Alarmed over the growth of these groups, President Jiang Zemin stated that "we must not underestimate it. If this problem is not solved, it will become a major social disaster." Later in 1999, several small groups of Falun Gong sat meditating in Tiananmen Square, silently protesting the banning of their movement, after which 111 members were arrested and charged with "disrupting state security and stealing state secrets."[42]

The implications of China's huge population have been variously interpreted under communism. During the Maoist era, population control was seen as a Western plot to weaken China's power, and Mao encouraged the birthrate to remain around three children per family. Deng saw this high rate of growth as a hindrance to economic development and introduced strong population control measures, resulting in the birthrate dropping to only 1.2 per family by the mid-1980s. By 2000, China's population totaled 1.2 billion people.[43] With each policy, China's leaders got what they wanted.

QUALITY OF LIFE ISSUES The dominant ethnic group, the Han Chinese, make up 92 percent of the population, and the government recognizes fifty-five other "official" ethnic groups in China. Literacy has improved in recent years but stood at a modest 82 percent in 2001 (90 percent for males and 73 percent for females). Fifty percent of China works in agriculture, GNP per capita in 2000 was $3,800, and China ranks in the medium range on the HDI, although higher than in previous years: 87th of 170 countries in 2001, improving from its 111th ranking in 1995.

More impressive is an average life expectancy of seventy-two (seventy for men, seventy-four for women). Much of China's recent economic growth has emerged from a ring of experimental regions along China's east coast. A variety of tax breaks, investment incentives, and foreign dealings are allowed in these Special Economic Zones (SEZs) which are not permitted in the rest of the country.[44]

But exactly what constitutes the rest of the country is a matter of great controversy because another macro-level Chinese society is considered by Communist China to have no legal right to exist as a state. The Republic of China (R.O.C.), also referred to as Taiwan or Formosa, has been overlooked by many countries on the world stage during the past fifty years. This is an island nation the size of West Virginia, located 120 miles off China's coast, which Kuomintang Party leader Chiang Kaishek fled to in 1949 when defeated by Mao Zedong's CCP in the civil war. Taiwan's role as a player among states is attributable largely to U.S. financial and military support. In the 1980s and 1990s, Taiwan achieved new status in world affairs as one of East Asia's newly industrialized countries (NICs) that have followed the Japanese path of export-led growth to prosperity. Taiwan's GDP per capita now more than doubles that of the CPR.

Another of the NICs, Hong Kong, is even more intriguing. A city-state jutting out from the Chinese coast, it was ceded to the British in 1842 under the Treaty of Nanking, owing to Chinese losses in the devastating Opium War. Hong Kong's 9 million polyglot inhabitants live in the world's most wide-open laissez-faire economy—and an affluent one at that, with GNP per capita of $19,000 in 2000. Whereas the CPR improved its mid-level rank in the 2001 HDI, Hong Kong could be found well into the high-level ranks, placing 24th among all states in quality of life (see Figure 11.4).[45]

Hong Kong also became a very nervous place as the year 1997 approached because the United Kingdom had agreed to return Hong Kong to Chinese control in that year. Although China promised to allow Hong Kong to keep its own political and economic system for another fifty years, many residents did not trust the CPR's leaders. Fresh memories of what happened in Beijing on June 4, 1989 (the Tiananmen Square massacre), continued to haunt many Hong Kong residents. Many affluent Hong Kong residents fled, mostly to Canada and the United States. Most residents remained, however, hoping that the glitter of their economic success will result in the small Hong Kong tail wagging the larger Chinese dog.

Figure 11.4
In 1997, the United Kingdom returned the vibrant economic dynamo of Hong Kong to Chinese sovereignty.

Semi-Collectivist Cultures

Russian Culture

As group-oriented Asian cultures, both Japan and China strike many North Americans as exotic. Russia is a Eurasian society with a mixed culture—partway between collectivist Oriental cultures and the United States' individualism. Russia is more than twice as large as either the United States or China, and its Siberian region alone dwarfs the United States. But the term "Eurasian" culture misleads, suggesting a smooth commingling of East and West. The Russian historical drama has featured bitter opponents, with the pendulum swinging violently from one extreme to the other, seldom coming gently to rest in the center. This tendency has left many Westerners thinking of Russian culture as rather schizoid in character.

SLAVOPHILES VERSUS WESTERNIZERS   The two irreconcilable forces in Russian culture are **Slavophilism** versus **Westernization**. The Slavophiles love that which is Russian, glorifying the dignity of Russia's proud 1,000 years of culture. Deeply rooted in the traditions of the Russian Orthodox Church, they see "Holy Russia" as morally superior to

Slavophilism ■ Russian nationalism in which Slavic cultural values are idealized as superior to Western values

Westernization ■ A recurrent minority thread in Russian history advocating reform to emulate advanced European cultures

Western materialism. Suspicious of Western individualism, their collectivist preferences show through in an old peasant proverb: "It is the tall blade of grass which first gets cut." The Russophiles have traditionally dominated both the inner sanctums of power and the hearts of the peasantry. Conservative status-quo forces in society have typically supported Slavophilism.

The gradual political modernization that occurred in some Western societies finds no harbor in the stormy sea that has been Russian history. The Westernizers, also known as Reformers, usually find themselves swimming against powerful tides in Russia. Cut off from the West for 250 years during the Mongol occupation unleashed by Genghis Khan, Russia missed out on the European Renaissance. This occupation left Russia one giant step behind Europe in science, education, and the arts. Russia has always faced a vexing dilemma: change or fall further behind your rivals. Little in Russian culture, however, facilitates piecemeal change—not autocratic political systems, not weak agrarian economies, not a Church under the thumb of dictators, and not fatalistic popular attitudes.

CHANGE FROM ABOVE Like a teakettle, Russia lies dormant for long periods and then suddenly erupts when enough steam builds to blow off the top. These eruptions have been the intermittent, violent rebellions littering the landscape of Russian history. Sometimes change has been imposed from above. Reform leaders such as Peter the Great, Catherine the Great, Alexander II, or Mikhail Gorbachev—trying to pull Russia up by its bootstraps—have met stiff resistance from the masses and entrenched elites.

Similar to European countries such as Britain, Germany, and France, Russia expanded into a colonial power in earlier centuries—except that while the Europeans used sea lanes to subjugate a colonial empire, the Russians traveled only the vast expanses of the Eurasian territory. Under both the Romanov tsars and communist commissars, many diverse ethnic groups fell under either Russian or Soviet control. Even today, there are twenty-one republics and seventy other ethnic groups within Russian territory agitating for greater freedom. If the rebellion-turned-civil-war in Chechnya were emulated in other parts of Russia, its map could begin to look like Swiss cheese.

No Russian reformer has ever matched the depth and scope of the eighteenth-century Westernizer, Peter the Great.

Source: Picture Desk, Inc./Kobal Collection.

RIFE WITH PARADOXES As a complex Eurasian culture, Russia is filled with paradoxes. One noted by journalist Hedrick Smith in *The Russians,* the best-selling book ever written on Russia, is the contrast between the "public Russian" and the "private Russian." In public places—concerts, markets, or buses—Russians tend toward the self-restraint and formality of many Orientals. But then a metamorphosis occurs around the kitchen table, where they become warm and emotional, informal and outgoing, somewhat like North Americans. A generous spirit causes Russians to love having guests and giving gifts. Hedrick Smith says this split makes them "both stoics and romantics," or, in the words of the late Russian emigré poet Joseph Brodsky, "like the Irish—in their poverty, their spiritual intensity, their strong personal relationships, their sentimentality."[46]

QUALITY OF LIFE ISSUES Although 120 ethnic groups coexist, 82 percent of the 145 million citizens are ethnic Russians. The population is shrinking at the rate of 0.4 percent annually and consists of three-quarters urban dwellers. Education is free and compulsory, with pockets of true excellence in theoretical sciences, math, language instruction, and engineering. As related in Chapter 10, some creative reforms have enlivened public education since communism collapsed. The literacy rate is 97 percent for females and close to 100 percent for males, making almost everyone able to read about the poor living conditions in Russia today.[47]

Among the worst situations is a health care system that has disintegrated. Those nostalgic for the days of communism in Russia find fodder for criticism in the present lack of availability of medical facilities and services. But the poor state of public medicine cannot alone account for a startling fact: Russia is the only industrialized country in which a sharp drop in life expectancy has occurred. Studies reveal that for males it fell from sixty-five years in 1980 to fifty-eight years in 1995. U.S. sociologist Murray Feschbach was long accused of hyperbole in his dire reports concerning health care in Russia. Feschbach now feels vindicated by multiple data sources that corroborate his negative assessments.[48] Environmental degradation, pollution, poor diet, rampant smoking, lack of exercise, obesity, alcoholism, criminal violence, and stress from a changing society have created a lethal cocktail for many Russians.

As mentioned in Chapter 10, almost all areas of Russian society suffered because of the nation's economic decline during the 1990s. One CIA report estimates that the economy contracted by a shocking 45 percent in the 1990s.[49] Russia's economy is semi-industrial, with the 2000 GNP per capita at $4,200 and an HDI ranking of 55th (medium-level among countries), down three places from its 1995 HDI.[50] After Boris Yeltsin's erratic tenure as president, economic conditions have improved considerably for many Russian citizens under his successor, Vladimur Putin.

SOCIETY IN TRANSITION When communism fell in 1991, the key question was: Can Russia make a successful transition to Western-style democracy and capitalism? At first, many scholars held optimistic views of Russia's prospects. Some political scientists and sociologists, in particular, marveled at the peaceful changes occurring in Russia and argued that for the first time, this new Russia qualified as a civil society. Accordingly, it was believed that Russia's well-educated urban population would not accept the antiquated ways of a peasant culture. These social scientists generally expressed much more hope for Westernization in Russia than their historian colleagues did.

Many academic historians look to Russia's peasant-dominated past and find little there to predict successful Westernization—although few go as far as Daniel Rancour-Laferriere, whose book *The Slave Soul of Russia* portrays a "butterfly national psyche" caught up in the "slave soul's self-defeating need to suffer." He writes that for 1,000 years, frustration, suffering, and unrealized human potential have characterized Russian culture, and that Russian masochism can be extinguished only by putting its peasant past to rest and progressing beyond it.[51] The dynamics of this issue of whether Russia can modernize successfully amount essentially to a contemporary variation on the age-old "Westernizers versus Slavophiles" theme. Prognosticators might benefit from the words uttered in 1939 by British statesman Winston Churchill concerning Russia: "I cannot forecast to you the action of Russia. It is a riddle wrapped in a mystery inside an enigma."[52]

Brazilian Culture

In some ways, Brazilian macro-culture parallels that of the United States: both are large, ethnically and racially heterogeneous societies that have been successful in forging national identities. In the United States, the ideas of American exceptionalism, America's world leadership, and the English language serve as centripetal forces to offset many centrifugal differences. In the Brazilian melting pot, the Catholic religion, the Portuguese language, racial tolerance, musical traditions, and passion for soccer all perform a similar role. In American scholar Joseph Page's *The Brazilians*, he delves into the subtleties of Brazilian-ness and emphasizes these four values as essential to the Brazilian character: (1) gigantism, (2) spontaneity, (3) tolerance, and (4) cordiality.

BRAZILIAN-NESS: GIGANTISM, SPONTANEITY, TOLERANCE, CORDIALITY Gigantism refers to a penchant for grandiosity and excess. The maxim that "bigger is better" stimulates few rejoinders among Brazilians, and gigantism typifies numerous public projects that proved long on ambition but short on results. The Portuguese term *desenvolvimento* is used in a derogatory way to describe failed pharaonic projects such as a massive hydroelectric project at Itaipu, the outsized dam at Tucuri, the world's largest soccer stadium (200,000 seats) built for the 1950 World Cup, and the carving of the capital city of Brasília out of inhospitable wilderness in 1960.[53] The cost of the Brasília project unleashed an inflationary spiral that wrecked Brazil's economy in the 1970s and 1980s. Brazilian grandiosity also has contributed to the abuse heaped on nature's bounty, not only in the Amazon Basin but also in industrial disasters such as Cubatão, considered the world's most polluted city in the 1960s (see Figure 11.5).[54]

Figure 11.5
While towering over its South American neighbors, Brazil has been described as a culture whose very Brazilian-ness impedes its full potential as a world power.

Source: From Maps on File, by Facts on File, Inc. Copyright © by Facts on File, Inc. Reprinted by permission of Facts on File, Inc.

Anyone who has marveled at the Brazilian-style soccer's gracefulness understands that spontaneity makes up another key element of the national mind-set. Playing the game creatively is almost as important to Brazilians as is winning, and Brazil is the only country to win five World Cups. Hedonism and sensuality are other components of spontaneity among Brazilians. Spontaneity also permeates many of the country's unusual combinations of different spiritual traditions. Brazilians seem bored by the planned lifestyle followed by North Americans and regard spontaneous experiences as more genuinely human.

A laudable history of social tolerance has enabled this heterogeneous nation to welcome immigrants more openly than the United States does. Immigrants come from Europe, the Middle East, and Asia (including the largest Japanese community outside of Japan: 1 million). In Brazil's population, 44 percent are of Portuguese or other European ancestry, 11 percent are black descendants of slaves arriving prior to 1880, 1 percent are indigenous peoples, and 44 percent are racially mixed. As a society with 500 years of experience in racial harmony, Brazil may have useful lessons for Americans to examine.[55] Finally, cordiality is understood by visitors to Brazil as another essential part of the national psyche. "They radiate an irresistible pleasantness, abundant hospitality, and politeness, especially to foreigners."[56]

The capital city of Brasília, carved out of the wilderness in five years, symbolizes Brazilian grandiosity.

However, even a culture's most endearing qualities possess a downside. The slogan commonly heard in Brazil, "Brazil, country of the future—a future that never comes," taps a feeling of unrealized potential. Spontaneity and hedonism, for example, don't foster a work ethic, and Joseph Page writes that "Brazilian-ness has contributed to the current plight of South America's ailing giant."[57]

SOCIOECONOMIC PROFILE No nation in the world has as many Catholics as Brazil, although many blend Catholicism with traditional African beliefs such as Candomble. Catholicism's influence has fostered moderately high fertility rates (2.2 births per woman), and its 175 million people rank it fifth in population in the world, exceeding the rest of South America combined. Fully 29 percent of Brazilians are youngsters under age fifteen, compared with only 15 percent under fifteen in Japan's aging population.[58] A much higher rate of population growth has been brought under control since the mid-1980s without direct governmental programs toward that end.[59]

Overall, Brazil's economy is the ninth largest and appears capable of advancing to a higher level after decades of troublesome high inflation and debt.[60] But distribution-of-wealth trends in Brazil have been toward "the rich getting richer and the poor getting poorer." The World Bank lists Brazil among middle-income countries, but maldistribution leads to 2 percent of its people holding 70 percent of the land and earning more income than the total earned by two-thirds of their fellow citizens. Conversely, the percentage share of income for the poorest 40 percent is only 8 percent, and estimates put chronic malnutrition in the country as affecting one-half of the populace.[61] The HDI similarly reflects weaknesses in the profile of this nation aspiring to regional leadership, ranking it sixty-ninth in quality of life during 2001.[62] Average life expectancy of sixty-three years breaks down to sixty-eight years for women and fifty-nine years for men.

Brazil was a colony of Portugal until gaining independence in 1822, while most of Latin America fell under Spanish colonial rule. Thus, caution should be exercised in using Brazil to typify the Latin American region. However, there are indeed qualities of the broader Latin culture that influence Brazilian life. **Machismo, militarismo, caudillismo,** and **personalismo** represent common cultural patterns in Latin America. These respective images all continue to affect the mental outlook of Brazil's elites as well as its masses.[63]

Machismo ■ A culture of proud and strong male leadership in all institutions

Militarismo ■ A historical legacy of military men as cultural and political heroes

Caudillismo ■ The consolidation of unbridled power in a few hands

Personalismo ■ Paternalistic relationships grounded in feudal agriculture, when the patron took care of his peons

RISK OF DUAL EXTINCTIONS Brazil's leaders have an awesome responsibility of trying to avert two forms of extinction: one we hear debated loudly in the West, and the other barely gets whispered. Emblazoned into Western consciousness is Brazil's stewardship over the world's largest rainforest, including the richest concentration of biodiversity. The other endangered resource—human rather than natural—is Brazil's stewardship over indigenous cultures threatened with extinction. Brazil's government identifies more than 200 indigenous tribes scattered across the globe's grandest jungle. Let's turn to one of those endangered cultures, the hunter-gatherer micro-culture known as the Arara people of the Uriri River basin, located in northern Brazil, near the mouth of the Amazon River. Theoretically, this region was officially protected by the government under the 1988 constitution, but little practical assistance resulted.

Hunter-Gatherer Micro-Cultures
The Arara Tribe of Brazil

The concept of culture contracts to the micro level of subcultures such as the Arara tribe, known to many outsiders as the "jaguar people." Like other indigenous peoples, the nomadic Arara tried for centuries to elude the control of Portuguese colonists and the influences of encroaching civilization. However, in 1950, after repeated efforts to find traces of the Arara tribe, the Brazilian government declared them extinct, seemingly closing the books on another irretrievable culture.

ENCROACHING CIVILIZATION But twenty-nine years later, the news media jumped all over a bizarre story. Three mineral prospectors were killed by wilderness tribesmen, and parts of their bodies were eaten. Arrows used to shoot the prospectors were examined and believed those of the long-lost Arara tribe. Representatives of Brazil's Indian Affairs Agency (FUNAI) were sent to investigate. In 1981, they returned with information about the Arara, including the first films of Arara daily life. The documentary film *The Tribe That Time Forgot* illuminates much about Arara life.[64]

The Arara complained to FUNAI anthropologists about decades of harassment and murder at the hands of whites; they also expressed concern about rapidly disappearing rainforests on which they depend. Only when cornered on an island, with nowhere to flee, did the Arara attack the Caucasian prospectors. Although normally pacific, the Arara believe they have a duty to defend themselves. According to their traditional beliefs, eating the organs of slain enemies will increase Arara strength, and severing foes' heads will prevent their spirits from going to heaven. More than killers, then, the Arara were seen by outsiders as cannibals. The news media squeezed every ounce of drama from this strange story.

But the FUNAI report also revealed a micro-culture notably harmonious and generous, at least within the confines of its own inner logic. The sixty-person Arara tribe can survive as nomadic hunters and gatherers only through cooperation of two types: (1) comity among all tribal members, and (2) oneness with nature's rainforests. The FUNAI team found no evidence of significant internal strife during many months of studying the Arara.

ARARA BELIEFS This cooperative ethic is socialized into tribal members via a powerful myth of atonement that teaches that their greedy ancestors once engaged in selfish behavior, which led to much violence. The gods of the forest, greatly displeased, then imposed a severe punishment—not only on the perpetrators but on their progeny as well. As penance, all tribal members are bound to cooperate unselfishly; also, all Arara ancestors become jaguars after death. To pay respect to the jaguar forever, tribal members paint their bodies with jaguar spots and cause no harm to any jaguar in the rainforest (thus the popular name of "jaguar people").

As in many animist religions, the Arara shaman fills a crucial role, mediating between the tribe and the spirit world, seeking balance and harmony. When animals are killed for food, rituals must be performed to appease the jungle spirits. The tribe also takes on any slain animal's offspring to raise as honored tribal pets. The Arara understand life as a series of exchanges, and they seek a natural balance as they blend into the rainforest, leaving hardly a trace to reveal their presence.

FUNAI REPORT AND FUNAI POLICY CHANGES Members of the FUNAI team were well-educated, and several anthropologists participated in the delegation. The FUNAI group subjected the Arara to unprecedented examination, and its official report helps to countervail the incendiary news reports about cannibalism. FUNAI's conclusions do not condone either killing or cannibalism. Yet these Brazilian officials do appreciate the desperate nature of the Arara's violent acts. An earnest, internally consistent, and somewhat naive set of Arara beliefs comes through in the FUNAI report.[65]

The Arara case led FUNAI in the 1980s to abandon its earlier policy of "assimilation" (many tribes people succumbed to the white man's diseases and vices). Malu Ochoa, head of an NGO called the Pro-Indian Commission, proclaims that "FUNAI's policy now is to protect them, to leave them alone, and it has been quite successful."[66] Nevertheless, in recent years, investigative reporters have filed stories chronicling decades of aggressive intrusion on Indian land by miners and loggers. With intruders ranging from small groups of miners (known as "porknokkers") to giant timber MNCs from Indonesia, Malaysia, and Japan (known as the "Asian invasion"), many incidents of violence against natives have been verified. In 1995, twenty Yanomami Indians were killed by Brazilian gold miners, and loggers looking for mahogany wood invaded the supposedly protected land of the Arara people and intimidated them with automatic rifles.[67]

The Baka Tribe of the Ituri River Forest

CAMEROON A continent and thousands of miles away live the Baka people in southeast Cameroon's rainforest. The Baka are one of relatively few surviving groups of "pygmies," a term used by anthropologists to identify tribes in which full normal growth for an average male is less than 59 inches (4 feet 11 inches). Located on the west coast of equatorial Africa, Cameroon is a sparsely populated nation of 12 million people, 1.1 million of whom live in Yaoundé, the capital city. Oil has recently been found, and exports have increased for timber and some light industry, lifting Cameroon ahead of its neighbors in the poorest region of Sub-Saharan Africa.

The average adult literacy rate is 60 percent, and the average life expectancy is only fifty-six years. GNP per capita is about $2,600, and Cameroon's HDI for quality of life ranks it 125th in 2001, right at the cutoff point between medium and low human development categories globally.[68] Although the Baka people live within Cameroon and are citizens of that country, they have no more identity with Cameroon than the Arara feel toward Brazil. The Arara and the Baka peoples both possess loyalty to their tribal groups of forty to sixty people. No larger social consciousness is relevant to their traditional lifestyles.

BAKA BACKGROUND At one time, the Baka had little contact with other tribes and spent the entire year living as rainforest nomads. Baka pygmies live in bands of 10 to 50 people, and a full tribe numbers as many as 1,000 or more people. Nowadays, the Baka and most other pygmies spend about four months of the dry season building huts outside of the settlements of cultivators, for whom they work as plantation labor. Cultivators generally work harder than do hunter-gatherers and therefore appreciate having hired help. Settled cultivator tribes normally do not have hunting skills and depend on the Baka for meat from the forest (usually antelope, gazelle, and monkey), which the Baka kill using poisoned arrows. Only the Baka know the herbal antidotes for these poisons. Roughly one-third of the Baka diet consists of these meats.[69]

Women gather fruits and vegetables but do not participate in hunting activities. However, in group decision making, women are full partners, and decisions are made in a full group around the fire. Because the Baka are extraordinarily peaceful, they hate and avoid violence. "If a dispute occurs, one of the fixed rules among the Baka is that those who quarrel badly must separate." The worst punishment meted out by the group is banishment, which is tantamount to a death sentence in the jungle if the expellee does not gain admittance to another group.[70]

BAKA–ARARA SIMILARITIES As seminomadic hunter-gatherers, the Baka exhibit many cultural similarities to their Arara counterparts from the Amazon Basin. Most obvious is that the Baka and Arara rely on extended families to organize their small societies. Equally critical to each of these preliterate societies is a deeply held belief in the need for cooperative harmony. Significantly, unlike most industrial societies, the Baka and Arara find it natural to passively blend into nature, rather than actively subjugating it. Also inherent in these cyclical and harmonious cultures is an animistic sense of fearing the spiritually potent natural world around them, resulting in a felt need to appease forest spirits.

In socializing the young into the conventions of their lifestyles, each relies on mythological storytelling, which provides entertainment as well as ethical codes of conduct.

Among the Baka and the Arara, the taking of life—either animal or human—occurs only when deemed necessary by these peoples, who are otherwise reluctant to do so. As in any society, a division of labor leads to differing social roles for various individuals, although these roles are much less specialized than in industrial societies. When the labor of a successful hunt is completed, both cultures hold celebrations with singing, dancing, and intoxicating beverages. The Baka and Arara both live sustainable lives.

BAKA–ARARA DIFFERENCES Nevertheless, at least four major differences exist between these two tribes. The Arara atonement myth, based on their ancestors' sin of greed, imposes a burden of guilt and includes punishment, which the more carefree Baka do not share. Although both tribes are internally pacific, the Arara have a greater proclivity for violence under siege, including ritual cannibalism under extreme pressure from outsiders.

The Arara also take more varied sexual partners. Accordingly, Arara women wear only a type of belt, called an uluri, made from tree bark. Wearing the uluri signals that an Arara woman is not sexually available. This custom makes paternity uncertain in many cases, expanding the role of the extended family, while weakening the immediate family, in child-rearing responsibilities.[71] Finally, although both tribes engage in subsistence hunting and gathering on a seminomadic basis, the Arara supplement these practices with their own horticulture, whereas the Baka do not.[72] As noted earlier with Japan and China, Western observers are capable of emphasizing real similarities or real differences between the Arara and Baka tribes. In addition to social reality having an objective dimension, social reality also has a subjective dimension that we influence through selective perception.

Islamic *Ummah:* Mega-Culture

Some identities even larger than macro-societies serve as the basis for a culture, and Islam is an example of a mega-culture. We examined Islam in Chapter 10 as a world religion, but here we recognize its sociocultural significance on the world stage at a time of efforts toward Islamic renewal. Muslim scholars suggest that all lesser forms of social identity have to fit within the superior identity of the Islamic global community, an "overriding invisible bond which unites all Islamic peoples of the world, the *ummah.*"[73]

Cycles of Islamic Renewal

Part of Islam's renewal has materialized from the ashes of the Cold War. Some Western writers have suggested that the disappearance of Soviet Communism as a psychological enemy has elevated the Islamic world as today's number one threat to Western values. The United States led the anti-Soviet Cold War, and some American opinion leaders have favored a similar role for the United States against Islam. Alarmist voices, however, can be heard in places other than the West. The Indian Hindu writer Anwar Shaikh warns that "Islam is an Arab National Movement which imposes Arabian cultural imperialism on non-Arabs through an unparalleled system of subtlety and sophistication."[74] Historically, Islamic renewals have recurred in broad cycles. The new one,

Located in Jerusalem, the Temple of the Rock is one of Islam's holiest sites.

however, differs from previous ones in two important ways: it is global in scope and multi-centered in organization.[75]

Western Muslim scholar Mir Husain elucidates six world events in recent decades that help to explain why Islam has risen to the forefront of Western awareness: (1) Iran's 1979 Islamic Revolution (spilling over to Pakistan and Sudan); (2) Islam's role in the mayhem of Lebanon's fifteen-year civil war; (3) the religious fervor of the Mujahedin rebels who inflicted 15,000 deaths on the Soviet Red Army, driving it out of Afghanistan in 1988; (4) its role in the 1981 assassination of Egypt's president, Anwar Sadat, in retaliation for his peace agreement with Israel; (5) its being a constant thorn in the side of Israeli-Palestinian relations in the Middle East; and (6) the hostility toward democracy expressed by Islamic factions in Algeria's domestic violence.[76]

The world Muslim population equals that of China—about one-fifth of humanity. The 100 million Muslims in India form the world's largest minority. Muslims represent a majority in fifty countries and a significant minority in sixteen others—mostly on the Asian continent, where Muslims constitute two-thirds of the population, and in Africa, where they make up more than one-quarter. Their locations place Muslim countries in proximity to seven strategic sea routes and to much oil—they possess two-thirds of the world's known reserves. And they represent ten of twelve members of the Organization of Petroleum Exporting Countries (OPEC).

Islam and Politics

One cultural "given" throughout Islamic history has been its fusion of religion and politics. As put by medieval Muslim philosopher Al-Ghazali, "religion and temporal power are twins." Not surprisingly, this confuses many Westerners, socialized under the quite different Christian dictum, "Render unto Caesar the things that are Caesar's, and unto God the things that are God's." In essence, Islam is a "nomocracy," or a system of rule by Divine Law. The Islamic perspective is that "the institutions of rule have a religious character because legitimacy comes from the ultimate ruler: Allah. Since the Prophet is prophet of Allah, principles of rule come directly from the Prophet."[77]

Contrary to the assumptions of many Westerners, the Islamic world contains much diversity. Professors John Esposito and John Voll analyze the unique Islamic experiences in Algeria, Egypt, Iran, Malaysia, Pakistan, and Sudan to argue that Islam is no monolith.[78] Some countries are modernized, others traditional; a few enjoy riches, while many struggle in poverty; some interpret the Koran strictly, others more loosely; some are pro-Western, but a few see the West as the Great Satan; a few are urban, most others are rural. No consistent pattern exists over the legality of selling alcohol, which the Koran forbids consuming, and no single Islamic country stands out as truly representative. Though not a monolith, the Islamic global identity *ummah* symbolizes a genuine mega-culture whose values resonate in the lives of 1 billion Muslims worldwide.

In Chapter 6, we discussed Samuel Huntington's controversial 1993 hypothesis that future international conflicts would derive less from nation-states and more from the clash of larger mega-cultures (civilizations). In a 2003 article in *The Atlantic Monthly*, Islamic Studies scholar Bernard Lewis updates the issue of clashing mega-cultures (Christianity versus Islam) in a post-9/11 milieu. Derived from Lewis' article, "I'm Right, You're Wrong, Go To Hell: Religions and the Meeting of Civilizations," Case Study 11.1 compares and contrasts the evolving relationship between these two largest monotheisms.

Case Study 11.1   "I'm Right, You're Wrong, Go To Hell"

Bernard Lewis, Princeton University Professor Emeritus of Near Eastern Studies, has written several books on Islam. In this article, he notes the commonality for Western modernists to "define ourselves primarily by nationality," with ancillary allegiances (such as religion) subsumed. Since 9/11, however, Lewis identifies a competing perception: "That of religion subdivided into nations, rather than a nation subdivided into religions." Furthermore, at one time, the meaning of the term civilized was intimately bound up with "us," or the way we did things, as opposed to "them," the uncivilized. Gradually, a less ethnocentric sense of civilization emerged, including the observation that all great civilizations rise and fall over time.

In the West, we use two related-but-separate terms: "Christianity" (a religion or system of belief and worship) and "Christendom" (civilization involving not only Christian elements but also non-Christian or even anti-Christian elements). However, when we discuss Islam in English, we use that same word for both its meaning as a religion and its meaning as a civilization, which fosters misunderstanding. One Western scholar tried to coin a new term to refer to the Islamic civilization only, "Islamdom," but failed. In Turkish, for example, no such confusion or ambiguity exists because that language distinguishes between the religion (Islam) and the civilization (Islamiyet).

Lewis describes significant ways in which Islam and Christianity are similar and significant ways in which they differ, and his essay ends with these words: "The clash between these two religiously defined civilizations results not only from their differences but also from their resemblances—and in these there may even be some hope for better future understanding."

He notes that Christianity and Islam are "the two religions that define civilizations," giving them much in common. Each has had its own variations of "triumphalism" (hard-line fundamentalism: "I'm right, you're wrong, go to hell") versus "relativism" (conciliatory tolerance: "I have my god, you have your god, and others have theirs"). Christianity and Islam are also similar in that they both occurred subsequent to Judaism; thus neither of them constitutes an original religion. During the prolonged religious war between them (jihad and/or crusade), a stalemate existed. Nevertheless, Christianity and Islam continued a significant level of communication, "Because the two are basically the same kind of religion. They could argue, debate, and hold disputations." This discourse remained mutually intelligible because they both clearly understood what the other meant by "You are an infidel, and you will burn in hell." Lewis notes that while the two religions' ideas about heaven differ somewhat, their hells seem strikingly similar. Had the enemy consisted of Hindus, Buddhists, or Confucians, such exhortations would have fallen on deaf ears.

From the outset, Christian Europeans had to learn foreign languages to communicate with one another and to understand each other's scriptures. After the seventh century, they had another incentive to look outwards: their holy places were under the control of Muslims, who could grant or not grant visitation rights. However, with Muslim holy places under Arab rule, their scriptures written in Arabic (which across their civilization was the language of government and commerce), they were good to go, or rather good to stay put.

Lewis contends that different civilizational needs largely drove "their attitudes towards each other." Early on, Europeans sought to learn the languages of the Middle East, developed a scholarly body of literature about Islam, and maintained the curiosity to learn more about "the other." However, Islamic civilization lacked comparable incentives, thus "displayed a total lack of interest in Christian civilization."[79] ∎

American Popular Culture: A Mega-Culture?

The Islamic *ummah* represents a mega-culture, but all mega-cultures do not need to be based on religious identity. Some observers have referred to a wholly materialistic form of social identity as a mega-culture: namely, American popular culture. U.S. pop culture is caricatured by critics as shallow commercialism, materialism, competition, individualism, pride, and self-absorption. American pop culture covers the gamut of personal expression and identity from processed food in fast-food restaurants; to rap and/or rock music; to casual clothing in the blue jeans, t-shirt, and ball cap mold; to entertainment technologies such as CDs, DVDs, and iPods; to video games; to Hollywood movies; to violent sports such as football.

As a three-way global hegemon, America ranks as a superpower not only militarily but economically and culturally as well. America has the vast resources that can market globally its movies, pop music, and hamburger restaurants. Its sizable population and the world's largest economy enable flooding American popular culture icons abroad. However, resentment inevitably follows as more traditional cultures feel threatened by the alluring imagery of Americana. Sophisticated film industries exist in many less-powerful countries, but their futures seem tenuous when confronted with Hollywood blockbusters. Critics object strenuously to what they perceive as nothing less than American cultural imperialism.

Digging for Cultural Essences

Intercultural communications specialist L. Robert Kohls has adapted a comparative cultures framework—originally known as the Kluckhohn Model—that has application to our present analysis. It involves five central questions aiming at the essence of any culture's value system, resulting in five cultural orientations:

The Five Questions and Orientations

1. What is the character of innate human nature?
   (human nature orientation)
2. What is the relation of persons to nature?
   (person–nature orientation)
3. What is the temporal focus (time sense) of human life?
   (time orientation)
4. What is the mode of human activity?
   (activity orientation)
5. What is the mode of human relationships?
   (social orientation)[80]

If applied thoughtfully, conceptual frameworks such as the Kohls Model help to describe, analyze, and contrast the essential tendencies of diverse cultures, perhaps leading to new insights and explanations.

The Kohls Model provides a range of three answers to each of the five questions essential to defining any culture. For the human nature orientation, the range includes the views that human nature is (1) basically evil, (2) a mixture of good and bad, or (3) basically good. Likewise, for the person–nature orientation, people are seen as (1) subjugated by nature, (2) in harmony with nature, or (3) masters of nature. With the time orientation, the choices suggest a culture that is (1) past-oriented, (2) present-oriented, or (3) future-oriented. When it comes to the activity orientation, we are looking for an emphasis on (1) being, (2) growing, or (3) doing. Finally, the social orientation can take the form of (1) authoritarian, (2) group-oriented, or (3) individualistic.

How does the Kohls Model (see Table 11.1) facilitate summarizing our comparative analysis of the eight cultures examined here? This table is based on the Kohls Model, derived and adapted from one developed by Kluckhohn and Strodtbeck; it indicates the range of responses to the five orientations.

Perusing these summaries ought to dispel notions of the United States as a cultural archetype. This point comes through poignantly on the social relationships dimension, where only the United States can be classified as individualistic. The only other culture that can be characterized as doing-oriented is Japan. Japan, and to a lesser extent Russia,

Table 11.1

KOHLS MODEL APPLIED TO NINE CULTURES

Orientations of Eight Cultures

	Human Nature	Person Nature	Time	Activity	Social
Japan	mix	master	future	doing	group
China	evil	harmony	past	being	auth
Russia	mix	master	present	being	group
Brazil	mix	master	present	being	mix
Arara	evil	harmony	present	being	group
Baka	good	harmony	present	being	group
United States	good	master	future	doing	indiv
Islamic *Ummah*	evil	master	past	being	auth

defy facile categorization in some orientations—Japan on the time dimension because of the seeming anomaly of an ancient culture of great historical depth blending rather harmoniously with a future-oriented and pragmatic work ethic.

Much more problematic today is Russia's perennial battle between its Westernizers and its Russophiles, a battle in which compromise and moderation often give way to strident militancy. Russia is changing rapidly; it may be heading in the direction of the United States (future-, doing-, and individual-oriented), but it is too early to tell. As small, animistic, hunting-and-gathering societies, the Arara and Baka share a sense of harmony with nature and with their fellows. The Arara atonement myth, however, casts a deep-seated spell of guilt and penance over its members that would appear quite alien to the more optimistic, secure, and carefree members of the Baka tribe.

Cultures: Rough Around the Edges

Cultural identity serves an important function by integrating individuals into groups that become societies. Chaos would seem the likely alternative to structured living in societies. But the very act of psychological identity—creating an "in-group" mentality—makes inevitable the existence of "out-groups." From this reality springs a host of problems. It might seem intuitively that cultures ought to fit as snugly as so many pieces in a jigsaw puzzle. However, cultures are not that neat and smooth. Rough around the edges, they rub up against one another, often producing sparks.

For example, in Denmark, it is common for parents to leave their babies in strollers out in the fresh air while they eat in a restaurant. On a sunny spring day in 1997, Danish citizen Xavier Wardauer and his wife did exactly that—but where they did it was not at home in Denmark but rather in New York City. While they were dining, their infant was picked up by city police, and the parents were ushered into jail, where they spent the next two frantic days. The Wardauers were arrested for child endangerment, an offense punishable by both a fine and jail time. Incredulous, they expressed love for their child, for whom they considered no danger to exist because they did this often at home. New York mayor Rudolph Giuliani defended the actions of the police and refused to intervene on behalf of the Wardauers. With whom do you agree in this clash of cultural values?

Danish parents commonly leave their infants in the sunshine while eating in restaurants.

Ethnocentrism versus Cultural Relativism

Ethnocentrism

So accustomed are people to the circumstances in which we are socialized that we often take them for granted. Anthropologists may possess the clearest understanding of a phenomenon stemming from this comfort level regarding one's own culture: **ethnocentrism.** This self-centered attitude produces a skewed sense of reality rising from the assumption that other cultures are not only different from ours, but inferior. Ethnocentrism has been called "a rigidity in the acceptance of the culturally alike and in the rejection of the culturally unalike,"[81] and the ethnocentric person has been accused of "following the path of least intellectual and psychological resistance." Sociologist Joan Ferrante points out that ethnocentrism can occur at quite harmless levels, such as Hindu vegetarians' considering the eating of beef to be sacrilegious, but it also can appear in more virulent forms, as in cases of **cultural genocide,** such as when Japan tried between 1910 and 1945 to destroy Korean culture.[82]

Cultural Relativism

According to anthropologists such as Carol and Melvin Ember, the best antidote to combat ethnocentrism is **cultural relativism:** "A society's customs and ideas should be described objectively and understood in the context of that society's problems and opportunities."[83] What was described in Chapter 9 as anthropology's holistic perspective

Ethnocentrism ■ Judging the customs of other cultures by one's own culture and concluding that others are inferior

Cultural genocide ■ A concerted effort by one society to destroy the integrity of another society's cultural practices

Cultural relativism ■ The fair-minded attitude that cultures are not better or worse, merely different

suggests that bits of foreign cultures should be considered only in conjunction with their broader milieu rather than piecemeal. Cultural relativism speaks to the scientist in all of us, imploring us to seek objectivity. It also asks us to respect cultural diversity and the right to be different. Anthropologist Dorothy Lee warns particularly against the effects of the ethnocentric myth that humans are necessarily better off in modern rather than traditional cultures.[84]

Each culture makes sense when viewed from inside its private logic. Only when outsiders make value judgments about other cultures do those cultures seem strange. Few concepts in social science are more defensible than cultural relativism. It carries the force of both moral suasion and sound logic. In one sense, cultural relativism symbolizes the societal counterpart to "You do your thing, and I'll do mine"—a quintessentially American aphorism. Conversely, only a rare social scientist would speak kindly of ethnocentrism as a guiding principle.

CHALLENGES FOR CULTURAL RELATIVISM Difficulties arise, however, in translating a vital concept such as cultural relativism from abstract analysis to concrete application. Humans hold deep-seated beliefs, and we often feel like traitors if we find ourselves abandoning them. The obvious moral dilemma arises when our ethical judgments about practices in other cultures come into direct conflict with a desire to adhere open-mindedly to cultural relativism. Is there a way to remain true to our values while respecting other cultures' right to march to the beat of their own drummer? Can we be good social scientists, yet remain true to our ethical moorings?

In a world of diversity, ethical codes vary greatly between societies. Many more examples of the cultural diversity mentioned earlier in this chapter could be cited: the Ik tribe in Africa legitimizes regular wife-beating; single daughters who shame the family by getting pregnant are routinely put to death in Iraq; drunk drivers can share the same fate in Bulgaria; in patriarchal India, ultrasound tests are used to identify female fetuses to be aborted; the Anasazi Amerindians once practiced cannibalism. These practices present serious challenges to the sensibilities of people socialized in Western societies. Similar ethical issues arise in Case Study 11.2, which examines the circumstances surrounding Lydia Oluloro's daughters.

Case Study 11.2   Lydia Oluloro's Day in Court

In 1994, Lydia Oluloro appeared before Judge Kendall Warren in a Portland, Oregon, court of law. A Nigerian by birth, Lydia Oluloro had been married, given birth, and then divorced in the United States. Mrs. Oluloro wanted cultural asylum in the United States for herself and her two young daughters because the U.S. Immigration and Naturalization Service was trying to deport them to Nigeria. She argued that her five-year-old, Lara, and her six-year-old, Shade, would be subjected to a "form of extreme hardship" if deported to Nigeria. The procedure she feared is variously called female circumcision, clitoridectomy, clitoral excision, infibulation, labiadectomy, or female genital mutilation. The words we choose to use matter, and in the case of this ancient ritual, the label we select reveals something about our attitudes.[85]

Commonly practiced in Africa, the Middle East, and Southeast Asia, this quasi-religious ritual has been performed on more than 80 million women, according to estimates by the World Health Organization.[86] The procedure is believed by different groups to reduce sexual desire, to encourage premarital virginity, to enhance female fertility, or to prevent infections of the clitoris.[87] In many cultures, an uncircumcised woman is considered impure and is not permitted to marry. The exact surgical procedure varies greatly by culture. Theoretically, after marriage, the opening is cut wider to permit intercourse, and some cultures leave it up to the husband to do so.

Some African traditionalists contend that this ritual serves as the female counterpart to circumcising adolescent males, and that the development of normal masculinity and femininity depend upon them. It is often thought that failing to do the procedure will result in the person being disinclined toward procreation.[88] A Kenyan anthropologist-turned-president, Jomo Kenyatta, argued that those who condemn female circumcision do so from prejudicial ignorance.[89] Another defender, Somali-born U.S. pediatrician Dr. Asha Mohamud, suggests that Americans should stop interfering in cultural matters that they misunderstand.[90]

Feminists see the practice as grossly violating human rights. Activist Gloria Steinem calls it an "international crime" that the United States would eradicate if it affected men.[91] Columnist Ellen Goodman calls it "child abuse" and claims that 6,000 adolescents in the world suffer through it—daily. Concerning Lydia Oluloro's daughters, Goodman writes: "One and then the other would have her clitoris and labia minor cut out, then be stitched leaving little room for urinating and menstruating—mutilated in the name of tradition."[92]

Back in that Portland courtroom, in the first decision of its type, Judge Warren ruled that forced genital mutilation violates basic human rights; he allowed the Oluloro family to remain in Oregon. Alice Walker's novel, *Possessing the Secret of Joy*, and a spin-off documentary film, *Warrior Marks*, mobilized new critics such as Representative Pat Schroeder (D-CO), who introduced legislation that passed Congress in 1997 outlawing the performing (or arranging) of female circumcision in the United States. ■

OTHER VOICES Other activists advocate different paths to reducing this ritual. One Sierra Leonean lawyer, Melron Nicol-Wilson, conducts grass-roots sensitization clinics using a health approach rather than a human rights approach: "I avoid the cultural rationales for the practice and concentrate on its health risks, creating a more comfortable atmosphere to discuss this highly charged issue." Nicol-Wilson says that the most common belief among villagers is that if circumcision is good enough for boys, it is good enough for girls. His rejoinder points out the far higher incidence of health problems associated with the female variation.[93]

So where does this controversy over female circumcision leave you in balancing one valid concept (cultural relativism) against a conflicting one (global human rights)? Do you believe Westerners should try to change such cultural practices in the world? If so, what types of measures seem most likely to succeed?

Winds of Sociocultural Change

One thing is for sure: sociocultural change occurs. Starting in the 1980s, futurist Alvin Toffler made a career of describing the impact of increasingly rapid change in the postindustrial world. Using the traditional sociological concept of culture shock, Toffler applied it to human difficulties in adapting to the social impact of unprecedented technological change in our lives.[94] Change can occur at any or all of the three levels of human endeavor examined in this textbook: micro, macro, and mega levels.

The impetus for social change can come from within or from without a given society. Cultures do not remain static for long, particularly when they come into contact with outsiders. External stimuli often result in useful adaptations, as with our modern system of numbers. This system did not originate in Europe but rather came to the West from India, by way of scholars in the Arab world. Few scholars would care to make a case for the old Roman numerical system as equal to the current one adapted from the Arabs.[95]

A potent external force stimulating change over the past 500 years has been that of Western society, which has managed to spread its influence to every region of the globe. The winds of change can blow either violently or peacefully. Some indigenous societies— such as the Aztecs discussed in Chapter 10, the Amerindian Sioux, and the African Zulus—were ripped asunder by the colonial sword quickly and bloodily. Other stronger and more resilient cultures, such as the Japanese or Chinese, were able to blend aspects of Western influence into their traditional lifestyles.

LINEAR AND CYCLICAL THEORIES OF CHANGE Sociocultural change may arrive in the guise of abstract ideas such as freedom; or it may appear more concretely through inventions such as the steam engine or the cell phone. Theories trying to explain the nature of sociocultural change approach the issue from two sets of assumptions: (1) change occurs in a linear, evolutionary manner, resulting in an "onward and upward" view of human progress;[96] or (2) change occurs in a cyclical, repetitive manner, resulting in a view of human existence today as fundamentally similar to our past.[97] Do you see either social scientism or social humanism as preferring one or the other of these two sets of assumptions about change?

SIX CAUSES OF CHANGE Tracking down the causes of something as elusive as sociocultural change is problematic. However, social scientists analyze the following six factors as significant. First, ideas and beliefs called ideologies include political values such as monarchy or democracy; religious values such as Islam or Buddhism; and social values such as individualism or collectivism. Ideologies tend to resonate largely in the realm of ideal culture rather than real culture. Second, ecological realities such as climate and geography affect sociocultural change. Changes in the natural environment, such as those at the end of the last Ice Age 11,000 years ago, result in profound alterations in human lifestyles.

Third, technological innovation starts with the processes of discovery and invention by the application of scientific knowledge to human existence. Just think of the endless ancillary changes that have accompanied new technologies such as the printing press, telephone, airplane, or atomic bomb. Fourth, conquest by war may be unrivaled in its spillover effects. Most of recorded human history has seen the presence of wars on the planet, and more than 100 million people were killed in the twentieth-century wars alone. Such massive dislocations produce spasms of change that redefine winners and losers in the game of life.

Fifth, migration has become increasingly important in the modern era, with more than 30 million refugees currently living in countries other than their own. Even a country such as Germany, which historically had taken few immigrants, has experienced a huge influx of more than 1 million Turks.[98] Sixth, social movements—a type of collective action—involve people and groups with similar agendas coming together to intentionally bring about specific kinds of change. The environmental movement in the United States has succeeded in promoting conservation and pollution control measures since its inception in the 1960s.

A form of change that interests anthropologists involves the dwindling number of indigenous cultures struggling to maintain their ancient lifestyles. Among these is an African tribal band whose hunting and gathering ways (like the Baka and Arara) remained stable for thousands of years, but which now finds itself struggling to maintain a semblance of its former identity, as described in Case Study 11.3.

Case Study 11.3   The Fading of the Kalahari !Kung

Formerly known as the Kalahari Bushmen, the nomadic !Kung were the first people to populate southern Africa (See Figure 11.6). Short in stature, nimble, with light-brown skin, they seemed well suited to the Kalahari Desert, where they hunted and foraged for a living in small bands of thirty to forty members. !Kung men hunted more than sixty animal species, while women worked with about a hundred edible plants. These native speakers of Khoisan, like all those of the San group, have a distinctive clicking pattern to their speech. Although they possess no written record, much oral history continues to pass from generation to generation. The !Kung also appear in the annals of other tribal groups and have left a visual legacy in the form of numerous faded cave paintings.

It has been said that while the Zulus epitomize the warrior tradition among southern African tribes, the other end of the spectrum is populated by the philosophical and spiritual !Kung. The outside world got to know the !Kung via South African filmmaker Jamie Uys's hit movie *The Gods Must Be Crazy* (1980). In this strange picture, an errant Coca-Cola bottle falls from an airplane; the Bushmen find the bottle, interpret it as a sign from the gods, and assign one of their

members the task of getting rid of it. One little Coke bottle causes big trouble in the lives of the bewildered foragers.

While most other foraging societies in the region were disappearing during the nineteenth and early twentieth centuries, the !Kung held firmly to the essence of their nomadic way of group sharing. A long-term anthropological study, the Harvard Kalahari Project, begun in 1951 provided considerable data about the process of change within this society. Anthropologists Richard Lee, Irven DeVore, John Yellen, and Lorna Marshall studied the group intensely. Professor Yellen's long-term analysis reveals that, as of the 1950s, they were still almost entirely hunter-gatherers, kept a leaderless group without anyone designated to adjudicate disputes, and remained committed to an unselfish culture of reciprocity.

In the 1960s, many more domesticated goats and cattle were being consumed than previously, and traditional animal-skin clothing was starting to give way to garments from outside; yet men still hunted with poisoned arrows and women still foraged for plants and roots on a daily basis. The 1970s, however, witnessed deeper social changes—marriages with members of the neighboring Bantu tribe, enlisting Bantu chiefs for adjudication, families planting

Figure 11.6
The micro-level culture of the Kalahari !Kung faces an uncertain future because of increased contact with outsiders.

Source: From Maps on File, by Facts on File, Inc. Copyright © by Facts on File, Inc. Reprinted by permission of Facts on File, Inc.

crops and eating domesticated cattle, fewer young boys learning bow-and-arrow hunting skills from their fathers, people hoarding material goods rather than sharing, and more people seeking privacy over traditional social intimacy. What explains such far-reaching changes to a society that was for so long impervious to external forces?

About 60,000 Bushmen still exist in Botswana, Namibia, South Africa, Angola, and Zambia. But a fundamental transformation has occurred among the !Kung in recent decades that imperils their future. According to John Yellen, the shift from a foraging to a mixed form of subsistence occurred not because of external force and not because of the failure of traditional foraging to feed the !Kung adequately.

An uncharacteristic materialism had begun eating away at the basis of !Kung culture: after they experienced regular access to material goods from outside, they began hoarding rather than sharing. Because an attachment to objects was alien to the beliefs of their society, people felt ashamed for not living up to their ideals of unselfishness. As the !Kung felt more embarrassed, they increasingly sought solace in privacy. Burgeoning materialistic values led the !Kung into this unfamiliar territory of cultural change and likely closer to the cultural graveyard. Because many elements of the !Kung story are similar to those described in the film *The Gods Must Be Crazy*, it seems to be an example of life imitating art.[99] ∎

Chapter Synopsis

The concept of culture can contract to include micro-cultures such as the Arara, then expand to incorporate macro-cultures such as Brazil, and can stretch still further to cover mega-cultures with a global reach, as with the Islamic *ummah*. A few macro-cultures, such as the collectivist-oriented cultures of Japan or China, are homogeneous. From the Western perspective, such Oriental cultures seem highly similar, as we notice lifestyles that are ancient, group-oriented, formal, socially responsible, respectful of elders, and abhorring the loss of face. Yet when viewed from within either of these cultures, differences seem more compelling—for example, China's rural populace, authoritarian communist government, less-developed economy, official atheism, Confucian traditionalism, moral Puritanism, rudimentary educational system, and efforts by the government to weaken family loyalties.

Relatively few macro-cultures are as homogeneous as Japan and China. More common are heterogeneous cultures. Russia's thousand-year-old Eurasian culture bursts with paradoxes born of striking diversity. Two philosophies have traditionally vied for dominance in this vast national space: Slavophilism (Russian ways are best) and Westernization (modernity is best). In the postcommunist era, Westernization has gained the ascendancy as Russia struggles after political democracy and an economic free market; but the traditional forces of Slavophilism continue to oppose wholesale Westernization. The Arab world is another region where Westernization remains controversial, and the resurgence of Islamic culture here creates another area with a confluence of strong cultural forces. History, geography, colonialism, religion, and economics have all contributed to a diverse cultural landscape defying Western stereotypes of a monolithic Islamic Middle East.

Culture can also contract to the level of micro-cultures, such as the Baka in Cameroon and the Arara in Brazil. Each relies on extended families, socializes its small society through storytelling, believes deeply in a spirit of social cooperation, blends seamlessly into the natural environment, and seeks to appease animistic forest spirits. As with the case of Japanese and Chinese cultures, it may seem to outsiders that these are remarkably similar hunting and gathering cultures. However, real differences exist: an atonement myth among the Arara people leads to a burden of guilt not present among the carefree Baka; the Arara have a proclivity toward violence when under siege not exhibited by the Baka culture; the Arara take more varied sexual partners than do the Baka, contributing to a wider sense of extended family responsibility; and the Arara supplement their hunting and gathering subsistence with horticultural activities alien to the Baka people.

FOR DIGGING DEEPER

Abuza, Zachary. *Militant Islam in Southeast Asia: Crucible of Terror*. Woodrow Wilson Center, 2003.

Adler, Nanci. *The Gulag Survivor: Beyond the Soviet System*. Transaction Publishers, 2003.

Bova, Russell, ed. *Russia and Western Civilization: Historical and Cultural Encounters*. Mitchell E. Sharp, 2003.

Burns, E. Bradford. *A History of Brazil*. Columbia University Press, 2001.

Chang, Kwang-chih. *Food in Chinese Culture: Anthropological and Historical Perspectives*. Yale University Press, 1977.

Christopher, Robert C. *The Japanese Mind*. Fawcett Columbine, 1984.

Esposito, John L. *Islam and Democracy*. Oxford University Press, 1996.

Ferro, Jennifer. *Russian Foods and Culture*. Rourke Press, 1999.

Fogel, Joshua, A. *The Cultural Dimension of Sino-Japanese Relations*. Mitchell E. Sharp, 1994.

Gordon, Andrew. *A Modern History of Japan*. Oxford University Press, 2003.

Harrison, Lawrence, and Samuel Huntington, eds. *Culture Matters: How Values Shape Human Progress*. Basic Books, 2000.

Hofstede, Gert Jan, and others. *Exploring Culture: Exercises, Stories and Synthetic Cultures*. Intercultural Press, 2003.

Hsu, Francis. *Under the Ancestors' Shadow: Kinship, Personality, and Social Mobility in China*. Stanford University Press, 1971.

Husain, Mir Zohair. *Global Islamic Politics*. HarperCollins, 2000.

Jenkins, Brian Michael. *Countering Al-Qaeda: An Appreciation of the Situation and Suggestions for Strategy*. Rand Corporation, 2002.

Jochim, Christian. *Chinese Religions: A Cultural Perspective*. Prentice Hall, 1986.

Kammen, Michael. *American Culture, American Tastes: Social Change and the 20th Century*. Alfred A. Knopf, 1999.

Kenyatta, Jomo. *Facing Mt. Kenya*. Secker and Warburg, 1953.

Kivelson, Valerie, and Robert Greene, eds. *Orthodox Russia: Belief and Practice Under the Tsars and Beyond*. Penn State University Press, 2003.

Lee, Dorothy. *Valuing the Self: What We Learn from Other Cultures*. Waveland Press, 1999.

Lewis, Richard. *The Cultural Imperative: Global Trends in the 21st Century*. Intercultural Press, 2002.

Molbech, Anette, ed. *The Indigenous World: 2002–2001*. Transaction Publishers, 2002.

Morishima, Michio. *Why Has Japan Succeeded? Western Technology and the Japanese Ethos*. Cambridge University Press, 1991.

Page, Joseph. *The Brazilians*. Addison Wesley, 1995.

Pyle, Kenneth. *The Making of Modern Japan*. Houghton Mifflin, 1996.

Rancour-Laferiere, Daniel. *The Slave Soul of Russia: Moral Masochism and the Cult of Suffering*. New York University Press, 1995.

Roberts, K., and S. C. Clark. *Surviving Post-Communism: Young People in the Former Soviet Union*. Edward Elgar Publishing, 2000.

Schneider, Ronald. *Brazil: Culture and Politics in a New Industrial Powerhouse*. Westview Press, 1996.

Smith, Hedrick. *The New Russians*. Random House, 1990.

———. *The Russians*. Ballantine, 1976.

Tobin, Joseph J., David Wu, and Dana Davidson. *Pre-School in Three Cultures: Japan, China, and the U.S.* Yale University Press, 1993.

U.S. Department of State. *Background Notes: Brazil*. Bureau of Public Affairs, 2007.

INTERNET

Arara Tribe:
http://www.socioambiental.org/pib/epienglish/arara/arara.shtm

Beliefs and Folklore:
http://home.about.com/culture

Bucknell Russian Studies:
http://www.bucknell.edu/x978.xml

Cultural Relativism:
http://www.scu.edu/ethics/publications/iie/v11n1/relativism.html

Cultural Studies Central:
http://www.culturalstudies.net/

The Hermitage Museum:
http://www.hermitagemuseum.org/

Islam in the World:
http://www.islamcpo.com/fazel/islamic.htm

Pygmies:
http://www.pygmies.info

Russian Gulag Online:
http://www.osa.ceu.hu/gulag/index.htm

Social Change Links:
http://www.abacon.com/sociology/soclinks/schange.html

World Factbook: Brazil, China, Japan, Russia:
https://www.cia.gov/library/publications/the-world-factbook

CHAPTER 12

Political Science: Who Gets What, When, and How

CORE OBJECTIVE

To understand political science's infatuation with power as the essence of politics both domestically and internationally.

THEMATIC QUESTIONS

- What is political science's take on cooperation and conflict as aspects of human nature?

- How are the core concepts of politics and government similar, and how do they differ?

- What are some of the key democratic features of the American political system?

- How does the American political system compare with others around the world?

The Stanislavsky Method of acting requires that performers find their way inside the feelings of characters they portray. Applied to the social sciences, this means trying to get behind the eyeballs of each discipline's perceptions. Political science's answer to the question of what matters most is straightforward: **political power.** Political actors may be individuals, NGOs, or larger entities such as states because the competitive process remains similar at the micro, macro, and mega levels.[1] The philosophical guru who helped to shape modern political science's fixation on power as the currency of politics was the Italian Renaissance thinker Niccoló Machiavelli.[2]

Idealists who prefer to think of human interaction as capable of rising above crass realities such as coercion and inequality often find the concept of power distasteful, whereas realists warm up to these notions more easily. Various psychological, biological, and cultural reasons have been offered to account for why some people come to exercise power over others, but no consensus exists. Closely tied to the role of power is its milder alter ego, namely political influence. To better understand power and influence, let's place them into proper context by discussing the pertinent concepts of politics and government.[3]

Politics and Government as Basic Concepts

One fundamental political science distinction is between **politics** and **government.**[4] Politics is a dynamic concept featuring human interaction entailing influence, manipulation, or coercion, whereas government is more of a static concept involving structures that involve predictable ways of doing things.

Political power ■ The ability of A (one actor) to get B (another actor) to behave in a manner in which B would not otherwise behave

Politics ■ Competition for scarce resources in society whereby people and groups attempt to maximize their interests

Government ■ The institutions of political life that involve accepted procedures for accomplishing the functions accorded to them in a society

Whether particular departments in academia call themselves departments of political science or departments of government often reveals the relative emphasis placed on either politics or government. Beginning in the 1960s, a school of thought called the *behaviorism* prioritized the study of human behavior using scientific methods, in sharp opposition to the traditionalists, who continued to concentrate on the bedrock institutions of government. Harvard's Samuel Huntington was one of the leading voices of the traditionalists, whereas behavioralism thrived in most land-grant state universities.[5] Both politics and government help to shape the competition for scarce resources at the heart of political science—as colorfully stated by a leading theorist (Harold Lasswell), who poses the key question as "Who gets what, when, and how?" In a similar vein, Michael Sego, inquires as to "Who gets the cookies?"; and Robert Dahl, who describes it as a matter of comprehending the authoritative allocation of values.

Political Ideologies

Political life is based on the existence of **ideologies**. As ideas in action, ideologies emerge around the edges of a core value such as equality or racial segregation that is shared by a group accepting this value as legitimate.[6] Ideologies serve to simplify the complex world around us and help us make sense of things. Certain ideologies defend the status quo, whereas others blithely attempt to tear down the status quo. Modern political ideologies that defend the status quo are called **conservatism,** and those that seek change for a better society are known as **liberalism.**

The political spectrum is typically used to compare and contrast individuals and groups espousing different ideologies. As suggested in Figure 12.1, the spectrum is usually divided into three sectors: the political center (home turf for moderates), the political left (home turf for liberals), and the political right (home turf for conservatives). The further we move away from the moderate political center and toward the extreme left or the extreme right, the more likely we are to find radical and violent groups willing to act either to bring about significant change (on the political left) or to oppose significant change (on the political right).

Ideologies ■ Doctrines, or beliefs, that provide a basis for collective action in society

Conservatism ■ Political philosophies congenial to preserving traditional values and the old, established order

Liberalism ■ Political philosophies advocating peaceful change rather than revolutionary ideas on one hand and the defense of inherited wealth and power on the other

Politics in Action

Berkeley political scientist Austin Ranney generalizes about what he calls three universal characteristics of the political process, whether local, national, or global in scope:[7]

- *Conflict.* Politics everywhere involve conflict, which is endemic to human existence, not an aberration.
- *Groups.* Political antagonists typically consist of groups rather than individuals. Humans are social beings who join together with others who think similarly when something significant is at stake.
- *Tactics.* To achieve their aims conflicting groups try to exert influence over the workings of government in these ways: lobbying, working inside political parties, mass propaganda, litigation, strikes, nonviolent civil disobedience, and violence.

Ranney also points out, however, that political conflict between competing groups for high-stakes outcomes does not normally amount to trench warfare. As philosopher Thomas Hobbes argued two centuries ago, the alternative to orderly decision making

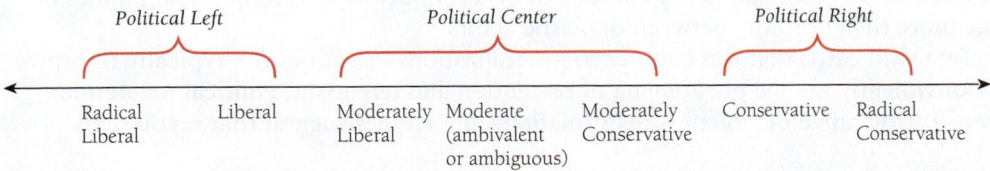

Political Left		Political Center			Political Right	
Radical Liberal	Liberal	Moderately Liberal	Moderate (ambivalent or ambiguous)	Moderately Conservative	Conservative	Radical Conservative

Figure 12.1

The Spectrum of Political Ideology

Case Study 12.1 The Politics of Medical Malpractice Lawsuits

Physicians and lawyers, two groups of well-educated, highly respected, and handsomely paid professionals, have been competing to influence the decisions of state legislatures concerning the proliferation of medical malpractice lawsuits. Most states allow for patients to initiate personal injury lawsuits if they believe that their doctors have failed to deliver accepted standards of medical care.

If they win their cases, patients may also win large awards often amounting to many hundreds of thousands of dollars or even higher in rare cases. In addition, patients in most states are able to initiate such cases on a "contingency fee" basis, meaning that if their lawyer wins the patient's case, a set percentage (often 30 percent or higher) goes to the lawyer, but if they lose the case, then the patient pays no legal fees whatever. This situation provides significant incentives for patients to take their physicians to court but few disincentives to do so. The result was a great increase in the number of medical malpractice cases filed in the 1990s.

The American Medical Association (AMA) represents the interests of physicians in these statehouse legal battles. What the AMA most wants to achieve through political activism is to convince state legislators to pass laws placing ceilings on the amounts juries can award to patients; reducing attorneys' fees; and establishing arbitration procedures intended to resolve grievances prior to formally entering the legal system as a court case. The AMA says that annual premiums have ballooned for physicians, and that in some specialties (such as obstetrics and neurosurgery) doctors pay more than $100,000 a year for insurance coverage. One bumper sticker found on some physicians' vehicles reads: "Feeling sick? See a lawyer," which sums up the feeling among doctors that the rise in malpractice cases is driven more by attorney greed than by genuine cases of malpractice. One difficulty faced by the AMA is that most state legislatures are populated by a disproportionate percentage of lawyers.

With huge outcomes at stake, the attorneys are also well represented in these legal battles. The Association of Trial Lawyers of America (ATLA) contends that all professionals must be held publicly accountable for their mistakes and for the damage done to victims. Anything less would amount to a travesty of justice. Because of the nature of what physicians do, the consequences are major, and, therefore, the relief granted to victims should likewise be significant. Only in this manner will irresponsible medical malpractice be deterred. The ATLA believes that doctors must accept society's means of holding them accountable.

The fact that both of these prestigious professions are affluent and well-educated does not preclude them from coming into direct political conflict when such important stakes are involved. Medical malpractice is one issue about which it is unusual to find many Americans feeling neutral. With which group do you tend to agree, the AMA or the ATLA, and why?[8] ■

---

in society would be an intolerable situation of "chaotic war of every man against every man."[9] The resolution of competing interests functions in many governments according to fairly civil rules of the political game, and Ranney uses a description of the battles waged in many American state legislatures during the 1990s between lawyers and physicians to illustrate the point, as capsulized in Case Study 12.1.

Political scientists identify different levels of political activity. The preceding case involves domestic (local, state, national) politics, which differs in some respects yet is similar in other ways, to the other level, known as international (between countries) politics.[10]

Both domestic and international politics include conflict between people whose interests are incompatible; involve groups actively struggling to get their way; entail issues that are essentially noncumulative (long-term animosities are reduced by shuffling alliances); and involve periodic resorts to violence.[11] Nevertheless, international politics differs from domestic politics in that the actors in international politics exhibit fewer overlapping memberships than do domestic actors (interest groups); the anarchic milieu of international politics lacks a central government; security is a more paramount value in international politics; and the values and beliefs of actors in international politics diverge more than do those between domestic actors.[12]

Political revolution ■ The overthrow of one political system in order to establish another political system

Two wild cards that run counter to generalizations about politics typically transpiring nonviolently are the phenomena of revolution and terrorism. **Political revolution** covers a wide range of violent transformations, but studies suggest that revolutions generally occur at times of rising expectations (when lives are improving); their success is lubricated by governments unresponsive to powerful groups; they are led by radicalized intellectuals; and often overthrowing the old regime is easier that legitimizing a new system that works.[13] Much like revolution, terrorism is a political act beyond the normal rules governing politics, except that it uses random acts of violence or threatened violence as a political strategy. Two decades ago, terrorism expert Paul Johnson provided three insights concerning terrorism. First, terrorists attempt to portray violence as legitimate political behavior. Second, terrorism is used not only by unofficial groups but also indirectly by governments. Third, although democratic governments universally condemn terrorist acts, their openness and limited police resources render them especially vulnerable to attack.[14]

Government

At the very least, governments seek to maintain order, protect individual and/or property rights, afford access to a justice system, and provide some vision of a common good. The institution of government represents one of the cultural universals because we find means of authoritative decision making in all cultures. From the Inuit Eskimos in the Canadian Arctic, to the Baka pygmies in Cameroon, to the Arara native Indians in Brazil, some form of legitimized authority exists. And the functions of government can be more specifically distinguished from other types of social institutions. In general, governments in places such as Japan, Russia, France, Canada, and the United States differ from nongovernmental organizations (NGOs) in the following ways:[15]

- *Comprehensive authority.* Rules and regulations set by government apply to all members of the society.
- *Involuntary membership.* Concerning most other social institutions, membership is a matter of choice, but membership in the state that is run by government is not.
- *Authoritative rules.* Codes of behavior set by private organizations may conflict with codes of other groups without automatic resolution, but with government, the means of conflict resolution are mandated.
- *Overwhelming force.* Only government entails a legitimate monopoly over coercion as the guarantor of social order.
- *Highest stakes.* The features of government listed previously mean that political stakes are among the highest stakes for which groups compete.

Classifying Governments

Some governments clearly realize these aims more capably than others, and the type of government affects its likelihood of success. The fundamental distinction in classifying types of governments involves the question of how power is distributed—in a *concentrated* manner or in a *diffuse* manner. **Democracies** distribute power diffusely and have spread around the world in the past 200 years, especially during the past three decades; today most of the powerful and affluent countries in the world qualify as democracies.

Democracies

There are no pure democracies in which all citizens participate directly in the decisions that order their public affairs. In an imperfect world, indirect democracy is considered more than acceptable. Indirect democracy means that someone represents our interests—and that someone may be an elected official, a political party, or a naturally existing group. Someone, somewhere, somehow must speak for us in order for indirect democracy to exist. Democracies safeguard their citizens' **civil liberties** as well as their **civil rights.**

Democracies ■ Governments based on formal or informal constitutions that protect citizens' rights and enable regular free elections

Civil liberties ■ Protecting individual citizens from governmental infringement on basic political freedoms such as assembly, petition, speech, and religion

Civil rights ■ The equal protection of freedoms such as equal voting rights, equal housing access, and equal employment opportunities for different groups within a society

Political scientists agree upon four principles as vital to a working definition of the concept of democracy:[16]

- *Popular sovereignty.* The ultimate decision-making authority rests with the people generally rather than with some segment of the people.
- *Political equality.* Sometimes expressed according to the formula, "one person, one vote," this means that citizens have an opportunity to participate politically in some way.
- *Popular consultation.* Officeholders must communicate with and remain responsive to the expressed wishes of the electorate.
- *Majority rule.* When significant disagreement exists on political issues, the government acts according to the wishes of the majority, while safeguarding basic minority rights.

The two main real-world models of democracy consist of the *parliamentary form* (epitomized by the United Kingdom), featuring a fusion of accountable governmental powers in one institution called the cabinet; and the *presidential form* (represented by the United States), in which democracy is sought by dividing up power between different governmental institutions: legislative (rule-making), executive (rule-administering), and judicial (rule-adjudicating). Both strategies, parliamentary and presidential, have established their bona fides as viable democratic systems. Some countries, such as France and Germany, possess democracies that blend the principles and practices of the parliamentary and presidential models. Europe, North America, Latin America, the former Soviet Union, and some parts of Asia can all be cited for the prevalence of democratic governments found in those regions today. Democracies ensure a voice for the people in some way, shape, or form. Typically that form consists of regular and free elections to hold elites accountable.

Dictatorships

Dictatorship ▪ Rule by a dominant strongman or clique; the antithesis of democratic rule

Traditionally, however, **dictatorship** was the prevalent form of government right up until the twentieth century. Dictatorship distributes power in a concentrated manner and is broken down into two variants, classified according to the level of control that the government exercises over society in general. *Authoritarian* governments are basically status quo–oriented and want to maintain the privileged status of a wealthy ruling class. Therefore, authoritarian governments have no ideological agenda to radically restructure society through mass mobilization.

Early human societies were small and uncomplicated, which facilitated the development of a form of dictatorship known as a *monarchy*—that is, a government ruled by a king or a queen passing along to a royal family the inherited right to rule. Many examples of authoritarian governments remain in Africa, the Middle East, and parts of Asia, and more than a few of them are monarchies. In sharp contrast, the twentieth century witnessed the rise of a virulent type of dictatorship known as *totalitarian* government.

Fascism found its most frightening expression in Adolf Hitler's Germany from 1933–45.

Totalitarian governments are led by a select political party that uses terror and the mass media to seek some radical restructuring of society according to an official ideology.[17] As its name suggests, totalitarian governments seek total control over their subjects. Best known in this category were the communist regimes in the former Soviet Union and eastern Europe, China and the other three communist countries still operating in a totalitarian fashion in 2007, and the fascist (national socialist) regimes that controlled Germany and Japan during the 1930s and 1940s. The track record of totalitarian governments suggests that they are far more dangerous to their neighbors' health and security than are authoritarian regimes.

American Government and Politics

Limited Government

Memories of repressive European governments were fresh in the framers' minds when they crafted the U.S. Constitution; thus, they were intent on delivering limited government to the shores of the New World. Constitutions represent serious business, and the infrequency with which America's has been amended testifies to the care with which it was drafted. The strategies devised by the founding fathers toward this end of controlling governmental power were ingenious.

Foremost is the principle of **federalism,** whereby the states were made independent of the national government in some respects. Power has clearly tilted in the direction of the U.S. national government at the expense of the states during the past two centuries. Yet, the framers succeeded in establishing a system far closer to the federal model they sought to emulate than to either of the other models of government: the unitary (centralized) authority of Great Britain from whence they came, or the confederate (decentralized) authority that embodied the Articles of Confederation in the United States from 1781 to 1787.

The Constitution provides that the national government has sole responsibility for certain tasks such as treaty-making, coining money, taxing imports and exports, and engaging in wars. Conversely, the states are accorded those residual powers not specifically delegated to the U.S. government nor prohibited by the Constitution to the states. Important among these have been the areas of social welfare, education, and police power. All local government derives its authority from the states.

Next comes the constitutional principle of the **separation of powers,** which is intended to prevent governmental tyranny by splitting power between three separate branches of the national government. Although tyranny is combated here by dividing power structurally, it is also combated functionally by a system of checks and balances enabling each branch to share power in ways that enable accountability through interdependence.

The office of the presidency heads the executive branch, allowing one individual clear authority to operate that branch. The president holds office for a four-year term after being elected by the American public (not by the legislature as in the parliamentary system) and is accorded impressive powers. For example, the president serves as chief foreign-policy–maker, commander-in-chief of the armed forces, political party leader, and the principal source of most legislation sent to the Congress for deliberation. As the power of the national government has steadily increased, so has the power of the president, who heads the most proactive branch of government.

The branch of government intended to be closest to the people was the legislature. The U.S. Congress is bicameral, and the 435 members of its lower body, the House of Representatives, represent narrow districts after election for two-year terms. The more prestigious Senate contains two senators per state who represent broader, statewide constituencies and have more job security because they are elected once every six years. The committee system rules in the U.S. Congress, and the way legislators rise to powerful positions as chairs of the standing committees is via the seniority system. This system rewards legislators from safe (noncompetitive) districts, who often become very old while holding these key positions. Although each committee chair is powerful in a given area of expertise, that power is shared with many other congressional leaders, precluding the kind of monopoly of authority that the president exercises over the executive branch.

The U.S. legal system includes parallel levels of both state and federal courts, although the jurisdictions relate to different kinds of disputes. Cases arising from state constitutions and from state legislation go to the state court system. National courts have jurisdiction over cases arising from the U.S. Constitution, statutes and treaties of the United States, conflicts between states, and issues of maritime law. The national (federal) court system includes three levels: ninety-four District Courts at the bottom rung; twelve Courts of Appeal above them; and at the apex, a U.S. Supreme Court, which mostly hears cases appealed from the lower courts.

Federalism ■ A governmental system wherein significant power is distributed to both the central government and to regional governments

Separation of powers ■ Government in which the legislative function of rule-making, the executive function of rule-enforcing, and the judicial function of rule-adjudication are divided up among three discrete structures

American Political Ideologies

Pragmatism ■ A political philosophy that considers the value of competing ideas and policies on the basis of their practical, tangible consequences

Many Europeans characterize American politics as minimally ideological because Europeans do possess more distinct ideological perspectives and political parties spanning the spectrum. Europeans perceive political **pragmatism** as the prevailing motif on this side of the Atlantic. Pragmatism has deep roots in twentieth-century America, especially in the writings of philosophers William James and John Dewey.[18] However, from the vantage point of American citizens, we have no shortage of intense political battles fought over specific issues in which the protagonists seem driven by ideological beliefs. For example, on an issue such as abortion rights, the positions of many individuals and groups can be predicted according to where they fall on the political spectrum.

Negative liberalism ■ A philosophy that sought to free people from oppression at the hands of unjust political, social, and economic systems

To the left of center we find modern American liberalism, which some scholars call positive liberalism to distinguish it from its antecedent in Europe during the 1700s and 1800s, **negative liberalism.** The term positive liberalism was coined in the 1930s to describe the New Deal programs initiated by President Franklin D. Roosevelt—programs designed to go beyond merely prohibiting infringement on civil liberties, such as those in the First Amendment of the U.S. Constitution, and provide comfort and shelter from life's considerable physical and economic travails during the Great Depression.[19] New Deal liberals believe in the idea of the welfare state in which the government should provide some degree of formal education and medical care as the bare necessities of human dignity.

Modern U.S. liberals also concur that government should maintain a separation between church and state, organized prayer should not be allowed in public schools, women have a right to choose to have an abortion, people should be able to read about and see movies that some others might consider pornographic, people's sexual preference is their own private business, taxes should be progressive (those with higher incomes pay higher percentages), and affirmative action programs are valid. Thus, modern American liberalism favors "considerable governmental intervention in people's economic affairs and minimum intervention in their moral, religious, and intellectual affairs."[20]

To the right of the political spectrum, we find modern American conservatism, which differs somewhat from its European antecedents in the 1700s and 1800s. Traditional conservatism accepted the notion that everyone had a proper place in the social hierarchy of rigid classes that existed for good reason and therefore needed to be guarded against radicals attacking the prevailing order.[21] Franklin Roosevelt's New Deal reshaped the agenda of U.S. conservatism around opposition to FDR's welfare state philosophy. Two related but distinctive emphases have characterized modern conservatism. The first is the economic philosophy first espoused by Adam Smith and modernized by American economists such as Milton Friedman who contend that the choices regarding the extent of government involvement in regulating private businesses range between little and none at all.

The second emphasis is less economic and more ethically oriented. Christian conservatives such as Pat Robertson suggest that government should act to protect traditional American values, stable families, monogamy, and heterosexuality. Government should also oppose abortion, which is an ethical issue, not a political one. Thus modern American conservatives favor "minimum government intervention in people's economic affairs and considerable intervention in their moral, religious, and intellectual affairs."[22]

And just how many Americans consider themselves to be moderates, liberals, and conservatives? Table 12.1 suggests that about one-quarter call themselves moderates, roughly one-fifth say they do not know their ideological proclivity, and among the remainder, at least twice as many consider themselves conservatives as consider themselves liberals. However, race, sex, and political party preference are variables that also affect ideological identity.

Democracy American-Style

Democracy is largely about being heard. In the United States, three major theories try to explain why this country should be considered a democracy. The traditional model says

Table 12.1

IDEOLOGICAL SELF-DESIGNATION (1998) IN THE UNITED STATES (BY PERCENT)

Group	Liberal	Moderate	Conservative	Undecided
U.S. total	15%	27%	36%	22%
Men	15	23	43	22
Women	16	30	29	25
White	15	26	39	20
Afro-American	15	30	14	41
Democrat	27	30	16	27
Republican	5	24	61	10
Independent	6	30	26	38

that democracy exists here because people have a say in public affairs by voting in free and fair elections, and is thus known as the *republican model*. The republican model depends largely on **political parties** to build bridges between citizens and public officials. The United States has a two-party system that is facilitated by the structure of our system and our political values, whereas the structure and values of European systems encourage multiparty systems. The American Democratic Party has since the days of the New Deal been a liberal to moderately liberal party, and the Republican Party has been a conservative to moderately conservative party, as those labels were defined previously.

Fundamental challenges to the republican model in the United States appeared as early as the 1950s and 1960s, when some critical thinkers challenged this traditional theory. Scholars argued that although it sounds good as an abstraction, in practice, the republican model falls short because our electoral units are so large that one person's vote doesn't mean much. Also, most Americans don't vote in most elections, in sharp distinction to European elections, where turnout is consistently higher. Robert Dahl became a leading proponent of our second theory of U.S. democracy, namely *pluralism*, which is very dependent on the role of **interest groups** as conduits of democracy. Dahl maintains that even if the electoral process is short on meaningful expression, fortunately, the naturally existing diverse groups to which Americans belong afford indirect ways for citizens to be heard in politics.[23] Before long, however, thoughtful critics were poking holes in both the republican and pluralist models by calling them extremely naive.

Sociologist C. Wright Mills was the first critic to systematically attack American politics as not only undemocratic but also downright elitist. Mills denounced what he saw as an interlocking conspiracy among governmental, business, and military elites whereby "big business gives money to politicians who vote massive defense spending, and the Generals award the contracts to big business." Laws, subsidies, and tax breaks all favor the rich, whose money makes politicians jump on cue. Mills saw this cozy form of elite bonding as wholly unfair and oblivious to the needs of common citizens, therefore at variance with republican and pluralist theories of democracy.[24]

During the 1960s and 1970s, however, some political scientists were able to square the circle of embracing the analysis of elitism with America as a democracy. Thomas Dye and Harmon Ziegler, in a book called *The Irony of Democracy*, argued that paradoxically the United States functioned as a democracy precisely because of the disproportionate influence of its elites. Their sketch of elites, however, differed fundamentally from that of Mills. Dye and Ziegler cited considerable data to show that while the average American paid lip service to the principles of democracy (such as freedom, equality, justice, and human rights), in reality, Americans' superficial attachment to these abstract concepts faded into meaninglessness as soon as it was tested in the real world.

For example, a research center at the University of Michigan has asked the following question of many citizens at many times: Do you believe in freedom of speech and the First Amendment? Nearly everyone answers "yes" to this. However, other questions

Political parties ■ Organized and legitimate bodies that carry labels of identity and nominate candidates for public office

Unilateralism ■ A competitive policy based on placing national self-interest above cooperation with other states as the foundation for dealing with the world

Interest groups ■ Associations that place pressure on governments to enact policies that those groups favor

appearing later in the survey test their commitment by asking whether a homosexual, a communist, or an anarchist should be allowed to speak in their neighborhood. The majority responds "no." Dye and Ziegler say that given the masses' shallow commitment to the values that make or break a democracy, it is fortuitous that elites are by and large not the money-grubbing conspirators that Mills suggests, but rather, well-educated people grounded in values of civility, tolerance, and open-mindedness. Under circumstances that combine masses that believe they have a voice in politics but don't actually, and elites who have a genuine philosophical commitment to the basic values that undergird the system, an imperfect democracy outlasts its critics. For the most powerful country in the world, being able to look itself in the mirror and believe that it is indeed a democracy is no small matter.

Public Opinion Polls and the Media

Political science is one social science in which number-crunching by both observers and participants occurs routinely. Public opinion polls such as the one cited previously attempt to gauge what citizens are thinking and feeling at any given time. Tons of data are at our fingertips in the Internet age, and scholars and practitioners dip into them freely. Polls are not always right; for example, nearly everyone predicted that Harry S. Truman would lose the 1948 presidential election, but he won it handily. However, methods have improved greatly since Truman shocked the nation. In selecting whom to sample, the two main techniques are called **quota sampling** and **random sampling.** Pollsters point out that public opinion is volatile, shifting abruptly with significant events; however, as time-bound attitudinal snapshots, polls have become increasingly sophisticated over the decades.

Quota sampling ■ Drawing a polling sample to match specific categories existing in the population

Random sampling ■ Drawing a polling sample at random with everyone having an equal chance of inclusion or exclusion

Politicians rely heavily on opinion surveys. President Bill Clinton's critics skewered him in the 1990s for resorting to polls so often that he became more the follower of polls than the leader of the nation. Yet when his popularity dropped very low toward the end of his first term, he turned to pollster Dick Morris, who devised a whole new policy emphasis that later salvaged victory from the jaws of defeat in Clinton's 1996 reelection bid. Does heavy reliance on polling dumb down the policy-making dialogue? If democracy is about giving a voice to the people, then what could be more democratic than polling?

Mass media ■ Modern means of communication reaching extremely wide audiences with their messages quickly and effectively

The role of the **mass media** is another topic that raises tough questions in the conduct of American politics. Some call the journalistic profession at the heart of mass media the Fourth Estate, placing it on a par with the three branches of government. Although the mass media are virtually limitless in scope, they are limited by operating as one-way streets: citizens who choose not to listen to a given message can easily change the station. Powerful television images in the 1960s of American soldiers returning to U.S. soil in body bags taught politicians, the military, and the media the impact that TV news coverage can exert on public opinion. Contemporary media are far more specialized than they were in the 1960s and aim their broadcasts at specific audiences according to variables such as income, education, and age.

In 2002, the ABC network boasted in a regular spot that "More Americans get their news from ABC than anywhere else." They might better serve the public with a preface saying, "for better or for worse," because television coverage tends to be episodic, jumping wildly from one sensational story to another with little follow-up or critical analysis—high glitz, low depth. Television has also raised the cost of political campaigns in the United States to embarrassing levels.

One fact that political scientists have verified is that the trust felt by Americans toward their government dropped precipitously from the 1960s to the 1990s. Some argue that the media's role in demythologizing U.S. presidents by exposing the seamy side of their private lives (such as the sex lives of John F. Kennedy and Bill Clinton) has contributed to this trend. Although the decline in trust has been a persistent one, some observers point to the triple tragedies of the 1970s as responsible for the decade of sharpest decline.

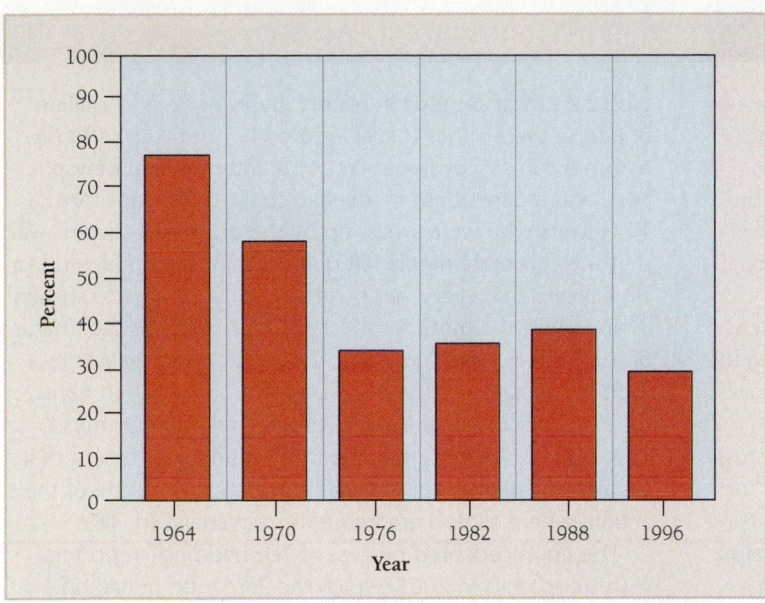

Figure 12.2
Americans' Trust in
Government (1964–1996)

First, there was the debacle of Vietnam, America's only lost war, and the domestic strife it engendered; second, there was the Watergate scandal, which resulted in the unprecedented resignation under pressure of Richard M. Nixon shortly after winning reelection by a landslide; third, there was the double-digit inflation that chewed up the American economy in the 1970s. Taken collectively, these disasters shook America's confidence in itself and engendered mistrust. But the pervasiveness of the mass media in our lives and the image of politicians as little more than poll readers also seems to engender mistrust. For a combination of reasons, Figure 12.2 reflects a pronounced loss of trust in government.

Equally troubling ancillary considerations arise when examining the pronounced diminution of public trust. As pointed out in Chapter 1, merger mania has struck all areas of American corporate life—the news business included. The media are supposed to act as guardians of public trust by engaging in critical thinking, asking the tough questions that hold policy elites responsible for their decisions.

Twenty-five years ago, more than fifty companies controlled America's mass media outlets. By 2006, that number had dwindled to a mere six: Vivendi Universal, AOL Time Warner, Disney, News Corp, Viacom, and Bertelsmann. Are corporate profits trumping the public's need to know when it comes to controversial matters of public policy? As nonelected power brokers beholden to the bottom line and their shareholders, are media elites even less dependable and trustworthy than political elites? Case Study 12.2 chronicles the work of one mass media "dissector" who leads the league in critical thinking skills.

Does the practice of "cross promotion" constitute a conflict of interest violating professional ethics? For example, *Time* magazine ran a cover story on tornadoes (twisters) the same week that Warner Brothers studio released it's hit film, *Twister* (considering that both the film company and the magazine are owned by the same parent firm, Time/Warner). Or, how much credence can be put into NBC television's coverage of any war when its parent company (General Electric) is the world's largest arms manufacturer?

The Politics of Race

We end our discussion of American politics by focusing on the issue that has plagued the United States since its inception: slavery's residual impact on society. How America has dealt with the descendants of African-American slaves is the nation's Achilles heel. The

Case Study 12.2   Dissectorville: Danny Schechter and the "Other" WMD

Media critics such as Danny Schechter argue that the revolving door interlocking directorate of elites in government, MNCs, news media, and the military-industrial complex means that elites who are supposed to be checking up on one another are actually in bed together. Among the chief victims in this bedmates situation is the informed public, which is crucial to both civil society and the practice of democracy. This case study focuses on Danny Schechter as a most curious fellow doing most curious things regarding the American media. Schechter brings thirty years as a journalistic insider and journalistic outsider to critical thinking on the tough questions that are about as popular with elites across the board as poison ivy. Schechter is a former producer for CNN News, ABC News, and 20/20, where he won two National News Emmys, as well as a 2001 Society for Journalistic Excellence in Documentary Journalism award. He also has written many books on journalism.

Schechter leads Globalvison.org, an international media company that for one decade has produced newsmagazines, televised specials, and documentary films. He also serves as editor and blogger-in-chief of MediaChannel.org, a media issues supersite bringing together investigative reporting from hundreds of organizations worldwide, and the largest online media issues network. MediaForDemocracy began in 2004 as a citizens' initiative to monitor mainstream news coverage of U.S. elections. Schechter calls himself the news dissector, and his virtual world of media monitoring and reform resources comes alive via Dissectorville (at *www.newsdissector.com*), with links to all his work. Each of these sites is identified in the Internet section at the end of this chapter.

Danny Schechter's biggest splash in the ocean of corporate media derived from his monitoring of exactly what the mass media were doing in the run up to the 2003 Iraqi War, a time when he "embedded himself in his living room fastidiously tracing the TV coverage on a daily basis." Seemingly the only person in the world trying to monitor precisely what was being reported where and how, he wrote thousands of words daily for MediaChannel.org, later collecting his columns, blogs, and research into a comprehensive book, *Embedded: Weapons of Mass Deception* (Prometheus Books, 2003), and the highly-acclaimed documentary film version of the WMD: Weapons of Mass Deception.

According to Schechter, there were really two simultaneous wars involving WMD: one was fought by armies of soldiers using bombs to protect the world from Saddam Hussein's supposed WMD. The shadow war was fought with cameras, satellites, armies of journalists, and sophisticated propaganda aimed at rationalizing the invasion, rallying public support for a consensual war, and marginalizing dissenters and skeptical souls.

Schechter suggests that "The war coverage sold the war even as it claimed to be just reporting it" (p. 10). The largest global anti-war protests in history involving tens of millions of people were either totally ignored or not taken seriously by American TV coverage. Websites, international newspapers, and independent media had to fill in the gaps for U.S. TV viewers who were swept up by the drumbeat toward war that the corporate media felt quite comfortable marching to. He believes that every war needs a popular theme to sustain it, and while the motif for the 1991 Gulf War was the image of the "video game," in 2003, the motif shifted to war as a "sports spectacle." "The news business is more than happy to oblige because war attracts viewers in large numbers." They also get caught up in the intoxicating excitement of it all, and for many reporters, war represents the scene of the action, where careers are frequently advanced (p. 18).

The unprecedented process of "embedding" reporters with troop units in 2003, which the Pentagon pulled off most adroitly, helped to coopt the news media. No wonder—if Schechter is right when stating "Overseen by 'public affairs specialists' and linked to TV news networks dominated by military experts approved by the Pentagon"— embedding amounted to a neat package (p. 19). Schechter notes that almost no one asked any questions about the genesis or financing of embedding, and if *Milwaukee Magazine* had not done so, it might have taken years to discover that it was the American taxpayer who picked up the hefty costs for the training of media personnel, transportation costs, and necessary equipment (p. 244). Writing in *Army Times,* Gulf War 1 veteran Ralf W. Zimmerman lamented that "We get either a sketchy tabloid report or the Pentagon's edited party line. Both are readily available and mainly strive to entertain the public or to whip up superficial patriotism" (p. 245).

American TV networks saw the war coverage as "their finest hour," giving it nonstop attention with new technologies revealing close-up access via embedded reporters. And not only did viewers in different world regions see different coverages, but so did Americans according to which channel they watched. For example, Fox News unabashedly provided 24/7 jingoism and repetition of the Bush Administration's story line, "attacking competing media outlets and correspondents who deviated in any way from the 'script' they were promoting" (p. 21). Fox gathered large audiences, creating what came to be known as the "Fox Effect," whereby channels such as MSNBC tried to "outfox Fox," who bullied any and all war critics, few as they were. Schechter summarizes a study measuring "frequency of misperception" among viewers relying on six different networks: The highest level of misperception came from Fox viewers (80%), whereas the lowest misperception was found among PBS viewers (23%). The three networks and CNN fell in between these two extremes: CNN 55 percent misperception, NBC 55 percent misperception, ABC 61 percent misperception, and CBS 71 percent misperception. ■

Case Study 12.3 Affirmative Action: Pro or Con?

By the 1970s, it was clear that while the GI Bill (which provided financial assistance enabling World War II veterans to attend college) had succeeded in educating some blacks, their education had not translated into comparable economic opportunities. Thus, liberals began to argue that it was necessary to level the racial playing field through affirmative action programs as an antidote to America's unsavory history of racial discrimination. Liberals also suggested that the idea of a "colorblind" society consisted of empty puffery, necessitating firmer action. Its proponents now contend that affirmative action has worked in measurable ways to improve the lives of many blacks.

Likewise, conservatives, both black and white, counter with criticisms of affirmative action's track record. What was intended as a short-term remedy has become entrenched bureaucratically and intellectually, resulting in a system of racial quotas tantamount to "reverse discrimination." Conservatives ask why whites should be penalized today for the errors of forebears whom they did not even know. They contend that the net effect has been to compromise standards, causing the recipients of affirmative action to wonder whether they really earned admission. Finally, critics say that those blacks who most need assistance, the poor underclass, end up no better off because the benefits accrue to those middle-class blacks who need them least.[25]

The U.S. Supreme Court has suggested that the goals of affirmative action are constitutionally acceptable, but that quotas requiring certain percentages of representation are not. That general principle is not an easy one for lower courts and legislatures to sort out. The Supreme Court has also upheld Proposition 209, passed by California in 1996, which mandates an end to governmental racial preferences. The matter is a very complicated one, and merely noting that liberals tend to favor it while conservatives tend to oppose it merely scratches the surface of the issue. With which side do you agree in the affirmative action debate? Is your self-perception on the liberal-versus-conservative spectrum consistent with the generalization that liberals like this policy and conservatives dislike it? ■

fallout from slavery leaves the United States vulnerable to accusations of hypocrisy regarding violations of its most cherished principles of freedom, justice, equality, and human dignity. America's history of discrimination against blacks is not unique, but its high ideals and superpower status make what happens here resonate globally.[26]

Inability in the nineteenth century to resolve the contentious question of whether slavery should be abolished or maintained made the Civil War (1861–1865) pretty much inevitable. Although that war's outcome resulted in the abolition of slavery, it could do nothing to solve a whole host of problems that survived in its wake. The black civil rights movement fought to gain equal voting rights, access to education, equal housing opportunities, use of public accommodations, and equal employment rights.

For a long time, what the civil rights movement desired was straightforward: a colorblind society providing equal opportunity to compete with whites. More recently, the movement has been split, with the more powerful faction demanding not just equal opportunity but equal results as well. Leaders such as the Reverend Jesse Jackson argue that 300 years of injustice can only be redressed by competitive advantages in the form of "compensatory racial preferences."[27] Only when black representation in colleges, law schools, and medical schools approaches 13 percent (its ratio in U.S. society) can justice be said to be real. This strategy of racial reparations through guaranteed results as opposed to open competition is addressed in Case Study 12.3 and is known as **affirmative action.**[28]

Affirmative action ■ Programs to remedy the negative effects of historical discrimination by increasing the percentage of blacks in desirable socioeconomic positions

Comparative Politics and Government

Political science contains three main content areas: American politics (discussed previously), comparative politics (covered here), and international relations (the subject of Chapter 13). In making the transition between American politics and comparative politics, we should keep the vital concept of *democracy* in mind. It represents the fundamental distinction separating modern governments. The point was made earlier that democracy has been expanding globally and that the most powerful states today have democratic governments. That good news must be tempered, however, with the bad news that the majority of people in the world today still do not enjoy the basic civil liberties and civil rights associated with democratic expression.

Freedom House, a New York City–based NGO, keeps track of the current condition of democracy in every country in the world. Figure 12.3 reveals that as of 2001, according to Freedom House, eighty-six of the world's states, comprising 41 percent of all humans, were classified as "politically free" (providing extensive civil rights and civil liberties). However, another fifty-eight countries, including 24 percent of the world's population, were classified as only "partly free." In the remaining forty-eight nations, home to 35 percent of humanity, governments restricted individual freedoms severely enough to warrant the lowest rating, "not free." Figure 12.3 fills in the blanks concerning the condition of democracy in specific countries and different world regions.

United Kingdom

Because the United States represents one of the models of democracy (presidential), it is important also to examine the United Kingdom, home of the mother of parliamentary systems. This small country is separated from Europe by the English Channel, a geographic fact that has greatly affected its history, providing a stable and peaceful incubator for democracy to develop gradually. A strong centralized government emerged in Great Britain much earlier than it did on the European continent, which enabled unification and a strong national identity to develop. Political stability constitutes the central motif of British history's evolution from a monarchy to a parliamentary democracy. The hub of the U.K. has for many centuries been London, which includes everything Americans associate with their government in Washington, the entertainment industry in Hollywood, plus Wall Street in New York City.

In 1066, William the Conqueror invaded from Normandy and set up a strong monarchy, with a feudal system creating a heredity nobility with special rights and duties vis-à-vis King William. These nobles benefited enormously from their official relationship with the monarch, but they reciprocated by paying taxes to the king, defending the realm from attack, and keeping the peace within their jurisdictions. When disputes arose between different nobles, these were resolved by a council of lords established by the king.

In 1215, the Magna Carta was signed—a formal document that empowered the noble barons to enforce their rights under a feudal contract with the king. After this, even the minor nobility had the right to representation in decisions on matters of taxation that affected them. By 1265, commoners were also given the right to be represented in the discussions of the town council, which came to be known as parliament. These relationships and procedures led gradually to the development of parliamentary government.

By the fifteenth century, during the reign of King Henry V, commoners could elect someone to serve as "speaker" by expressing their views as a petition to the king. Thus, in its early days, the Parliament represented an advisory council to the monarch and an informal sounding board for ideas to be floated. At this time, it was not perceived as a check against the power of the king. But over time, what had been the nobles' right to approve taxes evolved into a right of Parliament to originate all financial bills. Among the various struggles between monarch and Parliament, none was as dramatic as what occurred in 1629, when King Charles I dissolved Parliament and governed tyrannically.

In 1642, however, Oliver Cromwell led a revolution; Charles was beheaded, and Cromwell set up an ephemeral republic. Religion was also involved in the 1650 revolution; because of a doctrinal dispute with the pope, the Anglican Church replaced the Roman Catholic Church as the official religion in Britain. When James II, a Catholic, forced a showdown between himself and Parliament, he was deposed. But rather than abolish the

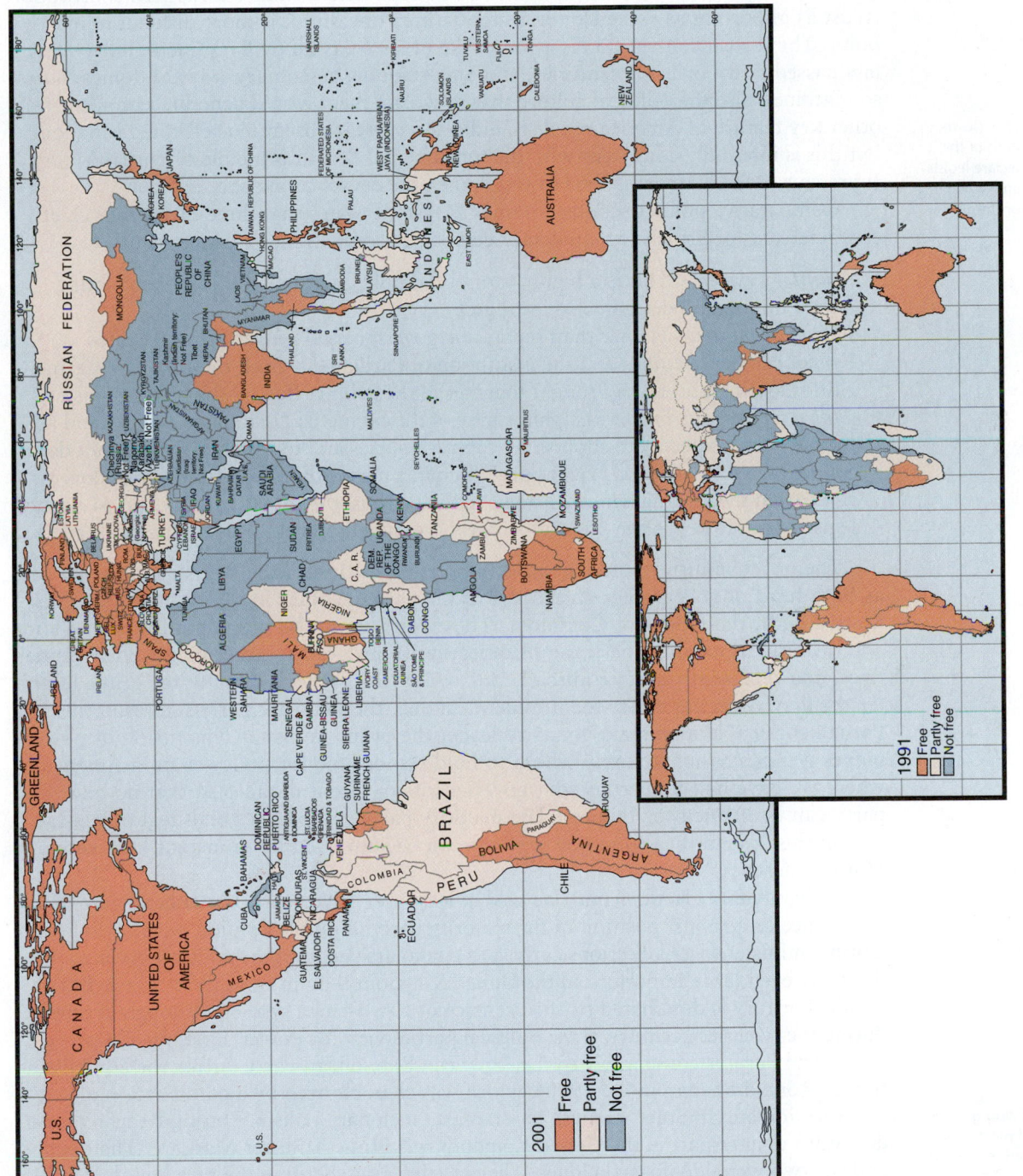

Figure 12.3

Political Freedom in Global Perspective

Source: Courtesy of Freedom House Inc., 2001.

monarchy, Parliament invited the king's Protestant daughter, Mary, and her husband, William, to share the crown. Their acceptance represented a recognition of parliamentary supremacy that no monarch since 1689 has dared to challenge.[29]

One key element of British parliamentary democracy that puzzles Americans is that the United Kingdom is also a constitutional monarchy with no written constitutional document and a monarch who is not involved in politics. Britain's unwritten constitution is just as important as is the United States' written one, but it is more difficult to pinpoint. The British constitution is a composite of laws passed by Parliament, judge-made law passed down over the centuries, and long-standing customary ways of doings things so ingrained into the political culture that to violate them would generate outrage. Another key feature of American system, **judicial review,** is absent in the United Kingdom, but this is internally consistent with the fundamental British principle of parliamentary supremacy: If Parliament is the last word, then the courts cannot be.

Judicial review ■ The power in the U.S. political system of the Supreme Court to declare legislation as unconstitutional when it conflicts with the Constitution

Comparative politics scholar Thomas Magstadt writes that three of the four chief characteristics of British parliamentary democracy seem strange to Americans:

- *A unitary system.* This is a highly centralized polity, with all authority emanating from London and delegated to local units.
- *Fusion of powers.* Rather than separating governmental powers, in the United Kingdom, they are united in the institution of Parliament. Both the rule-making and rule-enforcing duties are brought together in the cabinet (led by the prime minister).
- *Collective responsibility.* The philosophy of the cabinet is "united we stand," and all members are expected to support all cabinet policies and to resign if they cannot do so.
- *Strong two-party system.* Tight party discipline means that back-benchers seldom stray from their parliamentary leaders' policies; thus, the majority party can pass much legislation. However, the opposition party is entitled to grill the ruling party's leaders.

The prime minister holds the most powerful position in the British system, serving as both head of government and leader of the parliamentary majority in the main legislative body, the House of Commons. These roles allow the prime minister to appoint and dismiss cabinet members, establish legislative programs, direct major policy initiatives, and represent the state abroad. U.K. voters do not vote directly for prime minister the way Americans vote for president. Rather, the majority party's votes in the Parliament enable it to make its party leader the prime minister. This fusion of power makes it much easier to know whom to hold responsible for policy than in America, where we have had numerous split governments in recent decades so that no one party can be blamed for failures. The majority party can pass a great deal of legislation in this system, but its majority status can be subverted in an instant by a **vote of no confidence.**[30]

Vote of no confidence ■ The failure of a major policy of the prime minister to be approved in the House of Commons, resulting in new elections being called

Parliamentary elections must be held at least every five years, but either a vote of no confidence or a robust position of the majority party in public opinion polls often leads a prime minister to call elections early. Some scholars suggest that political polling is therefore even more important in the United Kingdom than in the United States. British political history is dominated by the presence of a two-party system, although at times during the twentieth century, three political parties vied for power. First, the Conservative (Tory) Party is comparable to the American Republican Party during the administration of Ronald Reagan in the 1980s, which was characterized by a combination of **privatization** and military strength based on staunch nationalism. During Reagan's presidency, his counterpart in the United Kingdom was Prime Minister Margaret Thatcher, and the two were ideological clones. The assertive Thatcher had the rare honor of leading the Conservatives to three straight election victories and held power until 1990, when she was replaced by a far milder party leader in John Major.[31]

Privatization ■ Ending governmental ownership of most major industries, and instead relying on laissez-faire principles of market competition

Second, the Labour Party is made up of the kind of disparate amalgam represented by the Democratic Party in the United States. Both initially grew out of labor unions and saw themselves as the party of the working class. However, the British Labour Party developed a socialist agenda typical of many European countries but alien to the American experience. An important force in British politics for most of the twentieth century, the Labour Party nearly destroyed itself during the 1980s and 1990s when it split into two factions. The left-wing faction gained the ascendancy and pushed radical policies such as *withdrawal from the European Union.*

The question of how deeply Britain wants to embed itself in the European Union has divided the country at each major juncture of integration. In the 1980s, a minority of moderate Labourites opposed the withdrawal initiative and formed a new Social Democratic Party closer to the center of the political spectrum than the radical Labourites. Just as it took a Reagan-like Margaret Thatcher to revitalize the Conservative Party in the 1980s, it took the emergence of a Clinton-like moderate, a market-friendly, youthful leader named Tony Blair, to later revitalize the British Labour Party. Blair was strikingly similar to his alter ego across the Atlantic, Bill Clinton, who branded himself a "New Democrat" (favoring pragmatism, market economics, and free trade) much like Blair, who labeled himself a "New Labourite," while initially pursuing a philosophy similar to Clinton's.[32]

Russian Politics

Quasi-democracy has spread in recent decades to new locations. One of these is Russia, where the process has been far from pretty. The seeds of democracy have had a difficult time growing in Russia's hardscrabble political culture. Although both Germany and Japan quickly developed successful democracies after their defeat in World War II, those political achievements were bolstered by an economic miracle that greased the skids for democracy (including massive U.S. aid).

When Vladimir Putin assumed power in 2000, Russia watchers were hoping that he would rule more efficiently than his predecessor.

Conversely, after the Soviet Union collapsed in 1991, Russia turned into an economic basket case, and really did not make steady economic progress until Vladimir Putin replaced Boris Yeltsin in 2000. First under Gorbachev and then under Yeltsin, Russia chose to pursue political democracy and economic capitalism simultaneously, which complicated matters considerably. Yeltsin was really not up to the task, and at the end of his presidency, his approval ratings fell to the single digits. Putin, however, was able to restore both order and economic growth and therefore the Russian people accepted many undemocratic practices that he instituted.

One problem is the absence of any semblance of democratic expression on the part of its citizens in Russia's history. From 1603 to 1917, the Romanov dynasty totally dominated Russian politics in one of the world's most rigid monarchies, known as Tsarism (after "Caesarism") to demonstrate its absolutism. Then for seventy-four years, Russia was ruled by an equally brutal communist government under the Soviet Union. The two leaders who constructed the character of Soviet Communism, Vladimir Lenin and Joseph Stalin, used the Communist Party (CP) as the "vanguard of the proletariat," and its tentacles reached into every aspect of Soviet life. This was dictatorship by an elite political party that crushed all opposition—both real and imagined. But because its leaders did not obtain legitimacy via free or fair elections, the CP needed some other vehicle to justify its monopoly of power. They found just what they needed in their adaptations of the socialist theories of Karl Marx, with his claims to have discovered immutable laws of "scientific socialism." The CP of Lenin, Stalin, and their successors used Marxist socialism as a secular religion to give their bloody regime a veneer of legitimacy.

The CP fabricated a fig-leaf system of meaningless elections in which only the official party candidate was on the ballot; the CP created governmental bodies that looked good on the surface, but were perfunctory in nature and dominated by the CP at every level; the CP also used terror, centralized authority, a monopoly over communications media, and a bureaucratized society to pull every last string. The CP created an elaborate hoax known as a "Potemkin village." In eighteenth-century Russia, Tsarina Catherine the Great ruled imperially, and her favorite advisor was Prince Grigory Potemkin, who contrived idyllic villages in the countryside to impress the tsarina as she rode past. These false fronts involved elaborate ruses to convince Catherine that conditions in rural Russia were far better than what really existed. Similarly, throughout the twentieth century, the

CP created the elaborate fantasy that because elections were held and government institutions existed, the Soviet Union was a democracy.

Joseph Stalin pulled the levers of power from the late 1920s until his death in 1953. Within three years, his successor, Nikita Khrushchev, had begun the formidable task of "de-Stalinization," or trying to exorcise the ghost of Stalin from Russian society. By the 1980s, the Soviet economy, still based on Stalinist principles of central planning and cradle-to-grave welfare benefits, was in very bad shape. Karl Marx's economic theories were dead wrong, and nowhere was that more apparent than in the Soviet Union. Into this formidable challenge stepped a formidable leader, the best-educated, most youthful, and politically flexible ever to emerge from the ranks of the CP. Mikhail Gorbachev set out to reform Soviet socialism, not to bury it, but his reforms ultimately hastened its demise.

The Gorbachev reforms can be broken down into three main parts: *perestroika* (restructuring of the moribund Soviet economy), *demokratizatsia* (democratization of the autocratic political system), and *glasnost* (openness, or transparency, regarding Soviet history, literature, and culture). It was *perestroika* that kept Gorbachev awake nights, and that was where his initial reforms focused in 1986, when he issued a list of thirty-eight changes to be introduced by 1990. Exactly how did Gorbachev seek to increase economic productivity? Through providing financial incentives, allowing individuals to moonlight for extra cash, loosening the ban on small private business ventures, decentralizing the management of 37,000 state-owned industries, allowing Soviet firms to deal directly with foreign companies rather than through the maze of red tape, facilitating joint ventures with foreign firms, and signaling that the regime was no longer hostile to the idea of private property. In 1988, a Law on Cooperative Enterprises allowed citizens to sell consumer goods for a profit at free-market prices, and thousands of new businesses sprang up overnight.

Viewed in the context of Soviet history, these were earth-shattering reforms that scared the devil out of mid-level CP bureaucrats, who had enjoyed a comfortable existence under communism. Along with other conservative forces in the military and the KGB (secret police), they bitterly opposed Gorbachev's initiatives as "too much, too fast." And to Gorbachev's surprise and chagrin, the late 1980s witnessed continued decline in the Soviet economy. His reforms, seen as too revolutionary by defenders of the status quo, were seen as ambivalent, halting, halfway measures by Western economists, who predicted they would fail. Gorbachev had managed to disrupt the centrally planned economy without establishing the conditions for a genuine market system to replace it.

Unable to deliver much economically, Gorbachev then tried to generate support for his efforts through *demokratizatsia* and *glasnost*. Measures aimed at *demokratizatsia* consisted of holding multi-candidate free elections beginning in 1989. Their novelty in Russia sparked much short-term excitement; I remember seeing citizens transfixed in front of store-front televisions as they watched genuine debate unfold in their newly democratized legislature. This new parliament expressed its own agenda in opposition to that of Gorbachev's CP, most notably demanding that the CP give up its monopoly of power—which it did in 1990, abetting the demise of the Soviet Union in 1991. The years 1987 to 1988 were the heyday of *glasnost,* as unprecedented public candor proved refreshing. Literature, film, art, and music, all long censored by the state, were suddenly unleashed on an astonished public. For example, Boris Pasternak's novel *Dr. Zhivago* and Tenghiz Abuladze's film *Repentance* (an allegory in which the ghost of Stalin continues reappearing as a Soviet nightmare) riveted the populace—at least for a short time. Gorbachev realized that the path of progress required a fundamental change in the social psychology of a nation of people who were unaccustomed to personal freedom. But although this was a necessary condition for modernization, it was not a sufficient one.

An abortive coup attempt by military, KGB, and CP hard-liners in August of 1991 eroded what little remaining support existed for Gorbachev. He was completely outshone during the crisis by an impulsive and courageous Boris Yeltsin, who physically confronted the forces of the coup plotters. By December 1991, the Soviet Union ceased to exist; it devolved into its fifteen independent states. The Russian Federation was the largest and most powerful of the successor states, and Yeltsin had already been elected as its president in

June of 1991. Ironically, Yeltsin had criticized Gorbachev for years for following a zigzagging economic policy, failing to hold the course of free-market reform—and precisely these same shortcomings were to characterize his decade in power (1991–1999). Relatively little progress was made toward a viable market economy during Yeltsin's presidency, but at least a few bright spots can be cited concerning democratization in the 1990s.

Regular competitive elections have become reasonably well established in post-Communist Russia, a new constitution creating governmental institutions was enacted in 1993, a nascent independent court system has been emerging, and a multiplicity of political parties exists. However, while fledgling democratic structures survived Yeltsin's reign, the decade was a disastrous one for the Russian people. Yeltsin instigated a confrontation with a recalcitrant legislature in 1993, and it ended with more than one hundred deaths. He allowed "Klondike capitalism" to develop when his oligarchical cronies fleeced state-owned industries and resources such as oil and gas, which were "privatized" surreptitiously. He operated what historian Nicholas Riasanovsky calls a "pyramid scheme whereby Russia paid for its failure to restructure effectively its economy by seeking ever-new international [IMF] loans to keep the machinery going."[33]

At least, that is, until August 1998. In that month, the financial world collapsed on Yeltsin's Russia, which suffered a financial disaster. Political scientist Steven Fish condemns Yeltsin for setting in motion a *"system of super-presidentialism"* at the expense of a competitive parliament.[34] As a volatile and high-strung person who seemed to rise to the occasion during crises but then disappeared between crises, and as a poorly educated individual for whom economics seemed like a foreign language, Yeltsin was ill-suited to lead Russia in the nineties. Add to this profile severe health problems, including alcoholism, and it seems amazing that Russia's fledgling democracy even survived the 1990s.

The 1993 constitution establishes a federal system, similar to the U.S. The Russian constitution looks good on paper, period. Like the French political system, a directly elected president appoints a cabinet (headed by the prime minister) to run the day-to-day business of the government, which must maintain the confidence of the parliament.

Both systems allow the president to dismiss the prime minister. The Russian president has a veto power over the legislature, which can then override his veto by a two-thirds vote in both houses, and the president can declare a state of emergency and rule by decree (as long as they avoid a two-thirds parliamentary vote to override). The parliament can impeach the president, a process that also involves Russia's Supreme Court and its Constitutional Court. The French system was fashioned during the presidency of General Charles de Gaulle in the 1960s, which was similar to Yeltsin's rule in the 1990s in that both leaders eschewed any direct association with any political party.

In 2002, all eyes were focused on former KGB officer Vladimir Putin, the successor to Yeltsin, who was elected in August 1999. How Putin rose meteorically to power speaks volumes about the wild gyrations of Russian politics. After the dissolution of the Soviet Union, Putin worked for five years under St. Petersburg mayor Anatoli Sobchak as a deputy mayor. When Sobchak lost his reelection bid in 1996, Putin found work in Moscow in Yeltsin's administration until 1998, when he was transferred to serve as director of the FSB (successor to the KGB). Then, in 1999, Yeltsin appointed Putin to the position of prime minister. As one more in a long line of short-term prime ministers, Putin's new position did not strike most analysts as a stepping-stone to the presidency. On December 31, 1999, six months before his term ended, Yeltsin resigned from office and abruptly appointed Putin as acting president until the next election.

Putin took full advantage of the opportunity by using the built-in advantages of incumbency (such as influencing the broadcast media). His style and personality were polar opposites of Yeltsin's—which was crucial because the public had grown quite weary of Yeltsin by this time. For example, Putin took a hands-on approach to prosecuting the war against Chechen rebels aggressively, whereas his predecessor had vacillated a great deal. Finally, he tapped the deep pockets of Yeltsin's rich cronies—the oligarchs.

Putin won the election handily and soon implemented a "vigorous campaign to reassert presidential power" over the three groups he believed had usurped central authority in the

1990s: the local elites out in the provinces, the legislators with whom he felt Yeltsin had compromised too easily, and the oligarchs (from whom he had just received large campaign contributions). The symbolic highlight of the centralization-of-power campaign was the arrest of one of the wealthiest oligarchs, Vladimir Gusinsky—head of NTV television and of a major gasoline firm—for embezzlement.

Most Russians loved this assertive display after Yeltsin's era of ineffectual leadership. U.S. scholar Steven Solnick, however, wondered whether Putin would be able to walk the fine line necessary to "create a central government that is strong enough to keep the country whole, yet limited enough to prevent a return to tyranny."[35] Another specialist in Russian politics points out that "for all his faults, Yeltsin tolerated the development of political opposition as an idea and institution. That is one part of Yeltsin's legacy worth preserving, and a major test of Putin's reforms is whether they will permit a legitimate opposition."[36]

Chinese Politics

An examination of Chinese politics follows logically here because what had been Soviet Communism up until 1991 was essentially still functioning in China as of 2007. When Mao Zedong and his Chinese Communist Party (CCP) won the civil war in 1949, a Soviet-style system was established. Mao ruled arbitrarily and brutally in another nation wholly lacking in democratic traditions. **Maoism** turned Marx's theory of economic determinism on its head by claiming that ideological zeal trumped all other considerations.

Maoism ■ The belief that human will could overcome all material barriers when bold leadership inspired the communist masses to action

Mao's first attempt to catapult China into the future, the Great Leap Forward in 1958, involved truly bizarre policies (such as backyard steel furnaces) that produced only a disastrous stumble backwards for China. By the late 1960s, another harebrained mass mobilization policy known as the Great Proletarian Cultural Revolution resulted in ideological witch hunts that once again left the country writhing in pain as its economy fell further behind the rest of the world. Mao lived as a recluse, rarely bathed or brushed his teeth, and basically lived in a fantasy world. Only after his 1976 death was Mao's totalitarian rule replaced by a more institutionalized authoritarian model in China. As under Soviet Communism, the CCP made and coordinated most public policy, and the governmental bureaucracy administered it.

Post-Mao China was led by Deng Xiaoping, who made a fantastic comeback after having been humiliated and imprisoned under Mao. Deng, not surprisingly, emphasized pragmatic policies rather than ideological conformity. A metaphor that he liked was that whether the cat is black or white does not matter; what matters is how well it catches mice. Deng opened China once again to the outside world, and during the 1980s and 1990s, its economy was one of the world's fastest growing. In the late 1980s, pleas for more free expression were heard in all communist countries, including China. A student democracy movement emerged that there at a spot known as Democracy Wall in Beijing became the focal point for posting political slogans. But in June of 1989, the Chinese leadership did what no other communist country any longer had the stomach to do: they turned military troops on peaceful demonstrators, killing the democracy movement and hundreds of peaceful demonstrators as well.

As of 2006, an unreconstructed CCP dictatorship continued to rule China. The key organs of parallel party and governmental authority are summarized in Table 12.2. This interlocking directorate enables the CCP to control and direct the government at the national level.[37] The main organ of the government in China is the State Council, headed by a premier, who is appointed by the president, but both premier and president are titular positions with no real political power. The key fact of life in Chinese politics continues to be that the governmental structure that parallels the CCP organization remains wholly dependent on the latter for direction.

The National People's Congress is similarly a lame parliament taking its marching orders from the Central Committee of the CCP. Since 1978, much has been made within China of the emergence of a "new legality" stemming from legal codes crafted since that date. Surprisingly, until that year, no actual system of criminal law existed in China.

Table 12.2

INTERLOCKING DIRECTORATE: CCP DIRECTS GOVERNMENT

Head of State: President Hu Jintao

CCP Organs	Government Organs
Executives	Executives
Chairman Jiang Zemin*	Premier Wen Jiabao
Politburo Standing Committee (7 members)	State Council Standing Committee (11 members)
Central Military Commission	Central Military Committee (Jiang Zemin)
Bureaucracy	Bureaucracy
Secretariat	State Council General Office
CCP departments	Government ministries
Judiciary	Judiciary
Discipline Inspection Commission	Supreme People's Court
Mass Membership Bodies	Mass Membership Bodies
Central Committee (344 members)	Congress Standing Committee (155 members)
National Party Congress (2,108 members)	National People's Congress (2,979 members)

Source: Adapted from *Nations and Governments: Comparative Politics in Comparative Perspective* by Thomas Magstadt (Wadsworth, 2006), pp. 308–11.

Even now, China does not possess what we would describe as a judiciary independent of the dominant CCP organs. The legal system favors the state and disfavors the individual accused of a crime, and the consequences of this skewed system can be severe because crimes punishable by death include smuggling, theft, and official corruption.

The conundrum of Chinese politics has caused many Western scholars to compare the relatively successful economic reforms undertaken in recent decades there to the destabilizing *perestroika* unleashed by Gorbachev in the former Soviet Union. The Chinese formula (essentially *perestroika* without *glasnost* or *demokratizatsia*) has resulted in impressive levels of annual economic growth, but its people are still suffering the ignominy of living in a totalitarian political system. On the other hand, while average Russians have failed to see the economic expansion they expected, and the number of people living in poverty has increased, they have a functioning system of free elections, can express themselves as never before in their history, can practice their religious beliefs openly after decades of Soviet repression, have freedom to travel the world over, and can brag about improvements in their revamped educational system. So who is better off, the Russians or the Chinese?

Japanese Politics

China and Japan are both East Asian countries, but their political systems could be located on different planets. For many centuries, Japan's political system consisted of a **shogunate**. It was not until 1853, when U.S. Commodore Matthew Perry's fleet of "black ships" pried open Tokyo harbor, that Japan extended an open door to the West. A decade of turmoil followed Perry's intrusion, and, in 1868, several traditional samurai warriors convinced the Tokugawa shogun to step down and enable the Meiji emperor to return to power. After the Meiji Restoration, Japan began to modernize quickly and sought to fill an Asian power void left by weak governments in Russia and China. In 1889, a bicameral parliament, the Diet, was established by a new constitution. The Diet was viewed as a personal gift from the emperor and had no real power.

In the 1920s, Japan was changed from an agricultural to an industrial society run by combines of samurai warrior families, *zaibatsu,* who had led the modernization drive since the Meiji Restoration. A brief democratic spark was lit in 1925 when universal

Shogunate ■ A feudal government based on heredity wherein political power is exercised by the leader (shogun) of a military clan

male suffrage was introduced along with political parties; however, their impact was minimal, for Emperor Hirohito rose to power the next year, and militarism rose right along with him. In 1931, the Japanese army, without governmental authorization, invaded neighboring Manchurian China. Japan's attack on U.S. forces at Pearl Harbor brought America into the war that Japan lost in 1945. General Douglas MacArthur both defeated Japan and then supervised its reconstruction, which was formalized with a new constitution in 1947. This document combined democratic principles from the British system and the American system. The Japanese emperor continued as a cultural figure with no political power (similar to the system in the United Kingdom). The pacifist nature of the 1947 constitution that renounces war and forbids Japanese forces being sent abroad is quite distinctive. This feature aided Japan's economic recovery because it meant the United States would protect Japan sufficiently for it to devote its resources to economic instead of military development.

Japan's government is parliamentary in nature, with the prime minister serving as the chief executive, selected by the majority party in the parliament (Diet). The office of prime minister looks good on paper but lacks the clout of its British counterpart, largely because in Japan's consensual political culture, the PM must devote much energy to negotiating compromises between competing factions in the majority party. That majority party in Japan for a long time has been the Liberal Democratic Party (LDP). More true to its British progenitor, collective responsibility also reigns in the Japanese cabinet. The bicameral Diet consists of the more powerful House of Representatives (511 members for four-year terms) and the less influential House of Councilors (252 members for six-year terms).[38]

In 1993, the LDP's thirty-eight-year run was broken when a brief coalition of splinter parties forced a vote of no-confidence against the LDP's prime minister, at which time, Japan's first socialist prime minister was chosen. Political problems in the late 1990s were closely tied to major economic woes during a decade that Japan spent largely in recession (while America recovered handsomely). In 1992, Japan's GDP was 60 percent of the U.S GDP, but a decade later, in 2002, it had fallen to 37 percent of the U.S. GDP. It has one of the world's fastest aging populations with almost no immigration to offset a falling birth rate. Many observers believe that while Japan was a major player in the last century, it is not likely to continue that status in this one.

The very political stability that had served Japan so well during its rise to economic superpower status in the previous two decades came back to haunt it in the late 1990s.[39] Long-entrenched, cozy linkages between business and government blocked Japan from undertaking the economic reforms that economists recommended: opening up the mostly closed economy to the world, infusing competition into a monopolistic banking system, reforming misleading accounting practices that hid losses, and lowering the top level of income taxes to allow homegrown wealth to accumulate. None of these measures was politically appealing, but the government of Prime Minister Ryutaro Hashimoto began in 1997 to address some of these reforms. Whether the Japanese political culture can adapt quickly enough to do the right thing economically is an open question.[40]

General Douglas MacArthur skillfully directed Japan's postwar transition to a capitalist democracy.

Brazilian Politics

If Britain is the mother of democracies, Russia a stumbling child, China a cynical octogenarian, and temperamental-but-charming Japan a robust teenager, then Brazil must be the under achiever among democracies—swinging back and forth historically between civilian and military rule. However, there are ways in which Brazil and other Latin American countries share some cultural tendencies with Asian countries. For example, Catholicism and a rigid class system in Latin America facilitate obedience to authority in much the same way as does Confucianism in China and some other parts of Asia.

Ever since Brazil gained independence from Portugal in 1889, the motto emblazoned on the Brazilian flag has been "Ordemo e Progresso" (Order and Progress), which says a lot about Brazilian history and political culture. The values of liberty and equality do not appear on the flag, and their presence in society is also scarce. Faith in a strong government that can deliver both order and progress (development) has typified Brazilian politics. Sometimes that strong state has been an elected civilian one, but almost as often it has been led by military generals who seized power without electoral niceties. But unlike military leaders in many other countries, the Brazilian generals have not followed status quo policies, but rather, they have been modernizers hoping to do a better job of realizing this giant nation's latent economic potential.[41]

It is no mere coincidence that the values of "order and progress" have appeared on Brazil's flag for more than a century.

In the early 1960s, the government of civilian President João Goulart presided over a steep rise in inflation and a moribund economy, so in 1964 the military staged a peaceful coup. Their subsequent policies for the next eighteen years amounted to a revolution from above. They delivered order, although at the expense of serious human rights abuses.[42] The military also delivered progress in the form of development: from 1965 to 1975, the economy averaged 10 percent annual growth, leading many observers to applaud the "economic miracle." However, this short-term expansion resulted from flawed strategies, including overreliance on foreign borrowing, heavy protectionism for 600 state-owned companies, and crash industrialization that virtually abandoned the agricultural sector. Double-digit economic growth in the preceding decade was followed by negative annual growth rates and hyperinflation (averaging 370 percent) in the next decade.[43]

Civilian rule returned to Brazil in 1985, and a new constitution was approved in 1988. Since then, Brazilian politics and economics have both matured more slowly and more responsibly. Brazil's constitutional democracy (as in the United States and Russia) is a federal republic featuring an elected president who towers in many ways over a bicameral legislature, the National Congress. It is the only truly federal system in Latin America, and Brazil's twenty-six states exercise real power in many areas. Its national congress is very similar in structure and function to the U.S. Congress, and there are dual state and national court systems (including a supreme court). The Brazilian president can rule by decree in periods of national emergency, exercise a line-item (partial) veto, and entirely draft the annual budget—powers that American presidents lack.[44]

One rough indicator of Brazil's progress in democratization lies in the emergence of new competitive political parties, of which there are now about one dozen. Electoral reforms undertaken in 1985 abolished the electoral college in favor of direct presidential election, eliminated literacy requirements for voting, and facilitated the creation of new parties. The main moderate parties are the Brazilian Democratic Movement Party (PMDB) and the Party of Brazilian Social Democracy (PSDB), the party of former president Fernando Henrique Cardoso. The top center-right party is the Liberal Front Party (PFL), and further to its right is the pro-business Brazilian Progressive Party (PPB). To the left of center can be found two parties that are both center-left, pro-labor, but non-Marxist—the Worker's Party (PT) and the Democratic Labor Party (PDT). Citizens have plenty of choices, but these recent parties all have shallow roots in Brazilian soil because here, as in all Latin American countries, the traditional political culture has been long on charismatic leadership but short on leadership based on institutions such as political parties.

Fernando Henrique Cardoso brought to the Brazilian presidency a sense of competency and integrity that the Brazilian people had longed for. As a former university professor, finance minister in a previous government, and skillful leader, Cardoso epitomized what the country needs. His two terms witnessed considerable progress economically and democratically, and he certainly left Brazil in far better shape than he had found it. However, it is important for that momentum to continue building, and the key person in the post-Cardoso era became Luiz Inacio Lula da Silva, or Lula for short. His 2002 election to the presidency handed a huge mandate for him personally; however, his left-of-center Worker's Party won nothing like a majority in the parliament (Chamber of Deputies); thus he was forced to fashion a coalition government in order to rule. Coalition governments can be difficult to maintain, and observers are hoping that Lula can emulate some of the considerable advances that Cardoso made for Brazil.

Chapter Synopsis

Each social science has a specific view of what matters most in human affairs. For political scientists, the use of power and influence to obtain scarce resources in conflictual situations is what resonates. Although cooperation represents part of humanity's repertoire, it is the nature of conflict that attracts the attention of political science. This discipline focuses on the dynamic concept of politics to glean insights about the use of power and influence, as well as studying how governmental institutions provide a stable environment for the political process to unfold.

The government of the United States serves as the chief model for presidential democracy in the world today. The American system uses a written constitution to establish limitations on governmental power and features both separation of powers and checks and balances to discourage tyranny. Some of the other key concepts discussed here are federalism, voting, the two-party system, interest groups, public opinion, and judicial review. The complexities of two controversial American political issues—medical malpractice legislation and affirmative action programs—are explored in case studies. Media critic Danny Schechter's examination of coverage leading up to the 2003 Iraq War challenges what he calls collaboration between the mainstream media and the U.S. Pentagon in a context where critical thinking was difficult to locate.

Democracy has been spreading globally in recent decades, and the most powerful countries in the world are currently democracies. However, the majority of people in the world still live under dictatorships. In addition to the American presidential model, the other prototype is the British system of parliamentary democracy. The British model is compared and contrasted with America's political system, as well as with the polities of Russia, China, Japan, and Brazil. All of these are influential countries, but only three are true democracies, two others aspire to that status, and one has refused to risk democratization.

FOR DIGGING DEEPER

Besson, Samantha, ed. *Deliberative Democracy and its Discontents*. Ashgate, 2006.

Bogdonar, Vernon, ed. *Politics and the Constitution: Essays on British Government*. Ashgate, 1996.

Bonnell, Victoria, and George W. Breslauer, eds. *Russia in the New Century: Stability or Disorder?* Westview, 2001.

Brown, Archie, ed. *Contemporary Russian Politics: A Reader*. Oxford University Press, 2001.

Burns, Bradford. *A History of Brazil*. Columbia University Press, 1980.

Chan, Alfred. *Mao's Crusades: Politics and Policy Implementation in China's Great Leap Forward*. Oxford University Press, 2001.

Chang, David Wen-wei. *China under Deng Xiaoping: Political and Economic Reform*. St. Martin's Press, 1991.

Cole, Matt. *Democracy in Britain*. Edinburgh University, 2006.

Colton, Timothy, and Michael McFaul. *Popular Choice and Managed Democracy: The Russian Elections of 1999 and 2000*. Brookings Institution, 2004.

Curtis, Gerald L. *The Logic to Japanese Politics*. Columbia University Press, 2000.

Dahl, Robert. *On Democracy*. Yale University Press, 1999.

Dreyer, June Teufel. *China's Political System: Modernization and Tradition*. AB Longman, 2006.

Domhoff, G. William. *Who Rules America? Power and Politics in the Year 2000*. Mayfield, 2000.

Finifter, Ada, ed. *Political Science: The State of the Discipline*. American Political Science Association, 2002.

Foner, Eric. *The Story of American Freedom*. Norton, 1998.

Font, Mauricio. *Transforming Brazil: A Reform Era in Perspective*. Rowman and Littlefield, 2003.

Freedman, Leonard. *Politics and Policy in Britain*. Addison Wesley Longman, 1996.

Goldman, Marshall. *The Piratization of Russia: Russian Reform Goes Awry*. Routledge, 2003.

Gordon, Andrew. *A Modern History of Japan: From Tokugawa Times to the Present*. Oxford University Press, 2003.

Gray, John. *Liberalism*. University of Minnesota Press, 1986.

Himmelstein, Jerome. *To the Right: The Transformation of American Conservatism*. University of California Press, 1990.

Hobbes, Thomas. *Leviathan (1651)*. Penguin, 1982.

Hrebenar, Ronald. *The Japanese Party System: From One-Party Rule to Coalition Government*. Westview, 1992.

Hunter, Wendy. *Eroding Military Influence in Brazil: Politicians Against Soldiers*. University of North Carolina Press, 1996.

Huskey, Eugene. *Presidential Power in Russia*. Sharpe, 1997.

Ivanov, Igor. *The New Russian Diplomacy*. Brookings Institution, 2002.

Karatnycky, Adrian, ed. *Freedom in the World: The Annual Survey of Political Rights and Civil Liberties, 2003–04*. Transaction Publishers, 2004.

Kuchins, Andrew. *Russia After the Fall*. Carnegie Endowment for International Peace, 2002.

Ladd, Everett Carl, ed. *America at the Polls 1998*. Roper Center for Public Opinion, 1999.

Larson, Stein U. *Theory and Methods in Political Science: First Steps to Synthesize a Discipline*. Columbia University Press, 2006.

Levine, Robert. *Brazilian Legacies*. Sharpe, 1997.

Liang, Zhang, Andrew Nathan, and Perry Link. *The Tiananmen Papers: The Chinese Leadership's Decision to Use Force Against Their Own People*. Perseus Books, 2002.

Lieberthal, Kenneth. *Governing China: From Revolution Through Reform*. W. W. Norton, 1995.

Malone, Daniel, and Yuen Foong Khong, eds. *Unilateralism and U.S. Foreign Policy: International Perspectives*. Center on International Cooperation Studies in Multilateralism, 2003.

Martinez-Lara, Javier. *Building Democracy in Brazil: The Politics of Constitutional Change, 1985–95*. St. Martin's Press, 1996.

McClain, James. *Japan: A Modern History*. Norton, 2001.

McFaul, Michael, Mikolai Petrov, and Andrei Ryabov. *Between Dictatorship and Democracy: Russian Post-Communist Political Reform*. Carnegie Endowment for International Peace, 2004.

Montefiore, Simon Sebag. *Stalin: The Court of the Red Tsar*. Weidenfeld and Nicholson, 2003.

Moynihan, Daniel Patrick. *Scorpion Tongues: Gossip, Celebrity, and American Politics*. Yale University Press, 1998.

Nassar, Jamal R., and Richard J. Payne. *Politics and Culture in the Developing World: The Impact of Globalization.* AB Longman, 2006.

Ndulo, Muna, ed. *Democratic Reform in Africa: The Impact on Governance and Poverty Alleviation.* Oxford University Press, 2006.

Nogee, Joseph. *Russian Politics: The Struggle for a New Order.* Prentice Hall, 1996.

Perry, Elizabeth. *Challenging the Mandate of Heaven: Social Protest and State Power in China.* Sharpe, 2001.

Pinkney, Robert. *Democracy in the Third World.* Lynne Rienner, 2003.

Pye, Lucian. *The Spirit of Chinese Politics.* Harvard University Press, 1992.

Remington, Thomas F. *Politics in Russia.* AB Longman, 2006.

Ross, Cameron, ed. *Russian Politics Under Putin.* Palgrave Press, 2004.

Schechter, Danny. *Embedded: Weapons of Mass Deception: How the Media Failed to Cover the War on Iraq.* Prometheus Books, 2003.

Schedler, Andreas, ed. *Electoral Authoritarianism: The Dynamics of Unfree Competition.* Lynne Rienner, 2006.

Shevtsova, Lila. *Putin's Russia.* Carnegie Endowment for International Peace, 2004.

———. *Yeltsin's Russia: Myths and Realities.* Carnegie Endowment for International Peace, 1999.

Spitzer, Robert. *The Politics of Gun Control.* Chatham House, 2004.

Stewart, John. *The British Empire: An Encyclopedia of the Crown's Holdings, 1493–1995.* McFarland, 1996.

Studlar, Donley. *Great Britain: Decline or Renewal?* Westview, 2002.

Thurston, Robert. *Life and Terror in Stalin's Russia, 1934–1941.* Yale University Press, 1996.

Tocqueville, Alexis de. *Democracy in America (1835).* Doubleday, 1969.

Trenin, Dmitri V. *Getting Russia Right.* Carnegie Endowment for International Peace, 2007.

Vanden Heuvel, William. *The Future of Freedom in Russia.* Templeton Foundation Press, 2000.

Veloso, Caetano. *Tropical Truth: A Story of Music and Revolution in Brazil.* Knopf, 2002.

Waller, Robert. *Almanac of British Politics.* Routledge, 1996.

Watts, Duncan. *British Government and Politics.* Edinburgh University Press, 2006.

White, David. *The Russian Democratic Party Yabloko: Opposition in a Managed Democracy.* Ashgate, 2006.

INTERNET

American Association of Public Opinion Research:
http://www.publicagenda.org

American Civil Liberties Union:
http://www.aclu.org/

Affirmative Action in the United States:
http://aad.english.ucsb.edu/docs/history-aa.html

American Political Science Association (APSA):
http://www.apsa.org

Asia Source:
http://www.asiasource.org/

Brazil:
http://countrystudies.us/brazil/82.htm

Brazilian Politics:
http://www.brazilbrazil.com/politics.html

British House of Commons:
http://www.parliament.uk

Center for the Study of Democracy:
http://www.csd.bg/

Cuban Missile Crisis:
http://www.hyperion.advanced.org/11046/

Classification of Governments:
http://www.cidcm.umd.edu/inscr/polity

Danny Schechter E-mail:
Danny@mediachannel.org

Democracy:
http://www.usinfo.state.gov/products/pub/whatsdem/

Democratic Socialism:
http://www.answers.com/topic/democratic-socialism

Election Resources:
http://www.electionresources.org

Election Statistics in Democracies:
http://www.dodgson.ucsd.edu/lij/

European Government Documents:
http://www.gksoft.com/govt/en/europa.html

Freedom, Democracy, Peace; Power, Democide, and War:
http://www2.hawaii.edu/~rummel/

Freedom House:
http://www.freedomhouse.org/

Government of the Russian Federation:
http://www.constitution.ru/en/10003000-07.htm

Human Rights Internet:
http://www.hri.org

Japanese Studies:
http://etext.lib.virginia.edu/japanese/

Latin American Politics:
http://lanic.utexas.edu/la/region/government/

Media Channel:
http://www.Mediachannel.org

National Election Studies:
http://www.electionstudies.org

Organization of Japanese Central Government:
http://www.jniosh.go.jp/icpro/jicosh-old/english/osh/mhlw/jpgovernment.html

Parliaments Worldwide:
http://www.gksoft.com/govt/

Political Resources:
http://www.politicalresources.net/europe.htm

Project Look Sharp:
http://www.ithaca.edu/looksharp

Russian Studies:
http://www.bucknell.edu/x978.xml

Supreme Court History:
http://www.supremecourthistory.org

Teacher's Guide to WMD the Film:
http://www.ColdType.net

U.S. Congress:
http://www.congress.org

Weapons of Mass Deception (WMD):
http://www.wmdthefilm.com/

Westminster Foundation for Democracy:
http://www.wfd.org/

White House:
http://www.whitehouse.gov

World Democracy Audit:
http://www.worldaudit.org

World Governments:
http://admi.net/world/gov

World Policy:
http://www.worldpolicy.org/globalrights/

CHAPTER 13

The State Challenged by New Actors

CORE OBJECTIVE

To trace the evolution of the state system, its legacy of warfare, and challengers to the state for human loyalties.

THEMATIC QUESTIONS

- How is the contemporary international scene heterogeneous?

- From what origin does the state system spring?

- What is the nature of warfare, and how is it changing?

- How has humanity attempted historically to control the ravages of war?

- What new actors are challenging the state for human loyalties?

Realism versus Idealism

Two broad ideologies, **realism** and **idealism**, underpin most people's views on specific issues of international politics. Personal preferences regarding these alternative views help shape our day-to-day opinions about complex issues arising in the complex world of public affairs. In skeletal form, realism and idealism can be contrasted on these dimensions:[1]

Idealism	Realism
optimistic about human nature	pessimistic about human nature
ethical emphasis	pragmatic emphasis
ideas are powerful	action is powerful
human rights vital to foreign policy	human rights tangential to foreign policy
national interest: doing good	national interest: seeking power
peace through cooperation	peace through strength

These ideological descriptions represent **ideal types.** You are unlikely to fit either category any more perfectly than you would fit the ideologies of liberalism or conservatism in American domestic politics. But this does not prevent ideal types from being useful to political analysis in both domestic and international contexts. Most social humanists lean in the direction of idealism's hopefulness, social conscience, and

Realism ■ Placing a premium on competitive national interest defined as power and suspicious of cooperative endeavors among states

Idealism ■ Believing that human reason can find ways to avert war and promote cooperation by finding common elements uniting all peoples

Ideal types ■ Archetypes or models, used in social science discourse to portray an image of some abstract concept

penchant for subjectivity. More scientistic colleagues, however, feel comfortable with realism's skepticism, action orientation, and objectivity. Yet each perspective has much to offer, and to reject one or the other wholly would destroy the balance essential to interpreting the complexities of international politics.

Traditionally, realism has represented the prevailing outlook, both abroad and in the United States. Idealism has proven resilient, however, and has gained the ascendancy for short periods. The devastation of major wars often encourages pacifistic responses congenial to idealism. In the United States, twentieth-century idealism first flourished under President Woodrow Wilson and into the 1920s following World War I. Its spirit later helped launch the United Nations after World War II, then thrived during Jimmy Carter's late-1970s presidency, and has more recently rebounded after the Cold War's demise and the aggressive policies of President George W. Bush.

Henry Kissinger's Realism

The most authoritative modern proponent of realism, Henry Kissinger, former secretary of state under presidents Richard Nixon and Gerald Ford, contends in his massive tome, *Diplomacy* (1994), that America needs less idealism and more *realpolitik*. According to Kissinger, the United States must define its vital interests conservatively, set clear priorities, and avoid getting bogged down in the ethnic and religious conflicts of the post–Cold War era: "Not every evil can be combated by America, even less by America alone." While recognizing that the world has changed significantly, he suggests that the basic determinants of world order do not change. World order will always spring from the "balancing of competing national interests," says Kissinger.[2]

Woodrow Wilson's Idealism

No comparable spokesperson epitomizes modern idealism. However, the twentieth century's first idealist voice was also its greatest: Woodrow Wilson. He once claimed that "America is the only idealistic nation in the world."[3] "Making the world safe for democracy," in his memorable phrase, demands much of the United States. Wilson strongly favored a world system based on **collective security.**

Collective security ■ The proactive approach to international peace based on a community of states willing to oppose potential aggressors

The first such experiment, the League of Nations, was Wilson's brainchild, but it ended in failure. Its post World War II successor, the United Nations, provided the international community with a viable global forum and benefited from the earlier experience of the League of Nations. Woodrow Wilson also believed that, for global democracy to succeed, the United States needed to support ethnic **self-determination.** This important idea is a logical international extension of the libertarian principles catalyzed by the French and American revolutions. The self-determination of peoples, an eminently laudable principle, often proves difficult to implement, as illustrated during the 1990s in places such as Yugoslavia and Russia.

Self-determination ■ The right of nations to shape their own destinies independently

Equally optimistic was Wilson's belief in an evolving international body of law, whereby states would come to accept universal rules of the game as desirable.[4] Among prominent political scientists recognizing the value of idealism is Charles Kegley, who in his presidential address to the International Studies Association suggested that "classical realism to the contrary, human nature is subject to modification and not permanently governed by an eradicable lust for power."[5]

Nation ■ A sizable group of people identifying with one another because of some perceived ethnic, religious, or racial commonalities

Ill-Fitting Nations and States

The idea of a **nation** is largely a sociological concept. However, often nations possess a political attitude and thus want their sense of identity recognized officially by other similar groups. From the political perspective, the entity ideally suited to mesh with the nation is the **state.** The popular term generally used to identify the state is *country*.

State ■ A political actor possessing sovereignty, territory, population, organization, and recognition from other states

In a perfect world, a distinct nation of people would blend smoothly with a legally recognized state and would exist neatly in a specific physical space. Taken collectively, these hypothetical entities would add up to a world full of **nation–states**. But it is only in relatively rare places such as Japan, France, China, or Poland that we find nation and state fitting snugly together in this ideal manner as **homogeneous** entities.

A Mostly Heterogeneous World

Japan's population is more than 99 percent ethnic Japanese, which is extraordinarily homogeneous for a country with 130 million people. Many nations of people, such as the Kurds, Palestinians, or Chechens, wait desperately for their own territory and representation in world affairs. Such dissatisfied peoples find themselves dispersed throughout countries where they feel like repressed minorities. The 25 million Kurds in places such as Iraq, Iran, and Turkey make up one of the largest such groups. Many Palestinians live as legal aliens in Jordan, Syria, or Egypt. The Chechens in the Caucasus Mountains of southern Russia have been so disgruntled as to fight a civil war against the Russian army. The great majority of states today consist of heterogeneous mixtures, as in Malaysia, the United States, India, Canada, and Brazil.[6]

Mel Gibson's Oscar-winning film *Braveheart* (1995) recounts the crosscurrents of loyalties that beset the movement for Scottish nationalism in the thirteenth century. In it, director Gibson also stars as the steadfast Scottish nationalist William Wallace, who is subjected to humiliation, treachery, torture, and execution for his defiance of an English king intent on subjugating the Scots. Although long identifying themselves as a nation, the Scots have never managed to make it on the world scene as a bona fide state. They have typically had to settle for minority status in a larger union led by an English majority. What, exactly, is the nature of the modern state that was referred to as England up until 1800, then as Britain, and more recently as the United Kingdom (see Figure 13.1)?

Nation–states ■ Sovereign political actor recognized by its peers as responsible for governing a cohesive group of people living on its territory

Homogeneous ■ Unified, cohesive; social groupings are often classified on a continuum from very homogeneous (unified) to very heterogeneous (diversified)

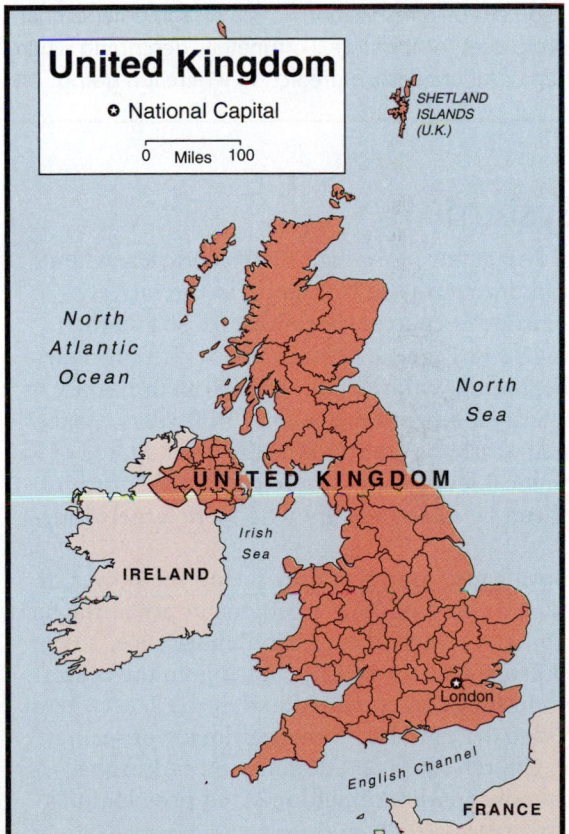

Figure 13.1
United Kingdom: Four Ethnicities, One State

Case Study 13.1 The United Kingdom: Four into One

What is properly known as the United Kingdom consists of four nations of people with a total population of 60 million: England, Wales, Scotland, and Northern Ireland. The largest and most powerful group, the English, managed by military and diplomatic means over many centuries to consolidate the four into one state. For citizens of the minority nations, this meant maintaining dual loyalties: the ethnic, religious, and linguistic identities lying close to their hearts, and the economic and security loyalty to a necessary evil in the form of the United Kingdom. People may not be capable of holding directly conflicting loyalties, but we seem capable of feeling divided identities between two or more groups.

In the southwest, Wales was the first nation to be formally linked to England, in 1284; Scotland to the north officially joined the union in 1707. The entire island of Ireland to the west was subdued by the 1800 Act of Union and remained so until 1921. Badly shaken by its losses in World War I, London then decided to accord independence to the lower three-quarters of the Irish island. The northern quarter has remained part of the United Kingdom as Northern Ireland. While most Welsh and Scots would like their nationalities to enjoy more independence from English influence, no serious threat of violence toward that end has materialized in many decades. But the saga of Northern Ireland has followed quite another script.

What local residents refer to innocuously as the "Troubles" has been a quarter-century cycle of bloodshed, recrimination, and retaliation between Catholic and Protestant factions. The Protestant majority in Northern Ireland are mostly Loyalists—meaning loyal to the British government and favoring Northern Ireland's remaining in the United Kingdom. The Glorious Revolution (1688–1689) officially elevated Protestantism to a status as the religion of Britain. By American standards, 300 years probably seems the equivalent of national eternity. For the British, it seems more like yesterday: witness the violence annually accompanying the celebratory parade down the streets of Belfast, Northern Ireland, in which the Protestants remind Catholics of their defeat in 1689.

Predictably, the Catholic minority feels much more affinity with their co-religionists to the immediate south in the independent Republic of Ireland. Many Northern Ireland Catholics are poor and consider themselves repressed minorities. Not surprisingly, some believe they have little to lose under such circumstances and consider that any change is likely to improve things. The Irish Republican Army (IRA) finds such minds fertile soil for planting their seeds of violent solutions to the problems of the Catholics.[7]

So, if most states are heterogeneous, and if even the most successful and affluent ones, such as the United Kingdom, are subject to prolonged domestic violence threatening their sense of unity, in what kind of general condition does that leave the state? The health of this aging actor—the most important on the world stage for the past 350 years—cannot be considered trivial. Some political scientists, such as Seyom Brown, see the present state as being in a "crisis of incongruence" and unlikely to emerge in robust condition.[8] Others, such as Hendrik Spruyt, consider the state more adept than other actors on the scene today at dealing with the complex changes required by globalization.[9] Such disagreements characterize prognoses for the state. Fortunately, describing where it came from is far easier than predicting where it is going. ∎

Emergence of the State System

Despite the state's domination of the world stage for more than three centuries, when contrasted with the full scope of the human drama, the state materialized relatively recently. The state system evolved in the European context, beginning loosely in the fifteenth century and coalescing around the 1648 Peace of Westphalia, which brought closure to the bloody Thirty Years War. Beginning with the fall of the Roman Empire in 476 A.D., power was exercised on two separate levels in Europe for 1,000 years. At the broad, all-European level, the pope's Roman Catholic Church was the chief source of political as well as spiritual power. On the local level, feudalism reigned in the form of fiefdoms, baronies, and principalities—all run by minor royalty who were largely independent within their own limited sphere.

By the fourteenth century, however, both papal central authority and the power of local royalty began weakening. Small fiefdoms could no longer provide safety in the light of new military inventions, especially gunpowder. Then, during the Renaissance, a new idea—individual freedom—swept across Europe like a tornado, challenging the central autocracy of the Catholic Church. These opposing forces culminated in the Thirty Years War (1618–1648). The 1648 Peace of Westphalia established the legitimacy of secular political authority and ended the Catholic Church's political domination of Europe. From these humble beginnings sprang the consolidation of fiefdoms and principalities into the modern state.[10]

The major nations conducting the negotiations at Westphalia and agreeing to respect each other's **sovereignty** were Sweden, France, Portugal, Spain, and the newly emergent Netherlands. The state's sovereign autonomy gradually enabled it to operate independently alongside other similar entities.

The weakening of the Roman Catholic Church as an all-European force led to intense state competition in this newly decentralized political environment. With sovereignty in hand, the state could compete at will over pieces of territory, economic assets, trade routes, or, later on, colonial possessions. Although these European countries worked out agreements to preserve peace, power was what counted most. All the states spent power as the main currency to pursue their interests. Competition for power has characterized state behavior internationally since the seventeenth century.

The state system was a European invention, and this region benefited greatly from its creation. African peoples, for example, have identified far less readily with states, mainly because colonial oppressors imposed states on them that were grossly at variance with traditional ethnic loyalties among nomadic Africans. Latin America may fall in between these extreme regional examples because Latin Americans benefited far less from the state system than Europeans but far more than did Africans. The history of the state system, therefore, is one of extremely uneven winners and losers.

Sovereignty ■ The legal concept asserting that countries are independent actors solely responsible for what transpires within their borders

War's Devastating Legacy

International competition has seen dramatic increases in both the number and severity of **wars**. Traditional international law legitimized wars to redress state grievances, but since World War II, modern principles have challenged war's legality. About 1,000 wars with a minimum of 1,000 deaths per war have been counted over the last 1,000 years (see Figure 13.2), forming an odd confluence of death around the number 1,000. At least 150 million people died in those wars—including 75 percent of them, an estimated 111 million, in the twentieth century alone.[11]

War ■ Organized mass violence conducted by societies

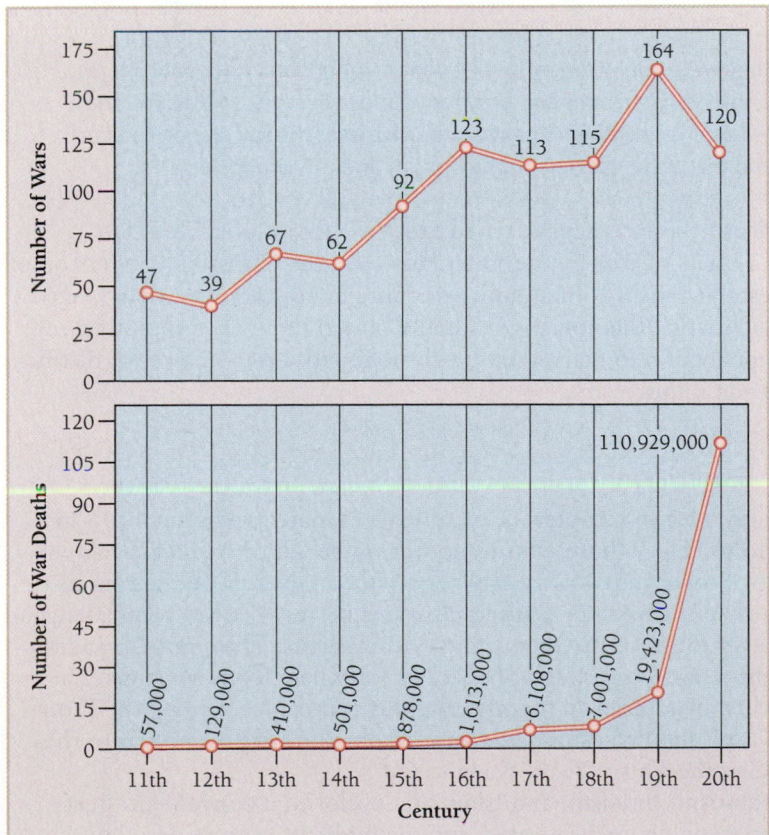

Figure 13.2
890 Years of War Death, 1110–1993
This figure shows the long-term trend in the rise of both the frequency and severity of war. Beginning in the year 1100, the number of wars by century has increased. Eckhardt's study, which only went through the end of 1989, fails to include subsequent ones. Even though incomplete, twentieth century wars produced 75 percent of the millennium's total.

Source: From p. 389 *International Politics on the World Stage* by John T. Rourke. Copyright © 1995 by Dushkin Publishing/Brown & Benchmark Publishers. Reprinted by permission of The McGraw-Hill Companies.

More than 50 million people died in World War II, 26 million of whom were Soviet citizens. America's greatest casualties were incurred in its Civil War, when it lost more than in World Wars I and II, Korea, and Vietnam combined. Internationalist George Kohn lists more than 1,700 entries in his *Dictionary of Wars,* which covers from 2000 B.C. up to 1980.[12] Another study, measuring things somewhat differently, concludes that during fifty centuries of human "civilization," war has been raging somewhere on earth 94 percent of the time. Since World War II, many smaller wars and internal conflicts have exploded, with a total of 127 wars from 1945 to 1991, an average of 2.8 per year, leaving only six years when a new war did not begin.[13]

Particularly since the breakup of the Soviet empire, civil disturbances have increased in number. One study identifies almost 150 significant ethnic, religious, or cultural conflicts from 1958 to 1976 alone.[14] The decade between 1985 and 1995 saw 2 million children die in wars; 1 million others were orphaned, and 12 million were left homeless, in an era when an unbelievable 90 percent of war deaths were made up of civilians, up from 50 percent a few decades before. From 1980 through 1988, the African countries of Angola and Mozambique lost 33,000 and 490,000 children, respectively, to war-related causes.[15] Such figures lend credence to Karl von Clausewitz's famous dictum, "War is a continuation of political commerce by other means."[16] Equally discouraging is the Morgenthau proposition, named after a well-known realist scholar, which says that "nations active in international politics are continuously preparing for, actively engaged in, or recovering from organized violence in the form of war."[17]

Religion and State Violence

Pacifist ■ Adhering to the biblical tradition of peacefully turning the other cheek, thus refusing to answer violence with counterviolence

War wasn't always considered such a routinely legitimate endeavor. Strong pre-Christian **pacifist** sentiments can be clearly identified, such as the passage from Isaiah in the Hebrew scripture, which advocates nations "beating their swords into plowshares and their spears into pruning hooks." More directly relevant to the European experience, however, is the moral imperative expressed by Jesus Christ in his Sermon on the Mount, from the New Testament:

> You have heard that they were told, "You must love your neighbor and hate your enemy." But I tell you, love your enemies and pray for your persecutors, so that you may show yourselves true sons of your Father in heaven, for He makes the sun rise on the bad with the good alike, and makes the rain fall on the upright and the wrongdoers.[18]

Until the fourth century, these passages carried great weight among Christian thinkers protesting against acts of war by the state. However, the Christian conversion of Emperor Constantine, establishing a Roman unity of church and state, greatly changed the role of Christianity. Christian theologians gradually buried the fifth commandment's ("thou shalt not kill") application to wars, coming gradually to settle on a set of distinctions between **just wars** and unjust wars.

Just wars ■ A distinction drawn in the monotheistic religions between legitimate and illegitimate resort to force by the state, based on explicit criteria

History of Just War Doctrine

As suggested in Case Study 11.1 in Chapter 11 relating to Bernard Lewis' essay, "I'm Right, You're Wrong, Go to Hell," those who wage war on behalf of one religion's empires against the infidels of other religions clearly believe themselves to be fighting just wars. The gradual evolution of Christian Church positions on war proved convenient for many Christian states eager to legitimize their military campaigns. The eight **Crusades** (1095–1291) were fought to recapture the Holy City of Jerusalem from Muslims. Later, the Crusades were matched by a series of bloody religious wars unleashed by the Protestant Reformation (1517), pitting Protestant against Catholic for a century prior to the Peace of Westphalia ending the Thirty Years War in 1648.[19]

Crusades ■ Intermittent holy wars fought between Roman Catholicism and Islam from the eleventh to the thirteenth centuries

Catholicism, Protestantism, Judaism, and Islam all developed a convenient "just war" concept. Principles gradually incorporated into the body of international law included *discrimination* (no civilian–soldier hostilities), *proportionality* (violence not exceeding injury suffered), *just cause* (good reason), and *option of last resort* (alternatives explored).

Over time, traditional international law developed into two separate bodies: the laws of war and the laws of peace, with a declaration of war necessary to activate the rules of war. The father of international law, seventeenth-century Dutch jurist Hugo Grotius, in his landmark work, *On the Law of War and Peace*, considered resorting to just war a normal means of redressing grievances after other approaches had failed. The 1991 Persian Gulf War, described in Case Study 13.2, was noteworthy for the effort devoted to framing it within the confines of just war doctrine by Bush I, and the 2003 Iraqi War equally noteworthy for not being framed in that manner by Bush II.

Case Study 13.2 Just War Doctrine: Bush I versus Bush II

Apparently believing that the United States would not intervene, in August 1990, Iraqi dictator Saddam Hussein unleashed his military forces against tiny-but-rich Kuwait, crushing it in a matter of days. This put Saddam in control of 20 percent of the world's oil reserves; it also placed him in a strategic position for a possible invasion of oil giant Saudi Arabia (see Figure 13.3).

Iraq, Kuwait, and Saudi Arabia

✪ National Capital

0   Miles   250

Figure 13.3
Operation Desert Storm, liberating Kuwait in 1991, was presented to the American public as a just war.

Saddam rationalized his aggression by claiming that Kuwait had violated limits on oil drilling set by OPEC; he said that Kuwait had engaged in oblique-line drilling, illegally stealing Iraqi oil; finally, Saddam argued that Kuwait was once part of greater Iraq, now returning home. The real reasons had mostly to do with oil, Iraqi access to the Persian Gulf, and enhanced power for Saddam in the Middle Eastern balance of forces.

The United States had sold military hardware to Iraq during the Iran–Iraq War (1980–1988). Presidents Ronald Reagan and George Bush had tilted toward Iraq with considerable aid. America had looked the other way when Saddam unleashed illegal chemical weapons in 1988 against Kurdish citizens in a northern Iraqi town, killing more than 5,000 of his own citizens. The U.S. ambassador, April Glaspie, had conveyed mixed messages during the summer of 1990 concerning the U.S. position on mounting Iraqi/Kuwaiti tensions. Given the absence of any clear U.S. criticism of Iraq's provocations or any statements of commitment to Kuwaiti sovereignty, Saddam assumed that President Bush would reluctantly accept an invasion of Kuwait as a *fait accompli.*

The U.S. President, Bush I, was energized by the crisis and reacted most adroitly. North America, Europe, and Japan were all dependent on Persian Gulf oil, and Bush and his advisors believed that Saddam could not be allowed to remain atop so much oil nor so close to Saudi oil—which, if captured, would give Saddam about half of the known global reserves. The economic effects of the Iraqi invasion quickly rippled across the world's oceans. Financial investors took a bath as the Wall Street stock market plunged in response to the invasion; all Americans felt concerned when gas prices jumped sharply at pumps across the United States.

Bush knew, however, that leading a democracy into war requires deft salesmanship, particularly with searing memories of the Vietnam debacle still vivid in America. One thing he did most effectively was to involve the United Nations directly in the decision making, carefully describing the crisis as one of the *United Nations against Iraq*, not merely the United States versus Iraq. With the Cold War over, no real Russian opposition to his efforts materialized, despite Russia's thirty-year alliance with Iraq. The U.N. also imposed an economic **embargo** against Iraq.

The most direct effects on Americans were economic ones, and Bush's secretary of state, James Baker, tried to sell a war against Iraq on the basis of the price of gas at the pump, but the public wants a loftier justification for war. Clear majority support for a U.S.-led war to liberate Kuwait did not materialize until President Bush carried the argument beyond financial self-interest to provide a *moral imperative based squarely on the concept of just war*, which Bush referred to often in public. He also brought Christian evangelist Billy Graham to his side while invoking the just war doctrine.

Although a small minority in Congress preferred economic sanctions to military action, after Bush demonized Saddam Hussein as "the worst dictator since Hitler" and justified war in Christian terms, momentum built for Operation Desert Storm. From January 17 to February 27, 1991, the U.S.-led coalition battered Iraq in two stages: (1) a massive bombing campaign and (2) a 100-hour ground attack that outflanked the Iraqis and easily compelled their surrender. Bush had fully involved the international community from the outset, and the coalition of twenty-six robust supporters that went to war fully believed they were doing the right thing in rolling back Saddam's naked aggression against Kuwait. Even countries such as Japan and Germany, forbidden by their constitutions from sending troops, wrote huge checks, and America ended up paying only 20 percent of war costs. The world community was clearly with America in 1991.

If the world community was clearly with America in 1991, that same world community was decidedly against American behavior leading up to Bush II's 2003 invasion and occupation of Iraq, deposing Saddam Hussein. The U.S. news media failed to report about street demonstrations abroad that were unprecedented in scope. If Bush I solved the puzzle of liberating Kuwait by working with allies from the bottom up to craft a popular multilateral solution, Bush II failed to establish any consistent justification for invading Iraq, crafting an unpopular unilateral solution arrived at from the top down.

Even America's closest allies skewered Bush II's headlong leap into the uncertain abyss of war. Why, they asked, was it suddenly so imperative to get rid of Saddam Hussein? It appears noteworthy that at no point during Bush II's hasty 2003 rush to war, and paltry planning to rebuild Iraqi society, did he address the *just war doctrine* that had permeated Bush I's justification for war in 1991 against the same country. ■

Embargo ■ Suspension of trade as a form of punishment against a state deemed to have violated international norms

Overkill ■ The capability to destroy an enemy many times over

Megaton ■ One million tons of nuclear TNT equivalency

A-bomb ■ Atomic bombs were nuclear fission bombs and served as the precursors of later hydrogen (H) fusion bombs

Kiloton ■ One thousand tons of nuclear TNT equivalency

Nukes and Other WMD

As if humanity's legacy of conventional warfare wasn't enough, the Cold War arms race created an unprecedented **overkill** situation in nuclear weaponry. The superpowers' combined stockpiles peaked at roughly 17 trillion tons of nuclear TNT equivalency, in the form of 33,000 warheads between them. Such firepower amounted to 1 billion times that of the U.S. atomic bomb dropped on Hiroshima in 1945.[20] Most of those missiles carried 1-, 3-, or, 5-**megaton** bombs. The Soviets actually tested a mammoth 50-megaton bomb in 1954.

Such mega-numbers are mind-boggling. As context, the Hiroshima **A-bomb** of August 6, 1945, was a 20-**kiloton** bomb that killed roughly 100,000 people. This 20-kiloton bomb represented a mere one-fiftieth of a 1-megaton hydrogen bomb. When the United States and the Soviet Union reached overkill capacity, British statesman Winston Churchill asked, "How many times do we need to make the rubble bounce?" What makes nukes a true dilemma is that even if we dismantle them all, humanity can never unlearn the science of how to remake them.

Cold–War Balance of Terror

The bizarre psychology of the nuclear standoff amounted to a mutual suicide pact. This balance of terror was meant to deter each side from attacking the other because any nuclear attack would be met with retaliation, destroying both superpowers. This superpower policy, officially called Mutually Assured Destruction (MAD), actually worked reasonably well; no nuclear war occurred between the Americans and the Soviets during the Cold War. However, this fact may contribute to the illogical belief that because it hasn't happened, it won't happen. With the Cold War now tucked away, it is tempting to underestimate the danger of not only nukes, but all forms of WMD.

It is also easy to forget just how seriously Americans and Soviets took the threat of nuclear war back in the 1950s and 1960s. Citizens and governments built fallout shelters and practiced civil defense drills to ease their fears. U.S. schoolchildren learned songs telling them to "Duck and Cover" if they heard the siren signaling nuclear attack. I remember a hopelessly inadequate 1962 fallout shelter in the basement of my parents' new home. Documentary films such as *Atomic Cafe* (1982) convey the palpable anxiety, as well as the absurd nature of many popular reactions to the threat.[21]

Americans tried mightily to avoid thinking about the possibility of nuclear war. The Hollywood film industry, often a barometer of popular attitudes, ignored nuclear war for the twenty tensest years of the Cold War. A few films in the 1950s were brave enough to imagine a post-holocaust world, although not nuclear war itself. Not until 1964—two years after the real-world warning provided by the Cuban missile crisis—did Hollywood look directly into the nuclear fireball. Stanley Kubrick's *Dr. Strangelove* and Sidney Lumet's *Fail-Safe* broke Hollywood's nuclear taboo in 1964.

U.S. Civil Defense drills at the peak of the Cold War used a catchy song called "Duck and Cover" to teach school children how to react to a nuclear attack.

Dr. Strangelove did so with unrelenting sardonic humor, making a mockery of the logic underpinning nuclear deterrence through MAD. The ending of *Dr. Strangelove* brings totally insane nuclear destruction. *Fail-Safe*, on the other hand, dissected the topic more coolly and hopefully, allowing rational heads to prevail. Although escalation to total annihilation was averted, the cities of Moscow and New York were destroyed by an unintended attack unleashed by a mechanical failure—pretty awful but not total Armageddon.

Post–Cold War Proliferation Problems

The superpowers, and the world, made it through the Cold War without such cinematic real-world calamities. Fear of nuclear confrontation has been eased by improved American–Russian relations, treaties reducing nuclear warheads, and the U.S.'s status as the only global military superpower. Polls show that most Americans do not worry about nukes very often. Yet good reasons exist for concern over **nuclear proliferation.** Whereas Ukraine, Kazakhstan, and Belarus (of the former Soviet Union) have turned their nuclear weapons over to the Russians, several regional rivalries could conceivably escalate to nuclear confrontations: India and Pakistan, Israel and its Arab neighbors, North and South Korea, or China and Taiwan.

Nuclear proliferation ■ The process whereby states not previously possessing nuclear weapons come to possess them

India became the first undeclared nuclear nation in 1974; Pakistan and Israel soon followed. In the 1990s, Iraq, North Korea, and Iran all tried to develop nuclear bombs: all undemocratic, secretive, and hostile toward the West. To most experts, the crux of post–Cold War security concerns consists of how to keep not only nukes but also biological and chemical weapons out of the hands of unpredictable dictators in countries such as North Korea and Iran. How has the international community generally gone about coping with such problems? Two main categories of responses have been employed in the past: (1) direct approaches tackling the issue head-on, usually via international treaty, or (2) indirect approaches that assume that weapons proliferation will take care of itself if other more basic issues are resolved.

Sometimes labeled "poor man's nukes," chemical and biological weapons round out the triple threat (nukes, biologicals, chemicals) of weapons of mass destruction (WMD). Not only are chemical and biological weapons cheaper and easier to produce, they also can be distributed in more diverse and unpredictable ways than can nukes. Then, compounding problems associated with all three WMD is the increasing number of states that possess significant missile capabilities. As pointed out in Chapter 1, in 2004, the Congressional Research Service published a study claiming that a total of nineteen countries then had missiles whose maximum range was 1,000 km; seven countries had missiles ranging up to 3,000 km; two states had missiles up to 5,500 km, and six had intercontinental missiles greater than 5,500 km (including North Korea).

Compounding the dilemma, we have to worry not only about states that might obtain and use WMD but also about nonstate actors such as Al Qaeda, Hezbollah, and Hamas. The complexity of these proliferation problems has led some observers to miss the Cold War's simplicity. President Bill Clinton and his successor, President George W. Bush, approached matters of national security in very different ways, with Clinton favoring a cautiously indirect approach (idealist in nature) and Bush generally adhering to a more aggressively direct approach (realist in nature).

Direct versus Indirect Approaches to Security Issues

Although Bill Clinton adhered mostly to a cautiously indirect approach to security during his presidency, in 1995, he did lead a successful campaign for permanent extension of the NNPT. In the 1990s, proponents of direct action sought to permanently extend the Nuclear Non-Proliferation Treaty (NNPT), initially established in 1970, for a twenty-five-year period. Ninety percent of all countries signed the NNPT, which requires non-nuclear powers to pledge not to seek these weapons. It does, however, allow nuclear powers to share resources for the peaceful use of nuclear energy, and it also binds non-nuclear states to allow unannounced inspections by the International Atomic Energy Agency (IAEA), such as those conducted in Iraq during the 1990s.

Another part of the treaty binds the nuclear powers to work toward setting a date for eventual nuclear disarmament. That has not happened. Idealists among us often favor exploring all avenues of human creativity to find ways of defusing the nuclear risk: arms control treaties, disarmament talks, international organizations to address the issue, and grass-roots efforts to change popular attitudes. Realists, however, skeptical of "do-gooders," often argue that such efforts are pointless, even delusional, because people and nations use power to enhance their own interests, not some abstract vision of the global good.

A variety of indirect ideas on beating the nuclear proliferation problem have also been advanced. Some argue that if the North–South economic gap can be controlled, it will remove much of the impetus for proliferation. Others suggest that encouraging democracy worldwide will help. An interesting thesis has been developed by political scientist Richard Rosecrance, who believes that countries that are capable of building a bomb will decide that doing so is not in their best interest.

According to Professor Rosecrance, "the genie is not yet out of the bottle" concerning nuclear proliferation, and a variety of factors other than the NNPT work against new countries taking the nuclear plunge. First, he says there are the many examples of "nuclear abstainers"—countries that definitely could have developed nukes but didn't—such as Canada, Switzerland, Sweden, Germany, Italy, Japan, Australia, Taiwan, and others. It was not seen as in their interests to undertake the expense and risk of nuclear weapons production. Equally notable is the case of South Africa—a recent demobilizer of its nuclear stockpile, consisting of six bombs, which have since been converted to civilian power projects.

Rosecrance believes that contemporary thinking about the utility of nuclear weapons has undergone a massive change since the Cold War. Whereas it was once believed that nuclear

World leaders gathered in New York City in 1995 to sign the permanent extension of the Nuclear Non-Proliferation Treaty (NNPT).

weapons would deter not only nuclear attacks but conventional ones as well, the history of the past five decades reveals that nuclear weapons have not effectively deterred conventional attacks. The new thinking, then, says that the possession of nuclear weapons is of "diminished utility." Threats to launch nuclear weapons are no longer believed, and with every passing year, what can only be called a "nuclear taboo" has taken firmer and firmer hold. In other words, if rival nations don't believe you will use your nuclear weapons, they are of little value to you. This line of reasoning leads to the conclusion that direct action to prohibit nuclear proliferation is unnecessary because nuclear weapons are no longer seen as particularly valuable to possess.[22]

One fly in the ointment of Rosecrance's analysis may be its assumption that nuclear proliferation will fade because national leaders will make the rational calculation that such weapons are not in the best interest of that country. Can you think of examples of national decision-makers who have made important decisions arguably quite irrational?

The Democratic Peace: Reason for Hope?

One reason to think that the state's future may outshine its war-torn past stems from recent studies positing a link between democracy and peace. These studies follow on the heels of a wave of democratization sweeping many of the world's regions. Samuel Huntington's *The Third Wave: Democratization in the Late Twentieth Century* traces more than thirty democratic transitions from 1974 to 1990, in what he calls the "third wave" of democratization in the world. Huntington is encouraged by both the diverse regions in which this has occurred and its peacefulness. U.S. State Department analyst Francis Fukuyama's optimistic 1989 essay, "The End of History," argued that the great twentieth-century ideological battle between dictatorship and democracy ended with democracy winning, and with no other viable competitors.[23]

In the 1970s and 1980s, democratic elections swept military dictators out of many Latin American countries. Among those deposed were Augusto Pinochet in Chile and Alfredo Stroessner in Paraguay. Communist president Daniel Ortega peacefully stepped down from power in Nicaragua when rejected by voters in 1990. In Africa, the 1990s saw unprecedented free elections in Benin, Cape Verde, Chad, Gabon, and Mauritania—not to mention the huge democratic changes introduced in the Republic of South Africa.

East Asian countries such as Taiwan and South Korea have also made democratic strides in recent years. In addition, Spain, Portugal, and Greece, the southern tier of the European Union, have strengthened the foundations of their democracies. An accusing finger sometimes gets pointed at the Middle East as impervious to this global trend. However, a book by three Canadian professors addresses democratization in the Middle East and concludes that although civil strife has caused democratic failures in Sudan, Algeria, and Yemen, democratization is underway in Egypt, Lebanon, Jordan, and Kuwait.[24] The most cataclysmic change, however, occurred in eastern Europe and the former Soviet Union from 1989 to 1991, where communism buckled like a ripe melon when squeezed by popular demands for free elections.

But why should a wave of democratization augur well for peace? Numerous studies make a strong case that the historical record demonstrates that democracies almost never fight with democracies.[25] Scholars find heartening the rigorous methodologies used in many of these studies, and political scientist Bruce Russett's survey concludes that this notion of a democratic peace is "one of the strongest conclusions that can be made about international relations."[26] For the first time in history, democracies have most of the military and economic power; fully 92 percent of the world's wealthiest countries are currently democracies.[27] Therefore, if democracy continues to spread, it is anticipated that fewer wars will occur in the future.[28] Journalist Thomas Friedman adds an entertaining wrinkle to the democratic peace discussion with what he calls the McDonald's factor: no two countries with McDonald's fast-food restaurants have fought one another. In 1997, Belarus became the one-hundredth country hosting the McDonald's MNC juggernaut.

Fall of the Berlin Wall in November 1989.

Is War Still Truly Legitimate?

Other scholars contend that the very idea of war is gradually being rejected, resulting in an antiwar global culture. One voice belongs to historian John Mueller, who brands war as a "thoroughly bad and repulsive idea, like dueling or slavery, sub-rationally unthinkable and therefore obsolescent."[29] Mueller attributes much of the new thinking about war to the end of the Cold War, equating the collapse of the Soviet Union to the "functional equivalent of World War III"—transfiguring both the distribution of political power and human thinking about war.[30]

Similarly, mathematician and peace researcher Anatol Rapoport suggests that many ideas lie dormant in human consciousness until the "ideational environment" becomes receptive to their germination. He believes that the time for peace has arrived.[31] The great physicist Albert Einstein, whose 1939 letter to President Roosevelt started the nuclear avalanche rolling, once quipped that "the unleashed power of the atom has changed everything except our modes of thinking."[32] Although Einstein's observation was undoubtedly once true, a popular book suggests that his desire to see creative thinking about war and peace is finally being realized around the world.[33]

Political scientist Donald Snow says that another hopeful development consists of the redefinition of national security taking place. During the Cold War, security was conceived strictly in terms of military defense. Today, a wider sense of human security includes a "psychological sense of safety"—incorporating ecological global issues such as the environment, population, food, and energy—fits into the equation of security.[34]

Confidence in a vigorous new spirit of individual empowerment on the world stage also finds expression in the writings of James Rosenau, who sees the information age contributing to "people power" where previously only passivity existed.[35] Similarly, political scientist John Rourke cites numerous examples of the personal empowerment of humble individuals as global players of consequence in the information age. Some of Rourke's examples include Rigoberta Menchu, a Guatemalan of Mayan descent who led a successful campaign to protect the human rights of indigenous peoples in her country. In 1992, her efforts were recognized with the Nobel Peace Prize. In Africa, an auto plant worker named Michael Werikhe conducts walkathons to protect the endangered black rhino. Sometimes wearing his pet python, Survival, he has collected over $1 million, with the funds being used to achieve international agreements protecting the black rhino.[36]

Traditional Prescriptions for Peace and Security

But what if the democratic peace fails to materialize, and nuclear abstainers become nuclear wannabes? What if some of the encouraging post–Cold War trends prove ephemeral? What strategies has the international community built up over the centuries to cope with war?

Traditionally, four methods have been advanced in behalf of international peace and security, two of them popular with realists and two favored by idealists. The two realist approaches, **balance of power** and collective security, share some conceptual underpinnings. Both emphasize a configuration of significant power as the key to deterring aggression.

The older of the two, balance of power, seeks fluid alliances to countervail the power of any country, or group of countries, that might threaten to upset the peace. Potential aggressors are deterred by alliances of committed countries joining together to

Balance of power ■ An equitable distribution of power between flexible international alliances countervailing one another to preclude domination by any aggressor

discourage aggression. The longest and most successful balance of power system prevailed during the century from the end of the Napoleonic Wars (1815) until the outbreak of World War I (1914).

The second realist formulation is the system of collective security, entailing not an alliance of balanced power but rather superior strength daunting enough to deter aggression even more assuredly than a balance of power. Collective security was first attempted by the League of Nations after World War I but quickly lost credibility when it failed to act against a tide of militarism sweeping over Germany, Japan, and Italy in the 1930s. The concept of collective security received a second chance with the 1945 creation of the United Nations after World War II. The five Allies of World War II (the United States, Britain, France, the Soviet Union, and China) formally carried their cooperation over to the Security Council of the United Nations.

George W. Bush took a decidedly aggressive, realist approach to foreign affairs even before September 11, 2001. Peace through strength had long been his mantra, and both he and his neoconservative foreign policy advisors (Richard Cheney, Donald Rumsfeld, Paul Wolfowitz, Scooter Libby) criticized Clinton for squandering America's military might with a timid agenda. All he needed was 9/11 to expand the hunt for Osama bin Laden and Al Qaeda into a global War on Terror (WOT) and the Bush Doctrine: pre-emptive war unprecedented in U.S. history, Afghanistan, Iraq, expansion of his war powers to curtail civil liberties in the U.S. and to maltreat suspected terrorist sympathizers internationally.

Idealists, however, think that realists are trying to navigate today's international waters using a rear-view mirror focused on outdated lessons. Idealists believe that there is a need for new visions, and two idealist recipes for peace are known as **arms control** and **international law.** Both arms control and international law use various forms of agreement between states as the basis of promoting international understanding. Whereas the realist methods share the notion of peace through strength, their idealist counterparts lean toward peace through mutual obligation.

Arms control proponents posit that the greater the number of sophisticated weapons available to a country, the more tempted it will be to use them. They fear that human nature seeks to use whatever weapons we have; therefore, we are better off agreeing with rival states to get rid of some of these temptations. The executive director of the Institute for Defense and Disarmament Studies, Randall Forsberg, contends that more than $100 billion annually could be cut from the U.S. military budget without endangering American security.[37] Some advocates of arms control go so far as to suggest the abolition of all WMD, or total disarmament.

The other idealist construct for peace, international law, is based on an analogy to domestic politics, where the role of law is robust. Just as it required time to build rule by law in civil societies, proponents of international law say that similar rules of the game are developing globally. International law may trail domestic law, but these are differences of degree, not differences of kind. Countries generally tend to obey the rules of the international game as spelled out in the body of international law. Richard Falk claims that the international community needs to revise its ideas of sovereignty, democracy, and security, aiming toward a "vision of humane governance."[38] Both of these idealist concepts invite derision from realists, who see them as distractions causing us to let down our guard. Peace through strength serves as the immutable realist principle.

Bill Clinton, in sharp contrast to George W. Bush, used American military might very sparingly during his tenure. In the few cases where

Arms control ■ An approach to peace suggesting that the regulation of levels and types of weapons can help to discourage resort to warfare

International law ■ An approach to peace relying on the body of formal and informal codes and rules as salutary influences discouraging violent state behavior

President Kennedy relaxes with three Army generals after the resolution of the Cuban missile crisis.

the Pentagon was brought in (Somalia, Haiti, Kosovo), relatively few American casualties occurred. His anti-terrorist efforts minimized the issue as a law enforcement matter, not the global WOT declared by Bush. Where Clinton put most of his effort was in making America a global economic hegemon, not the global military hegemony embraced by Bush. Breaking with Democratic Party tradition, Clinton pushed hard for free trade and brokered both NAFTA and the WTO in the middle of his unprecedented decade of affluence. His most influential advisors were economic gurus such as Robert Reich, Robert Rubin, and Lawrence Summers, in sharp contrast to the neocons pushing Bush in a different direction.

One of the most poignant case studies since World War II, the 1962 Cuban missile crisis, required elements of both realism and idealism to avert what nearly degenerated into thermonuclear war, as discussed in Case Study 13.3.

Case Study 13.3   High Drama: Eyeball-to-Eyeball Over Missiles in Cuba

Protagonists

- John F. Kennedy—U.S. president
- Nikita S. Khrushchev—Soviet general secretary
- Fidel Castro—Cuban prime minister since 1959 revolution
- "Executive-Committee Hawks"
- General Maxwell Taylor—Joint Chiefs chairman
- Dean Acheson—former secretary of state
- John McCloy—Wall Street lawyer
- Paul Nitze—State Department official
- Douglas Dillon—secretary of treasury
- "Executive-Committee Doves"
- Robert Kennedy—attorney general
- Robert McNamara—secretary of defense
- George Ball—undersecretary of state
- Ted Sorensen—presidential advisor
- Adlai Stevenson—ambassador to the U.N.
- Lewellyn Thompson—Soviet expert; ambassador at large
- Charles Bohlen—State Department Soviet expert
- Role players
- Valerian Zorin—Soviet ambassador to the U.N.
- Anatoli Dobrynin—Soviet ambassador to the U.S.
- Nicholas Katzenbach—deputy attorney general; formulator of the legal arguments justifying a blockade
- William Knox—Westinghouse president in Moscow, used by Khrushchev as conduit to U.S. government
- Rudolf Anderson—U-2 pilot shot down over Cuba on October 27, 1962

Prologue

Democrat John F. Kennedy won the 1960 presidential election partially by trying to out-Republican the Republicans: he demanded a "get-tough" policy with the Soviet Union, complaining of a supposed missile gap, with the United States behind. When Kennedy became president, however, his tough campaign rhetoric proved difficult to implement.

Months after assuming office, America's youngest president supported an attempt to liberate Cuba from Fidel Castro's control—the Bay of Pigs invasion, which turned into a total fiasco. Shortly thereafter, at his first summit meeting in Geneva, Switzerland, the inexperienced Kennedy allowed an aggressive Nikita Khrushchev to lecture him on U.S. policy, which the news media portrayed as JFK being bullied by Khrushchev.

In reality, the United States maintained a sizable nuclear advantage over the Soviets at the time. However, having won an election partly on the basis of a "missile gap," Kennedy could not credibly reassure an American public still worried about the Soviet Union's successful 1957 launch of the world's first orbiting "Sputnik." The psychological milieu was one in which Americans felt themselves in retreat, whereas the Soviets, epitomized by Khrushchev's "we will bury you [economically]" 1960 speech at the U.N., considered themselves the wave of the future. Against this backdrop of an insecure American mind-set vis-à-vis Russia, the Cuban missile crisis exploded.

Dramatic Plot

It all had to do with offensive missiles placed secretly in Cuba by the Soviets. The crisis lasted thirteen days for the Executive Committee (October 16 to October 28, 1962), an intentionally diverse group of advisors convened by the president to deal with the crisis. The public phase lasted only six days (October 22–28, 1962). After a week of secret Ex-Comm discussions, Kennedy went public with a televised speech explaining that the Soviets had placed "offensive nuclear missiles in Cuba" along with 20,000 of their troops.

A total of six response options had been considered by the Ex-Comm: (1) inaction (wait-and-see), (2) private diplomatic advances in search of a solution, (3) expressions of public outrage at the U.N., (4) a naval blockade around the island of Cuba, (5) a surgical air strike intended to wipe out missile sites only, and (6) a full-scale invasion of Cuba. After many days of heated debate, the surviving alternatives in the Ex-Comm were the air strike (favored by the "hawks") and the naval blockade (favored by the "doves"). On October 20, 1962, the Ex-Comm presented its views to the president: a majority favored the blockade, but a sizable minority preferred the air strike option.

A day later, Kennedy decided in favor of the naval blockade, issuing an executive order for action. Nicholas Katzenbach of the State Department developed the legal rationale for the blockade, justifying it by Article 51 of the U.N. Charter (collective self-defense) and an Organization of American States (OAS) vote in support of the blockade. Katzenbach suggested use of the less belligerent term "quarantine" because a blockade technically represents an act of war under international law.

By October 24, 1962, American naval forces began the actual blockade, ringing Cuba with nineteen U.S. vessels. That day, the world looked over the "edge of the precipice," as twenty Soviet ships with submarine escorts approached the quarantine line. With possible nuclear war hanging in the balance, eyeball-to-eyeball over missiles in Cuba, Khrushchev blinked: Soviet ships stopped in the water and, fortunately, headed back to the Soviet Union. The world released a collective breath of relief.

For the next four days, the two sides negotiated in an effort to end the crisis without undue humiliation for the Soviets. The final agreement involved dismantling the missile sites under the supervision of U.N. inspectors and returning them to Russia. Castro stated publicly that no new missiles would be accepted by Cuba, and the United States pledged never again to support an invasion of Cuba. A secret protocol also called for America to remove its missiles from Turkey as a quid pro quo for the Soviet missile removal in Cuba. Kennedy instructed his government not to present the outcome as a victory for the United States or as a surrender by Khrushchev.

Critical Analysis

President Kennedy believed in the importance of "process," or structuring decisions around rational procedures, and he deserves much credit for adhering to those principles in the Cuban missile crisis. He gathered an eclectic set of advisors in the Ex-Comm, listened carefully to all suggestions, avoided overreaction, and tried to place himself in Khrushchev's shoes (as kind of a Stanislavsky Method exercise) as he worked his way through this tense situation. He also learned from earlier mistakes in the Bay of Pigs invasion, when he blindly accepted the advice of military experts.

Most analysts agree that disaster would have resulted if JFK had followed the advice of "hawks" such as Dean Acheson, General Maxwell Taylor, and John McCloy (who demanded an air strike against Cuba). An air strike would

have killed some of the 20,000 Soviet troops, yet would have missed some of the numerous missiles already operational in October. Therefore, Khrushchev certainly would have been pressured at home to escalate the crisis, and the United States would have been left vulnerable to missiles capable of hitting cities in the eastern United States within five minutes.

Although JFK and the Ex-Comm deserve credit for keeping cool heads, they fare less well in assessments of their interpretation of Soviet motivations for placing missiles in Cuba in the first place. Kennedy and his advisors believed that Khrushchev was again testing JFK's mettle, as he had done at the Geneva summit, and that he was using the missiles to gain a strategic psychological advantage over the United States. However, long-classified materials now demonstrate that Khrushchev was motivated mainly by fear of a second American attempt at invading Cuba, or as he put it, "protecting the Cuban revolution."

Cuban intelligence had penetrated the CIA, obtaining a memo stating that if the United States could not "get rid of Castro by October of 1962, more drastic action would have to be taken." When Khrushchev received this information, he believed it meant another U.S. invasion of the island. The U.S. analysts rejected, out-of-hand, the possibility that Khrushchev's motivation might be defensive in nature. The United States believed—incorrectly—that it had clearly conveyed to Moscow that it had no intention of invading Cuba again.[39]

What long-term effects emanated from the Cuban crisis? Two major types of changes occurred, one psychological in nature and one more policy-oriented. In a psychological sense, the crisis forced the world to examine what it was loath to behold—the possibility of nuclear Armageddon. Staring into the nuclear fireball, humanity came to grips with the nuclear dilemma as the greatest of earthly enemies. Suddenly, the Soviets and Americans came to their senses about each other: they did not like each other's systems, but both were hostages to a form of nuclear blackmail. The bomb, not the Soviets, was the greater threat. On the policy front, this mental realignment quickly manifested itself in the form of a communications hotline, a partial nuclear test ban, regular summit meetings, expanded trade and cultural contacts, and a Nuclear Non-Proliferation Treaty (NNPT). The most dangerous phase of the Cold War era ended with the world intact.[40] ∎

New Actors Challenge the State

Some of the new Internet-age micro-level empowerment discussed earlier comes at the expense of states (countries). Almost imperceptibly, a parallel set of actors has emerged to challenge state leadership on the world stage. States once provided security for their citizens reliably enough to warrant undivided loyalty. No longer is this true. For one thing, the nagging insecurity of triple-threat WMD has shattered the once impermeable shell cushioning states and their citizens. Furthermore, contemporary definitions of security have expanded beyond the military dimension to incorporate broader notions of human security.

In addressing the troublesome range of diverse GIs examined in this text, the state system has proven rather ineffectual. Citizens often look elsewhere for solutions to ecological problems involving the environment, population, food, and energy, as they do concerning the protection of human rights and human security. Therefore, states have been forced to make some serious changes in recent years.

One thing that has not changed much, however, is the state's inherently competitive posture in the world. Close to 200 countries compete for power and influence in a world of scarcity, typically maximizing their interests at the expense of their rivals. Realists point out that this competitive model of international behavior advances humanity's efficiency and effectiveness. They see progress as energized by such a competitive process. The 350-year record of the state in ordering humanity's public affairs, say realists, has enabled more rapid and pervasive progress than any previous era of human history.

GIs and the Cooperative Motif

What, then, do idealists see as the essential problem? The short answer: solving today's GIs requires greater international cooperation, which states have not excelled at. The long answer is that states and their leaders see the world through inherently international (rather than transnational) lenses. State leaders consider the truly important matters in the world to be resolved between powerful countries such as France, the United Kingdom, China, Russia, the United States, and Japan. From their perspective, pleas for cooperation conceal efforts by poorer countries to steal the good life from powerful countries.

Such thinking works less well today than it did fifty years ago, idealists fervently believe. Idealists contend that ecological GIs do not respect national boundaries because they are genuinely global in scope. Deforestation, global warming, ozone depletion, and nuclear radiation affect everyone, not merely some nations or regions. In an age when aerosol spray cans and air-conditioning units in North America can cause skin cancer 12,000 miles away in Australia, new questions must be asked. Claiming that state competition only exacerbates global problems, idealists favor more cooperative endeavors.

Such increased cooperation could possibly come from existing states if they buy into the global paradigm soon enough. If they don't, some observers see the state's days of dominance in world affairs as numbered. As pointed out in Chapter 1, many people have begun shifting loyalties to new actors able to combat complex GIs. Let's reexamine some of these globally oriented entities challenging states on the world stage.

Nongovernmental Organizations (NGOs)

These are transnational entities that engage in activities crossing national boundaries and involve private, not public (governmental) participants. NGOs usually focus only on one or two issues and bring together people from around the world who think similarly. Strictly speaking, their activities are not considered international (between nations) but rather transnational (across national borders). The communications globalization revolution provides hardware in the form of fax machines, the Internet, e-mail, cell phones, and satellite transmissions that facilitates contact between like-minded average people everywhere. NGOs rely on information as their currency for influence.

Expanded communications have contributed to the proliferation of NGOs in recent decades. There were 5,000 NGOs by 1995, whereas only 795 existed in the year 1945, and 69 in 1900.[41] Cell phones represent the most recent vehicle for empowerment, and the CIA World Factbook estimates that about 1.8 billion cell phones were in use globally in 2004. The largest number were in the hands of Chinese citizens (335 million), second was the EU countries collectively (315 million), followed by the United States (194 million), Japan (91 million), Russia (74 million), Germany (71 million), India (69 million), and Brazil (66 million), rounding out the top ten in cell phone possession.

However, four other factors have increased the importance of NGOs: (1) the failures of states, (2) growing citizen concerns over human rights and ecological issues, (3) the end of the Cold War as the chief organizing reality of world affairs, and (4) the fact that although the demands on international organizations such as the U.N. have grown, their funding has not.[42] NGOs seek to fill in the gaps between human expectations and the performance of states.

Most NGOs have grass-roots origins, growing out of individual and small group contacts rather than macro-level initiatives. They epitomize the type of micro-level empowerment on the global scene detailed by scholars such as David Cortright, David Korten, and Craig Comstock.[43] Variously referred to as civil society, citizen summitry, track II diplomacy, or transnational participation, they all enable private individuals and groups to be heard on matters of public policy. NGOs' actions may be aimed at influencing governments, the U.N., or MNCs, and they often use information technologies to expose illegal or unethical behavior.

The "Dolphin Safe" logo is now a routine fixture on tuna cans.

A unique institution that has evolved over time is the Vatican, or the papacy of the Roman Catholic Church. An anomaly left over from the Middle Ages, when the pope was not only an all-European spiritual leader but an all-European political authority as well. The continued existence of "nuncios," or papal diplomatic representatives to more than 150 states gives the Vatican diplomatic clout. Theoretically nonpolitical, the Vatican exerted great influence concerning abortion at the 1994 Cairo Conference on Population. The Vatican was among the first to extend diplomatic recognition to the new state of Croatia when it broke away from Yugoslavia in 1992. A decade earlier, Pope John Paul II and President Ronald Reagan secretly conspired to support the Solidarity labor union undermining Polish Communism. Back to NGOs, the activities of two contemporary ones are described in Case Studies 13.4 and 13.5.

Intergovernmental Organizations (IGOs)

IGOs are international bodies set up by states to operate on their behalf for their common good. Unlike NGOs, these are public organizations. IGOs vary in scope, yet most tend to be either regional or global. Their functions also differ, although most concentrate either on military/defense issues or economic/social issues. The North Atlantic Treaty Organization (NATO) is a regional military/defense IGO, whereas the North American Free Trade Agreement (NAFTA) represents a regional economic IGO; the U.N. Security Council is a global military/defense IGO; whereas the World Trade Organization (WTO) serves as an example of a global economic IGO.

Case Study 13.4   The "Flipper" Factor

Dolphins are amazingly graceful and intelligent mammals for which many humans feel deep empathy. Not all dolphin species are endangered, but the fates of several have become inter-twined with the yellow-fin tuna fish. Scientists have gradually figured out why yellow-fin tuna have turned into world class hitch-hikers, and it has to do with the dolphin's impressive sonar capabilities.

Both the mammal and the fish in this case study are extremely fast, agile, and efficient predators. It turns out that dolphin sonar locates schools of fish, and the tuna tag along to share the feast de jour. Unfortunately for the dolphins, most commercial fishing ships traditionally used a narrow-gauged *purse seine* netting to catch the lucrative yellow-fin tuna fish, which is much in demand by consumers throughout the world.

Throughout the 1980s, both animal rights activists and environmentalist NGOs, such as the Sierra Club, agitated

against the large tuna-processing companies to end purse seine netting techniques that kill dolphins in the process of catching tuna. In 1986, an estimated 130,000 dolphins died this type of death. Protests, demonstrations, adverse publicity, and economic boycotts were used to put pressure on the guilty corporations to mend their ways, especially their nets. Nervous companies, experiencing slumping sales and bad press, responded to grass-roots pressures in 1990. StarKist, Chicken of the Sea, and Bumble Bee all created a bright red "dolphin-safe" logo signifying that their suppliers no longer use narrow-gauge netting. In 1992, Congress made the "dolphin-safe" logo a condition for sale in the United States, and by 1995, annual dolphin deaths had dropped to an estimated 3,200. Chalk one up for the NGOs (and for the dolphins).[44] ■

Case Study 13.5 The Rainbow Warrior

Given the risks of radiation poisoning, scientific groups such as the Union of Concerned Scientists have argued against further nuclear testing. However, France, one of the declared nuclear powers, conducted 130 atmospheric and underground tests after 1966 on the French Polynesian Pacific island of Mururoa Atoll. In the mid-1980s, Greenpeace was one of many NGOs protesting against France's tests. Greenpeace founder, Canadian David McTaggart, had a feud with French nuclear tests going back to 1972, when his first ship, the *Vega*, was rammed by a French naval vessel for harassment.

McTaggart founded Greenpeace in 1975 with the goal of nonviolent disruption of activities threatening either the environment or world peace. In 1985, he used his 145-foot sailing ship *Rainbow Warrior* for a series of well-publicized passes near Mururoa Atoll to embarrass the French government. Later that summer, scuba divers from the French secret service boarded the *Rainbow Warrior* while in port and set two bombs that exploded, sinking the vessel. Greenpeace photographer Fernando Pereira was still aboard and died. It also was learned that the French military had been spying on Greenpeace and infiltrating its operations for months.

World public opinion condemned the French attack against these peaceful protesters, and contributions to Greenpeace tripled in the wake of the incident, while the French lost a court battle that required $5 million in reparations to Greenpeace. In the interim, Greenpeace has become larger (5 million members), wealthier (a $150 million budget), more bureaucratic (offices in twenty-seven countries and a staff of 1,000), and more successful than anyone could have anticipated in 1975.

Critics, however, have accused it of "hit-and-run" tactics with no follow-up. Poor people in countries such as Argentina and Chile claim that Greenpeace causes unemployment by its efforts to get an international ban on yellow-fin tuna fishing. Conservatives describe it as a threat to capitalism, whereas leftist radicals say that Greenpeace had sold out to expand its own power. In the 1990s, Greenpeace was forced to look inward and reassess its mission, tactics, and image in the light of its rapid rise to stardom.

Despite organizational soul-searching and David McTaggart's departure, a new Greenpeace ship, *Rainbow Warrior II*, again confronted the French at Mururoa in 1992. This time, French commandos arrested its crew and impounded the ship. Another storm of criticism resulted in French president François Mitterand declaring a moratorium on nuclear testing. However, the saga was not over. In 1995, France's new president, Jacques Chirac, announced that it would resume nuclear tests at Mururoa, and Greenpeace responded by sending *Rainbow Warrior II* into French waters on the tenth anniversary of the 1985 explosion. The French then reacted by having 150 commandos board the vessel to remove its two dozen protesting passengers. The ongoing tension between Greenpeace and France symbolizes a broader struggle underway: the battle between NGOs and states for the hearts and minds of humanity.[45] ■

The Greenpeace NGO's ship *Rainbow Warrior*.

Political scientist Craig Murphy provides a comprehensive history of IGOs, concluding that they have benefited humanity by fostering industrial change under capitalism, facilitating transportation and communications developments, and promoting the ideals of internationalism.[46] During the Cold War era, military IGOs held center stage, but they have been shuffled aside somewhat amid new attention to economic IGOs more recently.

Similar to NGOs, IGOs grew in number and importance during the twentieth century, as shown in Figure 13.4. The 1815 six-member Central Commission for the Navigation of the Rhine is the oldest continuous IGO. The Universal Postal Union (UPU), another IGO tracing its roots well back into the nineteenth century, includes all states on earth. The World Health Organization (WHO) and the International Criminal Police Organization (INTERPOL) also boast high participation, with more than 170 members. In the year 1900, 30 IGOs existed; that number grew to 123 by the end of World War II, and to an impressive 272 by the early 1990s.[47]

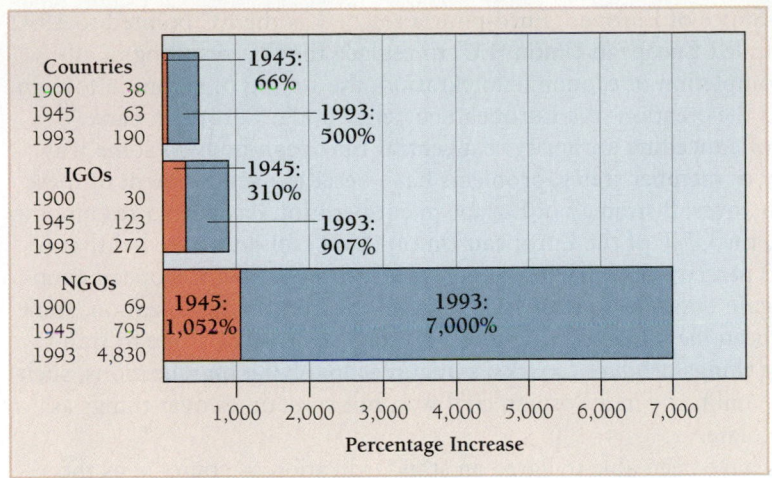

Countries		
1900	38	
1945	63	1945: 66%
1993	190	1993: 500%
IGOs		
1900	30	1945: 310%
1945	123	
1993	272	1993: 907%
NGOs		
1900	69	1945: 1,052%
1945	795	1993: 7,000%
1993	4,830	

1,000 2,000 3,000 4,000 5,000 6,000 7,000
Percentage Increase

Figure 13.4

Expansion of IGOs & NGOs 1900–1993
The number of IGOs and NGOs has expanded more rapidly than the number of countries. This figure shows the relative growth in percentages for countries, IGOs, and NGOs during comparable time periods.

Source: From p. 343 in *International Politics on the World Stage* by John T. Rourke. Copyright © 1995 by Dushkin Publishing/Brown & Benchmark Publishers. Reprinted by permission of The McGraw-Hill Companies.

From EEC to EC to EU

Regional economic cooperation is all the rage in the post–Cold War era, and Europe represents the prototype that others seek to copy. But how did Europe reach this enviable position? The answer can be found partly amid the burning rubble that was Europe at war's end in 1945. In addition to the carnage of more than 50 million war deaths, Europe's cities and its economies were decimated by World War II. As the culmination of centuries of bloody European wars, the Big One led creative thinkers to search for new ways to avoid a reprise.

Among the new ideas was **international functionalism**.[48] More direct approaches to averting war, such as the idealistic 1928 Kellogg-Briand Pact attempting to outlaw war by treaty, and the collective security alliance of the League of Nations, had failed. So why not try an indirect approach, asked the functionalists. If European nations could learn to cooperate on a piecemeal basis over softer cultural, economic, and social matters, maybe they could also learn to cooperate over harder political and military issues. Frequent interaction was intended by the international functionalists to improve relations, rendering conflict less likely. In the late 1940s, such idealism was derided by realists as pie-in-the-sky fantasy. Yet today, Europe is prosperous and pacific, and war seems inconceivable among Western European nations. How did this occur?

It occurred largely in three installments, issued in 1957, 1967, and 1986: the EEC, EC, and EU. Installment number one was the Common Market initiated by the 1957 Treaty of Rome. Two Frenchmen, Robert Schuman and Jean Monnet, spearheaded cooperation among France, West Germany, Italy, Belgium, the Netherlands, and Luxembourg (the inner six) to create a customs union called the Common Market, or European Economic Community (EEC). Modest in scope, the EEC reduced tariffs and other trade barriers among the inner six and set common policy for trade with outsiders. The EEC of the Treaty of Rome was in some ways the prototype for North America's customs union, NAFTA, in the 1990s.

Not only did the EEC succeed by growing successful economies among the inner six but also it fostered eagerness to build on its cooperative foundation. In 1967, the EEC merged with the European Coal and Steel Community (ECSC) and the European Atomic Energy Agency (EURATOM), forming a bigger and better organization known as the European Community (EC). Faced with stiff economic competition from the United States and military competition from the Soviet Union, the European countries realized that only through economic cooperation could Europe compete among the heavyweights. Growing to twelve members, the EC in the 1960s and 1970s also expanded into the creation of quasi-governmental institutions, such as the European Parliament, Council of Ministers, and the Commission.

The momentum of European cooperation continued to mount into the 1980s, culminating in the Single European Act of 1986, whereby members pledged to create what

International functionalism
■ Cooperation between states in nonpolitical areas, such as communications, trade, and travel, can spill over to render war between states less likely

Jean Monnet, one-half of the team crusading for a united Europe, more than fifty years ago.

some called a "United States of Europe." Euro-phoria reigned as the EC pointed to 1992 as the date for an expanded European Union (EU) to replace the EC, resulting in all-European passports, completion of economic integration, the setting of common foreign and defense policy, and the creation of a European currency and a European bank.[49]

Because every act of conceding authority to a central European body in some way reduces the sovereignty of member states, problems have beset the achievement of these ambitious goals. But the overall strategy of European cooperation has been a resounding success story. By 1996, the GNP of the European Union ($6.2 trillion) exceeded that of the United States by 20 percent ($5.3 trillion), and at least fifteen other European countries were pleading to gain entrance to this club. With all this central organization, some bureaucratization has been inevitable. Trying to get fifteen countries to agree to standardized ways of doing things produces sparks, sometimes involving big questions, such as whether to intervene militarily in a Bosnian civil war, but sometimes over things as simple as defining chocolate.

The EU's members have been able to agree on standardization as complex as the metric system of measurement. But the question of what in the EU may be called chocolate proved problematic. The EU Commission, which sets trade regulations for the EU, was faced with two viewpoints. The Belgians led one faction, with the head of its Godiva Chocolates company arguing that only 100 percent pure chocolate (made entirely of cocoa butter derived from beans imported from West Africa) should bear the name. The British headed a rival faction advocating looser standards, and a spokesman for Cadbury Chocolates urged the EU to "celebrate Europe's regional diversity" by allowing different types of chocolate (allowing manufacturers to replace up to 5 percent of the cocoa with cheaper vegetable oils). It took the EU Commission two years before accepting the looser definition.[50]

By far, however, the most important global IGO since WW II continues to be the United Nations. Let's examine some of the challenges facing the U.N. today and look more closely at its peacekeeping actions.

United Nations at the Crossroads

Chapter 1 contains background information about the basic functions of the U.N., an ever-evolving body responding to a world in flux. Because of U.S.–Soviet tensions from the 1940s to the 1980s, the U.N. was unable to act as decisively as intended by its founders. The threat of either a Soviet or American veto in the Security Council crippled the world body's role as an enforcer of the peace. Then, as communism disintegrated in the Soviet Union and eastern Europe, peace began breaking out all over, with the U.N. playing a pivotal role.

Although the U.N.'s biggest and boldest action occurred in 1991, authorizing the U.S.-led war to liberate Kuwait from Saddam Hussein's Iraqi invasion, many other vital U.N. actions also occurred: twenty-one new peacekeeping actions were undertaken between 1988 and 1994, almost twice as many as from 1948 to 1987. In 1995, U.N. peacekeeping troops operated in twenty countries, totaling more than 70,000 soldiers—fully six times the number active in 1992 (a trend that has continued unabated). Pakistan led the list of contributors with 7,000 troops, India was second, France third, and Bangladesh and the United Kingdom fourth and fifth, respectively. The United States ranked thirty-third, with 754 blue-helmeted U.N. peacekeepers in uniform.

A significant problem arose alongside the U.N.'s newfound relevance, however, because the increased demands for its services were not matched by increased funding from member states. In fact, its largest benefactor, the United States, was complaining about its financial burden (25 percent of the U.N.'s budget) and threatening to cut its contributions. Secretary-General Boutros Boutros-Ghali reminded members that the U.N. consists of the sum of its parts and is an IGO capable of doing only what its members empower it and fund it to do. It is not a world government.[51]

The U.N. celebrated its sixtieth birthday in 2005. However, in addition to receiving praise for past successes, the world body has been taking a beating from rich and poor countries alike. Topping the minimalist agenda of the MDCs has been their view that the U.N. spends too much money. Conversely, the maximalist agenda of the LDCs has called for an increase in its various services and therefore higher expenditures by the rich countries. Although most experts agree that some kind of U.N. reform is needed, a huge gulf separates the respective agendas of the rich states and the poor states.

The theme of administrative waste and inefficiency at the U.N. permeates the complaints of the major powers, especially the United States in recent years. They portray the world body, with its 15,000 employees, as a bloated Third World bureaucracy. In what sounded like a reprise of American electoral themes in the 1990s, "leaner and meaner" could have been the buzzword of the rich countries. They pay the lion's share of the U.N. budget, and their cost-cutting campaign has succeeded in reducing it by about 5 percent in recent years. A clear majority of U.N. members today are small, poor countries. Therefore, the reforms they favor entail a more aggressive role for the world body, which means more expensive programs. Heading their list of complaints in the late-1990s was the U.N. debt crisis, as the body was in the red to the tune of $3 billion, owing to nonpayment of dues, one-third of which resulted from American nonpayment. A decade earlier, the 5,000 blue-helmeted U.N. troops served under a peacekeeping budget that amounted to $600 million annually; but by 1995, those figures had risen to 60,000 troops at $3.6 billion annually. Third World countries have also argued for greater representation in the U.N.'s most powerful organ, the 15-member Security Council. When the U.N. began, it had 51 members, but today it contains 191, and small countries want restructuring to meet new realities.[52]

Which do you find more compelling, the cost-cutting argument of the large countries, or the debt resolution and restructuring priorities of the small members? Currently at a crossroads in its history, the world body can expand, or it can contract. In general, idealists within the United States tend to support a more robust U.N. role with increased funding, whereas realists see the U.N. as ineffectual and prefer a less ambitious world body.

More on Peacekeeping

The most serious strains between MDCs and LDCs at the U.N. derive from ever-expanding peacekeeping demands on the world body, namely deployments "to help countries torn by conflict to conditions for sustainable peace." This entails soldiers, military officers, police, and civilians from many countries to monitor peace processes that emerge in post-conflict situations. The Security Council is given the power by the U.N. Charter to undertake collective action and to dispatch troops serving under U.N. command. However, sometimes the Security Council chooses to get involved indirectly in a particular situation authorizing a regional IGO such as NATO or the African Union (AU) to intercede.

Violence within or between states represents a breeding ground for problems to worsen; therefore, the international community has learned that the risks of inaction generally turn out worse than the risks of action. The Rwanda genocide of 1994 serves as a classic case. Few modern conflicts remain truly "local" and often generate problems such as trafficking in arms, drugs, or people; terrorism; refugee flows; and environmental degradation. During more than fifty years of experience, U.N. peacekeeping has developed a unique sense of legitimacy based on proven outcomes. For example, when it moved into Bosnia in 1995, a genuine crisis existed, but a decade later, merely a faint echo remained. Troops serving under U.N. command are paid by their own governments according to their national rank and salary scale.

Typically under-sized and under-resourced, in the 1990s, several post-conflict situations remained actively dangerous, with both civilians and peacekeepers being killed. Therefore, the Security Council has, more recently, agreed to authorize what are called "more robust" rules of engagement in certain circumstances. Such mandates enable peacekeepers to use "all necessary means to protect civilians, prevent violence against U.N. staff and personnel, and deter armed elements from ignoring peace agreements." In

2006, mandates of this type were authorized for actions in Liberia, Kosovo, Burundi, Haiti, and the Ivory Coast, where they have been deemed successful. These 2006 reforms grew out of what was called "The Brahimi Report," a panel headed by former Algerian foreign minister Lakhdar Brahimi who was asked to assess the state of peacekeeping operations and to make recommendations.

The most crucial issue may be the relative effectiveness of U.N. peacekeeping operations. Many studies have concluded that these operations are generally "both effective and cost-effective," largely because the U.N. has a "built-in mechanism for globally sharing the financial, material, and personnel costs." Several historians have charted a strong inverse correlation between peacekeeping deployments and war casualties. One Rand Corporation research project looked at eight completed operations (Belgian Congo, Namibia, El Salvador, Cambodia, Mozambique, Eastern Slavonia, Sierra Leone, and East Timor), concluding that six of the eight were successful and stating more generally that U.N. peacekeeping is a "highly efficient means of placing post-conflict societies on the path to enduring peace and democratic government." (See *http://www.un.org/ Depts/dpko/dpko/faq/index.htm* for more about U.N. peacekeeping.)

Multinational Corporations (MNCs)

Like NGOs and IGOs, multinational corporations (MNCs) have grown in number and expanded their reach in ways uncongenial to states. Technological revolutions in transportation and communications have enabled MNCs to spread their commercial influence into all corners of the globe. Subaru Motors, Chrysler, Exxon Mobil, IBM, Texas Instruments, Samsung, and Fuji Film are examples of the seemingly endless list of global actors in this category. The essence of an MNC has been described as consisting of "a firm with production, marketing, and distribution facilities located in several countries, and highly flexible in moving around capital, goods and technology to match market conditions. It also 'thinks globally,' or has no specific [national] loyalty in making decisions."[53]

The MNC does, however, respond to one paramount motivation: profits. As the undisputed fuel driving the MNC engine, the profit motive leads it to shift its resources often, leaving it vulnerable to criticism by proponents of social justice. Fair play and human compassion sometimes get overwhelmed by a corporate fixation on the bottom line.

Critics and Defenders of MNCs

One scathing critic publicizing the MNC's global role has been David C. Korten, of the People-Centered Development Forum, a social justice NGO. Korten complains that states have allowed MNCs, often larger and wealthier than most countries, to function irresponsibly, with little public accountability. Of the world's one hundred largest economies, roughly half are corporations. Economic globalization has contributed to reducing antitrust actions taken by governments, allowing corporations to merge to the point of monopolization.

Korten says that any industry in which five firms control 50 percent of the market constitutes a monopoly, and that in the late 1990s, five firms did in fact control more than half the market in aerospace, automobiles, airlines, electronics, consumer durables, and steel. Five firms also controlled over 40 percent of global markets in oil, personal computers, and communications media. Korten sees this trend as damaging to both human rights and the environment.[54] Defenders of MNCs counter by arguing that their expansion contributes to improved global prosperity, economic efficiency, and the dissemination of democratic ideas to new areas. Do you consider it feasible that MNCs might someday replace states as the dominant actors in this century? Controversy invariably swirls around MNCs, which can operate for good or ill; but beyond debate is their impressive growth. Once the largest MNC in America, General Motors lost that position to Microsoft in the 1990s, although Microsoft was long embroiled in court battles in the United States and Europe, fighting charges that it constituted a predatory monopoly. Wal-Mart is another example of a seemingly implausible American giant among MNCs.

More than 10,000 MNCs now exist. Roughly 90,000 subsidiaries operate under the control of these 10,000 parent MNCs. Most remain based in a few locations: ninety percent of the top 500 MNCs operate out of North America, Japan, or Europe.[55] In recent years, however, both China and India have been breaking into that elite club. Many corporations once thought to be identifiable with one country have merged with firms from other countries, adding to the interdependent flavor of the global landscape—for example, Ford Motor Company with Mazda, and US Air with British Airways.

International Financial Institutions (IFIs)

The all-purpose U.N. includes six main organs and scores of other institutions as by far the most comprehensive IGO. Increasingly, however, institutions with more specific agendas are gaining attention at the global level. Among them are the international financial institutions (IFIs). Three main areas of economic and financial need arose after World War II, producing three major bodies aiming at global coordination. These relatively new activities in the areas of monetary policy, development lending, and trade have risen to great heights. The flow of international capital has turned into a flood, with tens of trillions of dollars crossing borders each year. Believing that the Great Depression of the 1930s resulted largely from unregulated economic warfare, the world's leaders gathered in 1944 at Bretton Woods, New Hampshire, to set up cooperative bodies.

Monetary Policy: The IMF

Early on, the main function of the International Monetary Fund (IMF) was currency stabilization—that is, bringing order to the process whereby dollars, yen, yuan, rubles, and euros fluctuate in value vis-à-vis one another. By the 1960s, the IMF turned more toward lending money to countries with problems related to their **balance of payments.** The IMF generally imposes stiff **austerity** requirements as a condition for lending. Fiscal austerity measures are generally politically unpopular at home. In addition to the IMF's operation at the global level, there are similar regional institutions, such as the European Monetary System and the Arab Monetary Fund.

Balance of payments ■ An annual accounting device used by states to assess external transactions such as trade, investments, and payments

Austerity ■ Fiscal belt-tightening measures undertaken by governments to receive loans from IFIs

Development Lending: The World Bank

In 2001, the World Bank involved all countries except North Korea and Cuba. Over the years, the World Bank has emerged as the leading source of long-term finance and policy advice for LDCs. It is made up of three divisions: (a) the International Bank for Reconstruction and Development (IBRD), making loans to medium-income countries; (b) the International Development Association (IDA), which specializes in low-interest loans to the poorest countries; and (c) the International Finance Corporation (IFC), helping private economic ventures in developing nations. The evolution of the World Bank is capsulized by a former director, Lewis Preston, who relates that it initially operated toward the reconstruction of Europe and Japan at the end of World War II. The World Bank later shifted more to lending for infrastructure development, and then into adjustment lending when the 1980s debt crisis hit Latin America and other regions very hard. In the 1990s, its mission focused more on rebuilding the former Soviet states.[56]

Free trade ■ The view that society benefits from allowing open and competitive trade to operate with no government intervention

Protectionist ■ Government should act to shelter domestic industries from foreign competition via restrictions such as tariffs, import quotas, and subsidies

Trade: GATT/WTO

The General Agreement on Tariff and Trade (GATT) similarly grew out of the post–World War II vision of economic cooperation at Bretton Woods. It functioned as the central mechanism regulating world trade for five decades. Its basic purpose was to promote **free trade** and in so doing to work against **protectionist** measures, especially

Tariffs ■ A tax placed by governments on imported goods, usually to raise revenues or to protect domestic businesses

taxes on imports known as **tariffs**. After World War II, there were so many economic basket cases littering the landscape that it was very much in the best interests of the United States to foster a new set of plumbing to facilitate the process of selling its goods and services internationally.

American leadership on behalf of free and open trade produced eight rounds of GATT talks, each expanding and refining the activities of this vital IFI. The last (the Uruguay Round) created an expanded successor to the GATT known as the World Trade Organization (WTO) in 1995. More than 135 countries participate in the WTO, comprising over 90 percent of world trade. As you will see in Chapter 15, the secrecy and exclusivity of this mighty triptych—the WTO, IMF, and World Bank—represent a huge target for those protesting publicly against inhumane aspects of what they describe as extant globalization "from above," working toward grass-roots initiatives to catalyze globalization "from below" in a more just future.

Chapter Synopsis

The values and purposes of the state system are Euro-centric because Europe is where it originated about 350 years ago. The catalyst enabling countries to supersede the authority of principalities and fiefdoms at the local level, and the authority of the papacy at the all-European level, was the termination of the bloody Thirty Years' War (Peace of Westphalia, 1648). States such as Sweden, Spain, Denmark, and France agreed on rules of the political game, especially the core principle of sovereignty.

Although the Peace of Westphalia helped reduce bloodshed in Europe, it did not end it. In fact, the system of sovereign states gradually created a body of international law enshrining the legitimacy of war as a means of redressing grievances. The human legacy concerning warfare is indeed a bleak one. Owing to the enhanced lethality of weapons, the twentieth century alone witnessed more than 100 million war deaths. Fortunately, some hopeful trends exist regarding war in today's world. For example, the theory of the "democratic peace" supports two contentions: (1) the historical record shows that democracies do not fight one another, and (2) a wave of democratization has swept the globe in recent decades. From the confluence of these two observations, it is predicted that the next century may prove more pacific than the last.

Four challengers to the state's domination of world affairs appear ready to exert greater influence: NGOs, IGOs, MNCs, and IFIs. These actors seem locked in a struggle with states to win the hearts and minds of humanity. No longer can it be assumed that countries claim the first loyalty of John and Jane Doe. States have lost prestige through inertia concerning a variety of intractable GIs, especially environment, population, food, energy, human rights, and WMD. In particular, many NGOs and IGOs offer agendas emphasizing cooperative ventures that are more attractive to educated global citizens communicating more freely in our brave, new, wired and cell phoning world.

FOR DIGGING DEEPER

Ahmed, Shamima, and David Potter. *NGOs in International Politics*. Kumarian Press, 2006.

Arend, Anthony, and Robert J. Beck. *International Law and the Use of Force*. Routledge, 2008.

Batliwala, Srilatha, and David Brown, eds. *Transnational Civil Society: An Introduction*. Kumarian Press, 2006.

Brown, Michael E., Sean Lynn-Jones, and Steven Miller, eds. *Debating the Democratic Peace*. MIT Press, 1996.

Brown, Seyom. *New Forces, Old Forces, and the Future of World Politics*. HarperCollins, 1995.

Croxton, Derek, and Anuschka Tischer. *The Peace of Westphalia: A Historical Dictionary*. Greenwood Press, 2001.

Durch, William, ed. *Twenty-First-Century Peace Operations*. U.S. Institute for Peace, 2006.

Fitzduff, Mari, and Cheyenne Church, eds. *NGOs at the Table: Strategies for Influencing Policy in Areas of Conflict*. Rowman, Littlefield, 2003.

Florini, Ann, ed. *The Third Force: The Rise of Transnational Civil Society*. Carnegie Endowment Publications, 2000.

Forsberg, Randall, William Driscoll, Gregory Webb, and Jonathan Dean. *Non-Proliferation Primer: Preventing the Spread of Nuclear, Chemical, and Biological Weapons*. MIT Press, 1995.

Gelvin, James L. *The Israel-Palestine Conflict: One Hundred Years of War*. Cambridge University Press, 2005.

Gordon, Michael R., and Bernard E. Trainor. *COBRA II: The Inside Story of the Invasion and Occupation of Iraq*. Vintage Books, 2007.

Heinrich, V. Finn, and Lorenzo Fioramonti. *CIVICUS Global Survey of Civil Society, Volume 2*. Kumarian Press, 2007.

Henderson, Errol A. *Democracy and War: The End of an Illusion?* Oxford University Press, 2002.

Huntington, Samuel. *The Third Wave: Democratization in the Late Twentieth Century*. University of Oklahoma Press, 1992.

Ivie, Robert L. *Dissent from War*. Kumarian Press, 2007.

Kagan, Donald. *On the Origins of War and the Preservation of Peace*. Anchor Doubleday, 1995.

Kennedy, Greg, and Andrew Dorman, eds. *War and Diplomacy: From World War I to the War on Terrorism*. Potomac Books, 2008.

King, Roger, and Gavin Kendall. *The State, Democracy, and Globalization*. Palgrave Press, 2004.

Kirchner, Emil, and James Sperling. *Global Security Governance: Competing Perceptions of Security in the 21st Century*. Routledge, 2007.

MacQueen, Norrie. *Peacekeeping and the International System*. Routledge, 2006.

Metz, Steven. *Iraq and the Evolution of American Strategy*. Potomac Books, 2008.

Moeller, Richard. *The Internet Guide for Students of World Politics*. Prentice Hall, 2006.

Mueller, John. *Retreat from Doomsday: The Obsolescence of Major War*. Basic Books, 1989.

Pierson, Christopher. *The Modern State*. Routledge, 1996.

Pugh, Michael, and Waheguru Pal Singh, eds. *The United Nations and Regional Security: Europe and Beyond*. Monterrey Institute of International Studies, 2003.

Rochester, J. Martin. *U.S. Foreign Policy in the 21st Century: Gulliver's Travails*. Westview Press, 2007.

Rosenau, James N. *Turbulence in World Politics: A Theory of Change and Continuity*. Princeton University Press, 1990.

Schoff, James L., and others. *Nuclear Matters in North Korea: Building a Multilateral Response for Future Stability in Northeast Asia*. Potomac Books, 2008.

Stephenson, James. *Losing the Golden Hour: An Insider's View of Iraq's Reconstruction*. Potomac Books, 2007.

Stoddard, Abby. *Humanitarian Alert: NGO Information and its Impact on U.S. Foreign Policy*. Kumarian Press, 2006.

Strayer, Robert. *Why Did the Soviet Union Collapse?* Mitchell E. Sharpe, 1998.

Tannenwald, Nina. *The Nuclear Taboo: The U.S. and the Non-Use of Nuclear Weapons Since 1945*. Cambridge University Press, 2007.

U.N. Publications. *Atoms for Peace: A Pictorial History of the IAEA*. United Nations, 2007.

U.S. Department of Defense. *The Armed Forces Officer*. National Defense University, 2007.

Vanhanen, Tatu. *Prospects of Democracy*. Routledge, 1997.

Weart, Spencer. *Never at War: Why Democracies Will Not Fight One Another*. Yale University Press, 1998.

Whitfield, Teresa. *Friends Indeed? The United Nations, Groups of Friends, and the Resolution of Conflict*. U.S. Institute of Peace, 2007.

INTERNET

Arms Control Association:
http:www.armscontrol.org

Bulletin of Atomic Scientists:
http://www.bullatsci.org/

Carnegie Endowment for International Peace:
http://www.ceip.org

Center for Nonproliferation Studies (CNS):
http://www.cns.miis.edu/index.htm

Center for Strategic and International Studies:
http://www.csis.org

CIA Publications and Reports:
http://www.cia.gov/library

Citation Style Guides for Internet and Electronic Sources:
http://www.library.ualberta.ca/guides/citations/index.cfm

CNN Custom News:
http://www.cnn.com

Cold War:
http:www.cnn.com/SPECIALS/cold.war/

Cuban Missile Crisis:
http://www.hyperion.advanced.org/11046/

Culture of Peace:
http://www.seedsofpeace.org

European Union:
http://www.europa.eu

Federation of American Scientists:
http://www.fas.org/

Foreign Affairs Online:
http://www.people.virginia.edu/~rjb3v/rjb.html

Foreign Policy Magazine:
http://www.foreignpolicy.com

Foreign Wire:
http://www.foreignwire.com

Institute for International Mediation and Conflict Resolution:
http://www.iimcr.org

Institute for the Study of Conflict, Ideology, and Policy:
http://www.bu.edu/iscip/

Maps on Other Websites:
http://www.lib.utexas.edu/Libs/PCL/Map_collection/map_sites/

Missile Threats and Responses:
http://www.cdiss.org/tempor1.htm

National Sovereignty Threats from Globalization:
http://www.globalpolicy.org/nations/soverindex.htm

Nonproliferation Topics (Carnegie Endowment):
http://www.ceip.org/files/nonprolif

North Atlantic Treaty Organization (NATO):
http://www.nato.int/

Nuclear Arms Race History:
http:www.nuclearfiles.org

Organization of American States:
http://www.oas.org/

Peace and Conflict Studies:
http://www.dir.yahoo.com/Social_Science/peace_and_Conflict_Studies

Peacekeeping Operations (UN):
http://www.un.org/Depts/dpko/home.shtml

Research and Writing:
http://www.ipl.org/teen/aplus/

Soviet Archive Exhibit (Library of Congress):
http://www.sunsite.unc.edu/expo/soviet//entrance.html

State Department Background Notes:
http://www.state.gov/www/background_notes/

United Nations Cyber School Bus:
http://www.un.org/pubs/cyberschoolbus/

United Nations International Law Commission:
http://www.un.org/law/ilc/index.htm

World Audit of National Scales:
http://www.worldaudit.org

World Bank:
http://www.worldbank.org

World Trade Organization:
http://www.wto.org

CHAPTER 14

Macroeconomics and U.S. Economic Hegemony

CORE OBJECTIVE

To analyze the means of subsistence devised by societies to produce, distribute, and consume goods and services.

THEMATIC QUESTIONS

- How have humans historically organized the production, distribution, and consumption of goods and services?

- In what ways is the discipline of economics different from other social sciences?

- Which theories of economics competed for dominance during the twentieth century?

- What special role has the United States played in the world economy since World War II?

- How does the idea that "bigger means better" fit into economics more comfortably than anthropology?

- What is the nature of the contemporary U.S. business climate?

Economics is one of the most quantitative social sciences. Methodologically, economics borrows heavily from its cousins in the physical sciences but has relatively little in common with the humanities. At some academic institutions, economics makes its home in the division of social sciences, whereas in others, it resides in the division of business because the content of economics naturally overlaps both business and the social sciences.

Economics and the Stanislavsky Method

By applying the Stanislavsky Method of analysis to each of the six social sciences, we seek to glean the essence of its distinctive perspective. For economics, it is the prism of the bottom line, or the value of money and other economic resources as means to ends deemed significant by people. "Bigger is better" might well be the motto of traditional economics. This motto embraces the expansion model of progress: in an economy that grows year after year, more and more goods and services are available for people, which is what everyone really desires.

This expansion model of progress, the heart and soul of economics, expresses value judgments diametrically opposed to the core values of another social science discipline. Applying the Stanislavsky Method of perceptual analysis to anthropology, we find a very different set of lenses. A fundamental belief in the anthropological perspective (addressed in Chapter 9) is the judgment that any society is as good as any other society and thus has a right to live according to its rules of the social game. Accordingly, anthropological lenses see a world inhabited by diverse societies choosing to operate in ways deriving from their experience. In the anthropological view, social scientists ought not impose Western-style thinking on others. We should not consider our assumptions about human existence as superior, even to pre-industrial ones.

Economics, however, assumes that human nature is the same everywhere: all peoples ultimately desire a higher standard of living (more and better goods and services). The dichotomous views of economists and anthropologists undergird the point made in Chapter 2 that although social sciences all examine human behavior, they do so from decidedly different angles. The major organization for economists in the United States, the American Economic Association (AEA), has more than 22,000 members. Half of them work in higher education, one-third work in business and industry, and most of the rest are on government payrolls. The AEA was founded in 1885 and incorporated in 1923. Its Website (listed at the end of this chapter) contains links to information about the organization, including membership, AEA publications, job openings, and news about its scholarly meetings.[1]

The Americanization of Economics

Intellectual historian Dorothy Ross considers economics, political science, and sociology the three "core" disciplines in the "Americanization" of the social sciences during the latter nineteenth and early twentieth centuries. Her analysis in no way demeans the modern contributions of the other three social sciences (anthropology, psychology, geography), but she thinks that the historical role of the three "core" disciplines (economics, political science, sociology) sets them apart as shapers of the "Americanized" social sciences: quantitative, methodologically rigorous, and empirical.[2]

In the American Gilded Age (after the Civil War and prior to World War I) an intellectual battle was waged concerning the proper scope and methods of the social sciences. Those emerging from French and German academic traditions (humanists) favored broad philosophical and historical analysis inseparable from ethical considerations. Their academic homes were in the small, church-supported private colleges that had typified American higher education since the late eighteenth century.

Their rivals, however, had just begun creating "professionalized" graduate departments in America's brand new universities. These social scientists acted as critics of the social humanists, who traced their intellectual lineage more to Britain than to the European continent. The social scientists' quest for natural-science–like methods of social research went farthest and fastest in the discipline of economics, where measurement blended seamlessly with the subject matter. They wanted an academic division of labor via professional disciplines able to improve the real world. No other social science fit this ambitious role as well as did economics.

One of the last of the generation of humanistic economists was Professor Edwin Seligman. Seligman's German-Jewish background was unusual because few Jews held academic positions during the Gilded Age in America. His roots, however, were in the wealthy and influential New York City community, and his voice in the economics debate was clear and distinctive; before long, however, it became a minority voice. Seligman criticized new quantitative approaches and published economic treatises steeped in ethical and historical arguments.

Gradually, Seligman's optimistic ethical idealism ran headlong into the chaotic world conditions leading to World War I, when the more detached, scientific, and professional voices of scholars such as Francis Walker took over the discipline of economics. Francis Walker's graduate courses in economics at Yale University taught that moral philosophy was anachronistic in the light of more powerful scientific tools of investigation, which he began describing as early as the 1880s in his *Political Economy* (1884). In retrospect, economics had less difficulty shedding its philosophical and historical identity and adopting the mantle of empirical science than did political science or sociology.

One century ago, the following issues competed at the cutting edge of economic discourse: (1) to what extent its *content* would maintain the philosophical and historical analysis of political economy or shift to narrower questions of human economic behavior; and (2) to what extent its *methods* would continue their humanistic orientation or change to more empirical techniques. Today, the discipline again faces change. Modern changes, however, revolve largely around economic globalization, including the emergence of a discipline melding the micro (individual), macro (national), and mega (global) levels of analysis. The main principles of economics resonate at all three levels.

Basic Concepts of Economics

The existence of universal human needs necessitates the creation of institutions to provide for those needs. High on the list of needs is a material means of subsistence. The results are institutions that produce, distribute, and consume both goods and services. At the hub of economics resides the question of how people go about coping with the fundamental problem of economic life: *scarcity*. The problem of scarcity stems from the juxtaposition of two realities: (1) the *infinite* range of goods and services that peoples desire; and (2) the *finite* resources available to obtain those goods and services.

Economics involves humans interacting to translate resources into goods and services aimed at meeting our economic *wants,* as well as our *needs,* and then distributing goods and services to those who will consume them. The scarcity of goods and services forces us to make difficult choices or to prioritize our desires from most to least important. These difficult economic choices involving what to produce, in what manner, and for whom can be left up to private individuals to decide for themselves, or they can be made collectively through some public forum.

Factors of Production

To satisfy human wants and needs, various resources contribute to producing goods and services. These **factors of production** include two types of human resources and two forms of nonhuman resources. **Labor** involves the physical and mental effort that workers bring to the economy. Owners of the means of production, who are usually represented by paid managers specializing in the day-to-day operation of business and industry, purchase labor from their employees. In addition to the labor provided by workers, owners and their managers bring the second human resource to the production process—**entrepreneurship**—the ability to conceptualize a business enterprise as well as the willingness to invest personal resources in the competitive marketplace.

The two nonhuman factors of production, land and capital, are more tangible in nature. Land includes natural resources such as water, forests, minerals, and property—all provided by nature. The other, capital, covers the gamut of equipment used in the process of production.

Factors of production ■ Resources committed to the creation of goods and services

Labor ■ Skills sold, by those who perform work, to managers and owners as their contribution to the production process

Entrepreneurship ■ A form of risk-taking inherent in the process of undertaking any new commercial enterprise in a market setting

A market involves people buying and selling goods and services. This open-air summer market in Boston, Massachusetts captures the hustle and bustle associated with markets.

Here we are talking about material objects such as buildings, tools, and machines. As nonhuman resources, land and capital contribute the nuts and bolts of the production process.

Markets: Supply, Demand, and Price

With scarcity as the basic economic dilemma, triggered by finite resources and expanding human wants and needs, it is no wonder that these forces play themselves out as exchanges in a competitive milieu known as the **market.** In preindustrial societies, economic transactions literally took place in centrally located marketplaces. Although most preindustrial societies have given way to industrial ones, we retain the label market to symbolize economic arrangements whereby people exchange goods and services. A vital component of markets is that they depend on the personal initiative of individual citizens to catalyze the production of the goods people want. Without direct regulation of the market, changes in the price of goods and services help to adjust production to consumption, and consumption back to production, in an economic feedback loop.

Markets depend greatly on the role of pricing because the price system determines who gets what and for how much in a market arrangement. Goods and services are **supplied** in the belief that people will want to buy them—in other words, that there will be a demand for them. **Demand** for goods and services consists of the willingness by people to buy something at a particular price. When the quantity demanded equals the quantity supplied, the market price for a given item is dictated by this convergence of supply and demand. The market price is sometimes called the **equilibrium price.** Willingness and ability to pay contribute to market prices, with demand, supply, and competition intersecting to identify the cost of goods and services.

However, powerful forces can sometimes intercede to distort the role of supply and demand in the pricing of goods and services. The competitive nature of the market may even be removed altogether by the existence of a **monopoly** over one or more commodities. Supply and demand have not been allowed to exercise their natural influence in the pricing of diamonds for a long time because of the international monopoly known as De Beers. The pricing of few other commodities has been subverted as successfully as diamonds, as described in Case Study 14.1.

In ancient times, the exchanges that took place in marketplaces often consisted of direct item-for-item transactions known as **bartering.** Exchange through barter had the advantages of simplicity, directness, and immediacy. For example, if you were proficient at making hunting knives, you might directly exchange them in the market for meat or for blankets. However, for bartering to work well, a double convergence of economic wants must occur: I must want your knife and you must want my blankets to satisfy us. When the number of bartering participants increases significantly, problems arise in the system.

In many early societies, a particular good was selected as a standard medium of exchange. On the Pacific island of Yap, large stone wheels were chosen. The ancient Greeks used cattle, whereas indigenous Americans relied on strings of beads called wampum. The introduction of **money** as a measurement of exchange provided a more durable, portable, and replicable medium, thus facilitating commerce greatly.[3]

National Economic Models

The most robust level of economic activity for more than three centuries has been the macro, or state, level. Three common models of national economic organization have been provided by the **command** government-directed model, the **capitalist** model, and

Diamonds—in all their radiant (albeit hyper-marketed and not-so-competitive) glory.

Market ■ Economic exchanges driven by competition, so that the forces of supply and demand determine the pricing of goods and services

Supply ■ The amount of a commodity needed to match demand in order to be sold at a certain price

Demand ■ The interest among people for a given commodity as an influence upon its price at a given time

Equilibrium price ■ The price of a commodity resulting from supply and demand countervailing one another in the marketplace

Monopoly ■ A market situation in which sale of a commodity is controlled by a single seller, thus frustrating the normal competitive dynamic

Bartering ■ The act of exchanging goods or services directly, without the use of money

Money ■ Currency issued by a government that acts as a means of exchange in establishing the price of goods and services

Command ■ An alternative approach to the capitalist economy that emphasizes central planning, governmental ownership, and production quotas for producers

Capitalist ■ An economic system favoring free-market forces, competition, and private ownership of the means of production

Case Study 14.1   The De Beers Diamond Empire

Most people believe that diamonds are much rarer than they really are. A hugely successful one-hundred-year monopoly and marketing campaign have created something of a deception—namely, the illusion that diamonds are extremely valuable; this perception has served to create its own reality. The marketing slogan "diamonds are forever" has created a powerful cultural imperative to buy diamonds as both good investments and as ritualistic gifts symbolizing love. But who has the power, wealth, and skill to create such a potent illusion for so long?

In the diamond industry, it is not a country or an IGO. Rather, it is the Oppenheimer family of South Africa, and its De Beers corporation—one of the most successful global **cartels** in history. This cartel is referred to as the Central Selling Organization (CSO), and it has succeeded where efforts to control the market in coffee, copper, tin, and steel have all failed. By controlling the production, pricing, and marketing of diamonds, De Beers has managed to manipulate the entire industry. Its most important achievement has consisted of co-opting potential rivals into joining the cartel, rather than competing with it.

By artificially limiting the supply of diamonds, the cartel stimulates demand that exceeds supply, which results in high prices for the diamonds available on the market. Diamonds are found where carbon is found, making them less rare than most people think. Vast deposits of diamonds have been mined in other parts of Africa and in Russia, Australia, and Canada. Thus far, De Beers has been able to entice these diamond suppliers to join the cartel rather than compete against it.

In the United States, such monopolistic practices are regarded as economically unhealthy, as well as being illegal under U.S. antitrust laws. However, De Beers has long gotten around this restriction by working through intermediaries in the American economy. This practice makes diamonds more expensive in the United States than they ought to be. In 1992, presidential candidate Bill Clinton vowed to do something about the diamond cartel. However, proving in court exactly what De Beers is up to is not easy, and the Clinton administration experienced frustration in its efforts to prosecute De Beers as well as other quasi-monopolistic enterprises such as Microsoft, skewing supply and demand. The Clinton administration scored its first big victory in 1996 when the mammoth agribusiness Archer Daniels Midland (ADM) lost an antitrust case and paid out $100 million in fines. The diamond cartel has also shown some signs of faltering on its own. In 2000, De Beers announced that it would begin to sell a large amount of its massive diamond hoard ($4 billion worth) and would concentrate instead on selling the stones from its own mines. ■

Cartel ■ An organization of producers interested in limiting competition and establishing high prices by manipulating shortages via low production quotas among members

Traditional ■ An economy based on simple exchanges of goods and services through bartering that is common among preindustrial societies

Individualistic capitalism ■ A variation on the theme of market economies that favors an entrepreneurial style of personal risk-taking and self-reliance

Communitarian capitalism ■ A market economy that combines entrepreneurship with emphasis on social responsibility

the **traditional** model. We stressed earlier that scarcity dictates tough choices required to answer the complex question of who gets what and how they get it.

In societies preferring collectivist forms of group decision making, the command model of central planning by an authoritative government developed in the twentieth century. When the Soviet Union led the world's thirteen communist countries, it was much easier to place the command face with the communist name, as the archetype of collectivism at work. The four communist countries left in 2008—North Korea, Vietnam, China, and Cuba—continued to exemplify the undemocratic, bureaucratic, and authoritarian nature congenial to the command economy.

The capitalist, free-market model has evolved in societies suspicious of extensive reliance on governmental authority. Capitalist economies give considerable latitude to the individual and rely on the forces of the marketplace (not government planners) to determine through supply, demand, and pricing exactly who gets what and how they get it. Figure 14.1 illustrates the distinction made between the more **individualistic capitalism** based on the pursuit of self-interest as found in the United States, the Netherlands, and United Kingdom, and the more **communitarian capitalism.** The latter model is dedicated to serving the interests of customers and society and is found in Japan, France, and Germany.[4]

The preindustrial economy continues to rely on hunting and gathering, horticulture, or pastoral means of subsistence and still exists in many smaller societies. However, the economic and political significance of these preindustrial societies is small in the modern world, and economists and political scientists generally leave the study of preindustrialism to anthropologists.

In reality, by the twentieth-century most macro-economies combined the command and capitalist models, with some leaning toward public control, and others leaning

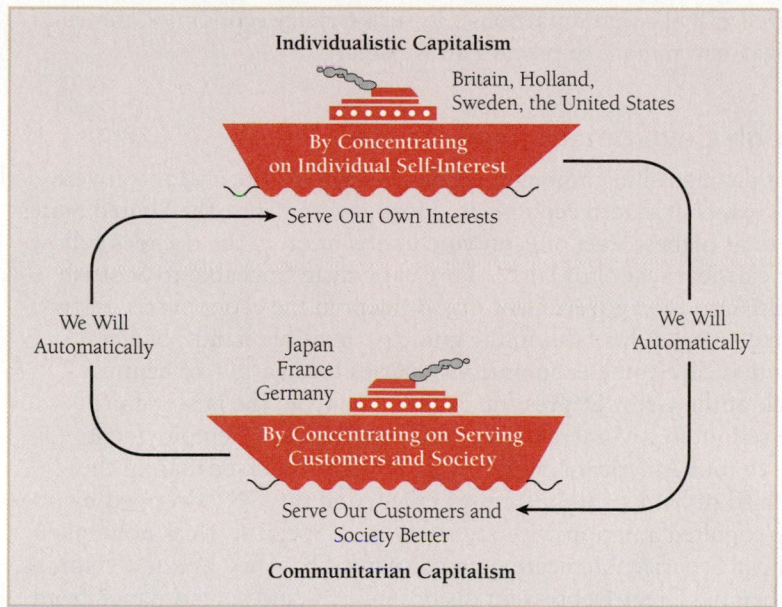

Figure 14.1

Individualistic and Communitarian Capitalism

Source: The Seven Cultures of Capitalism by Charles Hampden-Turner and Alfons Trompenaars. Copyright © 1993 by Charles Hampden-Turner. Used by permission of Doubleday, a division of Bantam Dell Publishing Group.

toward private market forces. The ownership of property in mostly capitalist economies such as the United States is primarily private, yet with some public ownership of property and a minimal amount of communal (private-group-owned) property. The global trend from the 1940s to the 1960s was toward a greater governmental role in the economy and governmental ownership of many industries, whereas the emphasis since the 1980s has shifted to greater reliance on private venues of economic growth, resulting in the privatization of many government-owned industries around the world.

Terms of trade ■ The relationship between the value of a country's imports and the value of its exports

Primary, Secondary, Tertiary Economies

Economists delineate other types of macro-economies besides the command versus capitalist dichotomy. One trichotomy relates to economic level of sophistication in production, distribution, and consumption of goods and services. Most LDCs remain mired in the *primary* economy's reliance on the production of goods extracted from the earth—agricultural products such as bananas and cocoa, and raw materials such as bauxite and tin. These undiversified economies share a colonial heritage and relatively low demand for their primary products, creating a **terms-of-trade** problem for poor countries such as Nigeria, Bolivia, and Sri Lanka. States relying on exporting primary products suffer declining terms of trade when prices of their imports rise faster than prices of their exports.

Tertiary economics, such as America's, feature the high-tech service sector. At the turn of the millennium, Microsoft, Inc., dwarfed all other companies in the expanding sophisticated services sector.

The *secondary* economy relies mostly on manufactured goods such as refrigerators, golf clubs, and furniture. Greece, Indonesia, and Hungary provide examples of mid-level economies much more productive than the LDCs but still lagging well behind the world's upper-tier economies. In places such as Canada, Germany, Switzerland, Japan, and the United States, macro-economies have evolved well beyond the industrial manufacturing of secondary economies. Today, they inhabit the high-tech information age of complex services such as bioengineering, medical services, computer software, and legal services (all

sped up by revolutionized global communications). In such *tertiary* economies, information has become a critical determinant of power and wealth.

How Much Is Enough Government Involvement?

Economists are fond of distinguishing among the household, the firm, and the government as the chief participants in macro economics. Most governments, the United States included, experienced their highest level of economic intervention in the decades following World War II. The classical school of laissez-faire capitalism traceable to Scottish philosopher Adam Smith criticized government involvement in the economy as dysfunctional. Classicists argued, instead, for faith in the guiding "invisible hand" of free-market forces—a view that captivated economic visionaries for nearly two centuries.

Great Depression ■ The prolonged and severe decline of a country's economy

However, the shock of the **Great Depression** (1930s) rendered the laissez-faire mantra of competitive self-interest vulnerable on numerous fronts. Unemployment climbed as high as one in four Americans, wages were 60 percent lower than in the previous decade, one-third of banks and businesses failed, and the GNP dropped by one-half. Massive suffering engulfed a nation without safety nets. Social services now taken for granted, such as Social Security, Medicare, unemployment benefits, and food stamps, simply did not exist when the Great Depression dislocated lives and spread havoc from Syracuse to Sacramento and everywhere in between. The viability of capitalism seemed dubious to many observers.

When a redistribution of income is needed in market economies with democratic expression available to the people, individuals and groups typically demand action to alleviate some of their suffering. The main agent of change combating the American Depression, President Franklin D. Roosevelt, redistributed income and introduced other palliatives. His aggressive New Deal policies were based on British economist John Maynard Keynes, who advocated increased governmental spending to prime the economic pump by creating jobs, thus starting economic recovery. Roosevelt created governmental programs and agencies, producing edifices of transportation and communications infrastructure across America. Governmental expansion continued unabated through the 1970s. Challenges to "big government" gained momentum with Ronald Reagan's election in 1980.

Economic Dysfunctions and Keynesian Prescriptions

Governments are generally called upon to intervene when the macro-economy is malfunctioning. Fortunately, most economic dysfunctions do not rival the Great Depression of the 1930s in scope or depth. A lesser decline, when the economy fails to grow for two or more consecutive quarters, is called a *recession*.

The inevitable ups and downs of economic productivity result in fluctuations known as the *business cycle*. Americans have been relatively well off in this respect as recessions have been recorded during only 20 percent of U.S. history. One of the tools available to government in fighting a recession is *fiscal policy*, having to do with taxing and spending revenues. Just as during the Great Depression, Keynesian theory calls for action to increase consumer demand during a recession. The prescription calls for government to add to the total demand by increasing its spending. It can also cut taxes or give rebates, providing consumers with more money to spend. Keynesian theory also calls for government to run a deficit, or take on debt, to prime the economic pump.

Inflation

Another form of economic malfunction, one that places a disproportionate burden on the poor (especially pensioners on fixed incomes) is *inflation*, characterized by rapidly rising prices and eroded purchasing power of the consumer's money. Inflation is often caused by demand growing faster than production of goods and services. There are two main variants of inflation. The first is *demand-pull inflation*, caused by an increase in aggregate demand. When President Lyndon Johnson increased spending on the Vietnam War in the 1960s from $100 billion to $144 billion in three short years without raising taxes or cutting government spending, he created a scenario for double-digit demand-pull inflation in the 1970s. High demand for military goods pulled the inflation rate up.

The other form of inflation, *cost-push inflation,* involves increased cost of a critical good pushing up the rate of inflation. A prime example of cost-push inflation grew out of the two oil shocks of 1973 and 1979 caused by the Organization of Petroleum Exporting Countries (OPEC). When the thirteen OPEC countries agreed to cut their production of oil supplies to the world, they pushed the price of crude oil from under $3 per barrel in 1973 to over $38 in 1979, contributing to cost-push inflation.

Russia's efforts under Boris Yeltsin to move from a planned central economy to a more capitalistic economy briefly triggered triple-digit inflationary rates (exceeding 100 percent) in 1997. Brazil, Bolivia, and Argentina in Latin America, as well as Israel in the Middle East, later experienced triple-digit inflation in the 1980s. The classic worst-case scenario, however, was Germany's skyrocketing inflation after World War I, which made the deutsche mark virtually worthless as a medium of exchange, forcing bewildered citizens to push wheelbarrows full of currency to purchase routine goods and services. America's double-digit inflation in the 1970s pales in comparison to these dysfunctions.

The Keynesian prescription for inflation is the opposite of that for recession: cut government spending and increase taxes. The reduction of government expenditures will lessen total demand and equilibrate it with supply once again. In addition to fiscal (tax) policy, government can also apply monetary policy in fighting recession and inflation. Monetary policy controls the flow of money and credit to influence economic performance. During a recession, government can relax controls on the flow of money, thereby encouraging banks to lend more money at lower interest rates. Conversely, during inflation, government can restrict the flow of money, thereby discouraging banks from lending money and causing them to lend at higher rates of interest when they do lend it.

Assessing Economic Performance

As global competition has forced macro-economies into higher levels of efficiency, methods for evaluating economic performance have demonstrated greater sophistication. The most common traditional measure was **gross national product (GNP)**. Since 1992, the United States has shifted to **gross domestic product (GDP)** as its main evaluative tool. However, the differences between GNP and GDP are relatively minor. Per capita (per person) measures of GNP and GDP also represent useful gross comparative data between countries, as do the rate of economic growth, level of price stability, level of consumer satisfaction, equitable wealth distribution, economic productivity (units of worker output), and **net national product (NNP)**.

Most economists consider these measures crucial to understanding complex modern economies such as that of the United States, where a mix of contrasting elements can exist side by side. For example, in the 1990s, GDP and price stability in America were excellent, but the trade deficit and federal debt were massive enough to trouble some economists. Social scientist scholars believe that without sophisticated statistics, one is left with little more than impressionism: judgments lacking standards of evaluation. In contrast, social humanists consider many of the numbers used by economists as too sterile.

A YARDSTICK FOR QUALITY OF LIFE Social humanists have welcomed a new measuring stick that economists bring to the task of assessment these days. The Human Development Index (HDI) is made available to the global community by the U.N. Development Program. In addition to including the traditional economic performance numbers, the HDI delves into the more subjective realm of assessing quality-of-life issues, imparting a sense of contemporary relevance to the standard number crunching involved in assessing macro economies. Canada has ranked first on the rank-ordered HDI list seven times, whereas no other country has achieved that recognition more than twice. Finally, it

Gross national product (GNP) ■ The total amount of goods and services produced by citizens of a country, either at home or abroad

Gross domestic product (GDP) ■ The total amount of goods and services produced within the borders of a country

Net national product (NNP) ■ The cost of machine depreciation subtracted from GNP

makes sense to ask how in the world did humanity arrive at a world dominated by so many complex and competitive macro-economies?

The Evolution of Complex Economies

Humans spent much longer living under the conditions of hunting and gathering societies than in any other means of subsistence. Neither those foraging societies, nor later pastoral (herding) societies, involved meaningful economic exchanges as defined previously. It was not until the advent of the Agricultural Revolution around 10,000 years ago that transactions involving goods and services began to typify human existence. As ancient civilizations such as those in Egypt, Persia, and China blossomed, new institutions took on the task of meeting basic social, political, and economic needs.

The Middle Ages

The revolutionary developments in producing, distributing, and consuming goods beyond the limited capabilities of agricultural societies occurred mostly in Europe. The ancient civilizations faded away with the fall of the Roman Empire in the fifth century A.D. During the Middle Ages—the following thousand years prior to modernity—the rural economies of Europe featured labor-intensive agriculture in the guise of feudalism. Peasants were little more than slave labor, legally bound to the land belonging to their wealthy and powerful feudal lords. Agricultural surpluses produced wealth for the landowning class, which prospered at the expense of the vast peasant class.

Mercantilism Replaces Feudalism

As political power in the seventeenth century rode the back of the rising state from the micro level to the macro level, so did economic power. This economic metamorphosis was known as *mercantilism,* which sought to use manufacturing-based trade as a vehicle for accumulating wealth for the state. Thomas Munn (1571–1641) was the best-known advocate for mercantilism, and his *England's Treasure by Foreign Trade* served as his main epistle. Not coincidentally, England was one of the leading beneficiaries of mercantilism, but Holland and France were other exemplars of the strategy. Under the Industrial Revolution that mercantilism encouraged, the merchant class of industrial owners replaced the feudal landed aristocracy as Europe's dominant class.

Sociologist Max Weber's 1930 treatise, *The Protestant Ethic and the Spirit of Capitalism,* traces the role of the Protestant Reformation in spiritualizing a set of values (thrift, savings, hard work) that facilitated the rise of an entrepreneurial class during the Industrial Revolution. Mercantilism thrived well into the nineteenth century but began to unravel earlier during the American rebellion against mercantilism's inherent unfairness to colonies. Mercantilism required **protectionist** trade policies to stuff the coffers of the state, and its death knell was sounded when the nineteenth century's most powerful country, Britain, staunchly advocated the exact opposite policy: **free trade.**[5]

Consensus exists among economists that the optimal policy benefiting the world as a whole is free trade, rather than the politically tempting policy of protectionism. Protectionism often results when a particular industry or business has the political clout to persuade legislatures to pass measures to help that industry survive, but such efforts usually cost the country's other consumers in the form of higher prices. Economist Dominick Salvatore goes so far as to write that "the most serious international trade problem facing the world today is the rising protectionism in industrial countries."[6]

Protectionist ■ The national government should shelter its domestic industries from foreign competition via tariffs, import quotas, and subsidies

Free trade ■ The greatest good flows from allowing free-market forces to operate as the government refrains from interfering with international trade

Market Economy Replaces Mercantilism

Mercantilism experienced other problems as well. It fostered extensive governmental control of the economy and viewed the macro economy as a mere vehicle for creating powerful countries. It wasn't much concerned about what might benefit individual citizens or the private sector of the economy more generally. Its narrow fixation on what was good for the state blinded it to the forces that make economies grow. The deftest autopsy on the corpus of mercantilist economics was performed by Adam Smith in his seminal work, *The Wealth of Nations* (1776). Most of what is now called classical economic theory derives from the brilliant analysis of Adam Smith. His laissez-faire injunction against governmental direction of the economy; the democratically based notion that individuals should be free to act in their best (and society's) interests; his description of the market being guided by an "invisible hand"; and his insistence on free trade over protectionism all establish him as a classical giant.

Nothing less than "the greatest good for the greatest number of people" was what Smith's free market was expected to deliver. The true believers who witnessed industrialization and market forces creating unprecedented economic growth among Europe's heavyweight states required no convincing. The accumulated wealth was, nevertheless, very unevenly distributed, leading to a nineteenth-century cottage industry in blasting the market for its dispassionate failure to offer assistance to the masses of poor and oppressed souls. Critics of the market economy's blind eye to suffering included numerous socialists, who shared a penchant for public rather than private ownership of property, a classless society, and a more equitable distribution of wealth.

Socialist Indictment of Markets

The most comprehensive expression of socialist principles flowed from the prolific pen of exiled German philosopher Karl Marx (1818–1883). Marx created a complex theory of historical evolution progressing through a series of stages culminating in a final perfect stage of economic abundance and classless equality. Writing in the mid-1800s, Marx claimed that the transition from one stage to the next derived from the clash of competing classes, which in the case of the capitalist stage of history meant the privileged bourgeoisie (owners) pitted against the impoverished proletariat (workers).

Marxism envisioned a violent revolution by the proletariat as the inexorable midwife of the birth of socialism over the decaying corpse of capitalism. Like other philosophers of the 1800s, Marx was profoundly influenced by Charles Darwin's contributions to scientific explanations of natural phenomena, and he set out to discover parallel laws governing social phenomena—hence his appealing-but-dubious claim that his theories bore the imprimatur of science and were rooted in "the iron laws of history."

Mixed Market Replaces Market Economy

Socialist challenges to market capitalism were substantial. Nevertheless, the market economy—which had brushed aside mercantilism and unleashed the resilient forces of supply and demand expanding the economic pie for those who succeeded—remained intact until the 1930s. It continues to exist today, although in a form greatly altered by twentieth-century cataclysms such as World War I, the Great Depression, World War II, and the end of the Cold War. The transition has moved from a market economy to a mixed-market economy.

All the largest economies in the world today fall into this category of mixed-market economy: they include both market forces and governmental institutions in the potpourri determining how goods and services get produced, distributed, and consumed. Figure 14.2 shows mixed-market economies along a continuum ranging from high market/low government to low market/high government.

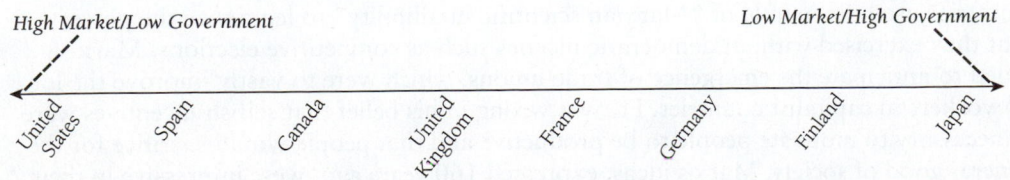

High Market/Low Government   *Low Market/High Government*

United States · Spain · Canada · United Kingdom · France · Germany · Finland · Japan

Figure 14.2
How much governmental intervention in the economy is desirable?

Neoclassical school ■ The advocacy of minimal governmental intervention in the economy coupled with a reduction of taxes to encourage spending

American economic thought has been influenced since the 1970s by a **neoclassical school** developed substantially at the University of Chicago. Since the 1930s, Keynesian economics had concentrated on the *demand side* of the economy: decrease government spending and restrict the money supply during inflation, then do just the opposite when fighting a recession. It was in the demand for goods and services that Keynes called on the government to intervene. Neoclassicists, also known as supply-side economists because of their focus on the once-ignored supply end of the equation, have become better known in the past four decades.

They prefer a laissez-faire market and counsel the government to reduce high taxes, which they see as serving as a disincentive for citizens to work hard. Supply-siders argue that lower tax rates will paradoxically bring in larger government revenues because people will spend and invest the money not taken in taxes, resulting in a boost for the economy. When Ronald Reagan took office in 1980, most of his advisors were supply-siders. He soon reduced taxes, which spurred economic growth and created jobs but also led to record federal deficits that continued to pile up on the debit side of the ledger. It also caused the rich to get richer and the poor to get poorer during the 1980s, as the top 5 percent of society saw their share of the economic pie increase by 14 percent while the lowest 20 percent simultaneously experienced a 12 percent decrease.[7]

Fading Communist Competitors

Communist economies ■ Based on nineteenth-century theories of socialist equality, these economies employed repressive political tactics that drove the command economy to unproductive extremes

The only genuine threat to the existence of Western-oriented, mixed-market economies in the 1900s came from the Eastern-oriented **communist economies,** which traced their philosophical roots to the previous century's socialist critics of capitalist heartlessness. But the diverse paths to collectivist equality advocated by socialist thinkers of the 1800s differed fundamentally from the monolithic systems that emerged in the twentieth century under the label of communism. Socialism always meant a key role for government in the economy, but socialism could be found coexisting with many different forms of political arrangements, from democratic to authoritarian. Communism, however, became synonymous with the fusion of state economic monopoly and political totalitarianism in one package, all under the control of the Communist Party.

During the Cold War, the Soviet Union and the Chinese People's Republic led thirteen communist countries in an internecine struggle against the enemy: Western democratic capitalism, epitomized by the United States and its allies. With 20/20 hindsight, it is tempting to take for granted the collapse of communism and Western capitalism's victory in the Cold War. It is tempting to believe that was the only way it could have turned out. But back when I first entered a college classroom in the 1960s, many of my professors and fellow students feared that the communist countries were winning the great race.

Only four communist countries remained intact in 2008: China, Vietnam, North Korea, and Cuba. Of these pillars of communism, only China can boast of an economy exhibiting impressive growth in recent decades, which it has achieved by abandoning most aspects of socialist economics while embracing principles of free-market competition. The obvious question is what happened to communism?

The Red Empire Awash in Red Ink

The short reply is that the communist countries derived their economic theories from Karl Marx, and Marx's analysis was dead wrong in many ways. The elites in communist countries used the mantle of "Marxian scientific infallibility" to legitimize the power that they exercised without democratic niceties such as competitive elections. Marx failed to anticipate the emergence of trade unions, which were to vastly improve the lot of workers in capitalist countries. He was wrong in his belief that selfish incentives were unnecessary to motivate people to be productive and that people would sacrifice for the general good of society. Marx's ideas, expressed 160 years ago, were impressive in their creative range and in their humanistic intent. But as supposedly infallible scientific laws and predictions, they failed abjectly.

Each of the countries that adopted communism imparted a unique national twist to the raw materials of Marxism. Therefore, we cannot simply blame Marx's naïveté for communism failing when so many people of my generation dreaded that it might succeed. Marx expected violent revolution to wipe away capitalism in the most advanced Western economies, such as France, Germany, and the United States. In actual fact, however, revolution in communism's name occurred only in feudalistic, preindustrial economies. In other words, conditions were already so poor in places such as Russia, China, and Vietnam that the communist systems set up there really had their work cut out for them.

By dragging their citizens through a wringer of oppression and sacrifice, some were able to achieve advances in production taken straight out of workers' hides. The Soviet Union proved particularly good at undertaking gargantuan public works projects, such as electrification dams or canals for shipping, and back when heavy industry was equated with economic vitality, the USSR fared reasonably well. However, when the West took a quantum leap into the brave new digital world, ossified communism proved incapable of stimulating the creative juices required to morph from industrialism to postindustrialism. People in communist countries had become good at taking orders but bad at taking either initiative or, worse yet, personal risks.

Under central governmental control, with its Five Year Production Plans, quotas became ingrained in the popular consciousness; the system enshrined the value of *quantity* but ignored product quality. The absence of competition in goods and services contributed little by little to a deterioration of manufactured goods made in communist countries. The lack of competition within each communist economy was then mirrored by a parallel lack of international competition because the unlucky thirteen avoided the global economy like poison ivy, opting to stay within the confines of their own economically incestuous trading network.

Communist countries were supposed to be more egalitarian than the money-grubbing capitalist alternative. But while these were relatively poor countries, not all shared in this poverty. What some referred to as a "new class" of Communist Party officials enjoyed luxuries that their fellow citizens could only dream of. Many factors led to the demise of communism as a global competitor, but the most crucial ones were economic in nature.

Some of the former communist countries are now called countries in transition (CITs) owing to the limbo that they find themselves in. Huge political skirmishes must play themselves out before issues as vital as how better to produce, distribute, and consume goods and services can be resolved peacefully. At the very least, a strong sense of insecurity pervades many CITs, and people generally abhor insecurity. A few CITs, such as Poland, Hungary, and the Czech Republic, have made the transition well and relatively quickly. Less fortunate have been CITs such as Russia, Romania, and Albania, where those living in poverty have risen dramatically while a tiny minority attains massive wealth, often illegally or unethically.

The Shadow Economy

One unscientific warning that any economy is in trouble consists of its **underground economy,** which in some CITs always was, and remains, pervasive. Also known as the *shadow economy* or *black market,* the underground economy is an unofficial, off-the-books network supplying goods and services that the official economy is unable or unwilling to provide. Tax avoidance serves as a potent incentive for many activities that are technically legal but are capable of being hidden or fudged. Baby-sitters, waiters, self-employed plumbers, domestics, consultants, and moonlighting lawyers find ways to underreport income bearing no paper trail. Rather different are the many economic wants that are met by goods and services hidden from public view owing to their illegality. Prostitution, illegal gambling, child labor, bribery, and trafficking in drugs can be as lucrative as they are unsavory.

Underground economy ■
That portion of a state's economy that goes unreported to the official economy, generally as a means of avoiding taxes

Table 14.1						
GROWTH IN ECONOMIC OUTPUT: THE 1980S AND THE 1990S						
	Percentage of Growth in GPD		Percentage of Growth in Agriculture		Percentage of Growth in Industry	
	1980s	1990s	1980s	1990s	1980s	1990s
Entire World	3.4%	2.5%	2.7%	1.3%	—	2.3%
High Income	3.4	2.3	—	—	—	—
Medium Income	3.3	3.5	3.6	2.0	3.7	4.3
Low Income	4.7	3.2	3.0	2.3	5.4	2.8

Source: World Bank Data Profile, Growth of Output, *http://www.worldbank.org/CPProfile.asp.*

The size of the underground economy varies from country to country, and its exact dimensions are difficult to measure for obvious reasons. In 1996, economist Peter Gutmann put the size of the American shadow economy at about $900 billion ($200 billion illegal, $640 billion legal, $60 billion in a gray area), or 13 percent of GDP, and slightly higher than the 10 percent figure often cited by researchers.[8] In 1996, the percentage was much higher in most CITs, hovering around 50 percent because the official economy simply was not supplying the goods and services consumers demanded. In the largest of the CITs, Russia, the postcommunist black market has been described as continuing to rival the aboveground economy at that time under Boris Yeltsin.[9]

Economic Globalization

As discussed in Chapter 1, all economies, regardless of type, location, or level of productivity, are intimately tied to the web of interdependence called globalization. The total volume of world trade during the past thirty years has increased more than tenfold. During the 1980s and 1990s, the increase in trade became a virtual tidal wave, with Japan, China, and the Asian NICs at the leading edge.[10] Considerable data attest to the vital role that increased trade has played in expanding global wealth (albeit very unevenly distributed) during these decades. Table 14.1 attests to the growth in economic output during the 1980s and 1990s.

The creation of a new international organization—the World Trade Organization (WTO)—in 1994 represented a watershed event. Its purpose is to facilitate trade between countries by lowering taxes on import, or tariffs, as well as other barriers to trade. The WTO replaces its predecessor, the General Agreement on Trade and Tariff (GATT), which existed from 1944 until 1994. The GATT's functions were similar to those of the WTO; however, the WTO possesses considerably greater scope regarding its functions, as well as far more clout to *enforce legal decisions* pertaining to trade disputes between countries.

The trend toward economic globalization is evident in numerous organizations other than the WTO. For example, the eight leading economic powers (referred to as the G-8) hold annual summit meetings to coordinate economic strategies. Record-level investments by foreigners in the American economy began in the 1980s and have continued to grow impressively. Many thousands of MNCs have stretched their broad wings over every corner of the globe in search of cheap labor, ways to diversify their operations, and new customers. Nevertheless, small family firms, empowered by the Internet and cell phones, now ply their goods and services worldwide. Multiple trillions of dollars routinely cross borders daily in the guise of foreign currency purchases. The metaphor of a shrinking world resonates more than ever.[11] Case Study 14.2 deals with the consequences of General Electric's 1999 decision to relocate the world's largest refrigerator plant from Bloomington, Indiana.

Case Study 14.2   Globalization: "GE Goes South"

JoAnn Wypijewski, former managing editor of *The Nation* magazine, writes about labor politics for CounterPunch. Excerpted from a longer article in *The Nation*, her piece "GE Goes South" describes a scenario all too familiar to North American blue collar workers: seeing their jobs heading south of the border to Mexico. In 1992, presidential candidate Ross Perot gained political traction by coining a phrase to accompany this aspect of globalization, namely "that giant sucking sound." In this case study, writer Wypijewski chronicles the saga of General Electric workers in Bloomington, Indiana.

Beginning in 1967, the largest building in the world producing refrigerators had been home to GE's side-by-side refrigerator/freezer manufactured exclusively in Bloomington. Called the "Cadillac of refrigerators," and selling for up to $2,499 retail, it epitomized excess in American home appliances. In 1999, the company was still producing them at a 24/7 clip of 230 an hour, 4,700 a day, 1.6 million annually. The plant's management stated that profits were down, and the IBEW union had to find $65 million in savings. When they did so, management reneged, saying that was insufficient, and half of the production would be shifted to Celaya,

Mexico, where wages averaged $2 an hour, compared to the $24 an hour IBEW union members were making in Bloomington. Shortly thereafter, 733 GE workers were laid off, and another cut lay around the corner.

Like many corporations, GE has diversified successfully. No longer so reliant on manufacturing, GE now ranks as the largest nonbank financial corporation, the biggest owner of planes, vehicles, and credit card debt. Between 1982 and 1997, the value of GE shares grew at an 11.5 percent clip. How else did GE manage to work such wonders? "It has moved production offshore, also engineering, and lately told its U.S. suppliers: companies that sell everything from screws to heavy machinery must move operations to Mexico or lose GE's business." Mastering the merger, GE made 125 acquisitions in 1999 alone, then in 2000, GE gobbled up Honeywell at a $45 billion cost. Ex-CEO, Jack Welch, widely considered the catalyst for the comeback in GE stocks, took $100 million with him when he left. Good for GE shareholders but very bad for GE workers in Bloomington and elsewhere. Thousands of "downsized" workers and their families face uncertain futures with few resources to retrain them for alternative employment.[12] ■

America and the Global Market
Economic Hegemony: The Pivotal 1990s

With a GDP of $9.6 trillion in the year 2000, the U.S. economy was by far the world's largest, triple that of its nearest competitor, Japan. The massive economy of the United States enabled GDP per capita to reach $34,260 in year 2000 and climb further to $40,100 by 2004. The American GDP per capita figure, however, ranked second to Luxembourg, which came in at $58,900 in 2004. Although that was very good news for Luxembourg's citizens, it does not translate into very much clout because it is such a small country. The United States continues to dominate the scene as a global economic superpower, yet that does not mean that America simply controls all aspects of the global economy.

Since World War II, the United States' pervasive influence has remained so pronounced as to warrant the label of an **economic hegemon,** similar to the preeminent British role during the nineteenth century. Nevertheless, major problems confront the American economy. For example, since 1985, it has typically faced federal budget deficits (the government spends more money annually than it collects). Until 1971, America had enjoyed **trade surpluses** throughout the twentieth century. However, by 1986, its **trade deficit** had ballooned to $170 billion owing to Ronald Reagan's tax cuts, where it hovered for about a decade, until being substantially reduced by Bill Clinton.

Irony oozes from the fact that conservatives most congenial to the Republican Party have traditionally favored fiscal austerity and limited governmental spending, criticizing Democratic Party rivals as irresponsible "tax and spend" liberals. Yet not only did the Reagan tax cuts produce unprecedented budget deficits, but after Clinton reduced the deficit, George W. Bush made the Reagan deficits look modest by upping the national debt to around $9 trillion in his second term.

In 1960, the U.S. share of world exports equaled 18 percent; by 1990, its share had declined to 12 percent, but then it rebounded very aggressively in the 1990s—the longest period of sustained economic growth in U.S. history. When the New York stock market

Economic hegemon ■ A dominant world power exercising great influence over the establishment of rules of the economic game

Trade surplus ■ A favorable balance of payments in which a country's economy exports goods more valuable than the goods it imports in a given year

Trade deficit ■ An unfavorable balance of payments in which a country's economy imports goods more valuable than the goods it exports

crashed in 1987, commentators were quick to blame the crash on globalization, and *The Wall Street Journal* pointed to the "cataclysmic power of the new global market."[13] Then when the stock market practically shot through the roof in the dot.com explosion of the late 1990s, globalization was hailed as a blessing rather than a curse.

How did the United States arrive at this exalted position as global economic hegemon? With all other major Western countries decimated by World War II, the United States emerged from that cataclysm as unrivaled director of the 1945 capitalist drama playing on the world stage. An entire system of global institutions was created at Bretton Woods to facilitate the free, open, international economy that would provide American businesses with economic partners in the years to come.

It was not until the 1970s that America really encountered robust economic competition. This hiatus allowed its production facilities, work ethic, and managerial style to ossify enough so that when countries such as Japan and Germany had regained their balance, they had a strong head of steam heading into the decade of the 1980s. At first ignoring their economic problems, many Americans sought to blame others for America's problems before finally getting down to the task of improving competitiveness in the 1980s, which succeeded amazingly well within a decade.

American corporations had prospered for most of the twentieth century under the model of *Fordism*, named after Henry Ford, who perfected the assembly line production strategy. The concept of **economies of scale** drove the assembly line, resulting in efficient mass production. For many years, bigger was always seen as better, which allowed some corporations to become rigidly bureaucratized. IBM, with its "Big Blue" image, seemingly unassailable for decades, served as a metaphor for U.S. business woes in general during the troublesome 1980s. IBM clung tenaciously to its commitment to large mainframe computers, failing to react to growing demand for small personal computers—which adaptable foreign firms captured with cheaper IBM clones. During a two-year stretch in the 1980s, IBM lost more than $13 billion. Top-heavy with upper management, Big Blue proved resistant to the changes occurring among many other MNCs.

Economies of scale ■
Production methods using size as a competitive advantage to produce more units of any commodity, thus enabling a company to reduce cost per unit and to increase profitability

Changing Corporate Culture

One thing that is certain about market economies is that they allow for considerable changes to occur. Since the late 1980s, the modus operandi for U.S. corporations has epitomized the motif of change. Widespread downsizing (firing) of personnel by giants such as IBM, Kodak, Xerox, and Texas Instruments was triggered by rapid technological change and foreign competition. Downsizing carries major human costs along with it, as lives have become dislocated in many corporations and industries.

Many companies were able to improve their bottom line via this strategy, yet by itself it was insufficient to restore their former successes. U.S. managers were somewhat slower in adopting long-term vision, flexibility, risk-taking, labor–management cooperation, as well as investment in research and development—but foreign competition spurred many of these changes to occur. So far-reaching are these adaptations that some observers consider these changes to have created a new form of corporate culture.

When a Japanese wake-up call blasted the big-three automakers out of bed in the early 1980s, management instinctively sought a quick, high-tech fix, in the form of robotics. Personified by GM CEO Roger Smith, who refused to heed the 1970s Japanese lesson that fuel efficiency sells, Detroit's managerial elite didn't seem to understand. The Japanese were making better-quality cars at the time because of employee–management communication, worker initiative, corporate loyalty, and production flexibility. Not, as Roger Smith thought, because they used robots.[14]

Corporate management at GM takes a real beating in Michael Moore's sarcastic documentary film, *Roger and Me* (1986). Presented through the eyes of a laid-off Flint, Michigan, autoworker, GM's Roger Smith comes off as aloof, inept, and obscenely overpaid. *Roger and Me,* the most popular documentary film ever at that time, tapped into a deep pool of frustration felt by American laborers struggling to cope with the economic dislocation caused by intensified global competition in the 1980s. One decade later,

Moore followed *Roger and Me* with an angry book in the same vein blasting corporate management, called *Downsize This!* (1996).

The fact that the intensity of international competition increased significantly from the 1970s, to the 1980s, to the 1990s, to the 2000s surely frustrated all Americans but none so profoundly as its blue-collar class (previously a bastion of Democratic support). Labor backlash proved problematic for the Clinton administration as it proposed both the North American Free Trade Association (NAFTA) and the World Trade Organization (WTO) treaties for congressional approval in 1993 and 1994, respectively.

Economic Nationalism

Some Americans are tempted to react to the competitive international economy with economic nationalism, or what two economists call "aggressive unilateralism."[15] Political pressures will always exist for protectionism to provide short-term solutions to long-term economic dislocations, but classical economists warn that countries embark on that path at their own peril. As a long-time champion of free trade and one that has cut many (but not all) tariffs dramatically since World War II, the United States might seem the likeliest country to resist adopting protectionist trade measures. Case Study 14.4, later in this chapter, addresses the issue of U.S. protection of cotton growers from the perspective of two African presidents whose countries are adversely affected.

However, all countries engage in some forms of protectionism. Despite its strong free-trade advocacy, the United States has "engineered import restrictions on an array of important products, including textiles, apparel, shoes, cars, carbon and specialty steel, machine tools, motorcycles, and semiconductors."[16] In 2002, president George W. Bush slapped a controversial 30 percent tariff on steel imports, which the EU and Japan immediately challenged in the WTO's legal system, and won.

One study concludes that the United States has increasingly used **nontariff barriers** to imports, with 29 percent of its goods being protected in 1996.[17] Another finds that protective trade measures added an average of 35 percent to the price of the affected products, and that every job saved through protectionism cost the U.S. taxpayer an average of $170,000.[18] Many economists counsel against widespread protectionism, not only because it raises the price paid by consumers but also because it often results in deteriorating product quality by removing market competition.

Nontariff barriers ■ Any of the varied means of protecting domestic industries from foreign competition other than import taxes

Beleaguered by foreign competition in the 1980s, the Harley-Davidson Company received congressional protectionism. A decade later, the company was doing all the right things to compete internationally on its own.

Legitimate Protectionism

Under special circumstances, however, limited protectionism may be warranted. For example, if it can be shown that a country is engaging in unfair trading practices, then some form of protectionism may be justified to level the playing field. Also, economists make an exception to the rule for "strategic industries" that manufacture items vital to national defense, for cutting-edge "infant industries" requiring help to get off the ground, and for Third World "diversification measures" intended to help LDCs move beyond their sole reliance on exporting few primary products.

However, after the protectionist door opens, it is often difficult to close it. Drawing the line separating valid from invalid claims for protection usually proves contentious in this highly politicized process. Case Study 14.3 concerning Harley-Davidson resonates well because it chronicles how a protectionist boost helped innovative owners and managers change their corporate culture in ways eluding many larger corporations. Harley-Davidson's enlightened policies brought it added efficiency and global competitiveness.

Case Study 14.3   Harley-Davidson's Hog-Wild Recovery

In the late 1970s, the American motorcycle company Harley-Davidson was wilting under a decade-long Japanese onslaught that was gobbling up market share. Then, under the astute direction of board chairman Vaughan Beals and company president Richard Teerlink, the company, on the verge of extinction in the early 1980s, turned itself around. By the mid-1990s, it became nearly impossible to find anyone saying anything bad in print about Harley-Davidson. What happened in the interim?

Harley-Davidson's success story results from a variety of factors. But the one that enabled the rest to follow was the protectionist legislation passed by the U.S. Congress in 1983, when it placed a hefty tariff on Japanese bikes imported into the United States. As the only U.S. motorcycle company, Milwaukee-based Harley was given some unusual breaks. But rather than becoming lazy and complacent, Harley did the things a competitive firm needs to do: cutting 40 percent of its workforce in 1982, modernizing management techniques, paring down its oversized bikes, emphasizing quality control, and devising more sophisticated marketing strategies.

As Harley celebrated its ninetieth anniversary in 1992, it produced the world's most-sought-after motorcycle. Unable to keep up with demand, in 1993, management decided not to risk loss of quality by overproducing and began more creative marketing of Harley accessories, rather than building too many bikes. Management has also ingrained a spirit of social responsibility into the corporate culture. Harley stock responded by returning 27 percent to investors in 1994. One marketing analyst exaggerates only slightly in claiming that "Harley-Davidson is possibly the best brand name in the United States. Coca-Cola is a good brand name, but people don't tattoo it on their bodies."[19]

In the late 1980s, Harley took another unusual step: it went to the U.S. Congress and asked for the removal of its protective tariff! Two decades after protectionist legislation, Harley is clobbering the Japanese competition with a high-quality product at a competitive price, not to mention successfully capturing the image of freedom, independence, and defiance so well ingrained into the American national identity. ■

The United States and WTO Ratification

Three American presidents, Ronald Reagan, George Bush, and Bill Clinton, all pushed for completion of the seven-year global trade negotiations known as the Uruguay Round (site of the talks) of the GATT arrangement, promoting it as beneficial to America. Because the United States was the world's largest trader and was considered to follow a relatively open trade policy since World War II, getting more restrictive traders to open up their markets seemed quite advantageous to these presidents. So why did Bill Clinton have such difficulty gaining congressional approval for the new GATT treaty in 1994?

Tentatively approved by 124 nations, formally endorsed by the G-8 economic powers as "fostering growth, generating employment, and increasing prosperity," the agreement needed Congress's approval to validate Clinton's signature on the document. On Capitol Hill, it encountered the same maelstrom of blue-collar backlash that had frustrated the NAFTA debate one year earlier. Like NAFTA, the GATT treaty had the procedural advantage of congressional "fast-track" status: it had to be voted either up or down, without amendments.

Laborers worrying about losing their jobs to cheap foreign wages were not the only opponents of the new GATT. Isolationists such as Pat Buchanan claimed that U.S. sovereignty would be infringed upon by the creation of a new trade bureaucracy (WTO) in Geneva. Some environmental NGOs, Greenpeace included, suggested that hard-fought ecological standards might be weakened by development-obsessed poor countries who would have a majority in the WTO. Protectionists such as Emil Innocenti, owner of a small textile-dyeing business in New Jersey, feared being put out of business by unnecessary regulations.

Senator Ernest Hollings (D-SC) wanted to save the jobs of hundreds of thousands of textile workers in his home state. Radical right-wing militia members predicted the WTO would help the "one-world conspiracy." Consumer activist Ralph Nader claimed that U.S. consumer rights could be endangered by the new WTO. Some local government officials pointed to the U.S.–Canadian trade pact as having already challenged a Minnesota tax exemption for micro-breweries as unfair to big Canadian beer makers.

Case Study 14.4 "Your Farm Subsidies Are Strangling Us"

On July 11, 2003, two African presidents published an op-ed piece in the *New York Times*: Amadou Toumani Touré, president of Mali, and Blaise Compaore, president of Burkina Faso. Their countries are among the poorest in the world, and like several others in West/Central Africa, their meager economies are dependent on one primary product, namely cotton. Fully 40 percent of export revenues and 10 percent of GDP in Mali and Burkina Faso depends on cotton. Not only is cotton vital economically to them, but socially as well, because it represents the social infrastructure of their very rural countries. This case study summarizes some of their criticisms of the WTO and U.S. policies.

Their African cotton is of the highest quality and relies on low-tech manual labor. In the United States and other cotton growers among MDCs, lower quality cotton is produced via large mechanized farms that employ few people and are known to damage the environment. In addition, production costs are fully 50 percent lower in Mali and Burkina Faso than is the case with American cotton. The two presidents point out that they understand the potential benefits of engaging in world trade. Comparative advantage is what countries are supposed to pursue, and both Mali and Burkina Faso's comparative advantage lies with cotton. However, they believe that they are prohibited from trading on a level playing field, and they have presented a proposal to the WTO to address the problem.

The problem, they contend, consists of U.S. subsidies that lead to global overproduction and distort the price of cotton. "From 2001 to 2002, 25,000 cotton farmers in America received more in subsidies ($3 billion) than the entire economic output of Burkina Faso, where 2 million people depend on cotton." Also, U.S. subsidies go to just 10 percent of its cotton farmers, so those 25,000 affluent cotton farmers contribute directly to the impoverishment of 10 million rural cotton workers in West/Central Africa.

As noted previously, the WTO possesses more power than did the GATT. Complaining to the United States has not garnered much empathy in the past. Therefore, these poor countries that are wholly dependent upon cotton in the world market turned to the WTO in 2003. They submitted a proposal for discussion at the next WTO meeting scheduled in Cancún, Mexico. It called for an end to unfair subsidies given by MDCs to cotton producers. In the interim, they have proposed that cotton-dependent LDCs be compensated for lost export revenues resulting from cotton subsidies in MDCs. In effect, they are asking for the WTO to see that free trade rules be applied not only to products the rich countries care about but also those that the poor countries care about. Several of the points made by these two African presidents share much in common with many of the critics protesting in the streets of various cities in recent years. ■

Lane Kirkland of the AFL-CIO also demanded stronger labor regulations in the global treaty. Surely it was no traditional liberal/conservative lineup that characterized the bloody fight over WTO approval. Case Study 14.4 reflects criticisms leveled in 2003 by the African Presidents of Mali and Burkina Faso that the WTO has failed to provide any semblance of a level playing field since its inception.

Most economists and consumer groups favored the new WTO. Michael Boskin, former chief economic advisor to President George H. W. Bush, argued that trade is "not a zero-sum game where one side must lose what the other gains. Expanded trade is a positive-sum game, a potential win–win for all sides." He also predicted that failure to approve it would be disastrous to the world economy, using the early 1930s—when protectionist tariffs reduced global trade by 75 percent, dooming the world to the Great Depression—as the worst-case scenario. A single-issue NGO, Alliance for GATT Now, calculated that it would add between $100 and $200 billion to the U.S. economy and create 1.4 million new jobs, while cutting tariffs by $744 billion worldwide. Alliance for GATT Now also said that the revised treaty would introduce new protection of intellectual property from piracy, where the U.S. had been burned by Chinese black-marketers selling movies and popular music.

The Enterprise Institute and the Heritage Foundation, conservative Washington think tanks, applauded the agreement for "bringing the rule of law to international trade." Concerning the opponents' fear of an arbitrary WTO bureaucracy stealing American sovereignty, economist Jeremy Rabkin argued that the WTO had no army to enforce decisions the United States might dislike and that any member could withdraw from the WTO on six months' notice. The WTO would have no direct power over a huge trading country such as the United States, although it might have a greater impact on smaller states. At the end of the struggle, President Clinton won congressional approval, creating the WTO, which went into effect on January 1, 1995. However, the depth of opposition to the WTO reflects the persistent anger felt by Americans adjusting to the vagaries of globalization.[20]

U.S. Trade Frustrations

In the economy-driven 1990s, President Clinton engaged in a strategy that could be called *trade brinkmanship*—that is, using the huge U.S. trade volume to intimidate problematic trade partners with the threat of trade sanctions, the way earlier presidents had used military brinkmanship to achieve political objectives. The United States was trying to rectify through trade brinkmanship its massive trade deficit, which had averaged around $170 billion annually for about a decade. When the value of a country's imports exceeds the value of its exports, it must pay for the difference in some convertible currency. If it becomes large and chronic, a trade deficit constitutes a drain on the rest of the economy, potentially inhibiting growth, savings, confidence, and investment.

Trade: Once a Means, Now an End in Itself

Having grown to tens of trillions of dollars annually, world trade has become essential to economic growth. Once used by powerful countries largely as a means toward other political or military ends, trade is now a coveted end in itself. Examples of past presidents using trade as a political club arise easily: President Kennedy imposing trade sanctions on Cuba to protest the communist Castro regime; MFN (most-favored-nation) trade status denied to North Korea and Vietnam because they were communist countries; President Carter levying trade sanctions against the Soviet Union after its 1979 invasion of Afghanistan; President Reagan's 1982 ban on trade with Libya for state-sponsored terrorism; President George H. W. Bush's continuation of trade sanctions against South Africa for its apartheid policies. However, when President Clinton decoupled human rights concerns from the issue of MFN status for China in June of 1994, he highlighted a shift already underway: playing political football with trade may no longer make good economic sense.

U.S. and Pacific Trade

Contemporary U.S. trade with Europe, the Americas, and the former Soviet Union proceeds fairly smoothly. The largest trade relationship in the world, between the United States and Canada, is a model of comity and mutual benefit. Canada typically runs a trade surplus in merchandise goods, balancing out a comparable U.S. surplus in services. In 1995, the two-way North American trade in merchandise goods alone was growing by $900 million per week.[21]

America's trading headaches originate mostly in Asia, home to nearly half the world's population and to most of its hottest economies. East Asia now has two economic giants, Japan and China. During the 1980s, most of America's complaints were voiced against Japan. America trades with more than 170 countries, but in the 1970s to 1980s, a majority of its trade deficit rested with Japan. Presidents Nixon, Ford, Carter, Reagan, and Bush all used behind-the-scenes diplomacy to address the problem, producing vague Japanese promises to open their markets wider to American products in the future.

Shaken by a record 1993 deficit with Japan of $60 billion, Bill Clinton decided to follow a more public, assertive, and quantitative path. He and his U.S. trade representative, Mickey Kantor, undertook a "results-oriented" policy: requiring measurable progress in market access of American goods, sector by Japanese sector. Demanding quantitative progress in thirty-one areas, including insurance services, medical equipment, telecommunications, and auto parts, they promised to invoke punitive tariffs on specified Japanese goods if results were not forthcoming.

To everyone's relief, the United States did not end up invoking sanctions, which can lead to disastrous trade wars. But no sooner would Japan meet one quota than the Clinton administration would impose another deadline for avoiding sanctions. Trade brinkmanship's tough line seemed popular with an American public otherwise unimpressed by Clinton's foreign policy record. However, trade brinkmanship (like military brinkmanship) involves significant risks. In the post-Clinton era, however, a Niagara of trade with China has exploded amazingly rapidly, creating comparable dilemmas for George W. Bush to manage.

Intellectual Property in China

Japan experienced a major recession in the 1990s, and America looked elsewhere to expand trade, but China had not yet filled that role under Clinton. It did so under George W. Bush, supplanting Japan as America's second-leading trade partner (after Canada). The issue of human rights abuses in the Chinese labor market that had divided the Clinton administration down the middle, did not phase the more business-oriented President Bush.

A most vexing problem faces the United States in trading with China, namely widespread piracy of copyrighted material. When I visited Beijing in 2006, the black market in Hollywood movie DVDs and music CDs was ubiquitous. These items were going on the street for about one-tenth their American price. America is experiencing rapid trade expansion in numerous export services—such as films, insurance, banking, computer software, and music. But policing this service sector has proven most frustrating in China. The current emphasis on service sector exports contrasts sharply with the merchandise trade in items such as cars, bicycles, and televisions that long characterized past American exports.

With 1.3 billion people and unprecedented economic growth averaging 8 percent annually, Communist China has become the "mother of all emerging markets," ranking second only to the United States in attracting direct foreign investment. Whereas some U.S. corporations—Gillette, Polaroid, Lotus, Lehman Brothers, McDonald's—are eagerly mining the Chinese gold rush, piracy has devastated the profits of many others. Former President Clinton's trade representative, Mickey Kantor, claimed that U.S. companies lost $1 billion in 1994 to copyright theft, with nearly 100 percent of the videotapes and 94 percent of the computer programs that were marketed in China sold illegally. More than twenty factories in southern China produce more than 75 million pirated CDs per year, mostly for the export market. The United States conducted extensive negotiations with China in the 1990s to tighten its intellectual property rights laws, but enforcement remained extremely lax.

Clinton followed a carbon copy of his earlier Japan trade policy with China as well. It consisted of (1) threatening trade sanctions if progress was not made in certain sectors; (2) negotiating to achieve specified standards by a certain date; and (3) reaching an eleventh-hour agreement, narrowly staving off sanctions and a possible trade war. With China, the demands included removing trade barriers to legally sold American films, music, and computer products to lower demand for pirated products; cracking down on illegal production (mostly in the form of CDs); and dropping barriers to agricultural products such as wheat and citrus fruits.

A 1995 deadline was set. Pending improvements, the United States pledged to impose punitive 100 percent tariffs on twenty-three categories of Chinese products, ranging from toys to watches to athletic shoes. Chinese officials promised to retaliate against American cigarettes, alcohol, and cosmetics, if necessary. Do you think a viable long-term trade policy can operate on the basis of threats, negotiations, and last-minute agreements?[22]

Normalizing Trade with Vietnam

President Clinton also addressed U.S. trade deficits with other Asian countries, such as Taiwan. Despite having only 20 million people, Taiwan enjoys a vibrant economy that then exported $26 billion in goods, for a trade surplus with America of about $9 billion.

In addition to playing trade brinkmanship with old partners, the Clinton administration looked to open new Asian markets for U.S. goods, especially in Vietnam.

Under the name of *doi moi,* Vietnam has been conducting its own limited Chinese-style market reforms, including opening the country to Western investment. Communist Prime Minister Vo Van Kiet had publicly expressed a most un-communist-sounding goal: "To make our people rich." Starting from a paltry base ($200 GNP per capita), Vietnam has a long way to go before rivaling the Asian economic miracles of South Korea, Taiwan, or Malaysia. However, it has a literate population of 60 million as well as assets such as oil and timber, and many MNCs are looking to expand there, including Mobil Oil, Coca-Cola, American Express, and United Airlines.

A major step toward Vietnam's economic renaissance was taken in 1994, when President Clinton lifted a thirty-year-old U.S. trade embargo. Only because of Vietnam's trading potential was Clinton willing to take the flak he received from veterans' groups for lifting the embargo. As an active protester against America's Vietnam War in the 1960s, President Clinton found himself vulnerable to criticism from military groups uncomfortable with his role as armed forces commander-in-chief. The Pentagon listed seventy cases of American soldiers who may have been captured alive during the war, but veterans' groups claim the real number is actually much higher. Until the Vietnamese government provides more help in accounting for MIAs, however, veterans' groups will remain critical of trading with Vietnam.[23]

U.S. Economic Climate and Institutions

In both human and nonhuman resources, America's raw materials for economic regeneration appear unrivaled. The United States is blessed with one-third of the world's coal reserves, even more of the world's natural gas, massive fresh water supplies, extensive forests, metals and ores in abundance, fertile farmland, and favorable weather conditions. Human resources among its 300 million citizens are no less impressive: cutting-edge high technology skills; rich entrepreneurial tradition; ranking near the top on the HDI; 2004 per capita GDP of $40,100; life expectancy of seventy-six years; abundant immigrant labor pool; and the most accessible higher education system in the world.

America's business climate is similarly conducive to economic success. Social values inherent in educational and other kinds of institutions favor a business orientation. The Protestant work ethic described by Max Weber virtually equates business success with divine approval. The political system is stable enough to encourage foreign investment in American enterprises. Private ownership of the means of production is higher than in other advanced economies, such as Japan or the European countries. Even many utilities, such as power companies, are extraordinary in their level of private ownership in the United States. When inevitable dips occur in the business cycle, U.S. governmental fiscal and monetary actions have proven adept at softening hardships. American values include strong backing for the economic system and confidence in its inherent capabilities.

American Regulated Capitalism

The modern U.S. economy provides a relatively free market. It leans toward capitalism more than do most other mixed-market developed countries. Its system might most aptly be described as regulated capitalism. Three forms of business organization characterize the American experience. The most important business type in the earlier stages of U.S. economic history was the *individual proprietorship,* which still ranks as the most common form, although its share of the market has waned. Often people will pool their resources and skills when establishing a business or when expanding or merging existing businesses, and the result is a *partnership.* Individual proprietorships and partnerships are more vital to the economies of Japan, France, and Italy, where small businesses play a big role, than in the United States, where large *corporations* rule the roost.

Corporate America

The legal status of a corporation is established by its receipt of a charter from the government, giving the corporate business a personal identity, conveying certain rights and duties. Like you and me, a corporation pays taxes and can be summoned into court for a lawsuit. Managerial expertise is the backbone of corporate structure, which in America tends to be quite large. At the apex of the corporation is the chief executive officer (CEO), the chairman of the board of directors, and senior vice-presidents. A power elite of relatively few people run America's corporations in a manner described by corporate lawyer A. A. Berle, Jr., as a "self-perpetuating oligarchy."[24]

America's corporate elites are also paid much, much better than their counterparts in other industrialized countries. A 1999 study reported that while CEOs in the 500 largest corporations averaged only 40 times what production workers made in 1980, by 1990 that figure had risen to 85 times, and in 1999, it was 419 times the average worker's wage.[25]

U.S. businesses typically exercise much more flexibility than their colleagues in Europe or Japan when it comes to most decisions related to their operations. Both the European and Japanese business cultures are less likely to accept the exercise of initiative by mid-level managers than is the case in America. Also considered abroad as relatively ruthless in pursuit of profit, American MNCs generate much negative press, some it certainly well earned, as in Case Study 14.5.

Case Study 14.5   Coca-Cola in India: Plachimada People's Victory

The tiny village of Plachimada lies in the Kerala province of India. A 2004 article by Vandana Shiva chronicles extraordinary events occurring in Plachimada two years earlier. Vandana Shiva is a physicist, ecologist, activist, and editor who directs the Research Foundation for Science, Technology, and Natural Resource Policy in India, as well as an NGO, Navdanya, committed to biodiversity conservation and farmers' rights.

In March 2000, the local government commissioned Coca-Cola to establish a plant to produce 1.2 million bottles of Coca-Cola soft drinks. A conditional license was issued for installation of a motor for drawing water on the Plachimada site. "However, the company started to illegally extract millions of liters of clean water from more than six bore walls installed by it using electric pumps in order to manufacture millions of bottles of soft drinks." Coke was drawing 1.5 million liters of water daily, and the water level fell from 150 feet to 500 feet. In addition to stealing water from the local community, this MNC was also polluting the remaining water reserves. All told, 260 bore wells of drinking water provided by the public authorities had run dry. When the local government requested details regarding their water usage, Coca-Cola ignored this directive.

The government then issued a "show cause notice" and cancelled Coke's license. The company responded with a failed attempt to bribe the governing council's president, A. Krishnan, with 300 million rupees. He refused the bribe and reported the illegal maneuver to authorities. In 2003, the district medical officer informed Plachimadans that their water supply was unfit for consumption. No longer able to draw water at home, the women walked miles daily for water supplies. Coke had unleashed a "water scarcity in a water abundant region, and the women responded with a '*dharna*' (sit-in)" on Earth Day 2003 accusing this MNC of "hydropiracy."

Later that year, a large rally was organized by a diverse alliance of supporters from the local area to global activists such as Maude Barlow and José Bové, at which time an ultimatum was presented to Coke officials. In February of 2004, under considerable political pressure from various quarters, the District Chief Minister ordered closure of the Plachimada plant. This action was also followed by court decisions supporting the closure. Author Shiva observes that "The Plachimada victory is a major step in reversing corporate hijacking of our precious water resources. It provides both inspiration and lessons for building water democracy in other parts of India and the rest of the world."[26] ■

Economic Sectors and Globalization

Some long-term problems facing the U.S. economy include underinvestment in infrastructure, rising medical costs of an aging population, and stagnation of family income for the lower economic groups (since 1975, nearly all the gains in household incomes in the United States have gone to the top 20 percent of households).

The American economy enjoyed an unprecedented run of prosperity during the 1990s, including the performance of its stock market. But the business cycle of ebb and flow has not been rescinded, and the United States was already sliding into recession when the events of September 11, 2001, dealt multiple blows to the economy. Any economy as large as America's consists of various segments known as *sectors*. What are the prospects for major sectors in the contemporary global milieu? Service, finance, and agriculture would seem to have all the tools to continue doing very well globally. The other two major sectors, however, labor and manufacturing, seem to face considerable troubles.

Referring to the United Stated a tertiary economy these days is not to exaggerate in any way because about 60 percent of GDP now derives from service-sector activities such as medical services, legal services, insurance services, education, and popular entertainment. No tangible goods are produced in the service sector. Traditionally accustomed to thinking of productivity in concrete terms of physical goods, Americans must adapt to the fact that high value is placed on the intangibles provided by modern service economies. The Information Technology (IT) revolution in India represents a good contemporary example of a country acutely aware of the huge potential for outsourcing service sector activities of various sorts.

The financial sector features institutions set up to intercede between borrowers and savers interested in transferring money between themselves. The world of finance is undergoing dramatic electronic innovations, speeding up every form of financial transaction and weakening national borders as barriers to global finance. Americans have created much of the software driving today's automatic teller machines (ATMs), enabling people to bank conveniently. The United States is well positioned to capitalize on the new world order in banking. The Federal Reserve System (better known as the Fed), where banks can deposit money and borrow, was founded in 1914 to regulate money and banking, making it one of America's earliest regulatory bodies. For many years, this vital body operated under the skillful tutelage of economist Alan Greenspan, who was replaced in 2006 by Ben Bernanke.

The third sector positioned to do well globally is the agricultural sector. One of the fundamental changes during American history has been the urbanization of the population. Now three-quarters urban, a century ago America was three-quarters rural, with the family farm as the basic socioeconomic unit. A clear majority of Americans labored on farms in those days; today, less than 2 percent work in agriculture. The family farm is out; huge corporations (agribusiness) using chemical-intensive methods, irrigation, GPS precision planting, and even genetic engineering of plants are in. The ecological costs of American agribusiness are sizable, as addressed in Chapter 4.

Sectors Challenged by the Global Market

The prospects for the manufacturing and labor sectors seem unlikely to rival those of the service, financial, and agricultural sectors any time soon. If you travel on U.S. Interstate 90 along America's northern tier between Buffalo and Chicago, you will witness some of the hollowing-out of America's rust belt since the 1980s. Such are the dislocations caused by a global economy in which manufactured goods are produced more cheaply in Brazil or Taiwan or Turkey.

The U.S. manufacturing sector has slipped to a mere 20 percent of GDP, and with aging factories, high labor costs, adversarial management–labor relations, and many new global competitors, it is hard to imagine the sector that produces tangible goods doing well again in America. The labor sector provides the workers required by enterprises to produce whatever kind of output they seek to distribute. Only about 15 percent of American workers today work in the labor sector.

American labor once experienced some impressive glory days. The growth in size and influence of labor unions in the 1930s was facilitated by popular sympathy for workers during the Great Depression, resulting in passage of the National Labor Relations Act of 1935, a law favorable to organized labor. Unions have enjoyed the right to collective bargaining in most states, providing some leverage in negotiations with management. The United Auto Workers (UAW), United Mine Workers (UMW), and the Teamsters (truckers) epitomized labor's higher-profile days.

The arrival of labor as a major player on the American political scene did not occur without courageous organizers taking great risks. John Sayles's gripping film *Matewan* (1987) uses a real-life company-directed massacre of striking West Virginia coal miners to illustrate the violent nature of unionism's baptism in America. Unions helped to convert the market economy from the brutal and impersonal enrichment of the few at the expense of the many into safety nets such as unemployment insurance, Social Security, Medicare, food stamps, and other benefits for the less fortunate.

If laborers represented the downtrodden underdogs in twentieth-century America, then MNCs constituted their oppressors in the public mindset. Although the practices of Coca-Cola in India (Case Study 14.5) seem pretty sleazy, for sheer grandeur, they pale in comparison to Case Study 14.6, which examines the Enron corporation in India before imploding upon itself in 2004.

Case Study 14.6 Enron in India: Mega-Malfeasance

Arundhati Roy, an Indian peace activist and prize-winning novelist studied architecture in Delhi but then went on to a career in film and literature. Roy writes about a schizoid ambivalence pervading contemporary Indian culture: India lives in several centuries at once, enabling it to both regress and progress simultaneously. She uses a hammerhead shark metaphor adroitly, noting "We greaten like the maturing head of a hammerhead shark with eyes looking in diametrically opposite directions." She expresses much suspicion about whether globalization could really be about wiping out world poverty, "or is it a mutant variety of colonialism, remote-controlled and digitally operated?" Whether modern-day Indians live in the city or the countryside answers such questions.

The impetus to privatize everything in sight has washed ashore in India like a tsunami, and the downside to globalization consists of Enron in India (the Houston-based natural gas company that undertook the first private power project in India, with disastrous results). In 1993, Enron signed a deal with the Congress Party-ruled government in the state of Maharashtra for a 740-megawatt power plant. From the outset, two opposition parties howled in protest against the deal as riddled with malfeasance and high-level corruption, including a lawsuit to thwart the pending deal. Two years later, these opposition parties used this as their only campaign issue in winning control of the Maharashtra state government and proceeded to annul the contract, charging that Enron had paid $13 million in bribes to gain this most astonishing contract, and called for a renegotiating committee to examine the problem, explains Arundhati Roy.

However, that government fell to a vote of no confidence, the previous party returned to head the state government and signed a fresh contract that Roy claims would "astound the most hard-boiled cynic" and represents the "most massive fraud in the country's history." The new contract exceeded the generous terms of the previous one and ended up with the Maharashtra state paying Enron a total of $30 billion, the largest contract ever in India. Enron ended up netting a cool $13 billion profit on the deal, amounting to a 30 percent return on equity (twice the legal limit in India). Yet, in 1997, the Indian Supreme Court refused to entertain an appeal against Enron in this matter.

As if the obscene profit netted by Enron and charges of mega-bribery plus the Indian Supreme Court's hands-off attitude were not enough, charges made by critics at the outset that Enron would not be able to deliver what it promised proved correct. The power generated by Enron turned out to be twice as expensive as its nearest competitor and seven times as expensive as the cheapest electricity available in Maharashtra. In 2000, the Maharashtra Electric Regulatory Committee ruled that no more power should be bought from Enron because it would be less expensive to pay Enron the contractually mandatory fixed charge for maintaining the plant than to continue to buy any more of its grossly overpriced power.

Industrialists in this state began producing their own power with private generators at a much cheaper rate. In January 2001, the Maharashtra government decided that it could no longer pay the maintenance fees to Enron, roughly the same time that a severe earthquake hit the region. Enron then invoked the counter-guarantee that if the fees were not paid, it would auction off the governmental properties named as collateral in the contract. ■

Corruption: America's New Corporate Culture Mutated?

When writing the second edition of this textbook, it appeared that despite some apparent excesses, much was right in how U.S. MNCs had responded in the 1990s to the challenges of globalization emanating from Japan and Germany in the 1980s. In 2006, however, it seems prudent to raise more serious concerns regarding corporate developments after the new millennium. Greed has surely run amok via widespread corruption scandals. Convictions or plea agreements have been reached with CEOs of the following corporations between 2000 and 2006: Tyco International: Dennis Kozlowski and Mark Swartz; WorldCom: Bernie Ebbers; Adelphia Communications: John Rigas and his son; HealthSouth: Richard Scrushy; Arthur Andersen Accounting: David Duncan; Enron: Kenneth Lay, Jeffrey Skilling, Andrew Fastow, and Michael Kopper. Of course, other examples could have been cited as well.

Among the books cited in the following bibliography appear several highly critical ones. Abraham Gitlow wants to know who is responsible for corporate corruption; Arianna Huffington examines the specifics of corporate greed and its relationship to American politics; Ella Shohat and Randy Martin describe a serious breakdown in the systems intended to provide corporate self-policing; also, Francois Vincke and Fritz Heimann offer concrete corporate best practices to combat ethically repugnant practices.

Each MNC corruption scandal illustrates significant problems. Let's examine Enron more closely, which grew from a small energy company in 1985 to the seventh-largest firm in America and the world's biggest energy trading MNC within a decade. At its apex, Enron employed 21,000 people in forty countries. Its meteoric rise in the late-1990s was matched by disaster shortly thereafter. In October 2001, it reported a $638 million third-quarter loss and $1.2 billion loss in shareholder equity. Simultaneously, the Securities and Exchange Commission began an inquiry into the firm's practices, and by December 2001, Enron had filed for chapter 11 bankruptcy as protection from legions of creditors. A criminal investigation started in 2005, culminating in one plea bargain agreement and two guilty verdicts on twenty-five of thirty-four charges against its two top officers.

That quickly, Enron ceased to exist; some of the reasons for its demise harken back to Enron behavior in India described earlier by Arundhati Roy. Relying upon what in the "go-go 1990s" was euphemistically referred to as "aggressive accounting measures," Enron was practicing falsified accounting: it lied routinely about profits, concealed debt in company accounts, and engaged in the kinds of shady dealings referred to in Case Study 14.6. So egregious were its misdeeds that not only did Enron disappear as a corporation but so did what had been the fourth largest accounting firm in America: Arthur Andersen, which had enabled Enron's hijinks.

CEO Kenneth Lay epitomized Enron's meteoric rise and demise.

The legend behind Enron's rapid rise to the pinnacle was Kenneth Lay, who had earned a Ph.D. in economics and taught for several years at George Washington University during the 1970s, where he honed his views about how energy markets should change to become more successful. Well known as an advocate of liberalizing gas and electric monopolies, in the early 1980s, Lay took over a small Houston gas company, and following a merger of local pipeline firms, Enron materialized in 1986. Enron's espousal of "pricing open markets and trading energy futures like other commodities" and its acumen for proselytizing others led *The Economist* magazine to describe Enron as "an evangelical cult with Mr. Lay as the messiah."

Lay himself was quoted as saying "We like to think of ourselves as the Microsoft of the energy world." After its 2001 bankruptcy, Enron's smoke and mirrors accounting procedures were scrutinized, and proved unsavory. Ken Lay was convicted in May of 2006, but died of a heart attack at age sixty-four before his sentencing date.[27]

How does such pervasive malfeasance occur in a sophisticated democracy with a free press? For answers, we turn to Joseph Stiglitz, critical thinker par excellence. Expert scholar and practitioner, this international economist is a widely published and prize-winning author. Stiglitz's 2002 article, "Corporate Corruption: The Conflicts of Interest Driving U.S. Financial Scandals Are Being Replicated on a Global Scale," includes useful insights.

Tax laws, unsound accounting practices, U.S. Treasury Department encouragement, stock options for CEOs, inappropriate incentives, mere appearances of wealth, conflicts of interest, and revolving doors all help to explain unprecedented corporate corruption running in some cases to several billions of dollars. "Because of tax advantages and inappropriate accounting practices—which received support from the U.S. Treasury under both Republicans and Democrats—firms were encouraged to reward their executives handsomely with stock options." This enabled great wealth on the part of executives without detracting from the company's bottom line, with no one appearing to bear the cost. This was, however, a grand mirage because "shareholder value was being diluted," writes Stiglitz.

He points out that in economics "incentives matter," but while functional incentives lead to genuine wealth creation, dysfunctional incentives lead only to "massive misallocation of resources." America suffers from the consequences of misallocation in that "over inflated prices have led firms to over invest." Existing dysfunctional incentives create the "appearances of wealth, not actual wealth." Auditing firms such as Arthur Andersen were making more money from consulting than from their auditing services, thus establishing a profound conflict of interest: they had significant incentives to go easy when auditing clients such as Enron and to assist in finding the loopholes in the law when consulting with those same clients. Enron wrote the book on improving the "appearance of profits," and Arthur Andersen aided and abetted.

Big problems regarding incentives, however, can be tracked back further to the Treasury Department, which had incentives "to urge continuation of the bad accounting practices," and which tends to respond to the interests of Wall Street, which benefited from the mirage as much as did CEOs. The accounting firms had incentives to prevent the SEC from acting to limit their conflicts of interest (as both auditors and consultants). Furthermore, the banks had incentives to lean on the Treasury to "repeal an act which required separation of investment and commercial banks."

Conflicts of interest also have plagued the IMF, which is supposed to be responsive to the needs of the LDCs, but in reality embraces the "ideology and interests of the financial community." The problem of "revolving doors" establishing interlocking directorates is something against which "many democracies have instituted rules," but these conflicts of interest permeate both the IMF leadership and that of the United States. In these ways, Stiglitz argues that an "intertwining of public and private incentives at both the national and global levels serves to distort public policy." Globalization critics who harp on the secretive nature of IFIs have a valid point, and the author recommends "sunshine as the strongest antiseptic."[28]

Chapter Synopsis

The quantitative nature of economics has facilitated the rigorous application of scientific methods. But because economic institutions are human institutions, unpredictability also bleeds through the mathematical models devised by economists. How humans deal with the scarcity of goods and services derives from both objective and subjective factors. In the twentieth century, command, capitalist, and traditional models dominated the competitive discourse concerning economic form and structure. In the historical evolution traceable to the early Middle Ages, feudalism eventually gave way to mercantilism, which in turn gave way to the market economy. In the wake of Marxian socialism's demise, the principal intellectual battle today is between two variants of the market economy: individualistic capitalism and communitarian capitalism.

Macro-level economics has generally dominated the scene during the heyday of the state for the past 350 years. Many objective measures of productivity have been devised to assess the performance of macro-level economies. Among them, GNP, GNP per capita, NNP, HDI, growth rate, balance of payments, and trade balance have been emphasized. New realities in recent decades, however, have wrought new thinking concerning the globalization of economics and the blending together of micro, macro, and mega levels of analysis as interdependent. In this context, international trade has occupied center stage as heated battles have been fought between the forces of free trade and protectionism. The domestic struggle in the United States over the NAFTA and WTO treaties typified this toe-to-toe shouting match that has profoundly affected economic winners and losers.

After World War II, the United States assumed the role that Britain had played during the previous century: global economic hegemon. Taking on new responsibilities, the United States created the Bretton Woods system of institutions intended to rebuild the world economy under the banner of free trade, with the United States poised to benefit from the highly competitive quality of its postwar goods and services. However, by the 1970s and 1980s, the hegemonic U.S. posture was being challenged by competitors from Europe and Asia.

In the 1990s, true hegemonic status again returned to America. As the world's largest, most diverse, and productive economy, it remains the single most important national player. Expanding its exports has been a major objective of recent U.S. administrations, and trade deficits with Asian competitors (mainly Japan and China) have become a serious political issue worrying recent U.S. presidents. Serial corporate corruption in recent years has led to many indictments and convictions of CEOs, raising serious questions about existing incentives in America's financial sector and the state of corporate ethics.

FOR DIGGING DEEPER

Acemoglu, Daron, and James A. Robinson. *Economic Origins of Dictatorship and Democracy.* Cambridge University Press, 2006.

Aronowitz, Stanley. *From the Ashes of the Old: American Labor and America's Future.* Houghton Mifflin, 1998.

Bellinger, William K. *The Economic Analysis of Public Policy.* Routledge, 2007.

Black, Jeremy. *Great Powers and the Quest for Hegemony: The World Order since 1500.* Routledge, 2007.

Bery, Suman, and others, eds. *India Policy Forum 2005–2006.* Sage Publications, 2006.

Burtless, Gary, and others, eds. *Globophobia: Confronting Fears about Open Trade.* The Brookings Institution, 1998.

Caprio, Gerard, and James A. Hanson, eds. *Financial Crises: Lessons from the Past, Preparation for the Future.* Brookings Institution Press, 2005.

Cohen, Benjamin J. *The Geography of Money.* Cornell University Press, 2002.

De Borchgrave, Arnaud. *Russian Organized Crime.* CSIS Books, 1996.

Demers, Jolle, and others, eds. *Good Governance in the Era of Global Neorealism.* Routledge, 2004.

Dobson, Hugo. *Japan and the G7/8: 1975–2002.* Routledge, 2004.

Epstein, Richard A. *Free Markets under Siege: Cartels, Politics, and Social Welfare.* Hoover Press, 2005.

Friedman, Milton. *Capitalism and Freedom.* University of Chicago Press, 1962.

Galbraith, John K. *The Culture of Contentment*. Houghton Mifflin, 1992.

Gilpin, Robert. *The Challenge of Global Capitalism: The World Economy in the 21st Century*. Princeton University Press, 2000.

———. *Global Political Economy: Understanding the International Economic Order*. Princeton University Press, 2001.

Gitlow, Abraham. *Corruption in Corporate America: Who Is Responsible? Who Will Protect the Public Interest?* University Press of America, 2005.

Gorga, Carmine. *The Economic Process: An Instantaneous Non-Newtonian Picture*. University Press of America, 2002.

Grieco, Joseph M., and G. John Ikenberry. *State Power and World Markets: The International Political Economy*. W. W. Norton & Co., 2003.

Henning, C. Randall. *Accountability and Oversight of U.S. Exchange Rate Policy*. Peterson Institute, 2008.

Hoekman, Bernard M., and Marcelo Olarreaga, eds. *Global Trade and Poor Nations: The Poverty Impacts and Policy Implications of Liberalization*. Brookings Institution Press, 2007.

Heilbroner, Robert L., and Lester C. Thurow. *Economics Explained*. Simon & Schuster, 1982.

Horvat, Branko. *The Political Economy of Socialism: A Marxist Social Theory*. M. E. Sharpe, 1982.

Hufbauer, Gary Clyde, and others. *Economic Sanctions Reconsidered*. Peterson Institute, 2008.

Huffington, Arianna. *Pigs at the Trough: How Corporate Greed and Political Corruption Are Undermining America*. Three Rivers Press, 2004.

Ikerd, John E. *Sustainable Capitalism: A Matter of Common Sense*. Kumarian Press, 2005.

International Monetary Fund. *World Economic Outlook 2006*. IMF Publication Services, 2006.

Korten, David. *The Post-Corporate World: Life After Capitalism*. Berret-Koehler Publishing, 2000.

Lawrence, Robert Z. *Blue-Collar Blues: Is Trade to Blame for Rising Income Inequality?* Peterson Institute, 2008.

Levitt, Steven, and Stephen Dubner. *Freakonomics: A Rogue Economist Explores the Hidden Side of Everything*. William Morrow, 2005.

Lorell, Mark, and others. *Going Global? U.S. Government Policy and the Defense Aerospace Industry*. Rand Corporation, 2003.

Lovell, Stephen. *Destination in Doubt: Russia Since 1989*. Palgrave Press, 2006.

Luttwak, Edward. *Turbo-Capitalism: Winners and Losers in the Global Economy*. HarperCollins, 1999.

Marcel, Valerie. *Oil Titans: National Oil Companies in the Middle East*. Chatham House, 2006.

McEachern, William. *Contemporary Economics*. South-Western Publishing, 2004.

Miller, Raymond. *International Political Economy: Contrasting World Views*. Routledge, 2007.

Mortensen, Jens. *WTO, Governance, and the Limits of Law*. Routledge, 2004.

Mulvey, Kathryn. "GE Can Be Beat: Grassroots Campaigns Against the Corruption of General Electric Company." *Multinational Monitor*, July 1, 2001.

Nafziger, E. Wayne. *Economic Development*. Cambridge University Press, 2005.

Noland, Marcus, and Howard Pack. *The Arab Economies in a Changing World*. Peterson Institute, 2007.

OECD. *Environmental Performance Reviews: China*. OECD Book, 2007.

Olson, Mancur. *Power and Prosperity: Outgrowing Communist and Capitalist Dictatorships*. Basic Books, 2000.

Peterson, Peter. *Will America Grow Up Before It Grows Old? How the Coming Social Security Crisis Threatens You, Your Family, and Your Country*. Random House, 1996.

Polaski, Sandra. *Winners and Losers: The Impact of the Doha Round on Developing Countries*. Carnegie Endowment, 2005.

Rustmann, F. W., Jr. *CIA, Inc.: Espionage and the Craft of Business Intelligence.* Potomac Books, 2002.

Shohat, Ella, and Randy Martin. *Corruption in Corporate Culture.* Duke University Press, 2004.

Smilov, Daniel, ed. *Political Finance and Corruption in Eastern Europe: The Transition Period.* Ashgate, 2007.

Smith, David, and Dorothy J. Solinger, eds. *States and Sovereignty in the Global Economy.* Routledge, 1999.

Sowell, Thomas. *Basic Economics: A Citizen's Guide to the Economy.* Basic Books, 2003.

Stalker, Peter. *Workers Without Frontiers: The Impact of Globalization on International Migration.* International Labor Organization, 2000.

Stiglitz, Joseph. "Corporate Corruption: The Conflicts of Interest Driving US Financial Scandals Are Being Replicated on a Global Scale." *The Guardian of London,* July 4, 2002.

Temin, Peter. *Lessons from the Great Depression.* MIT Press, 1989.

Tsai, Kellee S. *Capitalism Without Democracy: The Private Sector in Contemporary China.* Cornell University Press, 2006.

Vincke, Francois, and Fritz Heimann, eds. *Fighting Corruption: A Corporate Practices Manual.* ICC Publishing, 2003.

Vreeland, James R. *The IMF and Economic Development.* Cambridge University Press, 2003.

Weber, Max. *The Protestant Ethic and the Spirit of Capitalism.* Scribner, 1958.

Whelan, Charles. *Naked Economics: Undressing the Dismal Science.* Norton and Company, 2003.

INTERNET

American Economic Association:
http://www.vanderbilt.edu/AEA

Capitalism:
http://www.capitalism.org

Cato Institute: Benefits of Free Trade:
http://www.freetrade.org

Data Map of U.S.:
http://quickfacts.census.gov

Economic Sanctions and Incentives: Fourth Freedom Forum:
http://www.fourthfreedom.org/

The Economist:
http://www.economist.com

Export-Import Bank:
http://www.exim.gov

Federal Reserve System:
http://www.federalreserveonline.org/

G8 Information Center:
http://www.g8.utoronto.ca

Human Development Index Report:
http://hdr.undp.org/en

Internal Revenue Service:
http://www.irs.ustreas.gov

International Monetary Fund:
http://www.imf.org

International Trade Administration:
http://www.trade.gov

Justice Department Anti-Trust:
http://www.usdoj.gov/atr/overview.html

Max Planck Research Institute:
http://www.mpiew-jena.mpg.de

NAFTA:
http://www.fas.usda.gov/info/factsheets/NAFTA.asp

Profile of the World:
http://www.infoplease.com/ipa/A0004373.html

Statistical Abstract of the U.S.:
http://www.census.gov/compendia/statab

Third World Nations: Fair Prices for Their Products:
http://www.maketradefair.com

Treasury Department:
http://www.treas.gov

U.S. Students for Fair Trade:
http://www.usft.org

World Development Indicators 2006:
http://devdata.worldbank.org/wdi2006/contents/Section3_1.htm

World Bank:
http://www.worldbank.org

International Economics

CORE OBJECTIVE

To describe an international economic system in flux, major theories concerning its behavior, and perplexing aspects of the widening gap between MDCs and LDCs.

THEMATIC QUESTIONS

- Where and how does globalization manifest itself in the international economy?

- What considerations account for the transition from mercantilist to free-trade philosophies?

- What are the causes and possible cures for Southern Hemisphere poverty?

- In what ways did the end of the Cold War affect the workings of the international economy?

- How does the multi-faceted work of Jeffrey Sachs represent a coda tying together many of the North/South-related themes permeating this textbook?

The theme of globalization bubbles up through these pages as regularly as Old Faithful at Yellowstone Park. One of the most important examples of globalization is in the seamless economic web linking humans at every level of endeavor. Whether we examine the micro level, the macro level, or the mega level, dynamic market forces bind people together economically, reducing human isolation in the process. The traditional intellectual line dividing the domestic economy from the international economy has blurred considerably. These trends mean that your existence and mine are more deeply affected by economic happenings in faraway places.

Examining a few descriptive statistics about the world economy provides a backdrop for the analysis to follow. According to 2004 estimates, Global World Product (GWP) stood at $55.5 trillion, with per capita GWP $8,800, and a real growth rate of 4.9 percent for that year, led by China (9.1 percent), Russia (6.7 percent), and India (6.2 percent). The U.S. economy grew at a 4.4 percent rate. This global economic output consisted mostly of services (64 percent), followed by manufacturing (32 percent), with agricultural productivity considerably lower (4 percent).[1]

Also for 2004, the World Bank's World Development Indicators (WDI), its premier annual publication about development data, rounds out the world economic picture.

WDI notes that 2004's GWP growth figures were the highest in fifteen years. Whereas MDCs grew at an average rate of 3.4 percent in 2004, the LDCs grew at a "remarkable" rate of 7.1 percent, their highest rate of growth since 1970. East Asia and the Pacific grew the fastest, whereas Sub-Saharan Africa grew the slowest but nevertheless did grow.

Many of the fastest growing economies were oil and gas producers and exporters benefiting from significant increases in energy prices. Other primary products (such as metals, minerals, and agriculture) similarly witnessed unusually high growth. Also, global short-term interest rates fell sharply as central banks reduced rates, spurring economic expansion. The WDI report comments about the significance of five straight years of economic growth in Sub-Saharan Africa following two full decades of decline.[2]

We no longer have the option of considering events in distant places merely as "their problem," so let's examine some key topics of economic globalization tugging at our consciousness. We'll look at what has traditionally been called international economics, a process mostly involving orderly transactions between wealthy countries in the global North. Then we'll examine the more contentious economic agenda of "poor South against rich North," which generates plenty of sparks. First, however, providing a timeline that places contemporary international economics in historical context will assist these efforts.

International Economic Timeline

- 1500–1920: European powers colonize much of world
- 1750–1825: English Industrial Revolution accumulates great wealth in Britain
- 1839–1842: Opium War—Chinese fail to halt English sale of opium in China, increasing British power
- 1846: British Parliament repeals Corn Laws that provided protectionism
- 1848: Karl Marx's Communist Manifesto advocates proletarian revolution against oppressive bourgeoisie
- 1850–1900: growth in trade accompanies spread of Industrial Revolution to America and Europe
- 1860: Chevalier Treaty—MFN trade status created in Franco-British agreement
- 1870s: U.S. railroads transport American grain for sale in Europe, reducing prices and causing protectionist backlash
- 1870–1914: Gold standard of fixed exchange rates
- 1914–1918: World War I—system of international trade crumbles; France and Britain much in debt to United States
- 1924: Dawes Plan—monetary framework involving U.S. loans to Germany to pay reparations to France and Britain, who in turn pay the United States
- 1928: Fed jacked-up interest rates break the monetary cycle of the Dawes Plan, creating crisis in German economy
- 1929: Crash—U.S. stock market in October collapse
- 1930: Smoot-Hawley—high U.S. tariff leads to trade war and exacerbates economic failure
- 1939–1945: World War II—United States emerges from ashes of war as economic hegemon
- 1945–1973: Bretton Woods system—fixed rate gold/dollar exchange system bolsters U.S. role as leader of free trade
- 1946: World Bank—global lending role begins
- 1947: IMF—currency exchange rate stabilization begins
- 1947: GATT—global trade expansion via tariff reductions begins
- 1947–1991: Cold War aid—United States and USSR use economic aid as a tool to fight Cold War
- 1960: OPEC—Thirteen nations join oil cartel aiming to control world production (supply)
- 1960s–1970s: Nationalization—many poor countries take over MNC operations in their countries, increasing trend toward government ownership

- 1971: The Nixon shocks—United States withdraws from fixed conversion exchange system based on dollar; slaps on wage and price controls and protectionist trade measures
- 1973: Free-floating currency—U.S. unilateralism leads to collapse of Bretton Woods system
- 1973 and 1979: Oil shocks—OPEC production quotas lead to lower supply and great demand and price increases for "black gold"
- 1974: NIEO—poor countries organize their bargaining position with explicit agenda of complaints
- 1979–1983: Global recession—growing debt of Third World countries worsened by deep recession
- 1980s–1990s: Privatization—global trend shifts toward reduced government ownership and return of industries to the private sector
- 1991: Gulf War—United States leads military action to protect oil supplies, and allies pay most of the bill
- 1994: United States continues MFN trade status for China; NAFTA takes effect; the United States lifts trade embargo against Vietnam
- 1995: WTO—Uruguay Round of GATT succeeds in expanding GATT into the Geneva-based trade organization, the WTO, with provisions for further reduction of trade barriers
- 2001: September 11, 2001—The destruction of America's symbolic center of international economics, New York's World Trade Center, in a terrorist attack.
- 2003: Millennium Development Goals (MDGs)
- 2004: Paris 21 Conference on Statistical Capacity Building
- 2005: Helsinki Process of Globalization and Democracy

Evolution of the International Economy

In *A Concise Economic History of the World from Paleolithic Times to the Present,* Rondo Cameron chronicles the long and winding commercial road followed by the traders who have linked together all types of societies, from preindustrial to industrial to postindustrial, from near to far, since ancient times. Trade and exchange, whether by barter or monetary means, have played a vital part in the global drama. However, an exponential increase in trade and financial flow accompanied the Industrial Revolution that rippled from the shores of the British Isles during the eighteenth century. High agricultural productivity, a mobile labor market, and available capital allowed Britain to ride the engine of the Industrial Revolution all the way to status as the greatest naval and commercial power during the 1800s.[3]

The British landed gentry class of farmers had enjoyed the benefit of protectionist trade measures enacted on its behalf by Parliament. These tariffs, quotas, and other limitations on imported goods made such purchases more expensive for the general public but benefited the class of wealthy landowners. Britain's mercantilist trade policy had been well established for quite some time, and its agricultural elite must have been distraught and perplexed when Parliament repealed its protectionist barriers, known collectively as the *Corn Laws,* in 1846.

Political economist Robert Gilpin emphasizes the significance of England moving in the middle of the nineteenth century to a completely new economic policy based on the *market-oriented* classical economic formulations of Adam Smith and David Ricardo. Both of these classical economic theorists considered a free and open trading system the golden road to both economic gain and cooperative ventures in related areas.[4]

Britain and Free Trade

Given Britain's international clout at that time, when it started talking a new game of free trade based on market economics, other countries certainly listened. Most of them also took similar actions to ease existing trade limitations. As early as 1860, an important precedent was set with the Franco-British Chevalier Treaty, establishing most-favored-nation (MFN) trade status, making British textiles and stoneware cheaper in France, and making French wine and cheese less dear in Britain. According to Rondo Cameron, the next couple of decades witnessed the freest trade in Europe of any time prior to World War II. As discussed in Chapter 14, countries often use MFN status as either a carrot or a stick in efforts to influence the behavior of other states.

Most favored nation (MFN) ■ The granting of trading rules and conditions considered to be the norm for a state's trade partners

These early days of economic globalization occurred as a by-product of a trade explosion during the nineteenth century. The rapid growth of the United States, France, and Germany as viable competitors hoping to catch up with British power and wealth can also be linked to a general expansion of international trade. Various technological innovations added greatly to the expansion mania of the latter 1800s. For example, America's railroads enabled it to transport unprecedented quantities of grain and manufactured goods for export to European markets during the heady days of the U.S. post–Civil War Gilded Age. Technological innovation has always correlated with economic growth and the late 1800s were no exception to that rule.

While the international economy continued to grow all the way up until the outbreak of World War I in 1914, familiarity seems to have bred a season of discontent among countries suddenly linked together by trade. Political economist Steven Spiegel says that two main factors contributed to strife and to a return to more protectionist trade policies among the great powers: (1) competition for international markets had become intense because politically sensitive governments sought to shelter their at-risk industries; and (2) there was a resurgence of nationalistic pride in many countries, particularly Germany and Italy. With the new nationalism came increased expenditures for national defense; tariffs also came in handy raising funds for the military. Amid increasing disarray, the fixed exchange system known as the **gold standard** stood solid as Gibraltar, and all nations continued to peg the value of their currencies to gold until 1914.[5]

Gold standard ■ A fixed exchange rate system in which the values of different currencies around the world are set in terms of gold

World War I's Unfinished Economic Business

The great toll of World War I was measured not only in war dead and in altered political power equations among many nations but also in economic costs—which were staggering. The United States, serving as the "arsenal for democracy," was the only clear-cut major economic winner. As fighting drew to a close in 1918, America's industrial muscles were both flexed and bulging. The major defeated nation, Germany, faced crippling reparations payments to the two victors who demanded them: Britain and France. In turn, these two victors owed the United States more than $10 billion each in war debts.

An ingenious solution to this apparent dilemma was created in 1924, in the form of the **Dawes Plan,** essentially a win–win–win resolution of the impasse over postwar payments. U.S. sources lent money to Germany, which it used to pay its reparations to France and Britain, who then were able to pay their war debts to the United States. The cyclical monetary solution of the Dawes Plan, named after the U.S. Secretary of the Treasury who introduced it, worked until 1928. In that year, the American stock market was booming out of sight as a result of highly speculative investments.

Dawes Plan ■ A policy that recycled post–World War I payments from Germany to Britain and France, then to the United States and back to Germany in the form of loans

In response, the American institution responsible for monetary policy, the Federal Reserve Bank (Fed), became nervous over market speculation. It therefore decided to raise interest rates to slow down the market as well as the overall economy. Inadvertently, however, the Fed's move also frightened international investors, and the cycle of the Dawes Plan was broken, being replaced by economic nationalism, which made things decidedly worse. The German economy collapsed altogether amid **hyperinflation** and political instability. The New York stock market crashed in 1929, the Smoot-Hawley tariff was passed by Congress in 1930, and the gold standard had become a relic of the past by the time the Great Depression settled in for a disastrous decade during the 1930s.

Hyperinflation ■ An alarming rate of price and wage increases deemed perilous to a nation's economy because it undermines its currency and encourages wild speculation

Bretton Woods and American Hegemony

The dislocations of World War II were required to finally end the Depression and create a new global economic hegemon: the United States. The Bretton Woods system set up in 1944 served America's goals elegantly. It regulated trade under U.S. leadership and pushed the world toward freer trade, which proved especially beneficial to what had become the biggest market (America). A fixed exchange rate based on the dollar's value in gold at $35 per ounce stabilized financial exchanges after Bretton Woods. Global lending institutions helped to funnel U.S. economic aid to finance the rebuilding of allies and enemies alike (unlike post-WW I policy).

The three main international financial institutions (IFIs) established at Bretton Woods were intended to coordinate the global economy by influencing three related activities: setting monetary policy; providing development lending for needy countries; and expanding trade for just about everyone. Monetary policy became the purview of the new International Monetary Fund (IMF), which was to stabilize global currencies. The IMF would bring order to the process of deciding what in the world a dollar, yen, lira, or mark was worth. In some respects, the IMF came to be seen as a fire brigade coming to the short-term rescue of countries in need.

Somewhat related in function was the World Bank, which was charged with longer-term development financing and policy advice for LDCs. If the IMF was akin to a fire brigade, then the World Bank came to function as something of a global construction company. The third leg of the economic triangle drawn up at Bretton Woods was the General Agreement on Tariff and Trade (GATT), which was to promote free trade between countries by establishing global rules of the game. Its special mission was to reduce the protectionist barriers to trade (such as tariffs) that had proven so self-defeating in the 1930s.

All in all, these three IFIs performed admirably as vehicles for driving the brisk economic recovery that followed World War II. Variations on their themes continue to function reasonably well today but not without substantial criticism from many responsible quarters. Case Study 15.1 involves a former chief economist at the World Bank describing how heavy-handed meddling from the IMF can break some things in LDCs that are working well enough so that they do not need to be fixed.

Case Study 15.1   IMF/World Bank Clash over Ethiopian Policy

The IFI that has drawn the most sustained criticism for overdoing its assistance role is the IMF. Since the 1970s, when this "fire brigade" comes into poor countries with emergency loans to help them deal with economic crises, it has typically required austerity measures that impose procedures intended to ensure accountability (known as structural adjustment) but also can cause widespread suffering among the poor. Joseph Stiglitz, chief economist at the World Bank from 1997 to 2000, later described his frustration over narrow-minded bureaucratic procedures imposed by the IMF in Ethiopia, one of the world's poorest countries (see Figure 15.1).

In 1997, Stiglitz traveled to Ethiopia and spent much time there working with its prime minister, Meles Zanawi, for whom Stiglitz developed great personal and professional respect. Zanawi was trained as a medical doctor but also studied economics in England and understood macroeconomics particularly well. Stiglitz says that Zanawi was doing all the right things for Ethiopia's severely challenged economy. Under Zanawi's leadership, Ethiopia had zero inflation, economic output grew steadily during the 1990s, corruption had been rooted out and punished—and despite the country's having recently recovered from famine and civil war, Zanawi had sharply reduced the military budget in favor of an antipoverty program. Finally, Ethiopia's economy was looking good enough for Western countries to start sending foreign assistance once again.

Ex-chief economist Stiglitz says that leadership in poor countries just does not get much better than this and because the IMF is supposed to judge national performance by results, Ethiopia should have gotten an A+ when the IMF did its next audit. However, what happened was that the IMF suspended its aid to Ethiopia because Prime Minister Zanawi had embarked on some of his programs without consulting the IMF first. For his failure to consult properly, the IMF cut Ethiopia off from assistance it badly needed. In other words, the IMF had put bureaucratic process ahead of proven results. Normally, the World Bank, for which Stiglitz worked, does not grant its own aid to a country unless the IMF certifies that that country is in compliance with its guidelines. In this case, however, Stiglitz managed to convince his colleagues at the World Bank that the IMF's position was absurd, and the Bank tripled its lending to Ethiopia—which would not have happened without Stiglitz's personal experiences in Ethiopia.

Stiglitz argues that for better or for worse, globalization is here to stay—yet it must be made to function more justly, and IMF structural adjustment policies need to be revised. A huge majority of the world's poor countries are essentially disenfranchised from any debate concerning reforms to IFIs. The IMF in particular involves an elite circle of wealthy countries that make their decisions behind closed doors. Stiglitz contends that needed reforms include ending the secrecy

Ethiopia

✪ National Capital

0   Miles   200

Figure 15.1
Tiny Ethiopia is one of many sites where the IMF and World Bank have disagreed over lending policies.

Source: From *Maps on File*, by Facts on File, Inc. Copyright © by Facts on File, Inc. Reprinted by permission of Facts on File, Inc.

shrouding their decision-making processes, providing meaningful debt relief for the poorest countries, and dividing up power more effectively. Stiglitz writes that "in the U.N., five countries have a veto power over what happens. In the IMF, only one (the United States) can veto measures." Current practices of globalization from above, without comparable globalization from below, fans already-existing frustrations.[6]

U.S. foreign affairs journalist Helen Cobban has written probingly about many of the issues of accountability and governance raised in the preceding case about Ethiopia and the IMF. She says that the IMF's operating system is essentially the same as it was sixty years ago and needs drastic overhauling. Of the 182 member countries, the United States carries 18 percent of IMF voting power, whereas a country such as Ethiopia has a tiny fraction of 1 percent. All IMF decisions are made by a small twenty-four-member board, with only a few countries having permanent seats.

In 2000, the body was struggling over naming a new director, and all previous directors had been either American or European. Author Cobban sees how contemporary protesters in the streets can view the IMF as a "cozy rich man's club," and why their battle cry of "No globalization without representation" resonates with many young people globally, including in America. Cobban believes that the IMF can maintain its traditional role of providing financial stability to support the global trading system while developing a clearer mission "to provide special help in restructuring the finances of countries working seriously on poverty eradication and long-term economic growth in poor states."[7]

The three IFIs mentioned previously are, however, not the only organizations affecting global economic policy. The United States cooperates, albeit with elite countries only, in a multilateral forum of annual summits known as the Group of Seven (G-7) leading industrial powers (now called the G-8 since Russia was admitted).

In 1974, the formalization of the New International Economic Order (NIEO) provided an institutional base for poor countries' demands to rectify inherently unfair rules of the game for global economic competition. The NIEO faced a stiff challenge in the 1980s when both Ronald Reagan in the United States and Margaret Thatcher in the United Kingdom pushed hard for *privatization* in many LDCs that had earlier *nationalized* industries wholesale as part of their fight for independence. Principles of free-market economics enjoyed a renaissance under Reagan and Thatcher and have continued to reverberate through IFI policies ever since. ▪

Theory of International Trade and Finance

Trade

Nothing symbolizes globalization more poignantly than trade. A century or two ago, it was conceivable for a country to seek what economists call *autarky*, or economic self-sufficiency. Autarky is no longer a realistic goal. Because valued natural resources such as oil, gold, coal, forests, and water, as well as human resources such as education, technological skill, entrepreneurship, and cultural homogeneity are found sporadically around the world, societies find it mutually beneficial to trade for what they lack. It is not even necessary for a society to have an **absolute advantage** in making a product— say, sombreros in Mexico—to trade that item successfully. Economists claim that for the arithmetic to add up for Mexico to trade sombreros, it merely must posses a **comparative advantage** in sombrero production.

Classical British economist David Ricardo was the first to illustrate the mathematical justifications for comparative advantage, and thus, free trade. Every country benefits from exporting those goods in which it has a comparative advantage. Mexico may not be number one in sombrero production, but if churning out sombreros is what it does relatively well, then it should trade them for goods in which it has a comparative disadvantage—say, ice skates from Canada. "Mutual gains will lead to specialization in each country, making goods less expensive and production more efficient for both."[8] The idea of comparative advantage has become so well ingrained into classical economic theory that many economists now consider it to be a law rather than merely a theory. It surely has historically represented the most potent argument in favor of free trade.

But not everyone responds to the smooth logic of comparative advantage as a rationale for free trade. Its very antithesis, protectionism, often arises when pressure is placed on legislatures to enact laws shielding faltering domestic industries from foreign competition. Protectionism is a short-term political expedient often criticized by economists; nevertheless, political scientists accept it as an inevitable part of the human drama. On this issue, economists tend to embrace the spirit of what we have referred to as idealism, whereas political scientists often support protectionism from a realist outlook.

Although tariffs used to be the most common form of protectionism, the disastrous Smoot-Hawley tariff of 1930 gave all direct taxes on imports a bad name (it raised them as high as 60 percent). In 1933, retaliatory tariffs had cut world trade to a mere one-third of its 1929 level.[9] A half-century of U.S. cheerleading for the GATT treaty also encouraged tariff reductions, which have accompanied each successive round of the GATT.[10] Other, newer **nontariff barriers** (**NTBs**) are more subtle in creating an obstacle course for free trade. Trade restriction by setting high product *quality standards* to discourage imports has become common. For example, when California placed rigorous emission controls on all cars sold there, it made it impossible for autos from certain countries to meet those clean air standards.

Limits on the number of units of a given commodity can also cut down on imports. These import quotas may directly restrict the number of items a foreign company can sell in the United States, or they may negotiate for subtler kinds of limits. An example of the latter case occurred in 1980. With Detroit's Big Three taking a licking and barely ticking in the face of fuel-efficient imports, the U.S. government placed pressure on the Japanese to accept so-called **voluntary export restraints** (**VERs**), limiting the number of Japanese cars unloaded onto American docks.

Japan is a good example of another form of NTB, namely **subsidies.** These may consist of direct payments to domestic companies, or subtler tax breaks, or price supports that help local firms. If subsidies are substantial, they may even allow a company to sell its products abroad below the actual cost of production, a practice known derisively as *dumping.* When Japanese semiconductors were being sold very cheaply in the United States in the 1980s, American competitors complained loudly to President Ronald Reagan, who then accused Japan of dumping semiconductors on the U.S. market. The American companies claimed that the Japanese goal was to drive American producers

Absolute advantage ■ As related to the global division of labor, the ability of either a country or a firm to produce goods or services below the level of all competitors

Comparative advantage ■ Any country's economy benefits from engaging in trade where it has a relative (not absolute) advantage in efficiency producing some good or service

Nontariff barriers (NTBs) ■ Any of the varied means of protecting domestic industries from foreign competition other than excise taxes

Voluntary export restraints (VERs) ■ A form of indirect protectionism involving concealed coercive threats by the protecting country against a low-cost exporter

Subsidies ■ Monetary grants by countries to domestic producers to enhance their competitiveness against foreign companies

out of business and then raise prices sharply in a field with few competitors. Reagan succeeded in getting Japanese adjustments to the pricing of semiconductors.

Finally, we all know how effective marketing is in getting us to confuse our wants with our needs. MNCs wouldn't spend billions to advertise their products if it didn't work. By limiting the amount a foreign company can spend on marketing in the United States, such limits can help to contain the sales of foreign competitors such as Fuji film and Lowenbrau beer, thus extending a helping hand to U.S. companies such as Kodak and Samuel Adams.

Finance

Globalization is fostered by international exchanges of money just as surely as by trade. Daily international currency exchanges alone total in the trillions of dollars, as do electronic fund transfers. Because countries almost never trade by barter, money greases the skids for international exchanges of goods and services. The sheer volume of money flowing from country to country means that central banks, such as the Fed in the United States, have lost most of their ability to affect the relative value of currencies through large-scale buying and selling. They simply find it much harder today to use their monetary reserves to manipulate a meaningful percentage of the currency in circulation.

Each country has its own currency. For international business to operate smoothly, the relative value of the Mexican peso, Australian dollar, Chinese yuan, or Japanese yen must be readily calculable. Now there is also the euro, a new currency adopted by most of the European Union's members in 2002, figuring into the mix. There are two principal ways of determining currency values. The first is the **fixed exchange-rate system** in which currencies are set at specific rates. The fixed-rate system possesses the advantages of simplicity and predictability.

From 1870 until World War I, the fixed-rate system consisted of what was called the gold standard because, in theory, each currency at that time was convertible to gold. The idea of using gold as the basis for currency exchange was first broached by England as early as 1821. From 1945 to 1973, another fixed-rate method, the Bretton Woods system, was based on confidence in the U.S. dollar, rather than gold. What has existed since 1973 is a purely market-driven solution: the *floating exchange-rate system*, in which prices fluctuate on a daily basis like any other commodity: according to the intersection of the supply curve and the demand curve. The actual rate of a nation's currency is more naturally attuned to the overall strength of its economy in a floating-rate system than in the more arbitrary fixed-rate mechanism.

With globalized trade and finance, can banking be far behind? International lending by private banks totals in the tens of trillions of dollars annually. British banks typically lead the international lending parade to foreign borrowers. However, one particular British bank, Barings, may wish it had internationalized its operations somewhat more cautiously, as discussed in Case Study 15.2.

Fixed exchange-rate system
■ A financial mechanism that allows governments to agree on the prices (value) of their currencies at preestablished levels vis-à-vis one another

Case Study 15.2   The Barings Bank Saga

Like any other form of major change, global interdependence has produced good and bad alike. For Britain's oldest merchant bank, the venerable Barings, the downside degenerated into a nightmare. As one of the leading banks in the most aggressive country pursuing global lending and investment, Barings may have spread its international presence too thinly, too quickly. What was it that brought down the 232-year-old Barings bank? The irresponsible actions of a 28-year-old financial trader left largely unsupervised in Barings' far-off Singapore office.

Nick Leeson had been investing large sums of Barings money on the direction of the Japanese stock market, which he believed was going to go up in 1994 and 1995. But it went down, and down, and down. When all was said and done, young Leeson had invested $1.38 billion in unauthorized Barings money on his horrible hunch. He then spent frantic months forging documents, lying to superiors, and deceiving auditors in a futile effort to conceal his world-class theft. In the process, he tricked the Singapore exchange, known as SIMEX, into releasing $115 million in bogus earnings to his Barings account. Like a compulsive gambler loose at the racetrack, Leeson made bigger and bigger bets in an attempt to win back quickly what he had lost more gradually.

The damage to Barings' bottom line added up to a death sentence: losses of $1.38 billion. Even a two-century-old institution could not recover from that. British law does not allow a death sentence for people, so Nick Leeson did not have to fear the same fate that befell Barings. In 1995, Leeson pleaded guilty to two of eleven charges against him and received a sentence of six and a half years in prison. What is your opinion of the sentence Leeson received? Is six years and six months too little, too much, or appropriate for his crime?

How could such a thing happen? First, as alluded to previously, Barings seems to have grown internationally, apparently without holding its overseas employees accountable. Too much authority was accorded an inexperienced trader in stock futures, and too little attention was paid to clues of impropriety that popped up periodically. Secondly, we are not talking about cold hard cash transferred in hands-on meetings between real people. Rather, in this age of electronic finance, massive monetary transfers occur silently in nanoseconds from computer terminal to computer terminal, with no hard copy paper trail or verbal conversation between human beings. ◼

Theories of International Political Economy

Three broad theories dominate the landscape of the international political economy. We have encountered parts of each in earlier discussions. The three theories are economic idealism, economic realism, and economic Marxism. Politics and economics overlap in a major way at the global level, and each modern theory is grounded in that realization.

Economic idealism is sometimes called economic liberalism and owes its intellectual underpinnings to the eighteenth-century classical writings of David Ricardo and Adam Smith. Economic idealism considers trade barriers as debilitating obstacles to economic growth and advocates free trade instead. The arguments of both comparative advantage and laissez-faire constitute genuine articles of faith for economic idealism. Because the pure market operates as efficiently as human endeavor can aspire to, governments need to intervene only rarely, according to this theory.

A belief in the people's capability to recognize and act rationally on their best interests also lies close to the heart of idealists. Nations are considered little more than collections of such rational, wealth-seeking individual actors. It is people that create wealth, say the economic idealists.

Economic realism views the role of the national government as more active and vital than does idealism. Economic realism looks first to the power relations of states for clues as to appropriate economic policy for a given country at a given time. The relative power of states dictates what they can and cannot do in specific economic issue areas, such as trade. It is the state, not the individual, that economic realism sees as consistently acting rationally on the world stage; such rationality leads states to subsume economic policies to the quest for power, most often defined in military terms.

Prior to the nineteenth century, economic realism shaped the mercantilist belief that trade interests must serve the higher master of power politics. Economic realists feel comfortable with protectionism designed to promote the power status of the state in what is perceived as a hostile sea of sharks. The idea is that, without a strong national defense, the very existence of the country is naively left in jeopardy.

Just as strongly as economic realists are committed to the primacy of politics over economics, *economic Marxists* believe the exact opposite: economics shapes and directs all aspects of social existence, including politics. More specifically, it is the economic interests of competing classes that economic Marxists consider vital. Both the individual (idealism) and the state (realism) are viewed as minor actors when compared with the subtext battle between the dominant and oppressed classes in each society.

In capitalist countries, say the economic Marxists, the revolutionary working class, or proletariat, must rise up to overthrow the owners of the means of production—the bourgeoisie. The domestic working-class struggle for liberation gets transferred to the international level, where capitalist states have joined together to extend their subjugation of the poor to the global level. As a result of global oppression, the world has become divided into two broad categories: the core (rich North) and the periphery (poor South). Workers of the world should, and will, unite to overthrow their insensitive oppressors.[11]

Weighing in at well over $10 trillion annually, the U.S. economy serves as the symbolic target for attacks by economic Marxists. Proponents of this economic theory suffered a severe blow when communist systems in the Soviet Union and eight eastern European countries crumbled. Many economic Marxists still cling to their ideals, pointing a finger of blame at the clumsy application of Marxism, not at Marx's theories themselves. Because the United States is the only global economic and military superpower, let's look at some of the challengers facing it.

Current Economic Rivals: Japan and Germany

The Soviet Union acted as the rival military superpower during the Cold War, but there was no rival economic hegemon at that time. In 2006, there was neither an economic rival nor a military rival, but such judgments can change rapidly in a world of flux. Japan and Germany have risen to the top of the heap as potential challengers to American economic superpowerdom.

Many aspects of their modern stories seem strikingly similar. Japan and Germany both witnessed martial traditions gone haywire in the 1930s, culminating in aggressive state socialism, or fascism. More than defeated in World War II, they were humiliated into accepting unconditional surrender at the hands of the Allies. U.S.-germinated seeds—in the form of alien democratic principles—were planted, quickly took root, and developed stable institutional vines. The fertilizer that nourished this remarkable growth was in each case unmistakable: an economic miracle legitimizing the postwar systems created in Japan and Germany.

Fearing that militarism was buried deep in the soil of these cultures, the United States imposed pacifistic constitutions on its ex-enemies. Military maneuvers were limited to defensive operations on their own soil; nuclear weapons were prohibited; the countries were kept off the U.N. Security Council, both countries were tied to U.S. Cold War alliances against the Soviet Union; and their military budgets were limited. This allowed Japan and Germany to focus on economic, rather than military, competition while residing under the U.S. nuclear umbrella.

Forty years went by before Japan spent even 1 percent of its annual GNP on defense, while America was spending 7 percent and the Soviet Union about 20 percent on military matters at that time. Whereas the Americans and Soviets put their best and brightest young minds in quest of ever-more-sophisticated weaponry, their Japanese and German counterparts put resources into researching and developing manufactured goods and services for export. Before too many decades passed, World War II's vanquished had grown into economic giants.

World Bank figures reveal that in 2000, Japan and Germany ranked second and third to the United States, with GDPs of $2.95 and $2.1 trillion, and GNP per capita of $23,400 and $25,050, respectively. In 2001, Japan ranked ninth on the U.N.'s HDI for quality of life, and Germany ranked seventeenth. West Germany had been higher in most of these categories before it absorbed the former Communist East Germany in 1990. Japan briefly supplanted the United States as the world's largest foreign aid donor from 2002 to 2004, while Germany's status has been enhanced by its leadership in the powerhouse European Union. At the turn of the millennium, only these two national economies contended with the United States for superpower status.

Both cultures, however, remain divided over the same question: Should they become more assertive players on the world stage? In some ways, making money behind the scenes, while the United States led the charge during the Cold War, felt comfortable to the Japanese and Germans. Acutely aware of nationalistic excesses in their recent past, they seem not to trust themselves with too much power. When the United States led the 1991 coalition in the Persian Gulf War against Iraq, America wanted Japan and Germany to send military support personnel. They balked—choosing to open their wallets wider instead. Further, both powers warrant a position as permanent U.N. Security Council members, but neither has pushed aggressively for such a role.

Finally, each nation worries that its economic miracle consists of ephemeral smoke and mirrors; thus, they follow cautious policies while searching for a middle ground identity between the extremes of militarism and pacifism. Germany wonders about its ability to cope with spinoffs from national reunification: unemployment, inflation, a $100 billion price tag, and problems supporting immigrants. Although the international community sees Japan and Germany as poised for stardom, the protagonists themselves seem ambivalent about accepting marquis billing.

Looming Rivals: China, India, Russia, Brazil

Below the major economic powers in the G-8, we find a category of moderate economic powers, with GDP generally in the $200–600 billion range. In descending order, by GDP in billions of dollars, appear China, Brazil, Spain, India, Australia, the Netherlands, Switzerland, Sweden, Mexico, Belgium, and Russia. Among these moderate powers, four paradoxical high-potential underachievers stand out as plausible economic powers in the twenty-first century—namely, China, India, Russia, and Brazil.[12] All have large, diverse, and relatively well-educated populations, impressive natural resources, and influential roles in at least one global issue area—population for China, cutting-edge software development and English language skills for India, the largest rainforests for Brazil, and nuclear armaments for Russia—ensuring that their voices will be heard.

Thomas Friedman's analysis in Chapter 1 and Jeffrey Sachs' analysis in the "Coda" section of this chapter include strong statements about both China and India. They predict that those two countries are best prepared to rival America in the future because of the resources being placed into education (especially high-technology higher education), the emergence of dynamic middle classes for the first time in their histories, and endless numbers of young people empowered by the Internet to compete globally.

A final category defying easy numerical classification consists of the newly industrialized countries (NICs) of East Asia. These former colonial possessions, sharing the legacy of poverty common to Third World countries, have risen above the crowd in recent decades. Following the Japanese model of export-led growth, they have achieved flexible production through hard work, managed economies, American support, and a cultural emphasis on education. The result has been impressive economic growth in South Korea, Singapore, Taiwan, Hong Kong, and Malaysia. South Korea leads the group in total GDP, and Singapore leads in GDP per capita.[13]

The rapid pace of modern technological change has also produced economic winners and losers. In 1999, President Bill Clinton hosted a "National Digital Divide Summit" to explore ways of addressing the significant disparity between the "digital haves" in the global North, and the "digital have-nots" in the global South. Emerging from this effort was an online clearinghouse of news and resources concerning this problematic digital divide called the Digital Divide Network, which helps digital divide activists around the world communicate with one another. Membership is free and open and includes the Internet's largest e-mail forum for digital divide issues (see the Website at the end of this chapter). One seemingly routine technological innovation contributed significantly to the rise of the NICs discussed previously, located mostly in East Asia. This relatively quiet technological shift was not very glamorous and was largely ignored by the news media. However, international economists understand its significance: namely, the impact of **containerization** (see Case Study 15.3).

Containerization ■ The use of steel containers in commercial shipping to enhance its efficiency, security, and cost-effectiveness

Although the United States greeted the new millennium as an impressive global hegemon economically, militarily, and culturally, it still has plenty of problems. They include large trade deficits, record national debt, a growing disparity between rich and poor, 45 million people without health insurance, rampant corporate corruption, and an image of smugness repulsive to more than just Al Qaeda. As demonstrated in Case Study 15.1, America is being challenged to live up to its ideals of democracy and justice in global forums such as the IMF. Just about a century ago, Great Britain looked like an

Case Study 15.3 Containerization: The Quiet Revolution

Back in the seventeenth and eighteenth centuries, tiny Holland was the strongest trading country in the world. Part of Dutch riches derived from long domination of the Asian trade; Dutch vessels represented what amounted to state-of-the-art containerships of the time. Brisk East–West trade began mostly with Chinese tea, purchased by the ton for tea-loving Britons by the British East India Company. Other exotic spices of the Orient were soon in demand by the growing rich merchant class in the Occident.

But the determined Chinese were obsessed with British silver and would settle for nothing less. Not until England artificially created demand for a new commodity in China—opium—producing more than 12,000 Chinese addicts by 1836, did the British have a saleable commodity to leverage Chinese tea. Henceforth, tea and opium embraced one another in a devil's dance.

In our day, profits from East–West trade have shifted decidedly toward the Orient, with Japan, China, Taiwan, Malaysia, and South Korea leading the way. Cheap containers and cheap labor costs have boosted East Asian economies with a vengeance. This has been great for the East Asian NICs and has also been a boon for the 300 million American consumers. It has been disastrous, however, for several hundred thousand U.S. laborers working in industries such as textiles, televisions, steel, toys, or shoes.

World trade has been revolutionized through efficiency based on standardized containerships. Uniformity is the name of the transportation game today, as everything from computers to fish to toys traverses the seven seas in steel containers. The heaviest traffic steams nonstop across the Pacific Ocean between Seattle and Hong Kong, or Kobe and Vancouver, or San Francisco and Taipei. Eight million containers pass through Hong Kong's busy harbor each year.

Physically, these containers look just like the beds of the tractor-trailer trucks you see on U.S. interstate highways. Unloaded straight off ships, they are rolling across Interstates less than two hours after arrival. Hong Kong's Orient Overseas Container Lines (OOCL) now leads all shippers. If you look for the gold-colored OOCL logo, you will notice their containers bouncing across America.

But what exactly is so great about shipping via standardized metal containers? Well, they are secure from physical damage, completely sealable to foil thieves, interchangeable anywhere in the world, less expensive than other forms of transport, and uncommonly reliable. Containers make goods so maintenance-free that crews aboard commercial liners have been slashed to cut expenses in a highly competitive shipping business. Just a few years ago, there were more than one hundred shipping companies, but today, a mere few rule the waves. This relatively simple-looking new technology has transformed global shipping and has left big winners and losers in its wake.[14] ∎

---

unmatched global hegemon economically and militarily, but by the outbreak of World War I in 1914, that status had disappeared. So the United States' economic prowess should not lead to overconfidence since the age of globalization entails change, change, and more change.

Nonstate Threats to U.S. Economic Hegemony

Besides states as potential competitors, America's economic hegemony faces challenges from nonstate actors as well. They all contribute to a burden of frustration carried on America's shoulders. When compared with the prolonged economic stability that characterized the Cold War era, it almost seems as though economic heaven and hell have broken loose from their moorings simultaneously. Not only is everything different, but things are more unpredictable as well. The United States certainly has further to fall from its pinnacle of economic power than do rival countries, but it also feels a loss of control. Regarding the ecological GIs and human rights, NGOs have proven extremely influential. However, in the economic realm, almost certainly, the MNCs are the most notable nonstate actors challenging America.

Back to the Future: Markets Overwhelming State Policies

Economist Herman Schwartz's *States versus Markets* provides a broader historical understanding of trends in the global economy. Today, we witness market pressures overwhelming and frustrating state policies in many different contexts. Because the historical memory of many Americans seems to extend back no further than six decades to the end of World War II, this phenomenon of markets overwhelming state policies seems an unlikely one to many contemporaries. Professor Schwartz argues that it is nothing new but actually a shift back to the future—the way it was in the nineteenth century.

Countries had their greatest success in controlling international and domestic markets during the post–World War II era. But far from being normal, this successful state intervention represented a dramatic departure from historical processes of the global economy, according to Professor Schwartz: "The global economy is in fact moving back to the future, resembling more and more the global economy of the nineteenth century."[15]

Professor Schwartz's analysis points to the private sector, especially MNCs, as profoundly affecting the global economy. Other economists share his view that the weakening of states at the expense of MNCs is both inexorable and desirable. A decidedly different opinion, however, comes from globalization-from-below activists Jeremy Brecher and Tim Costello. They believe that a potent grass-roots movement against the consequences of deregulated globalization (from above) is growing, and they don't like the idea of states becoming more like spectators than movers and shakers in the global economy—precisely because they don't share the faith some economists have in MNCs.

MNCs' Critics

Brecher and Costello contend that MNCs care not one whit about environmental problems, human rights, or labor conditions. Yet, by competing to attract these "footloose corporations," unwitting communities encourage a disastrous "race to the bottom." According to these authors, the end result is that "the New World Economy is a disaster that has already happened." They see hope only in radical people's movements bubbling up simultaneously around the world to challenge corporate "globalization from above."[16]

What is it about MNCs that energizes leaders of LDCs and Northern Hemisphere activists such as Brecher and Costello to shower MNCs with a chorus of jeers? Fairly or unfairly, decade after decade, corporate executives have been portrayed unfavorably in Hollywood movies. Although Hollywood films mostly entertain, they also subtly influence our perceptions. Popular attitudes seem especially malleable regarding topics about which we know little—for example, what takes place in corporate boardrooms. Greedy, insensitive CEOs have made terrific celluloid villains. But Hollywood is not the main contributor to the image problems of CEOs.

Ex-Tyco International CEO Dennis Kozlowski is serving a long jail term for bilking more than $600 million from his company to support an outrageously decadent lifestyle.

Real life delivers its share of unscrupulous corporate leaders. The news media love corporate villains as much as Hollywood does. During the 1990s, corporate mogul Al Dunlap topped their list. His shtick consisted of taking over faltering corporations, downsizing as the only answer to cost reduction, turning quick profits for shareholders, and then repeating the formula elsewhere. In 1993, he took over the Scott Paper Company, eliminated 70 percent of upper management, and fired 11,200 employees, or 35 percent of Scott's payroll. By 1995, Scott was debt-free, and its shareholder stock had increased from $2.5 billion to $9 billion. In Dunlap's own words, "After twenty months of intense work I left Scott $100 million richer than when I arrived." Sunbeam then hired him to do the same.

For his slash-and-burn tactics, Dunlap earned two nicknames: "Chainsaw Al," and "Rambo in Pinstripes." Dunlap argues that a CEO's job demands putting shareholders first, not employees. Many critics dispute that it is really so simple. According to Joseph McCann, a business school dean: "This scorched earth policy benefits no one but Al Dunlap and a handful of shareholders." Management consultant Tom Peters believes that while corporate restructuring is necessary, Dunlap's quick-fix "chainsaw" approach fails to address underlying long-term problems and suffers from superficiality.[17]

Since 2000, things have only gotten worse regarding managerial behavior. The slew of criminal convictions and plea bargains referred to at the end of the previous chapter suggest that the term "corporate ethics" ought not be consigned to the oxymoron pile. Tyco International's Dennis Kozlowski was convicted in 2005 on twenty-two counts, including grand larceny, falsifying business records, securities fraud, and several other charges. He looted more than $600 million from his company to pay for lavish parties, valuable art pieces, and an opulent Manhattan apartment, including things such as $6,000 shower curtains. Kozlowski faced up to thirty years imprisonment after his four-month trial.

Equally disturbing practices have occurred in some U.S. chemical companies. Certain chemicals found to cause cancer and sterility, such as dibromochloropropane (DBCP), are banned in the United States. Yet companies such as Dow Chemical freely ship DBCP abroad to be used in Latin American countries by MNCs such as Standard Fruit as a bug-killing pesticide. Native workers inject DBCP into the roots of banana plants in places such as Nicaragua and Bolivia without knowing about its health hazards, and, in the 1990s, Dow Chemical and Standard Fruit were both facing class-action lawsuits.

The issue of U.S.-barred pesticides being exported for profit first gained notoriety with the 1981 publication of *Circle of Poison* by David Weir and Mark Schapiro, which traced a trail of pesticides exported to poor countries, used on crops, and then later unwittingly imported and consumed by Americans in products such as coffee, cotton, and bananas. An even more poignant warning of this danger appeared in the award-winning documentary film *Pesticides: For Export Only,* produced by Robert Richter, examining pesticide use in a tiny fishing village in Ghana.[18] But just when it seems tempting to paint the scarlet "V" for Villain on the chest of CEOs, along comes Aaron Feuerstein to complicate the corporate portrait (see Case Study 15.4).

Case Study 15.4   Humanist in Pinstripes: Aaron Feuerstein

A few decades ago, thriving textile factories provided good jobs for many workers in New England. Most of the factories have long since disappeared, as the American market has been flooded with imported clothes from countries with much lower labor costs than the United States. In 1981, it looked certain that Malden Mills in Lawrence, Massachusetts, would be chalked up as another textile mill down the tubes. When Malden Mills CEO Aaron Feuerstein was forced to file for bankruptcy protection, few experts expected his company to survive.

However, Aaron Feuerstein's approach to Malden's faltering status was a creative one: he invested heavily in research and development. The results were patents on two synthetic fabrics called Polartec and Polarfleece, designed for use in outdoor wear by pricey manufacturers such as L.L. Bean and Patagonia. These patented fabrics became much in demand, and Malden Mills seemed to have beaten the odds by doing well in a tough international clothing market. Feuerstein succeeded without the draconian measures used by Al "Chainsaw" Dunlap to improve the bottom line.

Malden Mills President Aaron Feuerstein, right, receives a warm welcome from his employees as he arrives on December 14, 1995, to announce that he will continue paying them while their burned-out factory is rebuilt.

Then, in December of 1995, a disastrous fire totaled the factory, putting Malden's 3,000 employees out of work at Christmastime. What could CEO Feuerstein possibly do? The factory's security director, Bob Fawcett, said: "Another person would have taken the insurance money and walked away. I might have done that. But he's [Feuerstein] not that kind of a person." After the December fire, Feuerstein surprised many people by announcing that he would pay all employees for a month—which at least got them through the holiday season. Then, mouths dropped when he did it for a second month. By the time Feuerstein forked out a third month's salary to all his workers, he had spent several million dollars covering the payroll of a company with an unpromising future. To say that his employees regarded him as a saint would not be hyperbole.

But it seems that CEO Feuerstein was more than a humanist with a checkbook—he was an excellent businessman as well. Before the fire, Malden Mills turned out 130,000 yards of fabric a week. A few weeks after the fire: 230,000 yards. Why did he do what he did? "I have a responsibility *to* the workers, both blue-collar and white-collar," said Feuerstein. "I have an equal responsibility to the community. It would

have been unconscionable to deliver a death blow to the cities of Lawrence and Methuen." When asked how most other CEOs differ from his approach, he replied that "I consider our workers as an asset, not an expense."

His religious beliefs come through when he quotes the ancient Hebrew scholar Hillel, who said, "In a situation where there is no righteous person, try to be a righteous person." You would have to read no further than the jacket cover of Al Dunlap's *Mean Business* to realize that a Grand Canyon of philosophical differences separates Aaron Feuerstein and Al Dunlap as corporate CEOs. That philosophical Grand Canyon might even rival the rich-versus-poor global chasm, which is the essence of the remainder of this chapter.[19] ■

North/South Polarization

The authors of *Dying for Growth: Global Inequality and the Health of the Poor* blame MNCs for contributing to the global fixation on economic expansion and mega-wealth for the few. They bring to life fourteen stories of real people that humanize cold statistics such as that one-fifth of the world's population live (and die) on less than a dollar per day.[20] Other sources inform us that while 75 percent of the world's people live in the LDCs, they produce a mere 20 percent of global GDP. The wealthiest 20 percent of the world's people earn $61 for every $1 earned by the poorest 20 percent. In the decade between 1985 and 1995, the gap between rich and poor countries grew by 15 percent.[21] The undeniability of the rich getting richer and the poor getting poorer has led many scholars to warn of global dangers around the corner. For example, international legal scholar Richard Falk writes that "ultimately, unmet economic problems may lead the poor to desperate politics versus the rich."[22]

Authors Richard Payne and Jamal Nassar provide historical data suggesting that the rich/poor gap is nothing new, predicting "the richest countries will maintain their lead over the poor countries for a long time." They point to studies indicating that the gap has widened in ways measurable during the past two centuries when comparing the richest 20 percent to the poorest 20 percent. In 1820, the gap was 3 to 1; in 1913, it was 11 to 1; in 1950, it was 35 to 1; in 1973, it was 44 to 1; in 1992, it was 72 to 1; and in 2000, it was 86 to 1.[23]

Thousands of poor people live in the shanty town around Shadipor Depot in Old Delhi, India.

The LDCs now total about 130 countries. Also called the Group of 77 (G-77), for their global organization that serves as a kind of alter ego of the G-7 rich states; this bloc has pushed a distinct agenda at international conferences. Its general program, known as the New International Economic Order (NIEO), calls for changing the rules of international economics to help poor countries develop, making the NIEO a sort of international version of the "affirmative action" programs found in the United States.

Very few rich countries have, however, stepped up to the plate to increase their assistance to the South. Even under a Democratic president, America cut its foreign aid during the 1990s. Responding to domestic austerity pressures after the Republicans won a congressional victory in 1994, President Bill Clinton's administration cut the $13.7 billion aid budget by 15 percent during his first two years in office. The U.N. asks rich countries to give 0.7 percent of GNP to foreign aid. America (and most other rich countries) keep promising to reach the 0.7 percent plateau in a future that never materializes. Only a few MDCs actually contribute 0.7 percent. In 1946, America was giving 1.75 percent, but by 1995, foreign aid had slipped to 0.117 percent of GNP.[24] American aid shrank even further under George W. Bush to less than 0.1 percent of GNP in 2004.

UNCTAD I and America

The first international conference devoted to North–South issues was the 1964 U.N. Conference on Trade and Development (UNCTAD I). Political scientist Richard Mansbach summarizes six demands that germinated at UNCTAD I and became codified ten years later at a special session of the U.N. They represent the crux of the G-77's agenda for reform:

1. Increasing state and IGO regulation of the activities of MNCs, including codes of conduct for MNCs.
2. Transferring technology as hardware and know-how from the computer-literate North to the computer-ignorant South.
3. Reforming trade rules to aid the development of poor countries, including preferential pricing for primary products exported by the South.
4. Providing debt relief for LDCs because their debt is a global issue affecting everyone. The debt burden of poor countries reached $1 trillion by the late 1980s.
5. Increasing economic aid (bilateral and multilateral) from rich to poor countries to meet the U.N.-designated level of 0.7 percent of GDP.
6. Revising voting procedures in IFIs such as the World Bank and IMF to give poor countries meaningful influence over decision making.[25]

The United States had had a long history of rejecting pleas from the LDCs to convene a global session for airing development concerns. But President John F. Kennedy was concerned in the early 1960s with promoting Latin American development as a counterweight to communism's entrenchment in Castro's Cuba. America's allies in Latin America advocated a global town meeting on development, and Kennedy's ambassador to the U.N., Adlai Stevenson, convinced the president to reverse the U.S.'s habit of opposing such a conference.

Although the United States went through the diplomatic motions at UNCTAD I, its hidden agenda consisted of placating the LDCs without agreeing to do anything. For the LDCs, by contrast, "this was considered the most important event since the founding of the United Nations." The LDCs particularly disliked one of America's pet institutions, the GATT, which poor countries saw as a "rich man's club" where they had minimal influence over trade decisions.[26]

The LDC position at UNCTAD I was presented by Dr. Raul Prebisch, executive secretary of the U.N. Economic Commission for Latin America. Prebisch described the terms-of-trade problem confronting LDCs and argued that they could never become competitive without big changes in the international economy. The remedies he favored were all opposed by the United States, especially price-setting for primary products, expanded foreign assistance, and reduction of agricultural barriers to imports put up by wealthy countries such as the United States, Japan, and France.

The LDCs failed in their efforts to unite prior to the conference, and they remained divided throughout the sessions over the resolutions that were discussed. Disunited, their rigid positions condemned them to ineffectiveness. For its part, the powerful U.S. delegation was equally inflexible, and thus no compromise agreements were reached. "The U.S. came with little to offer the G-77, and little is what they offered. Without active U.S. engagement in negotiating, few meaningful compromises were possible."[27]

The Cancún Conference

The United States had long feared starting down the slippery slope of legitimizing the G-77's agenda of **distributive justice** included in the NIEO. In 1983, a watershed event

Distributive justice ■ The view that great inequities in the global allocation of wealth between the North and South justify significant redistribution

occurred regarding America's role in the North–South dialogue. Under President Ronald Reagan, a conservative chief executive with little sympathy for the argument that the North owes poor countries a new start, the United States nevertheless found itself pressured from all corners to participate in the 1983 Global Conference on Poverty in Cancún, Mexico.

Rather than isolate itself, the United States entered the process, but did not concede anything to the idea that the United States owes distributive justice to anyone. However, its very presence made it more difficult to ignore the voice of the South. Today, the LDCs are better organized and more numerous than ever, and some of them exercise new clout because of the ecological resources (such as rainforests) in their possession.

U.S. participation under President Bush I in the 1992 Earth Summit in Rio de Janeiro similarly threatened to isolate America diplomatically concerning some vital environmental issues. As in Cancún, by virtue of its presence, America legitimized the direct North–South dialogue that it had been trying to avoid. Because the poverty gap has widened further, the LDCs and their demands for distributive justice will not soon disappear. Some philanthropic NGOs, such as the Panos Institute, seek to amplify the voice of LDCs sufficiently for their developmental concerns to be heard by northern MDCs, in structured dialogue.[28]

Occasionally, international cartels have similarly proved troublesome to the United States. Such producers' organizations try to control the supply and price of primary products by limiting competition. Their ultimate dream features a monopoly of global control over a given commodity. However, cartels are unstable in questing after unity among diverse countries, which is difficult to maintain. The temptation for a maverick country to break from established quotas to benefit from the increasing profits to its coffers will always hamper cartels. The prototype for Southern Hemisphere cartels during the twentieth century involved the supply and demand of oil, as described in Case Study 15.5.

OPEC's relative success has encouraged new cartels to spring up in uranium, gold, silver, diamonds, and fourteen other primary products. Growing in number, sophistication, and profit potential, cartels are likely, though sporadically, to produce the kinds of problems that the De Beers corporation (refer to Case Study 14.1 in Chapter 14) caused for the U.S. Justice Department's antitrust division during the 1990s. In 1994, President Clinton's head of antitrust activities, Anne Bingaman, "suffered a humiliating defeat after suing General Electric on charges it conspired with De Beers of South Africa to fix industrial diamond prices." Bill Clinton had pledged in his 1992 presidential campaign to break up powerful monopolies that his Republican predecessors had ignored, De Beers included.[29] Clinton's successor, George W. Bush, undertook no significant efforts against De Beers or any other major cartels.

Reliable Statistics, MDGs, and OECD

Every aspect of international economics depends upon the validity of the data involved, requiring the compilation, organization, and analysis of accurate statistics. Efforts have been made in recent years to coordinate support for "statistical capacity building," coalescing around the 2003 conference known as Paris21 and the 2004 Marrakech Action Plan for Statistics (MAPS). Shaida Badiee, Director of the Development Data Group, writes that "Statistics are crucial in the fight against poverty as essential starting points telling how many people live below the poverty line; how social, economic, and environmental conditions differ throughout regions; and what infrastructure, health, and education services are lacking across the world." A significant shift has occurred toward more *outcomes-based assessment* of programmatic success.[30]

Much of the impetus for more sophisticated statistics derives from the ambitious, time-specific, and measurable 2003 set of eight *Millennium Development Goals (MDGs)*:

- Goal 1: Reducing poverty and hunger
- Goal 2: Educating all children
- Goal 3: Empowering women

Case Study 15.5 OPEC Cartel's Leverage Against the MDCs

The Organization of Petroleum Exporting Countries (OPEC), founded in 1960, hoped to increase oil prices by limiting supply—thereby creating higher demand for their commodity. OPEC eventually grew to thirteen countries, mostly from the Middle East. From 1960 to 1973, OPEC's presence on the world stage was barely noticed by most countries. In 1970, a barrel of oil cost only $1.35, but not for long. When the October 1973 Yom Kippur (a major Jewish holy day) War broke out between Israel and its neighbors, OPEC's Arab majority convinced the others to impose an oil **embargo** intended to hurt Western states supporting Israel in this war. As world oil supplies dwindled, prices skyrocketed, as traced in Figure 15.2.

Some countries, such as Japan, which had earlier supported Israel, changed to a neutral position. OPEC countries produced two-thirds of global oil output in the 1970s, and prices jumped to an unprecedented $38 per barrel by the end of the decade. OPEC felt supremely confident as its coffers bulged with more than $1 trillion in 1970s **petrodollars**. As hard as the "oil shocks" of the 1970s hit the wealthy countries, in the long run, they hurt the LDCs more, contributing to their severe debt crisis in the 1980s and beyond.

If the story ended there, the OPEC saga would read as a huge cartel victory. Things were to change, however, in the 1980s. The eight-year Iran–Iraq War divided the OPEC countries, as did the 1991 Persian Gulf coalition against Iraq. Also, Western countries undertook serious conservation efforts, such as building fuel-efficient cars, thus reducing demand for OPEC oil. The inflated price of oil also spurred new suppliers, such as Britain, Mexico, and China. By the 1980s, oil prices settled at a more modest price in the mid-teens per barrel, where they remained for a long time. Accordingly, OPEC's political role in world affairs has been relatively limited since the heady days of its 1970s explosion.

OPEC will not soon sneak up on the rest of the world as it did in 1973, nor is it likely to match its former political influence. Yet when fortuitous circumstances arise, OPEC should be able to make life uncomfortable for its adversaries, at least temporarily. Although the United States is not as dependent on Persian Gulf oil as the Japanese or Europeans, it remains vulnerable by importing about half its petroleum needs; and OPEC may again unify sufficiently to produce difficulties for America. Ultimately, the world community (both MDCs and LDCs) will have to kick its addiction to petroleum and other fossil fuels and find sustainable means of generating energy, but the speed at which that cataclysm occurs seems impossible to predict.

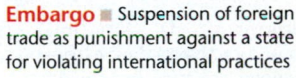

Embargo ■ Suspension of foreign trade as punishment against a state for violating international practices

Petrodollars ■ U.S. currency held by oil-producing countries that recycled petrodollars in Western financial institutions

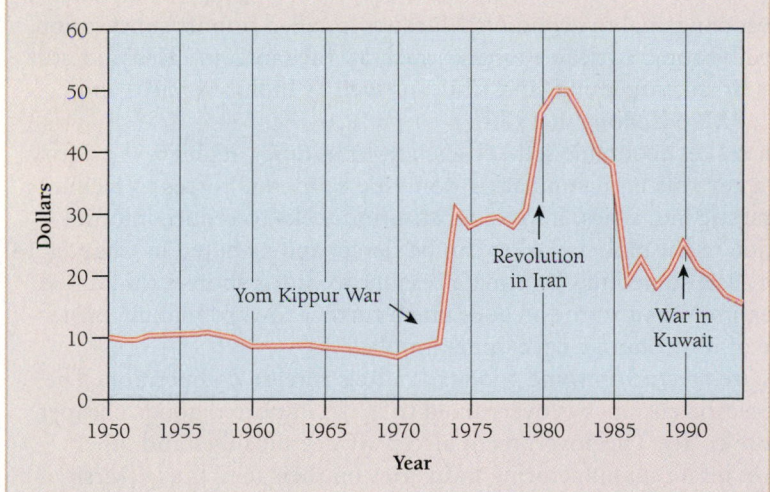

Figure 15.2

Real Price of Oil, 1950–1993, in Constant 1993 Dollars per Barrel

Source: Joan Spero and Jeffrey Hart, *The Politics of International Economic Relations* (St. Martin's, 1997), p. 286. Data from British Petroleum, *BP Statistical Review of World Energy* (London: 1993) and electronic database (London: 1992); Worldwatch estimates based on ibid., and on Department of Energy Information Administration, *Monthly Energy Review*, February 1994 (Washington, D.C.: Government Printing Office, 1994). ■

- Goal 4: Saving children
- Goal 5: Caring for mothers
- Goal 6: Combating disease
- Goal 7: Using resources wisely
- Goal 8: Working together

The most attention has been focused on goal 1, reducing poverty and hunger at specific levels of measurement. The "Coda" section ending this chapter delves into economist Jeffrey Sachs' efforts to establish an overarching paradigm for doing so. The 2006 World Development Indicators cited previously reports some progress in this realm: extreme poverty in LDCs fell from 28 percent in 1990 to 19 percent in 2002. This occurred even though population in LDCs during this time grew by 20 percent to more than 5 billion, leaving 1 billion in extreme poverty. Issued in 2003, the MDGs had been measured each year with a third monitoring report issued in 2006.

An IGO known for its excellent statistics, publications, country studies, attention to social issues, and aid programs is the Organization for Economic Cooperation and Development (OECD). Its membership consists of thirty states possessing successful market economies and democratic governments. Its Development Assistance Committee (DAC) facilitates aid programs, and it reported that in 2005 aid from OECD countries to LDCs rose to a record high $107 billion. This represents 0.33 percent of DAC members' GNP, up from 0.26 percent in 2004.

The largest gross amounts emanated from the U.S., Japan, United Kingdom, France, and Germany. However, the U.S.'s contribution amounted to less than 0.1 percent of GNP. The U.N. target of 0.7 percent of GNP was achieved only by Denmark, Luxembourg, Netherlands, Norway, and Sweden. The DAC report also referred to two "emerging donors," namely China and India, as new contributors. Also, Germany pledged to increase its aid from the current 0.28 percent of GNP to 0.51 percent in 2010 and 0.7 percent in 2015.[31]

Development Strategies

How do economists conceptualize the daunting task of economic development for the poor South? How have poor countries actually gone about trying to develop their economies? What policies have they followed in attempting to leave the ranks of the LDCs?

Import Substitution

Import substitution ■ An approach to economic expansion among less-developed countries that emphasizes protectionism and economic nationalism

The radical strategy most congenial to economic Marxists is called import substitution, which has been followed by some African countries such as Tanzania and Kenya; Latin American states such as Brazil, Argentina, and Chile; as well as India, Mexico, and China (up to the death of Mao Zedong in 1976).

Import substitution makes economic self-sufficiency, or *autarky,* its highest priority. The government plays a key role in manipulating domestic economic forces to facilitate the development of domestic industries. Import substitution seeks to reduce imports from MDCs. Competition in the global market can be fierce, and as noted in Chapter 14 in the Harley-Davidson case, sometimes legitimate reasons exist for short-term limited protectionism. However, import substitution goes much further toward making protectionism the cornerstone of its economic development policy.

High tariff barriers are erected on some goods to reduce foreign competition. The exchange rate of the domestic currency is overvalued to make imported goods cheaper and exported goods more costly. The government also provides subsidies and other forms of assistance to get infant manufacturing industries on their feet, thus diversifying the economic base. Finally, the production of more sophisticated capital goods for export is called for. However, this latter phase is difficult to achieve because it depends largely on high levels of foreign investment, which has by now been scared off through policies of economic nationalism.

In theory, many aspects of import substitution appeal to poor countries seeking to break free from a legacy of domination by wealthy countries. Despite a few short-term successes, import substitution policies have not fared well: in no country have they served over the long term to liberate a poor southern country from economic dependence or to create sustained economic development. In fact, economist Robert Alexander's analysis concludes that import substitution has usually resulted, ironically, in an increased dependence on capital and imports from northern industrial states.[32]

Import substitution represents extensive governmental interference in economic affairs, creating artificial domestic conditions, such as an overvalued currency, high tariff barriers scaring off imported goods and denying them to domestic citizens, a balance of payments deficit, and a growing debt burden. In short, import substitution has turned out to be more of an economic dead end than the royal road to independence envisioned by economic Marxists.

Export-Led Industrialization

The development strategy closest to the hearts of traditional economists is referred to as export-led industrialization, whose best-known practitioners have been the NICs (in and around East Asia). Steven Spiegel points out that "export-led industrialization seeks to promote development by working within, rather than against, the global economic system."[33] When governments such as China, India, Singapore, Malaysia, Taiwan, and South Korea have intervened in their own economies, it has been for the opposite purpose from countries such as Tanzania and Argentina, who have followed import substitution strategies.

The East Asian NICs have undervalued their currencies (rather than overvaluing them) to encourage exports—making their exported goods cheaper and imported goods more expensive. The results have been impressive over several decades of growth. Although other factors also help to account for the success of the NICs, many economists consider the export-led growth strategy as the key ingredient in the mix.

Export-led industrialization
■ An approach to economic expansion among LDCs that develops foreign markets for a state's manufactured goods

Collective Bargaining

A tongue-in-cheek slogan summing up import substitution might be, "Pull the curtains and bar the door, Katie," and for export-led industrialization, "If you can't beat me, join me." A third, more flexible strategy is called collective bargaining, named after the standard strategies employed by labor unions in domestic political economies. The sharply contrasting slogan of *collective bargaining* could be "One for all, and all for one." Just as unions use collective bargaining to improve their circumstances by organizing for effective negotiation, the term also fits the international scene, where poor countries want to redefine the rules of the game of international economics.

Today, membership in the G-77 is bulging at the seams. The logic here is that a unified voice representing a majority of humanity cannot easily be ignored. Therefore, the collective bargaining strategy simply says to poor countries: pool your resources to fight for reforms reflective of your interests. The NIEO discussed earlier shapes the contours of this substantive message. However, collective bargaining is a development strategy long on process but relatively short on content.

Although many poor countries still have faith in southern solidarity as a potent force, the unity of the 1970s existed partly because of special circumstances, such as the success of the OPEC cartel and the defensive posture of the United States, soul-searching after the Vietnam and Watergate debacles. Collective bargaining among the G-77 today looks somewhat like a medium in search of a message. This pool of nations shares poverty and a legacy of dependency, but that does not guarantee agreement on complex economic development issues.

Micro-Enterprise: A Creative Response to Poverty

As stated at the start of Chapter 14, economists see the world through perceptual prisms colored by the assumption that bigger is always better and that expansion equals progress. Period. Certainly the thinking of the major IFIs such as the IMF has shared these same perceptual prisms for a long time. There are, however, many creative examples around the world suggesting that sometimes small is not only beautiful but profitable as well. Various permutations of this notion revolve around the rubric of *micro-enterprise*.

What are micro-enterprises? The U.S. Agency for International Development (AID) defines micro-enterprises abroad as businesses with fewer than ten employees. Another definition commonly used is that of an enterprise in which both the business and the owner have low-level assets and incomes. Often micro-enterprises involve only one individual, and because of their smallness, they operate around the fringes of formal economies. Although small, these operations are numerous, and the AID has supported more than 10 million micro-enterprises in poor countries. Farming, basic food processing, handicraft production, repair services, dressmaking, and food vending constitute typical micro-enterprises.

In 1976, Dr. Muhammad Yunas founded the Grameen Bank in Bangladesh to give small loans to poor citizens so they could open their own businesses. Dr. Yunas did not realize that he had launched an experiment that would provide a minimalist prism as a counter-vision to the traditional maximalist lenses worn by expansionist economists. Grameen Bank has reversed conventional banking practice by removing the need for collateral and created a banking system based on mutual trust, accountability, and creativity. Grameen means "rural" in the local language. By 2004, Grameen's 1,267 branches had served 3.7 million borrowers, 96 percent of whom were women. In 2006, Muhammad Yunas won the coveted Nobel Peace Prize for his pioneering work.

One micro-enterprise incubator that has gained international attention resides in Bangalore, India, and is called the Association of Women Entrepreneurs of Karnataka (AWAKE). Technical assistance, management training, counseling and peer support, and financial assistance are given at AWAKE to women who participate in business activities. They make jewelry, clothing, electrical wiring, and computer software. One U.S. congressman who visited remarked that "AWAKE gave them the skills and capital necessary to build their own businesses, raise healthy families, and contribute to India's economic development."[34]

Another example of creative micro-enterprise is offered by the BancoSol in Bolivia, Latin America's first private commercial bank for the poor. Its sole owner, Bernardo Santa Maria, makes small loans of $25 to $300 to micro-entrepreneurs (such as street vendors and Native American artisans) who may want to hire short-term employees or buy materials for their small businesses. Mainstream banks cannot be bothered with such chump change. BancoSol is a profit-making business, not a charity or a governmental grant program. Señor Santa Maria's clients make weekly payments, and his fledgling bank boasts a repayment rate of 99 percent over five years of operation (eat your heart out, Citibank). BancoSol will not save the world, but it represents a meaningful response to the needs of poor people.[35]

A third example takes us back to the Asian subcontinent in a country bordering India—Bangladesh, one of the globe's poorest countries. In the town of Gorasin, the minimalist approach to local agriculture follows the precepts of a national NGO called the "New Agriculture," which promotes organic practices that are sustainable (which is really a very old form of agriculture). In the recent past, many residents of Gorasin suffered from health problems associated with pesticides that had been used by a foreign company. Burned by contemporary agribusiness in this highly personal manner, the town of Gorasin declared a "pesticide-free zone" and created an organic oasis (see Figure 15.3). Here

Figure 15.3

Microenterprises are alive and well in South Asia.

Source: From *Maps on File*, by Facts on File, Inc. Copyright © by Facts on File, Inc. Reprinted by permission of Facts on File, Inc.

crops such as eggplant, sugarcane, sponge gourds, sesame seed plants, and bamboo all grow without fertilizer, pesticides, or seeds imported from the West. By all accounts, the program is a roaring success.[36]

What was labeled in 1999 as the Battle of Seattle—involving violent protests against IFIs' vision of globalization from above and endless economic expansion—was fought largely over potential alternatives to the unsustainable exploitation of globalization thus far. The successes of micro-enterprises warrant hoping for future progress in poverty reduction. Another creative grass-roots project was developed recently in South Africa, as described in Case Study 15.6.

Case Study 15.6 Pursuing Economic Democracy in South Africa: Taddy Blecher and Free Higher Education for Poor Blacks

One decade after South Africa's 1994 peaceful transition from the apartheid dictatorship's racism to responsible democratic government under the African National Congress (ANC), observers were lauding the political miracle that had transformed this nation. Why? Because rarely does a disenfranchised majority of citizens assume power after decades of abuse by a white minority and establish a pacific, just, egalitarian rainbow nation; and almost never as quickly as what transpired in South Africa. In short, this diverse society had achieved remarkable progress in promoting and protecting the human rights of all of its citizens under an effective rule of law very rapidly.

But while South Africa was operating as an effective *political democracy*, observers worried because progress toward viable *economic democracy* had proven far more elusive. It was easier to guarantee freedom of speech, suffrage, and religion than to guarantee freedom from hunger, unemployment, and inflation. Leveling the playing field economically would clearly take longer to accomplish. However, many innovative young South Africans of all races sought ways of liberating an entrepreneurial spirit among poor blacks. One such dynamo was named Taddy Blecher. A liberal activist opposed to apartheid during his student days, Blecher had succeeded in the South African business world as a young man. He was considering big offers from American corporations to emigrate when he experienced an epiphany over what really mattered to him. Taddy's moving boxes were ready to ship to the United States when he decided that the new South Africa presented unique opportunities to do things helpful to the lives of others in need.

Not only would Blecher remain at home, but also he would give up his lucrative business career to work with poor black school children in the Alexandra township. He started a small educational NGO with the belief that "discipline and caring are the keys to education," initially fostering discipline by cracking down on tardiness among students, on which he took a hard line.[37] In Blecher's words, "Results shot through the roof. The Department of Education couldn't believe it. At the time, they issued a statement that if schools improved pass rates by 5 percent that deserved an award. We had school pass rates jumping by 40 percent."[38] This

NGO working so well in the townships he called CIDA (Community Individual Development Association), and CIDA's mission was soon to grow in both scope and ambition.[39]

Blecher realized that in South Africa only 3 percent of the black population went on to post-secondary education. His research staff also came to the conclusion that a 90 percent correlation exists between a nation's level of participation in higher education and its economic success.[40] Thus, his impressive success rate in exam scores and graduation rates was merely pumping more unskilled youngsters into an economy where unemployment was hovering around 28 percent.

What he settled on as a solution was the creation of a free, relevant business education for poor-but-talented township blacks, which is what CIDA morphed into. All CIDA students take an identical B.S. business curriculum, including entrepreneurship, leadership, accounting, and finance. But more importantly, CIDA's holistic philosophy holds that "businesses don't hire people with facts, they hire people with qualities," especially intangibles such as integrity, self-discipline, compassion, and team spirit.[41] Students and staff members all practice meditation twice daily for twenty minutes.

Funding comes from corporations such as Investec (which also donated the campus), Monitor, First National Bank, Dimensions Data, Corpcapital, and Microsoft. Courses are taught by corporate representatives, such as the accounting courses conducted by Price Waterhouse Coopers personnel. As to why South African corporations have suddenly gotten religion about the enlightened self-interest of funding business education for poor blacks, journalist Allister Sparks thinks that it has much to do with "a guilt reaction to their long consent [to apartheid] by silence."[42]

All CIDA graduates must return to their poor township communities to teach what they have learned to others for specified lengths of time. Blecher plans to expand CIDA throughout South Africa from its initial few campuses as a vehicle for real economic democracy in his home country. Other observers see even grander applications, such as "a solution to the problem of access to education in developing countries worldwide."[43] In 2002, Taddy received the Global Leader of Tomorrow Award from the World Economic Forum, presented in New York City. ■

Winners and Losers Among LDCs

For the time being, however, the prevailing economic paradigm accepts that growth is good, an assumption that pervades the analysis of Yale historian Paul Kennedy. He dissects "winners and losers in the economic development game" during the final third of the twentieth century and concludes that certain patterns are discernible. The key patterns that he sees are regional ones, and most striking among these regional patterns is the fact that, from the 1960s to the 1990s, the East Asian and Sub-Saharan African regions were headed in extremely different directions economically.

East Asian economies grew at a rapid pace, whereas many African economies became relatively poorer during this thirty-year period. Kennedy suggests that it is no coincidence that economic growth in East Asian countries has followed export-led industrialization strategies, whereas the African states examined have preferred import substitution policies.[44]

As symptomatic of the regional disparities cited previously, Kennedy compares South Korea and Ghana, two countries with similarly low GDP per capita in the mid-1960s. Both were agricultural societies that had suffered through lengthy periods of colonial domination. Having extensive natural resources seemed to augur well for Ghana when it gained independence in 1957, as did its status as a major exporter of cocoa. But after independence, it initiated import substitution policies, resulting in precipitous declines in cocoa exports. Ghana's policies were intended to replace reliance on agriculture with manufactured products, but this did not pan out. Ghana's GDP per capita fell from $500 in 1957 to $310 in 1983.[45] In 1995, Ghana ranked 129 of 174 countries on the HDI quality of life index, with average life expectancy of fifty-six years and a literacy rate of 61 percent.[46]

South Korea, by contrast, followed a policy of export-led industrialization. Its exports increased at a rate of 24 percent per year over these three decades. By the 1990s, South Korea had become ten times as prosperous as Ghana, and the world's thirteenth-largest trading nation. It ranks thirty-first among the world's nations on the HDI quality of life index, its people have a life expectancy of seventy-one years, a literacy rate of 97 percent, and GDP per capita of more than $10,000 annually.

Import substitution in Ghana versus export-led industrialization in South Korea offers a vivid contrast in strategies. However, Paul Kennedy recognizes that a number of other considerations were at work in these two countries as they careened in opposite directions from the 1960s to the 1990s. In Ghana, and in most of Africa, population has exploded, urbanization has produced disastrous overcrowding, women have been denied equitable life chances, national debt has piled up, traditional beliefs have remained unchallenged, and either wars or political instability have made havoc commonplace.

In marked contrast, most of East Asia, including South Korea, has valued education very highly, engaged in high national savings and low credit rates, fostered a strong political system, followed flexible mixed-economic strategies, and followed Japan as a regional role model.[47] Kennedy believes that other LDCs should learn lessons from the different paths taken by South Korea and Ghana, and their consequences. But Kennedy's assumption that growth is inherently good may represent one of the key intellectual battlegrounds for the twenty-first century. Another unabashed proponent of economic growth's benefits is Jeffrey Sachs, whose 2005 book provides a fitting conclusion to not only this chapter but this textbook in which the dilemma of the North/South gap has been highlighted throughout.

Jeffrey Sachs' career as an academic economist, author, consultant to numerous macro-level economies in crisis, Director of Columbia University's Earth Institute, and catalyst establishing the Millennium Development Goals (MDGs) as a template for all countries borders on the remarkable.

CODA: Jeffrey Sachs' Blueprint for Ending Extreme Poverty

Long-time Harvard professor Jeffrey Sachs was called upon in the 1980s and 1990s to serve as an economic consultant to several countries experiencing economic crises: taming hyperinflation in Bolivia; mapping out a highly successful transition to post-communism in Poland; frustration born of decidedly less successful interventions on behalf of Russia's economic basket case; picking up on and fine-tuning China's second decade of unprecedented economic growth; and advising capable Indian architects of reforms undertaken in 1991 based on lessons learned from these earlier experiences. Sachs had also spent much time examining conditions in more than one hundred of the poorest countries.

Sachs was later appointed as the first director of the Earth Institute at Columbia University, a multidisciplinary endeavor seeking to comprehend and defeat global poverty. Simultaneously, he was selected by Secretary-General Kofi Annan as Special Advisor regarding the U.N. MDGs. In *The End of Poverty: Economic Possibilities for Our Time,* Sachs provides the bold, holistic, contemporary blueprint for solving the conundrum of extreme poverty appropriate for concluding this text. Extreme poverty, he claims, kills 20,000 people every day. Bono, lead singer for U2 and development activist, has written the foreword to Sachs' book.[48]

How did wealth diverge so widely across the globe during the past two centuries? Why have one billion of the planet's citizens been condemned to lives in a "poverty trap" of disease, physical isolation, environmental stress, instability, and lack of access to capital, technology, medicine, and education? Jeffrey Sachs presents a clear plan to reduce extreme poverty by one-half in 2015 and eliminate it altogether in 2025. He describes how helping these poorest of peoples to "get a foothold on the first rung of the ladder represents the very hardest part of economic development." However, once achieved, this first rung enables an unprecedented modicum of control over their economic futures.[49]

Sachs explains why it makes not only good moral sense for the world's rich countries to care but also how such caring promotes our enlightened self-interest. The author's "Big Plan" criticizes the "piecemeal approach" characteristic of past efforts to solve the global poverty conundrum. Such compartmentalized efforts lacked holistic thinking, thus failing to make the big connections between the complex political, social, technological, educational, and economic systems that underpin extreme poverty. He details how the unparalleled advances in human well being during the 250-year Industrial Revolution provide humanity with the necessary resources to eliminate the extreme poverty trap. If only the United States would make good on its pledges to fund foreign aid at the U.N.-recommended level (0.7 percent of GNP), the author computes precisely the massive amount of aid that could be devoted to fighting poverty globally.[50]

Only a handful of rich countries have met their commitments to fund foreign aid at the 0.7 percent of GNP level. No real constituency lobbies for foreign aid in the U.S. Congress, and it represents a hard sell. American foreign aid fell by 15 percent during Bill Clinton's presidency, and under George W. Bush, it dropped further to less than 0.1 percent of GNP. Most of it goes to support U.S. geopolitical goals, not development aid. Although the public sector has little to brag about concerning foreign aid, the private sector has fortunately taken up some of the slack. The Bill and Melinda Gates Foundation decided to donate where they could do the greatest good for the greatest number of people, regardless of geography or politics. Bill Gates has stated that it was a U.N. Development Report that convinced him to pursue aiding the poorest of the poor. By 2006, the Gates' aid portfolio consisted of $30 billion, and was regarded as a prototype for best practices philanthropy. So impressed was fellow billionaire Warren Buffet that he decided to place all of his philanthropic aid into the Gates basket, in one stroke doubling the fund to $60 billion, amassing an unprecedented source of development aid.

The new millennium opened with the largest global town meeting ever convened: the Millennium Assembly, based at the U.N. site. A global statement forged at this meeting set forth "quantified and time-bound goals to reduce extreme poverty, disease, and deprivation." Eight MDGs were produced, the first of which dealt specifically with eradicating extreme poverty and hunger. The dislocating events of 9/11 then deflected considerable attention from efforts to end extreme poverty, but Sachs warns that "Terrorism has complex and varying causes and cannot be fought by military means alone. To fight terrorism, we will need to fight poverty and deprivation as well. A purely military approach to terrorism is doomed to fail."[51]

Jeffrey Sachs' efforts to advise the Bolivian government regarding hyperinflation in the early 1980s resulted in international publicity and similar consultations with four other Latin American states. In 1989, however, his status as economic superstar skyrocketed when recruited by the post-communist government in Poland. "No one knew what to do. The economy was broken; planning had collapsed; black markets, inflation, and extreme shortages were pervasive." He was asked to do what had never been done: construct a plan for this four-decade-long socialist economy to eschew central planning and adopt reforms for gradual conversion to a market-driven capitalist economy. Essentially a literate, homogeneous, urban country with sound infrastructure (roads, electricity, water and sewerage, sea and airports), Poland's leaders possessed a milieu built for eventual economic success. Although problems persisted for a couple of years, Germany and other European countries soon invested in Poland, which sped up the process greatly.[52]

After the Polish experience, Sachs was recruited by reformers in Mikhail Gorbachev's sprawling Soviet Union to assist them as well. But if the small and unified country of Poland were a resounding success, the USSR soon proved vastly more impervious to rational direction. The Soviet leader cut military spending in the late-1980s, but his country was suffering from consequences of the imperial overstretch of his predecessors (the USSR had been spending 20 percent of GNP on military matters, triple the American percentage). Sachs acted as economic consultant briefly for Gorbachev, and then for Boris Yeltsin, president of the largest successor state (Russia) for two years when the Soviet Union collapsed. Lessons gleaned by Sachs in Bolivia and Poland were tried, but Russia was an altogether different case.

Russia was large, heterogeneous, and primitive in several respects. Whereas Polish history was tied to Europe, Russia's was split between East and West (Eurasian). It was also more rural and dependent upon two primary products for foreign trade (oil and gas), with *state ownership of industry* more deeply engrained than Poland. Gorbachev had already spent four years trying economic reforms, "but the economy was not responding, other than falling deeper into black marketing, intensifying shortages, and spiraling inflation." Highly dependent on oil and gas exports for hard (convertible) currency, the Soviet economy reeled when the world price of oil dropped precipitously in the mid-1980s. The Soviets borrowed money from abroad and became caught in a scissors crisis of falling exports and rising debts. Sachs' plan for recovery was based on *convincing America and its allies to invest heavily in Russia,* but that effort failed. Exacerbating these matters was the poor health, corruption, and ineptitude of Russia's leader during the 1990s: Boris Yeltsin.[53]

After this stint with Russia, Sachs served as a consultant to the Chinese leadership starting in 1992. A proud and innovative culture for several millennia, China slid into near oblivion during the years 1500 to 2000. The first Chinese Communist leader, Mao Zedong, blamed China's problems on the decadent West and turned inward searching for self-reliance, including turning its back on world trade (economic nationalism). Mao's reign (1949–1976) produced a disastrous failed economy, with widespread starvation in the 1960s. Mao was a communist ideologue who believed that enough faith in the creed conquers all obstacles. His successor, Deng Xiaoping, learned from Mao's travails and followed a program of economic pragmatism while continuing to pay lip service to communist ideology as if it still mattered.

Deng's market-oriented reforms began in 1978, and the Chinese economy improved rapidly. "Liberalization of the farm sector freed up labor for the manufacturing export sector," and when China created free-trade zones, an export explosion stemmed from "labor-intensive exports in garments, textiles, footwear, plastics, toys, and electronic assembly." In a mere twenty years, China's exports in manufactured goods grew from just a few billion dollars to more than $200 billion by 2000. Sachs also observes that "China's reforms are reshaping the global economy and global politics. Soviet reforms in the 1980s (as well as changes in India in the 1990s) were no doubt inspired in part by China's successes."[54]

Sachs' status as guru of economic consultants also took him to India during the 1990s. From the seventeenth to the nineteenth centuries, India faced problems born of British colonial subjugation that Poland, Russia, and China did not confront. Economic growth during the British Raj in India was very low. Although the Brits did invest modestly in India's infrastructure, that was mostly aimed at serving the needs of the colonialists. Investment in educating native Indians was pitiful, and when independence occurred in 1947, the literacy rate was a lowly 17 percent. The Green Revolution in India during the 1960s and 1970s ended the cycle of mass starvation in India but sustained impressive economic growth did not occur until the 1990s, when import substitution policies were abandoned.

The architect with whom Sachs worked in India was the Minister of Finance, Manmohan Singh, a highly respected Oxford-educated economist. Many domestic skeptics predicted that India's history, extreme social divisions, and poor masses would doom efforts to grow its economy. The foundation on which India's economic miracle unfolded consisted of its Institutes of Technology (ITs), which had been turning out excellent software engineers and entrepreneurs for two decades. Companies such as Microsoft recruited them heavily and helped to spur foreign investment in a service-sector outsourcing revolution foreseen by almost no one. Like China, India relied successfully on export-led growth as a formula for achieving impressive annual growth rates between five and ten.

Jeffrey Sachs contends that much has been learned from these cases that can assist the very poorest countries in gaining a foothold on the ladder of development. And when we are looking for the poorest nations, the place to begin is Sub-Saharan Africa. Sachs concludes that most of the conventional wisdom about poverty in Africa consists of myths and faulty assumptions. He posits numerous solutions to Africa's economic dilemmas based on numerous visits from 1995 to 2005 reinforcing his faith in "the indomitable strength of the human spirit in the face of adversity."

Heading the list of myths is the pervasive notion that misrule and *political corruption serve to explain Africa's economic woes*. Extensive data, argues Sachs, dispute this mistaken belief. For example, well-governed countries in Africa such as Ethiopia, Ghana, Malawi, Mali, and Senegal fail to prosper, whereas high-corruption Asian governments such as Bangladesh, India, Indonesia, and Pakistan exhibit rapid economic growth. The colonial masters who dominated Africa argued that these relationships would lift Africa economically, but the result was just the opposite. Both the Soviet Union and the United States during the Cold War exploited old rivalries for their own purposes and undermined indigenous leaders who favored nationalism as a path to progress.

Sachs notes that he slowly came to recognize factors such as *lack of infrastructure, physical isolation from world markets, populations living in the interior without navigable rivers accessing the sea, disease, and drought as the most powerful explanations for Africa's lack of economic development*. Malaria and AIDS are two such diseases whose profound effects on African economies became clear to him only slowly. He notes, "I began to suspect that the omnipresence of disease and death had played a deep role in Africa's prolonged inability to develop economically."

Sachs thanks his medical colleagues for teaching him about bed nets, indoor spraying, and effective anti-malarial medicines as well, and others for teaching him about the efficacy of rural electrification, road building, and sanitary water. Such interventions must occur systematically and in a coordinated manner to break out of the *poverty trap*. The World Bank and IMF come under attack from Sachs for thirty years worth of draconian budget policies imposed on debt-ridden states that left them worse off than when these institutions entered the African scene. He calls these structural adjustment policies politically motivated and very weak on scientific evidence.[55]

The author recommends working toward what he calls *Enlightened Globalization* fostering democratization, multilateralism, science and technological discovery, sustainable development, and saving the poorest of the poor. He suggests that sufficient resources and intellectual understanding now exist to achieve these goals for the first time in human history and that the U.N. represents the best instrument to coordinate these complex endeavors. The rich countries like to donate most of their money via the World Bank and the IMF because they control the politics of these venues most directly. However, Sachs argues for the U.N. as the body most worthy of support. His book concludes with "Let the future say of our generation that we sent forth mighty currents of hope, and that we worked together to heal the world."[56]

Chapter Synopsis

Colonial exploitation and the Industrial Revolution enabled Europeans to establish massive wealth between the eighteenth and twentieth centuries. Much of international economics in recent decades has revolved around efforts to either dislodge (South) or protect (North) the pervasive legacy of highly concentrated wealth. Anticapitalist forces first coalesced around Marxism, yet its global demise has not weakened the resolve of LDCs to alter the maldistribution of wealth through reforms such as the NIEO. Although considerable international conflict over scarce goods and services surely exists, the majority of international economic exchanges occur in an orderly manner.

Various theories compete for dominance in the global milieu. Economic idealism, economic realism, and economic Marxism purport to describe and analyze the broad spectrum of international economics. The size of the international economy today raises the ante concerning monetary exchange rates, with winners and losers deriving from how the world community decides to go about exchanging one currency for another. Variations on *fixed and floating exchange rates* have existed during different historical periods. Exchange rates matter greatly because trade has exploded so dramatically. The successful Asian NICs has followed a script of managed trade emulating the Japanese precedent. Although David Ricardo's time-tested theory of comparative advantage remains an unassailable article of faith among most economists, political pressures for protectionism invariably arise, and the struggle between *free trade and protectionism* remains our constant companion.

No other international economic issue rivals the widening North–South chasm for staying power. For the South, nothing less than distributive justice is truly acceptable. In sharp contrast, the North wants to maintain its dominance. The two sides remain far apart, and the passage of time has done little to resolve their differences. Even among the LDCs unity is elusive. Should they pursue policies of import substitution, export-led growth, or collective bargaining? Paul Kennedy's comparison of two countries typifying regions heading in different directions (Ghana in Africa, South Korea in East Asia) provides grist for the analytical mill concerning this vexing dilemma.

Finally, economists assume that human progress results from economic expansion, making it an unassailable social good. This article of faith among economists has been attacked by those who believe that small can be not only beautiful but also profitable (e.g., micro-finance programs). The probing questions that characterize critical thinking must be applied to this vital issue for the twenty-first century. Jeffrey Sachs' recent book, *Ending Extreme Poverty: Economic Possibilities for Our Time*, is examined in depth as a coda bringing closure not only to this chapter but also to the North/South gap issue that permeates this textbook from beginning to end.

FOR DIGGING DEEPER

Ambrogi, Thomas. "Goal for 2000: Unchaining Slaves of National Debt," *National Catholic Reporter*, 36, no. 21, March 26, 1999, p. 3.

Anderson, Sarah, and others. *Field Guide to the Global Economy*. New Press, 2000.

Arias, Oscar. "Confronting Debt, Poverty, and Militarism: A Human Program of Support for the Developing World," *Journal of Third World Studies*, 17, no. 1, Spring, 2000.

Aaronson, Susan Ariel. *Taking Trade to the Streets: The Lost History of Public Efforts to Shape Globalization*. University of Michigan Press, 2002.

Barnet, Richard J., and John Cavanaugh. *Global Dreams: Imperial Corporations and the New World Order*. Simon & Schuster, 1994.

Bhagwadi, Jagdish. *A Stream of Windows: Trade, Immigration, and Democracy*. MIT Press, 1999.

Black, Jan Knippers. *Inequity in the Global Village: Recycled Rhetoric and Disposable People*. Kumarian Press, 1999.

Brecher, Jeremy, and Tim Costello. *Global Village or Global Pillage: Economic Reconstruction from the Bottom Up*. South End Press, 1999. British White Paper on International Development.

Eliminating World Poverty: Making Globalisation Work for the Poor. 2000, http://www.dfid.gov.uk/wp2006/default.asp.

Broad, Robin, ed. *Global Backlash: Citizen Initiatives for a Just World Economy.* Rowman and Littlefield Publishers, 2002.

Chossudovsky, Michel. *The Globalization of Poverty: Impacts of IMF and World Bank Reforms.* Zed Books, 1997.

Cline, William. *Trade Policy and Global Poverty.* Institute for International Economics, 2004.

Cortright, David, and George A. Lopez, eds. *Smart Sanctions: Targeting Economic Statecraft.* Rowman & Littlefield, 2002.

Daley-Harris, Sam, and Anna Awimbo, eds. *More Pathways Out of Poverty.* Kumarian Press, 2006.

Daly, Herman E., and John B. Cobb. *For the Common Good.* Beacon Press, 1989.

Davidian, Zaven N. *Economic Disparities among Nations: A Threat to Survival in a Globalized World.* SIPRI Publications, 1994.

Dowla, Asif, and Dipa Barua. *The Poor Always Pay Back: The Grameen Bank Story.* Kumarian Press, 2006.

Elias, Juanita. *Fashioning Inequality.* Ashgate, 2004.

Ensign, Margee. *Doing Good or Doing Well? Japan's Foreign Aid Program.* Columbia University Press, 1993.

Gaddy, Clifford, and Barry Ickes. *Russia's Virtual Economy.* Brookings Institution, 2000.

George, Susan. *The Debt Boomerang: How Third World Debt Harms Us All.* Stylus Publishing, 1991.

Grant, Richard, and Nijman, Jan, eds. *The Global Crisis in Foreign Aid.* Syracuse University Press, 1997.

Handelman, Howard. *The Challenge of Third World Development.* Prentice Hall, 2006.

Harrison, Graham. *The World Bank and Africa: The Construction of Governance States.* Routledge, 2004.

Henderson, Hazel. *Beyond Globalization: Shaping a Sustainable Global Economy.* Kumarian Press, 1999.

Hurrell, Andrew, and Ngaire Woods, eds. *Inequality, Globalization, and World Politics.* Oxford University Press, 1999.

Husted, Steven, and Michael Melvin. *International Economics.* University of Pittsburgh Press, 1995.

Isbister, John. *Promises Not Kept: Poverty and the Betrayal of Third World Development.* Kumarian Press, 2006.

Johnson, Chalmers. *Blowback: The Costs and Consequences of American Empire.* Owl/Metropolitan Books, 2001.

Jolly, Richard, ed. *Adjustment with a Human Face.* Oxford University Press, 1992.

Kanter, Rosabeth. *World Class: Thriving Locally in the Global Economy.* Kumarian Press, 1994.

Lancaster, Carol. *Foreign Aid: Diplomacy, Development, Domestic Politics.* University of Chicago Press, 2006.

Mehrotra, Santosh, ed. *Development with a Human Face.* Oxford University Press, 1999.

Mittelman, James. *The Globalization Syndrome: Transformation and Resistance.* Princeton University Press, 2000.

Obstfeld, Maurice, and Kenneth Rogoff. *Foundations of International Macroeconomics.* MIT Press, 1996.

Otero, Maria, and Elisabeth Rhyne, eds. *The New World of Microenterprise Finance.* Kumarian Press, 1994.

Payne, Richard, and Jamal Nassar. *The Politics and Culture in the Developing World: Implications of Globalization.* Longman, 2003.

Pomeranz, Kenneth, and Steven Topik. *The World That Trade Created: Society, Culture and the World Economy, 1400–the Present*. M. E. Sharpe, 1999.

Sachs, Jeffrey D. *The End of Poverty: Economic Possibilities for Our Time*. Penguin Books, 2005.

Schott, Jeffrey. *The WTO after Seattle*. Institute for International Economics, 2000.

Soros, George. *Open Society: Reforming Global Capitalism*. Public Affairs, 2000.

Spero, Joan, and Jeffrey A. Hart. *The Politics of International Economic Relations*. St. Martin's Press, 1996.

Thomas, Darryl C. *The Theory and Practice of Third World Solidarity*. Greenwood, 1995.

United Nations. *The Least Developed Countries Report 2007: Knowledge, Technological Learning and Innovation for Development*. U.N. Publications, 2007.

Upton, Barbara. *The Multilateral Development Banks: Improving U.S. Leadership*. Greenwood Press, 2000.

Veltmeyer, Henry, and Anthony O'Malley, eds. *Transcending Neo-Liberalism: Community-Based Development in Latin America*. Kumarian Press, 2001.

Warkentin, Craig. *Reshaping World Politics: NGOs, the Internet, and Global Civil Society*. Rowman and Littlefield Publishers, 2001.

Weatherby, Joseph, and others, eds. *The Other World: Issues and Politics of the Developing World*. Pearson Education, 2005

Wise, Timothy A., and Hilda Salazar, eds. *Confronting Globalization: Economic Integration and Popular Resistance in Mexico*. Kumarian Press, 2003.

Yong, Jim, and others, eds. *Dying for Growth: Global Inequality and the Health of the Poor*. Common Courage Press, 2000.

INTERNET

Association for Women's Rights in Development (AWID):
http://www.awid.org/

Bank Information Center:
http://www.bicusa.org

Bretton Woods Project:
http://www.brettonwoodsproject.org

Centre for Development and Population Activities:
http://www.cedpa.org/

Digital Divide Network:
http://www.digitaldividenetwork.org/

Economics Links:
http://www.progress.org/econolink

Global Exchange:
http://www.globalexchange.org/economy/rulemakers

Global Policy Forum:
http://www.globalpolicy.org

Institute for International Economics:
http://www.iie.com

International Development Exchange:
http://www.idex.org/

International Development Network:
http://idn.rtpi.org.uk/

International Monetary Fund (IMF):
http://www.imf.org

International Money Laundering Information:
http://www.imolin.org

Jubilee 2000:
http://www.jubileeresearch.org/jubilee2000

Microcredit Summit Secretariat:
http://www.gdrc.org/icm/summit/microcredit-summit.html

North-South Institute:
http://www.nsi-ins.ca/english/default.asp

One World:
http://www.oneworld.org

Poverty Net:
http://www.worldbank.org/poverty/

Protest.Net:
http://www.protest.net

Social Accountability 8000 Code:
http://www.cepaa.org/sa8000.htm

Society for International Development:
http://www.sidint.org/

Third World Conference Foundation:
http://www.twcfinternational.org/

Third World News:
http://www.thirdworldnews.com

UNITE! Trade Union:
http://www.unitehere.org

United Nations Conference on Trade and Development (UNCTAD):
http://www.unctad.org

United Students Against Sweatshops:
http://www.studentsagainstsweatshops.org/

U.S. Trade and Development Agency:
http://www.tda.gov/

U.S. Trade Representative:
http://www.ustr.gov

World Bank:
http://www.worldbank.org

World Trade Organization (WTO):
http://www.wto.org

WTO Action:
http://www.wtoaction.org

Chapter 1

1. Jan Aart Scholte, *Globalization: A Critical Introduction* (St. Martin's Press, 2000), p. 15.

2. Ibid., p. 3.

3. United Nations Development Program, *Human Development Report 1999* (Oxford University Press, 1999), Preface.

4. Hilary French, *Vanishing Borders: Protecting the Planet in the Age of Globalization* (W. W. Norton & Co., 2000), p. 6.

5. Ibid., pp. 6–7.

6. Global Policy Forum, "Defining Globalization," at *http://www.globalpolicy.org/globaliz/define/index.htm* (accessed March 4, 2008).

7. James H. Mittelman, ed., *Globalization: Critical Reflections*. Lynne Rienner, 1997, p. 230.

8. Thomas Friedman, *The Lexus and the Olive Tree: Understanding Globalization* (Farrar, Strauss, and Giroux, 1999), pp. xvi, 27.

9. John Bale and Joseph Maguire, *The Global Sports Arena: Athletic Talent Migration in an Interdependent World* (Frank Cass Publishers, 1994).

10. Thomas Friedman, *The World Is Flat: A Brief History of the 21st Century* (Farrar, Strauss, and Giroux, 2005).

11. Ibid., pp. 9–13.

12. Ibid., p. 110.

13. Benjamin Barber, *Jihad versus McWorld: How Globalism and Tribalism Are Reshaping the World* (Ballantine Books, 1996), p. 9.

14. Ibid., p. 215.

15. Ibid., p. 293.

16. Ibid., p. 8.

17. Helmut Anheier, Marlies Glasius, and Mary Kaldor, eds., *Global Civil Society 2004/05* (Sage, 2004).

18. United Nations Department of Public Information, "Basic Facts About the UN," at *http://www.un.org/aboutun/basicfacts/index.html* (accessed March 4, 2008).

19. Wikipedia, "The International Monetary Fund," at http://en.wikipedia.org/wiki/International_Monetary_Fund.

20. Wikipedia, "General Motors," at http://en.wikipedia.org/wiki/General_Motors.

21. American Museum of Natural History, "National Survey Reveals Biodiversity Crisis–Scientific Experts Believe We Are in Midst of Fastest Mass Extinction in Earth's History." Press release, New York: April 20, 1998.

22. Richard Leakey and Roger Lewin, *The Sixth Extinction: Patterns of Life and the Future of Humankind* (Anchor Books, 1995), p. 44.

23. French, p. 15.

24. Howard Frederick, *Global Communication and International Relations* (Wadsworth, 1993), p. 125.

25. Ben H. Bagdikian, *The Media Monopoly* (Beacon, 1994).

26. Herbert J. Schiller, *Information Inequality* (Routledge, 1996), p. 113.

27. Friedman, *The Lexus and the Olive Tree: Understanding Globalization*, p. 322.

28. Robert Joseph, "Nuclear Deterrence and Regional Proliferators," *The Washington Quarterly,* Summer 1997, p. 167.

29. Eugene Burdick and William Lederer, *The Ugly American* (W. W. Norton and Company, 1999).

30. George Ritzer, *The McDonaldization of Society* (Pine Forge Press, 1995).

31. David Rieff, "The Culture That Conquered the Earth," *World Policy Journal,* October 1994, p. 3.

32. Naomi Klein, *No Logo: Taking Aim at the Brand-Name Bullies* (Picador Press, 2000), p. 20.

33. Dani Rodrik, *Has Globalization Gone Too Far?* (Institute for International Economics, 1997), p. 1.

34. Friedman, *Lexus*, p. 268.

35. Amitai Etzioni, *The New Golden Rule: Community and Morality in a Democratic Society* (Basic Books, 1998).

36. Jeremy Brecher, Tim Costello, and Brendan Smith, *Globalization from Below: The Power of Solidarity* (South End Press, 2000), p. 16.

37. William Finnegan, "After Seattle: Anarchists Get Organized," *The New Yorker,* April 17, 2000, pp. 40–51.

38. Paul Schwartzman, "World Bank-IMF Protests Set This Week," at *http://www.washingtonpost.com/wp-dyn/articles/A48197-2005Apr12.html* (accessed March 4, 2008).

39. BBC News, "First WTO Protests in Hong Kong," at *http://news.bbc.co.uk/2/hi/asia-pacific/4517964.stm* (accessed March 4, 2008).

40. Jessica Woodroffe, World Development Movement, "States of Unrest: Resistance to IMF Policies in Poor Countries," at *http://www.greenleft.org.au/2000/back/423/22664* (accessed March 4, 2008).

41. Tarja Halonen and Benjamin W. Mkapa, "A Fair Globalization: Creating Opportunities for All," World Commission on the Social Dimension of Globalization, at *http://www.globalpolicy.org/globaliz/define/index.htm* (accessed March 4, 2008).

42. Dani Rodrick, *Has Globalization Gone Too Far?* (Institute for International Economics, 1997), p. 2.

43. Friedman, p. xvi.

44. Uday Mohan, "Bridging the Digital Divide," *News & Views,* International Food Policy Research Institute, September 2000, pp. 1–6.

45. Michael Glantz, "The Global Challenge," *The World & I, The Washington Times,* April 1997, pp. 24–31.

46. Ken Conca and Geoffrey Dabelko, *Green Planet Blues: Environmental Politics from Stockholm to Kyoto* (Westview Press, 1998), p. 11.

47. Stuart L. Pimm, "The Value of Everything," *Nature,* May 15, 1997.

48. Timothy C. Weiskel, "Unrestricted Population Growth?" *USA Today Magazine,* January 1995, pp. 38–40.

49. James Lindsay, ed., *Perspectives: Global Issues* (Coursewise Publishing, 1997), p. 19.

50. Jennifer Miller, "Before the Next Doubling," *World Watch Magazine,* January/February 1998, pp. 20–27.

51. Michael Tobias, *World War III: Population and the Biosphere at the End of the Millennium* (Continuum, 1998).

52. Max Singer, "The Population Surprise," *The Atlantic Monthly,* August 1999.

53. Lester Brown, Michael Renner, and Christopher Flavin, *Vital Signs 1998* (Worldwatch Institute, 1998), p. 16.

54. Ibid., pp. 16–17.

55. Scott Barbour, ed. *Hunger.* Greenhaven Press, 1995.

56. Thomas Fenton and Mary Heffron, *Food, Hunger, and Agribusiness* (Orbis Books, 1987), p. xvi.

57. William Bender, "How Much Food Will We Need in the 21st Century?" *Environment,* March 1997, pp. 7–11.

58. Brown, Renner, and Flavin, pp. 16–19.

59. BP Solar, "The Solar Biz," at *http://www.thesolar.biz* (accessed March 27, 2008).

60. Robert Fisher, "The Future of Energy," *The Futurist,* September/October 1997, pp. 43–46.

61. Vanessa Baird, ed., *New Internationalist.* October 1996, pp. 20–23.

62. Brown, Renner, and Flavin, pp. 19–20.

63. *New York Times,* August 24, 1991, p. A9.

64. Milton Leitenberg, "Assessing the Biological Weapons and Bioterrorism Threat" (Strategic Studies Institute, 2005), at *http://www.strategicstudiesinstitute.army.mil/pubs/display.cfm?PubID=639* (accessed March 4, 2008).

65. Center for Nonproliferation Studies, "Chemical and Biological Weapons Resource Page," at *http://cns.miis.edu/research/cbw/* (accessed March 4, 2008).

66. Michael Stebbins, "Introduction to Biological Weapons," Federation of American Scientists, at *http://www.fas.org/biosecurity/bw/intro.htm* (accessed March 4, 2008).

67. Stephen Schwartz, "Four Trillion Dollars and Counting," The U.S. Nuclear Weapons Cost Study Project, in George Lopez and Nancy Meyers, ed., *Peace and Security: The Next Generation* (Rowman & Littlefield, 1997), pp. 24–28.

68. John Deutch, "Combating the Threat of Nuclear Diversion," *USA Today Magazine,* January 1997, pp. 16–19.

69. Pervez Hoodbhoy, "The Myth of the Islamic Bomb," in Lopez and Meyers, eds., pp. 56–58.

70. Afghanistan, Algeria, Argentina, Armenia, Belarus, Bulgaria, China, Czech Republic, Egypt, Greece, India, Iran, Iraq, Israel, Kazakhstan, Libya, Netherlands, North Korea, Pakistan, Romania, Russia, Serbia, Slovakia, South Korea, Syria, Taiwan, Turkey, Turkmenistan, Ukraine, United Arab Emirates, Vietnam, Yemen.

71. J. Martin Rochester, *Between Two Epochs: What's Ahead for America, the World, and Global Politics in the 21st Century?* (Prentice Hall, 2002), pp. 123–26.

72. Biography, "Timothy McVeigh," *Arts and Entertainment,* April 20, 1996; "McVeigh Believes Millions Share His Views," *Associated Press Release,* April 22, 1996.

73. Rochelle Olson, "*Turner Diaries* Author: Dangerous or Revolutionary?" *Associated Press Release,* June 9, 1996.

74. *Patterns of Global Terrorism 1998,* U.S. Department of State, March 1998, pp. 1–2.

75. Rochester, p. 125.

76. Ann McElroy and Patricia Townsend, *Medical Anthropology in Ecological Perspective* (Westview Press, 1996), p. 332.

77. "Infectious Disease Rise Linked to Human Growth," *Popline,* 18, March-April 1996, p. 3.

78. Dennis Pirages, "Microsecurity: Disease Organisms and Human Well-Being," *The Washington Quarterly,* Autumn 1995, pp. 5–12.

79. David Brown, "The Long March Toward Stamping Out Infectious Diseases," *Washington Post,* June 2, 1997.

80. Michael D. Lemonick, "The Killers All Around," *Time,* September 12, 1994, pp. 62–69.

81. Mirko Grmek, *History of AIDS* (Princeton University Press, 1990), p. 13.

82. Pirages, p. 5.

83. Johan Galtung, *Human Rights in Another Key* (Polity Press, 1994), p. 72.

84. John T. Rourke, *International Politics on the World Stage* (McGraw-Hill/Dushkin, 2001), p. 486.

85. Dick Kirschten, "No Refuge," *National Journal,* September 10, 1994, pp. 2068–73; Myron Weiner, *The Global Migration Crisis* (HarperCollins, 1995); U.N. High Commissioner for Refugees, *The State of the World's Refugees* (Oxford University Press, 1995).

86. V. Hamilton, *World Refugee Survey 1999,* U.S. Committee for Refugees, 1999.

87. John Martin and Anne Romano, *Multinational Crime: Terrorism, Espionage, Drug and Arms Trafficking* (Sage Publications, 1992).

88. Martin Hodgson, "The Coca Leaf War," *The Bulletin of the Atomic Scientists,* May/June 2000, pp. 36–45.

89. Jerome McElroy, "The Caribbean Narco-Economy," *The Christian Science Monitor,* March 14, 2000.

90. Francis A. Beer, *Peace Against War: The Ecology of International Violence* (Freeman, 1981), p. 165.

91. Ambrose Bierce, *The Devil's Dictionary* (Dell Publishing, 1991).

Chapter 2

1. Robert C. Bannister, *Sociology and Scientism: The American Quest for Objectivity, 1880–1940* (University of North Carolina Press, 1987), p. 3.

2. Wikipedia, "Utopian Socialism," at *http://en.wikipedia.org/wiki/Utopian_socialism* (accessed March 4, 2008).

3. Wikipedia, "Marxism," at *http://en.wikipedia.org/wiki/Marxism* (accessed March 4, 2008).

4. Max Weber, *Roscher and Kneis: The Logical Problems of Historical Economics* (Free Press, 1975), p. 107.

5. Dorothy Ross, *The Origins of American Social Science* (Cambridge University Press, 1991), p. xiv.

6. Peter T. Manicas, *A History and Philosophy of the Social Sciences* (Basil Blackwell, 1987), p. 210.

7. Ross, *Origins,* pp. 55, 394.

8. Bannister, *Sociology and Scientism,* p. 3.

9. Kenneth R. Hoover, *The Elements of Social Scientific Thinking* (St. Martin's Press, 1980), p. 8.

10. Bernard Berelson, and Gary Steiner, *Human Behavior: An Inventory of Scientific Findings* (Harcourt, Brace, and World, 1970), p. 11.

11. Peter Senn, *Social Science and Its Methods* (Zephyr Press, 1983), p. 10; Stuart Chase, *The Proper Study of Mankind* (Harper and Row, 1975), p. 9; John and Erna Perry, *Contemporary Society* (HarperCollins, 1994), p. 3; Paul Weisz, *The Science of Biology* (McGraw-Hill, 1967), p. 14; Hoover, p. 3.

12. Carlo Lastrucci, *The Scientific Approach* (Schenkman, 1967).

13. Earl Babbie, *The Practice of Social Research* (Wadsworth, 1995), pp. 20–21.

14. Dava Sobel, "The Heretic's Daughter," *New Yorker*, September 13, 1990, pp. 52–59.

15. F. J. Roethlisberger and W. J. Dickson, *Management and the Worker* (Harvard University Press, 1939).

16. PBS, *Nova* #2812: "Sex Unknown," October 30, 2001, transcript, at *http://www.pbs.org/wgbh/nova/transcripts/2813gender.html* (accessed March 4, 2008).

17. John Darnton, "Scientists Confirm Identification of Bones as Tsar's," *The New York Times* (July 10, 1993), p. 9; "Anastasia," *Nova* (PBS video), 1995.

18. Brian Bergstein, "Class Project Frees Murder Convicts," *Associated Press*, June 15, 1996.

19. Anne Barnhardt Henderson and Sheila Phelan Wright, *The Social Sciences*, Handbook of the Undergraduate Curriculum, p. 301.

20. Mark C. Carnes, ed., *Past Imperfect: History According to the Movies* (Henry Holt, 1995), p. 7.

21. Stanislav Andreski, *Social Science as Sorcery* (St. Martin's Press, 1973), p. 11.

22. Elie Weisel, Interview on *The Charlie Rose Show*, PBS, November 10, 1995.

23. Abraham Kaplan, *The Conduct of Inquiry* (Chandler, 1970), p. xv.

24. Hayward R. Alker, *Rediscoveries and Reformulations: Humanistic Methodologies for International Studies* (Cambridge University Press, 1996), p. 1.

25. Gregory Pence, *Flesh of My Flesh: The Ethics of Cloning Humans* (Rowman & Littlefield, 1998).

26. M. C. Lewontin, in Gregory Pence, *Flesh of My Flesh*, p. 189.

27. Annas, p. 24.

28. Andrew Kimbrell and Bernard Nathanson, *The Human Body Shop: The Cloning, Engineering, and Marketing of Life* (Regnery Publishing, Inc., 1998).

29. Edmund Pellegrino, lecture, West Liberty State College, March 20, 2001.

Chapter 3

1. Aristotle, *Parts of Animals, Book I*, Chapter 5.

2. Walter McDougall, "You Can't Argue with Geography," Foreign Policy Research Institute Footnotes, September 2000, p. 2.

3. Arthur Getis, Judith Getis, and Jerome Fellman, *Introduction to Geography* (McGraw-Hill, 2002), p. 7.

4. Konstantin Stanislavsky, and Mermine Popper, *Creating a Role* (Theater Arts Books, 1989).

5. Andrew Goudie and Heather Viles, *The Earth Transformed: An Introduction to the Human Impact of the Environment* (Blackwell, 1998).

6. Getis, Getis, and Fellman, *Introduction to Geography*, p. 155.

7. World Wildlife Fund, "Southeast Asian Haze," *Associated Press Release*, September 28, 1997.

8. Jack Anderson and Jan Moller, "Once a Bonanza, Tiny Pacific Island Has Become an Ecological Disaster," *Wheeling News-Register*, May 6, 1997, p. 3.

9. "Introducing Huge Foreign Toad to U.S. a Big Mistake," *Associated Press Release*, September 21, 1996.

10. Mark Monmonier, *How to Lie With Maps* (University of Chicago Press, 1996).

11. In the late 1980s, many governmental and private-sector reports criticized the lack of international knowledge possessed by U.S. citizens at a time of global interdependence. Most cited geographic information as especially lacking. The Association of American Geographers believes that geography contributes to international understanding and a global perspective by emphasizing:
    a. The relationships of societies, cultures, and economies around the world to specific combinations of natural resources and of the physical and biological environment
    b. The importance of location of places with respect to one another, as depicted on appropriate maps
    c. The diversity of the regions of the world
    d. The significance of ties of one country with another through the flow of commodities, capital, ideas, and political influence
    e. The world context of individual countries, regions, and problems
    Source: H. J. De Blij and Peter O. Muller, *Geography: Realms, Regions, and Concepts* (John Wiley, 1994), p. 51.

12. Gerard Chaliand and Jean-Pierre Rageau, *Strategic Atlas: A Comparative Geopolitics of the World's Powers* (Viking Penguin, 1995).

13. Edward Aguado and James Burt, *Understanding Weather and Climate* (Prentice Hall, 2000).

14. Michael Glantz, *Currents of Change: El Niño's Impact on Climate and Society* (Cambridge University Press, 1996).

15. Michael Bradshaw and Ruth Weaver, *Physical Geography: An Introduction to Earth Environments* (Mosby, 1993), p. 211.

16. "Another Casualty of El Niño: Amazon Rainforests," Associated Press Release, October 9, 1997.

17. Susan Hardwick and Donald Holtgrieve, *Patterns on Our Planet: Concepts and Themes in Geography* (Macmillan, 1990), p. 296.

18. Melinda Bell, "Is Our Climate Unstable?" *Earth Magazine*, January 1994, pp. 24–31.

19. United Nations Human Development Index, "Human Development Report 2001" (Oxford University Press, 2001), at *http://www.undp.org/hdr2001*.

20. Susan Hardwick and Donald Holtgrieve, *Patterns of Our Planet: Concepts and Themes in Geography* (Macmillan, 1990), pp. 285–89.

21. John P. LeDonne, *The Russian Empire and the World, 1700–1917: The Geopolitics of Expansion and Containment* (Oxford University Press, 1997).

22. John P. LeDonne, *The Russian Empire and the World, 1700–1917: The Geopolitics of Expansion and Containment* (Oxford University Press, 1996).

23. Mikhail Lyubimov, Interviewed by the author on June 28, 1995.

24. Allen F. Chew, *An Atlas of Russian History: Eleven Centuries of Changing Borders* (Yale University Press, 1970); M. K. Dziewanowski, *A History of Soviet Russia* (Prentice Hall, 1994), Chapter 1: "The Geopolitical Personality of Russia"; James Gregory, *Russian Land, Soviet People* (Pegasus, 1968); W. H. Parker, *An Historical Geography of Russia* (Chatham Hoase, 1969).

25. John L. Allen, *Student Atlas of World Politics* (Dushkin, 1994), p. v.

26. Jared Diamond, *Guns, Germs, and Steel: The Fate of Human Societies* (W. W. Norton & Co., 1997), p. vi.

27. Ibid., p. 74.

28. Ibid., p. 186.

29. Malcom B. Russell, "When Will the Taps Go Dry?" in *The Middle East and South Asia: The World Today Series* (Stryker-Post, 2005), pp. 2–7.

30. Ibid.

31. Malcom B. Russell, "Black Gold: The Impact of Oil," in *The Middle East and South Asia: The World Today Series* (Stryker-Post, 2005), pp. 8–13.

32. Susan Cutter and William Renwick, *Exploitation, Conservation, Preservation: A Geographic Perspective on Natural Resource Use* (John Wiley, 1999).

33. Robert McCrum, William Cran, and Robert MacNeil, *The Story of English* (Elizabeth Sifton Books, 1986).

34. McCrum, Cran, and MacNeil, *The Story of English* (Elizabeth Sifton Books, 1986); James M. Rubenstein, *The Cultural Landscape: An Introduction to Human Geography* (Merrill Publishing, 1989).

35. Kevin Phillips, *The Cousins' Wars: Religion, Politics, and the Triumph of Anglo-America* (Basic Books, 1999).

Chapter 4

1. Julian L. Simon, *The Ultimate Resource* (Princeton University Press, 1996); Stephen Moore and Julian Simon, *It's Getting Better All the Time* (Cato Institute Publications, 2000).

2. Hilary F. French, "Can the Environment Survive Industrial Demands?" *USA Today Magazine,* January 1994.

3. Lester R. Brown, *The State of the World 1995* (W. W. Norton, 1995).

4. Mark Hertsgaard, *Earth Odyssey* (Broadway Books, 1999).

5. Garrett Hardin, "The Tragedy of the Commons," *Science,* 1968, pp. 1241–48; Garrett Hardin, *Living Within Limits* (Oxford University Press, 1993).

6. Dennis Meadows, Donnella Meadows, Jorgen Randers, and William Behrend III, *The Limits to Growth* (Universe Books, 1972).

7. George Sessions, ed., *Deep Ecology for the Twenty-First Century* (Random House), 1996.

8. Ibid.

9. Robert M. Torrance, ed., *Encompassing Nature: A Source-Book* (Counterpoint Press, 1999).

10. Lynn White, Jr., "The Historical Roots of Our Ecological Crisis," *Science,* 155 (1967), 1203–7.

11. Michael J. Strada, "Science, Religion, and Ecology Turn Eastward," *USA Today Magazine,* September 2001, pp. 58–60.

12. "Titanic: The Legend Lives On," *Arts and Entertainment Channel,* September 21, 1996.

13. Edith Brown Weiss, "Intergenerational Equity: Toward an International Legal Framework," in Nazli Choucri, ed., *Global Accord* (The MIT Press, 1993), p. 334.

14. William K. Stevens, "Humanity Confronts Its Handiwork: An Altered Planet," *New York Times,* May 5, 1992, p. B5.

15. Robert Taylor, "The Birth of Environmentalism," in *Ahead of the Curve,* excerpted in Environmental Defense Fund Web site, at *http://www.edf.org/content.cfm?contentID=809*

16. Lester Brown, *State of the World 2000* (W. W. Norton, 2000).

17. Gareth Porter and Janet Welsh Brown, *Global Environmental Politics* (Westview Press, 1996), p. 7.

18. Donald Wells, *Environmental Policy: A Global Perspective for the 21st Century* (Prentice Hall, 1996), p. 50.

19. Robert S. Stern et al., "Risk Reduction for Non-melanoma Skin Cancer with Childhood Sunscreen Use," *Archives of Dermatology,* May 1986, 122, no. 5, pp. 537–45.

20. Wells, *Environmental Policy,* pp. 44–48.

21. Hilary F. French, *Vanishing Borders: Protecting the Planet in the Age of Globalization* (W. W. Norton, 2000), p. 89.

22. John Rourke, *International Politics on the World Stage* (Dushkin McGraw-Hill, 1999), p. 550.

23. Wells, *Environmental Policy,* p. 162.

24. Marc Reisner, *Cadillac Desert: The American West and Its Disappearing Water* (Penguin, 1993).

25. Facts reported under each global issue are taken from these sources: Robert M. Jackson, ed. *Annual Editions: Global Issues, 95/96* (Dushskin, 1995); Paul Kennedy, *Preparing for the Twenty-First Century* (Random House, 1993), pp. 95–121; Charles W. Kegley and Eugene R. Wittkopf, eds., *The Global Agenda: Issues and Perspectives* (McGraw-Hill, 1995), Part 4—"Ecology and Politics," pp. 331–455; Wesley M. Bagby, *Introduction to Social Science and Contemporary Issues* (Nelson Hall, 1995), pp. 144–60; John T. Rourke, Chapter 18: "Sustainable Development," in *International Politics on the World Stage* (Dushkin, 1995), pp. 587–625; Hoyt Purvis, *Interdependence* (Harcourt Brace Jovanovich, 1992), pp. 307–33.

26. Jean-Paul Malingreau and Compton J. Tucker, "Large Space Deforestation in the Southeastern Amazon Basin of Brazil," *Ambio,* 1988, 17, p. 49; World Resources Institute, *World Resources, 1992–93* (Oxford University Press, 1994), pp. 118–19.

27. Warren Dean, *With Broadax and Firebrand: The Destruction of the Brazilian Atlantic Forest* (University of California Press, 1996), p. xv.

28. Edward O. Wilson, "Threats to Biodiversity," *Scientific American,* 1989, 261, no. 3, p. 112.

29. Wells, *Environmental Policy,* p. 63.

30. Peter H. Gleick, *The World's Water, 2000–2001* (Island Press, 2001).

31. Paul Simon, "Are We Running Dry?" *Parade,* August 23, 1998, p. 5.

32. Paul Simon, *Tapped Out?* (Welcome Rain Publishers, 1998).

33. Gleick, *The World's Water, 2000–2001.*

34. *The 20th Century,* "Black Tide: Nightmare Oil Spills," Arts and Entertainment Network, December 13, 1995.

35. Garry D. Brewer, "Environmental Challenges and Managerial Responses," in Nazli Choucri, ed., *Global Accord: Environmental Challenges and International Responses* (MIT Press, 1993), p. 300.

36. Gary Bryner, "Agenda 21: Myth or Reality?" in Norman Vig and Regina Axelrod, eds., *The Global Environment: Institutions, Law, and Policy* (Congressional Quarterly Press, 1999), pp. 157–89.

37. Porter and Brown, *Global Environmental Politics,* p. 111.

38. Paul Kennedy, *Preparing for the Twenty-First Century* (Random House, 1993), p. 96.

39. Daniel Prager and Valerie Thompson, *Findings of the Millennium Ecosystem Assessment: How Do the Poor Fare?* (World Resources Institute, 2005), at *http:// earthtrends.wri.org/features/view_feature.php?theme= 7&fid=61* (accessed March 4, 2008).

40. "World Population Clock," at *http://www.census.gov/ main/www/popclock.html* (accessed March 4, 2008).

41. Kennedy, *Preparing,* pp. 21–46; *New York Times,* April 30, 1992, p. A12; Charles W. Kegley and Eugene R. Wittkopf, "Population Pressures and the Global Habitat," in *The Global Agenda: Issues and Perspectives* (McGraw-Hill, 1995), pp. 367–80, "Population"; Steven L. Spiegel, *World Politics in a New Era* (Harcourt Brace College, 1995).

42. Wikipedia, "World Population," at *http://en.wikipedia. org/wiki/Population* (accessed March 4, 2008).

43. Kennedy, *Preparing,* p. 22.

44. Charles W. Kegley and Eugene R. Wittkopf, "Population Pressures and the Global Habitat," in *The Global Agenda: Issues and Perspectives* (McGraw-Hill, 1995), p. 370.

45. *2000 World Population Data Sheet,* Population Reference Bureau, 2000.

46. "The State of the World's Population," at *http://www. unfpa.org* (accessed March 4, 2008).

47. Nafis Sadik, *The State of The World's Population* (U.N. Population Fund, 2000).

48. United Nations Development Programme, 1997.

49. "The Fruits of Girls' Education," International Food Policy Research Institute, *News & Views,* December 1999, p. 2.

50. Philip Hauser and Leo Schnore, *The Study of Urbanization* (John Wiley, 1965).

51. Paul Lewis, "U.N. Sees a Crisis in Overpopulation," *New York Times,* April 30, 1992, p. A6.

52. John Weeks, *Population: An Introduction to Concepts and Issues* (Wadsworth, 1994).

53. Boyce Rensberger, "Damping the World's Population," *Washington Post Weekly,* September 12–18, 1994, pp. 10–11.

54. Timothy Weiskel, "Vicious Circles: African Demographic History as a Warning," *Harvard International Review,* Fall 1994, pp. 12–16.

55. Anne Nadakavukaren, "The Elusive Quest for ZPG: India's Family-Planning Program," in *Our Global Environment: A Health Perspective* (Waveland Press, 1993), pp. 110–12.

56. Food First/Institute for Food and Development Policy, "Democratizing Markets," at *http://www.foodfirst.org/ programs* (accessed March 4, 2008).

57. Neal Spivack and Ann Florini, *Food on the Table* (United Nations Association, 1986), pp. 24–53.

58. B. L. Turner and S. B. Brush, *Comparative Farming Systems* (Guilford, 1987).

59. Bruce Stutz, "The Landscape of Hunger," *Audubon,* Spring 1993, p. 54.

60. Per Pinstrup-Andersen, "World Food Prospects: Critical Issues for the Early Twenty-First Century," *2020 Vision Food Policy Report,* International Food Policy Research Institute, October 1999.

61. John Bongaarts, "Can the Growing Human Population Feed Itself?" *Scientific American,* March 1994, pp. 36–42.

62. E. Boserup, *The Conditions of Agricultural Growth: The Economics of Agrarian Change under Population Pressure* (Aldine, 1965).

63. Heidi Fritschel, "The Changing Outlook for Food Aid," International Food Policy Institute, *News & Notes,* November 1998, pp. 1–9.

64. United Nations Food and Agricultural Organization (FAO), at *http://www.fao.org/* (accessed March 4, 2008).

65. Robin Wright, "Hunger in the World: An Overview," in Scott Barbour, ed., *Hunger* (Greenhaven Press), pp. 12–15.

66. Dan Morgan, *The Merchants of Grain* (Viking Penguin, 1979).

67. Nabil Megalli, "Hunger versus the Environment: A Recipe for Global Suicide," *Our Planet,* 1992.

68. Bruce Stutz, "The Landscape of Hunger," *Audubon,* 1993, p. 54.

69. Orville Freeman, "Agriculture and the Environment: Meeting Global Food Needs," *The Futurist,* Winter 1993.

70. "What Causes Chronic Hunger?" *Freedom from Hunger,* at *http://www.freefromhunger.org/info/* (accessed March 4, 2008).

71. "Hunger Facts," *Freedom from Hunger,* at *http://www. freefromhunger.org/info/* (accessed March 4, 2008).

72. Dennis Pirages, *Building Sustainable Societies: A Blueprint for a Post-Industrial World* (Mitchell F. Sharp, 1996).

73. Charles Kegley and Eugene Wittkopf, "Fueling Growth: Oil, Energy, and Resource Power," in *World Politics: Trends and Transformation* (St. Martin's Press, 1995), pp. 333–68.

74. Daniel Yergin, *The Prize: The Epic Quest for Oil, Money and Power* (Simon & Schuster, 1991), p. 2.

75. Valav Smil, *Energy in World History* (Westview Press, 1994).

76. Colin Campbell and Jean Laherrere, "The End of Cheap Oil," *Scientific American,* March 1998.

77. "International Energy Database," at *http://www.eia.doe. gov/emeu/international/contents.html* (accessed March 4, 2008).

78. Rakesh Bakshi, "Country Survey: India," *Wind Directions,* April 1997.

79. Steven Nadel et al., *Lighting Energy Efficiency in China: Current Status, Future Directions* (American Council for an Energy Efficient Economy, May 1997).

80. "Survey for the Sustainable Energy Coalition," April, 1998.

81. Christopher Flavin and Seth Dunn, "Reinventing the Energy System," in Lester Brown, ed., *The State of the World 1999* (W. W. Norton, 1999), p. 23.

82. Nigel Hawkes et al., *Chernobyl: The End of the Nuclear Dream* (Vintage Books, 1987); Christopher Flavin, "Reassessing Nuclear Power: the Fallout from Chernobyl," *Worldwatch Paper 75* (Worldwatch Institute, 1987); Richard F. Mould, *Chernobyl: The Real Story* (Pergamon Press, 1988); "Chernobyl: Ten Years After," *Sixty Minutes,* CBS News, April 27, 1996.

83. Lester Brown, ed. *The State of the World 1999.* p. 31.

Chapter 5

1. Steve Lerner, *Eco-Pioneers: Practical Visionaries Solving Today's Environmental Problems* (MIT Press, 1998), p. 1.

2. Marvin S. Soroos, "The Tragedy of the Commons in Global Perspective," in Charles Kegley and Eugene Wittkopf, eds., *The Global Agenda: Issues and Perspectives* (McGraw Hill, 1991), p. 424.

3. United Nations Environment Programme, "Milestones," at *http://www.unep.org/Documents/Default.asp? DocumentID=287* (accessed March 4, 2008).

4. Associated Press Release, June 4, 1994, p. 2.

5. Daniel Sitarz, "Agenda 21: Toward a Strategy to Save Our Planet," in Kegley and Wittkopf, eds., *The Global Agenda,* p. 355.

6. Gary Bryner, "Agenda 21: Myth or Reality?" in Norman Vig and Regina Axelrod, eds., *The Global Environment: Institutions, Law, and Policy* (Congressional Quarterly Press, 1999), pp. 157–89.

7. Sierra Club, "Sierra Club 101: A Primer for New Volunteers," at *http://www.sierraclub.org/101/* (accessed March 4, 2008).

8. World Wildlife Fund, "About WWF," at *http://www. worldwildlife.org/about/index.cfm* (accessed March 4, 2008).

9. Greenpeace International, "About Greenpeace," at *http://www.greenpeace.org/international/about* (accessed March 4, 2008).

10. The Nature Conservancy, "About Nature Conservancy," at *http://www.nature.org/aboutus/* (accessed March 4, 2008).

11. "Earthjustice: Because the Earth Needs a Good Lawyer," at *http://www.earthjustice.org/* (accessed March 4, 2008).

12. United Nations Fund for Population Association, "International Conference on Population and Development (ICPD)," *http://www.un.org/popin/icpd2.htm* (accessed March 4, 2008).

13. United Nations Population Information Network (POPIN), "A Guide to Population Information on UN System Websites," at *http://www.un.org/popin/* (accessed March 4, 2008).

14. United Nations Department of Public Information, "Majority of World's Couples of Reproductive Age Are Using Contraception," at *http://www.un.org/esa/ population/publications/contraceptive2003/WallChart_ CP2003_pressrelease.htm* (accessed March 4, 2008).

15. Population Reference Bureau, "About the PRB," at *http://www.prb.org* (accessed March 4, 2008).

16. Population Connection, "Learn More, Take Action, Join or Give, Education, Legislation," at *http://www. populationconnection.org/* (accessed March 4, 2008).

17. The Population Institute, "The Population Institute: Home, Get Involved, Population Issues, Newsroom, Publications, Educating Communities," at *http://www. populationinstitute.org/* (accessed March 4, 2008).

18. Population Action International, "Condoms Count— Meeting the Need in the Era of HIV-AIDS," at *http:// www.populationaction.org* (accessed March 4, 2008).

19. Food and Agriculture Organization of the United Nations, at *http://www.fao.org/* (accessed March 4, 2008).

20. *Freedom from Hunger,* at *http://www.freefromhunger. org/* (accessed March 4, 2008).

21. *The Hunger Project,* at *http://www.thp.org* (accessed March 4, 2008).

22. "Mercy Corps—Be the Change," at *http://www. mercycorps.org/* (accessed March 4, 2008).

23. "Charity Navigator: Your Guide to Intelligent Giving," at *http://www.charitynavigator.org/index.cfm?bay= search.summary&orgid=4078* (accessed March 4, 2008).

24. *Africare,* at *http://www.africare.org/* (accessed March 4, 2008).

25. "Food Not Bombs Movement," at *http://www. foodnotbombs.net/* (accessed March 4, 2008).

26. "The Hunger Site—Give Food for Free to Hungry People in the World," at *http://www.thehungersite.com/cgi-bin/ WebObjects/CTDSites.woa/439* (accessed March 4, 2008).

27. Harry C. Blaney, *Global Challenges: A World at Risk* (Franklin Watts, 1979), pp. 170–75.

28. "Energy Quest: Energy Education from the California Energy Commission," at *http://www.energyquest.ca.gov/* (accessed March 4, 2008).

29. "Alliance to Save Energy," at *http://www.ase.org/* (accessed March 4, 2008). "Renewable Energy Resources in the World," at *http://energy.sourceguides.com/* (accessed March 4, 2008). European Wind and Energy Association, at *http://www.ewea.org/* (accessed March 4, 2008).

30. Eugene Linden, "Why You Can't Ignore the Changing Climate," *Parade,* June 25, 2006, pp. 4–7.

31. Kendall Stiles, *Case Histories in International Politics* (Pearson Education, Inc., 2004), pp. 169–182.

32. Lerner, "A Green Priest Preaches about the Need to Protect God's Creation," *Eco-Pioneer,* pp. 373–83.

33. Ari Goldman, "Churches Joining Green Movement," *New York Times,* May 21, 1992.

34. Albert Gore, Jr., *Earth in the Balance* (Houghton Mifflin, 1992), p. 12.

35. Lawrence Shames, *The Hunger for More* (Times Books, 1989), p. 43.

36. Vicki Robin recognizes Robert Muller, former assistant secretary of the United Nations, and now advisor to the New Road Map Foundation, for inspiring this concept.

37. Lerner, "The New Frugality Movement Promotes Living Better by Consuming Less," *Eco-Pioneers*, pp. 67–79.

38. Juliet Schor, *The Overworked American* (Basic Books, 1993); Amy Saltzman, *Downshifting: Reinventing Success on a Slower Track* (HarperCollins, 1991); Warren Johnson, *Muddling Toward Frugality* (Sierra Club Books, 1978); Frank Levering and Wanda Urbanska, *One Couple's Search for a Better Life* (Viking, 1992); Duane Elgin, *Voluntary Simplicity* (William Morrow, 1993).

39. Jerry Orabon, "Up on a Roof: Could Cities Ever Feed Themselves?" *New Age Journal*, November–December 1990, p. 38.

40. Lerner, "Urban Rooftop Agriculture," *Eco-Pioneers*, p. 160.

41. Ibid., p. 165.

42. Lerner, "Greenhouse Treatment of Municipal Sewage," *Eco-Pioneers*, p. 49.

43. Nancy Jack Todd and John Todd, *Bioshelters, Ocean Arks, City Farming: Ecology as the Basis of Design* (Sierra Club Books, 1984).

44. Lerner, *Eco-Pioneers*, pp. 277–86.

45. Ted Williams, "Courage Under Fire," *Audubon*, September–October 1998, pp. 36–45.

46. Lerner, "Redesigning Buildings and Building Materials for Environmentally Intelligent Architecture," *Eco-Pioneers*, p. 199.

47. Lerner, "Students Swap Protest for Practical Work Building an Ecologically Sustainable Campus," *Eco-Pioneers*, p. 255.

48. Sylvia Nasar, "It's Never Fair to Just Blame the Weather," *New York Times*, January 17, 1993.

49. B. Devall, *Simple in Means, Rich in Ends: Practicing Deep Ecology* (Peregrine Smith, 1988).

50. Anne Nadakavukaren, *Our Global Environment* (Waveland, 1995), pp. 649–51.

51. Margot Hornblower, "Next Stop: Home Depot," *Time Magazine*, October 19, 1998, p. 70.

52. Gareth Porter and Janet Welsh Brown, *Global Environmental Politics* (Westview Press, 1996), p. 144.

53. Paul Kennedy, *Preparing for the Twenty-First Century* (Random House, 1993), p. 339.

54. Paul Ekins, Mayer Hillman, and Robert Hutchison, *The Gaia Atlas of Green Economics* (Anchor Books, 1992).

55. Yusef J. Ahmed, Salah El Serafez, and Ernst Lutz, eds., *Environmental Accounting for Sustainable Development* (World Bank, 1989).

56. Jonathan Rowe, "Honey We Shrank the Economy," *Yes: A Journal of Positive Futures*, B1, Spring–Summer 1996, p. 29.

57. United Nations Human Development Report 2001, "Human Development Index," at *http://www.hdr.unpd.org* (accessed March 4, 2008).

58. Herman Daly, *Beyond Growth: The Economics of Sustainable Development* (Beacon Press, 1996).

59. Lerner, *Eco-Pioneers*, p. 389.

60. President's Council, *Sustainable America: A New Consensus for Prosperity, Opportunity, and a Healthy Environment for the Future* (U.S. Government Printing Office, 1996).

61. Marvin S. Soroos, "The Tragedy of the Commons in Global Perspective," in Charles Kegley and Eugene Witkopf, eds., *The Global Agenda—Issues and Perspectives* (St. Martins, 1995), pp. 429–32.

62. Donald Wells, *Environmental Policy, A Global Perspective for the 21st Century* (Prentice Hall, 1996), pp. 9, 15.

63. Timothy Swanson, *The International Regulation of Extinction* (New York University Press, 1994).

64. Richard Somerville, "Science's Role in Climate Change Policy," Institute on Global Conflict and Cooperation, *Newsletter*, Spring 1999, pp. 5–7.

65. Katherine Rizzo, "Polluters, Environmentalists Work Together," Associated Press Release, March 18, 1999.

66. Huey Johnson, *Green Plans: Greenprint for Sustainability* (University of Nebraska Press, 1995).

67. Lerner, p. 9.

68. President's Council, *Sustainable America: A New Consensus for Prosperity, Opportunity, and the Future* (U.S. Government Printing Office, 1996).

69. Terry Forrest Young and Vicki L. Golich, "Debt-for-Nature Swaps: Win-Win Solution or Environmental Imperialism?" *Pew Case Studies in International Affairs* (Georgetown University, 1993).

70. John Vandermeer and Ivette Perfecto, *Breakfast of Biodiversity: The Truth about Rainforest Destruction* (Food First Books, 1995), p. 14.

71. E. Bradford Burns, *A History of Brazil* (Columbia University Press, 1993).

72. Wilber A. Chaffee, *Desenvolvimento: Politics and Economy in Brazil* (Lynne Rienner, 1997).

73. S. Hewlett, *The Cruel Dilemmas of Development: Twentieth-Century Brazil* (Basic Books, 1980).

74. Page, p. 140.

75. Maria Willumsen and Eduardo Giannetti, eds., *The Brazilian Economy: Structure and Performance in Recent Decades* (North-South Center Press, 1997).

76. Siegfried Marks, ed., *Political Constraints on Brazil's Economic Development* (North-South Center Press, 1993).

77. Ronald Schneider, *Brazil: Culture and Politics in a New Industrial Powerhouse* (Westview Press, 1996).

78. Howard LaFranchi, "Spare the Ax, Spoil the Amazon," *Christian Science Monitor*, May 14, 1997, p. 9.

79. Interview by author with executive director of Brazilian NGO, *Mata Atlantica*, July 14, 1998.

80. Richard Leakey and Roger Lewin, *The Sixth Extinction: Patterns of Life and the Future of Humankind* (Anchor Books, 1996), pp. 59–67.

81. Page, pp. 276–82.

82. Ted Goertzel, *Fernando Enrique Cardoso: Reinventing Democracy in Brazil* (Lynne Rienner, 1999).

83. Information on Curitiba taken from lectures by officials speaking to the faculty group that I led in 1998, city of Curitiba literature, field visits, Joseph Page, pp. 488–92, and Barry Ames and Margaret Keck, "The Politics of Sustainable Development: Environmental Policy Making in Four Brazilian States," *Journal of Inter-American Studies and World Affairs*, 1997–98, pp. 31–43.

Chapter 6

1. Nicholas Humphrey, *A History of the Mind: Evolution and the Birth of Consciousness* (Copernicus Books, 1999).

2. Gordon Gallup, "The Mirror Test," at *http://philosophy.hku.hk/courses/cogsci/files/gallup-final.pdf* (accessed March 4, 2008).

3. Richard Leakey and Roger Lewin, *Origins Reconsidered: In Search of What Makes Us Human* (Anchor Books, 1992), p. 302.

4. Marc Pachter, "American Identity: A Political Compact," in Robert Earle and John Wirth, eds., *Identities in North America: Search for Community* (Stanford University Press, 1995), pp. 29–39.

5. Thomas Thorner, ed., *A Country Nourished on Self-Doubt: Documents in Canadian History, 1867–1980* (Broadview Press, 1996), p. xiii.

6. *Citizen's Forum on Canada's Future* (Supply and Services Canada, 1991).

7. Keith Spicer, "Canada: Values in Search of a Vision," in Earle and Wirth, eds., pp. 13–28.

8. Joseph Page, *The Brazilians* (Addison-Wesley, 1995), p. 8.

9. Jeffrey Gedmin, ed. *The Germans: Portrait of a New Nation.* American Enterprise Institute Press, 1996.

10. "The World's Richest Billionaires," *Forbes Magazine,* July 1996.

11. Raphael Ezekiel, *The Racist Mind: Portraits of American Neo-Nazis and Klansmen* (Viking, 1995), pp. 66–67.

12. Ibid., pp. 32–33.

13. Philip Gourevitch, *We Wish to Inform You That Tomorrow We Will Be Killed with Our Families* (Farrar, Strauss, 1998), Chapter 4.

14. Barry Jones, ed., *The European Union and the Regions* (Oxford University Press, 1995).

15. "Eurobarometer," *Economist,* September 9, 2000, p. 40.

16. Thomas Magstadt, *Nations and Governments: Comparative Politics in Regional Perspective* (Bedford/St. Martin's, 2002), pp. 165–71.

17. International Monetary Fund, 1998.

18. *New York Times,* November 19, 1993, p. A1.

19. World Bank, *World Development Report* (Oxford University Press, 1997).

20. United Nations, "Poverty Report 2000," at *http://www.undp.org/povertyreport/* (accessed March 4, 2008).

21. United Nations, "The Least Developed Countries," at *http://www.unctad.org* (accessed March 4, 2008).

22. International Monetary Fund, *World Economic Outlook, 1998*; World Resources Institute, *World Resources 1999* (Oxford University Press, 1999).

23. John M. Hamilton, *Entangling Alliances: How the Third World Shapes Our Lives* (Seven Locks Press, 1992).

24. Samuel P. Huntington, *Political Development and Political Decay* (Irvington Books, 1993).

25. Brian Beedham, "Islam and the West, the Next War, They Say," *Economist,* August 6, 1994, pp. 3–6.

26. Howard Rheingold, *The Virtual Community: Homesteading on the Electronic Frontier* (Addison-Wesley, 1993).

27. Joshua Quittner, "Mr. Rheingold's Neighborhood," *Time Magazine,* November 25, 1996, p. 99.

28. Kwame Anthony Appiah and Henry Louis Gates, eds., *The Dictionary of Global Culture* (Alfred A. Knopf, 1997), pp. ix–xii.

29. Jerel A. Rosati, *The Carter Administration's Quest for Global Community: Beliefs and Their Impact on Behavior* (University of South Carolina Press, 1991).

30. Martin Ira Glassner, *Political Geography* (John Wiley, 1993), pp. 10–13.

31. Robert Ardrey, *The Territorial Imperative* (Atheneum Books, 1966).

32. Mel Gurtov, *Global Politics in the Human Interest* (Lynne Reinner, 1994).

33. Kalevi J. Holsti, *Peace and War: Armed Conflicts and International Order* (Cambridge University Press, 1991), p. 283.

34. Gerald R. Pitzl, *The Northern Territories Controversy: A Four-Decade Stalemate Between Japan and Russia* (Georgetown University: Pew Case Studies in International Affairs, 1995); H. J. DeBlij and Peter O. Muller, *Geography: Realms, Regions, and Concepts* (John Wiley, 1994), pp. 159–160, 237.

35. Costas Melakopides, *Pragmatic Idealism: Canadian Foreign Policy, 1945–1995* (McGill-Queens University Press, 1998), pp. 4–5.

36. Costas Melakopides, p. 200.

37. Tom Keating, *Canada and World Order: The Multilateralist Tradition in Canadian Foreign Policy* (McClelland and Stewart, 1993), p. 22.

38. Costas Melakopides, p. vi.

39. Costas Melakopides, pp. 6–7.

40. Fen Osler Hampson, Michael Hart, and Martin Rudner, eds., *Canada Among Nations 1999: A Big League Player or a Minor League Player?* (Oxford, 1999), pp. 14–15.

41. Hampson, Hart, and Rudner, p. 21.

42. Hampson, Hart, and Rudner, pp. 46–56.

43. Costas Melakopides, p. ii.

44. Costas Melakopides, p. 30.

45. David Martin and T. Alexander Aleinikoff, "Double Ties: Why Nations Should Learn to Love Dual Nationality," *Foreign Policy* (December, 2002), pp. 80–81.

Chapter 7

1. David Gelman, "Why We All Love to Hate," *Newsweek,* August 28, 1989, p. 62.

2. Dennis Coon, *Introduction to Psychology: Exploration and Application* (West Publishing, 1995), pp. 2, 6.

3. Keith E. Stanovich, *How to Think Straight about Psychology* (HarperCollins, 1996), p. xiii.

4. Coon, *Introduction to Psychology,* p. 714.

5. Peter T. Manicas, *A History and Philosophy of the Social Sciences* (Wiley-Blackwell, 1991), p. 171.

6. Terrence Deacon, *The Symbolic Species: The Co-Evolution of Language and the Brain* (W. W. Norton, 1997), p. ix.

7. Geoffrey Masson, *The Making and Unmaking of a Psychotherapist* (Addison-Wesley, 1990).

8. Paul Gray, "The Man Who Loved Children," *Time Magazine,* March 30, 1998, p. 71.

9. Stanovich, *Psychology,* p. 1.

10. Association for Humanistic Psychology, "About Humanistic Psychology," at *http://www.ahpweb.org/aboutahp/whatis.html* (accessed March 4, 2008).

11. Aristotle, *Nichomachean Ethics, Book III,* Chapter 3.

12. David Elkind, *Erik Erikson's Eight Ages of Man* (New York Times Company, 1970).

13. Coon, *Introduction to Psychology,* p. 13.

14. Rodolfo Llinas, *I of the Vortex: From Neurons to Self* (MIT Press, 2001).

15. Vilayanur Ramachandran, "From Ramachandran's Notebook," at *http://www.pbs.org/wgbh/nova/mind/notebook.html* (accessed March 4, 2008).

16. Vilayanur Ramachandran and Sandra Blakeslee, *Phantoms in the Brain: Probing the Mysteries of the Human Mind* (William Morrow, 1998).

17. Terrance W. Deacon, *The Symbolic Species: The Co-Evolution of Language and the Brain* (Harvard University Press, 1996).

18. "Genomics 101: The Basics," Human Genome Project Information, at *http://www.ornl.gov/hgmis/publicat/primer2001/1.html* (accessed March 4, 2008).

19. J. Madeleine Nash, "The Personality Genes," *Time Magazine,* April 27, 1998, pp. 60–62.

20. Dean Hamer and Peter Copeland, *Living with Our Genes* (Doubleday, 1998), Introduction.

21. Steven Pinker, *How the Mind Works* (W. W. Norton, 1997), p. 24.

22. Ibid., pp. 31–36.

23. Peter D. Kramer, *Listening to Prozac* (Penguin Books, 1993).

24. Otto Klineberg, in Foreword to Marshall H. Segall, *Cross-Cultural Psychology: Human Behavior in Global Perspective* (Brooks/Cole, 1979), p. v.

25. Carol and Melvin Ember, *Cultural Anthropology* (Prentice Hall, 1996), pp. 284–90.

26. Donald E. Brown, *Human Universals* (Temple University Press, 1991).

27. Margaret Mead, *Coming of Age in Samoa* (Morrow, 1961).

28. Alice Schlegel and Herbert Barry III, *Adolescence: An Anthropological Inquiry* (Free Press, 1991), p. 44.

29. Ember and Ember, *Cultural Anthropology,* pp. 284, 289.

30. Blema S. Steinberg, *Shame and Humiliation: Presidential Decision Making on Vietnam* (University of Pittsburgh Press, 1996), p. 6.

31. John G. Stoessinger, *Crusaders and Pragmatists: Movers of American Foreign Policy* (W. W. Norton, 1985).

32. Sam Keen, *Faces of the Enemy,* documentary film (Catticus Corporation, 1986).

33. Robert Jervis, "Hypotheses of Misperception," *World Politics, XX* (1968), pp. 454–79; Kenneth Boulding, *The Image: Knowledge in Life and Society* (University of Michigan, 1956); Ole R. Holsti, Robert North, and Richard Brody, "Perceptions and Actions in the 1914 Crisis," in J. David Singer, ed., *Quantitative International Politics* (Free Press, 1968); Otto Klineberg, *The Human Dimension in International Relations* (Free Press, 1969).

34. Demosthenes, *Third Olynthiac,* section 19.

35. John T. Rourke, *International Politics on the World Stage* (Dushkin, 1995), pp. 139–40.

36. Walter S. Jones, *The Logic of International Relations* (HarperCollins, 1991), pp. 225–30.

37. Ibid, pp. 225–30.

38. "The U.S. Drops the Atomic Bomb on Japan, August 1945," *Intercom #106* (March 1985), p. 14.

39. Sam Keen, *Faces of the Enemy: Reflections of the Hostile Imagination* (Harper and Row, 1986).

40. "Thatcher Urges the Press to Help 'Starve' Terrorists," *The New York Times,* July 16, 1985, p. 3.

41. Walter Reich, *Origins of Terrorism: Psychologies, Ideologies, States of Mind* (Cambridge University Press, 1990).

42. John Dickerson, "Four for One," *Time Magazine,* March 14, 1994, p. 33; Laurie Mylroie, "Saddam and Terrorism: The WTC Bombing," *Newsweek,* October 17, 1994, pp. 30–32; Terence Samuel, "Man Said to be Key to World Trade Center Bombing Pleads Not Guilty But Blames Attack on Iraq," Knight-Ridder/Tribune News Service, February 9, 1995.

43. Jill Smolowe, "Enemies of the State," *Time Magazine,* May 8, 1995, p. 61.

44. Christopher John Farley, "America's Bomb Culture," *Time Magazine,* May 8, 1995, p. 56.

45. Robert Jay Lifton, Interviewed in Sam Keen's film, *Faces of the Enemy* (1987).

46. Christine Gorman, "Calling all Paranoids," *Time Magazine,* May 8, 1995, p. 69; James Coates, *Armed and Dangerous: The Rise of the Survivalist Right* (Hill and Wang, 1996).

Chapter 8

1. John Macionis, *Society: The Basics* (Prentice Hall, 1998), p. 3.

2. Arlene Levenson, "Atomic Bombings Called Top Story of Century," *Associated Press Release,* February 25, 1999.

3. Joel H. Rosenthal, "Fighting the Oxymoron Problem: The Study and Teaching of Ethics and International Affairs," *Forum,* Spring 1994, p. 3.

4. NBC White Paper, "The Decision to Drop the Bomb," *NBC News* (1965), 16 mm film; Michael J. Hogan, *Hiroshima in History and Memory* (Cambridge University Press, 1996); Donald Kagan, "Why America Dropped the Bomb," *Commentary,* September 1995; John Rawls, "Fifty Years After Hiroshima," *Dissent,* Summer 1995.

5. George F. Kennan, "Morality and Foreign Policy," *Foreign Affairs,* 1986, 64, p. 217.

6. Thomas Patterson and Dennis Merrill, eds., *Major Problems in American Foreign Relations* (D. C. Heath, 1995), p. 29.

7. Larry Berman, *Planning a Tragedy* (W. W. Norton, 1982); George C. Herring, *America's Longest War* (John Wiley, 1979); Doris Kearns, *Lyndon Johnson and the American Dream* (New American Library, 1976).

8. Paul Keal, ed., *Ethics and Foreign Policy* (Paul and Company, 1995).

9. Kenneth Thompson, "The Ethical Dimensions of Diplomacy," *Review of Politics*, 1984, p. 387.

10. John T. Rourke, *International Politics on the World Stage* (Dushkin, 1995), p. 207.

11. Douglas Johnston, ed., *Religion, the Missing Dimension of Statecraft* (Oxford University Press, 1994); David R. Smock, *Perspectives of Pacifism: Christian, Jewish and Muslim Views on Nonviolence and International Conflict* (U.S. Institute of Peace, 1995).

12. Mary Lean, *Bread, Bricks and Belief: Communities in Charge of Their Future* (Kumarian Press, 1995).

13. Gary H. Gossen, "Temporal and Spiritual Equivalents in Chamula Ritual Symbolism," in Lessa and Vogt, eds., *Reader in Comparative Religion*, pp. 116–28.

14. H. J. De Blij and Peter O. Muller, *Geography: Realms, Regions, and Concepts* (John Wiley, 1994), pp. 271–73.

15. Irving Aballa and Harold Troper, *None Is Too Many* (Random House, 1983), pp. v, 280.

16. Jack Donnelly, *International Human Rights* (Westview Press, 1993), p. 66.

17. Allister Sparks, *Beyond the New South Africa* (University of Chicago Press, 2003), p. 160.

18. Alex Boraine, *A Country Unmasked: Inside South Africa's Truth and Reconciliation Commission*. Cape Town (2003).

19. Sparks, p. 281.

20. Human Rights Watch, *Human Rights Watch World Report 1995* (Human Rights Watch, 1994), p. xiii.

21. Donnelly, *International Human Rights*, p. 104.

22. Ibid., pp. 32–39.

23. J. Milton Yinger, "Ethnicity," *Annual Review of Sociology*, 11, 1985, pp. 151–80.

24. United Nations Development Programme, *Human Development Report 1995* (Oxford University Press, 1995), p. 2.

25. Carol and Melvin Ember, *Cultural Anthropology* (Prentice Hall, 1996), p. 162.

26. Florence Hartmann, "Bosnia," in Roy Guttman and David Rieff, eds., *Crimes of War: What the Public Should Know* (W. W. Norton, 1999), p. 52.

27. Nader Mousavizadeh, ed., *The Black Book of Bosnia: The Consequences of Appeasement* (Basic Books, 1996).

28. Diane Orentlicher, "The Law on Genocide," in Guttman and Rieff, eds., *Crimes of War: What the Public Should Know*, pp. 153–57.

29. Brian Jones, Bernard Gallagher, and Joseph Falls, *Sociology: Micro, Macro, and Mega Structures* (Harcourt Brace), p. 414.

30. Paul Gauguin, *Noa Noa: The Tahitian Journal* (Dover, 1919 and 1985), pp. 19–20.

31. Betty Reardon, "Feminist Concepts of Peace and Security," in Paul Smoker et al., eds., *A Reader in Peace Studies* (Pergamon Press, 1990), p. 136.

32. Joan Ferrante, *Sociology: A Global Perspective* (Wadsworth, 1995), p. 411.

33. *Human Development Report*, pp. 50–71.

34. *Human Rights Watch World Report 1995* (Human Rights Watch, 1995), pp. 252–53.

35. Amnesty International. "Women in the Middle East: Human Rights Under Attack," *Amnesty International*, 1995, p. 3.

Chapter 9

1. Raymond Scupin and Christopher DeCorse, *Anthropology: A Global Perspective* (Prentice Hall, 1998).

2. Robert Jurmain, Harry Nelson, Lynn Kilgorem, and Wenda Trevathan, *Essentials of Physical Anthropology* (Wadsworth, 2001), pp. 14–15.

3. Raymond Scupin, "Language, Hierarchy, and Hegemony: Thai Muslim Discourse Strategies," *Language Sciences*, 10, no. 2, 1988, pp. 331–51.

4. Noel Boaz and Alan Almquist, *Essentials of Biological Anthropology* (Prentice Hall, 1999), p. 8.

5. Carol and Melvin Ember, *Anthropology* (Prentice Hall, 2000), p. xii.

6. *Sources*: C. Joyce and E. Stover, *Witnesses from the Grave: The Stories Bones Tell* (Ballantine Books, 1991); Christopher DeCorse, *The Record of the Past: An Introduction to Physical Anthropology and Archaeology* (Prentice Hall, 2000), pp. 4–5.

7. Jurmain et al., *Essentials of Physical Anthropology*, p. 15.

8. Alan J. Almquist, *Contemporary Readings in Physical Anthropology* (Prentice Hall, 2000), p. 2.

9. Stephen Jay Gould, "Darwin at Sea—and the Virtues of Port," in *The Flamingo's Smile: Reflections in Natural History* (W. W. Norton, 1985), pp. 347–59.

10. H. B. D. Kettlewell, "Industrial Melanism in Moss and Its Contribution to Our Knowledge of Evolution," *Proceedings of the Royal Institute of Great Britain* (1957), 36, pp. 1–14.

11. Jurmain, et al., *Essentials of Physical Anthropology*, p. 303.

12. Gaylord G. Simpson, *Tempo and Mode in Evolution* (Columbia University, 1944).

13. Stephen J. Gould and Niles Eldredge, "Punctuated Equilibrium Comes of Age," *Nature*, 366, pp. 223–27.

14. Richard Leakey, *The Sixth Extinction: Patterns of Life and the Future of Humankind* (Anchor Books, 1995), p. 40.

15. David Raup, "Extinction: Bad Genes or Bad Luck?" *New Scientist*, 14, September 1991, p. 47.

16. Steven Stanley, *Extinction* (Scientific American Library, 1987), p. 40.

17. Paul Wignall, "The Day the World Nearly Died," *New Scientist*, 25, January 1992, p. 55.

18. David Raup, "Changing Views of Natural Catastrophe," *The Great Ideas of Today* (Encyclopedia Britannica, 1988), p. 55; Walter Alvarez, *Rex and the Crater of Doom* (Princeton University Press, 1997).

19. Richard Leakey and Roger Lewin, *Origins Reconsidered: In Search of What Makes Us Human* (Anchor Books, 1992), p. 347.

20. Jacob Bronowski, *The Ascent of Man* (Little, Brown, 1973), p. 30.

21. Ian Tattersall, Eric Delson, and John Van Couvering, *Encyclopedia of Human Evolution and Prehistory* (Garland Publishing, 1988), p. 230.

22. Ember and Ember, *Anthropology*, p. 93.

23. Erik Trinkaus, "Pathology and the Posture of the La Chapelle-aux-Saints Neandertal," *American Journal of Physical Anthropology*, 67, 1985, pp. 19–41.

24. Jean Auel, *The Clan of the Cave Bear* (Bantam, 1981).

25. "Human Origins: Tootin' the Neanderthal Tusk," *Discover: The World of Science*, April 1997, p. 19.

26. "DNA Shows Neanderthal Difference," *Associated Press Release*, July 13, 1997.

27. DeCorse, *The Record of the Past*, p. 117.

28. Ember and Ember, *Anthropology*, p. 98.

29. John Halverson, "Art for Art's Sake in the Paleolithic," *Current Anthropology*, 28, 1987, pp. 63–89.

30. Rebecca L. Cann, W. M. Brown, and Allan C. Wilson, "Mitochondrial DNA and Human Evolution," *Nature*, 325, pp. 31–36.

31. Frank Spencer, "The Neanderthals and Their Evolutionary Significance," in Fred Smith and Spencer, eds., *The Origins of Modern Humans* (Alan R. Liss, 1984), pp. 1–50.

32. Ember and Ember, *Anthropology*, p. 98.

33. Frank Hole, "Origins of Agriculture," in Stephen Jones, Robert Martin, and David Pilbeam, eds., *The Cambridge Encyclopedia of Human Evolution* (Cambridge University Press, 1992), p. 376.

34. Jared Diamond, "The Worst Mistake in the History of the Human Race," *Discover*, May 1987, pp. 64–66.

35. Gordon V. Childe, *Man Makes Himself* (Watts, 1936).

36. Robert Braidwood and Gordon Willey, eds., *Courses Toward Urban Life: Archeological Considerations of Some Cultural Alternatives*. Viking Fund Publications in Anthropology No. 32 (Aldine Publishing, 1962), p. 342.

37. Ester Boserup, *The Conditions of Agricultural Growth: The Economics of Agrarian Change Under Population Pressure* (Aldine Publishing, 1965).

38. David Rindos, *The Origins of Agriculture: An Evolutionary Perspective* (Academic Press, 1984).

39. Mark Cohen, *Health and the Rise of Civilization* (Yale U. Press, 1989), pp. 112–13.

40. Boaz and Almquist, *Biological Anthropology*, p. 276.

41. Melvin D. Williams, "Racism: The Production, Reproduction, and Obsolescence of Social Inferiority," in Carol Ember, Melvin Ember, and Peter Peregrine, eds., *Research Frontiers in Anthropology* (Prentice Hall, 1995).

42. Richard O. Lewontin, "The Apportionment of Human Diversity," in Theodore Dobzhansky and William Steere, eds., *Evolutionary Biology* (Plenum Press, 1972), vol. 6, pp. 381–98.

43. Ember and Ember, *Anthropology*, p. 126.

44. Alison Brooks, Fatimah Jackson, and R. Richard Grinker, "Race and Ethnicity in America," *Anthro Notes* (National Museum of National History Bulletin for Teachers), 15, 3, Fall 1993, p. 11.

45. Pat Shipman, *The Evolution of Racism* (Simon & Schuster, 1994).

46. DeCorse, *The Record of the Past*, pp. 129–30.

47. P. W. Post, F. Daniels, and R. Binford, "Cold Injury and the Evolution of White Skin," *Human Biology*, 47, 1987, pp. 65–80.

48. Jurmain et al., *Physical Anthropology*, p. 320.

49. Kitty Ferguson, *Stephen Hawking: Quest for a Theory of the Universe* (Franklin Watts, 1991).

50. Stephen Jay Gould, *Rock of Ages: Science and Religion in the Fullness of Life* (Ballantine Books, 1999).

51. Carl Sagan, *Broca's Brain: Reflections on the Romance of Science* (Ballantine Books, 1993).

52. Edward O. Wilson, *Consilience: The Unity of Knowledge* (Alfred A. Knopf, 1998), p. 31; Frank Miele interview with Edward Wilson, "The Ionian Instauration," *Skeptic*, 6, no. 1, 1998, pp. 76–80.

53. Jurmain et al., *Physical Anthropology*, pp. 38–39.

54. Eugenie C. Scott, "Evolution and Creation: Current Controversies," in Boaz and Almquist, *Biological Anthropology*, pp. 20–21.

55. L. Petrillo, "A Lull Falls on Vista's Religious Battlefield," *San Diego Union-Tribune*, May 21, 1995.

56. Matt Cartmill, "Oppressed by Evolution," in Alan Almquist, ed., *Contemporary Readings in Physical Anthropology* (Prentice Hall, 2000), pp. 4–11.

57. Robert Blakely and Judith Harrington, *Bones in the Basement: Postmortem Racism in Nineteenth-Century Medical Training* (Smithsonian Institution Press, 1997).

58. Tessie Naranjo, "Thoughts on Two Worldviews," *Federal Archaeology*, Offprint Series, Fall/Winter, 1995, p. 8.

59. Timothy McKeown, "Ethical and Legal Issues, Complying with NAGPRA," in Rebecca Buck et al., eds., *The New Museums Registration Methods* (American Association of Museums, 1998).

60. M. Neil Browne and Stuart M. Keeley, *Evaluating Online Resources: Anthropology on the Internet* (Prentice Hall, 2001), p. vii.

Chapter 10

1. W. David Watts and Ann Marie Ellis, "Assessing Sociology Educational Outcomes: Occupational Status and Mobility of Graduates," *Teaching Sociology*, 17, July 1989, pp. 297–306.

2. Richard Schaefer and Robert Lamb, *Sociology* (McGraw-Hill, 1998), p. 7.

3. Brian Morris, *Anthropological Studies of Religion: An Introductory Text* (Cambridge University Press, 1987), pp. 264–72.

4. C. Wright Mills, *The Sociological Imagination* (Oxford University Press, 1959), p. 5.

5. Peter Berger, *Invitation to Sociology* (Anchor Books, 1963).

6. John Macionis, *Society: The Basics* (Prentice Hall, 1998), p. 3.

7. Emile Durkheim, *Suicide* (New York: Free Press, 1966 [1897]).

8. Robert Bannister, *Sociology and Scientism: The American Quest for Objectivity, 1880–1940* (University of North Carolina Press, 1987), p. 3.

9. Max Weber, *Roscher and Kneis: The Logical Problems of Historical Economics* (Free Press, 1975), p. 107.

10. C. Wright Mills, *The Power Elite* (Oxford University Press, 1956).

11. American Sociological Association, *Code of Ethics* (American Sociological Association, 1984).

12. Ralph Linton, *The Study of Man* (Appleton-Century-Crofts, 1936).

13. J. Milton Yinger, *Countercultures* (Free Press, 1982).

14. William Zellner, *Countercultures: A Sociological Analysis* (St. Martin's Press, 1995).

15. Russ Rymer, "A Silent Childhood," *The New Yorker*, April 13, 1992, pp. 64–81.

16. Karen Lipson, "Nell Not Alone in the Wilds," *Los Angeles Times*, December 19, 1994, pp. F1–6.

17. Lawrence Wright, "Double Mystery," *The New Yorker*, August 7, 1995, pp. 45–62.

18. J. Craig Venter, Interviewed on *The Charlie Rose Show*, Public Broadcasting System, March 6, 2000.

19. Joseph J. Tobin, David Wu, and Dana Davidson, *Pre-School in Three Cultures: Japan, China, and the United States* (Yale University Press, 1989), p. 94.

20. Edward O. Wilson, *On Human Nature* (Bantam Books, 1979).

21. Brian Jones, Bernard Gallagher III, and Joseph McFalls, Jr., *Sociology: Micro, Macro, and Mega Structures* (Harcourt, Brace, 1995).

22. Macionis, *Society*, p. 106.

23. Gerhard and Jean Lenski, *Human Societies: An Introduction to Macrosociology* (McGraw-Hill, 1987).

24. Raymond Mack and Calvin Bradford, *Transforming America: Patterns of Social Change* (Random House, 1979), pp. 12–22.

25. Melvyn C. Goldstein, "When Brothers Share a Wife," *Natural History*, March 1987, p. 39.

26. Ferdinand Mount, *The Subversive Family: An Alternative History of Love and Marriage* (Free Press, 1992).

27. William Jankowiak and Edward Fischer, "A Cross-Cultural Perspective on Romantic Love," *Journal of Ethology*, April 2, 1992, 31, pp. 149–55.

28. Elisabeth Bumiller, "First Comes Marriage—Then, Maybe, Love," in James Henslin, ed., *Marriage and Family in a Changing Society* (Free Press, 1992), pp. 120–25; Richard Weintraub, "A Bride in India," *Washington Post*, February 28, 1988.

29. Nelson H. Graburn, *Eskimos Without Igloos* (Little, Brown, 1969), pp. 188–200.

30. Carol and Melvin Ember, *Cultural Anthropology* (Prentice Hall, 1996), pp. 186–87.

31. Syed Zubair Ahmed, "What Do Men Want," *The Times of India*, January 28, 1994.

32. U.S. Bureau of the Census, 1996.

33. James Henslin, *Essentials of Sociology: A Down to Earth Approach* (Allyn and Bacon, 2000), p. 316.

34. *Statistical Abstract*, 1997, Table 59.

35. Naomi Gerstel, "Divorce and Stigma," *Social Problems*, 43, no. 2, April 1987, pp. 172–86; Frank Furstenberg, Jr., "The New Extended Family: The Experience of Parents and Children After Remarriage," Changing Family Conference XIII, Iowa City, IA, 1984; Amitai Etzioni, "How to Make Marriage Matter," *Time Magazine*, September 6, 1993, p. 76.

36. Richard Gelles, quoted in Roberta Roesch, "Violent Families," *Parents Magazine*, 59, no. 9, p. 75.

37. *Statistical Abstract*, 1997, Table 353.

38. R. J. Gelles and C. Pedrick-Cornell, *Intimate Violence in Families* (Sage Publications, 1990).

39. Schaefer and Lamm, *Sociology*, p. 405.

40. Macionis, *Society*, p. 314.

41. Henslin, *Essentials of Sociology*, pp. 312–13.

42. Ibid., p. 312.

43. R. Morin, "Across the Racial Divide," *Washington Post National Weekly Edition*, October 16–22, 1995.

44. Emile Durkheim, *The Elementary Forms of Religious Life* (Collier Books, 1961).

45. Edward B. Tylor, "Animism," in William A. Lessa and Evon Z. Vogt, eds., *Reader in Comparative Religion: An Anthropological Approach* (Harper and Row, 1979), pp. 9–18.

46. Bronislaw Malinowski, *Magic, Science, and Religion, and Other Essays* (Doubleday, 1948), pp. 50–51.

47. Emile Durkheim, *The Elementary Forms of the Religious Life* (Free Press, 1965).

48. Gary H. Gossen, "Temporal and Spiritual Equivalents in Chamula Ritual Symbolism," in Lessa and Vogt, eds., *Reader in Comparative Religion*, pp. 116–28.

49. Friedrich Engels and Karl Marx, *The Communist Manifesto* (Appleton-Century-Crofts, 1970 [1848]).

50. William Bridgwater, ed. *The Columbia Viking Desk Encyclopedia*. Viking Press, 1953.

51. Max Weber, *The Sociology of Religion* (Beacon Press, 1922).

52. Ernst Troeltsch, *The Social Teaching of the Christian Churches* (Macmillan, 1931).

53. John Andrew Hostetler, *Amish Society* (Johns Hopkins University Press, 1982).

54. Steven Tipton, *Getting Saved from the Sixties: Moral Meaning in Conversion and Cultural Change* (University of California Press, 1982).

55. Eileen Barker, *The Making of a Moonie: Brainwashing or Choice?* (Basil Blackwell, 1984).

56. Rodney Stark and W. Bainbridge, *The Future of Religion: Secularization, Revival, and Cult Formation* (University of California Press, 1985).

57. Wendy Gale Robinson, "Heaven's Gate: The End?" Paper presented at Journalism and Mass Communication Conference, Chapel Hill, NC, December 3, 1997, pp. 1–52, at *http://jcmc.indiana.edu/vol3/issue3/robinson.html* (accessed March 4, 2008).

58. R. C. Bush et al., eds., *The Religious World—Communities of Faith* (Macmillan, 1987), pp. 1–11.

59. Roger Schmidt, *Exploring Religion* (Wadsworth, 1980).

60. Walter Kaufman, *Religions in Four Dimensions: Existential, Aesthetic, Historical, and Comparative* (Reader's Digest Press, 1976).

61. Ainslie Embree, *The Hindu Tradition* (Vintage Books, 1972).

62. H. W. Schumann, *Buddhism: An Outline of Its Teachings and Schools* (Quest Book, 1974).

63. George Bedell, Leo Sandon, and Charles Wellborn, *Religion in America* (Macmillan, 1975).

64. Brian Wilson, *Religion in Sociological Perspective* (Oxford University Press, 1982).

65. Ninian Smart, *The Religious Experience of Mankind* (Charles Scribner's Sons, 1969).

66. Leften Stavrianos, *A Global History: The Human Heritage* (Prentice Hall, 1983).

67. John Esposito and John Voll, *Islam and Democracy* (Oxford University Press, 1996).

68. John Weeks, "The Demography of Islamic Nations," *Population Bulletin*, 43, no. 4, 1988.

69. Thomas O'Dea and J. O. Ariad, *The Sociology of Religion* (Prentice Hall, 1983).

70. Harvey Cox, *The Secular City* (Macmillan, 1971), p. 3.

71. Jones, Gallagher, and McFalls, *Sociology*, p. 516.

72. Robert Bellah and Philip Hammond, *Varieties of Civil Religion* (Harper and Row, 1980).

73. Will Herberg, *Protestant, Catholic, Jew* (Anchor Books, 1955).

74. Jones, Gallagher, and McFalls, *Sociology*, p. 517.

75. C. Wilcox, "Support for the Christian Right, Old and New: A Comparison of Supporters of the Anti-Communist Crusade and the Moral Majority," *Sociological Focus*, 22, no. 2, pp. 87–97.

76. C. M. Jacquet, ed., *Yearbook of the American and Canadian Churches* (Abingdon Press, 1985).

77. Randall Collins, *Conflict Sociology: Toward on Explanatory Science* (Academic Press, 1979).

78. Macionis, *Society*, pp. 337–38.

79. Samuel Bowles, *Schooling in Capitalist America* (Basic Books, 1976).

80. Putka, 1990.

81. Maureen Hallinan, *Handbook of the Sociology of Education* (Kluwer Academic Publishers, 2000).

82. Mehrangiz Najafizadeh and Lewis Mennerick, "Sociology of Education or Sociology of Ethnocentrism: The Portrayal of Education in Introductory Sociology Textbooks," *Teaching Sociology*, 20, no. 3, July 1992, pp. 215–21.

83. Ruth Benedict, *The Chrysanthemum and the Sword: Patterns of Japanese Culture* (New American Library, 1974).

84. Stephen Hayneman and William Loxley, "The Effect of Primary-School Quality on Academic Achievement Across Twenty-Nine High- and Low-Income Countries," *American Journal of Sociology*, 88, no. 6, May 1983, pp. 1162–94.

85. Carol Simons, "Japan's Kyoiu Mamas," in John Macionis and Nijole Benokraitis, eds., *Seeing Ourselves: Classic, Contemporary, and Cross-Cultural Readings in Sociology* (Prentice Hall, 1989), pp. 281–86.

86. Ben Eklof, "Russian Education: Transition or Collapse?" in Max Oksenfuss and Ann Blaisdell Rothery, eds., *The Peoples of Russia and China: Facing the Dawn of a New Century* (Pearson Custom Publishing, 1999), pp. 139–50.

87. Edward Dneprov and Ben Eklof, *Democracy in the Russian School* (Westview Press, 1993).

88. Jeanne Sutherland, *Schooling in the New Russia: Innovation and Change, 1985–1995* (St. Martin's Press, 1999).

89. Nicholas Riasanovsky, *A History of Russia* (Oxford University Press, 2000), p. 622.

90. Eklof, *Russian Education*, p. 145.

91. Roy Honeywell, *The Educational Work of Thomas Jefferson* (Harvard University Press, 1931).

92. NORC, *General Social Surveys, 1972–1994: Cumulative Codebook* (Roper Center for Public Opinion Research, 1994).

93. United States Bureau of the Census, 1996.

94. Pat Wingert, "The Sum of Mediocrity," *Newsweek*, December 2, 1996, p. 96.

95. Henslin, *Essentials of Sociology*, p. 290.

96. William Form, "Comparative Industrial Sociology and the Convergence Hypothesis," in Alex Inkeles, James Coleman, and Ralph Turner, eds., *Annual Review of Sociology*, 5, no. 1, 1979.

97. Gurutz Jauregui, "El Poder y la Soberana en la aldea global," *El Pais*, July 19, 1996, p. 11.

98. Henslin, *Essentials of Sociology*, p. 292.

99. Jones, Gallagher, and McFalls, *Sociology*, pp. 522–55.

100. George Bryjak and Michael Soroka, *Sociology* (Allyn and Bacon, 1996), p. 378.

101. Max Weber, "Power and Legitimate Authority," in Talcott Parsons, ed., *The Theory of Social and Economic Organization* (Free Press, 1947).

102. Max Weber, *Economy and Society* (Bedminster Press, 1968).

103. Robert Dahl, *Who Governs?* (Yale University Press, 1961).

104. Thomas Hobbes, *Leviathan* (James Thornton, 1881), p. 93.

105. Joan Huber and William Form, *Income and Ideology* (Free Press, 1973).

106. Thomas Ferguson, *Golden Rule* (University of Chicago Press, 1995); G. William Domhoff, *Who Rules America? Power and Politics in the Year 2000* (Mayfield Publishing, 1998).

107. Macionis, *Society*, pp. 155–56.

108. Bert Holldobler and Edward O. Wilson, *Ants* (Belknap Press, 1990), p. 355.

109. Jones, Gallagher, and McFalls, *Sociology*, pp. 346–50.

110. Seymour Martin Lipset and Richard Bendix, *Social Mobility in Industrial Society* (University of California Press, 1959).

111. H. Ganzeboom, R. Luijkx, and D. Treiman, "International Class Mobility in Comparative Perspective," *Research in Stratification and Mobility*, 9, 1989, pp. 3–79.

112. Michael Hout, "More Universalism, Less Structural Mobility: The American Occupational Structure in the 1980s," *American Journal of Sociology*, 14, 1988, pp. 293–318.

113. Nicole Benokraitis and Joe Feagin, *Modern Sexism: Blatant, Subtle, and Overt Discrimination* (Prentice Hall, 1995).

114. *Statistical Abstract, 1997*, Table 750.

115. Leonard Beeghley, *The Structure of Social Stratification in the U.S.* (Allyn and Bacon, 1996).

116. *Statistical Abstract, 1947; Statistical Abstract, 1998,* Table 725.

117. "Executive Pay," *Business Week,* 1997.

118. G. William Domhoff, *The Power Elite and The State: How Policy Is Made in America* (Aldine de Gruyter, 1990).

119. Donald Treiman, *Occupational Prestige in Comparative Perspective* (Academic Press, 1977).

120. Henslin, *Essentials of Sociology,* p. 182.

121. Dennis Gilbert and Joseph Kahl, *The American Class Structure: A New Synthesis* (Dorsey Press, 1993).

122. William Kelso, *Poverty and the Underclass: Changing Perceptions of the Poor in America* (New York University Press, 1995).

123. Daniel Patrick Moynihan, "Social Justice in the Next Century," *America,* September 14, 1991, pp. 132–37.

Chapter 11

1. United Nations, *Human Development Report 1996* (Oxford University Press, 1996), p. 61.

2. Mattei Dogan and Dominique Pelassy, *How to Compare Nations: Strategies in Comparative Politics* (Chatham House, 1984), p. 5.

3. Seymour Martin Lipset, *Continental Divide: The Values and Institutions of the United States and Canada* (Routledge, 1990).

4. William Kephart and William Zellner, *Extraordinary Groups* (St. Martin's Press, 1991).

5. John Gagnon, *Human Sexualities* (Scott Foresman, 1977).

6. Patrick Gray and Linda Wolfe, "An Anthropological Look at Human Sexuality," in William Masters, Virginia Johnson, and R. Kolodny, eds., *Human Sexuality* (Scott Foresman, 1998), pp. 650–78.

7. Birgitta Linner, *Sex and Society in Sweden* (Harper Colophon, 1972).

8. Steven Pinker, *How the Mind Works* (W. W. Norton & Co., 1997), p. 379.

9. Betty Mahmoody and Willima Hoffer, *Not Without My Daughter* (St. Martin's Press, 1988).

10. George Murdock, "The Common Denominator of Cultures," in Ralph Linton, ed., *The Science of Man in the World Crisis* (Columbia University Press, 1945), p. 124.

11. Stuart Chase, *The Proper Study of Mankind* (Harper and Brothers, 1956), pp. 84–85.

12. Robert Bellah et al., *Habits of the Heart: Individualism and Commitment in American Life* (University of California Press, 1985).

13. John Hewith, *Dilemmas of the American Self* (Temple University Press, 1989).

14. Daniel Yankelovich, *New Rules: Searching for Self-Fulfillment in a World Turned Upside Down* (Random House, 1981), pp. 82–85.

15. Gary Abrams, "American Youth: Is Selfishness Up?" *Los Angeles Times,* November 26, 1992, p. 12.

16. Robert C. Christopher, *The Japanese Mind* (Fawcett Columbine, 1984), p. 17.

17. Judith Valente, "They Steal from the Devastated," *Parade Magazine,* June 4, 1995, p. 5.

18. David Bayley, *Forces of Order: Policing Modern Japan* (University of California Press, 1991); Nicholas Kristof, "Guns: One Nation Bars Them, the Other Requires," *New York Times,* March 10, 1996, p. E3; Louise Shelley, *Review of Crime and Justice in Two Societies* (Brooks/Cole, 1992).

19. Karel van Wolferen, *The Enigma of Japanese Power* (Vintage Books, 1990).

20. Robert Whiting, *You Gotta Have Wa* (Macmillan, 1992), p. 25.

21. Illustrative of cultural differences between Japan and America is the PBS video *Baseball in Japan* (Bowling Green State University Films, 1994).

22. Edwin Reischauer, *The Japanese Today* (Harvard University Press, 1988).

23. Roberta Yates, "Overwork Blamed for Deaths of Japanese Businessmen," *San Diego Union,* May 6, 1990.

24. Ishihara in I. McArthur, "Plummeting Birth Rate Tied to Men's View of Marriage," *Japan Times Weekly International Edition,* August 12–18, 1991.

25. Evelyn Iritani, "Japanese Fleeing a Thick Glass Ceiling," *Los Angeles Times,* April 5, 1996, pp. A8–9.

26. Martin O'Neill, "The Half-Hour-a-Week Marriage," *Sunday Punch,* September 27, 1992.

27. Ruth Benedict, *The Chrysanthemum and the Sword: Patterns of Japanese Culture* (Houghton Mifflin, 1946).

28. Nathaniel B. Thayer and Stephen E. Weiss, "The Changing Logic of a Former Minor Power," in Hans Binnendijk, ed., *National Negotiating Styles* (U.S. Department of State, 1987), pp. 45–74.

29. U.S. Department of Education, *Japanese Education Today,* 1987, p. vi.

30. Edwin O. Reischauer, *The Japanese Today: Change and Continuity* (Harvard University Press, 1988).

31. *Human Development Report 1994: United Nations Development Programme* (Oxford University Press, 1994). The HDI uses 52 human development indicators to arrive at a composite ranking of 173 countries.

32. Michio Morishima, *Why Has Japan Succeeded? Western Technology and the Japanese Ethos* (Cambridge University Press, 1984).

33. Josha A. Fogel, *The Cultural Dimension of Sino-Japanese Relations* (Mitchell E. Sharpe, 1994).

34. Lena Sun, "China Seeks Ways to Protect Elderly," *Washington Post,* October 23, 1990, p. A1.

35. Gary Huang, "Daily Addressing Ritual: A Cross-Cultural Study," paper presented at the American Sociological Association, 1988.

36. James Henslin, *Essentials of Sociology: A Down-to-Earth Approach* (Allyn and Bacon, 2000), p. 262.

37. Kevin Kinsella and Cynthia Taeuber, *An Aging World* (U.S. Bureau of the Census, 1993).

38. Jay and Linda Matthews, *One Billion: A China Chronicle* (Random House, 1983).

39. Susan V. Lawrence, "The Legacy of the Red Guards," *U.S. News and World Report,* May 20, 1996, p. 40.

40. Joan Ferrante, *Sociology: A Global Perspective* (Wadsworth, 1995), pp. 265–73.

41. United Nations, *Human Development Report 2001* (Oxford University Press, 2001), p. 10.

42. *New York Times,* November 11, 1999.

43. "The World Factbook 2000—China," at *https://www.cia.gov/library/publications/the-world-factbook/* (accessed March 4, 2008).

44. Brigham Young University, "Culturgram '95: People's Republic of China" (David Kennedy Center for International Studies, 1995); United Nations Development Programme, *Human Development Report 1995* (Oxford University Press, 1995), p. 155.

45. United Nations, *Human Development Report 2001,* p. 79.

46. Hedrick Smith, *The Russians* (Ballantine Books, 1976), pp. 138–39.

47. "The World Factbook 2000—Russia," at *https://www.cia.gov/library/publications/the-world-factbook/* (accessed March 4, 2008).

48. Murray Feschbach, *Ecocide in the U.S.S.R.* (Harper-Collins, 1989).

49. "The World Factbook 2000—Russia," p. 7, at *https://www.cia.gov/library/publications/the-world-factbook/* (accessed March 4, 2008).

50. Brigham Young University, "Culturgram '95: Russia," (David Kennedy Center for International Studies, 1995); United Nations Development Programme, *Human Development Report 1995* (Oxford University Press, 1995), p. 155; United Nations Development Programme, *Human Development Report 2001,* p. 79.

51. Daniel Rancour-Laferriere, *The Slave Soul of Russia: Moral Masochism and the Cult of Suffering* (New York University Press, 1996).

52. Winston Churchill, radio broadcast, October 11, 1939.

53. Wilber Chaffee, *Desenvolvimento: Politics and Economy in Brazil* (Lynne Rienner, 1997).

54. Ronald Schneider, *Brazil: Culture and Politics in a New Industrial Powerhouse* (Westview Press, 1996).

55. E. Bradford Burns, *A History of Brazil* (Columbia University Press, 1993).

56. Joseph Page, *The Brazilians* (Addison Wesley, 1995), p. 9.

57. Ibid., p. 8.

58. The World Factbook 2000—Brazil, pp. 3–4.

59. David M. Kennedy Center for International Studies, "Culturgram '92: Brazil" (Brigham Young University, 1992), p. 2.

60. Harm De Blij and Peter Muller, *Geography* (Wiley, 1994), pp. 336–49.

61. The World Bank, *World Development Report 1990* (Oxford University Press, 1990).

62. United Nations Development Programme, *Human Development Report 2001* (Oxford University Press, 2001), p. 85.

63. Manuel G. Mendoza and Vince Napoli, *Systems of Society* (D. C. Heath, 1995), pp. 565–73.

64. John Miles, producer and director, "The Tribe That Time Forgot," *Nova,* videocassette AV#87122, 1994.

65. Ibid.

66. Andrew Downie, "A Century Later, Lost Amazon Tribe Reappears," *Christian Science Monitor,* August 29, 2000, p. 2, at *http://www.csmonitor.com* (accessed March 4, 2008).

67. Pratap Chatterjee, "Land Invasions in the Amazon," at *http://www.forests.org/archived_site/today/recent/1995/saviol.htm* (accessed March 4, 2008).

68. United Nations Development Programme, *Human Development Report 2001* (Oxford University Press, 2001), p. 156.

69. Baka Pygmies, at *http://www.pygmies.info* (accessed March 4, 2008).

70. "Reciprocal Arrangements: Pygmies and Cultivators," and "Pygmy Life," at *http://www.maricopa.edu/1dept/d10/asb/anthro2003/lifeways/diasporas/cultivators.html* (accessed March 4, 2008).

71. "Amazonian Indians: The Arara Tribe," at *http://www.socioambiental.org/pib/epienglish/arara/contact.shtm* (accessed March 4, 2008).

72. "Baka: People of the Rainforest" (PBS video), *Nova,* 1990.

73. Seyyed Hossein Nasr, "Society," *A Young Muslim's Guide to the Modern World* (Kazi Publications, 1993), at *http://www.fonsvitae.com/youngmuslim.html* (accessed March 4, 2008).

74. Anwar Shaikh, "The Arab National Movement," 1995, at *http://www.hindutva.org* (accessed March 4, 2008).

75. See Judith Miller, "The Challenge of Radical Islam," *Foreign Affairs,* 72, no. 2, Spring 1993; Steve Coll and David Hoffman, "Islam's Violent Improvisers," *Washington Post,* August 9–15, 1993, pp. 6–7; Robin Wright, *Sacred Rage: The Wrath of Militant Islam* (Simon & Schuster, 1985); Martin Kramer, "Islam vs. Democracy," *Commentary,* 95, no. 1, January 1993; Mark Juergensmeyer, *The New Cold War? Religious Nationalism Confronts the Secular State* (University of California Press, 1993).

76. Mir Zohair Husain, *Global Islamic Politics* (Harper-Collins, 1995), p. xi.

77. Seyyed Hossein Nasr, "Politics," *A Young Muslim's Guide to the Modern World* (Kazi Publications, 1993), at *http://www.fonsvitae.com/youngmuslim.html* (accessed March 4, 2008).

78. John L. Esposito and John Voll, *Islam and Democracy* (Oxford University Press, 1996).

79. Bernard Lewis, "I'm Right, You're Wrong, Go To Hell: Religions and the Meeting of Civilizations," *The Atlantic Monthly,* May 2003, pp. 36–42.

80. Brian Jones, Bernard Gallagher, and Joseph A. McFalls, *Sociology: Micro, Macro, and Mega Structures* (Harcourt Brace, 1995), p. 209.

81. Robert H. Clarke, "Lest Ye Be Judged: Ethnocentrism or Cultural Relativism," in Frank Zulke, ed., *Through the Eyes of Social Science* (Waveland Press, 1995), p. 238.

82. Joan Ferrante, *Sociology: A Global Perspective* (Wadsworth, 1995), p. 129.

83. Carol and Melvin Ember, *Cultural Anthropology* (Prentice Hall, 1996), p. 16.

84. Dorothy Lee, *Valuing the Self: What We Learn from Other Cultures* (Waveland Press, 1995).

85. Maynard Merwine, "How Africa Understands Female Circumcision," *New York Times,* November 24, 1993.

86. Mary Ann French, "A Practice Some Call Mutilation," *Philadelphia Inquirer,* January 17, 1993, pp. C1–3.

87. Kate Chalkley, "Female Genital Mutilation: New Laws, Programs Try to End Practice," *Population Today,* October 1997, pp. 4–5.

88. From Words of Domon Sage, Ogotemmeli, in Marcel Griaule, *Dieu d'Eau* (Librairie Artheme Fayard, trans. R. Clarke, 1966).

89. Jomo Kenyatta, *Facing Mt. Kenya* (Secker and Warburg, 1953), pp. 153–54.

90. Sophfronia Gregory, "At Risk of Mutilation," *Time Magazine,* March 21, 1994, p. 45.

91. Robin Morgan and Gloria Steinem, "The International Crime of Genital Mutilation," *MS Magazine,* March 1980, p. 98.

92. Ellen Goodman, "Setting a Precedent to Protect Little Girls from Mutilation," United Press Release, March 31, 1994.

93. Melron Nicol-Wilson, "Ending Female Genital Mutilation Without Human Rights: Two Approaches," *Human Rights Dialogue,* 2000, p. 8.

94. Alvin Toffler, *The Third Wave* (Morrow, 1980).

95. William Ogburn, *On Culture and Social Change* (University of Chicago Press, 1964).

96. Klaus Eder, "The Rise of Counter-Culture Movements Against Modernity," *Theory, Culture & Society,* 7, 1990, pp. 21–47.

97. Arnold Toynbee, *A Study of History* (Oxford University Press, 1946).

98. Myron Weiner, *The Global Migration Crisis: Challenge to States and to Human Rights* (HarperCollins, 1995).

99. John E. Yellen, "The Transformation of the Kalahari !Kung," *Scientific American,* April 1990, pp. 96–105; Richard B. Lee, *The !Kung San: Men, Women, and Work in a Foraging Society* (Cambridge University Press, 1979); "Safari Operator Working to Save Spirit of Bushmen," *United Press International,* April 12, 1987.

Chapter 12

1. James N. Danziger, *Understanding the Political World* (Addison Wesley Longman, 2001), p. 133.

2. William H. Riker, *The Art of Political Manipulation* (Yale University Press, 1976).

3. Roger Masters, *The Nature of Politics* (Yale University Press, 1989).

4. Samuel E. Finer, *The History of Government from the Earliest Times* (Oxford University Press, 1997).

5. Samuel P. Huntington, *Political Order in Changing Societies* (Yale University Press, 1969).

6. Karl Mannheim, *Ideology and Utopia* (Harcourt Brace, 1936).

7. Austin V. Ranney, *Governing: An Introduction to Political Science* (Prentice Hall, 2001), pp. 4–14.

8. Thomas Hobbes, *Leviathan* (James Thornton, 1881), p. 93.

9. Ranney, *Governing,* p. 6.

10. Hans F. Morgenthau and Kenneth W. Thompson, *Politics Among Nations* (Alfred A. Knopf, 1985).

11. Lewis F. Richardson, *Statistics of Deadly Quarrels* (University of Pittsburgh Press, 1960).

12. James N. Rosenau, *Turbulence in World Politics: A Theory of Change and Continuity* (Princeton University Press, 1990).

13. Crane Brinton, *The Anatomy of Revolution* (Vintage Books, 1965); Theda Skocpol, *States and Social Revolutions: A Comparative Analysis of France, Russia, and China* (Cambridge University Press, 1979); Charles Tilly, "Does Modernization Breed Revolution?" in Jack Goldstone, ed., *Revolutions: Theoretical, Comparative, and Historical Studies* (Harcourt Brace Jovanovich, 1986), pp. 47–57.

14. Paul Johnson, "The Seven Deadly Sins of Terrorism," in Benjamin Netanyahu, ed., *International Terrorism* (Transaction Books, 1981), pp. 12–22.

15. Ranney, *Governing,* pp. 26–30.

16. Ibid., pp. 95–99.

17. Carl J. Friedrich and Zbigniew Brzezinski, *Totalitarian Dictatorship and Autocracy* (Harvard University Press, 1956), p. 9.

18. William James, *Pragmatism* (Meridian, 1959).

19. John Gray, *Liberalism* (University of Minnesota Press, 1986).

20. Ranney, *Governing,* p. 87.

21. Roy C. Macridis, *Contemporary Political Ideologies* (HarperCollins, 1992).

22. Ranney, *Governing,* p. 88.

23. Robert Dahl, *Polyarchy: Participation and Opposition* (Yale University Press, 1971).

24. C. Wright Mills, *The Power Elite* (Oxford University Press, 1956).

25. Donald Kinder and Lynn Sanders, *Divided by Color: Racial Politics and Democratic Ideals* (University of Chicago Press, 1996).

26. Jesse Jackson, "Reparations Are Justified for Blacks," *Regulation,* September–October 1978, pp. 17–28.

27. Kathanne Green, *Affirmative Action and Principles of Justice* (Greenwood Press, 1989).

28. Adam Cohen, "A New Push for Blind Justice," *Time Magazine,* February 20, 1995, pp. 39–40.

29. Sydney Bailey, *British Parliamentary Democracy* (Greenwood Press, 1978).

30. Donley Studlar, *Great Britain: Decline or Renewal?* (Westview Press, 1996).

31. Dennis Kavanaugh, *Thatcherism and British Politics* (Oxford University Press, 1990).

32. Richard Rose, "Politics in England," in Gabriel Almond and G. Bingham Powell, eds., *European Politics Today* (Longman, 1999), pp. 78–137.

33. Nicholas Riasanovsky, *A History of Russia* (Oxford University Press, 2000), p. 622.

34. M. Steven Fish, "When More Is Less," in Victoria Bonnell and George Breslauer, eds., *Russia in the New Century: Stability or Disorder?* (Westview Press, 2001), pp. 15–34.

35. Steven Solnick, "Is the Center Too Weak or Too Strong in the Russian Federation?" in Valerie Sperling, ed., *Building the Russian State* (Westview Press, 2000), p. 137.

36. Eugene Huskey, "Overcoming the Yeltsin Legacy: Vladimir Putin and Russian Political Reform," in Archie Brown, ed., *Contemporary Russian Politics: A Reader* (Oxford University Press, 2001), pp. 82–97.

37. David Wen-wei Chang, *China Under Deng Xiaoping: Political and Economic Reform* (St. Martin's Press, 1991); Lucian W. Pye, *The Spirit of Chinese Politics* (Harvard University Press, 1992).

38. Ronald Hrebenar, *The Japanese Party System: From One-Party Rule to Coalition Government* (Westview Press, 1996).

39. Masaaki Kotabe, *Anticompetitive Practices in Japan: Their Impact on the Performance of Foreign Firms* (Greenwood, 1996).

40. Kazuo Sato, *The Japanese Economy: A Primer* (Sharpe, 1997).

41. Thomas Magstadt, *Nations and Governments* (St. Martin's Press, 2002), pp. 425–33.

42. Wendy Hunter, *Eroding Military Influence in Brazil: Politicians Against Soldiers* (University of North Carolina Press, 1996).

43. Danziger, *Understanding the Political World*, pp. 417–19.

44. Robert Levine, *Brazilian Legacies* (Sharpe, 1997).

Chapter 13

1. Martin Griffiths, *Realism, Idealism, and International Politics: A Reinterpretation* (Routledge, 1995).

2. Henry A. Kissinger, *Diplomacy* (Simon & Schuster, 1994).

3. Woodrow Wilson, address at Sioux Falls, South Dakota, September 8, 1919.

4. Woodrow Wilson, *War Message*, 65th Congress, Senate document no. 5 (Government Printing Office, 1971), pp. 3–8; David Callahan, *Between Two Worlds: Realism, Idealism and Foreign Policy After the Cold War* (HarperCollins, 1994); Martin Griffiths, *Realism, Idealism and International Politics* (Routledge, 1995).

5. Fred W. Riggs, "Thoughts about Neoidealism vs. Realism: Reflections on Charles Kegley's ISA Presidential Address," *International Studies Notes*, 19, no. 1 (Winter 1994), p. 1.

6. Eschel M. Rhoodie, *Cultures in Conflict: A Global Survey of Ethnicity, Sectarianism and Nationalism, 1960–1990* (McFarland, 1993); Walter Connor, "Nation-Building or Nation-Destroying," in Fred A. Sondermann, David S. McClellan, and William C. Olson, eds., *The Theory and Practice of International Relations* (Prentice-Hall, 1979).

7. James N. Danziger, *Understanding the Political World: A Comparative Introduction to Political Science* (Longman, 1996), pp. 136–38.

8. Seyom Brown, *New Forces, Old Forces, and the Future of World Politics* (HarperCollins, 1995).

9. Hendrik Spruyt, *The Sovereign State and Its Competitors: An Analysis of Systems Change* (Princeton University Press, 1994).

10. John T. Rourke, *International Politics on the World Stage* (Dushkin, 1995), pp. 35–42; John H. Herz, "The Rise and Demise of the Territorial State," *World Politics* 9, 1959, pp. 473–93; Karl Deutsch, *Tides Among Nations* (Free Press, 1979).

11. William Eckhardt, "War-Related Death Since 3000 B.C.," *Peace Research*, 23, 1991, pp. 80–85.

12. George C. Kohn, *Dictionary of Wars* (Anchor Doubleday, 1994).

13. Walter Jones, *The Logic of International Relations* (HarperCollins, 1995).

14. Eschel M. Rhoodie, *Cultures in Conflict: A Global Survey of Ethnicity, Sectarianism and Nationalism: 1960–1990* (McFarland, 1993).

15. "Two Million Kids Killed in Decade of Wars," *Associated Press Release*, December 10, 1995.

16. Karl von Clausewitz, *On War* (Princeton University Press, 1976), p. 147.

17. Hans J. Morgenthau, *Politics Among Nations: The Struggle for Power and Peace* (Knopf, 1978), p. 42.

18. Matthew 5:38–46, *The New Testament*, translation by Edgar J. Goodspeed (University of Chicago Press, 1948).

19. Seyom Brown, *The Causes and Prevention of War* (St. Martin's Press, 1987), p. 125.

20. *SIPRI Yearbook*, 1985, pp. 44, 52.

21. "The Atomic Cafe" (Thorn EMI video), 1982.

22. Richard Rosecrance, "Stuffing the Genie Back In," *IGCC Newsletter*, Fall 1995, pp. 4–5.

23. Francis Fukuyama, *The End of History and the Last Man* (Free Press, 1992).

24. Rex Brynen, Bahgat Korany, and Paul Noble, eds. *Political Liberalization and Democratization in the Arab World*. Lynne Rienner, 1995.

25. Joe Hagan, "Domestic Political Systems and War Proneness," *Mershon International Studies Review*, 38, no. 2, October 1994; David Lake, "Powerful Pacifists: Democratic States and War," *American Political Science Review*, March 1992; Dina A. Zinnes and Richard L. Merritt, "Democracies and War," in Alex Inkeles, ed., *On Measuring Democracy: Its Consequences and Concomitants* (Transaction Books, 1991).

26. Bruce Russett, *Controlling the Sword* (Harvard University Press, 1990), p. 123.

27. Max Singer and Aaron Wildavsky, *The Real World Order: Zones of Peace, Zones of Turmoil* (Chatham House, 1993).

28. Michael E. Brown, Sean Lynn-Jones, and Steven Miller, eds. *Debating the Democratic Peace*. MIT Press, 1996.

29. John Mueller, *Retreat from Doomsday* (Addison-Wesley, 1993), p. 214.

30. John Mueller, *Quiet Cataclysm: Reflections of the Recent Transformation of World Politics* (HarperCollins, 1995), p. 1.

31. Anatol Rapoport, *Peace: An Idea Whose Time Has Come* (University of Michigan Press, 1992).

32. Ralph E. Lapp, "The Einstein Letter That Started It All," *New York Times Magazine*, August 2, 1964.

33. Robert Elias and Jennifer Turpin, eds. *Rethinking Peace*. Lynne Rienner, 1994.

34. Donald Snow, *National Security: Defense Policy for a New International Order* (St. Martin's Press, 1994), p. 4.

35. James N. Rosenau, "The Relocation of Authority in a Shrinking World," *Comparative Politics*, 24, no. 3, April 1992, p. 266.

36. John T. Rourke, *International Politics on the World Stage* (Dushkin, 1995), pp. 142–44.

37. Randall Forsberg, "Wasting Billions," *Boston Review* (April–May 1994).

38. Richard Falk, *On Human Governance: Toward a New Global Politics* (Penn State University Press, 1995).

39. Interview with Pierre Salinger, former press secretary to President Kennedy; "Khrushchev," Biography, *Arts and Entertainment Channel,* July 26, 1995.

40. Gabrielle Brussel, "Cuban Missile Crisis: U.S. Deliberations and Negotiations at the Edge of the Precipice," *Pew Case No. 334,* Washington, DC: Georgetown University, 1993; James G. Blight and David A. Welch, *On the Brink: Americans and Soviets Reexamine the Cuban Missile Crisis* (Noonday, 1996).

41. Union of International Associations, *Yearbook of International Organizations* (K. G. Saur, 1994, vol. 4).

42. The Stanley Foundation, "The UN System and NGOs: New Relationships for a New Era?" (25th United Nations Issues Conference, 1994), p. 1.

43. David Cortright, *Peace Works: The Citizen's Role in Ending the Cold War* (Westview Press, 1993); David C. Korten, *Getting to the 21st Century: Voluntary Action and the Global Agenda* (Kumarian Press, 1990); Craig Comstock and Don Carlson, *Citizen Summitry: Keeping the Peace When It Matters Too Much to Be Left to Politicians* (J. P. Tarcher, 1986).

44. Annetta Miller, "Teaching an Old Fish New Tricks," *Newsweek,* August 16, 1993, p. 68; Ronald Powell, "Tuna Fleet's Departure Is Still Bitter Tale," *San Diego Union-Tribune,* August 28, 1994, p. B–1; "Today's Debate: Tuna vs. Dolphins," *USA Today,* December 28, 1996, p. 12A.

45. Peter James Spielmann, "French Navy Seizes Greenpeace Ship Near Nuclear Test Site in Pacific," *Associated Press Release,* July 11, 1995; Bob Ostertag, "Greenpeace Takes Over the World," *Mother Jones,* March–April 1991; Robert Hunter, *Warriors of the Rainbow: A Chronicle of the Greenpeace Movement* (Holt, Rinehart, Winston, 1979); Kenneth W. Stiles, "Greenpeace," in his *Case Histories in International Politics* (HarperCollins, 1995).

46. Craig N. Murphy, *International Organization and Industrial Change: Global Governance Since 1850* (Oxford University Press, 1994).

47. Union of International Associations, *Yearbook of International Organizations* (1994).

48. David Mitrany, *The Functional Theory of Politics* (St. Martin's Press, 1976).

49. Neill Nugent, *The Government and Politics of the European Union* (Duke University Press, 1994).

50. Mark Lawrence, "Bureaucratic War Waged Over Meaning of 'Chocolate'," *Associated Press Release,* November 23, 1995.

51. Richard Z. Chesnoff, "A Conversation with Boutros Boutros-Ghali," *U.S. News and World Report,* June 26, 1995, p. 44.

52. Enid Schoettle et al., *An Agenda for Funds: The United States and the Financing of the United Nations* (Council on Foreign Relations Press, 1995); Max Jakobsen, *The United Nations in the 1990s, a Second Chance* (United Nations Publications, 1993); Wendell Gordon, *The United Nations at the Crossroads of Reform* (Mitchell E. Sharp, 1994); "Who Are the UN Peacekeepers?" *Parade,* January 8, 1995, p. 18; Robert H. Reid, "Debts Challenge UN's Future," Associated Press Release, October 24, 1995; Charles J. Hanley, "UN Event Produces Few Answers," *Associated Press Release,* October 25, 1995.

53. Cathal J. Nolan, *The Longman Guide to World Affairs* (Longman Publishers, 1995), pp. 248–49.

54. David C. Korten, "Sustainability and the Global Economy: Balancing Market and Community Interests," *Surviving Together* (Winter 1994), pp. 3–5; David C. Korten, *When Corporations Rule the World* (Kumarian Press, 1995).

55. *Fortune,* July 25, 1994; "Ford Motor Corporation Circles the World," *New York Times,* April 22, 1994, p. D1; John T. Rourke, *International Politics on the World Stage* (Dushkin, 1995), pp. 68–69, 498–99.

56. FNS Regular Package Broadcast Interview, "The MacNeil Newshour Interview with Lewis Preston," Federal News Service, July 22, 1994.

Chapter 14

1. American Economic Association, at *http://www.vanderbilt.edu/AEA/* (accessed March 4, 2008).

2. Dorothy R. Ross, *The Origins of American Social Science* (Cambridge University Press, 1991), pp. xix–xx.

3. Fred Gottheil, *Principles of Macroeconomics* (South-Western, 1996), pp. 226–27.

4. Charles Hampden-Turner and Alfons Trompenaars, *The Seven Cultures of Capitalism* (Doubleday, 1993).

5. Cathal J. Nolan, *The Longman Guide to World Affairs* (Longman Publishers, 1995), p. 237.

6. Dominick Salvatore, *International Economics* (Prentice Hall, 1998), p. 9.

7. *Current Population Reports: Money Income of Households, Families, and Persons in the U.S.,* 1990, p. 202.

8. Gottheil, *Principles of Macroeconomics,* p. 117.

9. Anders Aslund, *How Russia Became a Market Economy* (Royal Institute of International Affairs, 1995).

10. Richard Robison and David Goodman, *The New Rich in Asia: Mobile Phones, McDonalds, and Middle Class* (Routledge, 1996).

11. Richard Stubbs and Geoffrey Underhill, eds., *Political Economy and the Changing Global Order* (St. Martin's Press, 1994).

12. JoAnn Wypijewski, "GE Goes South," in Paula Rothenberg, ed., *Beyond Borders: Thinking Critically About Global Issues* (Worth Publishers, 2006), pp. 490–92.

13. Sven Groennings, "The Changing Need for an International Perspective: The Global Economy and Undergraduate Education," *International Studies Notes,* Winter 1989, pp. 64–68; "Black Monday: What Really Ignited the Market's Collapse After Its Long Climb," *Wall Street Journal,* December 16, 1987, p. 1.

14. Hedrick Smith, "Challenge to America" (Films for the Humanities, 1994).

15. Jagdish Bhagwati and Hugh T. Patrick, eds., *Aggressive Unilateralism: America's 301 Trade Policy and the World Trading System* (University of Michigan Press, 1990).

16. Robert S. Walters, "U.S. Negotiations of Voluntary Restraint Agreements in Steel, 1984," *Pew Case Studies in International Affairs* (Georgetown University, Case 107, 1988), p. 1.

17. Donald P. Clark, "Recent Changes in Non-Tariff Measures Used in Industrial Nations," *International Trade Journal*, 1992, pp. 311–22.

18. Gary Hufbauer and Kimberly Elliott, *New York Times*, November 12, 1993, p. D1.

19. Fred W. Frailey, "Ralph Wanger Inside Interview," *Kiplinger's Personal Finance Magazine*, February 1995, pp. 100–105; Kevin Kelly, "The Rumble Heard Round the World," *Business Week*, May 24, 1993, p. 58; Jon Krakauer, "A Hog Is Still a Hog, But the 'Wild Ones' Are Tamer," *Smithsonian*, November 1993, pp. 88–90; Gary Slutzker, "Hog Wild," *Forbes Magazine*, May 24, 1993, pp. 45–46; Clint Willis, "Cash in on Companies That Are Hammering the Japanese," *Money Magazine*, April 1992, pp. 69–70.

20. Michael J. Boskin, "Pass GATT Now," *Time Magazine*, December 12, 1994, p. 137; Susan Dentzer, "Global Trade Meets James Bond," *Christian Science Monitor*, July 25, 1994, p. 45; Emil Innocenti, "GATT Could Destroy the Future of Small Business," *Newsweek*, November 21, 1994, p. 20; Amy Kaslow, "US Congress Dims Future of GATT," *Christian Science Monitor*, October 5, 1994, p. 1; Jeremy Rabkin, "Trading in Our Sovereignty?" *National Review*, June 13, 1994, p. 34.

21. Howard Banks, "Strong Trade Up North," *Forbes Magazine*, January 2, 1995, p. 35.

22. Sheila Tefft, "US, China Trade Clash Worsens," *Christian Science Monitor*, January 3, 1995, p. 9; Maria Shao, "China for Sale," *Boston Globe*, January 15, 1995, p. 1; Martin Crutsinger, "US Proposes to Impose Sanctions on Chinese Trade," Associated Press Release, January 1, 1995.

23. James R. Gaines, "Welcome to the Wild East," *Time Magazine*, April 11, 1994, p. 86; James Walsh, "Peace: Finally at Hand," *Time Magazine*, February 14, 1994, pp. 34–36.

24. A. A. Berle, Jr., *Economic Power and the Free Society* (Fund for the Republic, 1958), p. 14.

25. John Cassidy, "Wall Street Follies," *New Yorker*, September 13, 1999, p. 32.

26. Vandana Shiva, "Building Water Democracy: People's War Against Coca-Cola in Plachimada," *Znet Commentary*, May 13, 2004.

27. BBC News, "Enron Scandal at a Glance," August 22, 2002, at *http://news.bbc.co.uk/1/hi/business/1780075.stm* (accessed March 4, 2008); BBC News, "Ex-Enron Executive Pleads Guilty," August 21, 2002, at *http://news.bbc.co.uk/2/hi/business/2206365.stm* (accessed March 4, 2008); BBC News, "Andersen Guilty in Enron Case," June 15, 2002, at *http://news.bbc.co.uk/2/hi/business/2047122.stm* (accessed March 4, 2008); BBC News, "Kenneth Lay: A Fallen Hero," July 5, 2006, at *http://news.bbc.co.uk/2/hi/business/3875941.stm* (accessed March 4, 2008).

28. Joseph Stiglitz, "Corporate Corruption: The Conflicts of Interest Driving U.S. Financial Scandals Are Being Replicated on a Global Scale," *Guardian of London*, July 4, 2002, at *http://www.commondreams.org/views02/0704-02.htm* (accessed March 4, 2008).

Chapter 15

1. The World Factbook, "A Profile of the World," 2005, at *http://www.infoplease.com/ipa/A0004373.html*.

2. The World Bank Group, "World Development Indicators 2006," at *http://devdata.worldbank.org/wdi2006/contents/Section4_1.htm*.

3. Steven L. Spiegel, *World Politics in a New Era* (Harcourt Brace, 1995), pp. 284–85, 340–41.

4. Robert Gilpin, *The Political Economy of International Relations* (Princeton University Press, 1987), p. 31.

5. Spiegel, *World Politics in a New Era*, pp. 308–9.

6. Joseph Stiglitz, "Addis Ababa: Thanks for Nothing," *Atlantic Monthly*, October 2001, pp. 36–40.

7. Helen Cobban, "No Globalization Without Representation," *Christian Science Monitor*, March 9, 2000, p. 11.

8. Spiegel, *World Politics in a New Era*, p. 287.

9. Charles Kindelberger, *The World in Depression, 1929–1939* (University of California Press, 1973), p. 132.

10. Steven Husted and Michael Melvin, *International Economics* (HarperCollins, 1995), p. 227.

11. Spiegel, *World Politics in a New Era*, pp. 294–300.

12. S. M. Chiu, *China: The Next Economic Superpower* (Westview, 1996).

13. John Leger, "The Boom: How Asians Started the 'Pacific Century,'" *Far Eastern Economic Review*, November 24, 1994.

14. "Trade Winds, Trade Wars," *Seapower and Trade* (PBS series).

15. Herman Schwartz, *States versus Markets* (St. Martin's Press, 1994), p. 89.

16. Jeremy Brecher and Tim Costello, *Global Village or Global Pillage: Economic Reconstruction from the Bottom Up* (South End Press, 1994).

17. "Chainsaw Self-Portrait: Slash-and-Burn Executive Tells All," *USA Today*, August 30, 1996, pp. B1–2.

18. Diana Jean Schemo, "U.S. Pesticide Kills Foreign Fruit Pickers' Hopes," *New York Times International*, December 6, 1995.

19. Michael Ryan, "They Call Their Boss a Hero," *Parade Magazine*, September 8, 1996, p. 4.

20. Jim Yong Kim et al., eds., *Dying for Growth: Global Inequality and the Health of the Poor* (Common Courage Press, 2000).

21. John T. Rourke, *International Politics on the World Stage* (Dushkin, 1995), pp. 514–16.

22. Richard Falk, "What Went Wrong with Henry Kissinger's Foreign Policy," *Alternatives I*, 1975, p. 99.

23. Richard Payne and Jamal Nassar, *Politics and Culture in the Developing World: The Impact of Globalization* (Pearson Longman, 2006), p. 76.

24. Joseph Szlavik, "GOP Majority in Congress Means Less for Africa," *Associated Press Release*, March 22, 1995.

25. Richard Mansbach, *The Global Puzzle: Issues and Actors in World Politics* (Houghton Mifflin, 1994), pp. 344–51.

26. Carol Lancaster, "An Irresistible Force Meets an Immovable Object: The U.S. at UNCTAD I," *Pew Case Studies in International Affairs* (Georgetown University, 1988).

27. Ibid., p. 14.

28. *To Understand the World, Listen to Its People*" (Panos Institute, 1994).

29. Richard Lacayo, "The Promises and Perils of an Antitrust Chief," *Time Magazine,* February 27, 1995, p. 33.

30. Shaida Badiee, World Bank Development Data Group, "Building Statistical Capacity to Monitor Development Progress," at *http://www.worldbank.org/data* (accessed March 4, 2008).

31. "About OECD," Organization for Economic Cooperation and Development, at *http://www.oecd.org/about/* (accessed March 4, 2008).

32. Spiegel, World Politics in a New Era, p. 373.

33. Ibid., pp. 370–71.

34. Rep. Sam Gejdenson, "Micro-Credit Transforms Lives," *Front Lines,* June–July 2000, pp. 2–8.

35. Toronto Globe and Mail, February 20, 1992.

36. Bill McKibben, "An Alternative to Progress," *Mother Jones,* May–June 2001, pp. 79–84.

37. Allister Sparks, *Beyond the Miracle: Inside the New South Africa* (University of Chicago Press, 2003), p. 236.

38. Derek Watts, CIDA University, "Carte Blanche Interactive" (February 9, 2003), at *http://www.mnet.co.za/CarteBlanche/Display/Display.asp?id=2161.*

39. Alec Hogg, "Change Champions: Dr. Taddy Blecher," at *Moneyweb: http://m1.mny.co.za.mncc.nsf?0/C2256E70000443C2C42256F3800.*

40. "Ubuntu University Lifts Off" (November 18, 2003), at *http://www.safrica.info/ess_glance/education/ubuntu.htm* (accessed March 4, 2008).

41. Andrea Vinassa, "The Soul of Business in South Africa: Taddy Blecher Interview," p. 2, *CEO Torch Media,* at *http://www.workinfo.com/free/Downloads/243.htm* (accessed March 4, 2008).

42. Allister Sparks, p. 238.

43. "Ubuntu University Lifts Off," p. 1.

44. Paul Kennedy, "Preparing for the 21st Century: Winners and Losers," in *New York Review of Books,* February 11, 1993, pp. 32–44.

45. Ibid., p. 27.

46. Ibid., p. 124.

47. Ibid., pp. 204–12.

48. Jeffrey D. Sachs, *The End of Poverty: Economic Possibilities of Our Time* (Penguin Press, 2005).

59. Ibid., pp. 24–25.

50. Ibid., pp. 288–308.

51. Ibid., pp. 210–15.

52. Ibid., pp. 109–30.

53. Ibid., pp. 131–47.

54. Ibid., pp. 148–69.

55. Ibid., pp. 188–209.

56. Ibid., pp. 347–68.

Note: Page numbers followed by *f*, *i*, or *t* refer to figures, illustrations, and tables, respectively.

Student Notes